Gramophone

FILM MUSIC

GOOD CD GUIDE

Sales and distribution

North America

Music Sales Corporation
257 Park Avenue South,
New York, NY 10010, USA.
Telephone (212) 254 2100
Fax (212) 254 2013

UK and Rest of World Record trade

Gramophone Publications Limited
135 Greenford Road, Sudbury Hill, Harrow,
Middlesex HA1 3YD, Great Britain.
Telephone +44 (0)181-422 4562
Fax +44 (0)181-869 8404

UK and Rest of World Book trade

Music Sales
8/9 Frith Street,
London WIV 5T2
Telephone +44 (0)171-434 0066
Fax +44 (0)171-734 2246

Published by

Gramophone Publications Limited,
135 Greenford Road, Sudbury Hill, Harrow,
Middlesex HA1 3YD, Great Britain

RCA VICTOR

HOME OF SOME OF THE GREATEST FILM SOUNDTRACKS OF ALL TIME

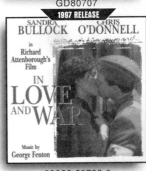

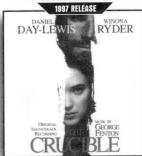

Editor	**Mark Walker**
Contributors	**Paul Cliff**
	Adrian Edwards
	Kevin Mulhall
	Paul Place
	Robert Seeley
	David Stoner
	Colin Touchin
	Mark Walker
	John Williams
	David Wishart
Production Manager	**Dermot Jones**
Designer	**Dinah Lone**
Design Assistant	**Janis Nicholls**
Advertisement Manager	**Paul Geoghegan**
Advertisement Co-ordinator	**Patti Alvarez**
Editorial Director	**Christopher Pollard**

Cover illustration Robin Cracknell
Printed in England by William Clowes Limited,
Beccles, Suffolk, NR34 9QE.

Contents

Foreword

David Arnold Composer

Since the first issue of the *Gramophone Film Music Good CD Guide* appeared last year, several hundred new films have been released, bringing with them several hundred new film scores. Countless opportunities for the finest composers in the world to create something amazing for us to listen to; opportunities for musicians and composers new to the genre to explore a different kind of music with different disciplines; opportunities for them all to create something in music that has never been heard before: new melodies, new technology, new instruments, new inspiration. Hundreds of compositions heard by millions of people in just about every country in the world, contributing to film music's internationally recognized status as one of the most dynamic and accessible forms of contemporary music.

It is very timely, therefore, that *Gramophone* has undertaken the daunting task of sifting through these scores to update what must be the definitive list of the greatest film music available. Whether you take the time to read the *Guide* from cover to cover, or occasionally browse through its pages, I am sure that you will come across something which will be a revelation to you. (The other thing I like about this *Guide* is that it is listed alphabetically by composer, which means I'm near the front!).

Introduction

Mark Walker Editor

The invisible on-screen presence of music in films has exercised a peculiar attraction for cinema audiences ever since the early 1930s when, for the first time, revolutionary new recording techniques locked sound and images together in an apparently indissoluble union. There had been music for films before then, of course, but the nascent art of the silent cinema accompanist – be it an orchestra, Wurlitzer organist or humble pianist – was swept away by the coming of sound. For a brief period, concerns about where the music was coming from threatened to undermine the efforts of those composers who discerned potential in the new medium; but showcase successes, like Max Steiner's oft-cited *King Kong* (1933), convinced the industry of the power and dramatic effect of musical underscore, and reassured nervous Hollywood moguls that audiences didn't, after all, worry about the hidden source of this extraordinary music. Extraordinary because of the novelty of its composition: musical films, being essentially an extension of the Broadway show format, quickly became a Hollywood staple (even if Busby Berkeley was taking previously unimaginable liberties with the format), but the concept of dramatic underscore – music specifically composed for, and shaped by, the narrative contours of the movie – was something new. Steiner, Korngold and their contemporaries were pioneers in what they fondly hoped was the dawn of a new art form.

What these early pioneers had not anticipated was the advent of the soundtrack album. Suites for the occasional concert performance or radio broadcast were sometimes prepared – although in Hollywood these were commonly viewed as an extension of the film's marketing campaign – but otherwise, all involved in the process imagined that once the music was recorded and 'dubbed' into the film, it would forever be just one element among many in the finished item. The control room of the recording studio on the day of the session was the first and last place this music would be heard on its own. The era of the long-playing record, and now of the compact disc, has changed that forever. Where even a few years ago it was rare for an album release to accompany anything but the biggest and most commercially-successful films, now it is routine; where the musically-inclined film buff was once restricted to sifting beneath dialogue and sound effects, now they can hear scores in their unadulterated form, joining by proxy as it were composer, producer and engineer in the studio's control room.

One curious result of this flood of soundtrack releases is that it is now quite possible – and sometimes even desirable – to enjoy a film composer's work without having to go and see the film for which it was written. What was once apparently subservient has now become independent, and its intrinsic musical worth is finally beginning to be acknowledged. A-list composers like Jerry Goldsmith, James Horner and John Williams have loyal fans who buy their soundtrack albums regardless of the merits or otherwise of the films in question. Occasionally, the soundtrack album seems to have a wider circulation than the film itself: David Arnold's *Last of the Dogmen* and John Scott's *The North Star* albums, for example, were much-praised by collectors, and arrived long before the movies' brief cinema releases. Although it remains broadly true, despite these exceptions, that the commercial viability of new score albums remains closely linked to box office performance (*Independence Day,* for example), there is a growing awareness in wider circles of the importance and value of past film music. If an unashamedly modern film composer like Hans Zimmer is unlikely to be hailed by the classical music fraternity as a kindred spirit, then at least the once-denigrated work of his forebears is now receiving overdue critical recognition: witness the recent recordings of film music from major classical labels, using internationally renowned orchestras and conductors (Sony Classical's Bernard Herrmann disc with the Los Angeles Philharmonic Orchestra under the baton of Esa-Pekka Salonen, for example). In addition to such high-profile projects clearly aimed at the broader classical market, much time, effort and money has been put into the loving restoration of the original soundtracks of great classics like Steiner's *Gone With the Wind* and Rózsa's *Ben-Hur*. Sadly, pitifully few of these originals survive, but thanks to the enterprising efforts of independent companies like Intrada, Marco Polo, Silva Screen and Varèse Sarabande we are now able to appreciate the considerable merits of many old scores in brand-new recordings.

The first edition of this book stressed the contribution of the composer, "that most neglected artist", and it is worth noting again that it is their work, as viewed through the medium of the soundtrack album, which this book seeks to celebrate. If a soundtrack album is to be considered as anything more than a memento of the film, it must be able to stand alone as a musical experience, without reference to the function of the score in the movie. Whilst film music must always retain strong visual associations, the soundtrack album allows us to isolate it and consider it as music. Re-recordings, such as those mentioned above, reinforce this view by removing the film score one step further from the film. Despite the sometimes appropriate and thoughtful use of pop songs in films (think of Scorsese or Tarantino, for example), the subsequent soundtrack albums, consisting as they do of an apparently miscellaneous collection of pre-existing songs, therefore have no place here.

Given the extraordinary diversity and stylistic range of film music both past and present, no attempt has been made within these pages to make absolute value judgments about the widely different pieces of music under consideration: each is taken on its own merits. The style and to some extent the content of any film score is determined by the nature of the film for which it is written, the composer is sometimes limited in the choices he can make, and the end result must always meet with the approval of those who have overall responsibility for the film. A score that uses synthesizers and electric guitars is not strictly comparable with one that employs a traditional symphony orchestra, but what they share – and what can make them both equally worthwhile listening experiences on CD – is an immediacy and directness, an ability to transport the listener to another place by purely musical means, the power to produce an emotional response. Thus, soundtrack albums as diverse as *Gone With the Wind*, *A Streetcar Named Desire* and *Crimson Tide* share common ground, and if their styles are strictly incommensurable, their emotive impact is not.

This year we are very pleased to publish the *Film Music Good CD Guide* in association with A&R Cambridge Ltd. (Arcam), a company whose many years of hi-fi expertise has been applied to the field of Home Cinema with critically-acclaimed results. As Keith Howard explains in his "Introduction to Home Cinema", the advent of Dolby Stereo and Surround-Sound systems for domestic use means that now it is not only possible to enjoy film music in the comfort of our own homes, but the movies as well.

JEAN-LUC GODARD
NOUVELLE VAGUE

with Alain Delon, Domiziana Giordano

The Complete Soundtrack
Music, sounds, dialogue

ECM New Series 1600/01
2-CD Set
Release: May 1997

Using the guide

Each review is prefaced with recording details, including

Film title(s) (date) **performers / conductor**. Issuing company (price) catalogue number (disc timing: recording mode).

The price codes are given simply as
Ⓕ Full
Ⓜ Mid
Ⓑ Budget
although the cost of discs will vary from one retail outlet to another, and from country to country.

A note on availability:

Although we have endeavoured only to list currently available recordings, discs are often deleted with lightning rapidity (and no advance warning), and the situation is further complicated by the status of many soundtrack albums as imports. Frequently a disc may be unavailable in the UK and Europe, but still be obtainable as an import from the USA. Less frequently, the reverse might be the case. Although these are inevitably somewhat less easy to obtain – and generally more expensive than domestic product – they form a significant part of the available recordings. In case of difficulty, the specialist dealers and mail order companies listed at the back of the book should be able to obtain most of the CDs mentioned in these pages. Persistence usually pays off, even in the case of deleted product.

Despite their wide availability, no illegitimate 'bootleg' recordings are mentioned here, as their inclusion might be taken as tacit approval of breach of copyright. Rare and limited editions have also been omitted, simply because they are either too difficult for the average record buyer to obtain, or – what is worse – far too expensive!

Editor's Top 40

A chronological selection of 40 landmark scores in the history of film music.

1933 **Max Steiner** King Kong.
Label X LXCD10

1935 **Franz Waxman**
The Bride of Frankenstein.
Silva Screen FILMCD135

1938 **Erich Wolfgang Korngold**
The Adventures of Robin Hood.
TER CDTER1066 / Varèse
Sarabande VCD47202

1939 **Max Steiner** Gone With the Wind.
Rhino 72269 / RCA GD80452

1941 **Bernard Herrmann** Citizen Kane.
Preamble PRCD1788

1942 **Erich Wolfgang Korngold**
Kings Row.
Varèse Sarabande VCD47203

1945 **Miklós Rózsa** Spellbound.
Flapper PASTCD7093

1951 **Alex North** A Streetcar Named
Desire.
Varèse Sarabande VSD5500 /
Capitol 95597

1953 **Alfred Newman** The Robe.
Arista 11011-2
Miklós Rózsa Julius Caesar.
Intrada MAF7056D

1954 **Louis and Bebe Barron**
Forbidden Planet.
GNP PR-D-001

1955 **Leonard Rosenman** East of
Eden.
Edel CIN2206-2

1956 **Victor Young**
Around the World in 80 Days.
MCA MCAD31134

1958 **Bernard Herrmann** Vertigo.
Varèse Sarabande VSD5759 /
VSD5600
Jerome Moross The Big Country.
Silva Screen FILMCD030

1959 **Miklós Rózsa** Ben-Hur.
Rhino 72197 / EMI
CDODEON18

1961 **Miklós Rózsa** El Cid.
Koch International 37340-2

1962 **Maurice Jarre** Lawrence of
Arabia.
Varèse Sarabande VSD5263 / Silva
Screen FILMCD036

1963 **Henry Mancini** Charade.
RCA 2755-2

1965 **Maurice Jarre** Doctor Zhivago.
Rhino 71957 / EMI
CDODEON1

1966 **Jerry Goldsmith** The Blue Max.
Columbia JK57890

1967 **Alex North** 2001.
Varèse Sarabande VSD5400

1968 **John Barry** The Lion in Winter.
Columbia CK66133

1969 **John Williams** The Reivers.
Columbia CK66130

1972 **John Scott** Antony and Cleopatra.
JOS JSCD114

1975 **John Williams** Jaws.
MCA MCLD19281

1976 **Jerry Goldsmith** The Omen.
Varèse Sarabande VSD5281

1977 (1980 & 1983)
John Williams Star Wars Trilogy.
RCA Victor 09026 68772-2 / 09026
68782-2 / 09026 68792-2

1978 **Leonard Rosenman**
The Lord of the Rings.
Intrada FMT8003D

1982 **James Horner**
Star Trek II: The Wrath of Khan.·
GNP Crescendo GNPD8022
Basil Poledouris
Conan the Barbarian.
Varèse Sarabande VSD5390 / Milan
11126-2
John Williams E.T.
MCA MCAD11494 / MCLD19021

1985 **Jerry Goldsmith** Legend.
Silva Screen FILMCD045
Bruce Broughton Silverado.
Intrada MAF7035D

1986 **Ennio Morricone** The Mission.
Virgin CDV2042

1989 **Patrick Doyle** Henry V.
EMI CDC7 49919-2

1992 **Elliot Goldenthal** Alien 3.
MCA MCAD10629

1993 **Randy Edelman** Gettysburg.
Milan 17008-2

1994 **David Arnold** Stargate.
Milan 24901-2

1995 **Michael Kamen**
Don Juan de Marco.
A&M 540 357-2

Editor's pick of 1996

The Editor selects his personal top ten
scores of last year

David Arnold
Independence Day
RCA Victor 09026 68564-2
"Arnold is so obviously captivated by the
movie's spectacle, his music shines with
passion and energy, and the listener
willingly shares the composer's
involvement."

Bruce Broughton
Carried Away
Intrada MAF7068
"This modest little score, a work of
intricate and fragile craftsmanship, will
reward those who seek it out with a few
precious moments of calm."

Patrick Doyle
Hamlet
Sony Classical SK62857
"The composer's previous Branagh
collaborations were impressive, but
Hamlet easily surpasses these
achievements."

Danny Elfman
Mission: Impossible
Point Music 454 525-2
"Elfman's offbeat rhythms and quirky
orchestration are abundantly apparent,
making this a fascinating example of his
distinctively eclectic style, and easily the
most inventive score of 1996."

Jerry Goldsmith
The Ghost and the Darkness
Hollywood HR62089-2
"Goldsmith merges the music of three
cultures in an epic orchestral score, one of
his best in recent times."

James Horner
The Spitfire Grill
Sony Classical SK62776
"An unexpectedly low-key piece of
Americana, this pastoral elegy to small-
town USA is Horner's most understated
and whimsical piece since *Field of
Dreams.*"

Michael Kamen
Jack
Hollywood HR62063-2
"The composer evidently enjoyed this
assignment: *Jack* is a score which tells us
as much about Kamen's own irreverent
sense of fun as the humour on screen."

Joel McNeely
Star Wars: Shadows of the Empire
Varèse Sarabande VSDE5700
"In a brave attempt to amplify the
episodic nature of a film score with the
pictorialism of a tone-poem, McNeely has
strived to portray musically some highly
visual scenarios."

Rachel Portman
Emma
Hollywood MH62069-2
"This screen adaptation of Jane Austen's
greatest – and most subtle – novel required
from its composer rare qualities of insight,
wit and gentle empathy. Rachel Portman's
score meets the challenge adroitly."

John Scott
The North Star
JOS Records JSCD120
"The broadly flowing, nobly heroic main
theme is typical of Scott's music."

Top *Scores* from emi

Dr Zhivago
O.M.P.S.
CDODEON 1

Meet Me In St Louis
O.M.P.S
CDODEON 2

Ziegfeld Follies
O.M.P.S.
CDODEON 3

Easter Parade
O.M.P.S.
CDODEON 4

Showboat
O.M.P.S.
CDODEON 5

North By North West
O.M.P.S.
CDODEON 6

Wizard Of Oz
O.M.P.S.
CDODEON 7

Lullaby Of Broadway
The Best Of Busby Berkeley
At Warner Bros.
CDODEON 8

The Best Of Gene Kelly
CDODEON 9

GiGi
O.M.P.S.
CDODEON 10

For Me And My Gal
O.M.P.S.
CDODEON 12

The Harvey Girls
O.M.P.S.
CDODEON 11

Erich Korngold
The Warner Bros Years
CDODEON 13

Singin' In The Rain
O.M.P.S.
CDODEON 14

Blow - Up
O.S.T.
CDODEON 15 / ODEON 15

Brigadoon
O.S.T.
CDODEON 16

Seven Brides For Seven Brothers
O.S.T.
CDODEON 17

Ben-Hur
O.S.T
CDODEON 18

The Band Wagon
O.S.T
CDODEON 19

An American In Paris
O.S.T.
CDODEON 20

That's Entertainment
The Best Of The MGM Musicals
CDODEON 21

Judy Garland
Collectors Gems From MGM
CDODEON 22

Kismet
O.S.T.
CDODEON 23

Al Jolson
Let Me Sing I'm Happy:
Al Jolson At Warner Bros.
CDODEON 24

Kiss Me Kate
O.S.T.
CDODEON 25

2001: A Space Odyssey
O.S.T.
CDODEON 28

Zabriskie Point
O.S.T.
CDP 7942172

Once you've experienced
Hi-Fi Home Cinema,
you won't settle for anything less

Over the years, we've all got used to better and better sound in the cinema. Just as, over the years, we've all got used to better hi-fi sound in the home.

So it's rather surprising to find that most home cinema systems, rather than displaying the best of both worlds, are something of a compromise.

Here at Arcam, our standards have always been higher than most. And whilst we found that home cinema systems always pack a punch, they lack the kind of finesse we'd expect from a really good hi-fi system.

As Britain's leading manufacturer of hi-fi separates, we therefore set our engineers the task of creating a home cinema system that delivered true hi-fi quality sound. We asked them to design a system which could deliver an Arnold Schwarzenegger punch, yet display the deftness of touch of Yehudi Menuhin. One which could throw you into the front line of battle just as easily as it could seat you into the front row of an intimate solo violin performance. Our patience was rewarded when they revealed the fruit of their labours... Hi-Fi Home Cinema.

Incorporating the latest four channel Dolby Pro Logic decoding circuitry, Arcam Hi-Fi Home Cinema gives you astonishingly realistic cinema surround sound. In addition to left and right channels, a powerful centre channel amplifier ensures you hear crystal clear dialogue located close to the viewing screen, irrespective of where you are seated. The surround channel incorporates variable time delay to optimise different room layouts and independent amplifiers to drive each rear speaker.

So now you don't ever have to compromise between hi-fi sound and home cinema sound. Whether it's the latest action movie or listening to a classical concert, with Arcam Hi-Fi Home Cinema you're always guaranteed the best seat in the house.

H I · F I   H O M E   C I N E M A

Arcam, Pembroke Avenue, Waterbeach, Cambridge CB5 9PB, England.
Telephone: (01223) 203203 (24 hours). Fax: (01223) 863384. e-mail custserv@arcam.co.uk

An Introduction to Home Cinema

by **Keith Howard**

Cinema is primarily a visual art, but not exclusively. Ever since the arrival of the 'talkies' in the late 1920s, sound has been a vital adjunct to the image on the screen. In fact, some of the most important developments in sound reproduction – stereo, for example – were originally conceived with film in mind, and deployed first in cinema auditoria. Today the major studios expend considerable time and effort on the recording and mixing of soundtracks, which are valued as an integral part of the complete movie experience. Home cinema's *raison d'être* is to reproduce this experience within people's own four walls; sound as well as vision. In fact it is the audio component – particularly multi-channel surround sound – which effectively defines home cinema, and distances it from simply watching a film on television.

The roots of home cinema lie in the mid-1970s with Dr Ray Dolby of Dolby Laboratories Inc. Dolby had by that time already made his name in the professional audio arena with his Dolby A-type noise reduction system, and with increasing fitment of the simpler Dolby B-type to high-quality cassette decks was well on the way to becoming a household name too. Cinema sound of the time was in the doldrums: although two-channel stereo soundtracks, often of good inherent sound quality, had been standard in the film industry for many years, cinema auditoria all too often dispensed them in screechy mono, with a high level of hiss generated by the optical soundtrack itself. Dolby recognized that his noise reduction technology could substantially improve matters, but also saw that there was a further advance waiting to be made. It was time film sound took the leap beyond stereo.

This was the era of quadraphonics in the hi-fi industry, with surround sound apparently poised to make multi-channel reproduction *de rigueur* in the modern home. If surround sound was to replace stereo in domestic audio systems – although in the event the presence of too many competing, incompatible and generally poorly conceived quadraphonic systems was eventually to scupper that development – Dolby reasoned that the same technology should also be present in the cinema. So he conceived Dolby Stereo: an integrated process of recording and reproducing film sound which combined noise reduction with surround sound to offer film makers an unprecedented combination of audio quality and versatility. Take-up of Dolby Stereo was gradual at first, but blockbusters like *Star Wars* (1977) and its sequels, which deployed the surround sound element to startling effect, sealed its success. Soon every major film release carried the double-D Dolby logo in its credits, marking a new era in cinema sound. Meanwhile an increasing number of cinema proprietors installed Dolby Stereo processors and extra loudspeakers in their auditoria so as to exploit this new potential.

At this juncture the idea of recreating cinema surround sound in the home wasn't even a twinkle in some visionary's eye. But during the mid-1980s it dawned on a few movers and shakers in the audio industry that the soundtracks on new film video tape and LaserDisc releases carried, like the cinema prints, a Dolby-encoded soundtrack. Dolby Stereo was conceived from the outset to be stereo compatible, so that film prints would reproduce satisfactorily in cinemas which had yet to install the decoding hardware.

Consequently there was no need for the film studios to create a bespoke soundtrack for domestic video media: the Dolby original would reproduce just fine in mono or stereo. To tap this serendipitous surround sound potential, a handful of hi-fi manufacturers began selling Dolby Stereo decoders for the home. Originally, to make them as inexpensive as possible, these lacked the sophisticated image-steering logic circuits of professional decoders, and were referred to as Dolby Surround decoders in order to distinguish them. Later, once the market potential for home cinema had been demonstrated, affordable integrated circuit 'chips' capable of full-house decoding were developed and thus Dolby Surround Pro-Logic came into being. (Though the names differ, Dolby Stereo and Dolby Surround Pro-Logic are essentially one and the same.) Today plain Dolby Surround decoders have been thoroughly supplanted by Pro-Logic types in almost every area of the home cinema market.

A Pro-Logic domestic decoder, like its professional cousin, generates four audio channels from the two encoded channels presented to it, which are normally reproduced over five loudspeakers distributed in front of and behind the listener. There are three front channels – left, centre and right – each of which usually earns its own loudspeaker, and a single surround channel for the rear, which is generally reproduced over a pair of loudspeakers in order to achieve a more diffuse surround sound effect. All three front channels carry a full audio bandwidth (nominally 20Hz to 20kHz) whereas the surround channel is band-limited to 7kHz. The role of the centre channel is to 'lock' dialogue to the screen across a wider listening area than two-channel stereo could provide, for which reason the centre loudspeaker has to be positioned close to the picture screen. As televisions are sensitive to external magnetic fields, this means that the centre loudspeaker must be magnetically screened. Often the left- and right-channel loudspeakers in a dedicated home cinema set-up will be screened too, though this is not essential if they are well spaced from the television tube. Though it is possible to mimic the presence of a centre channel using just the left and right loudspeakers – a common ploy in lesser home cinema systems – the result is not always as effective, particularly over a large listening area.

Multiple loudspeakers make a substantial impact on room aesthetics, so in many Pro-Logic systems the loudspeakers are made as small as possible to minimize their visual intrusion. This inevitably tends to limit their bass capability, but the consequent lack of low frequency extension and power can be compensated by adding a sub-

Typical Dolby Surround Pro-Logic layout with front left, centre and right loudspeakers plus a rear surround pair. The magnetically shielded centre channel loudspeaker is positioned as closely as possible to the television; the subwoofer is an optional feature.

woofer – a dedicated low-frequency loudspeaker whose positioning is generally not critical, so it can be placed wherever is convenient. Such a set-up is commonly referred to as a 'sat-sub' or 'sub-sat' system, comprising subwoofer and 'satellite' loudspeakers.

Various companies external to Dolby Labs have introduced developments on the back of Pro-Logic, ostensibly to add operational features and/or to compensate for the fact that listening conditions in the home do not exactly mimic those in a film theatre. Of these the most significant is Home THX developed by Lucasfilm – the company founded by *Star Wars* director George Lucas. Lucasfilm makes no home cinema hardware itself, but it does license equipment which meets its extended Pro-Logic specification. THX stands for Tomlinson Holman's eXperiment, Tom Holman of the University of California being the man hired by Lucas to investigate ways to improve Pro-Logic sound reproduction in the home. In the course of this work, Holman developed various enhancements of the Pro-Logic system which are incorporated in all THX-accredited home cinema products. The decoder itself has three additional circuit elements, designed to take into account certain characteristics of human hearing and the disparity in acoustics and system configuration between a cinema auditorium and the home. A fifth output channel is also provided carrying low-bass signals for a subwoofer. Elsewhere the principal changes are to loudspeaker directivity and positioning.

The first of the additional signal processing elements appended to a THX

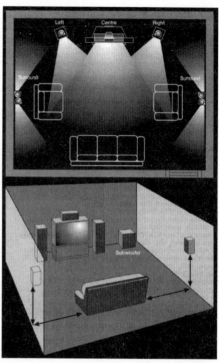

Typical Home THX configuration. Again there are five main loudspeakers but the two surround units have a dipole radiation pattern to improve diffusion, and are positioned roughly level with the listening position. A subwoofer is a standard feature.

decoder is called 're-equalization'. Because film soundtracks are intended for playback in large cinema auditoria where the seating and audience provide significant high frequency absorption, they tend to sound too bright and hissy if reproduced 'flat' in a domestic listening room. To counter this and restore the intended tonal balance, the re-equalization circuit applies a mild treble de-emphasis to trim back high frequency output.

In order both to provide the necessary audience coverage and to diffuse the sound reaching the listener from behind, the rear surround channel in film theatres is usually reproduced over a large number of loudspeakers, dispersed widely around the auditorium. In a home cinema installation, by contrast, the surround channel is usually reproduced by just two loudspeakers, so the element of diffusion is lacking. As a result the contribution of the surround channel is sometimes distractingly obvious. Within conventional Pro-Logic systems this problem is often addressed by pointing the surround loudspeakers away from the listener, sometimes up at the ceiling or into the room corners. Home THX provides a more elegant solution by means of a 'decorrelation' circuit which generates two, uncorrelated surround outputs from the single Dolby Stereo surround channel.

The last THX decoder addition is a 'timbre matching' circuit, the role of which is to prevent changes in perceived tonal balance as virtual sound sources move from a focused position within the forward sound field to a defocused position behind the listener, or vice-versa. The dedicated subwoofer channel actually achieves nothing more than might be differently implemented in a conventional Pro-Logic system, but at least it emphasizes the fact that many modern film sound effects rely on substantial low frequency content for their full impact.

In the course of his research, Holman additionally identified the significance of loudspeaker directivity – i.e. how the loudspeakers distribute sound off their principal listening axes. For the three front channels, wide horizontal directivity proved advantageous to provide the widest possible listening area, coupled with narrow vertical directivity to minimize the effect of floor and ceiling reflections on intelligibility. These requirements are formally specified within the Home THX standard. For surround loudspeakers, though, the requirements are very different, the most important factor in this case being effective diffusion of the surround channel information, as already described. To achieve this, THX surround loudspeakers are configured as dipole sources which radiate equally but in antiphase to the front and back, and have an output 'null' to their sides. Positioning the surround loudspeakers either side of the listening position places the listeners in this output null, so that they hear little or nothing from the loudspeakers directly. The sound has to be reflected from room boundaries first, thereby guaranteeing effective diffusion.

These comprehensive directivity requirements represent the most controversial aspect of Home THX. Intended specifically to improve the replay of film soundtracks, they are not equally well suited to music reproduction, whether in stereo or surround sound. As a result a number of hi-fi manufacturers who have incorporated the THX enhancements in their decoders have chosen not to follow through and manufacture THX-compliant loudspeakers, because they believe most of the home cinema systems they sell will be used in a dual role: to replay music as well as film soundtracks.

New developments

Though Dolby Pro-Logic remains the pre-eminent home cinema surround sound standard, not least because there is such a large back-catalogue of films with Dolby Stereo soundtracks, film sound has not stood still. There is now an entirely new cinema sound technology – also conceived by Dolby – which is gradually advancing the film industry, somewhat belatedly, into the realm of digital audio.

The new technology began life in the cinema as Dolby SRD, the D standing for 'digital' and the 'SR' for 'Spectral Recording' – a hark back to Dolby Stereo which, after starting out with A-type noise reduction, was in due course updated to incorporate SR, Dolby's latest and finest professional analogue noise reduction technology. Latterly Dolby has settled instead on the name Dolby Digital to describe both the professional and domestic variants of its new system, although this decision came rather too late to prevent the latter being widely referred to as either AC3 or 5.1-channel digital. Strictly, Dolby Digital is the name of the complete system, AC3 the name of the multi-channel digital encoding technology which underpins it, and 5.1-channel a generic description of digital surround sound technologies of this type, of which there are other examples than Dolby's. However, the terms tend to be used more or less interchangeably.

We all know from Compact Disc that digital audio is capable of providing improved sound quality in respect of distortion, noise and pitch stability – reasons enough for it to be embraced by the film industry. But there are other motivations for taking a step beyond Dolby Stereo, not least the limitations inherent in how its four audio channels are encoded. Dolby Stereo's quadraphonic ancestry was remarked on earlier. In a manner similar to the QS and SQ quad systems, it uses a matrixing technique to combine the four source channels – left, centre, right and surround – into two stereo-compatible channels on the film soundtrack. The decoder does its best to restore the four channels on playback but cannot separate them completely, any more than you could the gin from a martini. Once they have been matrixed in two channels, only a partial separation is possible. So the channels can never be reconstituted as the independent, 'discrete' entities they began as: in fact there are strict mathematical limitations on the channel separation that can be achieved. Dolby Stereo's image steering logic circuits were developed to minimize the consequences of this and ensure that the most important (loudest) sounds always emerge from the front centre channel, nearest to the picture screen. But this processing can only achieve so much, and renders Dolby Stereo a less than an ideal candidate for more general surround sound applications such as music recording. The solitary surround channel is an impediment here too since it prevents the formation of a focused virtual image behind the listener.

Dolby Digital entirely circumvents these old inherent limitations of Dolby Stereo. Its five full-bandwidth channels – left, centre and right front channels as before, plus two (stereo) surround channels – are truly discrete, as is the bandwidth-limited subwoofer channel which accounts for the remaining 0.1 channel. This not only makes Dolby Digital a superior cinema sound system: it also ensures it is much better suited to surround sound music recording. The one fly in the ointment here is that Dolby Digital's AC3 encoding – in order to accommodate all 5.1 channels in a digital data stream of half the capacity used by just one channel of CD sound – applies so-called lossy data compression. In plain

English, it throws away some of the signal – albeit those components it calculates would be inaudible anyway. This presumption is so alien to the traditional concept of high fidelity that, despite the remarkable results achieved, the hi-fi industry generally has indicated a preference for an alternative multi-channel standard of its own where the original signal is preserved intact. How much music recording will actually be performed in Dolby Digital therefore remains to be seen.

At the time of writing (January 1997) the only video carrier capable of offering Dolby Digital sound is NTSC (American) LaserDisc – there is insufficient space within the PAL equivalent to squeeze the AC3 soundtrack. However, this situation is due to change with the arrival of DVD (Digital Video/Versatile Disc), a CD-sized video medium – not to be confused with Video CD – which will carry both superior digital pictures and multi-channel digital audio. European DVDs are specified to use the MPEG Audio encoding system for their soundtrack – a broadly similar alternative to Dolby Digital (which will be used on US DVD releases). However, room exists on PAL DVDs for an AC3 data stream too, so which multi-channel digital audio technology will be favoured in practice is not certain. Of course, Dolby Digital and MPEG Audio require an entirely different breed of decoder to Dolby Stereo.

System configurations

The simplest way to create a Dolby Pro-Logic home cinema system is to buy a television set with on-board Pro-Logic decoding and amplification, and add the requisite satellite loudspeakers if they are not provided. This is generally the cheapest, neatest approach, but unsurprisingly does not exploit the full quality potential of surround sound. It also suffers the disadvantage of not being inherently upgradable – a costly limitation should you be bitten by the home cinema bug and want to make improvements.

Much superior results can be achieved by buying a Dolby Stereo-capable packaged audio system, or better still by extending a separates stereo hi-fi system. This can be done by adding extra loudspeakers and either an AV amplifier with on-board decoder circuitry, or a separate Dolby decoder and, if not incorporated, additional amplification. This separates route, as well as offering the ultimate sound quality potential, also enjoys the twin advantages of being the most versatile and readily upgradable. With a specialist retailer to guide you, you can assemble a separates home cinema system to fit your taste and pocket which will comfortably outperform any pre-packaged alternative.

Even if you don't watch films on video tape, LaserDisc or Video CD, a home cinema system is still worth considering because of the many broadcast films which have Dolby Stereo soundtracks, and the increasing number of television programmes which are recorded in Dolby Stereo. A wide choice of home cinema products is now available, across a broad range of prices – including AV amplifiers and decoders from Arcam, the well respected British hi-fi manufacturer that is the sponsor of this guide. Once you have heard hi-fi home cinema reproduced over a quality separates system, you will find it hard to live without – and joining the elite needn't cost silly money.

CDs recorded in Dolby Surround

Listing supplied by Dolby Laboratories

Arcam film classics

The following recordings are a personal selection by Arcam staff. We feel they represent a good section of well recorded and involving sountracks which will grace any collection

Luis Bacalov
Il Postino
CAM COS700-083 / Hollywood HW62029-2

John Corigliano
Altered States
RCA 3983-2
Hans Erdmann Nosferatu.
RCA 09026 68143-2

Erich Wolfgang Korngold
The Sea Hawk – Classic Film Scores
RCA 7890-2

Henry Mancini
Mancini in Surround
RCA RD60471

Sergei Prokofiev
Alexander Nevsky
RCA 09026 61926-2

Sergei Prokofiev
Ivan the Terrible
RCA 09026 61954-2

David Raksin
Laura, Forever Amber
The Bad and the Beautiful
RCA GD81490

Max Steiner
Adventures of Mark Twain
Erich Wolfgang Korngold
The Prince and the Pauper
RCA 09026 62660-2

Max Steiner
Gone With the Wind
RCA GD80452

Max Steiner
Now, Voyager – Classic Film Scores
RCA GD80136

Dimitri Tiomkin
Lost Horizon – Classic Film Scores
RCA GD81669

Franz Waxman
Sayonara etc
RCA 09026 62657-2

Franz Waxman
Sunset Boulevard – Classic Film Scores
RCA GD80708

Collections
Wanted Dead or Alive
CAM CVS900-020

David Arnold
Independance Day
(1996)

Patrick Doyle
Hamlet
(1996)

Jerry Goldsmith
The Omen
(1976)

Maurice Jarre
Lawrence of Arabia
(1962)

Jerome Moross
The Big Country
(1958)

Ennio Morricone
The Mission
(1986)

Alex North
A Streetcar Named Desire
(1951)

Leonard Rosenman
East of Eden
(1955)

Alan Silvestri
Forrest Gump
(1994)

John Williams
Star Wars trilogy
(1977, 1980, 1983)

The reviews

Richard Addinsell

1904-1977 England

Hailing originally from Oxford, Richard Addinsell studied at the Royal College of Music. He contributed music for André Charlot's theatrical revues, and in 1929, in collaboration with Clemence Dane who later co-scripted his first film, supplied incidental music for the Old Vic production of *Adam's Opera*. After a period of study in Europe, Addinsell returned to England in 1932 and scored the stage version of *Alice in Wonderland* (also with Dane), whose musical director was Muir Mathieson. Addinsell's career in films began with a brief stint as a contract composer for RKO in Hollywood; he was to write some 50 film scores in all, the first one being *The Amateur Gentleman* in 1936. Others included *Gaslight* (1940), *Love on the Dole* (1941), *Blithe Spirit* (1945), *The Passionate Friends* (1948) and *Scrooge* (1951), as well as *Dangerous Moonlight* (1941) for which he wrote the *Warsaw Concerto*. His song "I Found a Dream" from *The Prince and the Showgirl* (1957) was sung by Marilyn Monroe. Addinsell continued to write for the theatre, and was accompanist and co-composer for Joyce Grenfell. His last film score was *Life at the Top* in 1965.

Film Music BBC Concert Orchestra / Kenneth Alwyn.
    Marco Polo Ⓟ 8 223732 (68 minutes: DDD). Recorded 1994.
    Goodbye, Mr Chips (1939). The Prince and the Showgirl (1957). Tom Brown's Schooldays (1951). Fire Over England (1937). A Tale of Two Cities (1958) plus Invitation Waltz, The Smokey Mountains Concerto, The Isle of Apples, Tune in G, Festival, Journey to Romance.

The *Warsaw Concerto*, that glorious and sensationally popular pastiche of Rachmaninov from *Dangerous Moonlight*, may well be forever engraved on Addinsell's epitaph, but as this delightful CD makes clear, it is not a totally accurate reflection of the composer's true style. Effortlessly graceful and far less grandiose, much of the lilting material here was written for the stage or concert hall, though it is Addinsell's film music that lingers in the memory, his melodic gifts particularly well suited to the warm sentimentality of *Goodbye, Mr Chips*, one of his finest scores for which he provided a convincing school song, and *The Prince and the Showgirl*, an affectionate valentine to the Edwardian era. *Fire Over England* may lack the swashbuckling verve of Korngold but is still a splendidly colourful portrait of Elizabethan England, whilst the romantic sweep of *Tom Brown's Schooldays* and *A Tale of Two Cities* emphasize further this composer's impeccable and often under-valued craftmanship. **RS**

William Alwyn

1905-1985 England

Born in Northampton, William Alwyn studied at the Royal Academy of Music, where he was appointed professor of composition aged 21. His *Five Preludes for Orchestra* was premièred at the Proms in 1927. He composed five symphonies, two operas and many other works. A founder member of the Composers' Guild of Great Britain, Alwyn was awarded the CBE in 1978. His numerous film credits include *The Winslow Boy* (1948), *The Card* (1952), *A Night to Remember* (1958), *Carve Her Name with Pride* (1958) and *Swiss Family Robinson* (1960).

Film Music London Symphony Orchestra / Richard Hickox.
    Chandos Ⓟ CHAN9243 (72 minutes: DDD). Recorded 1993.
    Odd Man Out (1946). The History of Mr Polly (1949). The Fallen Idol (1948). The Rake's Progress (1945).

The music presented here, passionately and convincingly performed, demonstrates how a fine composer can write memorable, self-sufficient music over the whole emotional range, without compromising his strongly individual style. Recorded with an intensity and brilliance of orchestral balance and colour, Christopher Palmer's arrangements from the remaining piano sketches (some of the original scores having been destroyed in a clear-out at Pinewood Studios; although *The Fallen Idol* is completely original) allow us to enjoy examples of a major part of Alwyn's *oeuvre* (he wrote over 200 film scores). Chandos are to be commended on extending their recording of the symphonic, choral and chamber works of this wonderful composer to include these powerful examples – the *Finale* of the *Odd Man Out* suite is a fine symphonic movement which builds with impressive sustained intensity, whilst the *Mr Polly* suite shows the lighter side, a deft touch of pantomime and tongue-in-cheek, chipper vivacity. "The Panic and Flight" from *The Fallen Idol* has an urgent terror, superbly scored and structured; and the disc ends with the disarming catchiness of the rumba and calypso from *The Rake's Progress* which accompanied Rex Harrison in exile. A superb disc in every way. **CT**

David Arnold

b.1962 England

A native of Luton in Bedfordshire, David Arnold grew up on a diet of Hollywood epics and James Bond movies that decisively shaped his future as a film composer. At school he began playing recorder, moved on to clarinet and then took up the guitar. He played in orchestras and military bands, but despite some training in musical theory he acquired the greater part of his musical education playing in rock bands. Collaborating with aspiring director Danny Cannon, Arnold began his film music career scoring many of his friend's student pictures, when Cannon attended the National Film and Television School, and the composer learned a broad range of film-making techniques scoring films for other students – over 20 in less than two years – although he was never officially a student at the school (after *Stargate* he was, however, offered an honorary degree). Arnold's big break came when *Stargate* director Roland Emmerich heard his score for Cannon's first feature film, *The Young Americans* (1993). His second collaboration with Emmerich and writer/producer Dean Devlin, *Independence Day*, turned out to be the biggest grossing movie of 1996, with the soundtrack album entering the CIN classical chart at number two and receiving a Grammy Award nomination. His next Emmerich/Devlin project will be *Godzilla*. He has also co-written songs for, among others, Björk – a top ten hit with "Play Dead" from *The Young Americans* – and Shara Nelson, and produced several albums. He is the creative force behind the new James Bond song album to be released in 1997, arranging and producing all the music, which features artists such as Pulp, Iggy Pop and Shara Nelson. Before scoring a picture, Arnold likes to achieve an understanding of every aspect of the film's production through discussions with the creative personnel involved.

New review   ARCAM

Independence Day (1996) **Original Soundtrack / Nicholas Dodd**.
   RCA Victor Ⓟ 09026 68564-2 (51 minutes: DDD).

Broiling and churning overhead like storm clouds heavy with imminent rain, this thunderous score must be the most grandiose film music since, well, Arnold's previous collaboration with Dean Devlin and Roland Emmerich, *Stargate*. Whilst we reflect on the strange whim of fate that chose a young and almost unknown British film composer to be the saviour of the Hollywood epic, it is worth reminding ourselves that Arnold's music possesses in abundance a quality lacking in too many other scores by more experienced hands: sincerity. Arnold is so obviously captivated by the movie's spectacle, his music shines with passion and energy, and the listener willingly shares the composer's involvement. The devices he uses may be familiar, he may not be much of an innovator, but through his music he communicates his own enthusiasm and enjoyment. Here, the arrival of the aliens is portrayed with suitably portentous grandeur, the thrilling aerial dogfights are handled like an old Second World War movie, with bright major-key flourishes irresistibly reminiscent of Ron Goodwin and *633 Squadron* in particular, whilst his trumpet-led patriotic theme is a stirring example of Americana. By no means all the music heard in the movie, the album lacks some of the gentler pieces – for example the death of the First Lady – that would have prevented it from seeming a little too top heavy at times. One nice little detail to look out for, however, is the staccato string motif in "International Code" imitating the rhythm of a morse code message. Unlike *Stargate*, this disc was recorded in America, and the sparkling precision of the Sinfonia of London – especially their razor-sharp brass – and the clarity of the earlier recording at London's Air Studios is sadly absent.   **MW**

Last of the Dogmen (1995) **Original Soundtrack**, with the **London Symphony Orchestra / Nicholas Dodd**.
   EastWest Ⓟ 0630-11991-2 (36 minutes: DDD).

Last of the Dogmen is a minor work by this composer's standards, but it is unadulterated Arnold nevertheless: dark, pulsing basses and mellow, mid-range strings; the balletic interplay of woodwinds; the ominous growl of trombones, and the bright trumpet cutting through thick brass textures are all familiar. But most of all it is the richness, the sense of real depth to the orchestration – not so much actual counterpoint, rather gorgeously multi-layered harmonies – that is key to his style, what gives Arnold's scores the luxurious feel of film music's Golden Age. This is essentially a monothematic score: but what a theme! Warm like glowing coals in a hearth after the blaze has subsided; broad like the intoxicating vista from the summit of a mountain, the breathtaking reward of a hard day's climb. The appearance of this quintessentially romantic melody is punctuated by several powerful episodes which form a series of almost overwhelming climaxes. Here lies the album's only weakness: with over a third of the cues running for less than two minutes it has a tendency to play like a succession of grand emotional crescendos (at the end of the ravishing "Leaving Forever", for example, it is difficult to believe that there are in fact two more tracks left to go). Nevertheless, this is a score full of heartwarming radiance, clad in Arnold's luxuriant harmonic colours. The LSO – with their lush, uniform string sound – impart a sense of relaxed ease to the music.   **MW**

Stargate (1994) **Original Soundtrack**, with the **Chameleon Arts Chorus; Sinfonia of London /
Nicholas Dodd**.
Milan Ⓔ 24901-2 (65 minutes: DDD).

The impressive on-screen grandeur of *Stargate* is due in no small part to David Arnold's music.
Conceived on a grand scale, Arnold and orchestrator Nicholas Dodd succeeded in their attempt
to recreate that old-fashioned epic quality, which is at once so familiar, and so rarely achieved. In
an era when no self-respecting action/adventure movie is complete without splashing synthesizer
figures and crashing electronic percussion, Arnold's conscious homage to a Golden Age of big
orchestral writing is a bold move indeed. Given the film's mixture of Egyptology and Sci-Fi, it is
perhaps unsurprising that the composer draws heavily for inspiration on grand works like
Lawrence of Arabia, *Star Wars* and *Close Encounters* (with a hint of Ron Goodwin thrown in
along the way). The recording in the spacious acoustic of London's Air Studios contributes
greatly to the music's expansive feel. The music is colourful, bold in scope, and packed full of
memorable themes, making it both an auspicious Hollywood début for a talented young English
composer, and an unreserved recommendation for all those who like their music in Cecil B.
DeMille proportions.   **MW**

Also available:
The Young Americans (1993) Island 518 472-2 [mostly pop songs]

Sir Malcolm Arnold
b. 1921 England

Sir Malcolm Arnold studied trumpet, conducting and composition at the Royal College of
Music. Between 1942-1948 he was principal trumpet with the London Philharmonic Orchestra.
Film music accounts for only a small portion of his *oeuvre*, which also includes eight
symphonies, numerous concertos, string quartets and other works. Arnold's first score was
written for a documentary, *Avalanche Patrol* (1947) directed by Jack Swain. His most famous
film work was for David Lean: *The Sound Barrier* (1952), *Hobson's Choice* (1954), and the
Academy Award-winning *The Bridge on the River Kwai* (1957). His other scores include *You
Know What Sailors Are* (1953), *I am a Camera* (1955), *Dunkirk* (1958), *The Inn of the Sixth
Happiness* (1958), four *St Trinian's* films (1954-66), *Whistle Down the Wind* (1961) and *The
Heroes of Telemark* (1965). Arnold's decision not to score certain films has had important
repercussions for other composers: he turned down *Lawrence of Arabia* (subsequently taken up
by Maurice Jarre), and *The Blue Max* (Jerry Goldsmith). In addition, Arnold orchestrated and
conducted Walton's mostly-rejected *Battle of Britain* (1969) score.

The Bridge on the River Kwai (1957) **Original Soundtrack**, with the **Royal Philharmonic
Orchestra / Sir Malcolm Arnold**.
Columbia mono Ⓜ CK66131 (50 minutes: ADD). Includes *Colonel Bogey* (Alford), *I Give
My Heart To No One But You* (Arnold/Shand) and *The River Kwai March/Colonel Bogey*
(Arnold/Alford).

The uniquely British stiff upper lip is nowhere better exemplified than by the now immortal
whistled rendition of *Colonel Bogey*, accompanied only by the steady beat of marching feet.
Kenneth Alford's march, written in 1914 but resurrected for this film, is however only one
element of this score. Arnold's own "River Kwai March" is just as full of old-fashioned British
pluck; when it suddenly bursts into life for the first time in "Nicholson's Victory", the urge to
stand and salute is almost irresistible. Both marches are displayed to advantage in the superior
'pop' arrangement performed by Mitch Miller and His Orchestra, in which Arnold's "River
Kwai" is cleverly played in counterpoint to *Colonel Bogey*. Much of the remainder of Arnold's
score is built upon constantly shifting foundations, with the tense drama of the music
enhanced by a very dry mono recording. There is no smooth Hollywood-style sentimentality
here: spiky rhythms and jagged orchestral flourishes impart a sharply realistic – almost
noir-ish – edge.   **MW**

Film Music London Symphony Orchestra / Richard Hickox.
Chandos Ⓔ CHAN9100 (78 minutes: DDD). Recorded 1992.
The Bridge on the River Kwai (1957). Whistle Down the Wind (1961). The Sound Barrier
(1952). Hobson's Choice (1954). The Inn of the Sixth Happiness (1958).

Arnold's larger-than-life scoring and ebullient humour were tailor-made for the cinema, but
despite an extensive output this is the only CD to concentrate on his film work. *The Bridge on the*

River Kwai, Arnold's busy Oscar-winner written in just ten days, is chiefly remembered for giving Kenneth Alford's then 43 year-old *Colonel Bogey* a whole new lease of life, but though used to ironic effect on the soundtrack as a counter-melody to Arnold's own "River Kwai March", a bizarre copyright restriction means that the two pieces can now only be performed separately. On a more intimate scale is the florid, music-hall rumbustiousness of *Hobson's Choice*, in which an inebriated tuba and trombone bring to life the portly, stubborn character of Henry Hobson; and one of Arnold's own favourites, the enchanting *Whistle Down the Wind*, with its beguiling main theme and piquant orchestration. *The Sound Barrier Rhapsody*, Op. 38 reworks his soaring themes from the 1952 film into a cogent eight-minute concert piece, whilst *The Inn of the Sixth Happiness*, one of Arnold's most openly romantic scores (in which he uses, *à la Bridge*, the children's nursery rhyme "This Old Man" to counterpoint his own heroic main theme), brings this superb disc to a triumphant conclusion. **RS**

Georges Auric

1899-1983 France

When in 1930 Georges Auric wrote his first film score for Jean Cocteau's *Le Sang d'un Poète* he had known the poet, artist, novelist and director since his student years in Paris. Auric had been a member of Les Six, an informal group of French composers, also including Arthur Honegger, who had attempted to define a new style of French music under the aesthetic guidance of Cocteau. Cocteau saw the medium of film as a means of expanding his artistic vision, so when he came to direct his first feature it was natural that he should collaborate with Auric. They later worked together on *La Belle et la Bête* (1946), *L'Aigle à Deux Têtes* (1947), *Les Parents Terribles* (1948), *Orphée* (1949) and *Le Testament d'Orphée* (1959). In addition to his work with Cocteau, Auric provided music for many French, American and British films, including the Ealing comedies *Passport to Pimlico* (1949), *The Lavender Hill Mob* (1951) and *The Titfield Thunderbolt* (1952) as well as William Wyler's *Roman Holiday* (1953). His music for the theatre included numerous ballet scores, many of which were created for Diaghilev's ballet troupe, incidental music and one opera, *Sous le Masque* (1927). A disc of music from the Ealing films, featuring several of Auric's scores performed by the Royal Ballet Sinfonia, has been recorded by Silva Screen.

New review
La Belle et la Bête (1946) **Axios; Moscow Symphony Orchestra / Adriano**.
  Marco Polo Ⓟ 8 223765 (62 minutes: DDD) Recorded 1994.
Le Testament d'Orphée (1959) **Orphée** (1949) **La Belle et la Bête** (1946) **L'Aigle à Deux Têtes** (1947) **Original Soundtracks**, with dialogue.
  Auvidis Travelling mono Ⓟ K1506 (52 minutes: ADD).

Georges Auric was one of the finest composers ever to work in film. His commissions were international and varied – from Ealing comedies to Hollywood weepies – but Auric's evidently classical style distinguished all the films he worked on. His most enduring and possibly most rewarding collaborations were with the poet/film maker Jean Cocteau. Perhaps the crowning achievement for both of them was their telling of the tale of *Beauty and the Beast*. Cocteau's imaginative and innovative film prompted from Auric one of film music's masterworks, a massive score for orchestra and chorus that for some inexplicable reason has never been recorded or made available before now. Auric's music never loses its grip for a full 60 minutes; this reviewer was spellbound by the new Adriano performance – once the disc was playing it became inevitable to listen through to the end – a magical journey through a haunting netherworld, the orchestral pallete awash with brilliantly diverse hues, Auric's music ranging from delicate diminutive textures to swirling, storm-tossed eddies to vibrant fanfares. Period, mystery, love ... and death, are all present in Auric's masterly scoring. This new digital recording, set in a suitably huge acoustic, is thrilling and memorable, alive with atmosphere and true to Auric's intentions. A perfect reading of one of the truly great film scores.

Of companion interest is the issue on compact disc of extracts from the original soundtracks, inclusive of dialogue and sound effects, of the four Cocteau films scored by Auric. The emphasis is on the music but there are fairly lengthy dialogue sequences to contend with – fine if you understand French, but something of a distraction otherwise, although the dialogue is never less than mellifluous. The rather hoary thin sound of the original *La Belle et la Bête* makes one even more thankful for the new Adriano version, but even the aged sonics cannot dim the true lustre of the music. Throughout the album Auric's music – reflective, raucous, contemplative, celebratory – shines through, although in the final analysis this album can only be recommended for truly die-hard fans of the composer or completists. **DW**

Mark Ayres

b. 1960 England

London-born Mark Ayres spent his childhood in Tunbridge Wells. He studied Music and Electronics at Keele University where he was taught by Peter Dickinson, Roger Marsh and Tim Souster. After working for five years as a sound engineer on Breakfast TV, he became a freelance composer in 1984. His television credits include *Rockliffe's Babies* (1987), *Casualty* (1990) and three full-length scores for the final season of *Doctor Who* (1988-9). His association with the Doctor has continued on a number of documentaries and the direct-to-video production *Shakedown – Return of the Sontarans* (1994). Aside from television, he has also written music for video and CD-ROM projects. Scoring Scott Mitchell's short film *Seeds* (1993) led to him collaborating with the director again on their first full-length feature film, *The Innocent Sleep*. Mark Ayres also records extensively with Silva Screen, and has featured as performer and arranger on over 50 CDs.

New review

The Innocent Sleep (1995) **Original Soundtrack**, with **Lesley Garrett** (sop); **Chamber Orchestra of London / Nic Raine**.
Silva Screen Ⓕ FILMCD167 (59 minutes: DDD).

Although well known for his electronic scores for such television series as *Doctor Who*, *The Innocent Sleep* was Mark Ayres's first fully orchestral score, and a very capable effort it is too. Its beautiful main theme, "Il Sonno Innocente", performed by the lovely Lesley Garrett, is intended by the composer to act as a lament for the homeless. The text, based on Shakespeare (*Macbeth*), provides appropriate support for the melancholy four-note motif that effectively captures the loneliness and despair of the film's hero. The rest of the score is bleak in nature, with the jagged though never histrionic orchestrations reflecting the gloomy urban landscape of London and the many dangers contained within. Some of Ayres's action writing is rather biting and punctuated, and his suspense music has a chilling edge thanks to some neat sampled sounds from the synthesizers. That gorgeous main theme makes some welcome appearances throughout the score, but the composer is careful not to lessen its impact through repetition. A notable piece from a British composer for a British film. **PP**

Also available:
Doctor Who: The Curse of Fenric (1989) Silva Screen FILMCD087
Doctor Who: Ghost Light (1989) Silva Screen FILMCD133
Doctor Who: The Greatest Show in the Galaxy (1988) Silva Screen FILMCD114
Doctor Who: Myths and Legends (1991) Silva Screen FILMCD088
Doctor Who: Shakedown – Return of the Sontarans (1994) Silva Screen FILMCD718

Luis Enriquez Bacalov

b. 1933 Argentina

Pianist and composer, Luis Bacalov's career in the cinema has included collaborations with directors Federico Fellini, Pier Paolo Pasolini, Ettore Scola, Alberto Lattuada, Sergio Corbucci and Elio Petri. Although born in Buenos Aires he is now an Italian citizen. He began to study music aged five, and became a pupil of Arthur Schnabel. He made a particular study of South American folk music, and worked for Columbian radio and TV, before moving to Italy in 1959 and beginning a career as a film composeer. His first film score was *La Banda del Buco* (1960) and throughout the 1960s and 1970s he was responsible for scoring dozens of Spaghetti Westerns, bringing his own distinctive South American voice to films like Franco Giraldi's *Sugar Colt*, Sergio Corbucci's *Django* (both 1966), Damiano Damiani's *Quien Sabe?* (also 1966 – known in English as *A Bullet for the General*) and Peter Collinson's *Lo Chiamavano Mezzogiorno* (1973 – *The Man Called Noon*). His score for Pasolini's *The Gospel According to St Matthew* (1964) received an Academy Award nomination, but it was not until 1995 that Bacalov won an Oscar for his work on *Il Postino* – for which he also received the Italian Nastro d'Argento and Globo d'Oro Awards, and the BAFTA Award for Best Original Score.

New review

Il Postino (1994) **Original Soundtrack**, with the **Rome Sinfonietta / Luis Bacalov** (pf).
CAM Ⓕ COS700-038 (44 minutes: DDD) / Hollywood Ⓕ HW62029-2 / Polydor Ⓕ 162029-2 (68 minutes: DDD). Includes *Madreselva* (Canaro/Amadori). CAM disc includes *Despierta Ya* (Gensel/Bacalov); Hollywood/Polydor disc also includes readings of Pablo Neruda's poetry.

Every now and then the Academy of Motion Picture Arts and Sciences nominates a score that seems to be at odds with the other choices – and not always for a good reason. At other times the phenomenon turns into a welcome surprise, as it was in 1996 when Luis Bacalov won the coveted statue for Michael Radford's *Il Postino*.

Built upon fact and fiction, *Il Postino* documents the relationship between exiled Chilean poet Pablo Neruda (Philippe Noiret) and Mario Ruoppolo (the late Massimo Troisi), the postman who delivers his mail on a picturesque Italian island. Bacalov's score is a charming work that has been turned into a first-rate CD. Best known for his Italian Western scores, Bacalov has taken the opportunity to shift gears and drive towards a lyrical soundscape. This is essentially a one-theme score, the melody being simultaneously life-affirming and sad. Introduced in "The Postman (Titles)", the theme is performed with emotion by Hector Ulises Passarella on the Bandonéon. A more upbeat interpretation of the theme accompanies the postman's rounds on his "Bicycle". Variations of the theme are heard throughout the score, perhaps most memorably in the violin/piano dialogue between Riccardo Pellegrino and Bacalov in "Trio Version". A *habanera* is used in connection with "Beatrice," the postman's love interest. In this otherwise monothematic score, new material can be found in "Loved by Women". By the time the film reaches its ironic conclusion we come to understand the reason behind the tragic qualities of the main theme.

There are two versions of the *Il Postino* album. The CAM release is a straightforward presentation of the score with the bonus inclusion of a Bacalov-penned song not used in the film. A better choice is the Hollywood/Polydor release. This disc includes all of the score found in the CAM release plus a 29-minute, 15-track "Poetry and Music Suite" in which celebrity admirers of Neruda's art recite their favourite poems along with excerpts from the score. Apparently Julia Roberts heard about the movie and barged into the offices of Miramax co-chairs Harvey and Bob Weinstein armed with six of her Neruda collection. Before long, other Neruda fans like Sting, Madonna, Samuel L. Jackson, and Miranda Richardson became involved. The readings do not come across as a commercial gimmick. They feel like a series of loving interpretations by people who are clearly moved by the poet's visually charged imagery, whose chief subject is love. It's a shame, however, that the booklet notes offer no perspectives about the score or Bacalov. While the story of how the poetry suite came about is interesting, it should have been remembered that the score – which went on to win an Academy Award – is the *raison d'être* for the release. The CAM disc fares somewhat better in this regard, coming with a plot synopsis and a brief word about Bacalov and director Michael Radford. **KM**

Also available:
Il Grande Duello (1972) etc. Preamble PRCD120
Italian Western Scores Varèse Sarabande VCDS7015

see also Collections: **Wanted Dead or Alive**

Burt Bacharach
b. 1928 USA

A prolific and highly successful songwriter, Burt Bacharach was born in Kansas City, Missouri, but grew up in New York where he played in several jazz groups. He studied theory and composition at McGill University and the Music Academy of the West. He became Marlene Dietrich's musical director (1956-1958) and briefly teamed up with lyricist Mack David for the theme song of *The Blob* (1958), which was a Top 40 hit for The Five Blobs. From 1962, Bacharach and his most successful collaborator, lyricist Hal David, wrote several hit songs for Dionne Warwick. Their first film score together was *What's New Pussycat?* (1965) which also gave Tom Jones one of his most famous songs. They won an Academy Award for the song "Raindrops Keep Falling on My Head" from the film *Butch Cassidy and the Sundance Kid* (1969). After parting company with Hal David, Bacharach teamed up with Carole Bayer Sager, whom he married in 1982. Together they won a second Oscar for "Arthur's Theme" from *Arthur* (1981).

Butch Cassidy and the Sundance Kid (1969) Original Soundtrack / Burt Bacharach.
Spectrum ® 551 433-2 (28 minutes: AAD).

File under 'Nostalgia'. This is a work from that limbo period between the fall of Hollywood's monolithic studio system, with its in-house music departments, and the rise of a new era of freelance composers; music from those heady days before the intoxication of flower power brought on an unexpectedly bad hangover. Bacharach's dreamily sunny classic "Raindrops Keep Falling on My Head" ideally captures the lost innocence of that summer of love, and utterly dominates the remainder of the score, such as it is. Pleasantly tuneful, all of this music is written in such a way as to allow the cynical 1990s listener to pretend briefly that it is once again the dawn of the Age of Aquarius. The sweet-toothed sentiment of "Not Goin' Home Anymore", the scat-sung ditty "South American Getaway" and the mock-ragtime "The Old Fun City" all add up to a cheerful period-piece from an era which – strangely – seems more remote than the classically timeless Golden Age of Hollywood. **MW**

Casino Royale (1967) Original Soundtrack / Burt Bacharach.
　　Varèse Sarabande Ⓕ VSD5265 (34 minutes: AAD).

With a string of international pop hits behind him, it was inevitable that Bacharach would soon be courted by a 1960s Hollywood desperately seeking a 'cool' and 'happening' image. Though his career in the movies was brief, the results were always distinctively tuneful: the Oscar-winning *Butch Cassidy and the Sundance Kid* (1969) perhaps being the most famous, thanks largely to the evergreen "Raindrops Keep Falling on My Head". However, no other film score sums up the Bacharach sound or the swinging sixties quite so conveniently as *Casino Royale*. Although this overblown Bond spoof misfired spectacularly at the box office, the score did produce a groovy, stompingly memorable title theme performed by Herb Alpert and the Tijuana Brass, and the simmeringly sensual "The Look of Love", sung by that other icon of the 1960s, Dusty Springfield. The remainder of the score, a succession of wacky instrumentals (exemplified by "Home, James, Don't Spare the Horses", perhaps better known as "Bond Street"), may underline the film's lampooning with the subtlety of a sledge hammer, but it's great fun, especially in stereo that is still wonderfully vibrant. **RS**

Richard Band
b. 1957 USA

Richard Band comes from a movie family. His older brother Charles runs Full Moon, a production company specializing in straight-to-video releases. Father Albert Band worked with John Huston on *The Asphalt Jungle* (1950) and *The Red Badge of Courage* (1951). Richard lived in Italy for 11 years, touring as a flamenco guitarist. Back in the USA he played rock guitar before attending the Los Angeles Music Conservatory. He learnt about the movie business from an early age by visiting sets his father was working on. Band's first score was for *Laserblast* (1978), which was co-written with Joel Goldsmith (son of Jerry). He began a long-standing collaboration with his brother by scoring *The Day Time Ended* (1979), since when he has worked on many Charles Band productions. Band has therefore tended to concentrate on low-budget fantasy/horror flicks – what in pre-video days were known as B-movies.

The Resurrected (1991) Original Soundtrack / Richard Band.
　　Intrada Ⓕ MAF7036D (45 minutes: DDD).

A beefy orchestral score – supplemented by electronics – which delves progressively deeper into turmoil, *The Resurrected* employs all the clichés of the horror genre without sounding derivative. *Glissando*, *tremolo* and *pizzicato* strings, a moaning wordless chorus, repeatedly thudding chords – all the devices are familiar, but Band is inventive enough to produce something that manages to be fresh. The final, dark and desperate cues are the best, with subtle synthesized additions enhancing the sinister mood. The music is constantly shifting and apparently shapeless, deliberately lacking a recognizable theme to hold it together. There is a powerful feeling of mounting unease throughout. Rushing string figures in the penultimate cue ("Mutants") increase the tension. Not even during the lengthy "Final Battle" does the composer release this suspense, leaving the music to finish on an equivocal note. **MW**

Also available:
The Arrival (1991) Intrada MAF7032D
Castle Freak (1995) Intrada MAF7065D
The House on Sorority Row (1982) **The Alchemist** (1985) Intrada MAF7046D
Mutant (1984) Intrada MAF7052D
Re-animator (1985) **Bride of Re-animator** (1990) Silva Screen FILMCD082

Louis and Bebe Barron
b. 1920 and 1927 USA

Husband and wife team Louis and Bebe Barron were pioneers in the field of electro-acoustic music. Their early experiments with electronics eventually led to the construction of cybernetic circuits – based on the research of Professor Norbert Wiener at M.I.T. – in which electronic circuits were designed to mimic the psychological behaviour of lower life-forms. Each cybernetic circuit creates a different 'sound event' – in other words, individual circuits have their own unique 'voice'. Their first work using cybernetics was *Heavenly Menagerie* (1951).

Forbidden Planet (1956) **Original Soundtrack**.
  GNP Crescendo Small Planet ℗ PRD001 (40 minutes: AAD).

For its time, *Forbidden Planet* was a lavish Sci-Fi spectacle, with ground-breaking special effects and a plot based on *The Tempest* (although the Bard cannot claim credit for the unforgettable line "Monsters from the Id!"). It had an enormous influence on much later Science Fiction, from *Star Trek* to *Star Wars* – this is the movie in which a spaceship crew first reversed polarity – and was burlesqued in the rock musical, *Return to the Forbidden Planet*. The film also featured the first entirely electronic score for a mainstream film. So radical was the Barrons' soundtrack that it was described in the credits as 'Electronic Tonalities'. The score must have seemed nothing less than incredible to the original 1950s audience; and not even the advent of synthesizers has lessened the otherworldly impact of these weird cybernetic bleeps, gurgles and screams. Because each electronic circuit has its own characteristic sound, the Barrons were able to endow the film's characters with distinct *leitmotifs* – Robby the Robot's 'theme' clicks and whirs reassuringly; but the fearful tread of the invisible monster still has the power to terrify. Post-Cage, anything goes as music these days, yet *Forbidden Planet* still sounds fresh, excitingly different, and a lot more fun than Stockhausen. Stereo effect is exploited to the full, enhancing the surreal listening experience. As the composers' point out in the booklet, this is what your dreams sound like.   **MW**

John Barry
b. 1933 England

John Barry's love for movies was nurtured from a young age, as his father owned several local cinemas in their home town of York. As a teenager, Barry helped out in the projection booth. He had decided to become a film composer even before leaving school. After music lessons from a variety of teachers, including Dr Francis Jackson of York Minster and Bill Russo of the Stan Kenton Orchestra, Barry began his musical career playing in a big band. In 1957 he formed his own jazz outfit – The John Barry Seven – which soon achieved prominence through a succession of tours and TV appearances. Barry and his group collaborated with singer Adam Faith on his first major hit, "What Do You Want?", and on several subsequent hits. When Faith was offered the leading role in *Beat Girl* (1959) Barry, as Faith's arranger, was asked to write the score. After several minor film assignments, Barry was approached to arrange Monty Norman's James Bond theme for the first film in the series, *Dr No* (1962). He returned to James Bond as arranger and composer for the next installment, *From Russia with Love* (1963), and continued to be associated with the Bond movies until *The Living Daylights* (1987), scoring ten out of the 17 movies to date. Barry's songwriting talents were called upon for the opening credit sequences of his Bond assignments. The song "We Have all the Time in the World" from *On Her Majesty's Secret Service* (1969), sung by Louis Armstrong, was an unexpected UK hit a quarter of a century later when it was used in a Guinness advertisement. During the 1960s Barry won three Academy Awards: two for *Born Free* (1965 – song and score) and one for *The Lion in Winter* (1968). He received other Oscars for *Out of Africa* (1985) and *Dances With Wolves* (1990).

New review
The Classic John Barry, Volumes 1 and 2. **City of Prague Philharmonic Orchestra / Nic Raine**.
  Silva Screen ℗ FILMCD141/169 (79 and 78 minutes: DDD). Recorded 1993-5.
  FILMCD141 – Zulu (1964). Out of Africa (1985). Midnight Cowboy (1969). The Last Valley (1970). Eleanor and Franklin (1976). Hanover Street (1979). Born Free (1965). Chaplin (1992). Dances With Wolves (1990). Raise the Titanic! (1980). Indecent Proposal (1993). The Persuaders (1971). Robin and Marian (1976). Body Heat (1981). Somewhere in Time (1980). The Lion in Winter (1968). *FILMCD169* – High Road to China (1983). The Wrong Box (1966). The Ipcress File (1965). The Black Hole (1979). The Appointment (1969). The Scarlet Letter (1995). Monte Walsh (1970). The Knack (1965). Cry, the Beloved Country (1995). The Dove (1974). Walkabout (1970). Mary, Queen of Scots (1971). The Quiller Memorandum (1966). Deadfall (1968).

The diversity and distinctive musical style that has made John Barry's scores so consistently popular over the past three decades are well in evidence on these two volumes, which together make a very handy compendium of the major highlights of his prolific film career from *Zulu* (1964) right through to *The Scarlet Letter* (1995). Volume 1 features some of Barry's biggest commercial successes (such as *Out of Africa*, *Midnight Cowboy* and *Born Free*) along with less regularly-recorded but arguably more memorable triumphs like *The Lion in Winter* and *The Last Valley*, whose imposing epic grandeur makes an interesting contrast with Barry's more lyrical view of history in *Robin and Marian*, *Hanover Street* – a lushly romantic homage to the "Warsaw Concerto"-type score that was so much in fashion during the 1940s – and *Body Heat* with its simmeringly sensual theme for saxophone. The second volume contains even more valuable rarities, most notably the lovely Victorian-style waltz theme from *The Wrong Box*, a flavourful suite from one of Barry's rare Western scores, *Monte Walsh*, *Mary, Queen of Scots*, another of Barry's expressive historical scores, an animated selection from *The Dove*, and the highly dramatic "Romance for Guitar and Orchestra" from *Deadfall*, which ingeniously linked the intercutting of two separate sequences, a daring robbery and the concert attended by the robbery's victim. If the Prague orchestra are not always at ease with the composer's jazzier rhythms (*The Ipcress File*, *The Persuaders* and *The Knack*, for example, are rather stilted), they tackle the rest of his music with admirable enthusiasm. The sound is appropriately expansive, and each disc comes with lavishly informative booklets. **RS**

Dances With Wolves (1990) **Original Soundtrack / John Barry**.
    Epic Ⓕ 467591-2 (53 minutes: DDD).

Barry's epic, Academy Award-winning score is as broad and horizonless as the rolling plains it depicts. The pace is unhurried, the mood – for the most part – gentle. This is no conventional Western score. The music is based around a core of outstanding themes: in particular for the main character, John Dunbar, and Two Socks, the wolf. The ostensible love theme is a limpid piece for Dunbar and Stands With a Fist; yet, more importantly, what Barry has succeeded in capturing in his music is not so much the characters' love for each other, but their abiding love for the land. This is the spirit that informs the whole score with a real sense both of unfeigned affection and uplifting nobility. There is pathos, there is drama, but – most of all – throughout a series of simple, lyrical episodes, a feeling of awe inspired by natural beauty is ever-present. **MW**

From Russia With Love (1963) **Original Soundtrack / John Barry**.
    EMI Ⓜ CZ550 (37 minutes: ADD). Title song (Bart) performed by Matt Monro.

The release of the second Bond film in the autumn of 1963 left no one disappointed. The bigger budget did not, as happened later in the series, leave a gadget-conscious vacuum by figures who were mere cyphers. No one seeing it could surely forget Robert Shaw's blond thug or Lotte Lenya's redheaded assassin with shoes sprouting lethal knives. *From Russia With Love* inherited Monty Norman's original "James Bond Theme" from *Dr No*, and introduced what became an essential part of the series, a title song. The producers went for the man of the moment, Lionel Bart, who made a memorable contribution, suavely sung on the soundtrack by Matt Monro. Another first was the engagement of John Barry in what turned out to be a long line of Bond movies. His arranging and conducting skills were displayed to good effect, not least in his presentation of Bart's melody in the opening titles, where after the twice repeated orchestral fanfares, the melody was launched by strings over rhythmic background with percussion well to the fore. There was another musical first with his own "007 Theme". Like the "James Bond Theme", it was rhythmically propelled, possessing a characteristic 1950s tunefulness enlivened by some bright scoring for brass. Barry's use of bells and percussion, notably in "Spectre Island" foreshadowed later developments in his career with the more downbeat agent Harry Palmer in *The Ipcress File* (1965). A period piece, but for those around then, not to be missed. **AE**

Goldfinger (1964) **Original Soundtrack / John Barry**.
    EMI Ⓜ CZ557 (31 minutes: AAD). Title song (Barry/Bricusse/Newley) performed by Shirley Bassey.

Barry has frequently stated that this is his own favourite amongst the James Bond scores. Listening to Shirley Bassey delivering her scorching rendition of the famous theme song it is hard not to agree. The brash and brassy sound that Barry uses throughout is exactly right, and perfectly captures not only the spirit but also the look of the film. Everywhere there is gold, whether we are surveying a murdered Shirley Eaton covered in gold paint, or inside the glistening bowels of Fort Knox. In the depiction of all this, the brass section rises to the occasion splendidly. This is a wonderfully simple and direct score that Barry could only have written at that early stage of his career. The sophistication of later works would have been quite inappropriate. Unfortunately, the CD release is taken from the original USA vinyl version which means that, while having perfectly acceptable sound, four tracks from the UK vinyl issue are not included. **DS**

The Lion in Winter (1968) **Original Soundtrack**, with the **Voices of Accademia Monteverdiana / John Barry**.
    Columbia Ⓜ CK66133 (37 minutes: ADD).

The introductory spiky brass fanfares over a purposefully striding bass line herald a singularly memorable "Main Title" from John Barry's *oeuvre*. Anthony Harvey's film of James Goldman's play places us in the centre of the ruling family of the first Plantaganet reign during the twelfth century.

Barry feeds off the anger that blasts out of the script as Peter O'Toole tries to decide who amongst his offspring will carry the crown, using this as a springboard for his growling and ill-tempered score. A large portion of the music occurs during the fiery exchanges between the prinicipals but lighter moments come with three choir-only examples of cod-Gregorian chant. Dramatically, the choir is strongly represented in the opening and closing music, and particularly in the glorious sequence of Katharine Hepburn's arrival at the castle of Chinon. This work garnered a second Oscar for Barry for Best Original Score and it remains, perhaps, his finest overall work. The new mastering of Columbia's disc is a distinct improvement from the first CD release with an extended dynamic range.   **DS**

Zulu (1964) and other themes. **Original Soundtrack** etc / **John Barry**.
Silva Screen mono/stereo Ⓟ FILMCD022 (63 minutes: AAD).
Elizabeth Taylor in London (1963). From Russia with Love (1963). Four in the Morning (1965). 007 Theme. Fancy Dance. Arrangements – Kinky (Scott); Yesterday's Gone (Stuart/Kidd); No Tears for Johnny (Springfield/Hawker); Aliki (Hadjidakis); The Loneliness of Autumn (Calvi).

The very brevity that makes Barry's *Zulu* theme so effective probably also accounts for his decision not to re-record it since the original soundtrack version. The film contains only 16 minutes of score, with a further complement of Zulu dances and, of course, "Men of Harlech". Hence, this album has been sensibly structured as a compilation, featuring a varied selection from John Barry's extremely busy 1960s. The *Zulu* score is presented in its original mono form, with the addition of Richard Burton's voice-over; the strident, brassy motif that constitutes the main theme dominates the minimal amount of extra material. Everything in the 1960s had to have a pop version, so Barry obliged with his own upbeat arrangement of this powerful piece, oddly re-titled *Monkey Feathers*. Of the six Zulu dances included here, only two are authentically African, the others being written by Barry in a mid-1960s pop style. More straightforward are the selections from Barry's 1963 TV score *Elizabeth Taylor in London*, featuring a particularly delightful piece, the "London Theme". Sundry other examples of Barry's talents as a pop arranger – including two songs for the duo Chad and Jeremy and an early jazz composition by John Scott – round off this curious pot-pourri.   **MW**

Also available:
Beat Girl (1960) Play it Again PLAY001
The Best of James Bond EMI CDBOND007
The Best of John Barry Polydor 849 095-2
The Best of the EMI Years, Vols. 1-3 EMI CDEMS1497/1501/1555
Diamonds Are Forever (1971) EMI CZ554
Four in the Morning (1965) **Elizabeth Taylor in London** (1963) Play It Again PLAY002
Indecent Proposal (1992) MCA MCD10863
King Rat (1965) Columbia JK57894
The Man with the Golden Gun (1974) EMI CZ552
Midnight Cowboy (1969) EMI PRMCD6
Moonraker (1979) EMI CZ551
Moviola Epic 472490-2
Moviola II: Action and Adventure Epic 478601-2
On Her Majesty's Secret Service (1969) EMI CZ549
Out of Africa (1985) MCA MCLD19092
Peggy Sue Got Married (1986) Varèse Sarabande VCD47275
The Scarlett Letter (1995) Epic 483577-2
Somewhere in Time (1980) MCA MCAD31164
Thunderball (1965) EMI CZ556
Until September (1984) **Starcrash** (1979) Silva Screen FILMCD085
A View to a Kill (1985) EMI CDP7 46159-2
You Only Live Twice (1967) EMI CZ559

James Bernard

b. 1925 England

The son of a British Army officer, James Bernard was born in the Himalayas. After war service in the RAF he took the advice of Benjamin Britten, whom he had met in 1943, and studied at the Royal College of Music under the tuition of Herbert Howells. When he left the college, Britten asked him to assist with copying the vocal score for his forthcoming opera, *Billy Budd*. Bernard spent over a year working with Britten, during which time he also met Imogen Holst who continued to instruct him in composition. His first solo assignments were writing incidental music for BBC radio plays, and it was his work on these that attracted the attention of John Hollingsworth, music director for Hammer Films. Bernard's long-standing association

CLASSIC MOVIE MUSIC

SPACE AND BEYOND

The Ultimate Sci-fi
Movie Music Collection

28 Symphonic Suites & Themes
• 2001: A SPACE ODYSSEY
• CAPRICORN ONE
• SPECIES
• APOLLO 13
• THE RIGHT STUFF
• CLOSE ENCOUNTERS
• COCOON
• TAXI DRIVER
• STAR TREK – MOVIES & TV

New Dolby Surround Sound
Recordings
Over 140 Minutes of Music
plus Sound Effects
City of Prague Philharmonic
Conducted by Nic Raine
2CD: FILMXCD 185
2CASS: FILMXC 185

CINEMA CHORAL CLASSICS

An Album of the Most Beautiful
& Dramatic Choral Music Ever
Written for the Cinema
• JESUS OF NAZARETH
• KING OF KINGS
• THE OMEN
• THE MISSION
• THE LION IN WINTER
• EXCALIBUR
• THE ABYSS
• CONAN: THE BARBARIAN
  & OTHERS

New Dolby Surround
Sound Recordings
Over 70 minutes of Music
Crouch End Festival Chorus/
City of Prague Philharmonic
Conducted by David Temple
and Nic Raine
CD: SILKD 6015
CASS: SILKC 6015

WARRIORS
of the Silver Screen

Double CD Set of Heroic Themes
including Symphonic Suites & Themes
from
• TARAS BULBA
• THE VIKINGS
• PRINCE VALIANT
• BRAVEHEART
• ROB ROY
• HENRY V
• THE THIEF OF BAGDAD
• ANTHONY AND CLEOPATRA

New Dolby Surround Sound
Recordings
Over 140 Minutes of Music
City of Prague Philharmonic
Conducted by Nic Raine
2CD: FILMXCD 187

THE CULT FILES

The Ultimate Collection of
Cult TV & Film Themes
40 Classic Themes including
• THE X-FILES
• THE PRISONER
• THE SAINT
• THE PERSUADERS
• MISSION: IMPOSSIBLE
• ALIEN
• DOCTOR WHO
• THE AVENGERS

Over 140 Minutes of Music
Royal Philharmonic Concert Orchestra
and City of Prague Philharmonic
Conducted by Mike Townend
2CD: FILMXCD 184
CASS: FILMXC 184

HOW THE WEST WAS WON
Classic Western Film Scores I

Symphonic Suites & Themes from
• THE MAGNIFICENT SEVEN
• THE PROFESSIONALS
• HIGH PLAINS DRIFTER
• THE WILD BUNCH
• GETTYSBURG
• WILD ROVERS
• BUFFALO GIRLS
• HOW THE WEST WAS WON

Over 70 minutes of Music
City of Prague Philharmonic
Conducted by Paul Bateman
CD: FILMCD 173

LONESOME DOVE
Classic Western Film Scores 2

Symphonic Suites & Themes from
• HEAVEN'S GATE
• OLD GRINGO
• RED SUN
• RED RIVER
• THE OUTLAW JOSEY WALES
• SHE WORE A YELLOW RIBBON
• THE SONS OF KATIE ELDER
• LONESOME DOVE

67 minutes of Music
City of Prague Philharmonic
Conducted by Nic Raine
CD: FILMCD 176

with Hammer began with *The Quatermass Experiment* (1955 – known in the USA as *The Creeping Unknown*). He was to provide music for 23 Hammer films in all, as well as working on the first series of the TV spin-off *Hammer House of Horror*. In the 1980s, Bernard retired to Jamaica, but a revival of interest in his music encouraged him to prepare suites of his scores for CD release and move back to the UK. In 1996 he composed a new score for the 1922 silent horror classic, *Nosferatu* (the original was by Hans Erdmann – see separate entry).

New review

The Devil Rides Out The Film Music of James Bernard. [a]**Westminster Philharmonic Orchestra / Kenneth Alwyn;** [b]**City of Prague Philharmonic Orchestra /** [c]**Paul Bateman** ([a]pf); [d]**Nic Raine.** Silva Screen Ⓕ FILMCD174 (64 minutes: DDD). Recorded 1995-6.
  Kiss of the Vampire[a] (1962) She[a] (1965). Frankenstein Created Woman[bc] (1966). The Devil Rides Out[bd] (1968). Scars of Dracula[bc] (1970). Quatermass Suite[a] – The Quatermass Experiment (1955); X–The Unknown (1956); Quatermass II (1957).

If any one British composer was linked to a studio it would have to be James Bernard and Hammer – home of terror, fear and over-acting. In fact, many composers toiled for Hammer, notably under the aegis of conductor Philip Martell, but as Bernard got most of the best-known Dracula and Frankenstein assignments, his is the name that is most remembered. Silva Screen have already recorded a more mainstream album of Bernard/Hammer material (see below), so this disc takes a slightly different route by bringing together under one heading a selection of lesser-known scores. *She* is one of James Bernard's favourites, and it is easy to see why. Gone are the Gothic horrors of Transylvania, here is a timeless tale, based on H. Rider Haggard's novel, of a beautiful queen in a mythical African kingdom and her quest for the secret of eternal life. The score is free from all the bombastic excess that Dracula and co. had to have, and instead the music is rich, tonal and lyrical. Also worth noting is a seven-minute theme for "Christina" from *Frankenstein Created Woman*, and a five-minute "Love Theme" from *Scars of Dracula*. Amidst these scary movies some fine, delicate music was buried – and at long last it has been resurrected here. The recording succeeds in blending the three conductors and two orchestras together to make a musical whole without too much distraction. Notes from David Wishart and the composer, together with colour poster reproductions, add the finishing touch to this very varied album.   **JW**

Also available:
Dracula – Classic Hammer Scores (Philharmonia/Richardson) Silva Screen FILMCD714

See also Collections: **Horror!**

Elmer Bernstein
b. 1922 USA

Elmer Bernstein was trained as a pianist, but studied composition with Roger Sessions and Stefan Wolpe. He enlisted in the US Army Air Corps in 1942, where he arranged and composed music for Armed Forces Radio shows, working with Glenn Miller and his Army Air Corps Band. When he left the Army, Bernstein briefly returned to his original vocation as a concert pianist, before being asked by Norman Corwin to score a radio drama, which led in turn to offers from Hollywood. After scoring some minor pictures, beginning with *Saturday's Hero* and *Boots Malone* (both 1951), Bernstein was offered the chance to compose the music for Cecil B. DeMille's *The Ten Commandments* (1956) following the sudden death of original choice Victor Young. At the same time he wrote a groundbreaking jazz score for *The Man with the Golden Arm. The Magnificent Seven* (1960) and *The Great Escape* (1963) are probably his most enduringly popular scores. He received an Academy Award for *Thoroughly Modern Millie* (1967). Bernstein, along with contemporaries Alex North and Leonard Rosenman, was one of the first film composers to eschew the middle-European late romantic idiom in favour of a more modern, distinctively American style inherited in equal parts from Aaron Copland and from Jazz. Despite a dearth of good assignments during the 1970s and much of the 1980s, he has remained a major name in film music, with his work enjoying something of a renaissance in recent years. His classic score for *To Kill a Mockingbird* (1962) has been recently re-recorded by the composer with the Royal Scottish National Orchestra and will be released by Varèse Sarabande in 1997.

Elmer Bernstein Conducts Elmer Bernstein Royal Philharmonic Pops Orchestra / **Elmer Bernstein.**
  Denon Ⓕ CO75288 (66 minutes: DDD). Recorded 1993.
  The Magnificent Seven (1960). To Kill a Mockingbird (1962). The Man with the Golden Arm (1955). The Grifters (1990). Walk on the Wild Side (1962). Hawaii (1966). The Great

Escape (1963). Ghostbusters (1984). Hollywood and the Stars (1963). Rambling Rose (1991). Heavy Metal (1981). My Left Foot (1989). The Ten Commandments (1956).

The composer himself here provides a very useful overview of many of his major scores of the past 40 years (yes, incredibly, Elmer Bernstein has been composing for the movies for over 40 years). This collection distinctly demonstrates how Bernstein's current scores remain as vital as anything from his formative years: a recent outing like *The Grifters* comes over as gritty and consciously sleazy as the groundbreaking 1955 score for *The Man with the Golden Arm*; and *Rambling Rose* is as delicately woven and psychologically insightful as anything in the renowned 1962 score for *To Kill a Mockingbird*. The album is jammed with audience-pleasers – from *The Great Escape* to *The Magnificent Seven* – but there is a miscellany of other rarer selections, most notably Bernstein's brawny music for the animated Sci-Fi feature *Heavy Metal*, and the determinedly lush prelude for the television series *Hollywood and the Stars*. However, if this splendid album does have an undisputed highlight then it is the epic "Overture" for *Hawaii*, full to the orchestral brim with vibrant themes and motifs all uniquely and indelibly Elmer Bernstein. The performances are alert and enthusiastic, and tempos, for the most part, authentically akin to the original soundtrack sessions, whilst the recording by Keith Grant in the Henry Wood Hall is spacious and filmic (although Kenny Baker's spirited trumpet solo on *The Man with the Golden Arm* enters at an uncomfortably high level). Good to see one of the giants of film music delivering a giant of an album. **DW**

Genocide (1981) Original Soundtrack, with the Royal Philharmonic Orchestra / Elmer Bernstein.
Intrada Ⓕ FMT8007D (46 minutes: ADD).

A sense of righteous indignation characterizes this deeply-felt score, written to accompany a harrowing documentary on the Holocaust. Bernstein's music expresses the determined will of a people who, whilst being systematically exterminated, refused to bow their heads in defeat. A bold, attention-grabbing main theme immediately establishes the tone: not resignation, determination. The Nazis are portrayed both by a bitter rendition of "Deutschland über Alles", and a treading, ostinato theme for brass and percussion. Low, growling woodwinds – including cor anglais – colour the backdrop in shades of darkness. The score's emotional centrepiece is the brief cue "We Shall Outlive Them", in which a hopeful dance-like theme is passed from woodwinds to full orchestra, culminating in a magnificent display for French horns. Flute, harp, oboe and violin are given prominent solo passages, with the latter assuming a pivotal role in the heavily Jewish-inflected music for both "Be Strong and Brave" and "Liberation". After a moving finale, in which the Israeli national anthem is quoted, the principal theme returns defiantly. Respectful, stirring and compelling – one of the composer's very finest. **MW**

The Great Escape (1963) Original Soundtrack / Elmer Bernstein.
Intrada Ⓕ MAF7025D (33 minutes: ADD).

In case you were wondering, this score will remind you just what possessed you to listen to film music in the first place. Not even the whole score, the "Main Title" will do it all by itself. Remember: a rainy Bank Holiday afternoon, Dickie Attenborough, Steve McQueen, the motorbike chase, the cooler king – and that music. You can whistle it even now – but don't, because whistling such a grand march, with its melodic variety, ingenious counterpoint and rhythmic underpinning will spoil it. This is why film music is worth exploring: behind the whistleable tune there is the voice of an inventive, gifted composer at work: working at developing his initial melody, adding new motifs, structuring the whole into a potent musical experience. *The Great Escape* – like all good film scores – is a whole lot more than just a memorable whistle. Intrada's CD release has been carefully remastered from the original tapes. They prepared two transfers: one which eliminated all the background hiss and distortion; the other which preserved the 'presence' of the original. The latter was preferred – although this CD shows up its imperfections, the music blissfully overrides any technical deficiencies. Now, where did I put that catcher's glove? **MW**

New review

John Wayne Films, Volumes 1 and 2. Utah Symphony Orchestra / Elmer Bernstein.
Varèse Sarabande Ⓕ VCD47236 /64 (two discs: 41 and 36 minutes: DDD) Recorded 1985. *VCD47236* – The Comancheros (1961) True Grit (1969). *VCD47264* – The Shootist (1976). Cahill, United States Marshal (1973). Big Jake (1971).

Rugged and self-reliant, John Wayne was the personification of the Old West. His tough but always likeable screen image is admirably reflected in Elmer Bernstein's evocative Western scores. Bernstein's music is a vital, driving force in these films, producing a strong sense of forward motion through the use of energetic syncopation; brass and percussion colour rhythmic action sequences, whilst buoyant, big-hearted melodies speak of the widescreen splendour of the settings.

These two discs, splendidly performed and vividly recorded, give us the very best of Bernstein and Wayne. *The Comancheros* was their first film together: coming so soon after *The Magnificent Seven*, the music is unsurprisingly in a similar vein, with an arresting and entirely distinctive "Main Title" that seeks to rival its predecessor's famous main theme. There is plenty of action, Indians on the warpath driven on by Bernstein's pulsing rhythms, some trumpet-led Spanish interludes (again, like *The Magnificent Seven*), and a joyful, Copland-influenced dance ("McBaine and the Prairie"). *True Grit* is the better-known movie, Wayne's unforgettable portrayal of Rooster Cogburn winning him an Oscar. Bernstein's "Main Title" is more consciously a 'pop' piece, an instrumental version of the title song sung by Glen Campbell in the movie. The score proper makes much of this tune's infectious charm – given as solos to trumpet and violin – and the orchestration is lighter than *The Comancheros*, although exciting, onward-moving drama is never far away.

Big Jake and *Cahill, United States Marshal* continue the established Bernstein/Wayne tradition, providing more big tunes and blustering action, although with Wayne getting on in years, the composer's scoring becomes increasingly delicate, moving closer towards his preferred chamber-music style of writing. The jewel of this set, however, and arguably one of Bernstein's finest Western scores is the least typical. *The Shootist* was Wayne's last film, a poignant swan song to his career in which the suffering of the terminally ill gunfighter portrayed on screen was a mirror of the actor's own struggle with cancer. The music is expressive of the character's (and Wayne's) calm dignity, a proud "Main Title" summoning memories of past glory, reminding the listener of those sunnier earlier themes. The growing affection between the gunfighter and his landlady (Lauren Bacall) is gently handled in "Ride"; whilst the climactic shoot-out ("In the Fire") alternates fierce rhythmic figures with a low-key treatment of the main theme. The "Epilogue" presents a secondary theme for flute and piano which, in its depiction of the innocence of childhood, is reminiscent of *To Kill a Mockingbird*. *The Shootist* is a subtle and sensitive score – chamber music in all but name – but so powerful is its hold on the listener that it stands out as the very finest work in this fine collection of otherwise rousing Western music.**MW**

The Magnificent Seven (1960) **The Hallelujah Trail**[a] (1965) [a]**Arizona State University Concert Choir; Phoenix Symphony Orchestra / James Sedares**.
Koch International Ⓔ 37222-2 (64 minutes: DDD). Recorded 1993.

Perhaps this classic score should be renamed *The Magnificent Eight*, so famous is the main theme. It is pleasing to note, then, that the signature tune doesn't dominate the rest. Indeed, this music is a treasure trove of memorable moments: lilting Spanish-American dances rubbing shoulders with urgent action motifs. Reconstructed and edited by the composer and Christopher Palmer from Bernstein's original sketches (the orchestral parts having been lost or destroyed by the studio), *The Magnificent Seven* is a pure action score which makes satisfying listening in its own right. Sedares and his orchestra seem inspired by Bernstein's fecundity of invention, responding with energy to the constant forward momentum of the music (the enthusiastic percussion section deserve particular mention). The short choral overture from another western, *The Hallelujah Trail*, is in a similar – but far less memorable – vein, and divorced from the context of the film the trite lyrics are an additional handicap. **MW**

The Ten Commandments (1956) **Anonymous orchestra / Elmer Bernstein**.
MCA Ⓜ MCAD42320 (60 minutes: AAD). Recorded 1960.

Fresh from supplying a raw, strident jazz beat for *The Man With the Golden Arm*, Bernstein found himself travelling back several centuries to write this weighty, symphonic score for Cecil B. DeMille's widescreen version of the story of Moses. Taking over from the director's regular composer, Victor Young (who died during production), the 34 year-old Bernstein rose to the challenge of tackling his first film epic with spectacular results. In keeping with DeMille's Victorian, brightly coloured, Bible-in-pictures approach, the score is a rich selection-box of sumptuous melody and melodramatic incident; though unusually for this type of film, there is not a heavenly choir to be heard. Amongst the many highlights are a sturdy, noble theme for Moses, a lush, vampish string-laden one for Queen Nefretiri, several exotically-scored dances and two brilliantly rousing sequences describing the Exodus from Egypt and the parting of the Red Sea. **RS**

Also available:
The Babe (1992) MCA MCAD10576
Bulletproof (1996) Varèse Sarabande VSD5757
The Cemetery Club (1993) Varèse Sarabande VSD5412
Devil in a Blue Dress (1995) Columbia 481379-2 [mostly Jazz]
Frankie Starlight (1995) Varèse Sarabande VSD5679

The Good Son (1993) Arista 20th Century-Fox 110013-2
Last Man Standing (1996) Varèse Sarabande VSD5755
Lost in Yonkers (1992) Varèse Sarabande VSD5419
Mad Dog and Glory (1992) Varèse Sarabande VSD5415
Oscar (1991) Varèse Sarabande VSD5313
A Rage in Harlem (1991) Varèse Sarabande VSD5325
True Grit (1969) Capitol 32163

Peter Bernstein

New review
Bolero (1984) **Original Soundtrack**, with **Cynthia Millar** (ondes martenot); **Rome Studio Symphony Orchestra / Elmer Bernstein**.
Prometheus Ⓕ PCD124 (56 minutes: ADD).

John Derek's erotic, exotic movie starring his then wife, Bo Derek, had a very intriguing musical score, composed by Peter Bernstein and supervised and conducted by his father, Elmer, in Rome. Featuring a favourite Bernstein senior trademark, the ondes martenot, this is a melodious and at times dynamic score. Set amid the splendours of Spain, the opening track entitled "Bullero" is played with tremendous verve, vividly conjuring up the heat and – if you like that sort of thing – the excitement of the bullfight. This is a score of such variety that it is difficult to pick one particular track as representative: there is a belly dance, a cue called "Exstasy" (well, you can work that one out), and "Angel/Gypsy Dance" is performed by solo guitar. Out of the 23 tracks, two are actually composed by Elmer Bernstein, whilst some 12 cues make their first appearance on this new Prometheus CD (the remainder appeared on the original album release). As one might expect, Elmer Bernstein conducts with panache, and if one's attention lapses occasionally, well, there are always a few stills of Bo Derek on the sleeve to hold your attention. **JW**

Howard Blake

b. 1938 England

Born in London, Howard Blake spent his youth in Brighton, where he played the organ and sang operetta as a boy soprano. He won a scholarship to the Royal Academy of Music, where he studied piano and composition. For a time he earned a living as a projectionist at the National Film Theatre, becoming hooked on the magic of the cinema. As a successful session pianist, conductor and orchestrator he worked with such luminaries as Quincey Jones and Bernard Herrmann. It was Herrmann who recommended him to Laurie Johnson, then working on the TV series *The Avengers*; Blake took over from Johnson between 1968-9, taking on an increasing workload of television and film assignments at the same time. In 1971 he traded the bustle of London for the tranquillity of a watermill in Sussex, turning his back on commercial music to write concert works, before being tempted back into film scoring for Ridley Scott's first feature, *The Duellists* (1977). Blake was scheduled to score Scott's next movie, *Alien* (1979), but the studio preferred a more experienced hand and opted for Jerry Goldsmith. His large-scale symphonic score for *Agatha* (1979) was scrapped, as was most of his work on *Flash Gordon* (1980), which had music by Queen instead. He had to wait until *The Snowman* (1982) before scoring an overdue success. More recently, Blake has preferred to write for the theatre, notably the Royal Shakespeare Company. His Clarinet Concerto (1985) has been recorded on Hyperion (CDA66215), his Violin Concerto, "The Leeds" (1992) by ASV (CDDCA905 – a disc which also includes a suite from his score for *A Month in the Country*, 1987).

The Snowman (1982) **Original Soundtrack**, with **Bernard Cribbins** (narr); **Peter Auty** (sngr); **Sinfonia of London / Howard Blake**.
Columbia Ⓜ 40CDX71136 (58 minutes DDD).

More than a dozen years after the first screening on Channel 4 of this regular Christmas item, *The Snowman* retains all its magic and sparkle. This is wholly due to the skill and artistry of its composer, Howard Blake. Viewing the film is especially enjoyable because Blake's music is never overwhelmed by the dialogue track, it is allowed to carry the whole story. From the delightful – and now classic – "Walking in the Air" to the Scottish-style dance of the finale when our boy hero is transported to the Snowman's home, the music is well up to the task. On disc, aided by a superb performance from the Sinfonia of London under the composer's direction, it is quite possible to ignore the story of the Snowman as narrated by Bernard Cribbins, and just let Blake's marvellous and timeless score flow over you. **JW**

Sir Arthur Bliss

1891-1975 England

Born in London, Arthur Bliss studied at Rugby and Pembroke College, Cambridge, where he met Elgar. He studied conducting under Stanford at the Royal College of Music, and, after war service, became involved in London musical life, staging concerts and writing incidental music. After producing a series of experimental, avant-garde concert works like *Rout, Conversation* (both 1920) and *Colour Symphony* (1922), Bliss naturally used his first film score as an opportunity for further experiment. This was Sir Alexander Korda's *Things to Come* (1936) and the music was greeted as a landmark in the art of film scoring (much of it was written before the film was shot). He believed in the importance of music in films, but his few other forays in the genre were generally less successful. His music for Bernard Shaw's *Caesar and Cleopatra* (1945) was rejected, his score for Korda's *Conquest of the Air* (1938) was drastically cut. Bliss was knighted in 1950 and appointed Master of the Queen's Music in 1953.

Christopher Columbus (1949) **Seven Waves Away** (1956) **Men of Two Worlds** (1946)
    Silvia Capova (pf); Slovak Philharmonic Male Choir; Czecho-Slovak Radio Symphony
    Orchestra / Adriano.
    Marco Polo Ⓔ 8 223315 (50 minutes: DDD). Recorded 1990.

Whilst Adriano and the Czecho-Slovak Radio Symphony Orchestra might not have quite grasped the necessary idiom – and despite the recording being a mite hollow – they should still be congratulated for recording these rare Bliss scores, surely shaming British record companies who should have turned their attention to these fascinating pieces years ago. The rather staid 1949 Pinewood filming of *Christopher Columbus*, starring an imported Fredric March, benefited enormously from Bliss's ravishing score, alive with Spanish rhythmic devices, and particularly distinguished by a magisterial theme glorifying the voyage itself. The climax is one of the composer's characteristically rousing marches, celebrating Columbus's safe return from his incredible journey. The now-forgotten *Seven Waves Away* (which had Tyrone Power heroically handling a sinking cruise liner), presents Bliss in nothing less than balletic mood, with two stalwart *Allegros* and a distinguished *Marche funèbre* which could reasonably be wedged into *Checkmate*: three exacting self-contained musical exercises which also flawlessly evoke both the panic and the despair associated with disaster on the high seas. A suite from *Men of Two Worlds*, the tale of a Tanganyikan concert pianist returning from studies in England to Africa, allowed Bliss to experiment with indigenous African rhythms and motifs, culminating in "Baraza", a compact Piano Concerto thrusting with endemic African dynamism which, although brief, is as viable a work as anything in his classical canon. Indeed, if this disc demonstrates anything, it is that there is no convenient dividing line between Bliss's concert works and his compositions for the cinema. His music was always exceptional, whatever the medium, which makes the musical establishment's current disregard for him all the more disconcerting. **DW**

Also available:
Bliss Conducts Bliss [includes **Men of Two Worlds** (1946) **Things to Come** (1936) etc.] Dutton Laboratories CDLXT2051

See also Collections: **The Red Shoes**

Luiz Bonfa

b. 1922 Brazil

Antonio Carlos Jobim

b. 1927 Brazil

Bonfa and Jobim's interest in their native Brazilian music inaugurated the worldwide cult of the bossa nova via the influence of their score for *Black Orpheus*. Jobim – a composer, author, pianist and singer – has also written a significant body of songs, instrumental and orchestral works, as well as scoring the film *Copacabana Palace* in 1963.

Black Orpheus [Orfeu Negro] (1958) **Original Soundtrack**, with **Luiz Bonfa, João Gilberto,
    Antonio Carlos Jobim**.
    Verve Ⓜ 830 783-2 (54 minutes: AAD).

The film largely responsible for introducing the world to jazz samba. The bossa nova became one of the more endearing musical emblems of the 1960s and one that Hollywood embraced with relish, albeit several years after this award-winning film was released. The CD is a vibrant, pulsating souvenir of Brazilian Carnival, with many of the riotously percussive tracks recorded live in Rio. Most of the original material is by Jobim, though it is Bonfa's haunting main themes, "Samba de

VARESE SARABANDE

The Soundtrack Label

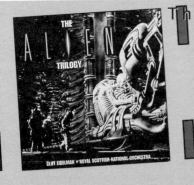

THE ALIEN TRILOGY
Music by Jerry Goldsmith
James Horner & Elliot Goldenthal
Royal Scottish National Orchestra
Cliff Eidelman
CD: VSD5753

LEGENDS OF HOLLYWOOD
Franz Waxman Vol 4
Queensland S.O. Richard Mills
CD : VSD5713

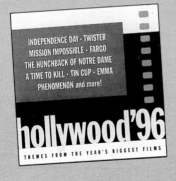

HOLLYWOOD 96
Various Artists
CD: VSD5764

AMERICAN BUFFALO & THREESOME
Music by Thomas Newman
CD: VSD5751

VARÈSE SARABANDE

DISTRIBUTED IN THE
UK BY PINNACLE

PINNACLE

Orfeu" and "Manha de Carnaval" (or "A Day in the Life of a Fool" as it became known in English), performed with wistful poignancy by a small group of eminent soloists, that make this score such a landmark. They swiftly became jazz/MOR standards and appear as a 13-minute bonus track (along with Jobim's "A Felicidade") at the end of the CD in a 1966 live performance by Bola Sete. **RS**

Bruce Broughton

b. 1945 USA

Los Angeles-born Bruce Broughton studied composition at the University of Southern California, where he attended classes in film music given by David Raksin; in addition, he also studied informally with Emil Söderström. The son of Salvation Army officers, some of his earliest music was written for Salvation Army bands. His professional career began at CBS Television working on shows like *Hawaii Five-O, Quincy, Gunsmoke, How the West Was Won* and *Dallas* (he has won several Emmy Awards for his continuing television work). After scoring some low-budget features, Broughton's first major motion picture assignment was the unconventional western *Silverado* (1985), for which he received an Academy Award nomination. A much-praised score for *Young Sherlock Holmes* (1985) followed. He has written several non-film works, including concertos for both Tuba and Piccolo, and most recently a Concerto for Horn and Strings commissioned by the Sinfonia of London. Other film-related projects include an orchestral score for a CD-ROM game, and music for Disney theme parks. An ongoing association with Intrada records has resulted in Broughton conducting their series of reconstructed classic film scores, the Excalibur Collection, which began with Miklós Rózsa's *Ivanhoe* (see Rózsa). He also plays an active role in the Society of Composers and Lyricists, and was its President for some time. All Broughton's scores are graceful, meticulously constructed, and share a distinctive clarity of orchestral texture.

New review
Carried Away (1996) **Original Soundtrack / Bruce Broughton**.
Intrada Ⓟ MAF7068 (36 minutes: DDD).

Moments of quiet reflection are rare in Hollywood, film music is usually required to exaggerate not understate, so the introspective creation of a mature and skilled composer like Bruce Broughton is to be received with particular gratitude. For the soundtrack collector, this disc must stand out as a delicate and subtly-patterned orchid in a garden otherwise filled with gaudy roses. Broughton's chamber-sized orchestration gives brief phrases, lyrical fragments, to solo woodwinds supported by equivocal, almost melancholic chords in the strings. The effect is contemplative, nostalgic, wistful. It is not until near the end that the music swells, the orchestra begins to move as one, and a shift from minor to major introduces a gently optimistic finale. This modest little score, a work of intricate and fragile craftsmanship, will reward those who seek it out with a few precious moments of calm. **MW**

New review
Homeward Bound (1993) **Original Soundtrack / Bruce Broughton**.
Intrada Ⓟ MAF7041D (31 minutes: DDD).

This remake of the 1963 Disney real-life adventure *The Incredible Journey* had the added bonus of a music score from Bruce Broughton, one of Hollywood's most talented composers. Here, amid the magnificent visual splendour of America's natural terrain, the composer finds a musical voice for the family of animals and their search for home. The score has multiple themes: guitar represents the pup, Chance, and the opening theme is established with support from the strings. In "The Journey Begins" the main theme is given luminous orchestral colouring, and developed in an expansive tone and style that all those aware of Broughton's music will instantly recognize. The five-minute "End Credit" sequence begins with the principal theme on solo trumpet before being taken up by full orchestra. This is Americana as seen by Bruce Broughton, not a warmed-over Copland, of the kind familiar from his other distinctively American scores like *Silverado* and *O Pioneers!*. **JW**

Honey, I Blew Up the Kid (1992) **Original Soundtrack / Bruce Broughton**.
Intrada Ⓟ MAF7030D (41 minutes: DDD).

Delightfully comic and highly virtuosic, Bruce Broughton's masterful Disney score sounds like ideal silent movie music. It has the perfect mixture of slapstick and pathos, humour and tenderness. Instead of Rick Moranis, picture Harold Lloyd or Buster Keaton. The chattering saxophones, with their rushing semiquaver runs; the brassy 1930s *Street Scene* manner; the sweetly sentimental 'love' theme, interrupted by frantically humorous interjections. The constant bustle of activity extends throughout the orchestra: a stomping piano-led version of the main theme in "Get Big Bunny", a brief Western-style diversion in "Clear the Streets!". As ever, Broughton's orchestral writing is a joy to hear. Frenetic cues like the racing "Car Flight", which throws around all the principal themes with reckless skill, must have tested the capabilities of the orchestra to the full: they respond flawlessly. "We think it is as good as they come!" says Intrada collectively in the booklet. Who could disagree? **MW**

O Pioneers! (1991) **Original Soundtrack / Bruce Broughton**.
Intrada Ⓟ MAF7023D (43 minutes: DDD).

Bruce Broughton's Emmy Award-winning television score is assuredly as much of a traditional Western as its big screen counterparts, Silverado and Tombstone, albeit one cast in a much gentler, affectingly pastoral mould. It is as if Broughton is deliberately sidestepping the reinvented Americana of Copland in search of a purer, more straightforward style. His beautifully fluid melodies have a beguiling folk-like simplicity which, decked out in his superbly transparent orchestral colours, could never be mistaken for pastiche. The hymn-like principal theme is infused with a gentle nobility that is quite captivating; whilst a tripping *allegro,* despite its fragile delicacy, is unmistakably the product of the same hand that crafted the pulsating rhythms of *Silverado*. The trumpet-led climactic rendition of the final hymn tune suggests unexpected parallels with quintessentially English works like Parry's "Jerusalem" or Holst's "I vow to thee my country" melody: works which share with Broughton's particular brand of Americana a noble and uplifting directness. Perhaps Broughton's early compositions for brass band are responsible for this trait in his music; if so, more film composers should serve their apprenticeships this way. **MW**

New review
Shadow Conspiracy (1996) **Original Soundtrack**, with the **Sinfonia of London / Bruce Broughton**.
Intrada Ⓟ MAF7073 (58 minutes: DDD).

When you give a composer like Bruce Broughton a film with intrigue, deception and murder, you can expect a score that brilliantly evokes all those elements and more. His score for *Shadow Conspiracy* does just that. Broughton has assembled a huge orchestra, notable for its percussion section which includes bongos, slit drums, bass drums, waterphones, cow bells, woodblocks, chimes, ratchets, rattles and snare-drum sticks. In addition, the composer utilizes cimbalon and contrabass trombone as he had before in *Tombstone*. This gigantic ensemble provides the fabric for a score that is at times elegant, mysterious, energetic, tormented, and above all, hypnotic. The music has astonishing weight and depth, thundering along with confident dynamism. The noble main theme incites notions of justice and state, whilst a short descending motif counteracts this with an uneasy impression of corruption. As the subject matter demands, there is a great deal of suspense material and it is here Broughton unleashes the full range of that mighty percussion section. Particularly satisfying is the fiercely modern action writing, punctuated and carefully-paced cues which excite through rhythm rather than volume. **PP**

Silverado (1985) **Original Soundtrack / Bruce Broughton**.
Intrada Ⓟ MAF7035D (46 minutes: DDD).

Broughton's first 'horse opera' features an exhilarating main theme, which, if the movie had been a bigger success, might have become as well known now as *The Magnificent Seven* or *The Big Country*. This really is a first-rate Western score, shot through with typical strokes of Broughton's distinctive melodic and harmonic style: in "The Getaway/Riding as One", for example, where the theme is triumphantly developed as a march; or the syncopated bass which underlies the opening of "On to Silverado". But, there is more to this score than just the one 'big' tune: fearsome, angry rhythms underscore clashes with the bad guys; ominous, shifting chords oppose the optimism of the sunny main theme. Conspicuous by its absence is any kind of love theme: the music is either discordant and disturbing or bold and brash. Broughton's enthusiasm for the project is tangible throughout: in the ceaseless driving pace of the music, and the sheer variety of texture, as a small nucleus of thematic material is put through orchestrational hoops. A law should be passed making the jubilant "End Credit" sequence mandatory on all future Western film music compilations. **MW**

Tombstone (1993) **Original Soundtrack**, with the **Sinfonia of London / David Snell**.
Intrada Ⓟ MAF7038D (67 minutes: DDD).

Bruce Broughton's *Tombstone* is a marvel: in this highly dramatic score, ably conducted by David Snell and played with some verve by the Sinfonia of London, Broughton finds something original to say whilst yet remaining largely within the familiar Western style of innumerable previous scores. He employs all the power that a big orchestra can give him, and adds some extra colour all his own, with

Hungarian cimbalon, Irish tin whistle, and French contrabass sarrusophone to counterbalance the more well-known Western devices. At some 67 minutes, it's almost too much music. If John Williams's score for *The Reivers* conjured up the open spaces of Southern landscapes, then *Tombstone* delivers the Wild West as aptly as Jerry Goldsmith did in *Hour of the Gun* (now there's a link for you!). If only Broughton could get more projects like this rather than some of the inane comedies he has recently scored. Still, talent will out, and I look forward to his future efforts with renewed interest. In the meantime, *Tombstone* will do very nicely indeed. Yes sir, very nicely indeed!   **JW**

Also available:
Homeward Bound 2: Lost in San Francisco (1996) Disney 60903-7
Infinity (1996) Intrada MAF7072
The Old Man and the Sea (1990) Intrada RVF6008

Roy Budd
1947-1993 England

Roy Budd began playing piano aged four, and performed at the London Palladium aged 12. He was a successful jazz pianist before becoming involved in writing for the screen with the film *Soldier Blue* (1970). This was followed by several scores the following year: *Flight of the Doves, Zeppelin, Get Carter, Kidnapped, Catlow* and *The Magnificent Seven Deadly Sins*. Working mainly in British cinema, Budd continued to score movies up to his death in 1993: his final project was a new score for the 1925 silent film version of *The Phantom of the Opera* – he died shortly before he was due to conduct the première screening of the film with his new score.

`New review`
The Phantom of the Opera (1925) **RTL Orchestra / Roy Budd**.
EMI ℗ [number to be confirmed] (DDD). Recorded 1993.

When Roy Budd passed away on 7th August, 1993 more than just a talented composer left us. Budd was a British link with the American style of jazz/symphonic composer capable of giving their jazz or orchestral themes a sense of depth and tremendous verve.

The Phantom of the Opera was more than just another assignment for Roy. He had read stories about the Lon Chaney film whilst collecting famous monster magazines as a young boy. From then on, his ambition was to write a score for the film. In 1989 he came across a film collector who had an original print, this he bought and lovingly restored to its full glory, using an experimental two-colour process and original tints of the film's original release. From the opening organ theme the listener can tell that Roy's ambition to write his masterpiece for this film has been realized. His "Phantom" theme is heard over the short opening credits, and it undergoes many changes throughout, agitated during the chase sequences and overtly romantic as the Phantom craves for the love of his life, his obsession, Christine. Listen also for the superb ballet music written for the establishing shots within the Paris Opera: luminous and enchanting it is a delight for the ear. The music is always cleanly presented and never over-orchestrated, so Roy's atmospheric and imposing score can always be heard in an unfettered way.

This was Roy Budd's last score, he died five weeks before the world première of the work at the Barbican in London. Listen and remember that this is indeed his greatest achievement, written with compassion and nobility. This disc is a fine tribute to a master composer at the height of his creativity.   **JW**

Geoffrey Burgon
b. 1941 England

When Geoffrey Burgon began his studies at the Guildhall School of Music, it was with the intention of becoming a jazz trumpeter. Composition, however, had always exerted a strong attraction and after a period working as a freelance trumpeter, he eventually gave up the instrument in favour of composing. But it was not until after seven lean years that his *Requiem* (1976) was performed at the Three Choirs Festival and won widespread acclaim. Television work followed, with *Dr Who, Testament of Youth, Tinker, Tailor, Soldier, Spy* , *Brideshead Revisited, Bleak House* (1985) and *Martin Chuzzlewit* (1995). Film projects include *Monty Python's Life of Brian* (1979), *The Dogs of War* (1980), *Turtle Diary* (1985) and *Robin Hood* (1991). He continues to divide his time between film, television and concert works. A disc of his choral works is available from Silva Classics (SILKD6002).

Brideshead Revisited The Television Music of Geoffrey Burgon. **Lesley Garrett** (sop); **Philharmonia Orchestra / Geoffrey Burgon**.
Silva Screen ℗ FILMCD117 (59 minutes : DDD). Recorded 1992.

Brideshead Revisited (1981). The Chronicles of Narnia (1988). Bleak House (1985). Testament of Youth (1979). Tinker, Tailor, Soldier, Spy (1979).

In *Brideshead Revisited* the music did not just comment on the drama, but flowed beautifully from scene to scene. The original album is still available, but here in six well-thought out cues, the main components are presented. *Testament of Youth*, one of the BBC's finest ever series, not only boasted a truly remarkable central performance by Cheryl Campbell, but a fine score from Geoffrey Burgon. Here his solo trumpet seems to mourn a lost generation. There was very little music in *Tinker, Tailor, Soldier, Spy*, but what there was counterpointed the drama superbly. In place of the boy chorister on the Original Soundtrack, Lesley Garrett here sings the famous "Nunc Dimittis" (the original actually got into the charts back in 1979). Music from *Bleak House* and *The Chronicles of Narnia* complete what must surely be one of the best ever albums of television music. **JW**

New review
Robin Hood (1991) **Original Soundtrack / Geoffrey Burgon**.
Silva Screen ℗ FILMCD083 (37 minutes: DDD).

A composer who is handed a film dealing with any aspect of the Robin Hood legend must have mixed emotions. On the one hand it is a marvellous opportunity for a composer to get his teeth into some high romance with an English period feel; on the other, so many previous films and television series have provided classic scores that are well-loved and respected. Erich Wolfgang Korngold, Hugo Friedhofer, Gary Hughes, Clifton Parker and Stanley Myers, to name but a few, have all risen to the challenge and written wildly different and varied scores. With this in mind, and knowing that another version of the same story was being filmed at the same time, with no one sure who would be first past the finishing post, Geoffrey Burgon's task could not have been an easy one.

Difficult it may have been, but with a composer of Burgon's stature the listener would never have guessed. John Irvin's film may have had a grittier edge than other Robin Hood movies, but the score is delicate and in turns exciting, without descending into a parody of Korngold as some other composers have done (and not just for this type of adventure movie). Burgon's style is unmistakable, be it for concert hall or film: strings, woodwinds and trumpets dominate. This score is highly romantic, as befitting the story of Robin Hood and Maid Marian, and their romance reaches a stylish climax in the lovely cue "Robin and Marian Reach Safety", scored for strings alone. Two cues, "The Outlaw Band" and part of the final track, utilize just percussion, whilst "The Attack on the Castle" is the most up-tempo piece, with fierce brass and swirling strings. Above all, the score sounds like typical Geoffrey Burgon: there can be no higher recommendation. **JW**

Also available:
Brideshead Revisited (1981) Music for Pleasure CDMFP6172

John Carpenter

b. 1948 USA

John Carpenter is better known as the director of cult movies such as *Dark Star, Escape from New York, The Thing* and the *Halloween* series. However, aside from editing and co-writing most of his own films, he also composes the music. Initially this seemed the best (and cheapest) way for a struggling young director to score his movies whilst retaining absolute creative control. Later, with bigger budgets to play around with, Carpenter occasionally hired other composers (Ennio Morricone for *The Thing*, Jack Nitzsche for *Starman* and Shirley Walker for *Memoirs of an Invisible Man*) but still continued to score many of his own pictures, often with the collaboration of synthesizer expert Alan Howarth. Carpenter has never received any formal musical training, despite his father being head of Kentucky University's music department. He cites Ennio Morricone and Bernard Herrmann – two composers noted for their eclectic orchestral style – as his main influences. Carpenter's synthesized scores are in their own way as distinctive as anything by either of these 'proper' composers.

New review
Big Trouble in Little China (1986) **Original Soundtrack**, with **John Carpenter** (synths).
Demon ℗ DSCD2 (46 minutes: DDD).

A lively Hollywood take on the popular fantasy Chinese cinema – visually stunning fables invariably involving heroes, demons and spirits – Carpenter's film was not well received on release, although it has since gone on to enjoy a cult reputation on video. Correspondingly, the soundtrack album has languished somewhat over the years because the music is in a different style from his more popular scores; this is a pity because it is a more approachable score. Carpenter takes his lead from the percussive nature of the Oriental originals but adds some rock 'n' roll touches of his own. The result is an energetic album which seldom affords any moments of relief, but is lighter in tone than his other scores. On the down side, this is a synth score and there are times when real percussion, strings and, possibly, a choir would have added meat to several undernourished sequences. Also, the score is light on melody which means that it is fun while it lasts but doesn't linger long in the memory. Part of that fun, however, is the title song, performed by The Coup De Villes, otherwise known as Carpenter and fellow writer-directors Nick Castle and Tommy Lee Wallace.   **DS**

New review

Escape from New York (1981) **Original Soundtrack**, with **John Carpenter, Alan Howarth** (synths).
   Varèse Sarabande Ⓕ VCD47224 (37 minutes: ADD).
Escape from L.A. (1996) **Original Soundtrack**, with various artists.
   Milan Ⓕ 40951-2 (34 minutes: DDD). Co-written with Shirley Walker.

Snake Plisken, that wonderfully arrogant anti-hero who spits out his dialogue like an annoyed Clint Eastwood with a sore throat, was the focus of attention in John Carpenter's cult hit, *Escape from New York*; and just about the only saving grace of the long-awaited sequel. Aside from this memorable character, the original movie also produced one of the director's most evocative scores. All of the typical Carpenter elements are here: a thudding heartbeat bass; hypnotically repetitive sequencer patterns worthy of any formally-trained minimalist; impressionistic splashes of synthesized sounds (a synth arrangement of Debussy's *Engulfed Cathedral* is entirely appropriate here). Carpenter doesn't so much write dramatic underscore as soundscapes to complement and enhance the action.
   The principal attraction of the second disc is Shirley Walker, who wrote over half of the score, and collaborated with Carpenter on much of the remainder. To begin with, Walker remains largely within the confines of the director's own idiomatic style, but greatly expands his limited tonal palette, making good use of a variety of solo instruments including violin, dulcimer and harmonica to flesh out Carpenter's brief themes. The original "Main Title" is reprised in a gloriously rocked-up arrangement which makes the most of its minimal content – the rest of the score never quite recovers from this powerhouse opening. The latter half of the album (entirely Walker's) relies increasingly on orchestra over and above the electronic percussion and effects. Oddly perhaps, the further Walker's orchestration moves away from Carpenter's own synth style, the less convincing the music is: stripped of Carpenter's distinctive contribution, by the end it becomes just another routine action/adventure score.   **MW**

Halloween (1978) **Original Soundtrack**, with **John Carpenter** (synths).
   Varèse Sarabande Ⓕ VCD47230 (34 minutes: ADD).

Like Hitchcock with *Psycho*, the director of *Halloween* thought he had a flop on his hands when a screening of his low-budget exploitation horror flick minus music and sound effects failed to impress. Instead of abandoning the film, Carpenter resolved to "save it with music". Like *Psycho*, after the music was added the movie was a runaway success (several less impressive sequels followed). The "Halloween Theme", an hypnotic 5/4 rhythm with a constantly repeating piano figure, has that Herrmannesque monotonous yet compelling quality. The remainder of the score is inevitably less memorable, much of it functioning simply to highlight one 'stinger' (a visual surprise) after another.   **MW**

New review

Halloween The Best of John Carpenter. **Daniel Caine, Derek Wadsworth** (synths).
   Silva Screen Ⓕ FILMCD113 (48 minutes: DDD).
   Assault on Precinct 13 (1976). Halloween (1978). Dark Star (1974). The Fog (1979). Big Trouble in Little China (1986). Escape from New York (1981). Prince of Darkness (1987). They Live (1988). **Ennio Morricone:** The Thing (1982). **Jack Nitzsche:** Starman (1984). Also includes "Bad to the Bone" (George Thorogood) used in *Christine* (1983).

The cult status of John Carpenter's films is almost matched by the cult status of the music he has written for them. Much of that music is included in new re-recorded versions on this disc. Carpenter works exclusively with electronics, employing minimalist and rhythmic techniques, and they have certainly given his scores a very unique sound. He is skilled in creating little fragmented motifs with a very strong hook, from which he assembles the uncomplicated structure of individual cues. In *Assault on Precinct 13* and *Escape from New York*, for example, Carpenter uses a simple bass line against a gritty and contemporary beat to convey the sinister danger of the stories. Broader and more ethereal timbres feature in *Halloween* and *Prince of Darkness*, evoking a spooky and occasionally nasty atmosphere. *Dark Star* and *They Live* embody more rock-centred rhythms. All of his music has a moody ambience, his simplistic and clear approach allowing the listener to appreciate the detail of

his invention. Carpenter sometimes hands over musical chores to other composers, and two of them, Ennio Morricone and Jack Nitzsche, are included here. Neither of their scores have the impact of Carpenter's creations no matter how much they try to mimic it. Electronic scores are often derided, but this is a compilation that shows just how effective synthesizers can be. **PP**

Village of the Damned (1995) **Original Soundtrack**, with **John Carpenter** (synths); **Dave Davies** (co-composer, guitars) and orchestra.
Varèse Sarabande Ⓕ VSD5629 (33 minutes: DDD).

John Carpenter's new film version of John Wyndham's novel *The Midwich Cuckoos* has the director/composer collaborating with ex-Kinks guitarist Dave Davies (who even gets some solos). The music, featuring the unusual addition of some 'real' intruments, is less self-consciously technical than some past scores, employing electronic instruments for the evocative sounds they are capable of producing, rather than just for their own sake. The eight-minute "March of the Children" might even have benefited from greater use of conventional orchestral forces: the typically minimal thematic material is stretched too far without more varied orchestration. A fuller, more expansive score than usual for Carpenter, with a greater emphasis on melody. **MW**

Also available:
Body Bags (1994) Varèse Sarabande VSD5448
Christine (1983) Varèse Sarabande VSD5240
Dark Star (1974) Varèse Sarabande VSD5327
The Fog (1979) Varèse Sarabande VCD47267
Greatest Hits, Vols 1 & 2 Varèse Sarabande VSD5266/5336
Halloween II (1981) Varèse Sarabande VCD47152
Halloween III: Season of the Witch (1982) Varèse Sarabande VSD5243
In the Mouth of Madness (1995) DRG DRG12611
Prince of Darkness (1987) Varèse Sarabande VCD47310
They Live (1988) Demon DSCD1

Tristram Cary

b. 1925 England

Born in Oxford, Tristram Cary's interest in electronic music was fostered by a stint as a radar operator during the Second World War. He studied conventional music at Trinity College of Music after the war, but gradually began to build his own studio of experimental electronic instruments. From the mid-1950s he won renown as an inventive composer primarily for radio, television and film: his scores include the classic Ealing comedy *The Ladykillers* (1955), and Hammer's *Blood from the Mummy's Tomb* (1971); several episodes of *Dr Who*, beginning in 1963 with "The Dead Planet". and numerous radio plays and series, including *The Technology of Music* (1984-7). Many of his earlier film scores employ conventional instrumentation, but his concert works utilize tape and computer music. In 1967, he founded the electronic music studio at the Royal College of Music; his own private studio is one of the longest-established of its kind in the world. The studio and the composer are now based at Adelaide University.

New review
Quatermass and the Pit (1967). **The Flesh is Weak** (1957). **A Twist of Sand** (1968). **Sammy Going South**[a] (1963). **Tread Softly Stranger** (1958). **Original Soundtracks** with [a]**Monica Sinclair** (contr).
Cloud Nine mono Ⓜ CNS5009 (78 minutes: ADD).

Ever since Miklós Rózsa employed a theremin in *Spellbound* (1945), film composers have been well aware of the expressive possibilities of electronic instruments, whether to suggest disturbed mental states – from alcoholism to serial killing – or the menace of hostile aliens. Tristram Cary went one stage further, using pure electronic sounds to enhance his already advanced and often atonal orchestral style. *Quatermass and the Pit* employs bursts of electronic noise amidst the chaotic and fearsome orchestral textures, blurring the distinction between music and sound effects. Much of Cary's score was dropped from the film and replaced by library music, making Cloud Nine's restoration doubly valuable. Elsewhere, Cary's orchestration is more conventional, even if the music remains forward-looking and at times 'difficult'. Monica Sinclair's wordless interjections in *Sammy Going South* impart an air of mystery to what is otherwise the most accessible and lyrical score featured here; *Tread Softly Stranger* is, by contrast, a work of almost unrelieved bleakness and ferocity. This first volume of a planned retrospective of Cary's film music is thus best sampled rather than played straight through from beginning to end. The mono sound, remastered from the composer's personal archive sources, is tolerably good throughout. **MW**

Bill Conti
b. 1942 USA

Born in Rhode Island, Bill Conti spent some time playing piano in bars alongside the Via Veneto in Rome before migrating to Los Angeles. He scored some minor pictures – *Harry and Tonto* (1974) and *Next Stop, Greenwich Village* (1976) – then came the overnight hit that shot Sylvester Stallone to fame in 1976, *Rocky*. That film was also the beginning of a long working relationship between Conti and director John G. Avildsen, for whom he has scored over a dozen films, including *The Karate Kid* trilogy (1984, 1986 and 1989). In between film assignments the composer has written title themes for television series like *Dynasty* and *Cagney and Lacey*. He regularly officiates as music director at the annual Academy Awards ceremony. Conti's music is not especially well represented on disc – that which has been issued is tuneful, enjoyable and extremely well-crafted.

The Adventures of Huck Finn (1993) Original Soundtrack / Bill Conti.
Varèse Sarabande ℗ VSD5418 (31 minutes: DDD).

Take a Walt Disney remake of a classic children's story, add the traditionalist approach, craftsmanship and charm of Bill Conti and this is the result: no surprises, no frills, just solid unfailingly delightful film music. The main theme is an infectiously jolly hoedown for full orchestra, which has a secondary theme vaguely reminiscent of Prokofiev's *Lieutenant Kijé* transplanted to the old West. This being a children's film, and a Disney production, dramatic moments are handled with a lightness which never obscures the clarity of Conti's orchestration. Delicate woodwinds share noble and affecting themes, whilst muscular, almost fugal, orchestral writing introduces rhythmic contrast. Conti's scoring is in a thoroughly classical manner. This charming score leaves the listener wondering why the composer is so underrated. **MW**

North and South (1985) The Right Stuff (1983) London Symphony Orchestra / Bill Conti.
Varèse Sarabande ℗ VCD47250 (38 minutes: DDD).

If you are a sucker for grand old-style Hollywood music – that manipulative, sentimental and derivative symphonic manner of the Golden Age – then these two Bill Conti suites will certainly appeal. *North and South*, a television mini-series, sounds just like the kind of thing Max Steiner was doing 50 years earlier. An achingly, overly romantic love theme and a rousing main theme, something like a cross between "You'll Never Walk Alone" and "Dixie", can't fail to please; whilst a classical piece for trumpet and orchestra, "A Close Call", is an unexpected bonus.

Conti's Academy Award-winning score for *The Right Stuff* is quite unashamedly derivative. It seems pretty obvious that the temp track consisted of "Jupiter" and "Mars" from Holst's *The Planets* (listen to "Breaking the Sound Barrier" and "Glenn's Flight"), and the first movement of Tchaikovsky's Violin Concerto (Conti's final cue, "Yeager's Triumph"). Despite all this borrowing, the score is packed full of drama, pathos and hummable tunes sumptuously clothed in old-fashioned Hollywood garb. The LSO perform with gusto, making this wonderfully old-fashioned disc an enjoyable antidote to all those cool, synthesizer-based new-fangled scores. **MW**

Also available:
Betrayed (1988) TER CDTER1163
Rocky (1976) Liberty 46081-2
Rocky II (1979) Liberty 46082-2
Rocky III (1982) Liberty 46561-2
Year of the Gun (1991) Milan 873 025

Michael Convertino
USA

Michael Convertino was educated at Harvard and Yale – he was a leading member of the Yale Jazz Band – and later at the Paris Conservatory. His diverse musical interests enabled him to play in a rock band and have an orchestral composition premièred at Carnegie Hall when he was aged 23. One of his very first film scores, *Children of a Lesser God* (1986) was nominated for an Academy Award. Subsequent scores include *The Hidden* (1987), *Bull Durham* (1988), *Bodies, Rest and Motion* (1993) and *Things to Do in Denver When You're Dead* (1996).

Bed of Roses (1996) **Original Soundtrack / Artie Kane**.

Milan Ⓕ 35739-2 (39 minutes: DDD). Includes *Independent Love Song* (Parker/Youle), *Ice Cream* (McLachlan), *Killing Time* (Harris/O'Brien) and *Nervous Heart* (Addison/Zimmerman).

For *Bed of Roses*, Michael Convertino is once again experimenting with mood and atmosphere as he did in *Children of a Lesser God*. Here he combines two orchestras (150 musicians altogether) to produce a broad depth of sound designed to evoke romance. Synthesizers augment the traditional orchestra, and prominent parts are provided for piano and woodwinds. Convertino utilizes several themes, notably a rather enticing motif which represents the sparkle and excitement of courtship, first heard in "Tuesday". A more melancholy theme is heard in "I Looked Up", delicately phrased for piano. However, as is often the case with this composer, it is the richness of his orchestration rather than the strength of his thematic material that makes his music so approachable. Much of *Bed of Roses* has an otherworldly aura; the fragility and honesty of his scoring is uniquely elegant and sophisticated. An enchanting soundtrack album, then, slightly marred by the inclusion of some distracting and unsympathetic source music that does little to enhance the score.   **PP**

Children of a Lesser God (1986) **Original Soundtrack / Shirley Walker**.

GNP Crescendo Ⓕ GNPD8007 (33 minutes: DDD).

Michael Convertino's score for the Academy Award-winning *Children of a Lesser God* is most unusual. The composer uses only strings, synthesizers and piano to create a dreamy and ethereal soundscape, an impression of magical romance. Other than the main and end titles, there are no particularly distinct themes or motifs. Instead, Convertino focuses on layering the synthesizers (synclavier), piano and string instruments to produce a warm, idyllic ambience that has a persuasive and quite hypnotic quality. The synths add to the strings a brilliant lustre, whilst solo piano evokes a more personal intimacy. Although never sentimental or melodramatic, Convertino is still able to inject passion into his music, with certain cues possessing a heady, even giddy thrust. Overall, though, this is a score of atmosphere, mood and colour.   **PP**

The Santa Clause (1995) **Original Soundtrack / Artie Kane**.

Milan Ⓕ 32364-2 (40 minutes: DDD).

One of the most enduring traditions in film music is the established custom that film comedy is treated in a serious and straight manner by the composer. When successfully adopted, this approach is intended to make the comedy funnier. Michael Convertino has taken this route with *The Santa Clause* and fashioned a score that is suitably festive and energetic, but also gentle and introspective. His main theme "Let's Go", a wildly vivid *scherzo*, has a pseudo-classical rhythm reminiscent of John Williams's theme from *Home Alone*, another Christmas story. Elsewhere however, Convertino treads less familiar ground. Most interesting is a rather dazzling theme that combines tambourine, echoey plucked strings, bells, and xylophone to produce a subtle but sure evocation of the Christmas spirit. The rest of the material veers towards rather cosy sentimentality, but Convertino manages to pull this back with a melancholy and unsettling tilt in his melodies. The approach may be musically simplistic and undemanding, but it prevents the score from becoming as facile and predictable as the film for which it was conceived. Not a major effort, but still a score that reveals at least some of the composer's personality and individual style.   **PP**

Also available:
Bodies, Rest and Motion (1993) Big Screen 924 506-2
Two Much (1996) Verve 529852-2

Ry Cooder   b. 1947 USA

Born in Los Angeles, Ryland Peter Cooder took up playing the guitar after losing an eye in an accident. His parents were both folk musicians, and he was initially taught by legendary bluesman Rev Gary Davis. Cooder formed the band Rising Sons with Taj Mahal before developing a successful career as a session musician, playing on albums by The Rolling Stones, Randy Newman, Little Feat and others. His friendship with film composer Jack Nitzsche enabled him to become involved in film scoring with *Performance* (1970). Although a master of many folk and blues styles, Cooder is best known for his distinctive slide guitar

EDEL AMERICA

the new name
in film music...

Jonathan First
Edel America Records, Inc.
729 Seventh Avenue, 14th Floor
New York, NY 10019
phone: 212-221-0600
fax: 212-944-3616

EDEL
AMERICA
RECORDS

e·a·r

playing – put to good use in the films *Southern Comfort* (1981) and *Paris, Texas*. Alongside his film work, Cooder has continued touring and recording, with an increasing emphasis on world music.

Geronimo (1993) **Original Soundtrack**, with **Kaigal-ool Khovalyg, Anatoly Kuular, Sayan Bappa** (throat singers); **Jones Benally** (Native American chant); **Ry Cooder** (gtrs) **/ George S. Clinton.**
Columbia Ⓕ 475645-2 (60 minutes: DDD).

Director Walter Hill's decision to employ Ry Cooder's distinctive gifts for *Southern Comfort* back in 1981 proved to be an astute move; it was only natural, then, that he should once again call on the same composer for his epic tale of the legendary American warrior. Departing from his traditionally spartan instrumentation, Cooder has woven a beguiling musical tapestry, which draws on Native American singing, folk textures and full orchestra. Assisted by arranger and orchestrator George S. Clinton, *Geronimo* is Cooder's most ambitious score to date. Much of the blustering orchestral music is reserved for the white man and his destructive ways, whilst the ethnic elements effectively portray the culture of the American Indians. The wistful principal theme is heard most attractively in a tender arrangement for solo cello; whilst Cooder's own distinctive guitar remains an important element (as in the lovely Spanish guitar piece, "La Visita"). Cooder does not pretend to be a fully-rounded film composer in the traditional mould, and sensibly hands over composition of certain elements – like "The Governor's Ball" for example – to his arrangers. Other selections were written in collaboration with the ethnic music performers, enhancing the score with a convincingly authentic feel that a 'proper' composer may have missed. **MW**

Paris, Texas (1984) **Original Soundtrack**, with **Ry Cooder** (gtrs); **Jim Dickinson** and **David Lindley**.
Warner Bros Ⓜ 7599-25270-2 (34 minutes: ADD). Includes *Cancion Mixteca* (Traditional) and *Dark Was the Night* (Blind Willie Johnson).

Perhaps even more than the murky swamps of Louisiana (*Southern Comfort*), the sun-bleached landscape along the Texas/Mexico border provided an ideal backdrop for Ry Cooder's laid-back slide guitar. Sparse instrumental backing throws the lead guitar into sharp focus: every nuance, every vibrato, every motion of Cooder's bottleneck is captured. Few guitarists could stand such close inspection; Cooder's performance is faultless, as ever. The principal theme, stated by guitar alone, sums up with a nonchalant slide and a casual string bend the whole mystery of southern blues. Harry Dean Stanton and Nastassja Kinski's lengthy dialogue, "I Knew These People", which is presumably intended to be poetic, proves instead to be a distraction from Cooder's instrumental accompaniment. His solo rendition of "Dark Was the Night" more than compensates. **MW**

Trespass (1993) **Original Soundtrack**, with **Ry Cooder** (gtrs, etc.); **Jon Hassell** (tpt); **Jim Keltner** (drums/perc).
Sire Ⓕ 9362-45220-2 (38 minutes: DDD). Includes *King of the Street* (Cooder/Keltner) and *Party Lights* (Jr. Brown).

Say farewell to the gentle folk music of the Deep South, this is hard-driven urban blues mixed with free-form improvisation. The contrast between this score and the same year's *Geronimo* (also directed by Walter Hill) could not be more pronounced. Here Cooder is joined by Jon Hassell, who extorts some truly tortured sounds from his trumpet, and virtuoso drummer Jim Keltner. The guitarist's unique floor slide (pictured in the booklet) produces the most enormous and atmospheric slide guitar textures imaginable. The music is highly experimental, which makes it an unrepeatable film score experience. There is nothing quite as accessible as a tune to be found, other than in the incongruous C&W song which closes the disc ("King of the Street", by contrast, is not a song as such, but includes dialogue snippets from the film arranged as 'lyrics'). Hardly average film music fare, but an undoubtedly exciting discovery for Cooder fans. **MW**

Also available:
Blue City (1986) Warner Bros 7599-25386-2
Crossroads (1986) Warner Bros 7599-25399-2
Johnny Handsome (1989) Warner Bros 925996-2
Last Man Standing (1996) Verve 533 415-2
The Long Riders (1980) Warner Bros 7599-23448-2
Music by Ry Cooder [compilation] Warner Bros 9362-45987-2

Stewart Copeland

b. 1952 USA

Although best known as the drummer with The Police, since the group disbanded in 1986 Stewart Copeland has created a career for himself as a composer both for film and stage. Born in Virginia, Copeland had played in Curved Air before joining up with Andy Summers and Sting in 1977 (he also recorded "Don't Care" under the name Klark Kent in 1978). Even before The Police disbanded, Copeland was pursuing solo projects, and had scored the film *Rumble Fish* in 1983. Other notable scoring assignments include *Wall Street* (1987), *Talk Radio* (1988), *Highlander 2: The Quickening* (1991) and the feature-length pilot episode for the Sci-Fi series *Babylon 5* (1993). In addition, Copeland has written the full-length opera *Holy Blood and the Crescent Moon* (1989) for the Cleveland Opera and the television operetta *Horse Opera*. He released the album *The Rhythmatist* in 1985, based on his interest in West African drumming, and formed the band Animal Logic in 1989.

New review
Rapa Nui (1994) **Original Soundtrack**, with **Vicki Randle, David Viloria** (sngrs); **Kealiíi O Nalani Choir / Stewart Copeland, Judd Miller, Ron Aston, Jonathan Sheffer**.
Milan Ⓕ 35681-2 (40 minutes DDD).

Rapa Nui endeavours to explain something of the mystery of Easter Island, drawing on scientific and anthropological research to fashion a plot both fascinating and bizarre. A standard symphonic score might well work here, but the effectiveness of the film is greatly enhanced by music of distinctly unusual timbres. Utilizing quasi-native chant, synthesizers, a raft of ethnic drums, earthy Indonesian flutes, and occasional standard instrumentation Stewart Copeland has created an extraordinary soundscape. Via mixing, looping, multitracking – and an expertise born of years of working on the best of rock and pop – he has invented a vital, pulsating, yet often lyrical score of the first order. The music drives on for 40 unforgettable minutes – more new age experience than standard film score. The music works well with the film; away from the movie it makes for stimulating listening.   **DW**

Also available:
The Pallbearer (1996) Hollywood 162058
Talk Radio (1988) **Wall Street** (1987) Varèse Sarabande VSD5459

Aaron Copland

1900-1990 USA

The son of Polish and Lithuanian immigrants, Aaron Copland was born in Brooklyn and was first taught to play the piano by his sister. He studied with various teachers in New York before moving to Paris aged 20 in order to learn from Nadia Boulanger. He soon developed his own individual style inspired by homegrown folk and jazz idioms. Copland forged a distinctively American sound in works like *Fanfare for the Common Man* (1942), and the ballets *Billy the Kid* (1938), *Rodeo* (1942) and *Appalachian Spring* (1944). His work for films was limited, not because of any lack of interest on the composer's part, but from a dearth of offers from Hollywood (each major studio had its own fully-functional Los Angeles-based music department) Copland remained in New York). Despite receiving an Academy Award for *The Heiress* (1949) Copland only wrote eight scores in total, and was never again asked to write a score in Hollywood (his final film was a New York-based production *Something Wild* in 1961).

Music for Films Saint Louis Symphony Orchestra / Leonard Slatkin.
RCA Ⓕ 09026 61699-2 (68 minutes: DDD).
The Red Pony (1949). Our Town (1940). The Heiress (1949). Music for Movies (1942). Prairie Journal: Music for Radio (1936).

This is a marvellous disc of gritty integrity, gorgeous phrasing, dynamic rhythm, and inventive magic. Wonderful music, conducted and played with great skill and devotion. Copland captures better than anyone the heart and nature of America, in musical images of immediacy and clarity: here are humour, tragedy, family values and traditional skills. Apart from the well-known *Red Pony*, it is a joy to discover *Prairie Journal*, a suite of music for radio, written in 1936 before he considered writing for film, and *Music for Movies*, five extracts from three scores (*The City*, *Of Mice and Men*, both 1939, and *Our Town*, 1940) deliberately arranged to have a life beyond the films which inspired them. There is also the world première recording of a suite from *The Heiress* (reconstructed by Arnold Freed) – music which earned Copland an Academy Award – restoring the original "Prelude", which the director William Wyler replaced in the film without the composer's knowledge. Thoroughly uplifting.   **CT**

See also Collections: **Music for Stage and Screen**

John Corigliano
b. 1938 USA

Born in New York, John Corigliano's mother was a·gifted pianist and his father was concert-master (leader) of the New York Philharmonic. He studied at New York's Columbia College, the Manhattan School of Music and privately with composer Paul Creston. He became a writer and programmer for WQXR radio and an associate producer of CBS Television's Young People's Concerts. He also worked as a rock music arranger for Kama Sutra and Mercury Records, and has since been appointed (1973) professor of music at Lehman College, City University of New York. Since 1986 he has been composer-in-residence of the Chicago Symphony Orchestra. Several of his compositions have been recorded, including his Clarinet Concerto (1977) and Symphony No. 1 (1990). Corigliano's 'clean' musical style is in the tradition of American composers like Copland, Harris and Bernstein; although his work is entirely unique. His microtonal, non-harmonic score for Ken Russell's *Altered States* (1980) received an Academy Award nomination, whilst his music for the film *Revolution* (1985) won the British Film Institute's Anthony Asquith Award. Corigliano's highly innovative style has influenced the work of his successful protégé, Elliot Goldenthal.

Altered States (1980) **Original Soundtrack / Christopher Keene**.
RCA Victor Ⓜ 3983-2 (40 minutes: ADD).

This incredible, hallucinatory score is an exercise in extremes: extreme dynamic range, extremely outlandish sonorities. Corigliano uses a percussion-heavy orchestra and two pianos re-tuned to play quarter tones. Rattling percussion, scampering brass, frantic woodwinds, and great crashing blocks of orchestral sound assault the listener; yet the music never descends into cacophony. Indeed, *Altered States* is as much capable of secretive whispers as it is of violent screaming. A thoroughly traditional and highly romantic "Love Theme" stands apart from the chaos, an oasis of calm serenity, whilst synthesizers add an extra dimension. By any standards, this is stunningly original music-making, and a demonstration that film scoring can produce works as bold and thought-provoking as any contemporary 'art' music. The commercial success of Corigliano's star pupil, Elliot Goldenthal, may go some way towards lessening the shock of hearing this music for the first time; it will not lessen the intoxicating effect of playing this disc. This is a true original. **MW**

Mychael Danna
b. 1958 Canada

The leading composer of music for Canadian films, Mychael Danna was born in Winnipeg. He received his music degree from the University of Toronto, where he won the Glenn Gould Composition Award in 1985. Much of his early success stemmed from his association with Atom Egoyan, the most critically acclaimed Canadian filmmaker of his generation. Danna's first film score, for Egoyan's *Family Viewing* (1987), was nominated for a Genie award by the Academy of Canadian Cinema and Television. Danna and Egoyan collaborated again on *Speaking Parts* (1989), *The Adjuster* (1991, selected as one of the ten best Canadian films by an international poll of critics at the 1994 Toronto Film Festival), a segment of *Montreal Sextet* (1992), and the telefilm *Gross Misconduct* (1992). Their association reached a peak with *Exotica* (1994), the winner of the International Critics' Prize at the 1994 Cannes Film Festival and the recipient of eight Genies including Best Picture, Best Director, and Best Music Score. Some of the composer's other credits are *Termini Station* (1989), *Cold Comfort* (1989), Bruce McDonald's *Dance Me Outside* (1994), and the highly-rated television series *Road to Avonlea*. He is also an internationally recognized recording artist, having created several popular instrumental concept albums inspired by the environment (*North of Niagara*). More recent international commissions include *Kama Sutra* (1996), John Greyson's *Lilies* (1996), Ang Lee's *The Ice Storm* (1997) and Atom Egoyan's film version of the Russell Banks novel *The Sweet Hereafter* (1997).

New review
The Adjuster[a] (1991) **Speaking Parts**[b] (1989) **Family Viewing**[b] (1987) **Original Soundtracks**, with [a]**Djivan Gasparian** (duduk); [a]**Mark Fewer** (vn); **Eve Egoyan** (pf); [b]**Esprit Orchestra / Alex Pauk**.
Varèse Sarabande Ⓕ VSD5674 (56 minutes: DDD).
Exotica (1994) **Original Soundtrack**.
Varèse Sarabande Ⓕ VSD5543 (50 minutes: DDD).

There are many well-documented examples of creative partnerships of director and composer but new ones are always worth exploring. That between Danna and Atom Egoyan is hardly new but the first disc is extremely useful in picking three scores from their 10-year association. The booklet notes for this compilation point out that it is planned as a companion release to the full soundtrack of *Exotica*, but it is actually a more interesting disc than that might imply. Danna's style with *The*

Adjuster is a combination of *Twin Peaks*-ian moodiness contrasted by some very affecting work for solo piano and violin. *Family Viewing* is not unlike Michael Nyman with its insistent repeating string rhythms, not so much menacing as disquieting, but again this is contrasted with a serene slow movement from a mock-Mozart piano concerto. The mesmeric Glass-like percussion of the cue "Talk Show" also acts as a neat stereo demonstration piece. *Speaking Parts* is the least interesting of the three scores but does exhibit more percussion ideas and moody string textures.

Exotica is by no means uninteresting being a collection of, well, exotic dances from the eponymous nightclub interleaved with more introspective piano-based cues. The performances on middle-Eastern instruments add sultry spice to the music that does appeal but ultimately it all wears a bit thin over 50 minutes. About 20 minutes of *Exotica* grafted onto the compilation album and you would have the ideal introduction to the world of Danna and Egoyan.   **DS**

Carl Davis
b. 1936 USA

Brooklyn-born Carl Davis has spent most of his working life in England. His family was musical, so Davis began studying at seven and was able to follow music scores by the age of nine. He studied at Queen's College, New York and the New England College of Music, and learned composition from Paul Nordoff and Hugo Kauder. His music for a revue called *Diversions* was seen by Jerome Robbins, who helped get it staged in Greenwich Village in 1959. Moving to Europe, Davis studied with Per Norgard in Copenhagen and worked with the Royal Danish Ballet. He arrived in London in 1961, and decided to stay. Following the success of *Diversions* at the Edinburgh Festival in 1961, Davis was asked by Ned Sherrin to write music for the satirical series *That Was the Week That Was*. He has composed copiously for both stage and screen, with extensive forays into televsion. He has been particularly associated with the revival of classic silent movies, especially the 'Thames Silents' commissioned by Jeremy Isaacs, writing several new full-length symphonic scores. In 1991 he collaborated with Paul McCartney on the *Liverpool Oratorio*, and frequently conducts concerts of music from films and shows. He is married to actress Jean Boht.

The French Lieutenant's Woman (1981) Original Soundtrack, with **Erich Gruenberg** (vn);
Kenneth Essex (va); **Keith Harvey** (vc) **/ Carl Davis**.
DRG Ⓕ CDRG6106 (38 minutes: AAD). Includes *Adagio* from Piano Sonata in D, K576 (Mozart).

Wheels within wheels. This score for a film within a film consists of two entirely distinct elements. The overridingly important musical style is a fervently passionate nineteenth-century romanticism, for which a string trio nucleus project the requisite anguish, longing and joy over a shimmering orchestral background. This expressively romantic mood is varied at times with a hint of an earlier classicism, reinforced by the Mozart extract. In total contrast are the score's contemporary elements, light pop pieces scored for electric guitars, keyboards and drums (arranged by Brian Gascoigne). Inevitably, the stylistic clash is a jarring one: in the context of the film this was exactly the point; on disc, however, the effect is simply to make the album seem disjointed. The problem is easily solved: programming out only three tracks (numbers seven, nine and 12) leaves the listener with a broodingly passionate, expertly constructed work to enjoy.   **MW**

Intolerance (1916) **Luxembourg Radio Symphony Orchestra / Carl Davis**.
Prometheus Ⓕ PCD105 (76 minutes: DDD). Composed and recorded 1990.

It would seem Carl Davis is not only a composer, he is also an industry: how else could he find the time and the muse to fulfil all that is asked of him, from conducting an enviable round of concerts to composing numerous film scores. Particularly taxing must be his work on the series 'Thames Silents' – restored classics from cinema's silent era – a roster which to date includes *The Thief of Bagdad, Ben-Hur* and *The Wind*. But even these venerated films are eclipsed by D. W. Griffith's awe-inspiring *Intolerance*. This remarkable film requires nearly three hours of continuous music, which has to evoke all the drama, all the tragedy, all the humanity of a vast panorama stretching from the time of ancient Babylon to the dawn of the twentieth century. The amount of work involved must have been monumental; and, except for a mock-baroque sequence evoking the court of Catherine de Medici, and some natty foxtrots illustrating the film's contemporary story, the scoring is massive. Permeating every episode is the commanding *Intolerance* theme, marching onward through history with a powerful inevitability which invites comparison with the mighty opening movement of Shostakovich's Seventh Symphony. Davis's score possesses an eminent classicism, not the aura of an average film score. There is something inherently distinguished about this music: it has a potency, an immensity, which commands attention. For this compact disc the score has been distilled to a generous 75 minutes. Every second of it is outstanding.   **DW**

Pride and Prejudice (1995) **Original Soundtrack**, with **Melvyn Tan** (fp) **/ Carl Davis**.
   EMI Ⓕ CDEMC3726 (55 minutes: DDD).

To describe this luminescent, scintillating score as pastiche is to imply no censure. *Pride and Prejudice* glows with an inner warmth that is all the composer's own, even though the style is entirely in keeping with the period setting. Examples of home-grown English music from the very end of the eighteenth century are pretty rare, so Davis has rightly turned to European models, more popular then as they are now. Beethoven's early Septet in E flat (1796) is avowedly the inspiration for some of the more intimate chamber pieces here; but the spirited vitality of Mozart informs the main theme and much of the rest. Davis is subtle with his material: a portentous *Prelude* in the cue "Rosings" alludes to the older baroque world of Handel, deliberately reflecting the old-fashioned stuffiness of its inhabitants; after we have heard the heroine on screen singing Cherubino's aria "Voi che sapete" from *Le nozze di Figaro*, the composer tells us of Darcy's state of mind by quoting it at the beginning of "Thinking About Lizzy": Davis has managed the difficult trick of adapting these influences to resemble a more straightforward English style. Melvyn Tan's crystal-clear fortepiano providing unaccompanied, Haydnesque 'Piano Summaries' for the beginning of each episode. Later cues, such as the eloquent "Darcy Returns", are deeply romantic in spirit, without anachronistically straying beyond the bounds of the era. This is an unfailingly delightful score which should be admired as much for its originality as for its brilliant use of period style.   **MW**

The Trial (1992) **Original Soundtrack**, with the **Czech Symphony Orchestra / Carl Davis**.
   Milan Ⓕ 873 150 (41 minutes: DDD).

The BBC's ambitious filming of Franz Kafka's *The Trial* may not have been an artistic hit, despite a Harold Pinter script, but Carl Davis certainly provided a model score. Dominated by two sterling themes – the first, a plaintive melody for accordion associated with the beautiful Leni and Josef's yearning for her; the other a devilish brass-led black waltz representing not only Josef's bizarre predicament, but also the grotesque legal system with which he has to grapple. A separate theme for the lawyer Huld is a near relation to the dark waltz typifying the legal process – Davis cannily informs us that for all his sympathetic council, Huld too is part of the unfathomable, repressive system. Elsewhere the scoring is stark, spare, disquieting; the orchestration is telling, with astute use of cimbalon and bass clarinet. As might be expected, this is overtly dramatic music. As fateful events start to impose more and more on the unfortunate Josef an insistent ground bass begins to permeate the score, creating an air of cold inevitability. This is music Kafka himself might have forged – it is so redolent of the tale, dense with foreboding and infused with anguish. Critics may have taken issue with some aspects of *The Trial*, but the musical score is an unqualified success.   **DW**

Also available:
Ben-Hur (1925) Silva Screen FILMCD043
Napoleon (1927) Silva Screen FILMCD149
Widow's Peak (1993) Varèse Sarabande VSD5487

John Debney

Born in Burbank, California, John Debney played guitar and piano from an early age. He studied music and acting at Loyola University, and took his degree in composition at CalArts. During his summer vacations Debney worked in the music library at Walt Disney studios (his father was a former Disney producer) and this led to a full-time job as a copyist, orchestrator and arranger with Disney. In addition, he wrote original music for Disney theme parks, including the EPCOT Center and EuroDisney. Debney became a freelance composer in the 1980s, working on television shows like *Cagney and Lacey*, *Fame* and *The Young Riders* – this latter earned him his first Emmy Award. He began an association with Hanna-Barbera Productions scoring the big-screen adaptation of their cartoon series *The Jetsons* (1990). For Steven Spielberg's Amblin Productions, Debney scored the Civil War mini-series *Class of '61* (1993) before winning another Emmy Award for his work on *SeaQuest DSV*. He was a late arrival to *Cutthroat Island* after original composer David Arnold parted company with director Renny Harlin. Recent scores include Harlin's *The Long Kiss Goodnight* and Peter Hyams's *Relic*.

New review
Cutthroat Island (1996) **Original Soundtrack**, with the **London Voices; London Symphony Orchestra / David Snell**.
Silva Screen Ⓕ FILMCD178 (70 minutes: DDD).

It has often been said that there is really only one way to score films of certain genres. John Debney wisely chose not to attempt to re-write the rule book in approaching this mammoth pirate epic, but instead penned a full-bodied orchestral score in the traditional style of Golden-Age composers such as Steiner, Newman, Korngold and Rózsa. Although Debney was never in any danger of emulating these past masters through mere imitation, he has nevertheless succeeded in writing a passionate orchestral *tour de force* with much heroism, adventure and flamboyance. Lovers of large-scale symphonic music will certainly enjoy hearing the 120 musicians of the London Symphony Orchestra rattling through gallant fanfares, lush romantic themes and hugely explosive action set-pieces. Indeed, *Cutthroat Island* is one of the most spectacular aural bombardments of recent times, although at 70 minutes even the most die-hard fans of this style of music are likely to become a little weary before the CD ends.   **PP**

New review
Eye of the Panther (1989) **Not Since Casanova** (1988) **Original Soundtracks / John Debney**.
Prometheus Ⓕ PCD140 (47 minutes: DDD).

A CD to join the burgeoning collection of discs available from this prolific up-and-coming composer showcases two scores which could not be more different. *Eye of the Panther*, a low-budget horror movie, has a score performed by large chamber orchestra. The emphasis is on strings, piano and solo woodwind instruments, with a respectable romantic theme woven amongst some stark and jagged material that is primarily tension-building. More interesting is the thoroughly romantic score for *Not Since Casanova* which boasts a highly memorable main theme. Although again performed by strings, piano and woodwinds, it has a much broader feel and depth. Debney positively bathes the listener in solo writing, particularly for piano and woodwinds, but it never becomes contrived or pretentious. Both scores are certainly worth a listen, although they suffer from a lack of any genuine passion.   **PP**

Also available:
SeaQuest DSV (1993) Varèse Sarabande VSD5565
Sudden Death (1996) Varèse Sarabande VSD5663

Georges Delerue
1925-1992 France

Born in Roubaix, Georges Delerue studied at the Paris Conservatoire under Henri Busser and Darius Milhaud. In 1948, Milhaud sent him to conduct at the Avignon Music Festival and this led to an offer to compose for the theatre. His prolific film career included several fruitful collaborations with directors Alain Resnais, Jean-Luc Godard and François Truffaut – *Hiroshima Mon Amour* (1958), *Le Mépris* (1963) and *Jules et Jim* (1962) for example – before inevitably expanding towards Hollywood (although Delerue did not move to Los Angeles until the year after he received an Academy Award for *A Little Romance*, 1979). In addition to scoring some 200 films, Delerue composed extensively for the concert hall, and was planning a cello concerto at the time of his death. (A new recording of Delerue's music for François Truffaut's movies is due for release as part of the new film music series on Nonesuch in 1997, featuring the London Sinfonietta conducted by Hugo Wolff).

Agnes of God (1985) **Original Soundtrack**, with the **Elmer Isler Singers; Toronto Symphony Orchestra / Georges Delerue**.
Varèse Sarabande Ⓕ VSD5368 (31 minutes: DDD).

One of Delerue's strongest characteristics was his seemingly effortless way of constructing melodies that instantly evoke a stong emotional response. *Agnes of God* is a religious film, or rather a film that examines religious belief, and as such is ripe material for a background score that plays on the emotions. While the opening and closing melody is highly emotive, and also one of his most lyrically beautiful compositions, it is the restraint that he exercises throughout the rest of the score that impresses. The strings playing sustained chords with occasional choral effects exerts a beatific calm that contrasts winningly with the main theme. So much so, that one finds oneself longing for the theme's return at the end; its simple rhapsodic charm acting as a cathartic release and so becoming all the more effective. The original album's presentation of assembling nameless cues into two *Symphonic Suites* over two sides is retained, but becomes somewhat pointless on CD. However, the addition of booklet notes is welcome. **DS**

New review

Jules et Jim (1962) **Une Aussi Longue Absence** (1961) **Le Mépris** (1963) **Hiroshima Mon Amour** (1958) **Viva Maria** (1965) **Original Soundtracks**, with dialogue.
Auvidis Travelling mono Ⓕ K1501 (47 minutes: DDD).

"Throughout the film, George Delerue's exquisite music – simple and fragrant – is part of the atmosphere; it is so evocative that if you put the music on the phonograph, it brings back the images, the emotions, the experience." These words from a review of Truffaut's *Jules et Jim* by critic Pauline Kael, whose pronouncements on film music have generally been amateurish, was this time an accurate description of Delerue's contribution to what is arguably Truffaut's best film.

Indeed, the late Delerue is perhaps best known as the main composer used by the directors of the French "New Wave" movement during the late 1950s and 1960s. Subtitled "Movies To Listen To", this disc lifts segments of music, dialogue, and songs directly from the original soundtracks of five "New Wave" films. For those who want to hear the music on its own, this approach will quickly become irritating. The disc seems to have been conceived in the mindset of an earlier, video-less era that saw soundtracks as the only way of recreating the original filmgoing experience. Now that films and soundtracks are widely accessible in form and variety, this production concept seems anachronistic. Still, the quality of the music is what matters most, and on this level the disc delivers.

Jules et Jim was one of the first European films to achieve success in America. The movie examines the friendship between the bourgeois Jules (Oskar Werner), the intellectual bohemian Jim (Henri Serre), and the feminist Catherine (Jeanne Moreau), whose independence and power is the lifeblood of the mens' lives but also their fund of despair. The three-movement suite includes the exuberant main title music, the bittersweet love music, and the bright, carnival-like waltz that connects the trio as a group. Moreau is heard singing "Le Tourbillon", while variations of the main themes round out the suite. The tragic ending of the film and the music stands in sharp contrast to the fun, optimistic opening. Henri Colpi's *Une Aussi Longue Absence* is represented by a short piece for French accordion and an unremarkable song. A more interesting score is the music for Jean-Luc Godard's *Le Mépris*. Here Delerue has composed several dark essays for strings to colour this tale of a marriage breaking up on the set of a Fritz Lang film. In the suite from Alain Resnais's *Hiroshima Mon Amour*, the music is buried beneath the dialogue between a French film actress (Emanuelle Riva) and a Japanese architect (Eiji Okade) in the midst of a post-war affair. The disc closes with 15 minutes from Louis Malle's *Viva Maria*, a fun romp about the exploits of two music-hall entertainers (Brigitte Bardot, Jeanne Moreau) who become involved with a revolutionary leader in Mexico. Delerue makes several concessions to the Mexican setting, although the folk-tinged music (an acoustic guitar adds to the feel) has been orchestrated primarily in a non-ethnic way. The suite from *Viva Maria* is marred slightly by the decision to dial-out the end ballad.

The booklet includes an anecdote by Henri Colpi, a brief biography of Delerue, and plot synopses of the films with cast and crew lists. This disc is a good buy for anyone who loves or wants to know more about the Delerue/New Wave era. On the other hand, completists and those who hate having their film music intruded on by dialogue have been warned. **KM**

The London Sessions, Volumes 1-3. **Anonymous orchestra / Georges Delerue**.
Varèse Sarabande Ⓕ VSD5241, VSD5245 and VSD5256 (53, 53 and 59 minutes: DDD). Recorded 1989.
VSD5241 – Platoon (1986). Rich and Famous (1981). Her Alibi (1989). Beaches (1988). Exposed (1983). Biloxi Blues (1988). A Little Romance (1979). Crimes of the Heart (1986). *VSD5245* – Steel Magnolias (1989). Interlude (1968). The Escape Artist (1982). The Pick-Up Artist (1987). A Tribute to François Truffaut. An Almost Perfect Affair (1979). Maxie (1985). Salvador (1986). *VSD5256* – Something Wicked This Way Comes (1983). The House on Carroll Street (1988). A Little Sex (1982). Maid to Order (1987). Man, Woman and Child (1983). Memories of Me (1988). Agnes of God (1985). True Confessions (1981).

During the final years of his life Delerue was almost exclusively appropriated by Hollywood, and these three commendable albums deal almost entirely with this later, extremely rich output – although his French heritage is represented by a suite of ten themes for Truffaut movies including *Jules et Jim* (1961) and *Day for Night* (1973). Delerue's freely flowing style was simple and winning, relying very much on strings and woodwind at the expense of brass, and with a minimum of percussion. There was always something of a baroque air about his music – and the melodic invention was forever ravishing. If there ever was a composer of amour, of adoration, of passion, then Delerue was he: *Her Alibi, Rich and Famous* and *Crimes of the Heart* are prime examples of music in a manifestly romantic idiom. But Delerue was also adept at human drama: his heartfelt, intimate, intensely personal scoring of *True Confessions, Salvador, Agnes of God* and *Platoon* invested these

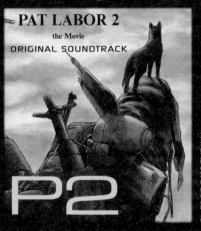

accomplished dramas with an added emotional dimension. Delerue's searing, fervent, but unused main theme for *Platoon* was replaced by Samuel Barber's *Adagio for Strings*. Inexplicably, Delerue had his entire score for the creepy childhood thriller *Something Wicked This Way Comes* rejected (the film was subsequently scored by James Horner); but thankfully we can now appreciate this music in an 11-minute suite, with the composer on this occasion employing some exceptionally spiky brass for his particularly unnerving prelude music. These albums, although omitting much of Delerue's earlier work, still manage to be representative of his consistent style. Whilst all three discs would seem essential, Volume 1 proves the most satisfying. Most of these recordings were made at Abbey Road Studios and are augmented with just the occasional Original Soundtrack offering.   **DW**

Platoon (1986) **Salvador** (1986) **Original Soundtracks**, with the **Vancouver Symphony Choir and Orchestra / Georges Delerue**.
Prometheus Ⓕ PCD136 (55 minutes: DDD). Includes *Adagio for Strings* (Samuel Barber).

Oliver Stone's compelling Vietnam drama gave a new lease of life to Samuel Barber's *Adagio for Strings*, in the process it consigned the greater portion of Georges Delerue's original score to oblivion. Of the seven tracks on this disc, only one – "Bunker to the Village" – can be heard in the film. Instead of being allowed to bring his own inimitable style to the picture, Delerue was required by Stone to write a theme so closely based on Barber's *Adagio* that it inevitably could not match the beauty and emotive impact of its model. At the same time, he was asked to record the Barber piece, making it painfully obvious that the director had already made up his mind which one he was going to use. Delerue's unused theme is interesting insofar as it follows the shape and flow of the *Adagio* without actually overtly quoting from it; but, in retrospect, it would have done Delerue no favours to have used it – imagine the glee of the critics as they lambasted the hapless composer for his unwilling plagiarism. The most effective parts of the score are those in which he was allowed a freer hand. There are several moments of tense drama in between the mock-*Adagio*; these are all the more notable for being completely unlike Delerue's habitual flowing melodies.

His previous collaboration with Stone, *Salvador*, was a happier one, resulting in an occasionally exciting, at times sombre, but often moving work. A rhythmic main theme forms a percussive backbone to the rest; a romantic love theme, first introduced in "At the Border", is gorgeously Spanish-tinged; darker, dramatic music dominates later episodes. The whole builds to a poignant "Finale" in which the lyrical "Love Theme" is fully stated in a choral and orchestral arrangement. Overall, a more satisfying work than the ill-fated *Platoon*.   **MW**

Also available:
Black Robe (1991) Varèse Sarabande VSD5349
The Borgias (1981) Prometheus PCD109
Cartouche (1961) Prometheus PCD104
The Conformist (1971) etc. DRG DRGCD32910
Le Dernier Metro (1980) **La Femme d'à Côté** (1981) Prometheus PCD113
Jules et Jim (1962) **La Cloche Tibéthaine** (1974) Prometheus PCD103
A Little Romance (1979) Varèse Sarabande VSD5367
Man Trouble (1991) Varèse Sarabande VSD5369
Rich in Love (1992) Varèse Sarabande VSD5370
Silkwood (1983) DRG DRGCD6107
Thibaud the Crusader (1967) Prometheus PCD114
Truffaut and Delerue DRG DRGCD32902
Two English Girls (1971) Milan 11846-2

see also Collections: **François Truffaut Films**

Pino Donaggio   b. 1941 Italy

Born in Burano, near Venice, Pino Donaggio began studying the violin at age ten, first in Venice then at the conservatory in Milan. Here he worked with conductor Claudio Abbado, who was also at the beginning of his career. In 1959, Donaggio interrupted his classical studies when he discovered Rock and Roll. His 1963 song "Lo che non vivo" sold 60 million copies around the world. Its English version, "You Don't Have to Say You Love Me", was performed by Dusty Springfield and Elvis Presley. Donaggio's first film score came in 1973 with Nicolas Roeg's eerie *Don't Look Now*. This score established Donaggio in Hollywood as a composer of horror and suspense – a trend confirmed by his long-standing association with director Brian De Palma, beginning in 1976 with the Stephen King adaptation *Carrie*. Alongside his Hollywood career, Donaggio continues to write music for home-grown Italian movies.

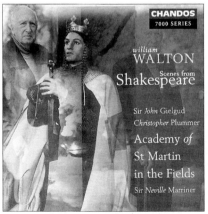

Brian De Palma Films Original Soundtracks.
Milan Ⓕ 19192-2 (47 minutes: ADD/DDD).
Carrie (1976). Home Movies (1978). Dressed to Kill (1980). Blow Out (1981). Body Double (1984). Raising Cain (1992).

This is a useful survey of the Donaggio/De Palma collaboration, even if the packaging is exceptionally tacky (but so are some of the movies), and the booklet note inaccurate (Donaggio has not composed the music for all of De Palma's films). *Carrie*, their first film together, typifies Donaggio's smooth, softly melodic reaction to scenes of horrific violence – as if Donaggio is writing against the images, rather than consciously creating 'mad' horror music. But, beneath the slick surface, there is an undercurrent of menace that can be heard throughout most of the extracts on this disc. The "Main Title" from *Home Movies* is an exception: it is an entertaining mock-classical *Minuet*, with added electric guitar and drums. *Blow Out* features some grandly gothic writing for brass; *Body Double* adds some romping synthesizers for extra special tackiness; whilst *Raising Cain* is an effectively bleak and chilling piece, to which moaning voices and saxophone briefly contribute an aura of sexiness. **MW**

Dressed to Kill (1980) Original Soundtrack / Natale Massara.
Varèse Sarabande Ⓕ VCD47148 (41 minutes: ADD).

Brian De Palma's shameless remake of Hitchcock's *Psycho* did not – for the most part – tempt Donaggio to follow Bernard Herrmann's lead. Instead he produced a surprisingly romantic 'Shower scene', relying on lush unison strings and heavenly voices for its effect. The subdued atmosphere evoked here only occasionally reminds us this is a horror score: "Death in the Elevator" and "The Forgotten Ring" – with their choppy, stabbing string motifs – are the only places where Donaggio nods in Herrmann's direction. Otherwise, his emphasis is more on the erotic than the horrific – responding to De Palma's voyeuristic images, his melodies are warmly sensual, not discordant. That said, it is those scenes of dramatic tension – like "The Transformation" – in which the score really comes to life. **MW**

Also available:
The Barbarians (1987) Intrada MAF7008D
Colpo di Coda (1993) CAM COS016
Don't Look Now (1973) TER CDTER1007
Dove Siete? Io Sono Qui (1993) CAM COS018
Morte in Vaticano (1982) CAM CSE033
Never Talk to Strangers (1995) Edel CIN2244-2
Raising Cain (1992) Milan 10130-2

Patrick Doyle

b. 1953 Scotland

Patrick Doyle attended the Royal Scottish Academy for Music and Drama, where he studied piano and singing, graduating in 1974. He acted in and wrote music for several theatre and radio productions before joining Kenneth Branagh's Renaissance Theatre Company as actor, composer and musical director in 1987. When Branagh's film version of *Henry V* (1989) went into production, Doyle got the chance to write his first film score. The result – also a first for conductor Sir Simon Rattle – proved to be a significant factor in the film's success. Doyle's status as one of the most original and inventive composers currently active in movies has been assured ever since. In addition to expanding his work with other directors, the Doyle/Branagh partnership has continued to flourish, resulting in memorable scores for *Dead Again*, *Much Ado About Nothing*, *Frankenstein* and *Hamlet*. In addition, he has provided incidental music for the Renaissance Theatre Company's Shakespeare radio recordings. Doyle the actor and singer can be seen and heard in both *Henry V* and *Much Ado About Nothing*. He has also written a song-cycle for choir and orchestra, "The Thistle and the Rose" (1990) for the Queen Mother's 90th birthday. His usual orchestrator is Lawrence Ashmore.

Dead Again (1991) Original Soundtrack / William Kraft.
Varèse Sarabande Ⓕ VSD5339 (32 minutes: DDD).

A prototypical Patrick Doyle score (if such a thing exists), *Dead Again* contains many elements which were to reappear in subsequent works. The urgent ostinato rhythms punctuated by shrill brass in the opening sequence are recalled on a grander scale in *Frankenstein*; the nostalgic love theme echoes Doyle's delectable *Much Ado About Nothing*; the operatic climax has the driving urgency of *Needful Things*. String-led monochrome orchestration shades the remainder in the manner of Hollywood *film noir*. An unmistakably characteristic work. **MW**

Exit to Eden (1994) **Original Soundtrack / David Snell**.
Varèse Sarabande ℗ VSD5553 (33 minutes: DDD).

Something of a change of direction: written about the same time as *Frankenstein*, Doyle's score for this sex comedy is admittedly a less well-moulded creation. An insistent Latin American-style beat gives a new twist to Doyle's usual idiom during the opening cues, and its recurrence throughout the score is always welcome ("Get with the Programme" being perhaps the best example). "The Arrival" introduces a mock grand march, which then makes way for the first of several 'love' themes, led by solo piano and flute. These and other up-tempo jazzy numbers are the least plausible parts of the score, simply because they are the least like Doyle's personal style. An oddity, but not without interest. **MW**

New review
Une Femme Française (1995) **Original Soundtrack**, with **Jill Gomez** (sop) **/ David Snell**.
WEA ℗ 4509-99630-2 (37 minutes: DDD).

One of the composer's lesser-known works, Patrick Doyle's light and breezy orchestral score for *Une Femme Française* evokes all the charm and romance of France. Refreshingly he does this without ever resorting to pastiche of that country's unmistakable musical sound. Instead he imbues his melodies with a sprightly dash to evoke the spirit of elegance and sophistication so often associated with French culture. The vibrant allure of cosmopolitan society is beautifully captured in his title theme, a tautly written *scherzo* for large string ensemble. In contrast is the delicate theme for the French woman of the title, which forms the basis of much of the score. This receives some exquisite and often surprising treatments, ranging from solo saxophone to solo piano. The highlight of the score, however, is the five-minute cue "Une Femme Francaise". Here Doyle employs a heart-stopping wordless soprano voice in conjunction with airy strings, in a dazzling stand-alone piece that splendidly develops his addictive love theme with almost dreamy lethargy. An undemanding but simply enthralling score. **PP**

New review | ARCAM
Hamlet (1996) **Original Soundtrack**, with **Plácido Domingo** (ten) **/ Robert Ziegler**.
Sony Classical ℗ SK62857 (76 minutes: DDD).

For sheer bravura, Kenneth Branagh's *Hamlet* was the film event of 1996. The four-hour movie – a complete account of the play with every dot and comma included – is the best of Branagh's three Shakespeare films to date. Filmed amidst the baroque splendour of Blenheim Palace, *Hamlet* is elevated by wonderful acting (American box-office stars and British thespians form the ensemble) and the first-rate music score by Patrick Doyle. The composer's previous Branagh collaborations were impressive, but *Hamlet* easily surpasses these achievements.

Doyle's eclectic, accessible score reflects Branagh's desire to present the argument for optimism in Elsinore – though the all-encompassing tragedy and Hamlet's brooding melancholy are not sacrificed. There are three major themes, two of which are weaved into "In Pace", sung with emotion by Plácido Domingo. In keeping with Hamlet's continuing search for peace, the Prince's theme is simple. The best variations can be found in "What a piece of work is a man" and "I loved you once". The composer's haunting theme for Kate Winslet's Ophelia is introduced in "Oh, what a noble mind". The third theme is for Claudius, the ostensible cause of Hamlet's problems. With its restless forays into twentieth-century harmonies and use of a string quartet, Claudius's material (first heard in track 14, "Now could I drink hot blood") is a departure from the rest of the score. Other moments worth visiting include the opening wedding fanfare, the ten-minute description of "The Ghost", a lively composition for the players, the wonderfully understated "To be or not to be" and the powerful choral finale. The sound quality is excellent and the booklet contains revelatory notes by Doyle and Branagh. **KM**

Henry V (1989) **Original Soundtrack**, with the **City of Birmingham Symphony Orchestra / Sir Simon Rattle**.
EMI ℗ CDC7 49919-2 (59 minutes: DDD).

When this version of *Henry V* was first released comparisons inevitably were made with the Olivier classic from 1944: a generation may have grown up in the meantime, but there were those who still asked what right Branagh had to encroach on such hallowed territory? As we know, his version turned out to eschew the pomp and ceremony of Olivier's morale-boosting interpretation, for a tougher, darker line, more truthful to the play.

Just as daunting was the job of the composer – how could he match the effectiveness of Walton's music? This was Patrick Doyle's first film score and to date, I think, his best. He began with the invaluable asset of a director who knew exactly what he required. In his notes, Branagh states how he wanted the film "to move people to every possible extreme of emotion", encouraging his composer to adopt "the epic approach ... whilst at the same time observing 'Shakespeare's golden word'". A daunting task for a first-timer. Doyle and his orchestrator, Lawrence Ashmore, took a symphonic approach, and came up trumps. This is an exhilarating and often moving score. Most touching are those scenes describing the death of Falstaff with its air of Elgarian *nobilimente*, and the stoic string theme whose accompanying trills suggest the flying pennants mounted atop the encampment at Agincourt. Nor could the listener fail to be stirred by the anthem "Non nobis, Domine" (sung on screen by the composer), particularly the middle section where the melody is taken up by the orchestra to thrilling effect. The wooing of Katherine, with its little *portamentos* for the violas portraying the youthful French Princess, is a gem. The first class recording does full justice to the splendid playing of the CBSO under Sir Simon Rattle. What a shame they don't venture into this world more often.   **AE**

Indochine (1992) **Original Soundtrack / William Kraft**.
Varèse Sarabande Ⓕ VSD5397 (52 minutes: DDD).

Indochine's score is as lush and verdant as the film's Vietnamese backdrop. Doyle writes for a large string orchestra, sensitively augmented by familiar low woodwind and brass. The result is a sultry, languorous sonority which contrives to be somehow oriental whilst remaining firmly grounded in thoroughly occidental romanticism. The composer's gift for warm, legato melody is everywhere apparent. A main theme of truly epic stature is subjected to ever-changing variation, revealing it in many different guises: anguished, sullen, uplifting. Flute, clarinet and oboe articulate a poignant secondary theme, whilst blaring trumpets and horns add dynamism. A sumptuous musical treat, as gorgeous to listen to as the film is to watch.   **MW**

A Little Princess (1995) **Original Soundtrack, with the New London Children's Choir / David Snell**.
Varèse Sarabande Ⓕ VSD5628 (50 minutes: DDD).

Indian ragas, baroque-style canons and 19th-century waltzes vie for attention in this inventive patchwork score, all of them unified by Doyle's distinctive gift for pungent harmonies and subtle orchestral colouring. A sitar and Indian percussion adds an exotic element; harp and synthesizer intertwine in playful canon; a string quartet is classically restrained then bursting with romantic passion; the mournful tone of a clarinet creates pathos, as a choir chants the traditional Indian greeting "Om Namaste". *A Little Princess* shows Doyle exploring new worlds in his music. Singing poems by William Blake and the composer's own lyrics, the choir and soloists are an integral part of the scoring. Abigail Doyle affectingly carries the central, sentimental song, "Kindle My Heart" (although the close miking is unflattering) backed by quasi-Indian harmonies. The whole is exotic, tender, exhilarating. A fresh perspective on a composer who never seems to run out of surprises.   **MW**

Mary Shelley's Frankenstein (1994) **Original Soundtrack / David Snell**.
Epic Ⓕ 477987-2 (70 minutes: DDD).

Patrick Doyle's music and Kenneth Branagh's vision brought Shakespeare to life for a new generation, before the same team attempted to reanimate a more gothic legend. If the movie was less successful than it should have been, the music remains one of Doyle's finest achievements, a non-stop aural bombardment of overwhelming proportions, exactly right for such a melodramatic subject.

The exquisite love theme – a discarded setting of Byron's "So we'll go no more a'roving" – is the central element of the score, illuminating all subsequent themes much as the hidden light source in a painting by Joseph Wright of Derby. It is a soaring, lyrical melody which, as an expression of doomed passion, is truly romantic in spirit. During the first creation scene both film and score are literally galvanized into life. This short cue makes maximum use of Doyle's large orchestra, particularly the massed brass and percussion. In a supercharged sequence only two minutes long, accompanied by pounding drums, fiendish horn trills and blazing synthesized organ chords, the score's other major motifs are introduced: a wailing 'Madness' theme; an ominous 'Fate' theme. Doyle does not treat these themes as *leitmotifs* to be introduced whenever a particular character or subject appears, instead he uses them to represent in music the swirling emotions which the characters on screen are experiencing: passion, obsession, despair, terrible rage. The grand and gothic music for *Frankenstein* is a living, breathing creation of its composer; however, unlike the film's subject, the themes are not stitched together to form the whole, but grow organically from it.   **MW**

Mrs Winterbourne (1996) **Original Soundtrack / Mark Watters**.
Varèse Sarabande Ⓕ VSD5720 (33 minutes: DDD).

Taking a brief sabbatical from heavyweight adaptations of literary classics, Patrick Doyle's score for this recent comedy is refreshingly lightweight. Some easy listening jazz and suave big band numbers mix comfortably with more up-tempo and characteristic orchestral cues. A propulsive energy, given a gentle jauntiness by the relatively small orchestra, drives the music along in places: a dramatic piece like "Dead Steve" is reminiscent of a scaled-down *Frankenstein*. The principal theme, on the other hand, is warm-hearted and sentimental in the same touching manner as that of *A Little Princess*. The final cue, "Connie's Song", a limpid violin solo, displays the composer's superb gift for melody as effectively as anything in his larger-scale assignments. Not a score likely to attract the same attention as *Hamlet* or *Sense and Sensibility*, but an attractive example of Doyle's art nevertheless. **MW**

Much Ado About Nothing (1993) **Original Soundtrack / David Snell**.
Epic Ⓕ MOODCD30 (59 minutes: DDD).

A glowing achievement from Doyle, one in which he blends the burnished hues of the Tuscan countryside with his own inimitable style. As with *Henry V*, it is Shakespeare's words which serve as the bedrock upon which the composer builds his radiant musical edifice. "Sigh no more, ladies", one of the most popular of all the bard's lyrics, is the foundation: we first hear it spoken (by Emma Thompson), before the tune is given full orchestral treatment during the uplifting "Overture", which encompasses all the score's major themes. Doyle's "Sigh no more" is a setting of which any composer since Dowland might justly be proud. The composer's pleasant baritone can be heard singing both this song and the regretful "Pardon, Goddess of the Night". These separate melodies dance together throughout the score, sometimes with the carefree joy of rustic festivity; sometimes with the melancholy aspect of a lover scorned. The gulling of Beatrice and Benedict (Branagh and Thompson) presents a delightful set of chamber variations on "Sigh no more"; the abortive wedding, with rapidly shifting moods and textures, takes both themes and twists them to great dramatic effect. The product of a warm, open-hearted composer, *Much Ado About Nothing* is Patrick Doyle's sunniest score. **MW**

Sense and Sensibility (1996) **Original Soundtrack**, with **Jane Eaglen** (sop) **/ Robert Ziegler**.
Sony Classical Ⓕ SK62258 (43 minutes: DDD).

Although near contemporaries, Mary Shelley and Jane Austen had rather different ideas about the art of novel writing; Patrick Doyle's recent career neatly mirrors this disparity. First came *Frankenstein*, an imposing gothic edifice wherein the story's already theatrical melodrama was exaggerated to suitably monstrous proportions; now for *Sense and Sensibility* his own stormily romantic musical temperament has been softened – gentrified even – by the addition of much elegant classicism, and a degree of emotional restraint of which Miss Austen would have heartily approved. Informed throughout by appropriate period mannerisms, Doyle has not, however, elected to follow the example of Carl Davis's skilful pastiche score for *Pride and Prejudice*: here the idiom may emphasize period refinement but it remains recognizably Doyle's own, some vivacious country dances and classical *Adagios* notwithstanding. Only Jane Eaglen's grandly operatic soprano strikes an oddly anachronistic note in the two expressive songs, where actress Kate Winslet's simple and unaffected rendition in the film seemed much more appropriate. Another fine work from this versatile composer, though in marked contrast to *Frankenstein* it perhaps errs too far on the side of understatement. **MW**

Also available
Carlito's Way (1993) Varèse Sarabande VSD5463
Into the West (1993) Sony SBK89049
Needful Things (1993) Varèse Sarabande VSD5438

George Duning

b. 1908 USA

Born in Richmond, Indiana, George Duning studied at the Cincinnati Conservatory of Music before beginning a career as a trumpet player (both jazz and classical). He made arrangements for the Kay Kyser band during the 1940s, and started to orchestrate film scores. After service in the Navy, Duning started working for Columbia Pictures; his first score was for a Dick Powell movie, *Johnny O'Clock* (1946). He went on to write scores for over 250 movies, and receive five Academy Award nominations, the first one for *Jolson Sings Again* (1949). *From Here to Eternity* (1953) and *Picnic* (1955) picked up another two nominations. The theme from *Picnic* had lyrics added by Steve Allen and became a hit song. His usual orchestrator was Arthur Morton, who later worked closely with Jerry Goldsmith. From the 1960s onwards, Duning wrote mainly for television, contributing to series like *Star Trek, The Partridge Family* and *The Big Valley*. Duning retired from film scoring in 1983, but still writes occasional chamber works.

Picnic (1955) **Original Soundtrack / Morris Stoloff.**
  MCA Ⓜ MCAD31357 (47 minutes: ADD).

Duning is one of the many Hollywood veterans who worked solidly through the 1940s and 1950s and yet gained little recognition for his efforts. He possessed a spry and easy style, often leaning towards light jazz, that was particularly well suited to romantic comedies, though he was equally at home with grittier subjects. *Picnic* combines elements of both and is probably the best example of his work, its warm and sunny love theme describing the small Kansas town in which William Inge's story is set as well as the yearning sensuality of Kim Novak's character. But the ingredient that made the original LP such a big seller in its day (peaking at number six in the American Billboard chart) is Duning's deft and bewitching blending of this theme with the standard "Moonglow", a deceptively simple device that spawned a huge number of cover recordings though none can rival the shimmering magic of the original. **RS**

Randy Edelman

b. 1947 USA

Born in Teaneck, New Jersey, Randy Edelman began writing songs when he was a teenager. He studied pre-med at the University of Cincinnati but always knew he wanted to pursue a career in music. Whilst in Cininnati, he established a reputation as an arranger for several local bands, and this led to him being hired by James Brown as an orchestrator. Edelman moved to New York in 1970 where he worked as a staff-writer for CBS, continuing his musical activities on Broadway (he played keyboards in a production of *The Boy Friend*) and also working as an arranger and conductor. He began to record his own albums – over a dozen altogether – having hits in the UK with the songs "Uptown, Uptempo Woman" and "Concrete and Clay". Success as a songwriter and arranger led to work with artists as diverse as Abba, The Carpenters, Barry Manilow (for whom he wrote "Weekend in New England"), Bing Crosby, Patti LaBelle and Olivia Newton-John. He also toured with The Carpenters and played keyboards for Frank Zappa and the Mothers of Invention. Edelman began his involvement in dramatic scoring as far back as 1972's *Outside In* (the year he relocated to Los Angeles). Television work followed, including *Blood Sport* (1973), *Ryan's Four* (1983) and *Dennis the Menace* (1987). Other feature film assignments included *Executive Action* (1973), *Ghostbusters II* (1989) and *Drop Dead Fred* (1991). Much of his subsequent film work was for comedies, exploiting his ability to pen light, snappy melodies, sometimes backed by a driving pop beat (as in *My Cousin Vinny*, 1992, for example). Recently, however, scores like *Last of the Mohicans* (1992), *Gettysburg* (1993), *Citizen X* (1995), *Dragonheart* (1996) and *Daylight* (1996) have demonstrated that he is also at home with larger-scale, action scores. In 1995 he was commissioned by NBC Television to write a theme for the National Football League – this is now played at the beginning of every NFL game and during the Super Bowl. Edelman tends to favour a rich mixture of standard orchestra and synthesizers, giving his scores an unmistakably full-bodied sound. Ralph Ferraro is his usual orchestrator.

Beethoven (1991) **Original Soundtrack / Randy Edelman.**
  MCA Ⓕ MCAD10593 (39 minutes: ADD).

Edelman's second collaboration with director Ivan Reitman resulted in a warm, likeable score mercifully free from too many of the 'pop' cues that have marred some of his other comedy scores. What applies to the earlier *Kindergarten Cop* can on the whole also be said of *Beethoven*. A jolly, piano-based main theme conjures up the frolics of the eponymous pooch without ever becoming overly saccharine. This unpretentious little tune, cast in a deliberately 'classical' style, forms the backbone of the score, with a pleasantly sentimental secondary theme adding contrast. A faster slapstick motif has the composer manfully resisting (most of the time) the inevitable temptation to turn it into a jokey rendition of the opening bars of Beethoven's Fifth. Unlike *Kindergarten Cop*, however, the 'action' cues, similarly interspersed throughout, seem less well integrated with the lighter comedy themes. Enjoyable and undemanding. **MW**

FiRST
FOR
FiLM SCORiNG

Contact: ALiSON BURTON

Air Studios, Lyndhurst Hall, Lyndhurst Road, Hampstead, London NW3 5NG
Tel: +44 (0)171 794 0660   Fax: +44 (0)171 794 8518   www.airstudios.com

Citizen X (1995) **Original Soundtrack / Randy Edelman.**
  Varèse Sarabande Ⓔ VSD5601 (30 minutes: DDD).

A darker, more subdued score than we are used to from Edelman, HBO's television thriller *Citizen X* is nevertheless a good example of his non-comedy style. Typically lush synthesizer textures merging seamlessly with the 'standard' orchestra are here coloured with an ominous hue; woodwinds and horns evoke a mournful atmosphere; a stabbing staccato motif with halting counter-subject in the basses is cold and disquieting. The music contains two principal themes: an elegaic, hymn-like theme which opens the disc ("A Heavy Burden"), and a tender, wistful melody first presented in "Two Comrades Embrace", where clarinets then French horns state the theme before it is taken over by full orchestra. In between, brooding chordal passages and the distant pounding of thunderous timpani keep the score edgy and unsettling. With few dynamic contrasts, and an overall dirge-like feel, *Citizen X* is an unusually moody work which clearly shows Edelman's ability to handle much more than just comedy. **MW**

New review
Dragonheart (1996) **Original Soundtrack / Randy Edelman.**
  MCA Ⓔ MCD11449 (46 minutes: DDD).

Dragonheart was a recent attempt to revive the genre of Sword and Sorcery epics. It failed dismally, becoming little more than a vehicle for some self-indulgent CGI effects. Randy Edelman's score fares better. He uses a standard symphonic setup, with the now routine addition of synthesizers. His main theme, heard in the opening cue "The World of the Heart" and later in "Wonders of an Ancient Glory", permeates the whole score. It is a good, robust theme and can stand the treatment: majestic and well detailed it is given an observant and sympathetic reading from the studio orchestra. As might be expected, more than one cue is up-tempo and full of action, with snarling brass leading some barnstorming orchestral writing. Tracks like "Enion" and "Mexican Standoff", on the other hand, have a more acoustic, almost ethnic feel (although there is little in the way of 'period' music) giving the whole album a balance that some scores for similar movies lack. One of the better scores of 1996. Shame about the movie. **JW**

Gettysburg (1993) **Original Soundtrack / Randy Edelman.**
  Milan Ⓔ 17008-2 (57 minutes: DDD).

Gettysburg is an epic of almost Homeric proportions, concentrating as it does on the characters and motivations of the principal commanders during those few decisive days in 1863. Amidst the set-piece battles like Chamberlain's defence of Little Round Top or Pickett's Charge, Edelman's score reminds us of the shared sense of honour which united the combatants, and the bloody conflicting loyalties that divided them. Given just six weeks to write some three hours of music (an apt and interesting parallel to *Gone With the Wind*), the composer was nevertheless sufficiently inspired by the subject to produce a lush, sweeping score with a rich variety of themes. Although he typically relies heavily on synthesizers to fill out the orchestral textures, surprisingly, in the context of such a meticulous historical re-enactment, their use never seems anachronistic: indeed, when we have heard real fifes and drums on screen, their transformation by Edelman into the synthesized realm has an almost magical effect. The most effective moments are introspective, not dramatic – "General Lee's Solitude" or "Killer Angel" for example – but even the battle music is expressive less of war's brutal physicality than of the bitter convictions which pit friend against friend, brother against brother. Edelman has made a worthy contribution to a noble film. **MW**

The Indian in the Cupboard (1995) **Original Soundtrack / Randy Edelman.**
  Sony Classical Ⓔ SK68475 (54 minutes: DDD).

This is a delightful consolidation of Edelman's past work, containing nothing that will surprise but much that will please his many admirers. Here are the jovial, foot-tapping tunes we have come to expect; those moments both of lighthearted action and convincingly tense drama; and – most immediately apparent – several sincerely-scored episodes of quiet lyricism clearly recalling his triumphant *Gettysburg*. Lush orchestral strings thickly overlaid with synths are something of a trademark, and are once again employed to good effect here. The full orchestral treatment of the end credit sequence is a grand summation not just of this score, but of the all this composer's work. Whilst *Gettysburg* remains unsurpassed, this is a safe bet for Edelman's fans. **MW**

Kindergarten Cop (1990) **Original Soundtrack / Randy Edelman**.
Varèse Sarabande Ⓟ VSD5305 (38 minutes: DDD).

Listening to *Kindergarten Cop* it is easy to see why Edelman is so often typecast as a composer of romantic comedies: the main themes are fresh and light without ever seeming twee; the mood is sentimental without becoming schmaltzy; above all, this is charming, heart-on-the-sleeve music-making without any sign of insincerity. The opening 'childish' school theme scored for piano backed by Edelman's characteristic mix of luxurious synths and orchestral strings is a warm, tender melody which quickly develops a playful turn in "Children's Montage". Solo piano is a strong element in the score, particularly effective in the "Love Theme", sensitively orchestrated by Mark McKenzie (the remainder of the score was orchestrated by Greig McRitchie). There are enough dramatic moments in the film for Edelman to diversify his score. The penultimate track, "Fire at the School", for example, is as effective a piece of tension-building drama as might be found in one of his more serious movies. These darker action cues sprinkled liberally throughout help prevent the music from ever seeming too frothy or superficial. A well-balanced, pleasing score – perhaps only the John Williams of *Home Alone* does this sort of thing better. **MW**

While You Were Sleeping (1995) **Original Soundtrack / Randy Edelman**.
Varèse Sarabande Ⓟ VSD5627 (38 minutes: DDD).

A jaunty, jazzy piano-led opening, followed by a quirky danceable melody in "Peter's Family", and then a sensitive "Love Theme" puts us firmly in romantic comedy territory. Sandra Bullock's first starring feature is familiar material for Edelman. But then he does this kind of thing so well. For those who prefer a more symphonic approach to film scoring, *While You Were Sleeping* will not appeal as much as Edelman's more serious assignments; however, the pop elements are not overdone, and – as always – Edelman's irresistible charm conquers all reservations. Not one of the composer's best, but a characteristically light and breezy score nevertheless. **MW**

Also available:
Angels in the Outfield (1995) Hollywood 161608-2
The Distinguished Gentleman (1992) Varèse Sarabande VSD5364
Daylight (1996) MCA UND53024
Dragon: The Bruce Lee Story (1993) MCA MCAD10827
Last of the Mohicans (1992) see Jones, Trevor
The Mask (1994) Tristar WK66646
My Cousin Vinny (1992) Varèse Sarabande VSD5364
The Quest (1996) Varèse Sarabande VSD5716

Cliff Eidelman
b. 1964 USA

Born in Los Angeles, Cliff Eidelman studied violin from the age of eight, and learned jazz guitar, before continuing his musical training at Santa Monica City College, where he completed a ballet score, *Once Upon a Ruler* and *Celebration Symphony Overture in Three Movements*. He later enrolled in the music department of the University of Southern California. Remarkably, he received his first film commission before graduating. This was for *Magdalene* (1988), which proved successful enough to attract further film assignments. As well as motion pictures, Eidelman has been active in television, scoring episodes of *Tales from the Crypt* and the TV films *Judgment* (1990), *Backfield in Motion* (1991), *The Final Days* (1989), and for HBO *Dead Man Out* (1989) and *If These Walls Could Talk* (1996). In addition to composing and conducting his own scores, Eidelman has conducted the Seattle Symphony Orchestra in recordings of classic film scores (see Collections: "Blood and Thunder") and the Royal Scottish National Orchestra on a disc of selections from the *Alien* trilogy (Varèse Sarabande VSD5733) plus a collection of music from Shakespearian films, which includes his concert suite *The Tempest* (Varèse Sarabande VSD5752). Other concert works include *Suite for Orchestra* (1986), *Five Pieces for Violin and Piano* (1987) and *The Creation Symphony* (1995). As one of a rising generation of young composers, Eidelman's music is steeped in the traditions of Hollywood. Mark McKenzie – now forging his own career as a composer – orchestrated his earlier scores.

Christopher Columbus: The Discovery (1992) **Original Soundtrack**, with the **Seattle Symphony Orchestra / Cliff Eidelman**.
Varèse Sarabande Ⓟ VSD5389 (43 minutes: DDD).

This is just the kind of assignment Miklós Rózsa would have been given in the 1950s: he would have filled his score with authentic fifteenth-century fragments, and it would still have sounded just like all his other music! Cliff Eidelman eschews such historicity, even going so far as to set his version of "Come, O Come, Emanuel" in English. Yet Eidelman's grand choruses, and his broad orchestral treatment fondly recall the epic sweep of Rózsa's historical scores. Divided into four distinct 'Acts', Eidelman's ambitious work depicts Spain, The Sea and The West Indies with different musical shadings. His Spanish music is grand and regal; the Sea is open and expansive; the West Indies are nominally ethnic. The hymn-like main theme, which reappears in different settings throughout, unifies the whole. Eidelman has clearly enjoyed this rare opportunity to write large-scale music after the manner of Hollywood's epic past. **MW**

Magdalene (1988) **Original Soundtrack**, with the **Munich Symphony Orchestra / Cliff Eidelman**. Intrada Ⓕ MAF7029D (45 minutes: ADD).

Eidelman's largely impressive début relies a little too heavily on the quoted phrases from Mozart's *Requiem* for it to be fully satisfying when removed from the context of the movie – the opening cue, "The Revolution", not only begins with Mozart's "Rex tremendae", but seems to borrow from *Don Giovanni* as well. The first phrase of the "Lachrymosa" forms the basis for several of Eidelman's cues, although he chooses to set the words of "Kyrie eleison" instead. These quibbles aside, the remainder of the score is a delight, with wistful, tender themes for the eponymous prostitute and her ill-chosen lover Father Mohr. Clarinet and piano develop the romance, initially echoing a typically Mozartian *Adagio*. Then, more gothic shading is introduced, with the music becoming increasingly poignant, as in "Freedom in Salzburg". The beautifully romantic finale conquers all lingering reservations. A jolly baroque pastiche in "The Archbishop's Entertainment" – marred only by some uncertain solo violin playing – sounds more like Bach than Mozart. Is it being too pedantic to complain that a film set during the French revolution uses Franz Gruber's "Stille Nacht", which was not written until 1818? **MW**

New review
Now and Then (1995) **Original Soundtrack / Cliff Eidelman**. Varèse Sarabande Ⓕ VSD5675 (34 minutes: DDD).

Leski Linka Glatter's teen-to-adulthood drama set between the years 1970 and 1995 treads the familiar path of many such films. As might be expected, the director opts for the usual mix of pop standards to give the film its period feel. Contrary to some director's notions, however, such songs alone cannot supply a film with its emotional content or style: this is where the specially-commissioned score comes into its own. Cliff Eidelman's music for *Now and Then* employs a delicate balance of strings, piano, woodwinds and an exquisite use of harp. None of the cues on the album are very long, but each seems just right (sometimes we bemoan the lack of extended cues, but there is a need for neat, shorter tracks as well). "Sam's Dad Leaves" contains fine writing for strings, whilst "It's a Girl", with its concentrated emotional intensity, recalls the late Georges Delerue at his very best. A good, functional score, then, showing the continuing maturity of Eidelman, building on the promise we first heard in *Triumph of the Spirit* (1989). No earthshaker, but a pleasant, intimate score which the listener warms to easily. **JW**

Picture Bride (1995) **Pablo Sepulveda** (pan pipe/bamboo fl); **Seattle Orchestra / Cliff Eidelman** (pf). Varèse Sarabande Ⓕ VSD5651 (30 minutes: DDD).

When is a film score not a film score? When it is not used in the film for which it was written. Then it becomes something else, something with an aura of mystery and magic: a film score that has no visual connections, no extra-musical associations. It exists as a contradiction: film music that is 'pure' music. Cliff Eidelman's rejected score for *Picture Bride* – described here as "music inspired by" the film – happily stands on its own. It is a charming piece, a work wrapped in calming mists, with gentle themes reaching out like wispy tendrils, surrounding and enveloping the listener. Smooth, legato strings and the refined, ethereal texture of pan pipes and bamboo flute evoke an atmosphere of meditative tranquillity, without ever becoming static or repetitive. The composer's solo piano rendition of his music brings this short, but satisfying disc to a tender conclusion. Matthew Peak's striking cover art is an additional delight. **MW**

A Simple Twist of Fate (1994) **Original Soundtrack**, with the **Los Angeles Master Chorale / Cliff Eidelman** (pf). Varèse Sarabande Ⓕ VSD5538 (28 minutes: DDD).

By degrees sentimental, sombre and dramatic, *A Simple Twist of Fate* is a better work than the romantic comedy-type packaging suggests. Eidelman's main theme is an attractive song-like melody (the title of one cue, "Floating on Air", seems to fit the tune perfectly). This theme carries the weight of the score, although such a short running time does not allow it to ever become unwelcome. It is performed by the composer in a delightful, low-key version for solo piano at the end of the disc. Other motifs have a somewhat sinister edge – murmuring woodwinds and *tremolo* drums in "Prelude to Tanny's Fate", low strings and wordless voices in "Into the Light". The traditional tune, "Red is the Rose" – here arranged Country-style by Eidelman – might be better recognized in Britain as "Loch Lomond".   **MW**

New review

Star Trek VI: The Undiscovered Country (1992) Original Soundtrack / Cliff Eidelman.
MCA Ⓜ MCLD19348 (45 minutes: DDD).

The score that gave Cliff Eidelman his first taste of major league success is still his best-known work. You might think director Nicholas Meyer was taking a risk by selecting a relatively unknown composer, but he was in fact repeating a tactic that had paid off handsomely a decade earlier when he hired the then almost untried James Horner to score his first big movie, *Star Trek II: The Wrath of Khan*. If Eidelman's subsequent career has not yet matched the meteoric rise of Horner's, it is not for want of real ability. Eidelman's approach to *Star Trek VI* wisely does not attempt to match the strong thematic basis of previous *Trek* scores, even at the cost of making his music less instantly attention-grabbing than some of its predecessors. Instead, the composer creates a darker mood, colouring his orchestration with sombre percussion and synthesizers in tense and atmospheric cues like "Assassination" and "Escape from Rura Penthe". Although Meyer in the booklet indulges in a touch of hyperbole by comparing Eidelman to Puccini, the director's desire for an "operatic" score did allow the composer the luxury of some extended set-pieces, like the eight-minute climax, "The Battle for Peace", in which he is able to spend time building suspense instead of having to jump right in *fortissimo*. Conceiving the principal theme as a brooding, sober alternative to earlier *Star Trek* marches is a good idea, but it is too apparently modelled on Holst's "Mars" by way of Danny Elfman's *Batman* to be completely effective (*The Planets* was the director's unoriginal first choice for scoring the film). A secondary 'Enterprise' theme sounds a more optimistic note, although Eidelman replaces the usual "to boldly go" heroics with a gentle hint of nostalgia – this time when Alexander Courage's original fanfare is introduced during "Sign Off" it has a fitting ring of finality. Another such opportunity to hear Eidelman's talent for strong and vivid dramtic writing is long overdue.   **MW**

New review

Untamed Heart (1992) Original Soundtrack / Cliff Eidelman.
Varèse Sarabande Ⓕ VSD5404 (26 minutes: DDD).

Sometimes scores for love stories can be as sickly and sentimental as the films themselves, and equally nauseating on disc. One would expect more from a sophisticated composer such as Cliff Eidelman, and *Untamed Heart* does not disappoint. From the outset, the listener is aware of the composer's sympathetic and subtle approach to this love story, and the results are no less moving than some of the more melodramatic scores written for this type of movie. Of particular note are the opening and closing credits which feature a spellbinding theme for female voices, strings, harp, clarinet, flute and piano. Opening with a feathery choral refrain, it moves through several solo-instrumental variations, notably violin, before returning to the mystical-sounding chorus, interspersed with resonant harp. The music that falls between these intriguing pieces is ever so delicately paced, again relying on solo instruments, principally piano and clarinet. The wonderful opening theme returns occasionally to impart a strangely otherworldy aura. The pace changes only once for a sporty and contemporary piece featuring drums and piano to evoke plenty of youthful vigour and energy, but otherwise this is a relaxed and refined work which is just all too short.   **PP**

Also available:
Triumph of the Spirit (1989) Varèse Sarabande VSD5254

Danny Elfman   b. 1953 USA

As a teenager, Danny Elfman wanted to be a film-maker, not a film composer. Despite never having played a musical instrument until he was 18, Elfman taught himself music, and formed a music theatre troupe. His highly individual musical training took the form of transcribing Louis Armstrong and Cab Calloway numbers from the soundtracks of Max Fleischer cartoons. Elfman later moved from music theatre to rock, forming the band Oingo Boingo. His involvement in film scoring came about as a result of director Tim Burton seeing the band, and deciding Elfman was the right choice to score *Pee-Wee's Big Adventure* (1985). This was the first of a spectacularly successful series of Burton/Elfman collaborations – *Beetlejuice* (1988), *Batman* (1989), *Edward*

Scissorhands (1990), *Batman Returns* (1992), *The Nightmare Before Christmas*, and latterly, *Mars Attacks!* (1997). The composer has forged a unique musical style, best described simply as 'Elfmanesque', which can also be heard in his television themes for *The Simpsons* and *Tales from the Crypt*. His lack of formal musical training, by imposing no restrictions on what can and cannot be done, and allowing him to follow his own instincts, has proved his greatest asset. More recent assignments such as *Dolores Claiborne* (1995), *To Die For* (1995) and *Mission: Impossible* (1996) chart the development of his maturing style, showing the composer developing and refining his individual manner. Oingo Boingo's guitarist Steve Bartek is his regular orchestrator.

Batman (1989) **Original Soundtrack**, with the **Sinfonia of London / Shirley Walker**.
 Warner Bros Ⓔ 7599-25977-2 (55 minutes: DDD).
Batman Returns (1992) **Original Soundtrack / Jonathan Sheffer**.
 Warner Bros Ⓔ 7599-26972-2 (70 minutes: DDD). Includes *Face to Face* co-written and performed by Siouxsie and the Banshees.

The awe-inspiring grandeur of Elfman's music proved to be the perfect complement to Tim Burton's gothic vision. Its impact is undiminished on disc: both these scores are marvellous examples of Danny Elfman's inimitable style. The Batman theme – a brooding modal motif developed into a powerful march – looms over the entire original score: a dark, potent force just like the movie's hero. It forces submission from all else whenever it appears, as in the "First Confrontation", where it battles with opposing rhythmic brass flourishes and chopping string figures. The Joker and his minions dance to creepy rhythms, which occasionally hint at the influence of Bernard Herrmann. The Joker's own 'theme' is a burlesque waltz, heard in full during the climactic "Waltz to the Death". Virtuoso work-outs for the brass section bring out the very best in the Sinfonia of London – perhaps the finest recording orchestra for film scores – notably in the powerful action cues like "Attack of the Batwing", and during the superbly heroic "Finale". Organ and chiming bells add a further gothic dimension to the Cathedral scenes. Elfman also makes good use of two additional themes, subtly intertwining them with his own music: "Scandalous" by Prince and Stephen Foster's "Beautiful Dreamer".
 Batman Returns is in many ways even better than the first score. It certainly has more variety, both thematically and texturally. The original Batman theme no longer dominates: this time around it has to contend with additional competition. Slinky, *glissandi* strings characterize Catwoman; a bleak lullaby, featuring clarinet and saxophone evokes the sinisterly comic Penguin. Wordless chorus, celesta, xylophone and harp – amongst others – add spice to the orchestrations. Overall, the tone is several shades darker. Less action-dominated, this score is as closely related to the quirky, spooky *Nightmare Before Christmas* as it is to *Batman*. Just try the quintessentially 'Elfmanesque' "Cat Suite" or "Batman vs. the Circus" to hear the similarities. The Hollywood studio musicians, although very capable, can't quite match the blistering intensity of the Sinfonia of London's brass section. The song "Face to Face" is a rare example of the successful integration of a promotional pop song into the movie: co-written by Elfman, it is an attractive musical relation to the rest, not a blatant, musically irrelevant marketing tool. **MW**

Beetlejuice (1988) **Original Soundtrack / Bill Ross**.
 Geffen Ⓜ GED24202 (37 minutes: DDD). Includes *Day-O* (Burgie/Attaway) and *Jump in Line* (DeLeon/Bell).

An archetypal 'Elfmanesque' work, *Beetlejuice* begins with a whizz and a bang, and fizzes and crackles all the way to the end. Over pounding pianistic accompaniment, Elfman weaves his spell – employing a dizzying array of instruments and styles, his music hops and skips, dances a jig, runs a race, careers madly about, and generally behaves with an air of anarchic lunacy. The 'Gothic' sonority of an organ is used to burlesque effect; the scraping of a fiddle is deliberately 'devilish'; xylophones rattle like dancing skeletons. You never know what mock-grotesque musical gargoyle might be lurking just around the next corner. Hilarious, but with a sharp edge of unpredictability that also makes it delightfully dangerous. **MW**

Dolores Claiborne (1995) **Original Soundtrack / Richard Stone**.
 Varèse Sarabande Ⓔ VSD5602 (30 minutes: DDD).

Predominantly sombre and restrained in mood, this score, with its novel use of texture – all are shades of grey – and its experimental forays into dissonance, marked the beginning of a new, more mature phase in Elfman's career. Gone are the manic outbursts, the frantic cavorting, the wicked, irreverent humour of his Tim Burton collaborations. What has been substituted, however, is even more fascinating, more absorbing. An insistent violin solo in "Vera's World" – over piano and strings – is a psychological study in itself: jumpy semiquavers, *pizzicato*, slurring and double stopping, then a solemn, legato melody. Divided strings playing acidic harmonies conjure a bleak atmosphere of growing tension. This is the score in miniature. Listening to the composer build this tension until it is finally released in the chaotic ferocity of "Getting Even" and "Eclipse" provides us with a far darker, far deeper view of Danny Elfman than the bold, but largely two-dimensional character studies of his Tim Burton movies. *Dolores Claiborne* is indeed a seminal work.   **MW**

`New review`
Edward Scissorhands (1990) **Original Soundtrack / Shirley Walker**.
    MCA Ⓜ MCLD19303 (49 minutes: AAD). Includes *With These Hands* (Silver/Davis).

Providing a vital contribution to Tim Burton's strangely beautiful, oddly moving modern day fairy-tale is one of Elfman's most heart-warming and exquisitely crafted scores. Though its graceful elegance is far removed from the grandiose gestures of, say, *Darkman* or *Batman*, Elfman's admiration for the music of Bernard Herrmann is well in evidence in the surging brass and rippling harp figures of vibrant, animated cues like "Castle on the Hill" and "Cookie Factory". There are also some typically quirky, Elfmanesque moments of humour, most notably in "Edwardo the Barber" where amorous Spanish rhythms and a Paganini-like *scherzo* underline the exotic hair styles created by Edward's bizarre scissorhands. However, it is Elfman's shimmering, waltz-like main theme and the luminous love theme, embroidered in delicate string textures and the pure, silvery tones of a wordless boys' choir, that imbue this film with such a wondrous and almost palpable sense of magic.   **RS**

`New review`
Mission: Impossible (1996) **Original Soundtrack / Artie Kane**.
    Point Music Ⓕ 454 525-2 (53 minutes: DDD).

After *Batman Returns*, Danny Elfman remarked somewhat ruefully that he never wanted to compete with sound effects on that scale again, so it was a little surprising to find his name attached to this big action blockbuster. A late replacement for Alan Silvestri's rejected first attempt, Elfman's take on *Mission: Impossible* is, however, more in the spirit of Lalo Schifrin's original music for the television series than the noisy, all-action scores at which Silvestri excels. Elfman borrows from Schifrin an aura of tension, the music of intrigue and secret agents, which is effectively developed during some lengthy and atmospheric set-pieces; the acidic string writing – familiar from the outstanding but underrated *Dolores Claiborne* – is uniquely his own. Schifrin's original theme appears at the beginning and end in a rock-solid arrangement, but Elfman uses another authentic cue, "The Plot", to better effect, weaving it in and out of his own music during several key scenes. Otherwise, the score is largely devoid of any identifiable themes or melodies, although Elfman's offbeat rhythms and quirky orchestration are abundantly apparent, making this a fascinating example of his distinctively eclectic style, and easily the most inventive score of 1996.   **MW**

Music for a Darkened Theater **Original Soundtracks**; Various conductors.
    MCA Ⓕ MCAD10065 (73 minutes: AAD).
    Pee-Wee's Big Adventure (1985). Batman (1989). Dick Tracy (1990). Beetlejuice (1988). Nightbreed (1990). Darkman (1990). Back to School (1986). Midnight Run (1988). Wisdom (1986). Hot to Trot (1988). Big Top Pee-Wee (1988). The Simpsons (1989). Alfred Hitchcock Presents: The Jar (1986). Tales from the Crypt (1989). Face Like a Frog (1987). Forbidden Zone (1980). Scrooged (1988).

Of all the young composers to enter the movies over the last few years, the career of Danny Elfman has been the most remarkable. Confidently embracing the big orchestral sound of Hollywood's Golden Age together with a quirky, fairground humour, it is easy to understand why these dynamic scores have gained such a cult following. This CD is a bumper roller-coaster ride through his greatest hits as far as 1990, taken from the original recordings and annotated by the composer himself. From the surging intensity of *Batman, Darkman* and *Nightbreed,* through the country rock of *Midnight Run* and *Wisdom,* to the outlandishly lugubrious *Beetlejuice* and *The Simpsons,* each track demonstrates Elfman's burgeoning talent and his flair for producing orchestral fireworks. Best of the bunch, however, is arguably *Pee-Wee's Big Adventure*, his first orchestral score and an endearingly madcap tribute to two of his major influences: Nino Rota and Bernard Herrmann.   **RS**

Sommersby (1993) **Original Soundtrack / Jonathan Sheffer, Thomas Pasatieri**.
    Elektra Ⓕ 7559-61491-2 (51 minutes: DDD).

A subdued, darkly romantic score, *Sommersby* marks a change of direction for the composer. The ebb and flow of dense strings, plaintive solos for trumpet and clarinet and delicate guitar accompaniment immediately indicate that this score is not 'Elfmanesque' in the sense we have come to understand. The style may be different, but the personality behind the music is still discernible: in the folksy "Welcoming" or "At Work", or the bewitching "Return Montage" for example – the instrumentation has changed, but the interplay of different textures is familiar. The romantic love theme suffers from over-use towards the latter part of the score, although this was apparently a decision made at the insistence of the studio after the movie was re-edited (hence the need for a second conductor). *Sommersby* nevertheless remains an attractive work, full of brooding passion, and far more subtle than some of the composer's earlier scores.   **MW**

New review

To Die For (1995) **Original Soundtrack**, with **Warren Fitzgerald** (gtr); **John Avila** (bass); **Brooks Wackerman** (drums); **Little Gus and the Suzettes / Richard Stone**.
Varese Sarabande Ⓟ VSD 5646 (43 minutes DDD). Includes *Wasting Away* (Nailbomb), *Nothing From Nothing* (Billy Preston), *All By Myself* (Eric Carmen), *Sweet Home Alabama* (Lynyrd Skynyrd), *Wings of Desire* (Strawpeople) and *Season of the Witch* (Donovan).

A 43-minute album bulging with an eclectic rag-bag of songs (nice to have Donovan's "Season of the Witch", though) with Danny Elfman's score coming in at just under 20 minutes – but don't be discouraged, this is vintage Elfman, with resounding echoes of *Edward Scissorhands* and *The Nightmare Before Christmas*. Like his previous work, this is a marvellously quirky listening experience. Elfman knows how to put a score together – unafraid to merge disparate elements to achieve his outlandish ends. This music is often witty, sometimes wacky, even fetchingly off the rails in places. Elfman really exists in his own peculiar musical twilight world; here he concocts some of Hollywood's most devilish music, drawing on the best of the past (he openly acknowledges a debt to Bernard Herrmann and Nino Rota) but filtering all through rare experiment to arrive at scores which are often musical oddities – charming, idiosyncratic, or just plain peculiar. *To Die For* is a prime example. Forget that this music originates in a darkly humorous tale of an ambitious, nay, homicidal television anchorwoman and just enjoy Elfman's zany indulgences for their own sake. This score is akin to a musical kaleidoscope: just revel in the fluctuating colours and patterns. **DW**

Also available:
Article 99 (1992) Varèse Sarabande VSD5352
Black Beauty (1993) Giant 4568-2
Darkman (1990) MCA MCAD10094
Dick Tracy (1990) Sire 7599-26264-2
Extreme Measures (1996) Varèse Sarabande VSD5767
The Frighteners (1996) MCA MCAD11469
Nightbreed (1990) MCA MCAD8037
Pee-Wee's Big Adventure (1985) **Back to School** (1986) Varèse Sarabande VCD47281

Hans Erdmann
1887-1942 Germany

Hans Erdmann Timotheus Guckel was born in Breslau. He studied violin, theory and composition and took his doctorate in music. Whilst still a student he worked as a conductor in Breslau's theatres, but was then called up for military service during the First World War. In 1921 he became artistic director of the Prana Film Company: his first score was *Nosferatu* (1922). In addition, Erdmann worked as a music critic and edited a journal devoted entirely to film music; he also ran a course in film composition at the Berlin Conservatoire. He continued writing scores with the advent of the new 'talkies' including Fritz Lang's *Das Testament des Dr Mabuse* (1932).

Nosferatu (1922) **Brandenburg Philharmonic Orchestra / Gillian B. Anderson**.
RCA Victor Ⓟ 09026 68143-2 (77 minutes: DDD). Reconstructed by Gillian B. Anderson and James Kessler. Includes *Overture* to *Der Vampyr* (Marschner). Recorded 1995.

Friedrich Murnau's silent horror classic *Nosferatu* was originally premièred in the Marble Hall of the Berlin Zoo. A select audience, all presumably extravagantly costumed in preparation for the fancy-dress ball which was to follow, were treated to the *Overture* from Heinrich Marschner's 1828 opera *Der Vampyr* before a viewing of the film accompanied by a full-sized symphony orchestra. Hans Erdmann's lavish, specially composed score has since been lost, although his *Fantastisch-Romantische Suiten* derived from the film are still extant, as is his handbook of film music which also contains themes used in the film. It is these sources that Gillian Anderson and James Kessler have drawn upon to reconstruct Erdmann's work; a performance of the restored music was conducted along with a screening of the film in August 1994. Appropriately sub-titled "A Symphony of Horror", Erdmann's score could at almost any point be mistaken for mainstream nineteenth-century symphonic repertoire: the composer's musical vocabulary pre-dates the decadent romanticism of Richard Strauss (which might have been more in keeping with the film) and looks back to the earlier works of Beethoven and Mendelssohn. Only rarely does Erdmann infuse sinister passages with a

FARRINGDONS
RECORDS

Farringdons Records
are happy to supply
any of the soundtracks
listed in this book*

Please call our
International
Mail Order Service on
Tel: (00) 0171 626 2805
Fax: (00) 0171 626 2891

*subject to availability

Farringdons Records:
64-72 Leadenhall Market London EC3V 1LT
Telephone 0171 623 9605
Royal Festival Hall South Bank Centre London SE1 8XX
Telephone 0171 620 0198

heavily chromatic, almost atonal atmosphere. Wagner's singularly prescient contribution to the art of film scoring – the *leitmotiv* – is gainfully employed by Erdmann, whose use of a handful of memorable themes associated with specific characters imparts a distinctive shape to a score that would otherwise not have any particularly striking features. Although this is undoubtedly a fascinating – and extremely rare – glimpse into the musical world of the silent era, Erdmann's score ultimately lacks the coherence of genuinely dramatic, descriptive film music, which was not to really arrive until Max Steiner's *King Kong* a decade later. Fulsome booklet notes and a solid, impressively recorded performance considerably enhance the appeal of this unusual disc.   **MW**

George Fenton

b. 1949 England

George Fenton's professional career began as a freelance guitarist, playing on several recordings, as well as for English Music Theatre, the Festival Ballet and others. He has pursued composition full-time since 1974, working primarily for film, television and theatre, although he has written several concert works including *Birthday*, a children's opera. Beginning with music for Peter Gill's *Hitting Town* (1974), his television credits include plays and features such as *Bergerac, Shoestring, The Monocled Mutineer* – for which he received a British Academy Award – and *The History Man*; documentaries *Life in the Freezer, Beyond the Clouds*; and innumerable signature tunes, for example the BBC's *Nine O'Clock News, The Money Programme, Newsnight* and *Telly Addicts*. He won an Ivor Novello Award for his contribution to the 14-hour serial *The Jewel in the Crown* (he picked up another in 1987 with the score for Sir Richard Attenborough's *Cry Freedom*). Five of Fenton's many film scores have been nominated for an Academy Award: *Gandhi* (1982–co-written with Ravi Shankar), *Cry Freedom* (1987–best song and best score), *Dangerous Liaisons* (1988) and *The Fisher King* (1991). He has collaborated successfully with Attenborough, most recently on *Shadowlands*. Fenton is a founder member of the Association of Professional Composers, and lectures occasionally at the National Film School.

The Company of Wolves (1984) **Original Soundtrack / George Fenton.**
TER Ⓔ CDTER1094 (40 minutes: ADD).

The adult fairy-tale world of Angela Carter is brought astonishingly to life by Neil Jordan much aided by a complex music score. Fenton's adroit mix of orchestra and electronics is a work worthy of much attention and constant plays. It successfully combines appealing tunes of childhood innocence with the atmospheric sounds of childhood fears and nightmares. Fenton also mixes in natural sounds, for instance, his own breathing, with the music giving an altogether dreamlike quality to the whole enterprise. This works well in the cue "The Boy and the Devil" where the sampled and treated breathing forms a distinctly menacing bass line over which a solo bass flute performs. The idea is simple enough but it is most effective. The addition of rustic folk tunes, a Beethoven String Trio given a macabre turn and a gorgeous piece of Debussy-like impressionism, "One Sunday Afternoon", all magically work together to produce a most affecting album. It is a pity that the film has not received more attention for it is a marvellous example of film-maker and composer working in real harmony.   **DS**

New review
High Spirits (1988) **Original Soundtrack**, with **Catherine Bott** (sngr); **Dermot Crehan** (vn); **Paul Brennan** (uillean pipes); **Graunke Symphony Orchestra / George Fenton.**
GNP Crescendo Ⓔ GNPD8016 (53 minutes: DDD)

George Fenton's music for Neil Jordan's ghostly comedy *High Spirits* positively overflows with boundless energy and enthusiasm, an abundance of themes, and some richly-textured orchestration. The music is composed in an Irish idiom, and this accounts for its jaunty, rollicking thrust. Solo fiddle, Uillean pipes and wordless female voice give this distinctively Irish music a feel that is at once earthy, otherworldly and mystical. The swirling main theme, performed by fiddle with cacophonous orchestral backing, evokes almost unstoppable lunacy and high-jinx. The bittersweet love theme possesses an uncanny ethereal quality courtesy of the elegant female voice. Moments of intimacy and fragility are interspersed with bombast and comic chaos. Pure joy from beginning to end.   **PP**

New review
Mary Reilly (1996) **Original Soundtrack**, with the **London Symphony Orchestra / George Fenton.**
Sony Classical Ⓔ SK62259 (45 minutes: DDD).

During its making, there was much speculation about Christopher Hampton's reworking of the Jekyll and Hyde story for director Stephen Frears. In the end, the film came and went with barely a murmur but luckily Sony saw fit to release the soundtrack. This is a darkly romantic score where the string section of the LSO are very prominent: violin solos throughout that add a plaintive lament for the tragic aspects of the story. Focusing on the character of Mary Reilly, a servant in Jekyll's household, the film is at pains to stress her naiveté and innocence. The music helps a great deal here – a simple, almost child-like melody can be heard in the "Opening Credits" as a violin solo but under it are malevolent swirling movements from the lower strings suggesting dark forces at work. The whole score is like this – constant struggles between light and dark, innocence and corruption, good and evil. Inevitably, there is no resolution and the disc's almost unrelieved gloom may deter some from repeated listening. This would be a pity for there is much to admire here. It would have been so easy to plaster the film with bombast but Fenton seldom raises his voice and the score is free from traditional horror film music trappings. The cues are thoughtful, eloquent statements of the inner turmoil faced by the protagonists. A good score worth persisting with, but you might need to play something more cheerful afterwards.   **DS**

New review

Memphis Belle (1990) Original Soundtrack / George Fenton.
  Varèse Sarabande Ⓔ VSD5293 (44 minutes: DDD). Includes *I Know Why* (Warren/Gordon).

A lilting string arrangement of "The Londonderry Air (Danny Boy)" followed by a full orchestral statement of the principal themes leave the listener in no doubt as to where Fenton's intentions lie. Heroism in the face of adversity, the pain of tragic and senseless loss, a nostalgia for times past but all underpinned by a lightness reflecting the youthful recklessness of American pilots in World War II-stricken England. As is often the case with Fenton's scores, a deep emotional vein can be heard running through the work that reveals itself gradually on repeated plays. A particular highlight of the score is "The Final Mission", a stirring, heartfelt piece which accompanies the visually arresting sequence of massed bombers slowly rumbling into the sky. The seven-minute "End Title" suite is similarly a gorgeous summation of all that has gone before and makes for a deeply satisfying conclusion. Fenton's music underlines the emotions, but the source cues determine the time in which these emotions are played out. The three tracks, one of them a cosy Glenn Miller original and the others arranged and re-recorded by Fenton, are well placed in the running order so as not to detract from the dramatic heart of the score. The album actually ends with a peculiar vocal performance of "Danny Boy" given a contemporary arrangement: although this track doesn't ruin the mood of the disc, it certainly doesn't help it either.   **DS**

Shadowlands (1993) Original Soundtrack, with the **Magdalen College Choir, Oxford / Grayston Ives; London Symphony Orchestra / George Fenton**.
  EMI Angel Ⓔ CDQ5 55093-2 (47 minutes: DDD). Includes *O Little Town of Bethlehem* (Trad. arr. Fenton), *Once in Royal David's City* (Gauntlett/Mann), and *Summer is Icumen In* (Anonymous).

Dignified and restrained, with no concessions to Hollywood-style sentimentality, *Shadowlands* is a determinedly 'English' film score. In a series of brief, sensitively scored sketches, Fenton depicts the timelessness of Oxford collegiate life: the beautiful age-old hymn "Veni Sancte Spiritus" (actually newly written), the 1920s chintz and china of "The Randolph". For once, the source music fits this ambience perfectly, with the famous Magdalen College May morning song "Summer is Icumen In" a delightful addition to Fenton's original score. Only during the finale does Fenton let his music soar, and here it becomes most obviously Elgarian: a heartening theme which grows to an unfeignedly impassioned climax. *Shadowlands* is a subtle and refined work, but most assuredly one which repays attentive listening.   **MW**

Also available:
August (1996) Debonair DEBCD1002 [with Anthony Hopkins]
The Crucible (1996) RCA Victor 09026 68666-2
Cry Freedom (1987) MCA MCAD6224 [with Jonas Gwangwa]
Dangerous Liaisons (1988) Virgin CDV2583
Final Analysis (1992) Varèse Sarabande VSD5356
The Fisher King (1991) MCA MCAD10249 [includes songs]
Heaven's Prisoners (1996) Debonair DEBCD1004
In Love and War (1996) RCA 09026 68725-2
Land and Freedom (1995) Debonair DEBCD1001
White Mischief (1987) TER CDTER1153

Brad Fiedel

b. 1951 USA

New Yorker Brad Fiedel hails from a distinctly musical family. His great-grandfather was leader of a family orchestra in Eastern Europe, his grandfather was a violinist who played for silent movie orchestras in New York, his father was a pianist and composer, his mother a dancer and choreographer (not to mention the cousins ...). His parents ran a school for performing arts, so young Brad naturally learned piano and began writing songs with his father at the age of five; by age seven he had composed his first original piece. As a teenager he wrote music for modern dance classes and worked as a musician and composer whilst still at high school. In 1972 he began working as a songwriter for Paul Simon's DeShufflin' Music, and also became New York City University's first resident dance composer. He wrote early scores for educational films, and toured with Daryl Hall and John Oates before scoring John Howard's first feature *Apple Pie* (1975). Moving to Los Angeles, Fiedel got his big break with James Cameron's original *Terminator* movie. Other credits include *Blink* (1993), *True Lies* (1994), *Johnny Mnemonic* (1995) and *Eden.*

The Terminator (1984) **Original Soundtrack**, with **Ross Levison** (electric vn); **Brad Fiedel** (synths).
    Edel ℗ 0022082CIN (72 minutes: ADD).
Terminator 2: Judgment Day (1991) **Original Soundtrack**, with **Brad Fiedel** (synths).
    Varèse Sarabande ℗ VSD5335 (54 minutes: DDD).

Relentlessly mechanistic, containing only one principal theme, and much that functions more like sound effects than music, these scores will be some people's worst nightmare. However, the very unrelenting machine-like style has a fascination, even when removed from the visuals that gave it a context. The familiar *Terminator* theme – a short but instantly recognizable synth motif built over a hypnotic percussion rhythm – is Fiedel's only concession to melody. A brief interlude in the first score, with electric piano momentarily augmenting electronics, simply restates this main tune as a substitute "Love Theme". Ross Levison's electric violin adds haunting ambience, and a much-needed extra sonority to the electronic palette.
    The second score has a fleshed-out version of the original theme, and some powerful additions in the form of new motifs (but not tunes) associated with the T-1000. There is a sinister mechanical 'breathing' effect signalling the presence of the super-Terminator; and a dynamic percussion-led 'running' motif which cannot fail to set the pulse racing. Edel's fully remastered release – sub-titled 'The Definite Edition' – contains the original score in its entirety, with the welcome addition of booklet notes giving background information on both film and score. Despite this entirely laudable completism, I suspect all but dedicated *Terminator* enthusiasts will find 72 minutes excessive. **MW**

Also available:
The Big Easy (1987) Spectrum 551 159-2
Blink (1993) Milan 191 902
The Real McCoy (1993) Varèse Sarabande VSD5450
True Lies (1994) Epic 476939-2

Robert Folk

b. 1950 USA

New York-born Robert Folk's early musical interests were songwriting and rock music. However, aged 18 he began serious studies at the prestigious Juilliard School. Folk remained at the school for a decade, composing, conducting and teaching piano in his spare time, eventually graduating with a doctorate. Despite intending to stay on as a member of the Juilliard faculty – and with an impressive list of concert works already behind him – Folk suddenly got sidetracked and found himself in Hollywood. His first film score was a low-budget independent movie called *The Slayer* (1984), but he also scored two of that year's biggest comedy hits, *Bachelor Party* and *Police Academy* (Folk subsequently scored all of the sequels). Unfortunately, Folk became a victim of his own success and was typecast as just a comedy composer. However, the obvious quality of his work is now beginning to pay dividends, with an increasingly busy and diverse workload.

Arabian Knight [**The Thief and the Cobbler**] (1994) **Original Soundtrack**, with **Bobby Page, Steve Lively, Andrea Robinson, Arnold McCuller** (sngrs); **London Symphony Orchestra / Robert Folk**.
    Milan ℗ 35730-2 (45 minutes: DDD). Lyrics by Norman Gimbel.

Reunited with animator Don Bluth – for whom he previously scored *Rock-a-Doodle* (1990) and *Troll in Central Park* (1993) – Robert Folk has delivered a full-sized symphonic work clearly after the mould of James Horner's similar assignments, and including several Disney-style pop songs *à la* Alan Menken. This is unashamedly old-fashioned, Hollywood-style scoring. That the melodies are pleasing and the orchestrations unchallenging is only to be expected; Folk is too good a composer, however, to slavishly follow the lead of others. *Arabian Knight* has enough lively, swashbuckling moments, and is flavoured with just the right amount of 'Arabic' instrumentation to grab the attention and hold it throughout. The extremely saccharine quality of the four songs – combined with some jarring stylistic differences to the underscore – will prompt many listeners to skip those tracks. Some unusually uncertain playing from the LSO's brass section mars what is otherwise a slick performance. **MW**

New review

Lawnmower Man 2: Beyond Cyberspace (1996) **Original Soundtrack**, with the **Sinfonia of London / Robert Folk**.
Varèse Sarabande Ⓕ VSD5698 (65 minutes: DDD).

After an early hit with *Police Academy* (1984), Robert Folk fell victim to Hollywood typecasting and spent much of the next decade scoring a series of increasingly inane comedies. Thankfully, Folk's career seems now to be diversifying, even if the calibre of assignments he is being offered remains decidedly undistinguished. *Lawnmower Man 2* – another desperate attempt to cash in on the current Virtual Reality fad – may have sunk faster than *Raise the Titanic* at the box office, but the score is worthy of more notice. This is unashamed Hollywood action movie music: simple, ostentatious, overblown, in your face. In other words, great fun. What sets Folk's work apart, however, is his ability to pen real melodies, not just dislocated action 'themes'. There is a warm vein of melodic interest running through this score, and consequently an unexpected suggestion of pathos in places – "Jobe's Theme" for example – which helps the listener make sense of the many splashy, bombastic set-pieces. The Sinfonia of London – especially their blisteringly powerful brass section – give another exemplary performance, capably handling all of the music's frantic gear changes. At over an hour it is perhaps too much to take in all at once, but I found repeated listenings to be increasingly rewarding. **MW**

Selected Suites Original Soundtracks, with the **London Symphony Orchestra; National Philharmonic Orchestra; Royal Philharmonic Orchestra; Los Angeles Philharmonic Orchestra; Munich Opera Orchestra; Berlin Radio Symphony Orchestra; Paris Opera Orchestra / Robert Folk**.
Knightsbridge/Intrada Ⓕ RF2001 (two discs, 155 minutes: DDD).
Arabian Knight [The Thief and the Cobbler] (1994). Toy Soldiers (1991). The Never Ending Story II (1990). Tremors (1990). Troll in Central Park (1993). Miles from Home (1988). The Planets. Can't Buy Me Love (1987). Police Academy (1984). To Dream of Roses – ballet.

The Selected Suites are from ten Original Soundtracks, and comprise over 150 minutes of 'big' film music. That is to say that Folk fashions his scores to get the maximum out of a large orchestra, and is not frightened to come at you with all guns blazing. Listening to the first three suites alone will leave you exhausted: animated fantasy with *The Thief and the Cobbler*, teen-*Die Hard* heroics in *Toy Soldiers*, and more fantasy – live-action this time – with *The Never Ending Story II*. Not all the suites are as frantic as these. *Troll in Central Park* has a sparkling and perky Christmas-like sheen; *Miles from Home* radiates with a pastoral charm; and *Can't Buy Me Love* is contemporary romance, but in their own way they are all very intense scores. The best way to approach these discs is to listen to each suite separately, then have a break before going on to the next one, thus avoiding music fatigue. What will emerge is the realization that Folk is a truly under-rated composer, and you begin to wonder why he hasn't worked on better-known films (only four of the films represented here have been released in the UK). Perhaps this will change in the future. Certainly his command of the orchestra is astonishing and if, on occasion, the actual material fails to impress, the presentation always does. The orchestras listed comprise some of the finest in Europe, but since they are not allied to the actual titles, it is impossible to know who is performing what. Which leads to another gripe: the packaging. Given that so little is known about the composer and the majority of these films, it is woefully inadequate. The music may be plentiful, but information about it is not. In spite of poor presentation, this is an important collection of work and one that is well worth seeking out. **DS**

Also available:
Beastmaster 2: Through the Portal of Time (1992) Intrada MAF7019D
In the Army Now (1994) Intrada MAF7058D
Maximum Risk (1996) Varèse Sarabande VSD5756
Toy Soldiers (1991) Intrada MAF7015D
Trapped in Paradise (1994) Varèse Sarabande VSD5555

Christopher Franke

b. 1942 Germany

Born in Berlin, Christopher Franke studied composition at the Berlin Conservatory and performed in the jazz/rock group Agitation Free. He was instrumental in setting up a sound studio at the Conservatory where he gave classes in improvisation. This project ultimately became the basis for the Berlin School of Electronic Music, where Franke met Edgar Froese and Peter Baumann. Franke joined their innovative band, Tangerine Dream, for the 1971 album *Alpha Centauri*. He recorded 36 studio albums with the Dream, and over 30 film scores up to 1988, when he left to pursue a solo career encompassing studio recordings, live performances, and of course, film scoring. Film soundtracks with Tangerine Dream include *Risky Business* (1983), *Firestarter* (19⁀4), and the American version of Ridley Scott's *Legend* (1986). Franke's solo work has concentrated mainly on scoring television features and series such as *The Tommyknockers* (1993), *Walker: Texas Ranger* (1993) and *Babylon 5*. He is the founder of the Berlin Symphonic Film Orchestra, and has his own recording studio in Hollywood where he is now based.

Babylon 5 (1993-4) **Original Soundtrack**, with the **Berlin Symphonic Film Orchestra / Christopher Franke** (synths).
Sonic Images ℗ SI8502-2 (58 minutes: DDD).
Chrysalis. Mind War. Parliament of Dreams. The Geometry of Shadows.

This disc presents music from the first and second series of the ambitious Sci-Fi show arranged into extended suites by the composer. The muscular "Main Title" appears in both the original ("Chrysalis") and re-orchestrated ("Geometry of Shadows") versions (for the third series, Franke created a new, more militaristic theme). The rhythmic energy of the original underpins much of the remainder of the disc. Franke can make a lot of noise with his synthesizers: pounding rock drumbeats overlaid with swooping, crashing patterns of sound; enormous string chords and rushing sequencer patterns. He can also produce delicate, ethereal textures that are quite enchanting (his Minbari music in "The Geometry of Shadows" for example). The stunning recording sometimes makes this disc more of an audiophile experience than a musical one; nevertheless, the grandness of Franke's musical vision might properly be labelled 'symphonic', despite the near-total absence of orchestral instruments other than in their sampled form (the Berlin Symphonic Film Orchestra is dominated by the impressive bank of synthesizers pictured on the album sleeve). Complete with glossy booklet, this is an irresistible purchase for devotees of the series, and much more exciting than many of the more conventional *Star Trek* TV scores. As we go to press, a second volume of music from the third and fourth series has just been released by Sonic Images. **MW**

Also available:
New Music for Films Varèse Sarabande VSD5393
Night of the Running Man (1995) Super Tracks STCD500
Universal Soldier (1992) Varèse Sarabande VSD5373

Hugo Friedhofer

1901-1981 USA

One of the most under-valued of the 'great' film composers, Hugo Friedhofer won the admiration of his peers, if not of the wider musical establishment outside Hollywood. Born in San Francisco of a musical family, he began playing the cello aged 13, but dropped out of school three years later. He worked at various jobs and studied painting at the Mark Hopkins Institute before deciding to pursue music as a career. Work as a cellist was gradually superseded by arranging and orchestrating. With the advent of sound pictures, Friedhofer moved from arranging music for theatre orchestras to Fox Studios in Hollywood. Between 1930-1943 Friedhofer arranged and orchestrated over 60 films, beginning with the musical *Sunny Side Up*. In 1935 he moved to Warner Brothers, although Fox music director Alfred Newman frequently asked for his services. Friedhofer began a long-standing association with Erich Wolfgang Korngold by orchestrating Korngold's first Hollywood project *A Midsummer Night's Dream* (1935). But Friedhofer's main interest was composition, and in 1937 he scored *The Adventures of Marco Polo*. By 1943, Friedhofer had abandoned his career as an orchestrator – with the single exception of Korngold's scores – and embarked on full-time composing. He won an Academy Award for *The Best Years of Our Lives* in 1946, and was nominated a further eight times. Despite his work being considered as particularly fine by his colleagues, Friedhofer's fortunes declined along with the old studio system. His last full-length score was for *Private Parts* in 1972. In his later years he taught composition informally at his home, and thus had a wide but largely unrecognized influence on a later generation of film composers.

INTRADA
Is a label featuring . . .

- Composers that include Jerry Goldsmith, James Horner, Bruce Broughton, Elmer Bernstein, Basil Poledouris, Christopher Young, David Newman, Craig Safan, Leonard Rosenman, John Scott, Lee Holdridge, Laurence Rosenthal and Miklós Rózsa.

- Great film scores that include -- TOMBSTONE (Broughton), THUNDERHEART (Horner), QUIGLEY DOWN UNDER (Poledouris), SILVERADO (Broughton), PLANET OF THE APES (Goldsmith), A PATCH OF BLUE (Goldsmith), FIRST BLOOD (Goldsmith), RAMBO III - The complete 76 minute score (Goldsmith), THE GREAT ESCAPE (Bernstein), THE WIND AND THE LION (Goldsmith), THE LAST STARFIGHTER (Safan), RIO CONCHOS (Goldsmith), IVANHOE (Rózsa) and JULIUS CAESAR (Rózsa).

INTRADA
Also is a retail soundtrack shop with . . .

- A *FREE* monthly mail-order catalog. Send us your name and address, and we will be happy to send you the latest volume. All orders are handled promptly and are fully guaranteed.

- A large inventory of soundtrack CDs on all labels, including all current releases, Intrada titles at discount prices and hard-to-find imports.

INTRADA

1488 VALLEJO STREET • SAN FRANCISCO, CALIFORNIA 94109
TEL: (415) 776-1333 • FAX: (415) 776-2666 • e-mail: intradanet@aol.com
http://members.aol.com/intradanet/intrada.htm

An Affair to Remember (1957) **Original Soundtrack**, with **Marni Nixon** (sop); **20th Century-Fox Orchestra and Chorus / Lionel Newman**.
Epic Ⓜ EK57568 (39 minutes: AAD). Includes *An Affair to Remember*, *You Make It Easy to Be True*, *The Tiny Scout* and *Tomorrowland* (Warren/Adamson/McCarey).

It was the success of *Sleepless in Seattle* (1993) with its flashbacks to *An Affair to Remember* that no doubt rekindled interest in this lightweight soundtrack to a high style soap opera starring Cary Grant and Deborah Kerr. Hugo Friedhofer composed the incidental music for several key scenes in the film. These include a luminously scored love scene in Villefranche, where we first hear the couple's theme song, and the crucial one at the Empire State, where they've agreed to meet six months later, following a shipboard romance. The sombre mood, with bells tolling somewhere in the distance, mirrors Grant's anxiety, as he waits in vain for Deborah Kerr to turn up. Here the score refers again to the movie's theme song, one of four songs by Harry Warren with lyrics by Harold Adamson and the film's director Leo McCarey. The potentially awkward situation of having a songwriter contributing a hoped-for chart success to a score by another distinguished hand was averted in this instance by Friedhofer's admiration for Warren's "beautiful, flexible melody", which Vic Damone introduced over the credits and turned into a hit record. Warren's other contributions are "You Make it Easy to Be True", a pretty melody harking back to his Busby Berkeley days, "The Tiny Scout", and another optimistic ditty "Tomorrowland", with Marni Nixon again doing her Anna Leonowens vowels for Deborah Kerr. No one knew better how to conduct such a confection than Fox's own Lionel Newman, who always drew the sweetest sounds from his home orchestra. **AE**

This Earth is Mine[a] (1959) **The Young Lions**[b] (1958) **Original Soundtracks**, with[a]**Universal-International Orchestra / Joseph Gershenson**; [b]**20th Century-Fox Orchestra / Lionel Newman**.
Varèse Sarabande Ⓕ VSD2-5402/3 (two discs, 79 minutes: AAD).

This very generous coupling, at least by soundtrack standards, brings together two contemporaneous scores by one of Hollywood's least known figures. Friedhofer's death in 1981, which passed unnoticed by The New York Times, prompted American jazz critic, Gene Lees, to write a most affectionate study of the composer, collected in the volume Singers and the Song. Friedhofer spent many years as an orchestrator before coming into his own as a composer with *The Best Years of Our Lives*. Much of his work is not available on disc, making this issue all the more treasurable. *The Young Lions*, based on Irwin Shaw's acclaimed Second World War book, was a major Fox CinemaScope movie, shot in black and white, a rare event in 1958. The score, as Kevin Mulhall's fulsome notes relate, moves between major and minor keys. The former mode conveys the characters of the two American soldiers, one in strict dance tempo, the other hometown America, whilst the big events – the "North American Battle", "Berlin Aftermath" with its Valhalla quotation, and even the march of the "Main Title" – are sombre in tone. A gentle bluesy melody for strings conveys the third principal character, a Nazi who questions his Party's philosophy when reality dawns. A Parisian interlude brings with it the key to Friedhofer's art – here are the perfect orchestral balance, the beauty of line and sensitivity in scoring that were so admired by his contemporaries. *This Earth is Mine* was a lush melodrama set in the vineyards of California and shot in luxuriant Technicolor. Once again restraint is the key note, even in the treatment accorded the "Main Title", the melody of which is not by Friedhofer. This is sung by Bob Grabeau, with music by Jimmy Van Heusen and lyrics by Sammy Cahn – information missing from this CD release, although it was properly credited on the original LP. **AE**

Also available:
The Adventures of Marco Polo (1937) **The Rains of Ranchipur** (1955) **The Lodger** (1944) **Seven Cities of Gold** (1955) (Moscow SO/Stromberg) Marco Polo 8 223857

Peter Gabriel

b. 1950 England

Born in London, Peter Gabriel rose to prominence as lead singer of progressive rock group Genesis. He left the band in 1975 to pursue a solo career that has been characterized by experiment, increasingly featuring a combination of music and visuals (his 1993 album *Xplora* was released on CD-ROM) and an emphasis on non-Western musical styles. He sponsored the first WOMAD (World of Music and Dance) festival in 1982. Gabriel's first film score was for Alan Parker's *Birdy* (1984), and he also supplied the music for Martin Scorsese's controversial *The Last Temptation of Christ*.

New review

Passion – music from **The Last Temptation of Christ** (1988) Various artists, including **Peter Gabriel, Shankar** and **Mahmoud Tabrizi Zadeh**.
Real World Ⓕ RWCD1 (76 minutes: DDD).

An audio collage of ethnic music recorded in various locations around the world and Peter Gabriel's own original music for the film, *Passion* is part soundtrack album, part experimental World Music album – hence its release on Virgin's Real World label, set up to promote the work of WOMAD. For Gabriel's many fans little needs to be said, here is pop music's arch-innovator continuing to assimilate the music of different cultures within his own sophisticated electronic environment. Duduk, tabla, Ney flute and surdu are sampled, processed and interpreted by Fairlight and Prophet 5 synthesizers. Wordless (but not voice-less), there are no catchy hit tunes like "Sledgehammer" here, and the music, built upon persistent North African rhythms, has little in the way of a common thematic basis: instead, most tracks are carefully structured units based upon particular rhythmic patterns or improvisations (the few exceptions including "Of These, Hope" and "With This Love", the latter a melting theme for cor anglais). For soundtrack collectors, this is something of an out-of-the-ordinary experience (but then, Martin Scorsese never did go in for normal Hollywood fare) – although now that the Armenian duduk and other like 'exotic' instruments regularly crop up in contemporary film scores (Grame Revell's *The Crow*, for example), its uniqueness is somewhat diminished. The score bears few of the hallmarks normally associated with film music, an impression enhanced by Gabriel's reworking of much of the music specifically for this album release (which is why the title is not simply *The Last Temptation of Christ* – original soundtrack). Therefore it is perhaps best described simply as a spendidly evocative Peter Gabriel album, which, like all of his others, defies easy categorization.   **MW**

Also available:
Birdy (1984) Charisma CASCD1167

Philip Glass

b. 1937 USA

Born in Baltimore, Philip Glass's minimalist style influenced several pop artists, including Mike Oldfield, Brian Eno and David Byrne. Glass took his master's degree at New York's Juilliard School before studying in Paris. He discovered Ravi Shankar and the refreshing delights of Indian music, finding them an antidote to the academic European avant-garde (he transcribed Shankar's music for the film *Chappaqua*). He has written four avant-garde operas, including *Einstein on the Beach* (1976), and several film scores. He became the first composer since Stravinsky to sign an exclusive recording contract with CBS (now Sony), and founded the Point label to issue contemporary music, including his *Low Symphony* based on David Bowie's 1977 album. In 1997 he will be scoring *The Secret Agent*, an adaptation of Joseph Conrad's novel directed by Christopher Hampton, and Martin Scorsese's *Kun Dun* – a Disney-distributed film about the life of the Dalai Lama.

Koyaanisqatsi (1982) **Original Soundtrack**.
Island Ⓜ IMCD98 (47 minutes: ADD).

The impact of this individual score is as stunning on disc as with the film. Most remarkably, the sense of human exultation in the face of the mechanical and mundane is intensified by the almost rigid calculation of the rhythmic overlaying technique which Glass uses here, particularly in the longest track "The Grid", to overwhelming and brilliant effect. In the first and last tracks, the deep bass voice announcing the title (a Hopi Indian word) has a calming and chilling effect at the same time – summing up the film's thesis that our late twentieth-century world can simultaneously beguile and terrify us. Performances and recording are first-rate – a thoughtful, and thought-provoking disc.   **CT**

Mishima (1985) **Original Soundtrack / Michael Riesman**.
Nonesuch Ⓕ 7559-79113-2 (46 minutes: DDD).

In his booklet notes, director Paul Schrader describes Glass as being the only composer for this biographical film of Japanese novelist and playwright Mishima. It was an interesting choice because Glass's film scores, though few, have been for documentary features, whereas *Mishima* is a narrative drama. However, the constantly propelling nature of this type of music, with its arresting title theme, is an ideal force that makes for compelling cinema. The opening – in which the soft sounds of wind-chimes give way to a full statement of the main theme, underlining the poetry and artistry of the man is quite splendid. This contrasts with the more purposeful, militaristic sounds depicting the disciplines of the samurai warrior which Mishima and his supporters followed. Glass has taken these elements, which work together within the dramatizations of Mishima's novels in the film, and produced a completely gripping album. **DS**

Also available:
Anima Mundi (1988) Nonesuch 7559-79329-2
Film Works (1988) Nonesuch 7559-79377-2
Powaqqatsi (1988) Nonesuch 7559-79192-2
The Thin Blue Line (1988) Nonesuch 7559-79209-2

Ernest Gold
1921 Austria

Born in Vienna, Ernest Gold studied piano with his grandfather, and began writing music when he was five. He studied at the Vienna State Academy before emigrating to the USA in 1938. In New York he worked as an accompanist and studied harmony with Otto Cesana. Gold took to writing songs, having an early hit with "Practice Makes Perfect" (1940). He wrote several concert works before moving to Hollywood in 1945 and fulfilling his ambition to write film scores, beginning with *The Girl of the Limberlost* (1945). His score for *Exodus* won him an Academy Award. He also wrote the musical *Solomon* (1968), and became the first film composer to have his name on Sunset Boulevard's Walk of Fame.

Exodus (1960) **Original Soundtrack**, with the **Sinfonia of London / Ernest Gold**.
 RCA Ⓜ 1058-2R (34 minutes: ADD).

Although the theme to *Exodus* has been subjected to many wildly different interpretations over the years (Pat Boone even added lyrics to it), there is still something undeniably moving about the original version; its purposeful nobility seemingly rooted in the turbulent history of the Jewish people. The theme's popularity made the LP a big seller throughout 1960 (staying at number one in the American Billboard chart for 14 weeks), and if the remainder of the score is not quite so powerful, it remains an excellent, well-crafted example of big-budget film scoring. **RS**

Elliot Goldenthal
b. 1954 USA

New Yorker Elliot Goldenthal is one of the most original composers currently working in Hollywood. A student of John Corigliano who also studied with Aaron Copland, Goldenthal took his Masters Degree in composition at the Manhattan School of Music. Since then he has written music in a variety of genres: *Juan Darien – a Carnival Mass*; musicals *The Transposed Heads* and *Liberty's Taken*; incidental music for several Shakespeare productions; *Shadow Play Scherzo*, written in honour of Leonard Bernstein, and *Fire Water Paper – A Vietnam Oratorio* (recorded by Sony Classical, SK68368). He is currently working on a full-length opera, *Grendel*, based on the story of Beowulf's monstrous adversary. Goldenthal scored the films *Cocaine Cowboys* (1979) and *Blank Generation* (1980), but his first major Hollywood venture was *Drugstore Cowboy* (1989), closely followed in the same year by *Pet Sematary*, a low-budget Stephen King adaptation. It was his stark and compelling score for *Alien 3* (1992), however, that brought him wider recognition. His eclectic style defies easy categorization, although it might not be unfair to cite Bernard Herrmann as his closest filmic ancestor. Goldenthal described his approach to the film *Cobb* (1994) as "composition as collision", and this might be an appropriate description of his music generally. In the normally conservative world of film music Goldenthal's uncompromising modernity can seem shocking, but it is always tempered by a latent romanticism which adds emotional depth to the more chaotic elements of his music. Robert Elhai usually collaborates on orchestrations.

Alien 3 (1992) **Original Soundtrack**, with **Nick Nackley** (alto) **/ Jonathan Sheffer**.
 MCA Ⓔ MCAD10629 (50 minutes: DDD).

Alien 3 is a snarling, growling, spitting nightmare of a score. Brass instruments scream and groan like tormented souls; synthesizers screech and scurry like swarming insects; strings sigh and lament for the soon-to-be departed. This is music that will haunt your dreams. Goldenthal begins by emphasizing the mournful nature of the film, with a boy soprano dolefully intoning "Agnus Dei" (a warning that the characters will become lambs to the slaughter?). When the Alien attacks, Goldenthal's music assaults us too, although he reserves his most brutal musical onslaught for the prisoners' attempted rape of Ripley ("Wreckage and Rape"). When the creature is eventually destroyed ("The Entrapment"), cascading violin figures break through this otherwise unrelenting mood of fear, grief and despair, providing the only moment of relief and hope in the score. The final noble "Adagio" is a voiceless reiteration of the "Agnus Dei", an elegy to the triumph of the spirit over the flesh. The album is thoughtfully sequenced to make the best musical sense, rather than simply following the film's order. *Alien 3* is a dark, turbulent and disturbing score. In short, unforgettable.   **MW**

Batman Forever (1995) Original Soundtrack / Jonathan Sheffer.
    Atlantic Ⓟ 7567-82776-2 (44 minutes: DDD).

Goldenthal demonstrated with *Demolition Man* that he was more than able to cope with the absurdities of comic-strip film making. Having his youthful vigour and extraordinary way with an orchestra let loose on a Batman film has resulted in a score of dazzling variety and inventiveness. What leaves one really breathless is the detail and sheer diversity of the orchestrations. It sounds like a large orchestra augmented by extra percussion and synthesizers, but there is so much going on that you have almost to listen in sections just to take it all in. The central *Batman* theme, dotted throughout the album in various guises, is strongly heroic and martial; but the range of styles on display is equally impressive. Gotham City nightlife is presented as a pugnacious boogie, and there are dances for the villains in the form of a risqué rumba, fearsome foxtrot, wicked waltz and terrifying tango. Best of all, a brief suite of science-gone-mad music for Jim Carrey's pre-Riddler persona E. Nygma. Binding all these disparate elements into a cohesive whole is Goldenthal's unique musical voice, a voice that can be eloquent and soothing in the score's quieter moments (of which there are some), but can exhibit a frantic and ferocious madness when required. There is frequently the sense that this music is hurtling towards some endpoint that only the composer knows, and it is this element of danger that makes his scoring so invigorating. The clarity of the recording is simply stunning.   **DS**

Cobb (1994) Original Soundtrack, with **Elliot Goldenthal** (pf) / **Jonathan Sheffer**.
    Sony Classical Ⓟ SK66923 (43 minutes: DDD). Includes *Life is a Ball Game* performed by Sister Wynona Carr.

Releasing a film about notorious American baseball legend Ty Cobb in the middle of the country's first ever nationwide baseball strike could guarantee only one thing: total box office disaster. Whatever the merits of the film might have been, however, the soundtrack album is an experience that should not be neglected. A typically eclectic mixture of styles, *Cobb* could not be the handiwork of anyone save Elliot Goldenthal. The disc opens with the composer's own earthy rendition of "There is a Fountain Filled with Blood" which unexpectedly segues into a tender, chamber-like set of variations. A brooding romantic theme is followed by sleazy New York jazz. A breezy ragtime piano tune (played by the composer) struggles against crashing, dissonant orchestral chaos. Some soundtrack albums jump from one cue to the next with no regard to musical continuity, but not *Cobb*. These short cues, despite – or because of? – their diversity fit together with a weird neatness. Listen to how the sequence from track nine (the mysterious "Winter Walk") through to track 13 (the thrilling "Reno Ho', Part II") forms a perfectly-connected suite. The score closes with "The Beast Within" from *Alien 3* (presumably cribbed for the temp track), which is cleverly prevented from seeming out of place by ensuring that the penultimate track, "Cobb Dies" is in the same tempo and key, with near identical orchestration. Only after such a crazy, exhilarating journey of the mind could Sister Wynona Carr's bluesy baseball-as-religious-metaphor song "Life is a Ball Game" make perfect sense!   **MW**

Demolition Man (1993) Original Soundtrack / Jonathan Sheffer.
    Varèse Sarabande Ⓟ VSD5447 (30 minutes: DDD).

A relentless assault on the senses brimming over with delicious macabre humour, *Demolition Man* must be the most original, exhilarating and funny action score ever written. With track titles like "Subterranean Slugfest" and "Obligatory Car Chase" (the latter twisting the bleakness of *Alien 3* to its own purposes) we can guess that the composer's tongue is set firmly in cheek. As ever with any Goldenthal creation, the listener never knows what might be around the next corner: a grandiose and powerful orchestral build in the opening "Dies Irae" (for once with no voices) gives way with a startling crash to a racing synthesizer figure punctuated by wailing brass, before resolving the opening theme in even grander fashion. A grimly amusing "Machine Waltz" is followed by a distinctly Bernard Herrmann-inspired piano ostinato in "Defrosting". "Musuem Dis Duel" and "Subterranean Slugfest" pit synthesized effects against orchestra in a wild death dance. Every brief cue segues perfectly into the next maniacal episode with the kind of crazy logic only to be found in Goldenthal's work. 'Subtle' is not an adjective that readily springs to mind.   **MW**

Heat (1996) **Original Soundtrack**, with the **Kronos Quartet / Jonathan Sheffer, Stephen Mercurio**. Warner Bros Ⓟ 9362-46144-2 (74 minutes: DDD). Includes music by Passengers (Brian Eno/U2), Terje Rypdal, Michael Brook, Einstruzende, Moby, Lisa Gerrard and Brian Eno.

Goldenthal's most visceral and contemporary music for film to date is also his most sombre and despondent. Devoid of his crackling writing for brass, Goldenthal relies on strings, vocals (his own), electric guitar, steel cello, drums and synthesizers. Whilst never lacking emotion, the score evokes a strong sense of alienation and unease, primarily through the use of minimalist motifs. There is little warmth in the score which instead chooses to incite notions of anarchy and impotency by abandoning traditional forms of musical development. In the opening title track, "Heat", for example, Goldenthal juxtaposes a throbbing drum beat with an icy solo violin, solo voice and psychedelic electric guitar to produce an ever-increasingly chaotic swell of sound with no apparent theme or direction. Goldenthal develops these ideas throughout the score in cues that never appear to have a tangible musical conclusion.

The score makes up barely half of the CD's 74-minute running time, the remainder consisting of source cues by such varied artists as Brian Eno, U2 and Lisa Gerrard. Unusually these songs perfectly enhance and even mirror the score, producing a uniquely balanced and satisfying listen. **PP**

Interview With the Vampire (1994) **Original Soundtrack**, with the **American Boychoir / Jonathan Sheffer.** Geffen Ⓟ GED24719 (49 minutes: AAD). Includes *Sympathy for the Devil* performed by Guns 'n' Roses.

Director Neil Jordan's first choice of composer, George Fenton, had his score rejected by the film's producers, but despite being a last-minute replacement, Goldenthal's attempt was good enough to earn him an Academy Award nomination. A highly chromatic choral setting of "Libera Me" for boys' voices and viola da gamba sets the gothic tone, followed by an overtly romantic, distinctly Mahlerian main theme in "Born to Darkness". Subsequent cues take the listener on a chaotic journey from wild, off-kilter eighteenth-century pastiche, through mournful romanticism to the utmost rigours of modernity. The composer demonstrates his mastery of form and content, mixing these disparate elements with rare skill (a solo harpsichord introduces "Lestat's Recitative", for example, before the music inflates to Wagnerian proportions). Characteristically frenzied outbursts, familiar from past scores, arise naturally from the prevailing mood of gothic romance, never seeming out of place or gratuitous. The composer has pointed out a couple of sly jokes in his Latin settings: during "Abduction and Absolution" he slyly alters the words from "Libera me, Domine, morte aeterna" to "vitae aeternae" – save me from everlasting life – and quotes "Lux aeternam*"* from the *Requiem Mass* (a little musical joke: vampires notoriously dislike light!). Another example of Goldenthal's uniqueness. **MW**

Michael Collins (1996) **Original Soundtrack / Jonathan Sheffer**. Atlantic Classics Ⓟ 7567-82960 (47 minutes: DDD). Includes *She Moved Through the Fair* (Traditional) and *Macushla* (McMurrough/Rowe).

On April 24 1916, Patrick Pearse, Michael Collins, and 150 armed men took over the General Post Office in Dublin and formally proclaimed the Dail Eireann. The rebellion was thwarted, the leaders were shot, and years of colonial and guerilla warfare ensued. These events and others are depicted in Neil Jordan's much-anticipated *Michael Collins*. Jordan has decided to treat the story as part of the Golden Age biopic tradition. Although quintessentially Irish, the director wants to draw universal values from Collins's story. This might explain his decision to emigrate to New York for the film's music score. Although there are Irish elements in the score, Elliot Goldenthal has adapted his own composing style to the requirements of the story. His ensemble includes orchestra, choir, electronics, vocals, and special instruments such as low whistle, Uilleann pipes, hammer dulcimer, solo violin, trumpet, and piano. "Easter Rebellion" has a haunting, ethereal quality combined with a broad, dramatic sound (recapitulated later in "Elegy for a Sunday" and "Civil War") that cries with importance. "Fire and Arms" is a *scherzo* for strings and brass, while "Train Station Farewell" introduces the waltz for Kitty. This eloquent theme, first heard as piano solo (and in a trumpet over strings arrangement in "Boland's Return"), is a perfect evocation of another time and place. "Winter Road" is typical of the action/suspense music in the score, with one section of the orchestra trying to outrun the next. Fortunately, Goldenthal's discipline and Jonathan Sheffer's conducting keeps the musicians on the same page. "Train to Granard" and "Home to Cork" sees the composer working with more familiar Irish sounds. Collins was eventually killed after signing a 1921 treaty that established the Irish Free State as a self-governing British dominion. In "She Moved Through the

Fair," the sweet, wistful voice of Sinead O'Connor haunts a scene in which Collins is murdered by Republican forces. Meanwhile, Jordan movingly cross-cuts the action with shots of Kitty trying on a wedding dress that she will never wear. "Funeral/Coda" is a broad, majestic set-piece that opens with a hymn for strings followed by a dramatic, descending motif for full orchestra. Mid-range fiddling and upper string harmonies fill the *fff* soundscape as the lower spectrum of the orchestra vibrates with intensity. **KM**

Pet Sematary (1989) **Original Soundtrack**, with the **Zarathustra Boys' Choir; Orchestra of St Luke's / Steven Mercurio**.
Varèse Sarabande Ⓕ VSD5227 (32 minutes: DDD).

Although a relatively early example of his film work, retrospectively this B-movie horror score is recognizably Goldenthal-esque: grim dissonances work against a predominantly bleak romantic backdrop; boys' voices wordlessly intone a lullaby from hell. Hitchcock and Herrmann would have been amazed by "The Return Game", in which Goldenthal extorts more hair-raising sounds from the string section than *Psycho*. All of this composer's scores are unforgettably distinctive experiences – *Pet Sematary* is no exception. **MW**

New review
A Time to Kill (1996) **Original Soundtrack / Jonathan Sheffer**.
Atlantic Classics Ⓕ 82959-2 (37 minutes: DDD).

Based on the novel by John Grisham, *A Time to Kill* deals with the complexities of racial prejudice and the inadequate attempts of the American justice system to emasculate it. Goldenthal seems to thrive on stories rooted in conflict and uses them to set musically opposing styles against each other in a literal tug-of-war. The 'Southern' locale of the film is represented by harmonica, penny whistle and dulcimer against a dense block of strings. Justice and the quest for truth is suggested by an unconventional fanfare theme, whilst the story's love interest is cemented with a seductive saxophone-based theme. The architecture of the score harmonizes each of these elements but, more often than not, throws them towards each other in a dissonant and deeply moving symbiosis that is, as usual with Goldenthal, fiercely modern and impressionistic. In "Consolation", for example, screeching saxophone is pitched toward strings in a virtuoso display of aggression; "Abduction" features that unmistakable Goldenthal sound of brass blaring at their lowest registers amidst a jumble of crashing anvil and timpani; whereas "Justice Wheel" and "Victory Fanfare" boast rather more optimistic and less cynical renderings of the justice theme with a bizarre Copland-like twist. Many continue to be excited by Elliot Goldenthal's determination to write 'pure' music within the confines of film. *A Time to Kill* is a perfect example of his passion for casting aside convention and pushing forward the boundaries of modern music without ignoring the relevance and success of what has gone before nor the demands of the drama. **PP**

Also available:
Golden Gate (1993) Varèse Sarabande VSD5470

Jerry Goldsmith
b. 1929 USA

It has been estimated – I don't know by whom – that every minute of every day a film or television programme accompanied by Jerry Goldsmith's music is being shown somewhere in the world. One of the most prolific composers active today, Goldsmith's progressive approach to film scoring has won him the admiration of his peers, unprecedented critical acclaim, and a legion of admiring fans. Born in Los Angeles, he studied piano with Jakob Gimpel and composition with Mario Castelnuovo-Tedesco. Goldsmith continued his musical training at Los Angeles City College, and attended Miklós Rózsa's film music classes at the University of Southern California. His professional career began humbly enough, as a clerk/typist in the music department of CBS; but his persistence soon landed him assignments providing music for radio and television dramas. Many of these scores were recorded live, thereby requiring Goldsmith to indulge in a certain amount of ad-libbing (he played piano, organ and novachord in the small ensemble) whilst on air – a difficult but invaluable education for an aspiring film composer. His first feature film was *Black Patch* in 1957. His reputation was increased by work on television series like *Gunsmoke, The Twilight Zone* and *Thriller*. These led to his first major film, *Lonely Are the Brave* (1962). Notable successes followed with *The Blue Max, Planet of the Apes* and *Patton* (1970). Goldsmith has always been a forward-looking composer, keen to experiment with new techniques and new technology – he has consistently advocated the introduction of electronic instruments as part of the standard orchestra – and often utilizes an eclectic mix of instruments in his scores. His non-film work has included a cantata, *Christus Apollo* (1969), and several ballet scores. He regularly conducts concerts of film music. He ascribes his fecundity to discipline and mastery of his craft. His usual orchestrator is Arthur Morton, although Alexander Courage (composer of the original *Star Trek* theme) has also collaborated with him. Goldsmith's reputation today has never been higher, although he has yet to win a second Academy Award to sit alongside the one he received for *The Omen* in 1976. Nobody quite knows how, but he continues to produce serious, original, top-quality film music at a prodigious rate.

Alien (1979) **Original Soundtrack**, with the **National Philharmonic Orchestra / Lionel Newman**.
Silva Screen Ⓜ FILMCD003 (36 minutes: ADD).

There is a distant coldness about this music which makes Goldsmith's depiction of pure fear all the more convincing. Of all film music – from Waxman's *Bride of Frankenstein*, through Herrmann's *Psycho*, to Goldsmith's own *Planet of the Apes* and *The Omen* – there is nothing quite so coldly, clinically terrifying as *Alien*. The orchestra never express anything so warm as a melody: although the haunting main theme is heard in snatches throughout, it is an expression of foreboding, not hope. Fearful, growling wind instruments cry out in horror; *glissandi* strings are like nails being scratched over a blackboard; percussive outbursts terrorize the unwary listener. This is why Goldsmith is so admired: he seizes upon the essence of a movie, divines exactly what the heart of it is, and produces an absorbing, realistic musical depiction of its soul. Director Ridley Scott may not have understood (he rejected several cues recorded here, and replaced the "End Title" with extracts from Howard Hanson's *Romantic* Symphony), but for anyone listening to this disc, the message is clear: be afraid, be very afraid.   **MW**

Bad Girls (1994) **Original Soundtrack / Jerry Goldsmith**.
Milan Ⓔ 22054-2 (39 minutes: DDD).

An invigorating Western score, *Bad Girls* is also an exemplary demonstration of Goldsmith's approach to composition. From the musical material found in an initial melody – first stated tenderly in the opening cue "The John" – Goldsmith meticulously constructs the rest of his score. The second cue, "The Hanging", leads us straight into a kinetic action motif with an off-kilter rhythm, which turns out to be based on the previous melody. This syncopated rhythm played directly against the opening tune is wittily stated in "Jail Break". Thus the music continues, ever inventive, fresh and exciting, but always thematically linked: the continuing development of a musical argument. This is why Goldsmith's scores (even the mediocre ones) are always worth listening to: he is a superb musical architect. *Bad Girls* is by no means mediocre, with a succession of highly dramatic scenes, inventively orchestrated (acoustic guitar and synthesizers added to the 'standard' instruments) and clothed in an attractively non-clichéd Western idiom.   **MW**

Basic Instinct (1992) **Original Soundtrack**, with the **National Philharmonic Orchestra / Jerry Goldsmith**.
Varèse Sarabande Ⓔ VSD5360 (44 minutes: DDD).

Sultry and sinister, sexy and solemn, *Basic Instinct* is loaded with ice-cold eroticism. A languorous principal theme, supported by the soporific ebb and flow of strings, contains swirling undercurrents which restrain any hint of romance. Goldsmith contrives to give his orchestra an orgasm during "Pillow Talk", but the chilly undertow makes this a distinctly fake climax. Another orgasm comes in the final cue: briefer, more passionate, still lacking emotion. There is a driving, dramatic edge to some of the score, but the overall impression is one of icy sensuality – an apparent contradiction resolved only by Goldsmith's masterly depiction of the characters' inner lives. There might be sex on screen, but Goldsmith's music tells us what is really going on. As pure music, the score is a study in passion without sentiment.   **MW**

The Blue Max (1966) **Original Soundtrack**, with the **National Philharmonic Orchestra / Jerry Goldsmith**.
Columbia Ⓜ JK57890 (63 minutes: ADD).

Listening to *The Blue Max* is the closest you will ever come to experiencing the terrifying exhilaration of aerial combat without actually joining the Air Force. Goldsmith's 'flying' theme raises us by dizzying interval leaps up into the clouds; dense contrapuntal textures throw us into the thick of a dogfight; virtuosic orchestral aerobatics leave us giddy and breathless. There is more: a passionate, yet unsentimental "Love Theme"; a great deal of grandiose, yet sombre militarism. The longest cue, "Retreat", is an enormous fugal *Passacaglia* for full orchestra, developed over a reiterated bass figure. This score has acquired a reputation amongst Goldsmith's legion of admirers as one of his very finest. Its reputation is well-deserved. Columbia's welcome reissue of the complete score contains several source music tracks which were featured in the film, including "Deutschland über Alles" and J. Strauss II's *Artists' Life*. Interesting as they are, Goldsmith's grand *tour de force* needs no assistance to qualify as an essential purchase. **MW**

New review

Chain Reaction (1996) Original Soundtrack / Jerry Goldsmith.
Varèse Sarabande Ⓕ VSD5746 (31 minutes: DDD).

Densely orchestrated, with a colourful and varied palette of contemporary sound, *Chain Reaction* is one of Goldsmith's busiest action scores. The typically complex ensemble Goldsmith employs here includes a vast amount of clanking electric and acoustic percussion, bells, anvil, electric guitar, xylophone and piano, in addition to the standard orchestra. The composer also indulges in a large and mesmerizing contingent of synthesizers. As with most Goldsmith action scores, the music evolves from a tiny fragment of thematic material, here a strident four-note motif, which is stated, developed, and re-sequenced in an infinite number of ways. This technique gives even the weakest Goldsmith score almost total coherence. The opening and closing cues feature a warm, though quite masculine theme for brass amidst a wash of strings derived from the original motif. The action set-pieces, "Ice Chase", "System Down" and "Open Door", are unruly and bombastic, whilst suspense tracks such as "Assassins" and "No Solution" are rather more subdued. **PP**

New review

Chinatown (1974) Original Soundtrack, with Uan Rasey (tpt) / Jerry Goldsmith.
Varèse Sarabande Ⓕ VSD5677 (31 minutes: AAD).
Includes *Easy Living* (Robin/Rainger), *I Can't Get Started* (Gershwin/Duke) performed by Bunny Berigan and His Orchestra, and *The Way You Look Tonight* (Fields/Kern).
City Hall (1996) Original Soundtrack / Jerry Goldsmith.
Varèse Sarabande Ⓕ VSD5699 (30 minutes: DDD).

Jerry Goldsmith was allotted just ten days to write and record his score for Roman Polanski's 1974 *colour noir*. It is entirely characteristic of this composer that in the white heat of inspiration he was able to create one of his most admired works. *Chinatown* is set in 1933 Los Angeles, but aside from some period source music included on the album, the score is distinctly modern: four pianos and four harps struck and plucked percussively, atonal strings and an eclectic ensemble of percussion instruments. The unsettling rasp of the *güiro* which helps to emphasize this score's fundamentally rhythmic nature was employed recently in John Ottman's music for *The Usual Suspects* (1995) to underline that movie's debt to convoluted 1970s thrillers like *Chinatown*. Goldsmith's only fully developed melody is the "Love Theme", a languid, jazzy trumpet solo which might have begun life in one of the original black and white *films noir*. This first CD release is a faithful repackaging of the LP, including the original sleeve design, although the poor sound has not been remastered. A very brief score, but a classic all the same.

More than two decades later Goldsmith is still the composer of choice for detective thrillers filled with political intrigue and devious plot twists. Reunited with director Harold Becker, for whom he previously scored *Malice*, Goldsmith's *City Hall* adopts a jazz-inflected approach somewhat reminiscent of his mentor Alex North. The bluesy principal theme, terse yet expressive, is the only melodic interest: all else is developed from it, whilst ostinato timpani and piano rhythms relentlessly force the pace during moments of drama. As with many of his recent scores, the instrumentation is conservative when compared with experimental works like *Chinatown* – even the synthesizers are relegated to a supporting role – but *City Hall*, if not vintage Goldsmith, is an effectively moody piece nevertheless. **MW**

New review

Executive Decision (1996) Original Soundtrack / Jerry Goldsmith.
Varèse Sarabande Ⓕ VSD5714 (29 minutes: DDD).

Executive Decision is a robust and indefatigable action score with a heavy militaristic feel which echoes, though never emulates, the composer's past triumphs in the action field. The score is notable for some particularly bright brass writing and is a good example of Goldsmith's justly famous transparent string sound. He imbues the score with a military feel primarily through the use of snare-drum, echoing trumpet, cymbals, timpani, electric percussion and synthesizers. Most of the material is 'slow-burning', with Goldsmith drafting in his stop-start suspense style, resulting in some deliciously intriguing rhythmic interplay between different sections of the orchestra. The longer cues, "All Aboard" and "Drill Team" are the most successful in this respect, the latter almost smouldering with danger and conspiracy. **PP**

First Blood (1982) **Original Soundtrack / Jerry Goldsmith.**
Intrada Ⓕ FMT8001D (40 minutes: ADD).

Rambo: First Blood Part II (1985) **Original Soundtrack / Jerry Goldsmith.**
Colosseum Ⓕ CST34 8005 (45 minutes: DDD).
Rambo III (1988) **Original Soundtrack**, with the **Hungarian State Opera Orchestra / Jerry Goldsmith.**
Intrada Ⓕ RVF6006D (76 minutes: DDD).

Even from a composer renowned for the sheer physical masculinity of his music, these three *Rambo* scores must rate as supremely macho. A brutal insistence on rhythm and a calculated preference for the often harsh timbres of brass and synthesizers characterize the music. The only principal melody, "It's a Long Road", is a solitary, wistful theme used to delineate the Rambo character as a man at odds with his surroundings.

A deceptively delicate opening to *First Blood* introduces "It's a Long Road", which appears in full at the end of the disc in both vocal (sung by Dan Hill) and instrumental versions (the original "End Title" not used in the film). Throughout a succession of increasingly dark and violent episodes – punctuated by ostinato synth motifs and dazzling virtuoso brass – no other developed tunes are allowed to compete; no hint of softness is allowed to intrude.

The second and third installments of the increasingly silly *Rambo* trilogy continue and develop this trend. Some of the most effective episodes on the second disc are moments of tension, when the forward-marching rhythm is interrupted and Goldsmith's orchestration produces a fragmentary, halting dialogue between the synths and other instruments. Otherwise, the score is ingeniously constructed from variants of the main theme. The third movie saw fit to dispense with most of Goldsmith's score – which is a pity, because it must have been just about the best thing the film had going for it. Intrada enterprisingly sought out the original master tapes from the scoring sessions in order to prepare this release. "It's a Long Road" is reprised once more, this time set against some wild rhythmic motifs inspired by the movie's Afghanistan locale, and a surprisingly warm theme introduced in "Questions". The action is a long time coming, but when it does arrive the pummelling orchestral writing is characteristically – and satisfyingly – testosterone-driven. Only Basil Poledouris (*Conan, RoboCop*) can match this sort of thing (as he demonstrated by parodying Goldsmith's *Rambo* style in *Hot Shots! Part Deux*). **MW**

First Knight (1995) **Original Soundtrack / Jerry Goldsmith.**
Epic Ⓕ 480937-2 (40 minutes: DDD).

Although *First Knight*, the most recent screen version of the Arthur-Guenevere-Lancelot triangle, failed to revive the costume adventure genre at the box office, Jerry Goldsmith's magnificent music certainly captured the spirit and orchestral splendour of the finest epic scores from Hollywood's Golden Age. Bristling with excitement and blazing with colour, this is the composer's own dazzling homage to Rózsa's *El Cid* or Newman's *Captain from Castile*. All the classic elements are here, a resplendent brass fanfare for King Arthur, an ardent love theme (the string writing almost Barry-like in its plaintive simplicity), a liberal dose of stirring action cues (notably "Raid on Leonesse"), and the one ingredient no self-respecting epic can be without, a large choir. Their dramatic chanting makes a thrilling contribution to the lengthy and superbly-constructed cue "Arthur's Farewell", as well as "Camelot Lives" in which Goldsmith's expert blending of each of the score's components brings the disc to a noble and highly satisfying conclusion. **RS**

The Ghost and the Darkness (1996) **Original Soundtrack**, with the **National Philharmonic Orchestra / Jerry Goldsmith.**
Hollywood Ⓕ HR62089-2 (53 minutes: DDD).

Jerry Goldsmith has a particular penchant for assimilating the music of many cultures into his own unique musical language. This has resulted in scores with English and Irish colouring and, most notably, scores influenced by music from Latin America, the Far East and the Middle East. In *The Ghost and the Darkness* Goldsmith develops this skill further by merging the music of three cultures in an epic orchestral score, one of his best in recent times. The rich and exotic orchestration includes African and Hindu chanting (both live and sampled), and an array of percussion and synthesizers. The main theme encapsulates the score's three major ideas: the chanting and African percussion, a grand English theme for brass, and an Irish counter-melody. The combined effect is a soaring and lyrical theme that perfectly captures the spirit of both the African landscape and the film's two major characters. This tantalising fusion of styles makes for some unusual and breathtaking action cues, genuinely haunting moments of suspense and more upbeat renditions of that splendid main theme. The synthesized colouring featured is some of the most elaborate and imaginative Goldsmith has ever utilized. **PP**

Hour of the Gun (1967) Original Soundtrack / Jerry Goldsmith.
Intrada Ⓕ MAF7020D (32 minutes: ADD).

Jerry Goldsmith had already established some rootin' tootin' Western credentials with *Lonely Are the Brave* (1962), *Rio Conchos* (1964) and the remake of *Stagecoach* (1966) prior to scoring John Sturges' ambitious, earnest, downbeat examination of the aftermath of the infamous Gunfight at the OK Corral. Whilst Goldsmith responded admirably to the challenge of a decidedly serious Western, the album disconcertingly starts with a foot-tapping, up-tempo version of the film's main theme: an overt commercial nod to United Artists Records, who originally released the album in 1967, but a step removed from the overall tenor of Goldsmith's score. The film's "Main Title" sequence – the fateful long walk to the OK Corral – certainly establishes a grim tone: an inexorable *marche funèbre*, with Goldsmith's taut theme, shorn of the mercenary properties of the opening track, reiterated by differing sections of the orchestra and relentlessly building to a reverberating climax. Later, the solemn tonality is amplified by the music typifying murderous attacks on Wyatt Earp's two brothers and the sensitive scoring detailing Doc Holliday's rapid decline into terminal illness. But, more sprightly passages do intervene, most notably "The Painted Desert", infused with Coplandesque colour, and "Whose Cattle", a frenzied mêlée of Mexicana. This is a classic Western score characterized by Goldsmith's uncannily expert orchestration, and here the radical use of percussion particularly impresses. As a bonus the music is stunningly recorded, with the present mastering bringing the resonance of the nearly 30-year old tapes virtually up to modern digital standards. **DW**

Legend (1985) Original Soundtrack, with the **National Philharmonic Chorus and Orchestra / - Jerry Goldsmith**.
Silva Screen Ⓕ FILMCD045 (71 minutes: AAD).

Legend is arguably one of Goldsmith's finest scores, the film's lavish, fairy-tale visuals inspiring him to create a rich and incandescent soundscape quite unlike any of his other work. The whole score is wonderfully pictorial, with Goldsmith effortlessly conjuring up a rustic land of goblins, fairies, unicorns and demons right before our eyes. Amongst the many ravishing moments are a merry fairy chorus, a yearning love song for the heroine, and a sumptuous Ravelian waltz that ends in a sudden moment of horror. Inexplicably, Goldsmith's score was excised from the American print (and the video release) and replaced with the electronic tinkerings of Tangerine Dream, a fact that makes this captivating and highly rewarding CD (which also includes a host of material omitted from the original LP) even more valuable. **RS**

The Omen (1976) Original Soundtrack, with the **National Philharmonic Chorus** [ARCAM] and **Orchestra / Lionel Newman**.
Varèse Sarabande Ⓕ VSD5281 (35 minutes: AAD).

To date, Goldsmith has only once received the Oscar for Best Score: but what a score! *The Omen* pretty much set the standard in horror film music and has seldom been bettered. Frequently confused with "O Fortuna" from Orff's *Carmina Burana*, the opening "Ave Satani", scored for orchestra and chorus, never fails to send genuine chills down the spine with its grim paean of praise for the devil. Other highlights include "Killer's Storm" which details the spectacular death of Patrick Troughton's character, who expires by having a church tower's lightning conductor skewer him to the ground during a fierce storm. Here, the choir shout and cheer demonically over the thumpingly shrill orchestra – an unnerving cue even when listened to in broad daylight. The malevolent whisperings during "The Demise of Mrs Baylock", the tension-building in "The Fall", the ferociousness of "The Dog's Attack" are further examples of the work of a really superb choir. This is very much their album, and if they are not on every cue the cumulative effect of their presence gives the impression that they have been. The quieter moments of the score are no less effective, serving to humanize the narrative, and – in the sequencing of the album – functioning as moments of welcome respite from the malignant onslaught of the rest of the music. It was a great relief when the CD appeared in 1990, for until then all that had been available was a rare and pricey vinyl pressing of dismal quality. The disc reveals textures within the score that had previously been unheard, so now you can hear all the music, and not have to undergo major limb surgery to acquire a copy. **DS**

Leonard Rosenman

music from **East of Eden** and
Rebel Without a Cause

The London Sinfonietta,
conducted by John Adams

CD 7559 79402-2

Georges Delerue

music from the films of
François Truffaut
including **Jules and Jim**,
Shoot the Piano Player and
Two English Girls

The London Sinfonietta,
conducted by Hugh Wolff

CD 7559 79405-2

Alex North

music from **A Streetcar
Named Desire, Spartacus**
and **The Bad Seed**

The London Symphony Orchestra,
conducted by Eric Stern

CD 7559 79446-2

Toru Takemitsu

music from **Rikyu, Harikari**
and **Face of Another**

includes performances by
The London Sinfonietta,
conducted by John Adams

CD 7559 79404-2

A new film music series
from Nonesuch Records,
coming this Spring

NONESUCH

Marketed and distributed by Warner Classics UK.,
28 Kensington Church Street, London W8 4EP.
A division of Warner Music. A Time Warner Company.

STAR TREK
Technical Specifications

Original Soundtracks on GNP / Crescendo

STAR TREK FIRST CONTACT

Music by Jerry Goldsmith
CD: GNPD 8052 / CASS: GNP 8052.4

STAR TREK GENERATIONS

Music by Dennis McCarthy
CD: GNPD 8040 / CASS: GNP-5 8040

STAR TREK 30TH ANNIVERSARY SPECIAL

Music by Jerry Fielding, Dennis McCarthy,
Jerry Goldsmith, Ron Jones, Jay Chattaway
CD: GNPD 8053 / CASS: GNPD 8053.4

THE ENTIRE GNP / CRESCENDO STAR TREK CATALOGUE
IS DISTRIBUTED IN THE UK THROUGH

SILVA SCREEN RECORDS LTD
261 ROYAL COLLEGE STREET
LONDON NW1 9LU
TEL: 0171 284 0525
FAX: 0171 482 2385
EMAIL: INFO@SILVASCREEN.CO.UK

Outland[a] (1981) **Capricorn One** (1977) [a]**Original Soundtrack**, with the **National Philharmonic Orchestra / Jerry Goldsmith**.
　GNP Crescendo Ⓕ GNPD8035 (79 minutes: AAD).

In the genealogy of Goldsmith scores, *Outland* must surely rank as the successor to *Alien*, and – to stretch the analogy perhaps too far – *Capricorn One* might be seen as the predecessor of *Star Trek*. If *Outland* – a remake of *High Noon* in space – is in places a much beefier action score, it shares with *Alien* a stark and unearthly coldness that is at once unsettling, and wonderfully impressive. There are moments of warmth to be found here – moments of brief respite – but the overall, oppressive menace is never far away. *Capricorn One*, which depicts a stage-managed Mars landing and its disastrous consequences for the unwilling 'astronauts', is hardly less demanding, with a typically dense and spiky "Main Title" presaging an intensely dramatic score. This is not the optimistic vision that is *Star Trek*, but an altogether more cynical view of man's conquest of space. Neither score is quite as instantly memorable as either *Alien* or *Trek*, but both are so replete with invention, so rich with orchestral detail that they stand out as marvellous examples of Goldsmith's astringent, dramatically motivated approach to film scoring. (Both scores also suffer from the inclusion of just one duff track each: an unconvincingly 'sexy' synth cue in *Outland* – which was dropped from the film – and a rather dated 1970's-style pop arrangement of the love theme in *Capricorn One*). Two such strong scores on one disc make for great value, although the sheer scale and attention-demanding difficulty of Goldsmith's music makes listening to both in one sitting a real test of stamina. GNP's presentation is – as always – superb.　　　　　　　　　　　　　　**MW**

Planet of the Apes (1968) **Original Soundtrack / Jerry Goldsmith**.
　Intrada Ⓕ FMT8006D (31 minutes: ADD).

Vicious, brutal, and utterly without humour, the raw power of Goldsmith's score remains a landmark in the annals of film music. This is a timeless creation: the sounds Goldsmith extorts from his orchestra (with no electronic instruments added) are as unearthly and frightening now as they were nearly 30 years ago. In order to achieve the desired effects, the composer re-deployed his conventional forces: French horns had mouthpieces removed whilst air was blown through them; clarinets played no notes, just clicked the keys. Additionally, an enhanced percussion section included piano, xylophone, vibra slap, cuika, stainless steel mixing bowls and so on. The chilling wail of a Ram's horn cuts through the orchestral mania in "The Hunt" – a centrally important cue which has been restored for the first time on Intrada's reissue. Remastered from the original session tapes, the sound quality is admittedly somewhat less than perfect. Nevertheless, this is a reminder of just how inventive and original a good film score can be. **MW**

New review
Powder (1996) **Original Soundtrack**, with the **National Philharmonic Orchestra / Jerry Goldsmith**.
　Hollywood Ⓕ HR62038-2 (35 minutes: DDD).

Jerry Goldsmith's main theme for *Powder* shimmers with beauty, youth and innocence and speaks of a yearning for self-discovery. It also has a dark mystical quality, suggestive of magic and the supernatural. Goldsmith's ability to capture the spirit of a film and its characters in a single theme has rarely been so potently executed. *Powder* is a gentle and introspective work which, for the most part, forgoes brass and percussion in favour of strings, woodwinds, harp and synthesizers. The gorgeous main theme is present in almost every track, heard in a number of variations and often performed by solo instruments, as in the cue "Steven and the Snow". The music is warm and delicately paced, though never sentimental. The theme reaches its zenith in the final track, "Everywhere", a full orchestral rendition that soars with emotion. The score's darker moments feature deafeningly deep brass and synthesizers in a particularly disturbing and powerful combination.　　　　　　　　　　　　　　**PP**

QB VII (1974) **Original Soundtrack / Jerry Goldsmith**.
　Intrada Ⓕ MAF7061D (35 minutes: ADD).

Jerry Goldsmith's score for this mammoth blockbuster of a TV mini-series was in parts far superior to the images it accompanied. Goldsmith uses fanfares for the court scenes, whilst Hebrew influences are paramount in the chilling Holocaust sequences; the whole culminating with the powerful "Kaddish for Six Million", in which the Jewish prayer for the dead is sung 'purely', as Goldsmith puts it in the sleeve notes, against being sung 'abstractly' in "The Holocaust". This first issue on CD sadly contains no additional music, despite there being some superb cues in the mini-series, now seemingly lost (particularly the finale of the very last episode where Goldsmith's music majestically soared with the camera angle). That said, we must be grateful to Intrada for making this classic TV score available to an even wider audience.   **JW**

Rudy (1993) **Original Soundtrack / Jerry Goldsmith**.
　　Varèse Sarabande Ⓕ VSD5446 (37 minutes: DDD).

The complexities of American College football, and the passions it inspires, may perplex viewers of this movie outside of the USA, but the spontaneous joy inspired by Jerry Goldsmith's sincere and heart-warming score will require no explanation. This is music which unashamedly wears its heart on its sleeve, but with such beguiling melodies no listener will be able to resist the overt emotional manipulation. A simple, lyrical main theme for flute, and a stirring jig-like tune combine to stir emotions appropriate to a film dealing with the trials and triumphs of an aspiring football player: desire, elation, and above all, hope. Atypically, *Rudy* eschews synthesizers, relying instead on standard orchestral forces and sheer charm to carry the listener along. This delightfully unpretentious score is one of this composer's most consistently rewarding albums, and one of the most unfailingly charming film scores of recent years.   **MW**

The Secret of NIMH (1982) **Original Soundtrack**, with the **National Philharmonic Chorus and Orchestra / Jerry Goldsmith**.
　　TER Ⓕ CDTER1026 (48 minutes: ADD).

Goldsmith was on a creative high during the early 1980s, and this fertile score for Don Bluth's animated feature has become one of his great favourites. Though in many ways a companion piece to *Legend,* the two scores are actually quite different: whilst the former is cloaked in a shimmering web of magic, *NIMH* is more forthright, bringing Bluth's family of mice to life and a sense of real danger to their adventures without ever resorting to the cute clichés normally associated with this type of film. True, there is a choir, but here it invokes more the spirit of Claude Debussy rather than Walt Disney.   **RS**

Star Trek: The Motion Picture (1979) **Original Soundtrack / Jerry Goldsmith**.
　　Columbia Ⓜ CK36334 (40 minutes: ADD).
Star Trek V: The Final Frontier (1989) **Original Soundtrack / Jerry Goldsmith**.
　　Epic Ⓕ EK45267 (42 minutes: DDD). Includes *The Moon's a Window to Heaven* (Hiroshima).

It is easy to forget quite how powerful and effective Goldsmith's original *Star Trek* score really is after getting used to hearing that grand "Main Title" performed in the watered-down *Next Generation* TV version. Here is the genuine article: an enormous, sweeping virtuoso performance, with huge orchestral themes countered by rolling waves of synthesized sound. The "Main Title" – an almost impossibly grand fanfare – is refashioned to form the noble Enterprise theme: the highlight of the score – and of the film – is the first view of the remodelled starship, with this achingly beautiful theme first played by delicate strings, then building to a full orchestral crescendo. V'ger's music groans with ominous synths over broad string arpeggios, suggestive of incomprehensible vastness. Goldsmith's score thunders and echoes like the musical depiction of a great subterranean cavern.
　　The composer's return to the series for *Star Trek V* reprises his original themes – yet they sound so fresh as to make the lack of them in the previous films seem doubly regrettable (why do filmmakers seem unable to grasp the importance of musical continuity?). The opening transition from the original "Main Title" to a gorgeous, expansive tune for trumpet and strings is a delight in itself sufficient to recommend this disc. An arresting brass motif, and a tender pastoral melody for strings and synthesizers – both first encountered in "The Barrier" – form the basis of much of the new music. The sincerity of Kirk's theme in the opening scene contrasts with the slightly hollow quasi-religious motif which underscores Sybok's mistaken quest. The warlike Klingon theme returns on several occasions: in the all-action "Without Help" it is heard wrestling with an energetic rendition of the original main theme. Attempts to write futuristic pop songs are always a dismal failure, and "The Moon's a Window to Heaven" – based on a theme which appears in the cue "Open the Gates" – is no exception.   **MW**

New review
Star Trek: First Contact (1996) **Original Soundtrack / Jerry Goldsmith**.
　　GNP Crescendo Ⓕ GNPD8052 (51 minutes: DDD). Includes *Magic Carpet Ride* (Steppenwolf) and *Ooby Dooby* (Roy Orbison).

Star Trek: First Contact is the eighth entry in the film series and the first to feature the cast of *The Next Generation* on its own. In a surprise move, producer Rick Berman – whose philosophy of burying washes of music in a wall-of-sound mix has irritated many in the past – hired Hollywood legend Jerry Goldsmith, no stranger to the *Star Trek* universe, to compose the score.

Whereas the heroic, awe-inspiring *Star Trek: The Motion Picture* announced the beginning of a new human adventure, *First Contact* is composed from a standpoint of experience and maturity. Goldsmith's music suggests that, at this point in the space-time continuum, mankind has come to terms with its place in the cosmos – a status brought into focus by an intense battle with the Borg. To provide continuity, Goldsmith has revived glimpses of Alexander Courage's theme for the original television series and his own Klingon motif and main theme from the first film (later used, of course, as the theme for *The Next Generation* series). The score, however, is not a hodgepodge of previously witnessed material. While the functional emphasis of the music superficially resembles his work on *Star Trek V*, Goldsmith has given us a beautiful new theme. Introduced by French horns over decorative winds and warm strings in "Main Title", the hymnal, serene melody is most beautifully presented in"First Contact". Electronics are used to represent the feared Borg (three of the tracks are composed by synth expert Joel Goldsmith, the composer's son). *Star Trek: First Contact* might lack the number of great moments in some of Goldsmith's other work, but this is a fine, polished score.   **KM**

Total Recall (1990) **Original Soundtrack**, with the **National Philharmonic Orchestra / Jerry Goldsmith**.
Varèse Sarabande Ⓟ VSD5267 (41 minutes: DDD).

A muscular score for a muscular Schwarzenegger picture, *Total Recall* begins with a futuristic twist on an earlier Arnie vehicle, Basil Poledouris's *Conan the Barbarian* – pounding percussion overlaid with unison French horns (a gripping variation of this motif is heard in the penultimate track, "End of a Dream"). A hopeful, legato melody for orchestra in "The Hologram" is introduced by electronics, and soon lost in the ensuing drama. There follows a succession of frenetic action cues, all displaying that distinctive, pellucid orchestration which mixes synthesizers and a percussion-heavy orchestra with perfect clarity. Impressionistic splashes of electronics merge seamlessly with lush string chords. These come to the fore in the finale, "A New Life", in which the broad, expansive melody is grandly reprised. Loud, non-stop Goldsmith magic.   **MW**

The Wind and the Lion (1975) **Original Soundtrack / Jerry Goldsmith**.
Intrada Ⓟ MAF7005D (39 minutes: ADD).

Goldsmith's Moroccan adventure is a dizzying mix of passion, romance and breathtaking action. His expansive love theme ("I Remember") is surrounded by angular motifs – based on Moroccan rhythmic patterns – which rush whirlwind-like across massed percussion and brass. This virtuosic 'Arabic' music never entirely swamps the love theme, however, which recurs in a variety of tender variants. Ferociously masculine cues – of the kind Goldsmith alone seems able to produce – like the thrilling "Raisuli Attacks" infuse the score with furious energy. This is an intoxicating, exhausting work in which both the heat of battle and the ardour of love are vividly brought to life by the vigorous immediacy of Goldsmith's scoring.   **MW**

Also available:

Angie (1993) Varèse Sarabande VSD5469
Bandolero! (1968) Intrada VJF5003D
Cabo Blanco (1980) Prometheus PCD127
Congo (1995) Epic EK67266
Criminal Law (1989) Varèse Sarabande VSD5210
Damien: Omen II (1978) Silva Screen FILMCD002
Explorers (1985) Varèse Sarabande VSD5261
Extreme Prejudice (1987) Intrada MAF7001D
Fierce Creatures (1996) Varèse Sarabande VSD5792
The Final Conflict (1981) Varèse Sarabande VSD5282
Forever Young (1992) Big Screen 24482-2
Gremlins (1984) Geffen GED24044
Gremlins 2: The New Batch (1990) Varèse Sarabande VSD5269
High Velocity (1977) Prometheus PCD134
Hoosiers [Best Shot] (1986) TER CDTER1141
Inchon (1981) Intrada FMT8002D
Islands in the Stream (1976) Intrada RVF6003D
King Solomon's Mines (1985) Intrada FMT8005D
Leviathan (1989) Varèse Sarabande VSD5226
Lionheart (1987) Varèse Sarabande VSD5484
Love Field (1992) Varèse Sarabande VSD5316

MacArthur (1977) Varèse Sarabande VSD5260
Malice (1993) Varèse Sarabande VSD5442
Masada (1986) Varèse Sarabande VSD5249
Matinee (1992) Varèse Sarabande VSD5408
Medicine Man (1992) Varèse Sarabande VSD5350
Mr Baseball (1992) Varèse Sarabande VSD5383
Mom and Dad Save the World (1992) Varèse Sarabande VSD5385
Papillon (1973) Silva Screen FILMCD029
Poltergeist II (1986) TER CDTER1116
Psycho II (1983) Varèse Sarabande VSD5252
Ransom (1974) **The Chairman** (1969) Silva Screen FILMCD081
Rio Conchos (1964) **The Artist Who Did Not Want to Paint** (1965) Intrada RVF6007D
The River Wild (1994) RCA 07863 66459-2
The Russia House (1990) MCA MCAD10136
The Shadow (1993) Arista 18763-2
Supergirl (1984) Silva Screen FILMCD132
Twilight's Last Gleaming (1977) Silva Screen FILMCD111
Warlock (1988) Silva Screen FILMCD038

Ron Goodwin

b. 1925 England

Born in Plymouth but educated at the Guildhall School of Music in London, Ron Goodwin learned piano and trumpet and worked for several music publishers as copyist and arranger. He formed his own orchestra for radio performances in 1951, and arranged for band leaders Stanley Black, Ted Heath and Geraldo. He regularly conducts concerts of his music and other popular classics around the world, and broadcasts with the BBC Concert Orchestra. He scored his first film in 1958, *Whirlpool*, and has written over 60 scores, mostly for British movies. Notable successes include *Where Eagles Dare* (1969), Alfred Hitchcock's *Frenzy* (1972 – a replacement for Henry Mancini's rejected score) and *Battle of Britain* (1969). This latter largely replacing Sir William Walton's score. Famous Goodwin themes, like those for *633 Squadron* (1963) and the Miss Marple films have become standards in concerts of film music. In 1994 he received the Ivor Novello Award for Life Achievement in Music.

The Miss Marple Films Odense Symphony Orchestra / Ron Goodwin.
Label X Europe ℗ LXE706 (73 minutes: DDD). Recorded 1992.
Miss Marple Films – Murder She Said (1961); Murder at the Gallop (1963); Murder Most Foul (1964); Murder Ahoy (1964). Lancelot and Guinevere (1962). Force Ten from Navarone (1978).

There's a mystery to be solved. Miscellaneous cues from all four Margaret Rutherford *Miss Marple* films are here jumbled together, with no corresponding track titles, and with the liner notes offering no clues as to which is what or what is which, or indeed how long anything is. There are no timings in evidence either, so the listener needs to be a Miss Marple or a Hercule Poirot just to fathom what each cue might be. But the music is attractive, led by the jaunty "Miss Marple Theme", a light music hit for Ron Goodwin in the 1960s, and a brilliant invention – just how did Goodwin decide on such a sprightly motif for the septuagenarian Margaret Rutherford? Overall the 21-minute suite (disconcertingly split into two tracks and not one as indicated on the sleeve) is pleasing without being particularly distinguished. Goodwin provides sterner stuff for *Lancelot and Guinevere*, director and star Cornel Wilde's admirable if bloody retelling of the Arthurian legend; the great misguided love is characterized by a radiantly realized theme which ranks as one of the composer's most profound, and whilst Goodwin never quite summons the gravitas or the regal splendour a composer like Walton could have brought to the subject, the score is nevertheless impressive, crammed with a miscellany of court fanfares, gallops and rousing battle motifs. Again, the listener has to guess what each of the cues in this generous 25-minute suite might correspond to in the film. Goodwin certainly ranks as one of the very best creators of theme tunes, and *Force Ten from Navarone* has a potent main title march which vies with *633 Squadron* (1963) and *Where Eagles Dare* (1969) for the award of most demonstrative Ron Goodwin theme. But whilst the vigorous march provides a sturdy skeleton, the remainder of the score is only meagrely fleshed out with some rather mundane cues. Goodwin may be one of cinema's most expert creator of themes, but much of his 'incidental' film music is underdeveloped and routine. Performances and recording are excellent.   **DW**

Also available:
British Light Music (New Zealand SO/Goodwin) Marco Polo 8 223518

Dave Grusin

b. 1934 USA

Born in Littleton, Colorado, Dave Grusin studied piano at the University of Colorado and the Manhattan School of Music. He became music director for Andy Williams, before beginning his own recording career. His film scoring assignments took priority following the success of the *The Graduate* (1967). Other notable scores include *Heaven Can Wait* (1978), *On Golden Pond* (1981) and the Academy Award-winning *The Milagro Beanfield War* (1988). Grusin co-founded the jazz-fusion record label GRP along with drummer Larry Rosen (Grusin/Rosen Productions) in 1976, which has released recordings by artists like Chick Corea and Gary Burton, as well as Grusin's own jazz and film projects.

New review

The Bonfire of the Vanities (1990) **Original Soundtrack / Dave Grusin**.
Atlantic ℗ 782177-2 (44 minutes: DDD).

Many of the composers who learnt their craft in that now revered time known simply as 'the sixties' have not been well served at all by the compact disc revolution. Even if they are still active in the medium, their older scores do not seem to be on any record company's list of prime reissues, whatever the merits of the music. One such composer is Dave Grusin, whose scores have always had a high degree of integrity and a high degree of listenability away from the movies for which they were written. *The Bonfire of the Vanities* is no exception: Grusin's score is a delight of itself without regard to the movie. The "Overture" is a witty, gradually building theme in which all the Grusin trademarks of style, orchestration and melody are neatly woven together. The principal theme itself, with its lovely clarinet solo, is a gem. Whilst this album contains its fair share of extremely short cues – the 59-second "Concorde" sounds like a brief excerpt from *Three Days of the Condor* – these do not detract from the fact that this is an extremely imaginative and charismatic score, and a testament to the creative genius of Dave Grusin. **JW**

New review

The Cure (1995) **Original Soundtrack / Dave Grusin**.
GRP ℗ GRP98282 (43 minutes: DDD).

One thing that Dave Grusin always brings to the table is class and sensitivity. With a subject matter like *The Cure*, the filmmakers couldn't have hired a better composer. The film is the story of a friendship between two young boys, one of whom acquires AIDS through a blood transfusion. Surprisingly, the early sections of Grusin's score are upbeat. "Battleship" and "Shopping Cart Ride" are fun and lively, while the Penny-whistle playing of Jim Walker in "Candy Montage" helps turn it into a piece of sunny, Southernesque pop. Later, Walker brings out the recorder in "Gathering Leaves" and the alto-flute in "Bedtime/Big Changes". Grusin evokes the blues with guitars in "Mississippi Montage" and "Make Mine a T-Bone" (the soloists are Dean Parks and George Doering). The score works best, however, in tracks like "Going Home", where the composer's idiosyncratic style of lyrical piano and string writing takes centre stage. There is more than one theme in the score, but the main melody is heard initially in an abbreviated version in "First Visit." Composed for an ensemble of strings, winds, bells, piano, guitar, harp, harmonica, and electric bass, the atmosphere comes across as an *On Golden Pond*-ish exercise in mid-range sincerity. Grusin achieves this effect without making one false dramatic step along the way. Of course, as there is no cure for AIDS, things must eventually turn downbeat. In "Requiem" and "Last Visit" Grusin applies his own piano playing over warm, sympathetic strings. The final track, "Down the River/End Credits," gives the film and the disc the requisite sense of closure. **KM**

The Fabulous Baker Boys (1989) **Original Soundtrack / Dave Grusin**.
GRP ℗ GRP20022 (44 minutes: DDD). Includes *Makin' Whoopee* (Donaldson/Kahn), *My Funny Valentine* (Rodgers/Hart), *Do Nothin' Till You Hear From Me* (Ellington/Russell), *Moonglow* (Hudson/DeLange/Mills) and *Lullaby of Birdland* (Shearing).

The combination of Dave Grusin and this film, with its subject matter of music and musicians, is a marriage made in musical heaven, for it is one where this composer's strengths are utilised to the very best advantage. Grusin's deceptively easy style, backed by many key names in contemporary jazz, obscures the fact that his pieces are dramatically right for the mood and character of the film. Six of the 11 tracks are Grusin's score, all of which stand up perfectly well as attractive works. The rest comprises one big band number from The Duke Ellington Orchestra, and two vintage recordings from The Benny Goodman Quartet and The Earl Palmer Trio. Lastly, there are two vocal contributions from the real star of the film and this album, Michelle Pfeiffer. In the film, her rendition – unforgettably clothed in red velvet and draped over a piano – of the

admonitory "Makin' Whoopee" elicited much comment. The lack of the visual element may dispel some appeal, but, with Grusin on solo piano, it remains a beautifully delivered song. Her rendition of "My Funny Valentine" is no less enchanting. Perfect. **DS**

New review

The Firm (1993) **Original Soundtrack**, with **Dave Grusin** (pf).
>GRP Ⓕ GRM20072 (49 minutes: DDD). Includes *Stars on the Water* (Crowell), *M-O-N-E-Y* (Lovett), *Never Mind* (Howard), *Dance Class* (Narell) and *Start it Up* (Ford).

John Grisham is so successful that multi-million dollar film deals are made before his books are even finished. In these highly commercialized times it is nice to report that Sydney Pollack's film version of Grisham's *The Firm* is a well-acted, fairly solid adaptation that stretches the genre's boundaries in an unanticipated area: the music score. Not that Dave Grusin wasn't a likely candidate to widen the envelope. It's just that the composer's approach caught this reviewer off guard. The film stars Tom Cruise as a Harvard Law School graduate who joins a prestigious Memphis law firm, only to discover that there are some horrible secrets lurking beneath the polished surface. Instead of an obvious approach involving some combination of orchestra and electronics, Grusin has composed a score for solo piano. Yes, Grusin is widely known as a virtuoso pianist. And no, this is not the first time that a score has been written for solo piano. But given that Grisham novels have not exactly resulted in a cache of great musical memories, this decision is a risk-taking venture. Pollack's presence probably helped: the director and the composer collaborated successfully (and at times ambitiously) before on *Three Days of the Condor* (1975), *The Yakuza* (1975), *Bobby Deerfield* (1977), *The Electric Horseman* (1979), *Absence of Malice* (1981), *Tootsie* (1982), and *Havana* (1990).
>Grusin's music evokes the Memphis setting in a general, atmospheric manner. The score is disciplined, even as arranged for compact disc. There are no self-indulgent blow-fests, partly because of the film timings but also because Grusin knows exactly how long each piece should be. Indeed, one of the pleasures of this disc is the balance achieved between the separate but interdependent pleasures created by structure and improvisation. This is established with "The Firm," a pro-active romp that kicks things off boisterously. Tracks such as "Memphis Stomp" and "Ray's Blues" are self-explanatory. A lovely, beautiful theme for "Mitch and Abby" is a piano miniature that makes Grusin seem like film music's answer to Chopin. "The Plan" returns us to the busy mood of the opening track, while "Blues: The Death of Love and Trust" is an introspective composition that threatens but ultimately fails to break out of its major/minor, optimistic/blues ambivalence. A recurring feature of the composer's style, the music sounds as if Grusin had Jack Baker flown in from Seattle as a guest soloist. In "Mud Island Chase" Grusin uses every aspect of the piano, both inside and out, to create harp, percussion, and other effects. The music itself is a daring, discordant variation of "The Firm." Grusin's left-hand plays ominous figures and ostinatos while the right-hand provides colour and harmonic interest. The final selection ("How Could You Lose Me?/End Title") features a recapitulation of the love theme and some more Memphis stomping. The score runs about 30 minutes, the rest of the disc being filled with songs from the back catalogues of MCA and GRP. The songs support the Memphis setting, but are of secondary interest to Grusin's work. **KM**

Havana (1990) **Original Soundtrack / Dave Grusin**.
>GRP Ⓕ GRP20032 (43 minutes: DDD).

Robert Redford's homage to *Casablanca* is a good case of forget the film and put on the CD. Grusin's music is, as one might expect, full of Hispanic flavour and tinged with jazz, all wrapped up with his superb musicianship. The "Main Title" contains a wonderful trumpet solo by Arturo Sandoval, and indeed all the tracks have many fine soloists. Just listen to "Cuba Libre (Se Fue)" to understand that this is a work of a world-class film composer. Sadly, Grusin rarely tackles the calibre of film assignments he used to, perhaps with other interests he doesn't need to; but when he does – like his recent score for *The Cure* (1994) – he can deliver the goods like no one else. If his jazz background seems off-putting, just listen to *Havana* and discover that Grusin is one of the top five or six composers working in Hollywood. **JW**

Also available:
Mulholland Falls (1996) Edel 0022592CIN
The Orchestral Album GRP GRD97972

Christopher Gunning
b. 1944 England

Born in Cheltenham, Christopher Gunning studied composition, orchestration, piano and percussion at the Guildhall School of Music, where he was taught by Edmund Rubbra and Richard

Rodney Bennett (he orchestrated parts of Bennett's *The Buttercup Chain*, 1970 and *Nicholas and Alexandra*, 1971). Early film assignments include *Goodbye, Gemini* (1970) and *Hands of the Ripper* (1971), but much of his subsequent work has been in television. In 1990 he won the "Best Original Television Music" BAFTA Award for *Agatha Christie's Poirot*. Other television scores include *The Big Battalions, Day of the Triffids, Middlemarch, Porterhouse Blue, Rogue Male, Yorkshire Glory* and the recent television adaptation of *Rebecca* (1996).

New review

Karaoke and **Cold Lazarus**[a] (1996) **Original Soundtracks**, with the [a]**London Symphony Orchestra / Christopher Gunning**.
Silva Screen Ⓟ FILMCD181 (76 minutes: DDD). Includes *A Teenager in Love* (Pomus/Shuman), *Your Cheatin' Heart* (Hank Williams), *Pennies from Heaven* (Johnston/Burke), *Hush, Hush, Here Comes the Bogey Man* (Lowton/Benson), and *Will There Be Any Stars in My Crown?* (Sankey/Sweeney).

Christopher Gunning's scores for Dennis Potter's final television works represent the very best of British television music. Music for television is often viewed as the poor relation of film music, but Gunning's scores for *Karaoke* and *Cold Lazarus* would meet the standard for any feature film. For *Karaoke*, Gunning has fashioned a score that is best described as schizophrenic: the main theme, performed by prickly saxophone against plucked strings, synthesizers and piano, is desperate in nature, perfectly reflecting the chaotic state of mind of the story's central character. Two tracks totalling ten minutes are represented from this score with the rest of the CD, aside from a few source cues, devoted to *Cold Lazarus*.
For this futuristic tale of political unrest, social decay, sexual deprivation and corruption, Gunning has composed a sparkling traditional orchestral score in the grand big-screen manner, a rare occurrence for television. His music is based around a dark but exhilarating three-note theme which captures the whole soul of the story at a stroke. It is sonorous, seductive and spacious, but tinged with a melancholy edge which suggests the anxiety and cynicism of Potter's hellish vision. Gunning treats us to some enchanting variations of his theme, ranging from swirling full orchestral *tuttis* to delicate cello solos. There is also some gritty and ferocious action music to be savoured. The score is rounded off by a dazzlingly optimistic finale, which thunders with blissful splendour. A truly magical score. **PP**

When the Whales Came (1989) **Original Soundtrack**, with **Catherine Bott** (sop) **/ Christopher Gunning**.
Silva Screen Ⓟ FILMCD049 (38 minutes: DDD). Includes *Daniel's Theme* composed by Ruth Rennie.

This clear and clean recording of an evocative score proves what a fine composer Gunning is: a superbly balanced performance with excellent vocal and instrumental solos, this has an epic feel, with an emotional range following the chronology of the film. The haunting use of solo soprano, whale song, flute, violin, and harmonica over a full symphony orchestra is masterfully controlled. Recalling Holst, Vaughan Williams and Britten in their nature music, but always consistently individual, Gunning's score has a wonderful majestic sweep of timelessness, combined with the detailed presence of folk music elements (some written by the mother of one of the cast). This is a most enjoyable disc, which stands well without its visual partner. **CT**

Georg Haentzschel
1907-1992 Germany

Born in Berlin, Georg Haentzschel studied at the Stern Conservatory before working as pianist/arranger for some of the city's dance orchestras. He assisted composer Theo Mackeben on the Berlin Radio Hour before moving into film scoring. Haentzschel also produced a considerable amount of light orchestral music for radio orchestras. During the Second World War he directed the German Dance and Light Music Orchestra. After the war he took up a post as composer and conductor for West German Radio in Cologne.

Film Music Cologne Radio Orchestra / **Emmerich Smola**.
Capriccio Ⓟ 10 400 (70 minutes: DDD). Recorded 1992.
Via Mala (1944). Annelie (1941). Münchhausen (1943). Robinson Soll Nicht Sterben (1957). Emil und die Detektive (1955). Meine Kinder und Ich (1955). Hotel Adlon (1955).

Although practically unknown outside his native Germany, this disc makes a charming introduction to Haentzschel's film work. If few of his films will be familiar to an English-speaking audience his refined, symphonic style is immediately recognizable; the flowing, elegantly romantic melodies from

Via Mala, Annelie and *Hotel Adlon*, for example, very reminiscent of the music emanating from English studios like Gainsborough during the late 1940s. Also of note is his gorgeous use of massed strings, harp and a solo soprano to convey Robinson Crusoe's exotic island paradise for a 1957 version of Daniel Defoe's story. Affectionately performed, beautifully recorded and a guaranteed delight from beginning to end. **RS**

Richard Harvey
b. 1953 England

Richard Harvey was born in Enfield, Middlesex into a musical family, his father, Raymond, being a recorder player and composer. Whilst studying at the Royal College of Music he met Brian Gulland and together they formed the eccentric and innovative folk/rock band Gryphon, releasing their first album in 1971. During his time with the band, Harvey became interested in composing for theatrical productions and film (the title track of their second album, "Midnight Mushrumps", was based on a ballet score). After Gryphon disbanded in 1977, Harvey joined an agency specializing in writing music for television commercials; here he met British film composer Stanley Myers with whom he collaborated on *The Martian Chronicles* (1980), *Lady Chatterley's Lover* (1981) and *The Honorary Consul* (1983). Aside from those reviewed below, his scores for British television and film include *Death of an Expert Witness* (1982), *House of the Long Shadows* (1983), *Steaming* (1984), *First Among Equals* (1987), *Inside Story* (1988) and *The March* (1991). In addition to his music for the screen, Harvey has composed a Viola Concerto, an oratorio, *The Plague and the Moonflower*, and *Concerto Antico*, a guitar concerto for John Williams (available on Sony Classical SK68337).

New review

G.B.H. (1991) **Original Soundtrack / Richard Harvey**.
Demon Ⓕ DSCD4 (70 minutes: DDD). Written in collaboration with Elvis Costello.

Elvis Costello is to be admired for the way he has embraced many aspects of music, from his days with The Attractions to his work with the Brodsky Quartet and Ann-Sophie von Otter. He has always had an interest in film and TV scoring and his partnership with Richard Harvey has been very fruitful. Harvey has always been a master of musical clarity and understatement, as witnessed by his 'solo' scores for *Game Set and Match*, *The Assam Garden*, *Doctor Finlay* and *Defence of the Realm*. So, quite where one composer's work begins and the other ends is impossible to discern because by and large this score contains all the usual Harvey hallmarks, especially in the extensive use of the haunting viola of Roger Chase, although there are additional rock and jazz riff quotes. As a background score to Alan Bleasdale's hard-hitting images it worked brilliantly but as an album, apart from the main themes, it tends to be rather dull and repetitive, especially over a far too lengthy 70 minute playing time. Some judicious editing would have made for a better listen. **PC**

New review

Shroud for a Nightingale The Screen Music of Richard Harvey. **Original Soundtrack**s / **Richard Harvey**.
Silva Screen Ⓕ FILMCD172 (79 minutes: DDD).
Shroud for a Nightingale (1983-95). Hostages (1992). The Assam Garden (1984). Doctor Finlay (1993). G.B.H. (1991). Defence of the Realm (1985). A Small Dance (1991). Doomsday Gun (1994). Jake's Progress (1995). The Wimbledon Poisoner (1994). To Each His Own (1991). Dancing With the Dead (1990). Shape of the World (1990). Deadly Advice (1993). Game, Set and Match (1988).

The screen music in the title of this excellent compilation refers to Richard Harvey's film *and* television music. It is a truism that when television music is average it is mediocre indeed, but less well known is that when it is good it is inspired. Luckily for the listener, Richard Harvey's music falls into the latter category. *Shroud for a Nightingale* is actually a composite title for music written for the P. D. James Inspector Dalgeish mysteries, the wonderfully expressive viola theme, so eloquently played by Roger Chase, was heard in all seven of these TV adaptations to date. *Hostages* was a Granada TV movie about the Beirut hostages, so the music is unnerving, uneasy and infused with a Middle Eastern style. Ethnic music also appears in two documentaries: *Dancing With the Dead* and *The Shape of the World*. The two collaborations with Elvis Costello, *G.B.H.* and *Jake's Progress*, are especially interesting, but all the selections weave their own special magic. The final piece, the Len Deighton thriller *Game, Set and Match* is superb, again featuring the talents of Roger Chase.

In truth, this compilation barely scratches the surface of Richard Harvey's amazingly consistent output, and it is to be hoped that more volumes will follow. Meanwhile, we hopefully await the release of his masterpiece, *The Plague and the Moonflower*, an oratorio written with Ralph Steadman. Then the classical world would know what the television viewer has known for years: that Richard Harvey is one of our finest composers. **JW**

Also available:
Jake's Progress (1995) Demon DCD14 (with Elvis Costello)

Isaac Hayes

b. 1942 America

Born in Covington, Tennessee, Isaac Hayes played piano in Memphis clubs, fronted several bands – including Sir Isaac and the Doo-Dads – and recorded some singles before signing for Stax Records in 1964. He collaborated with David Porter on several successful songs, forming the group Soul Children as a vehicle for their compositions. Hayes went solo in 1967 with the album *Presenting Isaac Hayes*. His soundtrack for the 'blaxploitation' *Shaft* is often cited as Hayes's best work: the theme won an Academy Award, and became a hit single, reaching number 13 in the UK charts as late as 1985 (performed by Eddy and the Soul Band). Two later films, *Three Tough Guys* and *Truck Turner* (both 1974), were less successful and Hayes has since intermittently continued his solo career.

Shaft (1971) **Original Soundtrack / Isaac Hayes**.
Stax Ⓔ CDSXD021 (70 minutes: AAD).

Isaac Hayes's victory in winning the Academy Award for Best Song of 1971 with his "Theme from Shaft" was a breakthrough in more ways than one. He was the first black composer to win such an award from the Hollywood music establishment – even such a household name as Quincy Jones had never won, though ironically, it was he who suggsted Hayes for the *Shaft* assignment. In fact it would have been hard for the Academy to overlook *Shaft* as it had been a number one single and album chart topper, won Grammy Awards and been recorded by artists as diverse as Percy Faith and Sammy Davis Jr (who presented Hayes with his Oscar). More than 20 years on, *Shaft* now sounds like a period piece, but is nonetheless enjoyable for that. The groovy main theme still sounds both cool and funky, with raw hip sexual biplay and choral injections of "Shaft!" making for a true original. Other tracks mix a sleek uptown quality redolent of cocktail bar and disco with an urban streetwise knowhow. MGM did so well out of *Shaft* that it spawned two sequels, *Shaft's Big Score* and *Shaft in Africa* – would it be wishful thinking to imagine the first sequel's title was a timely tribute from an MGM executive to Hayes who contributed so much to the MGM coffers?! **AE**

Bernard Herrmann

1911-1975 USA

The most radical and innovative film composer of his day, Bernard Herrmann was almost single-handedly responsible for dragging the infant art of film scoring into the twentieth century. Of all American film composers, his contribution to their craft remains unsurpassed. Born in New York, Herrmann took violin lessons as a child. He studied composition at New York University with Percy Grainger and Philip James; and became a fellowship student at the Juilliard School. Whilst at the Juilliard, Herrmann formed the New Chamber Orchestra, and made a policy of conducting concerts of rarely programmed pieces (including works by his close friend Jerome Moross). Aged 22 he joined CBS to write, arrange and conduct music for educational radio broadcasts. He also became staff conductor of the CBS Symphony Orchestra. In 1936 Herrmann joined forces with the precociously brilliant Orson Welles, becoming musical director of the famous Mercury Theater radio shows (which included the infamous *War of the Worlds* broadcast). Already Herrmann had developed his distinctive approach to dramatic scoring, consciously seeking out the most effective sounds by bold orchestral experimentation (Herrmann's music relies much more on orchestrational colour than almost any other composer's; melody is subservient to tone). When Welles moved to Hollywood to make *Citizen Kane* in 1940, he brought Herrmann with him. After the fiasco of *The Magnificent Ambersons* two years later, Herrmann went on to work with other directors, notably Alfred Hitchcock. He won an Academy Award for *All That Money Can Buy* (aka *The Devil and Daniel Webster*) in 1941.

Herrmann was a thoroughgoing iconoclast, responsible for redefining the cinema's use of music. He consistently refused to acknowledge a distinction between writing for films and for the concert hall. However, he never abandoned his career as a conductor or as a composer of concert works, and wrote several non-film works, including a symphony (recorded both by the composer, Unicorn-Kanchana UKCD2063, and by James Sedares, Koch 37224-2) and an opera, *Wuthering Heights* (UKCD2050/2). As a conductor, Herrmann was dedicated to championing new composers – he was one of the first to 'discover' the music of Charles Ives, gave many American premières of English works, and many British premières of American works (a committed Anglophile, he moved to London in 1972). Herrmann bitterly resented the critical derision heaped upon the pejorative appellation of 'film composer'. If he had lived a little longer he might have seen that derision turn to praise. But, it was not to be. The critical fraternity's acceptance came too late. Tragically, he died just at a time when his work was being rediscovered by a new generation of filmmakers and musicians.

Citizen Kane (1941) **Rosamund Illing** (sop); **Australian Philharmonic Orchestra / Tony Bremner**.
Preamble Ⓕ PRCD1788 (43 minutes: DDD). Recorded 1990.

There is no doubt that Orson Welles's *Citizen Kane* established untold precedents in the movie industry, and that Bernard Herrmann's singular score was in itself epoch-making. Hollywood's prevailing musical vogue for late romanticism was rudely displaced by Herrmann's spare, vital mode of composition which immediately implemented new standards for film scoring. Herrmann's musical palette was more select, more austere, yet strangely more expressive than much contemporary American film music. His score for *Kane* – here recorded in its entirety in a scholarly interpretation – of necessity employs pastiche: particularly notable is Herrmann's masterly evocation of the 1920s in the cues "Galop" and "Kane's Return"; and also "Salaambo's Aria", an ardent evocation of late nineteenth-century Franco-Oriental opera. Then consider the brilliant theme and variations of "Breakfast Montage", with each modification becoming more agitated, more complex as Welles utilizes rapid dissolves to illustrate the disintegration of Kane's marriage. But, if this score, exceptional from beginning to end, has one timeless, indelible sequence, then it is the opening montage depicting Kane's palatial home, Xanadu: with its glowering brass and festering woodwind, death and decay trail audibly in the musty air. This is music in an individually modern idiom, neoteric without reference to earlier innovators like Schoenberg; here Herrmann is creating his own specific musical landscape. The score is very ably recreated by conductor Tony Bremner, who artfully doesn't impose his own will on the music, matching Herrmann's original intentions and tempos. The recording, set in a fairly close acoustic, also perfectly seems to complement this classic score. **DW**

New review

Classic Fantasy Film Scores Original Soundtracks / Bernard Herrmann.
Cloud Nine mono Ⓕ ACN7014 (72 minutes: ADD).
The Three Worlds of Gulliver (1960). Mysterious Island (1961). The Seventh Voyage of Sinbad (1958). Jason and the Argonauts (1963).

Although usually remembered and revered for writing darkly dissonant, almost mono-thematic music for directors such as Alfred Hitchcock, this compilation of classic fantasy film scores reveals that Bernard Herrmann was also responsible for some frighteningly imaginative and colourful music that employed a more vivid and impressionistic musical vocabulary. All four scores on this disc exhibit the familiar and rather intense dramatic power that characterized scores such as *Vertigo*, *Psycho* and *Obsession*, but they also embody a lighter and more tonal lyricism. *The Three Worlds of Gulliver* evokes a rather grandiose vision of eighteenth-century England. As with all four scores, Herrmann utilizes a palette of mind-blowing proportions, with chimes, tambourines, trombones, celesta, toy trumpets, vibraphone, muted trumpets, strings and woodwinds combining to produce a uniquely tailored sound. In *Mysterious Island* the composer uses an even larger ensemble, including eight blaring French horns, to produce an impossibly dense and cacophonous sound of undulating aggression. For *The Seventh Voyage of Sinbad*, Herrmann embraces colourful oriental timbres, particularly in the spritely *fandango*-like "Overture", in an ensemble that includes whip and castanets. And finally, for *Jason and the Argonauts*, a pulsating theme is driven with bass drum, timpani and tam-tam amidst macabre rhythms and chilling *scherzos*. The weight, depth and volume of Herrmann's orchestrations may be overwhelming at first, but one cannot fail to be awestruck by the sheer scale of the composer's vociferous orchestral approach. **PP**

The Day the Earth Stood Still (1951) **Original Soundtrack**, with **Sam Hoffman** (theremin) / **Bernard Herrmann, Lionel and Alfred Newman**.
Arista 20th Century-Fox Ⓕ 11010-2 (36 minutes: ADD). Includes *20th Century-Fox Fanfare* (Alfred Newman).

With the high-pitched whine of a theremin, Bernard Herrmann ushered in the modern Sci-Fi era. Even in today's high-tech synthesizer age, Herrmann's bizarre assemblage of electronic and conventional instruments still has the power to create an unearthly ambience. The theremin may now seem like a cliché of the genre (its use parodied, for example, in Howard Shore's *Ed Wood*) but in Herrmann's multi-layered orchestration it retains its weird freshness. The background is all important: low brass, delicate harp figures, two pianos playing an octave apart, three organs. Four tubas depict the lumbering robot Gort. Only a brief interlude in "Arlington" and "Lincoln Memorial" is consciously terrestrial; elsewhere the music turns our thoughts to the unimaginable void between the stars. Fox's lovingly-restored recording, which comes complete with lavish booklet and picture disc, is another notable addition to their series of classic scores. The stereo sound is remarkably fresh and clear. Incidentally, Herrmann conducted most of the score, with the Newmans taking over whenever the composer wanted to check the orchestral balance in the control room. **MW**

Fahrenheit 451 Seattle Symphony Orchestra / Joel McNeely.
Varèse Sarabande Ⓕ VSD5551 (34 minutes: DDD). Recorded 1994.
Fahrenheit 451 (1966). The Man in the Gray Flannel Suit (1956). Tender is the Night (1962). The Ghost and Mrs Muir (1947). Anna and the King of Siam (1946).

Taking a break from his own career as a film composer, Joel McNeely has chosen to emphasize Herrmann's more romantic inclinations for his conducting début. Reportedly, director François Truffaut asked for a 'futuristic' score to accompany Ray Bradbury's nightmare totalitarian vision, Herrmann gave him a beautifully simple, radically conservative one instead. *Fahrenheit 451* opens with an emotionless "Prelude" and an automaton's march for the "Fire Engine"; but as the suite develops, the music begins to wear an increasingly passionate aspect. The finale is a warmly romantic, slightly equivocal portrait of hope for the future. This new recording presents a fuller version of the score than the suite prepared and conducted by the composer in the 1970s. The remainder are a well-chosen selection of moments from rarely-heard Herrmann scores, all of which stress the composer's romantic side. A mini-suite from *Anna and the King of Siam*, which incorporates Siamese sources in a Western context, is the only other multi-movement work on the disc; the "Andante cantabile" from *The Ghost and Mrs Muir* is perhaps the loveliest item. McNeely conducts with a warmth and sympathy that was sometimes absent from the composer's own recordings. Detailed booklet notes are a welcome addition; the short running time is the only caveat. **MW**

New review
Film Scores [a]**Ambrosian Singers; Royal Philharmonic Orchestra / Elmer Bernstein**.
Milan Ⓕ 14081 (69 Minutes: DDD). Recorded 1992.
Citizen Kane (1941). The Devil and Daniel Webster (1941). The Man Who Knew Too Much (1956)[a]. Psycho (1960). The Wrong Man (1956). Vertigo (1958). North By Northwest (1959). The Bride Wore Black (1967). Fahrenheit 451 (1966). Taxi Driver (1976).

There have been a plethora of Bernard Herrmann compilations released over the past few years but this is one of the most adventurous – one predominantly concerned with Herrmann's fruitful collaborations with a sterling roster of leading directors: Alfred Hitchcock, Orson Welles, François Truffaut and Martin Scorsese. Here we have the première recording of the jazzy latin-American coloured prelude from *The Wrong Man*, masterly suites from *The Bride Wore Black* and the sultry saxophone-led *Taxi Driver* (both arranged by Christopher Palmer); some old faithfuls – including *Citizen Kane* and *North By Northwest* – and even some oddities: Herrmann himself, from a radio interview, extolling the merits of film music; and the splendid bonus of composer Arthur Benjamin's *Storm Clouds Cantata*, originally written for Hitchcock's 1935 version of *The Man Who Knew Too Much* but suitably adapted by Herrmann for the 1956 remake. Benjamin's tempestuous soundscape is wholly in keeping with Herrmann's own sometimes wild musical vision. Playing and recording are outstanding, although Bernstein's tempi are quite often measured – and whilst the love music from *Vertigo* perhaps flowers even more sensuously via a more leisurely treatment, the "Prelude" from *Psycho* needs a touch more pace and venom than afforded here to be wholly effective. However, a must-have disc for all Herrmann *aficionados* or converts – and for movie music buffs in general worth the cost price alone for Arthur Benjamin's *Cantata*. **DW**

New review
The Film Scores Los Angeles Philharmonic / Esa-Pekka Salonen.
Sony Classical Ⓕ SK62700 (76 minutes: DDD). Recorded 1996.
The Man Who Knew Too Much (1956). Psycho (1960). Marnie (1964). North By Northwest (1959). Vertigo (1958). Torn Curtain (1966). Fahrenheit 451 (1966). Taxi Driver (1976).

You know the Herrmann recording renaissance has reached epidemic proportions when Sony Classical decides to get in on the act. The good news is that "The Film Scores" is an excellent, wide-ranging listen that tries hard to bring the composer's work to the targeted classical-crossover market. You can't go wrong with these scores, even if the programme is overly prejudiced towards the Hitchcock collaborations, although in all fairness these works were the most commercially successful pictures of the composer's career. The disc opens nicely with the "Prelude" from *The Man Who Knew Too Much*. "A Suite for Strings" from *Psycho* has a vitality missing from other recorded performances, although Salonen's take of "The City" is far too languid. Eleven minutes from *Marnie* include the love theme and the hornpipe, while the ubiquitous *fandango* from *North By Northwest* makes yet another appearance. The three-movement suite from *Torn Curtain* is a pleasant surprise (recorded before by Silva Screen – see below). This was the project that ended the Hitchcock/Herrmann association (the studio demanded the removal of the score in favour of a pop score that ultimately didn't materialize). As Alex Ross's notes tell us, the scoring is for 16 French horns, 12 flutes, nine trombones, two tubas, and strings (primarily cello and bass). The complete suite from *Fahrenheit 451* lacks the warmth of the McNeely/RSNO version (see above), but the performance is exemplary. The disc concludes with Christopher Palmer's concert suite, "A Night Piece for Orchestra with Obbligato Alto Saxophone" from *Taxi Driver*. The composer felt that he was moving in a new direction with this jazz-tinted music ("Blues"), but the score does have its share of traditional Herrmannisms ("Bloodbath"). The three-note 'madness' motif from *Psycho* ("Finale") closes the piece, although a fourth note that produces a perfect cadence deviates from the unresolved ending of Herrmann's version.

There are times when Salonen creates the impression that he has never seen any of these films or heard other recorded interpretations. And if Salonen has, he has apparently decided that everyone else's perceptions are offbase. The most glaring point where he loses his footing is in the "Scene d'Amour" from *Vertigo*. Instead of conjuring insatiable passion, we get a somnolent take that lasts 6'49". In comparison, the Herrmann/NPO version lasts 5'32", the original Mathieson version is 5'04", while the McNeely/RSNO recording runs 5'09". This problem isn't enough to discredit what is an ideal disc for those who want to introduce themselves to Herrmann's art.   **KM**

The Ghost and Mrs Muir (1947) **Royal Philharmonic Orchestra / Elmer Bernstein.**
Varèse Sarabande Ⓕ VCD47254 (42 minutes: ADD). Recorded 1975.

The magical pull of this music has as much to do with its association with the film as any qualities within the music, for this is a much-loved and well-revered Hollywood classic. It is a film of almost timeless charm and appeal, and, in its romantic aspects, completely moving and sentimental in the best way. Herrmann's wistful score plays no small part in all this, and one could argue that, as enjoyable as this disc is, the music weaves its strongest spell in the context of the film. It is as strong a moving force as the spirit of Rex Harrison; the composer combines his themes for the charm of the innocent but wilful heroine, the picturesque isolation of the cottage, the turbulent sea and the troubled irascible ghost in ways guaranteed to soften the hardest of hearts. It is a work of simple and unaffected beauty, and this recording – prepared 28 years after the event and lovingly assembled by Fred Steiner – brings together all the major cues. If the 1975 orchestra doesn't match the opulent sound that Hollywood orchestras had, and Bernstein's tempos, although generally fine, aren't always spot-on, then this can all be forgotten in the emotional high that the music itself brings. Detailed notes by Steiner add greatly to the enjoyment.   **DS**

New review
Great Film Music National Philharmonic Orchestra / Bernard Herrmann.
Decca Phase Four Ⓜ 443 899-2 (72 minutes: ADD). Recorded 1974-75.
Journey to the Centre of the Earth (1959). The Seventh Voyage of Sinbad (1958). The Day the Earth Stood Still (1951). Fahrenheit 451 (1966). The Three Worlds of Gulliver (1960).

One of Bernard Herrmann's greatest strengths as a composer was his ability to orchestrate: his boundless ability to create unique, imaginative instrumental combinations that translated into previously unexplored musical/dramatic associations. A compendium of music from his fantasy films, reissued from the "Fantasy World of Bernard Herrmann" album, with the added bonus of his Gulliver suite grafted from the "Mysterious Film World" LP, this disc is the perfect context to explore Herrmann's skills as an orchestrator.

There is nothing conventional about the selections on the disc – unless you consider Herrmann's decision to score *Journey to the Centre of the Earth* with woodwinds, brass, percussion, harps, four electric organs, and one large cathedral organ to be normal. In the original album notes (removed from the reissue in favour of comments by Kenneth Chalmers), the composer explained his decision "to evoke the mood and feeling of inner Earth by using only instruments played in low registers." Organs create a good deal of atmosphere in "Atlantis," while the antique Serpent instrument lends its distinctive sonority to the climactic fight sequence. A standard symphonic ensemble was used to provide an air of familiarity in *The Seventh Voyage of Sinbad*, but even here the composer was able to experiment. In "The Duel With the Skeleton," Herrmann uses brass, trumpets, woodblocks, castanets, and xylophones to represent the clanking of bones. The innovative spirit continues with the music for Robert Wise's cautionary classic *The Day the Earth Stood Still*. To create an otherworldly effect, Herrmann wrote music for electronic violin, electronic bass, two theremins (absent from this recording), four pianos, four harps, and about 30 brass players.

When François Truffaut hired Herrmann to score *Fahrenheit 451*, the director asked the composer to write futuristic music that would preview the sounds of the twenty-first century. Herrmann

disagreed, optimistically thinking that the grey, emotionless world of the book would eventually revert to a serenity that had been lost and that simplicity and beauty would triumph. Orchestrated for strings, harp, and percussion, his music ranges from the impressionistic "Prelude" to the strident "Fire Engine" composed for the book police. "The Road and Finale," described by Herrmann as "a song of humanity," is the perfect embodiment of sadness and beauty. It is regrettable that Herrmann was prevented from recording his entire suite. Those who wish to hear it should turn to the RSNO/McNeely or LAPO/Salonen recordings (see above).

The disc is rounded off with a suite from *The Three Worlds of Gulliver*. Different orchestral ensembles and styles are used to denote the worlds encountered by Jonathan Swift's hero. England is satirized with pastiche compositions, while Lilliput is represented by charming miniature compositions featuring harp and celeste. Finally, Brobdingnag is coloured with grand, lumbering motifs designed to match the physical profiles of its inhabitants. This suite is thought by some to be a cinematic "Nutcracker"; others feel that the pastiche, established immediately in the pseudo-serious "Overture," wears thin despite being dramatically proper. Regardless of one's opinion, this is an excellent disc overall, with good sound quality that has survived the ravages of the past two decades. **KM**

New review
Great Hitchcock Movie Thrillers London Philharmonic Orchestra / Bernard Herrmann.
Decca Phase Four Ⓜ 443 895-2 (47 minutes: ADD). Recorded 1968.
Psycho (1960). Marnie (1964). North By Northwest (1959). Vertigo (1958). The Trouble With Harry (1955).

This was the first of 12 recordings Herrmann conducted for Decca in the late 1960s/early 1970s. It was an oasis for Herrmann admirers who had suffered for years without having much of his film music available – the only scores released previously were *The Egyptian* (with co-composer Alfred Newman), *Vertigo*, and *The Seventh Voyage of Sinbad*. So it must have been a relief when this LP – now remastered for CD – arrived in stores. Of course, it was released just two years after the destruction of what is arguably the greatest director/composer association of all time (the *Torn Curtain* fiasco). When it came time to select the contents of his inaugural London album, Herrmann did not allow any lingering hurt or anger to override the fact that his work for Hitchcock was in desperate need of preservation. The result was a compilation of excerpts from five of his seven scores for the "master of suspense".

Let's state the obvious right away: this is some of the finest film music ever written. The disc begins with a 14-minute, nine-cue suite from Herrmann's all-strings, "black and white" score for the infamous psychological shocker *Psycho*. Unfortunately, Herrmann's conducting of the suite is slow and ponderous – the opening credit music lacks the raw, edgy "Allegro (Molto agitato)" of the original film sessions. No matter, the entire disc is a revelation, which continues with the richly romantic suite from *Marnie*. This was one of the few times Herrmann chose to headline his love theme, although an exciting hornpipe written for a fox hunt sequence serves as a welcome contrast. Even more rousing is the kaleidoscopic *fandango* fashioned for *North By Northwest*. Then there is a three-movement suite from *Vertigo*, the film generally considered to represent the summit of the Hitchcock/Herrmann canon. It opens with the dreamy "Prelude," moves on to the habanera composed for "The Nightmare", and concludes with the score's main highlight: the romantic, cathartic "Scene d'Amour". The disc concludes with a suite from *The Trouble With Harry*, the composer's first score for the director. Bearing the subtitle "A Portrait of Hitch", the suite is pastoral, lyrical, and humorous – the perfect accompaniment for this black comedy about a corpse that causes problems for a small New England community.

To give this release anything but the highest rating would be an act of heresy. Besides celebrating the history-making Hitchcock/Herrmann works, the disc is, in the words of the late *Films in Review* critic Page Cook, "a soaring affirmation of the distinct joy of merely being alive". Yes, it's true that Joel McNeely's 1995 recording of *Vertigo* with the Royal Scottish National Orchestra surpasses both the Herrmann and Muir Mathieson interpretations. But that doesn't diminish the importance of this disc. Herrmann's renditions of his scores stand on their own as testaments to the spirit of film music's most uncompromising warrior. **KM**

Jane Eyre (1944) Original Soundtrack / Bernard Herrmann.
Arista 20th Century-Fox Ⓟ 11006-2 (65 minutes: ADD). Disc also includes **Raksin:** Laura (1944) **Original Soundtrack / Alfred Newman.**

Jane Eyre was Herrmann's first score for 20th Century-Fox, where he spent much of his early career, and his darkly obsessive music, with its gentle, but anxious theme for Jane and tormented one for Rochester, added immeasurably to the dank claustrophobic atmosphere of this best-known version of the Charlotte Brontë novel. If the 13-minute suite prepared by the composer for Decca in 1970 (available on Decca's "Music from Great Film Classics") is still the most potent way of appreciating this music (there is also Marco Polo CD of the entire score – see below), there is a certain thrill about hearing the composer's performance for the original soundtrack. What makes this CD so extra special, however, is the wonderful coupling. David Raksin's alluring theme for *Laura* (which, unbelievably now, was very nearly replaced by "Summertime" or "Sophisticated Lady") is one of the few film themes to withstand countless repetition, and certainly in its original context, where it is treated to a series of masterly variations, including several evocative 1940s dance band arrangements, it is never less than beguiling. Considering the age of these recordings, the sound is really very impressive.   **RS**

New review

Jane Eyre (1944) **Slovak Radio Symphony Orchestra / Adriano**.
    Marco Polo Ⓕ 8 223535 (68 minutes: DDD). Recorded 1994.

Bernard Herrmann's decision to write the music for Robert Stevenson's film adaptation of Charlotte Brontë's *Jane Eyre* was a defining moment in his career. It yielded an excellent score, recharged his interest in the Brontë sisters (culminating in the creation of his 1951 opera *Wuthering Heights*), and marked the beginning of a 19-year association with 20th Century-Fox. Herrmann was hired to score *Jane Eyre* after negotiations with Igor Stravinsky fell through. Fortunately, the composer was no stranger to the story, having previously scored a Mercury Theatre production for radio. In scoring the film version, Herrmann relied upon low winds, brass, and muted strings. In an article for the New York Herald Tribune, Paul Bowles praised the score for its "Gothic extravagances and poetic morbidities". Others have described the score as "conventional", because of its standard symphonic assumptions and the use of the *leitmotif* system. The score certainly demonstrates Herrmann's emphasis on the vertical element of composing, and his desire to employ short motifs rather than fully developed melodies.

The "Prelude" introduces two of the three major motifs. The first is a passionate motif representing the love between Jane and Rochester, played by the violins over a horn ostinato. The second is a pastoral, sad theme for Jane heard initially as an oboe solo. "Rochester" exposes us to the third theme, a seven-bar offering for brass. An exercise in beautiful moodiness, Herrmann's score also contains secondary material. This includes a five-note motif for "Thornfield Hall" and a sprightly gallop orchestrated for violins, clarinet and snare drum first played in "Jane's Departure". This piece sounds like something that could have been used in *Citizen Kane*, although darker variations of the gallop appear here and there. Another ominous mood is summoned in "The Fire", with a piano ostinato, snare drum rhythm and dissonant strings, adding their intense sonorities to the drama. When Jane and Rochester are reunited at the end ("Jane's Return"), Herrmann resists the temptation to indulge in excessive romanticism.

One leaves the listening experience in astonishment, knowing that this was only the composer's fourth film score. While it does not reach the level of *Citizen Kane* (1941), *The Devil and Daniel Webster* (1941), or *The Magnificent Ambersons* (1942), the score for *Jane Eyre* is definitely a minor masterpiece. For its fine presentation, decent sound quality, completist philosophy, and polished performance by the Slovak Radio Symphony Orchestra, this compact disc earns high marks. Swiss-born conductor Adriano recorded all of Herrmann's 29 cues and assembled them into a 21-track recording. The disc also includes music not used in the film. In his programme notes Adriano informs us that the performance in the film (Alfred Newman allowed Herrmann to conduct the score – a rare event) differs from the composer's own manuscript directions. He goes on to write that this release is not an "archaeological restoration" but "a new rendering, still conforming to original intentions." As an interpretation Adriano has made a compelling musical statement, one that should please the most discriminating Herrmann admirer. For those who can't live without Herrmann's own interpretation they can turn to the Arista CD release of the original soundtrack, reviewed above.   **KM**

Mysterious Island (1961) **Original Soundtrack**, with the **London Symphony Orchestra / Bernard Herrmann**.
    Cloud Nine Ⓕ ACN7017 (43 minutes: ADD).

Famous collaborations with Orson Welles and Alfred Hitchcock notwithstanding, Herrmann arguably produced some of his most pungent and distinctive music for the three-dimensional fantasies of animator Ray Harryhausen. Beginning with *The Seventh Voyage of Sinbad* (1958), and continuing through *The Three Worlds of Gulliver* (1960), *Mysterious Island* and *Jason and the Argonauts* (1963), Herrmann and Harryhausen brought a succession of screen monsters vividly to life. Herrmann's highly eccentric use of orchestral colour was the ideal accompaniment to Harryhausen's bizarre creations: the amazed joy of generations of schoolchildren amply attests to their success. *Mysterious Island* – filmed in "Superdynamation"! – exemplifies Herrmann's unrivalled compositional gifts, as well as demonstrating his total immersion in these stories: his music always carries with it complete conviction, even when depicting the horrific antics of a giant chicken. Each fantastic episode is given a fresh and unexpected perspective by Herrmann, from a helter-skelter balloon flight to the attack of an enormous octopus. Each episode is a fully-developed musical *tour de force*, containing every novel ingredient the composer could muster. Here is Herrmann's unique genius in a nutshell (or should that be giant eggshell?): there simply was – and still is – no one else who could have penned that maniacal fugue for "The Phorarhacos". Cloud Nine's splendid release – with full booklet-notes and colour illustrations – has been remastered from the original stereo session tapes (the film used a mono soundtrack), although reels containing the Giant Bee sequence are missing. An essential purchase for Herrmann *aficionados*. **MW**

North By Northwest (1959) **Original Soundtrack, with the MGM Studio Orchestra / Bernard Herrmann**.
Rhino Ⓕ 72101/ EMI Ⓕ CDODEON6 (65 minutes: ADD).
North By Northwest (1959) **London Studio Symphony Orchestra / Laurie Johnson**.
Unicorn-Kanchana Ⓜ UKCD2040 / Varèse Sarabande Ⓜ VCD47205 (38 minutes: DDD). Recorded 1979.

Herrmann's striking "Main Title" device, with its endlessly reiterated rhythm varied only by kaleidoscopic orchestral colouring, produces the impression of a frenetic *danse macabre*. This agile, *fandango*-like principal theme has a propulsive energy which serves to accelerate the music towards its fearsome climax atop Mount Rushmore. There is momentary relief to be found in the tender "Conversation Piece" – an independent movement in its own right – otherwise Herrmann's score plays like a hyper-active ballet.

It seems strange that, while the combination of Herrmann and Hitchcock is one of the most famous in film music history, the Rhino/EMI disc is actually the first available soundtrack album from any of their films (not counting a pirate disc of *Marnie*). Up until now, everything else has been a re-recording for album release. Laurie Johnson's 1979 recording is a highly satisfactory performance of the major parts of the score. Unfortunately, the UK release on Unicorn was made from the single microphone technique popular at the time which all but obliterated the detail in the score. Much better is the Varèse Sarabande USA release of the same performance which was mastered from the multi-track back-up tapes, so that, literally, all is revealed. If you already have that, then it could be argued there is no need to acquire the soundtrack album, other than the fact that there is more music and it is the authoritative original conducted by the composer. Quite apart from the exhilarating "Main Title" it is undoubtedly an exciting score – perhaps even more so than you may remember from seeing the film – and the 65-minute running time soon zips by. The addition of non-Herrmann source cues adds the final touch of period appeal. The sound on the Rhino/EMI disc is very good (and in stereo), with the accompanying booklet being a textbook example of presentation. At first sight, the disc seemingly offers 50 short tracks, but they are grouped intelligently together so that all the linked cues flow together. **DS**

Psycho (1960) **National Philharmonic Orchestra / Bernard Herrmann**.
Unicorn-Kanchana Ⓜ UKCD2021 (58 minutes: ADD). Recorded 1975.

It is the stuff of legend: how Hitchcock wanted the shower scene without any music, how he was dissatisfied with the result, how Herrmann suggested he might want to try ... this is, after all, one of the few pieces of film music to pass into popular imagination. The strings-only orchestra; the agitated bird-like pecking rhythms; the shrieking terror of the shower scene – achieved without electronics or any gimmicks, just violins – the horrendous descending chords as blood spirals into the plughole. So film music is just background music? Away from the movie, the score is undoubtedly a difficult listening experience. It is not overly dissonant, not excessively loud, nor is it disjointed or fragmented. It is difficult nevertheless: the blank monochrome sound; the unsettling edginess of it all; the unrelenting insistence on fear. There is one colour, one emotion throughout: terror. Nothing else. As such, even the composer's greatest admirers will baulk at playing this disc *too* often. But, it remains a central work in Herrmann's corpus – even if this, the composer's own reading, is excessively ponderous – and as such should not be neglected. Just remember: don't listen alone. **MW**

Taxi Driver (1976) **Original Soundtrack / Bernard Herrmann, Dave Blume**.
Varèse Sarabande Ⓕ VSD5279 (31 minutes: AAD).

This score was recorded at Burbank Studios on December 23rd, 1975. The composer, tired but satisfied when the session ended, returned to his hotel, his thoughts already turning to the next assignment. He must have been pleased that after years of neglect his career was undergoing something of a revival. By morning he was dead. Martin Scorsese's *Taxi Driver* was his last film.

As the streets of New York literally steam before our eyes and Robert De Niro's unholy avenging angel cruises through the filth and depravity that so oppresses him, Herrmann's disturbingly sultry alto saxophone theme penetrates the stench of moral decay like the sickly-sweet breath of a gloating demon. In isolation this theme is innocuous enough – an ultra-laid back bluesy solo – but when combined with Scorsese's menacing images and the composer's distinctive harmonic backdrop – snare drum crescendos, low brass chords – it is transformed into something charged with fear and foreboding. The soundtrack album is awkwardly divided into two parts: tracks six to ten are the score, conducted by the composer on that fateful day; tracks one to five, on the other hand, consist of Herrmann's blues theme arranged by Dave Blume in an up-tempo jazzy 1970s manner somewhat at odds with the composer's grim portrait of degeneracy and obsession. Doubtless the sparseness of the score necessitated such an arrangement for the original LP release, although the advent of CD should have allowed a better coupling (perhaps with the composer's penultimate score, Brian De Palma's *Obsession*?). For those not wanting to put up with the disadvantages of the soundtrack album, Christopher Palmer's effective concert suite of the music, *A Night Piece for Orchestra*, has been recorded elsewhere. **MW**

The Three Worlds of Gulliver (1960) **Original Soundtrack**, with the **London Symphony Orchestra / Bernard Herrmann**.
Cloud Nine mono Ⓕ ACN7018 (47 minutes: ADD). Includes *Wonderful Gulliver* and *Gentle Love* (George Duning/Ned Washington).

"When once you have thought of the big men and little men, it is very easy to do all the rest" said Samuel Johnson disparagingly of Swift's novel; 200 years later some filmmakers seemed to agree. A terrible Hollywood bowdlerization of English literature's greatest satire (what happened to the other worlds?), *Gulliver* nevertheless gave Herrmann plenty of fantastic creations and situations to exercise his fertile invention. His splendid "Overture" and the following minuet, "Wapping Market", are more than just vague baroque pastiches – in tone and texture they are such convincing recreations of mid-eighteenth century English music that Thomas Arne would not have been ashamed to claim them as his own (Herrmann's Anglophilia was well-informed). The delicate, miniature music for "The Lilliputians" (celeste and toy trumpets in "The Emperor's March"); the slow tempos and growling basses for the gigantic Brobdingnagians are shot through with a thoroughly Swiftian irony. On one account alone Hollywood is forgiven: if the scriptwriters hadn't introduced a female lead, then Herrmann would not have had the opportunity to write such an affecting tender love theme. The two sugary songs featured in the film (not by Herrmann, of course) are included for the sake of completeness even though the vocal mix of "Gentle Love" has been lost – but are just a distraction from the score. The mono sound is very clear. A typically lavish booklet is just one more reason to rush out and buy this wonderful disc. **MW**

Torn Curtain The Classic Film Music of Bernard Herrmann. **City of Prague Philharmonic Orchestra / Paul Bateman**.
Silva Screen Ⓕ FILMCD162 (75 minutes: DDD). Recorded 1995.
The Man Who Knew Too Much (1956). Cape Fear (1962). Citizen Kane (1941). On Dangerous Ground (1951). Obsession (1976). The Snows of Kilimanjaro (1952). Taxi Driver (1976). The Ghost and Mrs Muir (1947). Psycho (1960). Vertigo (1958). Torn Curtain (1966). Ray Harryhausen Fantasy Film Suite – The Three Worlds of Gulliver (1960); The Seventh Voyage of Sinbad (1958); Mysterious Island (1961); Jason and the Argonauts (1963).

Silva Screen's Prague recordings are improving before our very eyes (or ears, rather), and this disc displays a surer grasp of the repertoire than that of some disappointing earlier issues, even if the Prague ensemble are no match for Salonen and the Los Angeles Philharmonic on the new Sony recording (see above). Here is a fascinating collection of Herrmann, both familiar (*Vertigo*) and unknown (*On Dangerous Ground*), which does not make the mistake of concentrating on Hitchcock scores at the expense of other equally fine works. That said, perhpas the most interesting item is a suite from Herrmann's rejected score for Hitchcock's *Torn Curtain* receiving a welcome first recording here – it has since been recorded again by Salonen – whilst the Ray Harryhausen suite is an inspired coupling. Only the Prague orchestra's interpretation of *Psycho* is horrendous for all the wrong reasons, and could well have been omitted altogether. Booklet notes and presentation are typically first-rate, making this a good introduction to Herrmann's world. **MW**

New review
Vertigo (1958) **Original Soundtrack / Muir Mathieson**.
Varèse Sarabande mono/stereo Ⓕ VSD5759 (65 minutes: DDD).
Vertigo (1958) **Royal Scottish National Orchestra / Joel McNeely**
Varèse Sarabande Ⓕ Ⓘ VSD5600 (63 minutes: DDD). Recorded 1995.

Dreams and reveries haunt Hitchcock's *Vertigo*, and they find their musical expression in Herrmann's mesmerizing score. Now universally acknowledged as their finest collaboration, the film's superficially calm exterior hides a dark and volatile centre – a mirror to the director and composer's opposing natures: the cool, controlled Hitchcock, the tempestuous, unpredictable Herrmann. Uncomfortably unresolved cadences – that repeating motif in the "Prelude" never goes anywhere, it just exists – and the unsettling caress of insistent harp and strings – the touch of a deformed hand concealed in a velvet glove – define the music's dreamlike unreality. Its principal highlights have received numerous airings, becoming standardized as a neat trio: the insistent, swirling "Prelude", the dawning horror of "The Nightmare" and the tragic Wagnerian romance of the "Scene d'Amour", but not until now have we been privy to the complete score; and just like the number nine bus, you wait 38 years then two come along at once.

As a result of a musicians' strike in Hollywood, the score was recorded in London and Vienna, with Muir Mathieson conducting. Afterwards, Herrmann expressed dissatisfaction with the result, although he was apparently content at the time. The lengthy principal cues were recorded in London in stereo, but the Vienna sessions were in mono. Mathieson re-recorded a truncated 34-minute version of the music with his Sinfonia of London for Mercury's soundtrack album release, and that has long been the only reasonably authoritative recording, until 1995 when Varèse Sarabande turned their attention to the score.

Producer Robert Townson's original plan was to issue a moden recording of the full score, using as far as possible Herrmann's original tempi. Joel McNeely and the Royal Scottish National Orchestra give a splendidly sympathetic and expressive interpretation, revealing colours and subtelties in the music not to be heard either in the film or on Mathieson's Mercury album. Upon its release in the summer of 1996, it seemed clear that McNeely's disc – aided by a warm, full-blooded recording – would stand unchallenged as the score's definitive version. Then, Townson located the 1958 master tapes and decided to issue a disc of the original soundtrack to coincide with the film's re-release. Uniquely, I think, the same label now has two near-complete recordings of the same score.

The original differs from McNeely's glowing account in respect of a few minor details – notably three brief but previously unrecorded cues, including "Mission Organ", which replaces "The Graveyard" (heard on McNeely's disc) , as the tapes for that cue had degenerated beyond repair (these restored cues account for the longer running time). Overall, however, Mathieson and McNeely's interpretations are broadly similar, with tempi closely matched, although Mathieson seems less expansive, less heart-on-the-sleeve in the grand romance of "The Beach" or the "Scene d'Amour". The unfortunate switch between mono and stereo, and the dry, boxed-in sound of the original also works in McNeely's favour. Of course, serious collectors and Herrmann *aficionados* will want both discs, if only for the additional tracks. For my part, and notwithstanding the apparently authoritative lure of the original, I think it will be McNeely's version to which I will return most often. **MW**

Also available:
Cape Fear (1991) [arr E. Bernstein] MCA MCAD10463
Classic Film Scores (National PO/Gerhardt) RCA GD80707
It's Alive 2 (1978) Silva Screen FILMCD074
Music from Great Film Classics (National PO/Herrmann) Decca Phase Four 448 948-2
Obsession (1975) **The Devil and Daniel Webster** (1941) **Welles Raises Kane** Unicorn-Kanchana UKCD2065
Prince of Players (1955) **Garden of Evil** (1954) (Moscow SO/Stromberg) Marco Polo 8 223841

Lee Holdridge

b. 1944 Haiti

Born in the Haitian city of Port-au-Prince, Lee Holdridge studied the violin in Costa Rica, before deciding to become a composer and moving to Boston aged 15. In 1962 he enrolled at New York's Manhattan School of Music and began composing rock songs, chamber music, incidental music for the theatre and scores for short films. He moved to Los Angeles in 1973, and began his film career there collaborating with singer Neil Diamond on *Jonathan Livingston Seagull* (1973). Notable feature film scores include *The Beastmaster* (1982), *Splash* (1984) and *Old Gringo* (1989). Holdridge has worked primarily in television, with recent TV movie credits including *Heidi* (1993), *Buffalo Girls* (1995) and *The Tuskeegee Airmen* (1995). He has also written several concert works including concertos for viola, piano and two for violin, as well as a one-act opera, *Lazarus and His Beloved* (1974).

New review
One Against the Wind (1991) **Original Soundtrack / Lee Holdridge**.
Intrada ℗ MAF 7039D (32 minutes: DDD).

One Against the Wind tells the not unremarkable story of Mary Lindell – played by Judy Davis who won a Golden Globe for her performance – who whilst living in Paris during the early days

of the Second World War managed to smuggle to safety Allied fliers shot down by the Nazis. A rich tableau, then, for composer Lee Holdridge to weave his special magic. A composer of integrity and experience, he has come up with a suitably dramatic score, martial in places, as in the cues "Mary in Danger", "Escape" and "Captured and Wounded"; more intimate and personal in others, "Simple Acts of Courage", "Reunion and Finale". Throughout, Holdridge's music captures all the emotion of this true story, and infuses the final production with a style that was missing on screen, but can be savoured on disc.   **JW**

Also available:
Film Music Varèse Sarabande VCD47244

Arthur Honegger

1892-1955 Switzerland

Born in Le Havre, Arthur Honegger studied at the Zurich Conservatory and the Paris Conservatoire. His first major work, a Violin Sonata, was published in 1918. After the First World War Honegger was for a time a member of *Les Six*, a group of composers committed to promoting French music under the guidance of Jean Cocteau. Although Honegger's work encompasses a variety of genres he was a self-confessed film buff, and wrote some 40 film scores for French cinema between 1923 and 1951. Particularly notable is his early collaboration with director Abel Gance on the silent epic *Napoléon* (1927). He stated that film scoring differs from other musical composition in that it relies on contrast, not continuity. It was Honegger who inspired the young Miklós Rózsa to try his hand at film scoring, partly in order to have an opportunity to write dramatic music, but mostly as a way of paying the bills!

Film Music Bratislava Radio Symphony Orchestra / Adriano.
Marco Polo Ⓟ 8 223134/3466/3467 (three discs: 63, 59 and 60 minutes: DDD). Recorded 1987-1993.
8 223134 – Les Misérables (1934). La Roue (1922). Mermoz (1942). Napoléon (1927).
8 223466 – Farinet (1938). Crime et Châtiment (1934). Le Deserteur (1939). Le Grand Barrage (1942). L'Idée (1934). *8 223467* – Mayerling (1936). Regain (1937). Le Démon de l'Himalaya (1935).
Les Misérables (1934) Bratislava Radio Symphony Orchestra / Adriano.
Marco Polo Ⓟ 8 223181 (59 minutes: DDD). Recorded 1989.

This series of recordings is of much historic interest, revealing idiomatic and stylish playing, well controlled and balanced by the conductor, who also provides enlightening and thorough programme notes. The orchestra sounds best on the latter two discs (recorded 1992-3), but always provides convincing and expressive playing. The first disc begins with five slightly adapted extracts from *Les Misérables* (1934) which display the despair, dirt, and deprivation plus the humour and indomitable spirit of Hugo's novel. A four-minute "Overture", the only surviving music from *La Roue* (1922), Gance's melodrama, the subject of which is the railway, clearly provided Honegger with inspiration for his later sound experiment, *Pacific 231*, with which it shares motivic material. *Mermoz*, a film by Guny conceived as a vindication of the eponymous French aviator, inspired Honegger to produce one of his most brilliant and dissonant scores, rather experimental, but undeniably imaginative in its images of flight and scenery. Eight tracks from *Napoléon*, Gance's milestone of film history, aim to present as far as possible the composer's intentions, although it can never be known how the score was originally performed with the film, since Honegger left the pit infuriated with Gance's constant re-editing. Of the two other compilation discs, both have much to commend and recommend; in particular, the two symphonic movements of *Le Démon de l'Himalaya* (the first is as impressive as any of his symphonic structures in the concert music) and the two suites from *Regain*; but for me the most enjoyable of all this fascinating set is that featuring *Farinet, L'Idée*, etc. for here we have some of the most powerful and imaginative writing which stands up on its own as superb composition. There is also some marvellous ondes martenot playing by Jacques Tchamkerten. Honegger used this instrument several times in the film scores, though less in his concert works, and his orchestration throughout is a delight. The best of all is the 25-minute complete score for *L'Idée*, which refers to Milhaud's *La Création du Monde*, and Stravinsky, but has a sense of rightness that is all its own.

The 'complete' *Les Misérables* (according to the booklet, this recording omits two or three minor sections, but adds music not incorporated in the final cut, and features an orchestration by the conductor of one section from the soundtrack itself, the manuscript having vanished) is a wonderfully evocative and consistently ennobling score – a fine disc.   **CT**

James Horner

b. 1953 USA

Born in Los Angeles, James Horner spent his early years in England, and attended the Royal College of Music. Back in his native California, he obtained his Masters degree in music at the University of Southern California before taking his doctorate in theory and composition at UCLA. In 1980, while teaching at the University, Horner was approached by the American Film Institute to score a short film called *The Drought* – his original desire to write avant-garde concert works was quickly replaced by a newly discovered passion for film composing. He was lured away from academic studies to the wordly environs of Hollywood, where he scored several B-movies for Roger Corman's New World production company, including *Humanoids from the Deep* and *Battle Beyond the Stars* (1980). It was here that he first met several aspiring directors, including Ron Howard and James Cameron. His thrilling score for *Star Trek II* (1982) launched Horner into the mainstream. His 1986 score for Cameron's *Aliens* received an Academy Award nomination, as did the song "Somewhere Out There" – written with Barry Mann and Cynthia Weil – from the film *An American Tail* (1986). 1989's *Field of Dreams* got another nomination, whilst *Glory* from the same year won a Grammy award. With Ron Howard he has scored several outstanding success including *Cocoon* (1985), *Willow* (1988) and *Apollo 13* (1995). Many of his scores make use of ethnic instruments such as shakuhachi and pan pipes, something of an innovation in that he employs them to suggest specific moods, not just as a means of adding 'exotic' colour. Horner's services are in constant demand, making him one of the most popular and successful composers currently active in Hollywood.

Aliens (1986) **Original Soundtrack**, with the **London Symphony Orchestra / James Horner**. TER Ⓕ CDTER1115 / Varèse Sarabande Ⓕ VCD47263 (41 minutes: ADD).

In between the otherworldly coldness of Goldsmith and the unearthly skitterings of Goldenthal, is James Horner's more conventional, action-orientated *Aliens*. The score opens and closes with an atmospheric "Main Title" modelled on Goldsmith's original, which also contains the closest thing to a recognizable melody. Thereafter, the listener is plunged into a series of tense musical episodes, wherein brooding suspense and hard-driven drama alternate. *Glissandi* strings and discordant brass wail in suitably 'Alien' fashion, building to some appropriately cacophonous climaxes. With hints of *Star Trek* and other scores, these fiery, combative sequences play like a thrilling compendium of Horner's work, both past and future (this is a composer who is notoriously loathe to abandon a good idea after just one use). Horner's *Aliens* may lack the striking originality of the *Alien*s 1 and 3, but its volatile drama supported by solid orchestral writing make it a representative example of his style nevertheless. **MW**

New review

Braveheart (1995) **Original Soundtrack**, with the **London Symphony Orchestra / James Horner**. London Ⓕ 448 295-2 (78 minutes: DDD).

A good director knows that in the epic you can find the personal, a fact not lost upon Mel Gibson in his Oscar-winning film *Braveheart*, the story of thirteenth-century Scottish warrior William Wallace and his inspirational resistance against King Edward I. Horner's personal style is characterized by long-line themes, unobtrusive mood-producing soundscapes, kinetic action cues, and the anachronistic deployment of ethnic instrumentation. What Horner rarely does is provide emotional and psychological insights into the characters and the story. Nevertheless, *Braveheart* is a pleasant surprise and reveals itself to be one of the composer's best efforts. His peers must have felt the same way – Horner was rewarded with an Oscar nomination.

The score is performed by the London Symphony Orchestra along with the Choristers of Westminster Abbey and instrumental soloists such as Tony Hinnegan (Kena and whistle), Erich Rigler (Uilleann pipes), and Mike Taylor (Bodhran drum). Horner himself gets involved, integrating his piano and Ian Underwood's synthesizers into the tapestry. After the atmospheric "Main Title," the score begins to detail the developing romance between Wallace and Murron (Catherine McCormack). The Celtic-flavoured "The Secret Wedding" is a highlight. Murron is murdered early in the film, but the love music returns when Wallace romances the French-born Queen of England (Sophie Marceau). The score assumes a more sweeping profile when it is performed by high-range strings in "For the Love of a Princess". Horner's approach to scoring the battle scenes does away with the complex orchestrations and compositional structures of, say, Alex North or Jerry Goldsmith, but violent incidents like "The Battle of Stirling" and "Falkirk" do have their share of savage, percussive moments. The highlight of the score is "Freedom/The Execution, Bannockburn", in which the composer offers three major elements: a moving elegy for strings with pipe colourations as Wallace cries in defiance and death, an anthem for the freedom fighters played by the French horns in counterpoint (featured earlier in tracks like "Sons of Scotland"), and an orchestral/choral recapitulation of the love music used to reunite Wallace with his deceased love. The scene shifts to Bannockburn, where Wallace's memory is preserved by a powerful statement of the opening Celtic motif and the noble anthem.

There has been some controversy revolving around Horner's decision to use Irish Uilleann pipes instead of Scottish bagpipes, but as a composer Horner probably preferred the greater range, dynamics, and flexibility of the Irish pipes as compared with their Highland counterparts. If the argument of artistic licence fails to persuade, then consider the fact that the events of *Braveheart* happened long before Highland pipes as we know them today came into existence. In any event, this is an excellent (if slightly overlong) disc.   **KM**

Casper (1995) **Original Soundtrack / James Horner**.
   MCA Ⓕ MCD11240 (73 minutes: DDD). Includes *Remember Me This Way* (Foster/Thompson) performed by Jordan Hill, and *Casper the Friendly Ghost* (David/Livingston) performed by Little Richard.

Any big screen children's fantasy these days almost inevitably attracts the services of James Horner. His velvety orchestral textures and unchallenging melodies lend themselves perfectly to depicting the childlike wonderment that these films – usually through ever more elaborate special effects – strive to evoke. For *Casper*, Horner modifies his habitually smooth style with some interjections of Danny Elfmanesque gothic quirkiness (tuba, sax, harpsichord and organ all play their part), as well as flavouring with some of his own favourite big band jazz. Otherwise this is strictly by-the-book Horner: full-bodied, gorgeously lyrical, old-fashioned. The central theme, "Casper's Lullaby", is truly a tear-jerker, marred only by the nagging feeling that Horner can churn out this sort of thing before breakfast.   **MW**

Field of Dreams (1989) **Original Soundtrack / James Horner** (synths).
   Novus Ⓕ 3060-2 (51 minutes: DDD).

Jim Thatcher's haunting French horn solo rises over subdued synthesizer, before a folk-like piano lullaby introduces us to Horner's gentlest, most evocative score. The low throbbing of electronic chords, and a short keyboard motif act as a musical signature for the supernatural events surrounding Kevin Costner's cornfield. The "Old Ball Players" practise their game to the strains of some decadent, bluesy jazz. Tommy Tedesco's restrained guitar solo in the title track, "Field of Dreams", is a particular highlight. The lengthy penultimate cue, "The Place Where Dreams Come True", might rely a little too heavily on Copland, but in reprising all the principal themes, it nevertheless forms a delightful climax to a score wreathed in misty nostalgia.   **MW**

Glory (1989) **Original Soundtrack**, with the **Boys' Choir of Harlem / James Horner**.
   Virgin Ⓕ CDV2614 (43 minutes: DDD).

Ed Zwick's moving Civil War tale elicits a sympathetic response from Horner, whose understated, unmilitary score is quite glorious. A noble theme consisting of broad intervals inspired by Prokofiev's *Ivan the Terrible*?), and a sombre regimental trumpet voluntary form the basis of the score. When they are intoned by the wordless boys' voices the effect is at once melancholy and uplifting. Backed by a marching drumbeat, the contrast is deliberately disconcerting. Playing in counterpoint against a typical military marching tune, the music reinforces the mood of noble sacrifice. Subtle gradations of subdued orchestration more than compensate for the lack of thematic variety. An emotional watershed is reached in "Preparations for Battle" in which, after the main theme is given to muted French horn, strings evoke a pastoral atmosphere, rising to an impassioned choral, then orchestral, restatement of the theme, which unexpectedly dissolves into chaos. The climactic charge is accompanied by an entirely new, insistent Latin choral theme: a mournful *Carmina Burana*.   **MW**

New review
Jumanji (1995) **Original Soundtrack / James Horner**.
   Epic Ⓕ 481561-2 (51 minutes: DDD).

If there are no surprises in store here for those familiar with Horner's work, this is nevertheless a score with plenty of variety, full of exciting and unexpected twists and turns. Middletown America is characterized by a gently pastoral melody in the "Main Title", before its tranquility is rudely disturbed by hordes of invading, computer-generated animals: stampeding elephants, vicious hornets and criminally-inclined monkeys. The music keeps pace with the ensuing mayhem, with a good deal of large-scale orchestral writing in the vein of this composer's other action/adventure scores, some gleefully chaotic monkeying about – shades of Danny Elfman – and a sinister theme for "The Hunter". But throughout the emphasis remains on typically expansive melodies: because Horner keeps his focus on the players, not the unpredictable dangers of the game, the score retains a warmth and charm. The only unwelcome element are the shrill tones of pan pipes and bamboo flute that have become such a self-imposed cliché. Not a great, but a characteristic James Horner score. **MW**

The Pagemaster (1994) **Original Soundtrack**, with **Universal Voices; London Symphony Orchestra / James Horner**.
 Arista 20th Century-Fox Ⓕ 11019-2 (63 minutes: DDD). Includes *Dream Away* (Warren) and *Whatever You Imagine* (Horner/Mann/Weil).

James Horner seems to have become the animation industry's favourite composer, supplying his own brand of sweeping, romantic music for big screen cartoons like *An American Tail* (1986), *The Land Before Time* (1988) and *Once Upon a Forest* (1992). With *The Pagemaster* he has created a magical musical kingdom, expressly designed to be explored by kids of all ages. Horner certainly knows where to seek inspiration: *The Pagemaster* is clearly modelled on – but does not copy – established classical works like *Peter and the Wolf* and *The Sorcerer's Apprentice*. The music strives to capture a sense of childlike wonder and excitement: Adventure, Fantasy and Horror are all depicted in bright, primary colours. There are two principal themes interwoven in this colourful orchestral tapestry: a skipping, 'Peter' theme for the protagonist, and the "Whatever You Imagine" melody. The journey of the jaunty theme throughout a series of striking tableaux is the score's great strength. There is a variety of incident: impressionistic splashes of colour when the eponymous Pagemaster appears; the encounter with an unexpectedly jazzy clarinet in "Meeting Adventure and Fantasy"; the sinsister 'Horror' motif (a repeating three-note phrase) which leads us to a terrifying depiction of Dr Jekyll and Mr Hyde; the transformation of the travelling theme into a heroic horn fanfare in "Towards the Open Sea"; the swashbuckling Pirate music, and so on. As with its close relation, John Williams' *Hook*, *The Pagemaster* is a must for the excitable, wide-eyed child in all of us. **MW**

The Rocketeer (1991) **Original Soundtrack / James Horner**.
 Hollywood Ⓕ HR61117-2 (57 minutes: DDD). Includes *Begin the Beguine* (Porter) and *When Your Lover Has Gone* (Swan).

Horner's flying theme – a lyrical, legato melody backed by swirling strings – is perhaps his most delightful creation. It illuminates the score with its radiant optimism; and the composer is characteristically unwilling to conceal the light of his find under a bushel. A secondary love theme – "Jenny" – is scarcely less attractive: the two themes are constructed so as to complement one another. The pulsing action music, which sometimes threatens to outstay its welcome, is reminiscent of Horner's *Star Trek* scores, but the glowing main theme always returns to save the day, becoming increasingly brash as the music progresses. The final cue, "Rocketeer to the Rescue/End Title" forms a perfect miniature suite of the score's highlights. The two authentic 1940s songs (presumably arranged by Horner) fit neatly into the musical scheme. If you only wanted one Horner score in your collection, this might be the one to pick. **MW**

`New review`
The Spitfire Grill (1996) **Original Soundtrack / James Horner**.
 Sony Classical Ⓕ SK62776 (50 minutes: DDD).

An unexpectedly low-key piece of Americana, this pastoral elegy to small-town USA is Horner's most understated and whimsical piece since *Field of Dreams*, and a welcome change from his more familiar large-scale bluster. Opening with a languid "Main Title", scored for piano and French horn, the music develops a vein of quiet lyricism, in which solo piano and ethereal solo flute stand out over shimmering support from the strings. Several attractive and entirely idiomatic folk tunes, featuring prominent parts for guitar, fiddle and mandolin (thankfully, no pan pipes) enhance the score's unpretentious appeal – try the authentically bluegrass "Open for Business" for example – although none of these folk elements depart from the score's overall sense of tranquility. Horner begins to open things out about two-thirds of the way through as he introduces a delicious theme in "Reading the Letters" which looms large over the remainder of the score, climaxing quietly in a tender finale "...Care of the Spitfire Grill". A subtle and haunting work of lyrical understatement. **MW**

Star Trek II: The Wrath of Khan (1982) **Original Soundtrack / James Horner**.
 GNP Crescendo Ⓕ GNPD8022 (45 minutes: AAD).
Star Trek III: The Search for Spock (1984) **Original Soundtrack / James Horner**.
 Silva Screen Ⓕ FILMCD070 / GNP Crescendo Ⓕ GNPD8023 (43 minutes: DDD).

James Horner's musical contribution to the *Star Trek* movies was second only to Jerry Goldsmith's. Horner's two scores are the work of a highly-skilled musician at the beginning of his career, eager to make an impact. He succeeded. *The Wrath of Khan* superbly captures the film's militaristic tone – "Captain Horatio Hornblower in Space" was the film's brief – with explosive moments of high drama, a lyrical main theme, and moments of great pathos. Horner uses Alexander Courage's original *Star Trek* fanfare sparingly – something which cannot be said of some later scores in the series. His own heroic main theme is introduced with a rousing brass flourish, and underlaid by rapid string arpeggios: its appearance – during "The Enterprise Clears Moorings" for example – is always thrilling. An ominous, muscular theme for Khan and his cohorts is the musical antagonist – against an ever-quickening ostinato beat both themes fight it out in "Battle in the Mutara Nebula". Spock's death scene (the end of "Genesis Countdown") is scored with rising, anguished violins in counterpoint to a tender rendition of the main theme. Leonard Nimoy's voice is heard during the dolorous "Epilogue" (over a subdued version of the Courage fanfare – an emotional moment for all Trekkers), before the main themes are gloriously reprised for the end credits.

The Search for Spock introduces a few new features, whilst retaining much of the music from the second film. The expansive principal theme is a more richly-scored version of Spock's epitaph from the previous movie. Horner's Klingon music is jagged and tribal, related in style yet distinctively different from Goldsmith's in *Star Trek: The Motion Picture*. Some of the livelier action scenes from *Wrath of Khan* are reprised, this time with the Klingon theme as agressor, until things become increasingly mystical with the introduction of Vulcan music – the 'Spock' theme in disguise – delicately scored for synthesizers, strings and harp. An impassioned climax is reached during "The Katra Ritual"; before a synthesized rendition of Alexander Courage's *Star Trek* melody (not the usual opening fanfare) leads us back into the main theme. Inevitably less original than Horner's first *Trek* assignment, this is nonetheless an ideal companion. **MW**

Willow (1988) **Original Soundtrack**, with **King's College Choir, Wimbledon; London Symphony Orchestra / James Horner**.
Virgin ⓜ CDV2538 (73 minutes: ADD).

The movie was derided as a sub-*Star Wars* Lucasfilm production: cynics might be tempted to categorize James Horner's score in the same manner. But, the cynically-inclined generally don't listen to film music (it's too openly emotional for them) and the rest of us who enjoy wallowing in rip-roaring, rumbustious, epic scores will not blame *Willow* for having all the right ingredients. If, in places, these ingredients make a rather flaccid soufflé, the listener will still find plenty to get his teeth into. "Willow's Theme" is the central element of the score: a racing, tumbling fanfare, with an attractively lyrical bridge for strings. "Elora Danan" has the other, gentler, more spiritual theme (complete with a choir faintly echoing the "Credo" from Janáček's *Glagolitic Mass*). There are growling brass aplenty, and the by now familiar Horner trademarks – shakuhachi (Japanese bamboo flute) and pan pipes – to warn us whenever the bad guys are on the scene: "Tir Asleen", for example, is how Prokofiev might have written *Alexander Nevsky* if he had thought about using pan pipes! Performed with a reverence normally accorded a famous symphony (but Beethoven never wrote for shakuhachi), *Willow* is a grand, perhaps overlong, indulgence. Treat yourself. **MW**

Also available:
An American Tail (1987) MCA MCAD39096
An American Tail 2: Fievel Goes West (1991) MCA MCAD10416
Apollo 13 (1995) MCA MCD11241
Balto (1995) MCA MCAD11388
Brainstorm (1983) Varèse Sarabande VCD47215
Clear and Present Danger (1994) Milan 22401-2
Cocoon 2: The Return (1988) Varèse Sarabande VSD5211
Courage Under Fire (1996) EMI CDC8 53105-2
A Far Off Place (1993) Intrada MAF7042D
Gorky Park (1983) Varèse Sarabande VCD47260
The Land Before Time (1988) MCA MCAD6266
Legends of the Fall (1994) Epic 478511-2
Once Around (1991) Varèse Sarabande VSD5308
Patriot Games (1992) Milan 74321 10150-2
Ransom (1996) Hollywood 162086-2
Swing Kids (1993) Milan 74321 14210-2
Thunderheart (1992) Intrada MAF7027D
To Gillian on Her 37th Birthday (1996) Epic EK67866
Unlawful Entry (1992) Intrada MAF7031D
We're Back! A Dinosaur Story (1993) MCA MCAD10986

James Newton Howard

b. 1951 USA

James Newton Howard studied music at the University of Southern California, and at Santa Barbara's Music Academy of the West. This classical training notwithstanding, he became progressively more involved with pop music during the 1970s, playing with the band Mama Lion and even releasing his own solo album *James Newton Howard and Friends*. At this time he also worked as a session pianist and arranger, ultimately joining Elton John's band in 1975-6 and 1980-1. He was to team up with John once again as orchestrator and conductor for his 1986 tour. Howard simultaneously developed a career as a record producer, working with Cher, Randy Newman, Chaka Khan and many others. His first film score – *Head Office* – came in 1986. Since then, his services as a composer have been in constant demand. Howard's music is refreshingly filmic, owing no debt to any other stylistic models.

The Fugitive (1993) **Original Soundtrack**, with **Wayne Shorter** (sax) **/ Marty Paich**.
Elektra ℗ 7559-61592-2 (42 minutes: DDD).

With few concessions to easy listening, and much that is typical of innumerable other contemporary action scores, *The Fugitive* nevertheless distinguishes itself as a superior example of the genre. A pulsating blend of orchestra and electronic instruments, topped with Wayne Shorter's sultry sax, it has all the right elements without resorting to cliché. Moments of drama – and there are many – are handled with verve, as in "Kimble Dyes His Hair", for example, where the composer blends jazz rhythms with driving orchestral motifs; or during the excitement of "Helicopter Chase", in which larger-than-life orchestral gestures crash and thunder over a synthesizer background. The disc compensates for the score's general lack of melodic interest by including a concert version of "The Fugitive Theme", scored for piano (played by the composer) and sax. **MW**

Waterworld (1995) **Original Soundtrack**, with the **Los Angeles Master Chorale / Artie Kane**.
MCA ℗ MCD11282 (69 minutes: DDD).

A late recruit to a notoriously troubled production (Mark Isham being the original choice), James Newton Howard was obviously inspired by the dynamism of his friend Kevin Costner's watery adventure. Without once straying beyond the boundaries of contemporary action/adventure conventions, *Waterworld* still manages to press all the right thrill buttons. A heroic fanfare for Costner's stoical main character underpins moments of derring-do, as in the second cue, "Escaping the Smokers". Otherwise, there are few surprises, but plenty to enjoy: grandly-conceived synth and orchestral string figures, heart-pounding percussion, awe-inspired vocalese from the chorus, the now obligatory breathy flute/pan pipe *à la* James Horner, and some chaotic brass *à la* Elliot Goldenthal. All great fun. Marisa Chandler's wordless soprano, supported by bell-like synths during "Swimming", is a delightfully delicate respite from the action. **MW**

Wyatt Earp (1993) **Original Soundtrack**, with the **Hollywood Recording Musicians Orchestra / Marty Paich**.
Warner Bros ℗ 9362-45660-2 (61 minutes: DDD).

Disastrously overblown as the movie was, Howard's score is luckily saved from the same fate by its variety and exuberance. True, in places it becomes blustering and exaggerated, but generally the music evokes a sweeping Western panorama without becoming too infected by the humourless confusion of the film's narrative. There is much to savour here: a grand main theme, summoning up widescreen vistas of the prairie; a rousing gallop in "The Wagon Chase"; a regretfully tender love theme in "The Wedding". Light and folksy Americana gives way to tension-building drama as the score progresses – the famous gunfight in "OK Corral", the unsettling "Kill 'em All". Howard keeps our interest in the disc's final third, introducing much new music: celebratory for "Dodge City"; disturbing and histrionic for "Indian Charlie". Overall, a fine example of the modern Western score. **MW**

Also available:
Alive (1993) Hollywood HR61454-2
Diggstown [Midnight Sting] (1992) Varèse Sarabande VSD5379
Dying Young (1991) Arista 21695-2
Grand Canyon (1991) Milan 262 493
Guilty By Suspicion (1991) Varèse Sarabande VSD5596
Junior (1994) Varèse Sarabande VSD5558
Just Cause (1995) Varèse Sarabande VSD5596
Outbreak (1995) Varèse Sarabande VSD5599
Primal Fear (1996) Milan 35716-2

Prince of Tides (1991) Columbia CK48627
Restoration (1995) Milan 35707-2
The Saint of Fort Washington (1993) Varèse Sarabande VSD5444

Jacques Ibert

1890-1962 France

Born in Paris, Jacques Ibert originally wanted to become an actor, but went on to learn composition at the Paris Conservatoire with Paul Vidal. His diverse output – which includes works in almost all genres – had a significantly dramatic bent, as Ibert believed in linking music with the other arts. Two of his seven operas were written in collaboration with Arthur Honegger. Early in his career Ibert earned a living playing the piano for silent films, as well as writing popular music under the pseudonym William Berty. He worked on numerous radio scores and some 30 films, although not all these were full-length scores. One of his last film assignments was the ballet *Circus* which he wrote for Gene Kelly in MGM's *Invitation to the Dance* (1956).

Macbeth (1948) **Golgotha** (1935) **Don Quichotte**[a] (1933) [a]**Henry Kiichli** (bass); **Slovak Radio Symphony Orchestra / Adriano**.
Marco Polo Ⓔ 8 223287 (77 minutes: DDD). Recorded 1989-90.

Jacques Ibert, like his friends Honegger and Auric, was able to supplement his concert income with a number of choice film commissions. The three scores on this enterprising disc are all as fundamental and integral as Ibert's celebrated concert works, and in the case of *Macbeth*, avant-garde even by the composer's own standards. But whilst Orson Welles's film – one of the most idiosyncratic of all Shakespearian adaptations – remains a cult perennial, the other two films represented are rare to the point of extinction, so their music has to be judged purely on its own merits – which are considerable. Julien Duvivier's 1935 *Golgotha*, a reverent account of Christ's last days, inspired Ibert to create one of the cinema's most extraordinary early scores; whilst in Hollywood the contemporary idiom was overridingly late-romantic – and in Britain Bliss and Walton were only just starting to write neo-classical film scores – here was Ibert, composing music for a historical subject, and employing two ondes martinots and a saxophone amongst his unusual orchestrations. The centrepiece of the score celebrates Palm Sunday – an outpouring, a cascade of musical joy, 13 minutes of extraordinary symphonic revelry – whilst the antithesis is discovered in the music for Calvary: intense anguish realized primarily through the unusual medium of the ondes martinot.
When director G. W. Pabst cast the Russian bass Fedor Chaliapin as his *Don Quichotte* in 1933, he thought some dramatic songs might be appropriate, and having considered Milhaud and Ravel, settled on Ibert to write them. The five settings are presented here in their première performance – alternately lusty, romantic and mournful, they deserve to enter contemporary classical repertoire. It is a mystery as to how Orson Welles prevailed on Republic Studios to import Ibert to Hollywood to score *Macbeth*, given Los Angeles was full to the rafters with composers, both homegrown and emigré. But Welles was right. Ibert's music, bubbling, like the witch's cauldron, with weird invention, brings a unique unsettling ambience to the whole film. His main theme, a bizarre march, never settles for being forthright or steady on its feet (which might previously have been considered a prerequisite for a march). For the witches string harmonics are augmented by a most unusual breathing choir; and the throne-room sequence preceding Banquo's death is occasion for a substantial bass tuba solo. Not only is this an uncommon score but it also stands as one of Ibert's most advanced compositional exercises. Whilst this orchestra and conductor, dedicated to recording all manner of intriguing film music, have often not been quite at home with certain idioms, here they excel in outstanding performances.   **DW**

Mark Isham

b. 1951 USA

Renowned jazz trumpeter Mark Isham scored his first film, *Never Cry Wolf*, in 1983. Previously he had played trumpet with the San Francisco and Oakland Symphony Orchestras, rock music with the Sons of Champlin, avant-garde with Art Lande and The Rubisa Patrol, and progressive jazz with Group 87. His experiments with electronic instruments were an important factor in landing his first film assignment (*Never Cry Wolf*, 1983), and he has utilized synthesizers in later scores such as *The Hitcher* (1986) and *Fire in the Sky*. Collaborations with director Alan Rudolph include *Trouble in Mind* (1985), *Made in Heaven* (1987) and *The Moderns* (1988). Many of his scores are jazz-based, with the composer adding his own distinctive trumpet playing (*Cool World,* 1992 and *Mrs Parker,* 1994, for example). He has also worked in television, providing amongst others the theme for *Chicago Hope*. Ken Kugler usually orchestrates and conducts.

The Browning Version (1994) **Original Soundtrack**, with **St Mary's Choir School Choristers, Reigate / London Metropolitan Orchestra; Ken Kugler**.
Milan Ⓟ 21301-2 (37 minutes: DDD).

Sustained string chords overlaid with delicate harp and piano; expansive unhurried melodies; wordless boys' voices – all evoke the cloistered atmosphere of an English public school. A subliminal bass drum pattern occasionally hints at deeper passions, but for much of the score all is orderly and proper in Isham's school. Only when the solo trumpet finally breaks free from confining string-based orchestration during the last track does the mood lift perceptibly. Barrington Pheloung's Oxford-based *Inspector Morse* scores have a similar ambience, even though Isham is more distinctively American, more Barber than Delius. A quiet and subdued work that repays repeated listening. **MW**

Fire in the Sky (1993) **Original Soundtrack / Ken Kugler**.
Varèse Sarabande Ⓟ VSD5417 (41 minutes: DDD).

An eerie and disturbing score that abandons Isham's customary restraint. Synthesizers and electronic sounds depict the terrifying ordeal of alien abduction in graphic detail; the orchestra is left to handle more mundane events, albeit in typically dispassionate fashion. Three long cues in the middle of the album prevent the electronic assault on the senses from seeming just too disjointed for comfort, although at over 12 minutes "Evil Spirits from the Sky" is (intentionally) a difficult and uncomfortable experience. Certainly not easy listening, *Fire in the Sky* is an ideal counterbalance for Isham's usual jazz tendencies. **MW**

New review
The Hitcher (1986) **Original Soundtrack**, with **Mark Isham** (electronics/flugelhorn); **Kurt Wortman, Bongo Bob Smith** (percussion); **Bill Douglass** (bass).
Silva Screen Ⓟ FILMCD118 (42 minutes: DDD).

Although Mark Isham has written several tonal and richly melodic scores, he is best known for his more avant-garde efforts, of which *The Hitcher* is the most often cited. This is a complex and surreal mood piece with an emphasis on sound rather than form. The barren and foreboding main theme is directionless and isolating, written for a lonely flugelhorn pitted against layers of smooth but unsettling electronics. This surfaces throughout the score and serves as something of an antidote to the more aggressive material. Isham serves up some quite noisy action music, purely minimalist in form and featuring throbbing electronic chords, biting electronic and acoustic percussion, and other metallic sounds. The pace is relentlessly terrifying and becomes increasingly cacophonous. Synthesizer technology has changed considerably since this score was recorded, and the music does tend to sound somewhat dated in places. It is however an interesting example of a score that attempts to break the traditional Hollywood mould. **PP**

New review
Nell (1995) **Original Soundtrack / Ken Kugler**.
London Ⓟ 444 81 8-2 (49 minutes: DDD).

In Michael Apted's *Nell*, Jodie Foster plays a young woman who has never experienced the modern, so-called civilized world. Nell's world – a rejection of Western patriarchal structures and moral codes – is revealed to be an ideal place for one of film music's master creators of mood to work in. In scoring the film Mark Isham wanted to provide a musical profile of Nell's inner world and her physical environment. The score is a blissful blending of the acoustic and the electronic, with further colours added by recorder, dulcimer, percussion, piano, and guitar. The disc opens with "Welcome to Robbinsville," a spirited dance that is only reprised one other time on the disc. The melody is subtitled "Theme from Nell," although the actual theme for the character does not appear until later. This folk-like tune, performed by the strings without vibrato, evokes the rural locale in which Nell lives – the only one she has ever known. In "The Woman in Grey", Isham switches to his non-classical, New Age style perfected in several of the composer's earlier scores. This ethereal, expansive cue creates the feeling that Nell lives in a place where time remains suspended, as opposed to the pace of the industrialized world. More classically-styled material arrives in the form of a theme for "Nell". Written for solo flute with a floating string accompaniment, this is a beautiful offering that captures the purity of the character. Other memorable arrangements of the theme can be found in "Donana Kee" and the concluding track, "Don't Weep for Nell". Isham sets up dissonances when the influence of the modern world begins to intrude. These moments are few, however, being limited to tracks such as "Trees in the Wind" and "A Glass Wall". In addition, Isham has provided several thematically unrelated musical fragments that add variety to the score. In these passages the primary orchestrations are flute over strings or electronics (or both), as in

"Swimming and Popcorn" and "Milly". In summary, *Nell* is a haunting combination of New Age and lyrical orchestral scoring achieved with an economy of means. At 49 minutes, the disc is neither a minute too long or too short. **KM**

Of Mice and Men (1992) **Original Soundtrack / Ken Kugler**.
Varèse Sarabande ℗ VSD5371 (35 minutes: DDD).

A poignant and affecting score which makes no attempt to imitate Aaron Copland's 1939 original. Brass instruments have been largely eliminated from an ensemble which emphasizes strings and woodwinds. Piano and 12-string acoustic guitar play a prominent role in creating a folk-like ambience, although Isham's characteristically understated non-jazz style never allows the music to become 'folksy' (track 8, "Buckin' Barley", for example is too cool and sophisticated to be mistaken for authentic Country music). The main theme, in true parsimonious Isham manner, is built upon a repeating three-note figure which is deliberately restrained from ever becoming overly romantic or sentimental. A low-key, jazz-free score of great subtlety. **MW**

New review
Quiz Show (1996) **Original Soundtrack**, with **Mark Isham** (tpt) **/ Ken Kugler**.
Hollywood ℗ HR62000-2 (48 minutes: DDD). Includes *Moritat* (Weill/Brecht) .

Mark Isham Jazz trumpeter and Mark Isham film composer combine in this score to demonstrate just how versatile a musician he is. This is not so much a film score as a great jazz album with a few cues of background music. Isham has surrounded himself with fabulously versatile players including David Goldblatt (piano), John Clayton (bass), Bob Shepard (sax) and Conet Candoli (trumpet) to creat jazz cues totally in keeping with the period of Robert Redford's clever film. Even Isham's arrangement of the Kurt Weill/Bertolt Brecht title song "Mack the Knife" – performed by Lyle Lovett – never seems out of place. Not an album for the hardcore soundtrack collector, but nevertheless a fine example of dazzling and dynamic music. **PC**

A River Runs Through It (1992) **Original Soundtrack / Ken Kugler**.
Milan ℗ 12469-2 (58 minutes: DDD).

A beguiling mixture of Americanas, Coplandesque folk and trad jazz, *A River Runs Through It* shows Isham exploiting his compositional strengths. This predominantly orchestral score is typically reserved – Isham is not prone to 'Hollywoodizing' the emotional content of his music – but warmhearted nevertheless. Themes are constructed from brief, repetitive melodic fragments and motifs which are given extra interest by varied dynamic treatment and subtle orchestration: piano, flute, harp and even uilleann pipes (played by John Isham). The score suffers from an excess of its virtue, insofar as Isham's musical parsimony, whilst not pandering to the listener with facile tunes, sometimes fails to give the ear enough diversity. Only the opening and final cues are overtly melodic. The few jazz numbers – confined to the first half of the album – are swinging and old-timey, most of them authentic, not composed by Isham. Thankfully, they do not smother the underscore. **MW**

Also available:
Cool World (1992) Varèse Sarabande VSD5382
Home for the Holidays (1995) Mercury 528 871-2
Last Dance (1996) Hollywood HW62055-2
Little Man Tate (1991) Varèse Sarabande VSD5343
Miami Rhapsody (1995) Hollywood 62004-2
The Moderns (1988) Virgin CDV2530
Mrs Parker and the Vicious Circle (1994) Varèse Sarabande VSD5471
The Net (1995) Varèse Sarabande VSD5662
Point Break (1991) MCA MCLD19327
The Public Eye (1992) Varèse Sarabande VSD5374
Romeo is Bleeding (1994) Verve 521 231-2
Time Cop (1994) Varèse Sarabande VSD5532

Maurice Jarre

b. 1924 France

Born in Lyon of Russian descent, Maurice Jarre did not 'discover' music until the relatively late age of 16. Realizing that he was too old to take up the piano, Jarre was advised to join an orchestra as a percussionist. He went on to attend the Paris Conservatoire, where he studied composition with Jacques de la Presle, Louis Aubert and Arthur Honegger. He also took courses in ethnic music – lessons that would come in useful in his film career. After graduating, Jarre became arranger and conductor for the Jean Louis Barrault Theatre Company, then Music Director of the Théâtre National Populaire (where he composed his first theatrical scores). In 1952, his first original film score *Hôtel des Invalides* – was the beginning of a fruitful collaboration with director Georges Franju which lasted throughout the 1950s. Jarre wrote several avant-garde film scores, ballets and concert works during this time. His international reputation was secured in 1962 when he was asked to score David Lean's *Lawrence of Arabia*. Attempts to engage the services of such notables as Malcolm Arnold, William Walton, Benjamin Britten and Aram Khachaturian had proved unsuccessful, and Jarre was forced to complete the score in just four weeks. The result won him his first Academy Award; and Jarre scored all of David Lean's films thereafter, winning further Oscars for *Doctor Zhivago* (1965) and *A Passage to India* (1984). During a prolific career, Jarre has scored over 200 major films. He is the father of synthesizer showman Jean-Michel Jarre.

New review

The Damned [La Caduta degli Dei] (1969) **Una Stagione all'Inferno** (1971) **In Nome dei Miei** (1983) Original Soundtracks / Maurice Jarre.
  DRG Ⓕ 32906 (two discs: 135 minutes: AAD).

This double CD collection features three of Maurice Jarre's lesser-known orchestral scores, the most important being the music composed in 1969 for Luchino Visconti's *The Damned* – the grim saga of the power struggle of the Von Essenbeck family in Nazi Germany. Heavily edited, with Dirk Bogarde's brilliant portrayal left largely on the cutting-room floor, *The Damned* still remains a remarkable piece of cinema and possibly Visconti's greatest achievement. Jarre's score is one of his most inventive being largely low-key and understated with quirky and unusual melodies that have an uneasiness and instability bordering on the bizarre – highly appropriate for the subject matter involving incest, murder, scheming and sexual perversion!

A Season in Hell (*Una Stagione all'Inferno*) on the other hand is not one of this composer's better scores. This little seen Nelo Risi film of 1971 was set in Africa and starred Terence Stamp and Jean-Claude Brialy as the French poets Paul Verlaine and Arthur Rimbaud. Jarre obviously still had his music for David Lean's *Ryan's Daughter* (composed the year before) in his system as "Rosy's Theme" (in ethnic guise) makes an unwelcome appearance in the opening and closing titles. Great use is made of the local colour in the exotic arrangements but the melodic material is weak and insubstantial with the exception of an attractive love theme "To My Best Loved Friend".

Jarre has never been enamoured with the rushed production values of television dramas, yet two of this greatest scores have been composed for this medium, *Jesus of Nazareth* (see below) and *For Those I Loved* (*In Nome dei Miei*). This latter title takes up all of the second disc. Robert Enrico's rather tame World War II drama about the horrors of the Holocaust benefited greatly from Jarre's masterful underscoring – music rich in variety with marches, waltzes, folk dances and moments of anguish and torment.

Overall, a fine collection of Jarre's rarer film music. By and large the CD transfers are good although some distortion is noticeable in *The Damned*. Fine sleeve notes by film music historian Didier Deutsch are a bonus, although DRG's artwork is rather garish. **PC**

Doctor Zhivago (1965) Original Soundtrack / Maurice Jarre.
  Rhino Ⓕ 71957 / EMI Ⓕ CDODEON1 (70 minutes: ADD).

Despite producing one of the best-selling soundtracks ever (157 weeks in the American *Billboard* chart), this Oscar-winning score has received a lot of bad press over the years, due no doubt to the saccharine vocal version of "Lara's Theme", "Somewhere My Love", a song impossible to avoid on the radio during the late 1960s. True, it is not the most complex film score ever written (Jarre, in fact, had only six weeks to compose and record nearly two hours of music); indeed, with its obvious Russian-isms (massed male choir and balalaikas galore) it could easily have been written for an MGM epic of 1935 rather than 1965. And yet, in spite of the often rudimentary structure, its sumptuous, heart-on-sleeve romanticism, performed with absolute conviction, is still capable of sweeping the listener away on a sea of violins. The score isn't all "Lara's Theme" either. There's the surging, passionate melody that introduces it in the "Main Title", several lilting waltzes, and a scintillating *troika* (even though it does tend to sound more like a sleigh ride through old Peking at times). Presented for the first time almost complete, with fabulous sound and many out-takes, this is widescreen romance at its most irresistible. **RS**

New review

Ghost (1990) Original Soundtrack / Maurice Jarre.
  Milan Ⓕ 34278-2 (46 minutes: DDD).

This release has been marketed as a "Fifth Anniversary" edition with two bonus tracks – why there is the need to celebrate so soon after the film's release, especially as the bonus tracks don't amount to much musically, is beyond me. Maurice Jarre's score is certainly one of his best of recent years, and is very successful in combining a large orchestral pallete with a mass of synthesizers, even if it does not match his earlier triumphs of *Lawrence of Arabia, Doctor Zhivago* and *Jesus of Nazareth*. No small measure of the film's unexpected success was due to the use of the 1960s Righteous Brothers hit "Unchained Melody" (originally composed by Alex North for the 1955 movie *Unchained*). Jarre's own "Love Theme" is not quite in the same class but it does complement North's well-known melody with its luscious and romantic scoring and has just the right hint of mystery and otherworldliness. The rest of the score is serviceable but not particularly distinctive. Good recorded sound by ace Hollywood engineer Shawn Murphy. **PC**

New review

Jesus of Nazareth (1977) National Philharmonic Orchestra / Maurice Jarre.
RCA Ⓕ OST131 (40 minutes: AAD).

Jarre's remarkable music for Franco Zeffirelli's highly-praised TV production is surely one of the composer's masterworks. This worthy companion to Rózsa's *King of Kings* and Newman's *The Greatest Story Ever Told* is perhaps closer in spirit to the restrained, compassionate approach of Newman rather than the blazing ecclesiastical fervour of Rózsa's ornate epic, though the rippling, gently pastoral quality of much of Jarre's writing and his extensive use of ethnic instrumentation (particularly for "Salome's Dance") ultimately creates a genuinely exotic atmosphere that is quite unlike either of its predecessors. If the cues "Annunciation", "Three Kings" and "Jairus' Daughter" are perhaps the emotional highlights, dominating the score is the majesterial main theme, an unforgettably potent Hebraic statement that seems to encapsulate the power and the passion of Christ's life and times. (Incidentally, on the original Pye album Robert Powell recited the Beatitudes, but on this Italian reissue Christ's words are spoken in Italian by Pino Colizzi). **RS**

Lawrence of Arabia (1962) Original Soundtrack, with the London Philharmonic ARCAM
Orchestra / Maurice Jarre.
Varèse Sarabande Ⓕ VSD5263 (37 minutes: ADD).
Lawrence of Arabia (1962) Philharmonia Orchestra / Tony Bremner.
Silva Screen Ⓕ FILMCD036 (51 minutes: DDD). Recorded 1989.
Includes *The Voice of the Guns* (Kenneth Alford).

Jarre's famous single-line melody has become indelibly fixed in our collective consciousness as the musical epitome of Arabia. It is one of those rare and precious creations which instantly transports the listener – any listener – to that exotic land. The unbelievably vast expanse of sand, the unbearable intensity of the sun, the marauding Bedouin: Jarre depicts them all with the romanticized vision of T. E. Lawrence. His "Overture" – which forms a mini-suite of the whole – is a near-perfect example of film music: arrestingly bold, pungently evocative, and quite unforgettable. Beyond the main theme, the score still has much of interest, albeit often less immediately striking. However, a percussion-heavy orchestra, flavoured with ondes martenot and cithara, creates a uniquely spicy sound more than sufficient to compensate for several routine and uninspired passages. Two competing versions of this score are available, although really serious collectors will surely not hesitate to acquire both. The remastered Original Soundtrack would normally be considered an automatic first choice, were it not for the quality of Silva's extended issue, featuring several cues not on the original album, new orchestrations by Christopher Palmer (under the guidance of the composer), and a handsome full-colour booklet. Tony Bremner does not attempt slavishly to reproduce all tempos and dynamics, and even substitutes a synthesizer for the cithara. The result is yet more proof that good film music can exist independently of the film: it does not supplant the original Varèse disc, but must at very least be considered as an equal alternative. **MW**

Lean By Jarre Royal Philharmonic Orchestra / Maurice Jarre.
Milan Ⓕ 10131-2 (49 minutes DDD) Recorded 1992.
Lawrence of Arabia (1962). Doctor Zhivago (1965). Ryan's Daughter (1970). A Passage to India (1984). Remembrance. Offering.

Three Oscars out of four assignments with just one director is pretty good going. Here, in a musical tribute to David Lean, Maurice Jarre leads the RPO in a breathtaking musical ride through four films, plus two new pieces not available elsewhere. *Remembrance* is a dramatic orchestral *tour de force*, with emphasis on percussion and woodwinds. *Offering* is a more reflective tribute that is worthy of repeated listening. *Doctor Zhivago* is of course much, much more than just "Lara's Theme" and in a ten-minute suite, all principal themes are explored. The same could be said of *Lawrence* – everyone knows the tune, but there's a lot more to it than the oft-parodied theme. This recording is very, very good considering it was recorded live at The Barbican, London. A well-edited video tape and Laserdisc of the same concert are also available (Milan 11844-3/6). Maurice

Jarre is still writing effective scores, but most of his finest work was done in the 1960s and early 1970s. This is a welcome reminder of how good a composer he really is. **JW**

New review

Mad Max: Beyond Thunderdome (1985) **Original Soundtrack**, with the **Royal Philharmonic Orchestra / Maurice Jarre**.
GNP Crescendo Ⓕ GNPD8037 (44 minutes: DDD). Includes *We Don't Need Another Hero* (Britten/Lyle) and *One of the Living* (Knight).

Mad Max III was possibly Jarre's last great symphonic score before he decided to concentrate on the electronic ramblings which mark much of his work of the past ten years. As always with Jarre the scoring is exotic with a vast array of percussion instruments plus organs, multiple pianos, saxophone and no less than three ondes martenots and, most suitably, an Australian didgeridoo. The original album was initially planned as a double LP – in fact this master exists somewhere in EMI's vaults – but bowing to the commercial interests of the record label only 25 minutes of this massive score made it to the finished disc with another 17 minutes of the disc comprising of the two songs "We Don't Need Another Hero" and "One of the Living", performed by Tina Turner, plus an instrumental mix of the backing-track for "We Don't Need Another Hero". Fortunately, all the major elements of Jarre's score have been preserved in the three extended cues in this 'edited' version: the wild and manic music for Aunty's (Tina Turner) domain "Bartertown"; the playful theme for "The Children" and the barbarity of the final chase in "Coming Home". Jarre's martialling of the immense orchestral forces (ably assisted by Christopher Palmer) has never been better, and whereas other film composers use the ondes martenot as a solo instrument Jarre, ever since *Lawrence of Arabia*, has preferred to use this instrument for its mysterious and otherworldly effect. The performance by the Royal Philharmonic Orchestra is exemplary aided by dynamic digital engineering by Dick Lewzey at CTS Studios. **PC**

Maurice Jarre at Abbey Road Royal Philharmonic Orchestra / Maurice Jarre.
Milan Ⓕ 262 321 (57 minutes: DDD). Recorded 1991.
Georges Franju Suite. Behold a Pale Horse (1964). Ghost (1990). Witness (1985). Jacob's Ladder (1990). Prancer (1989). Gorillas in the Mist (1988). Fatal Attraction (1987). Moon Over Parador (1988). Dead Poets' Society (1989). A Passage to India (1984).

This compendium usefully covers highlights of Jarre's career from 1958 to 1990. His penchant for elusive themes (and even "Lara's Theme" is a surprisingly odd little tune) is well evidenced in his enchanting music for *Ghost, Fatal Attraction*, and most vividly, *Jacob's Ladder*; this being one of a clutch Jarre scored for synthesizer ensemble, but here, and very happily, we are treated to an atmospheric orchestral version of the main theme. We also get memorable symphonic arrangements of two other synthesizer scores: *Fatal Attraction* and *Witness*, the latter's "Building the Barn" – one of Jarre's best inventions – here decked-out in marvellous Coplandesque colours supplied by Christopher Palmer. But the disc's true focal point is its least known material: music from four films by Georges Franju arranged into a continuous 16-minute suite. Here Jarre takes pride in his former profession as a percussionist in the thrilling drum-led score for *La Tête Contre les Murs* (1958), and presents in his music for *Judex* (1963) the unusual instrumental mix which would later come to typify his work and so distinguished his music for *Lawrence of Arabia*. The Abbey Road acoustic is used to fine advantage in a showcase recording which serves the composer well. **DW**

New review

The Message[a] (1976) **Lion of the Desert**[b] (1981) **Original Soundtracks**, with the [a]**Royal Philharmonic Orchestra**; [b]**London Symphony Orchestra / Maurice Jarre**.
Silva Screen Ⓕ FILMCD060 (77 minutes: ADD).

Whilst many of Maurice Jarre's admirers will feel that his Oscar-winning scores are his best and most successful efforts, like many other composers some fine music is to be found in his lesser-known scores. Here on a disc with a very generous playing time are two rare examples of Jarre's epic style back to back. *The Message* tells the story of the prophet Mohammed and the birth of Islam in the seventh century; whilst *Lion of the Desert* is the tale of twentieth-century Libyan patriot Omar Mukhtar and his 20-year long struggle to free his country from the occupying forces of Mussolini. Neither score is a far cry from *Lawrence of Arabia*, but both stories are told from the Arabic point of view, with no Western leanings, as Jarre points out in the booklet notes, and the music is constructed with this very much in mind. His famous use of percussion is well to the fore, as might be expected from such heady tales, but *Lion of the Desert* especially has many quieter moments. All the famous Jarre trademarks are here: just turn up the volume and let it wash over you. This is a disc that proves there is much more in the Maurice Jarre canon than just his scores for Sir David Lean. **JW**

A Walk in the Clouds (1995) **Original Soundtrack / Maurice Jarre.**
  Milan Ⓕ 28666-2 (35 minutes: DDD). Includes *Crush the Grapes* and *Mariachi Serenade* (Brouwer/Arau).

Director Alfonso Arau's professed admiration for "Lara's Theme" stimulated Jarre to recreate the lush romanticism exemplified by his earlier David Lean collaborations. *A Walk in the Clouds* has all the attractive, immediately appealing characteristics of vintage Jarre. There is a passionate waltz-like main theme, some danceable South American interludes, and a hint of melodrama; all lightly scored, and never over-sentimentalized. The gentle romance of "First Kiss", for example, which reveals the true nature of the main melody as a gorgeous love theme, is never cloying. The two songs by Cuban-born Leo Brouwer enhance the Latin-American flavour, without detracting from Jarre's delicious score. **MW**

Witness (1985) **Original Soundtrack**, with **Electronic Ensemble** (Michael Boddicker, Randy Kerber, Stewart Levin, Michel Mention, Chris Page, Pete Robinson, Clark Spangler, Nyle Steiner, Ian Underwood) **/ Maurice Jarre.**
  TER Ⓕ CDTER1098 / Varèse Sarabande Ⓕ VCD47227 (30 minutes: DDD).

The action of *Witness*, if you recall, is played out against the backdrop of the shy, fervently religious and utterly technophobic Amish community; a community in which no infernal modern machines are suffered to invade their quakerish seventeenth-century idyll. Odd then that Maurice Jarre should produce an entirely electronic score. After *Blade Runner* (1982, coincidentally also starring Harrison Ford) this sort of moody, impressionistic synthesizer style enjoyed a certain vogue, and Jarre's *Witness* undoubtedly contains more than a hint of Vangelis. It is by no means a bad score for all that, with glowering synths voicing sombre chords to create an air of sinister menace; although it always remains warmer and more likeable than the dissonant gloom of *Fatal Attraction*, for example. The score's central element – that of the film too – is, however, "Building the Barn", a sequence during which the mood lightens considerably. This is a fully self-contained composition somewhat resembling a baroque Passacaglia, albeit one played in the lushest, most romantic manner imaginable. A celebratory anthem, it cries out for orchestral treatment, although it had to wait for Christopher Palmer's arrangement to achieve what surely must be its preferred form. Even entirely synthesized, this cue is still the score's strongest, most memorable feature, and certainly constitute's the principal reason for buying this disc. **MW**

Also available:
Classic Film Music (City of Prague PO/Bateman) Silva Screen FILMCD158
Dead Poets' Society (1989) **The Year of Living Dangerously** (1982) Milan CDCH558
Gorillas in the Mist (1988) MCA MCAD6255
Jacob's Ladder (1990) Varèse Sarabande VSD5291
Mosquito Coast (1986) Fantasy FCD21005-2
The Night of the Generals (1966) Intrada FMT8004D
No Way Out (1987) **The Year of Living Dangerously** (1982) TER CDTER1149
Only the Lonely (1991) Varèse Sarabande VSD5324
The Professionals (1966) Silva Screen STD5002
Shadow of the Wolf (1993) Milan 35634-2

Laurie Johnson
b. 1927 England

Laurie Johnson had already published several light orchestral works before he was 18, and had composed and arranged music for several big band leaders including Ambrose, Ted Heath and Geraldo before beginning formal studies at the Royal College of Music. He has concentrated on film and television work since the 1950s – composing over 400 scores – but has also found time to write concert works like his *Symphony (Synthesis)*, a rare fusion of jazz and classical music (available on Unicorn-Kanchana UKCD2057). In addition, he has written music for the shows *Lock Up Your Daughters* (with lyrics by Lionel Bart) and *The Four Musketeers* (lyrics Herbert Kretzmer). Active as a producer as well as a composer, he has also developed business interests in film production companies.

First Men in the Moon (1964) **Original Soundtrack / Laurie Johnson.**
  Cloud Nine Ⓕ ACN7015 (46 minutes: ADD).

The orchestration of this score is brilliantly considered to capture as alien a sensation as possible: almost every standard woodwind instrument is exploited in its extreme register at some point, and the use of muted brass and of string effects, not to mention scintillating percussion, adds great impact

Other titles from **Gramophone Publications**

Gramophone Musicals Good CD Guide
The only book of its kind, this guide explores the glorious heritage of musical theatre. It contains biographies of featured composers and lyricists together with some 400 CD reviews of shows, films and recitals.

£9·95

Gramophone Classical Good CD Guide
The 1997 edition of this well-established publication is the largest and most comprehensive to date. The guide is a must for every music lover, recommending the best classical recordings currently available.

£15·99

Gramophone Jazz Good CD Guide
This essential jazz companion contains over 1,600 reviews, recommending the best recordings by all the major jazz artists. Eighteen top jazz critics, from Britain and the USA, give a broad range of opinions on this increasingly popular area of music.

£15·99

Gramophone Opera Good CD Guide
Designed for the opera aficionado and for the music lover wishing to explore this exciting art form, the *Gramophone Opera Good CD Guide* offers hundreds of recommendations for the best opera recordings currently available. The first edition will be published in June 1997.

£12·95

Gramophone magazine
With contributions from the world's most respected critics and reviews of around 200 new classical CDs every month, *Gramophone* is recognised as the best classical music magazine in the world. It is published monthly and includes a free CD.

Single copy **£3·95**
UK annual subscription **£44·20**

International Opera Collector
IOC is the only publication for the collector of opera recordings, past and present. It contains a judicious mix of contemporary and historical articles and provides a forum for debate on issues of interest to the opera aficionado. *IOC* is published four times each year.

Single copy **£4·00**
UK annual subscription **£16·00**

International Classical Record Collector
ICRC is the quarterly music magazine that covers all aspects of collecting classical music recordings from the past, from cylinders and 78s to analogue LPs and historic reissues on CD.

Single copy **£4·00**
UK annual subscription **£15·20**

Gramophone Opera 75
Gramophone Opera 75 brings together reviews of 75 great opera recordings selected by *Gramophone* magazine's Editor. Each page is devoted to a different opera and features writing by some of the finest judges of operatic recordings this century.

£5·95

Gramophone explorations 1
The classical music of the Nordic and Baltic countries
Written by the world's leading experts on Nordic and Baltic music, *Gramophone explorations 1* includes nearly 50 articles and interviews covering all aspects of the repertoire and recording artists, and is accompanied by a compilation CD illustrating the wealth of recordings currently available.

£6·95

These publications are available through newsagents, bookshops and record stores, or direct from the publishers.

Gramophone Publications Limited
135 Greenford Road, Sudbury Hill, Harrow, Middlesex HA1 3YD, Great Britain
Telephone +44 (0)181-422 4562 **Fax** +44 (0)181 869 8400
E-mail subs@gramophone.co.uk

to this impressive composition. The transfer cannot, however, disguise the rawness of the original sound; nevertheless there is enough depth to show the imaginative scoring in a very favourable way. The Victorian scenes are lovingly recreated, and the Moon Beast, Selenites, and Sphere have effective and identifiable themes, well worked and well developed. Enjoyable, though dated. **CT**

The Rose And The Gun The Music of Laurie Johnson. Various orchestras / **Laurie Johnson**. Fly Ⓜ FLYCD103 (46 minutes: ADD/DDD).
The Lady and the Highwayman (1989). A Hazard of Hearts (1990). A Duel of Hearts (1992). A Ghost in Monte Carlo (1990). The Avengers (1965). The New Avengers (1976). Tiger Bay (1959). Hot Millions (1968). When the Kissing Had to Stop. Shirley's World (1971). I Aim at the Stars (1960). This is Your Life (1968). Jason King (1971). First Men in the Moon (1964). The Professionals (1977).

Laurie Johnson, one of the few British film composers successfully to emulate the gleaming sound of his Hollywood counterparts, is sadly under-represented on CD and so this collection makes an invaluable introduction to a master tunesmith. Incredibly versatile, Johnson is equally at home with costume drama (as illustrated by the surging opulence of his music for four TV films made from the quivering romances of Barbara Cartland), or the more contemporary world of cops and robbers (the polished big band sound of *The Avengers* and the funky bass line of *The Professionals* conveniently summing up the prevailing musical styles of each decade). Other highlights on this very satisfying CD include the glamorous theme for *This is Your Life* and three delightfully contrasting excerpts from the film *Hot Millions*. **RS**

Also available:
The Avengers, etc. Varèse Sarabande VSD5501

Quincy Jones
b. 1933 USA

Born in Chicago, but growing up in Seattle, Quincy Jones sang in a gospel quartet aged 12 before studying trumpet at Boston's Schillinger House. He worked in New York as a freelance arranger and composer and toured Europe with the Lionel Hampton band. He worked for Barclay Records in Paris in the late 1950s where he studied composition with Nadia Boulanger. Back in New York he became head of A&R at Mercury Records, and continued arranging for artists including Frank Sinatra and Tony Bennett, as well as recording his own albums (more recently he has worked with Michael Jackson amongst others). In 1961 he scored his first film, *Boy in the Tree*, but it was Sidney Lumet's *The Pawnbroker* (1965) that established him as a film composer. He has since scored over 40 films and written extensively for television, writing themes for shows such as *Ironside* (1967). Feature film scores include the Oscar-nominated *In the Heat of the Night* (1967) and *The Color Purple* (1985).

New review
The Pawnbroker (1965) **The Deadly Affair** (1966) Original Soundtracks / Quincy Jones. Verve Ⓟ 531 233-2 (68 minutes: AAD).

During the 1950s, the jazz-influenced scores of Alex North and Elmer Bernstein helped to change the sound of Hollywood film music forever. The following decade, the film scores of Quincy Jones would further shape and refine this sound, thus bringing film music into a ground-breaking new era far removed from its late-Romantic symphonic roots. This superb CD presents two of Jones's most notable scores from this period (both, coincidentally, written for director Sidney Lumet) and is an excellent demonstration of Jones's huge talents as both composer and arranger. As Rod Steiger's powerful dialogue on "How Come You People" illustrates, *The Pawnbroker* was the harrowing tale of the title character's moral disintegration in the slums of Harlem after seeing his family murdered by the Nazis during the war. The searing jazz of cues like "Harlem Drive" and "Rack 'em Up" (expertly performed by such eminent soloists as Freddie Hubbard, J. J. Johnson, Oliver Nelson and Elvin Jones) provided a powerful adjunct to the film's unrelenting bleakness, while in direct contrast, the shimmering harpsichord and strings of the "Main Title" paint a beautifully limpid reminder of happier times. The bossa nova and the beguiling Brazilian melodies of Antonio Carlos Jobim were captivating the world throughout the 1960s, and for the spy thriller *The Deadly Affair* Jones adopted these insistent, hypnotic rhythms to create an unusual and hugely effective air of mystery and suspense. The entire score makes for compelling listening; its appeal best summed up by the spellbinding, ravishingly-orchestrated main title (credited as "Main Theme – Version 1" on the track listing). **RS**

Also available:
The Color Purple (1985) QWest 925389-2

Trevor Jones England

Trevor Jones was inspired by movies early, so much so that he had decided at the age of five that he wanted to write film music. His family background was theatrical, so his ambition was encouraged. He won a scholarship to the Royal Academy of Music and studied conducting, composition and orchestration. Whilst working for the BBC after graduating, Jones developed a Film and Media music course with Wilfrid Mellors of York University. Jones then enrolled at the National Film School and scored several student films. Highlights of his career to date include collaborations with director Jim Henson on *The Dark Crystal* (1983) and *Labyrinth* (1986), and John Boorman's *Excalibur* (1981).

Cliffhanger (1993) **Original Soundtrack**, with the **London Philharmonic Orchestra / David Snell**.
   Scotti Bros Ⓕ 514 455-2 (51 minutes: DDD).

Some excellent playing from the London Philharmonic, conducted by David Snell, provides the best element of this disc. The recording, however, doesn't give enough depth to the bass, and the whole is a little insubstantial. Too often the melodic motifs (either *Dallas*-like trumpet or conventional violin romantic) are accompanied by unimaginative harmonic progressions, but the rhythmic excitement for the tenser moments later in the film is well captured, with some particularly fine horn playing. The fight music is good, and the last track is, as often, an extended and effective structure, which most of the cinema audience would miss as they walk out during the credits. **CT**

New review
In the Name of the Father (1993). **Original Soundtrack**, with the **London Philharmonic Orchestra / David Snell**.
   Island Ⓕ 518 841-2 (51 minutes: ADD/DDD). Includes *In the Name of the Father, Billy Boola* and *You Made Me the Thief of Your Heart* (Bono/Friday/Seezer), *Voodoo Chile* (Hendrix), *Dedicated Follower of Fashion* (Davies), *Is This Love* (Marley) and *Whiskey in the Jar* (Lynott/Bell/Downey).

In the Name of the Father is Jim Sheridan's dramatically riveting adaptation of the Gerry Conlon book "Proved Innocent". The film opens with the title song – an intense, percussive piece whose unfocused lyrics and hallucinatory music mirrors the lifestyle of the hedonistic main character. Before long the listener discovers that the soundtrack for the film is one of those rare instances where the songs perform a legitimate dramatic function. And thanks to the collaborative efforts of score composer Trevor Jones and song writer Gavin Friday, we have a disc where songs and score work together as a coherent listening experience.
   The soundtrack is divided into newly composed songs, original score, and licensed songs that are retro-fitted to enhance the period mood. All three parts are given equal weight in the playing time and are interspersed nicely throughout the sequencing. "Billy Boola," as sung by Friday and U2's Bono, is another illustration of the main character's wayward attitude. All of this changes when the police intervene, forcing him to embark on a crusade for justice. At this point Trevor Jones's score assumes a greater role. A nice blend of acoustic and electronic materials, Jones creates the requisite amount of tension and foreboding. "Interrogation" vibrates with electric guitar wails, washes of synthesized sound, drones, and percussive passages. The music is very effective in creating a sense of hopelessness about the situation. There is no outrage in the score – that comes from the intensity of the performances, notably Emma Thompson's as the lawyer who defends the family. The gloomy mood continues with "Walking the Circle", although the cue segues to a piano solo that introduces a tonal, vaguely melodic section. After a brush with atonality, "Passage of Time" delivers a theme first hinted at in the previous score track. Divided into six-note sections, the darkly lyrical theme helps a father and son reconcile a strained relationship, and leads the way to the eventual overturning of the injustice. The functional demands made by the narrative do not allow Jones the opportunity to create entirely self-contained pieces. One is impressed, however, with the effect that he is able to generate. The vocal highlight of the score, if not the entire soundtrack, is "You Made Me the Thief of Your Heart". This is a haunting ballad sung with anger and love by Sinead O'Connor, an artist who has never been afraid to express either emotion. **KM**

The Last of the Mohicans (1992) **Original Soundtrack / Daniel A. Carlin, Randy Edelman**.
   Morgan Creek Ⓕ 517 497-2 (55 minutes: DDD). Includes additional music by Randy Edelman, and *I Will Find You* (Brennan).

Michael Mann's films are highly kinetic entertainments which boast a very impressive feel for what works visually and aurally. They are never less than stunning to look at but always display a confident and assured use of music. Mann applies an MTV-style approach to this film where important sequences, usually a chase of some description, are heavily underlined with music almost to an exclusion of natural sound. Jones responds to the visual splendour with a robust score based on original melodies and gaelic reels that counterpoints the on-screen action. Away from the film, his music comes across as a series of darkly tinged period dances. The additional music by Randy Edelman which occupies the second half of the disc acts as a more solid underscore and is of less immediate interest as far as listening goes although one cue, "The Courier", is a stand-out item. The disc finishes with a brief Clannad song which is in keeping with the general tone of the rest of the score. **DS**

Also available:
Angel Heart (1987) Island IMCD76
Criss Cross (1992) Intrada MAF7021
Gulliver's Travels (1996) RCA 09026 68475-2
Kiss of Death (1995) Milan 280 202
Labyrinth (1986) EMI CDFA3322
Mississippi Burning (1988) Spectrum 551 100-2
Richard III (1996) London 828 719-2
Sea of Love (1989) Spectrum 550 130-2

Michael Kamen

b. 1948 USA

A formally trained classical musician, Michael Kamen is one of those rare talents equally comfortable writing in either pop or classical styles. He studied the oboe at the Juilliard School of Music, New York, where he formed one of the first rock/classical fusion groups, The New York Rock and Roll Ensemble. He later wrote several ballet scores, and collaborated successfully with many major names in the pop world, including Bob Dylan, Eric Clapton, Kate Bush, The Eurythmics and Pink Floyd (for whom he orchestrated and arranged *The Wall*). Singer Bryan Adams has featured on several recent Kamen film scores, beginning with their co-written hit "(Everything I Do) I Do it for You" from *Robin Hood, Prince of Thieves* (1991). The composer's first orchestral score was for the Sean Connery film *The Next Man* (1976) – it was also his first attempt at conducting, due to his forgetting to hire a conductor for the recording sessions! Kamen's first major Hollywood assignment was David Cronenberg's compelling adaptation of Stephen King's bestseller *The Dead Zone* (1983). His collaboration with director Terry Gilliam on the surrealistic *Brazil* (1985) was described by the composer as "my most completely satisfying participation in film". Although a New Yorker by upbringing, Kamen has lived in London for many years. He continues to fit writing concert works into his hectic film-scoring schedule, and still finds time to play the oboe as a part-time member of the London Metropolitan Ensemble.

Brazil (1985) **Original Soundtrack**, with the **National Philharmonic Orchestra / Michael Kamen**.
Milan Ⓜ 11124-2 (39 minutes: ADD). Includes "Brazil" (Ary Barroso) performed by Kate Bush.

Any fan of Terry Gilliam's dark, visionary film will derive much pleasure from this release. In order to convey the anarchy and controlled disorder that is *Brazil*, Kamen has pulled together a dazzling array of musical styles, sound effects and dialogue clips. The chief delights are the uses of the well-known title tune, or parts of it, that occur during the story. Whether it is the orchestra gradually building the familiar rhythm over the sound of typewriters or the lilting arrangement that is used in Jonathan Pryce's dream-flying sequences, the choice of this particular lightweight and completely inconsequential song seems absolutely right. It is as if the very fact that it is such a nonsense piece enhances the grim nature of the narrative by strong contrast. An interesting point is that, originally, Pryce's first dream contained Kate Bush performing a vocal version of the song over the lush orchestral background. In the final film, only the orchestra is heard but on the disc the Kate Bush version is used, making it something of a must for Kate Bush fanatics. **DS**

The Dead Zone (1983) **Original Soundtrack**, with the **National Philharmonic Orchestra / Michael Kamen**.
Milan Ⓜ 23976-2 (43 minutes: DDD).
"Please, please stop playing the piano ...You're scaring me and my family to death, we're having nightmares, we can't sleep ... Please stop." This reaction from Michael Kamen's long-suffering neighbour was the composer's first indication that his *Dead Zone* score, currently being thrashed out on the piano, was indeed the blood-chilling work it should be. Still, despite the cold veneer, there is warmth to be found at the heart of this music: a bittersweet central theme evokes the nostalgic regret of lost love. Stark strings and mournful horns, sparse woodwinds and harp elsewhere conjure visions of a wintry landscape. The dark sonority of low-pitched woodwinds in particular defines the bleakness of this soundscape. Kamen's first major Hollywood score skilfully exploits orchestral resources to produce a powerfully disturbing work. Hints of Bernard

Herrmann in places ("Alone" for example) do not detract from Kamen's original vision – the austere depiction of loneliness and fear is all his own. This CD release was delayed for over a decade: all the more reason then to savour retrospectively such an outstanding début.   **MW**

Die Hard 2: Die Harder (1990) **Original Soundtrack**, with the **Los Angeles Motion Picture All Stars Orchestra / Michael Kamen**.
  Varèse Sarabande Ⓟ VSD5273 (41 minutes: DDD). Includes *Finlandia* (Sibelius).

Film music has often been accused of plundering the classics, but Michael Kamen's first two *Die Hard* scores do so with an insouciant shamelessness that can only be admired. The original adapted "Ode to Joy" from Beethoven's Ninth Symphony as the theme for the (German) bad guys; the second movie needed only the even flimsier excuse of a snowy backdrop to raid Sibelius's nationalistic tone-poem *Finlandia*. Admittedly, Kamen uses his source sparingly, restricting himself for the most part to quoting its opening few bars, then treats us to a complete rendition of the piece at the end of the album. Kamen's own contribution is much greater than the above implies: his loud, arhythmic, often intricate scoring is here undiluted by any contributions from other hands, like Eric Clapton (*Lethal Weapon*) or Robert Kraft (*Hudson Hawk*). As the original *Die Hard* score has yet to be (legitimately) issued on CD, and the third film's album is an unhappy mix of sundry pop songs and several cues apparently was dropped from the movie, this disc must stand alone as representative of Kamen's action movie credentials.   **MW**

Don Juan de Marco (1995) **Original Soundtrack**, with the **London Metropolitan Orchestra / Michael Kamen**.
  A&M Ⓟ 540 357-2 (46 minutes: DDD). Includes *Have You Ever Really Loved a Woman?* (Adams/Lange/Kamen).

A score redolent of Latin-American passion, Kamen's *Don Juan de Marco* has all the tempestuous sensuality of its obvious model, Bizet's *Carmen*. Under the banner of the London Metropolitan Orchestra, Kamen has assembled a group of superbly talented soloists, including guitarists Julian Bream and Paco de Lucia (not forgetting the composer's brother Paul), violinist Christopher Warren-Jones, and cellist Caroline Dale (who is also a member of the London Metropolitan Ensemble). Together, their performances contribute to making this disc a delightful listening experience. Featuring radiant solos for each of his star players, and scored throughout with a delicacy that belies his reputation as just an 'action' movie composer, Kamen's music shimmers gracefully as if in the heat of a sultry afternoon sun. Following Bizet's example he gives us his own "Habanera", alongside other sensuous Latin textures. There is a romantic cello theme, some virtuosic Spanish guitar playing, soaring violin, and exquisite filigree writing for oboe-led woodwinds in the finale. The whole glows with an inner warmth and vivacity that is only too rare in much recent film music, and flows so naturally there is scarcely anything appreciably filmic about it. If Kamen had written nothing before or since, his reputation would be assured by this score. It is a work of lasting beauty and joy that deserves the widest possible exposure.   **MW**

New review
Jack (1996) **Original Soundtrack**, with the **L.A. All Star Orchestra / Michael Kamen**.
  Hollywood Ⓟ HR62063-2 (38 minutes: DDD).

A sentimental comedy from the director of *Apocalypse Now* and *The Godfather* must have seemed an unlikely box office winner (even starring Robin Williams); but one person evidently sympathetic to Coppola's attempted change of direction was Michael Kamen, who knows all about typecasting, having spent many years scoring a succession of bombastic action movies. At any rate, the composer demonstrably enjoyed this assignment: *Jack* is a score which tells us as much about Kamen's own irreverent sense of fun as the humour on screen. Comedy film scores tend to avoid self-consciously 'zany' music in the belief that jokes work best when not underlined by wacky effects. Kamen, rebel that he is, will have none of this, and throws everything he can into the mix, including bells, whistles and kazoos (performed, the booklet tells us, by "The Little Man's Chowder and Marching Society Band and Orchestra"). Fortunately, because Kamen is a good and sensitive musician, this wackiness always serves the music, never swamps it. The opening "Jack Conga", swiftly followed by "Jack Scherzo", introduce Jack's sprightly theme clothed in a dizzying variety of multi-coloured orchestrations that are thrown around the orchestra with reckless abandon. Solo instruments, including trumpet, cello and French horn, have a prominent role throughout, and for once the booklet credits individual performers. Later cues are less playful, with a marked increase in the sentiment quotient; but, thankfully, after a worryingly saccharine cue entitled "Back to School (What Do I Want to Be When I Grow Up? Alive!)" the final "Valedictorian (Life is Fleeting)" is stirring and heart-warming without overdosing on the syrup.   **MW**

Mr Holland's Opus (1996) **Original Soundtrack**, with the **Seattle Symphony Orchestra; The London Metropolitan Orchestra / Michael Kamen**.
London Ⓕ 452 065-2 (68 minutes: DDD). Includes "Allegretto" from Symphony No. 7 (Beethoven), First movement from Concerto for Three Harpsichords in C, BWV1064 (Bach) and *Cole's Song* (Kamen/Lennon/Clayton).

This was a project obviously close to the composer's heart – the story of a music teacher whose dreams of writing the great American symphony are apparently undermined by his commitment to teaching, but who in the end discovers that the inspiration he has given his students is more than ample compensation. Michael Kamen, a passionate advocate of accessible, popular music (be it Bach or Bon Jovi) could hardly have found a film more in keeping with his own outlook. The centrepiece of his score is the "Opus" itself, an eight-and-a-half minute mini-symphony which switches near the end from a big romantic orchestral work – in effect a suite of the rest of the score – to a statement of the principal theme over a driving pop beat. It is this latter 'pop' section which forms the rather anticlimactic climax of the movie, which is a shame because it is by no means the best music in the score. The underscore proper has many moments of wit and charm, with a plentiful infusion of touching sentiment. Mr Holland's theme is energetic and attention-grabbing, the overt repository of the music's emotional content; other themes are less extrovert, the tender "Iris and Glen" for example, or "Cole's Tune", a moving flute solo. Kamen has some fun skating around the classics, as in "Rush to Hospital" – subtitled "While parents listen to Beethoven" – which includes a frantic skit on the *Emperor* Concerto, and the delightful montage sequence "Practice, Practice, Practice". Mr Holland is no proponent of avant-garde techniques, and the score's tone mirrors that of the classical excerpts specially recorded for the film. Julian Lennon's contribution puts Kamen's theme to better use than most movie spin-off songs.   **MW**

Robin Hood, Prince of Thieves (1991) **Original Soundtrack**, with the **Greater Los Angeles Orchestra /Michael Kamen**.
Morgan Creek Ⓕ 511 050-2 (60 minutes: AAD). Includes "(Everything I Do) I Do it for You" (Kamen/Adams/Lange) performed by Bryan Adams, and "Wild Times" (Kamen/Lynne) performed by Jeff Lynne.

Michael Kamen made his mark as a composer well-suited to splashy, big budget action thrillers like *Die Hard* and *Lethal Weapon*; and with *Robin Hood* he obviously relishes the opportunity of pointing up the mayhem in period dress by recapturing the full-blooded Korngold sound of the Errol Flynn classic. If the sheer panache and imagination of his illustrious predecessor is missing, a sequence such as the galloping opening with Robin's theme ringing out from burnished brass is still mighty impressive (incredibly beefy sound adding to its impact). And though it's difficult to hear Maid Marian's theme without being reminded of the resistible but highly successful pop song it became, Kamen's original setting is certainly very appealing.   **RS**

Also available:
Circle of Friends (1995) ZTT 0630-10957-2
Die Hard With a Vengeance (1995) RCA 09026 68306-2
Hudson Hawk (1991) Varèse Sarabande VSD5323
Last Action Hero (1993) Columbia 473990-2
Lethal Weapon 2 (1989) WEA 925985-2
Lethal Weapon 3 (1992) WEA 7599-26989-2
Licence to Kill (1989) MCA MCAD6307
Shining Through (1992) Milan 262 742
The Three Musketeers (1993) Hollywood HR61581
101 Dalmatians (1996) Walt Disney WD699402

Yoko Kanno   Japan

Born in Miyagi on Japan's main island, Honshu, Yoko Kanna began playing the piano at an early age. Moving to Tokyo, she began writing songs and jingles for make-up adverts, and has averaged about 200 such songs a year. In 1994, Shoji Kawamori, creator/director of the Japanese animation series *Macross* (first aired in 1982), approached the composer with a view to writing songs for a new venture to be called *Macross Plus*. The quality of Kanno's work was so good that Kawamori asked her to provide symphonic underscore for the movie, and eventually most of the original songs were replaced by this material. Aside from *Macross Plus*, Kanno has also scored the series *Esca Floné of the Skies*, again for Kawamori.

New review

Macross Plus (1994-5), Volumes 1 and 2. **Original Soundtracks**, with **Yoko Kanno** (keybds); various artists; members of the **Israel Philharmonic Orchestra / Anthony Inglis**. Demon Ⓕ DSCD12/13 (two discs: 52 and 50 minutes: DDD).

Japanese animation offers a world of fantastic storylines, dazzling visual style and kaleidoscopic presentation. The latter particularly applies to the two discs making up the soundtrack to this particular epic. The first disc features orchestral tracks that wouldn't sound out of place in a Hollywood score – dramatic action cues, stirring martial music and contrasting tender romantic melodies; whereas the second disc contains more pop-based elements. But even here, diversity rules. Hi-tech synth pop tracks are followed by Ry Cooder-style guitar; heavy rock, Satie-like piano, French vocals and frenetic voice sampling all have a part in this score. Although lavishly illustrated, neither disc gives hint as to what *Macross Plus* might be about, but at least the music is fun. The strangeness of having the song lyrics printed in French and Japanese only adds to the odd feeling of enjoying something but not being sure what it is. For these are highly entertaining discs; both contain music of a wide variety of styles and sounds, all immaculately performed. Not for all tastes, perhaps, but this is bold, energetic scoring unconfined by the limits of conventional film music. Music from Japanese animation is poorly represented in the UK, but if this is a representative example, then let us have more. **DS**

Eleni Karaindrou Greece

Born in Teichio, a mountainous area in the Roumeli region of central Greece, Eleni Karaindrou recalls being surrounded from the very beginning with music: sometimes folk music or Byzantine church music, sometimes the 'music' of the wind, rain and snow amongst the mountains. She developed an interest in films after her family moved to Athens, living next door to an open-air cinema. Between 1953-1967 she studied piano and theory at the Hellenikon Odion, Athens; but was then forced to leave the country by the military Junta. Settling in Paris, Karaindrou began to study ethnomusicology, as well as orchestration and conducting. Returning to Athens in 1974, she formed the Laboratory for Traditional Instrumentalists. Her first film score, *Wandering*, came in 1979. Karaindrou has worked with directors Christoforo Christofis (*Wandering* and *Rosa*, 1982), Lefteris Xanthopoulos (*Happy Homecoming, Comrade*, 1986) and Theo Angelopoulos (*The Beekeeper*, 1986, *Landscape in the Mist*, 1990, *The Suspended Step of the Stork*, 1991, *Ulysses' Gaze*, 1995). She also holds a Masters degree in History and Archaeology, and has written extensively for the theatre as well as for Greek cinema.

The Suspended Step of the Stork (1991) **Original Soundtrack** with **Vangelis Christopoulos** (ob); **Dimitris Vraskos** (vn); **Christos Sfetsas** (vc); **Nikos Spinoulas** (hn); **Ada Rouva** (hp); **Andreas Tsekouras** (accordion) **/ Lefteris Chalkiadakis**. ECM Ⓕ 511 514-2 (36 minutes: AAD).

Ulysses' Gaze (1995) **Original Soundtrack**, with **Georgia Voulvi** (voice); **Vangelis Christopoulos** (ob); **Kim Kashkashian** (va); **Christos Sfetsas** (vc); **Socratis Anthis** (tpt); **Vangelis Skouras** (hn); **Andreas Tsekouras** (accordion) **/ Lefteris Chalkiadakis**. ECM Ⓕ 449 153-2 (60 minutes: ADD).

Karaindrou's work for director Theo Angelopoulos, as exemplified by these two discs, is far removed from the standard heart-on-the-sleeve romanticism of Hollywood; but, it is emotionally direct and broadly accessible music nevertheless. Both of these scores share an intimacy of scale and intent, with a string orchestra gently supporting solo performers. In *Ulysses' Gaze* these soloists rarely play together as if members of a chamber ensemble – more often they are each given a single-line melody against a backdrop of string chords. Even in *The Suspended Step of the Stork* there is little interaction between the principal musicians. Karaindrou's music has a deliberately abstract quality absent in traditional film scores: it does not follow action or dialogue, but attempts to seek out some unseen or unspoken aspect of the film. Technically, this is achieved at least in part by her 'theme and variations' approach, which allows her to leisurely state and develop a central melody unhampered by the necessity of hitting certain filmic cue points. However, freed from some of the restraints that shape other scores, Karaindrou's work is thereby robbed of an important element: drama stimulated by action or dialogue. Consequently, both scores are extremely static in nature, with little or no change of mood or pace. Most of the music consists of elaboration or restatement of core themes, and the tempo remains *adagio* throughout.

The interplay of oboe and strings in *The Suspended Step of the Stork* has an almost Vivaldian directness that is most appealing; yet Karaindrou's generally aimless manner might best be compared with that of Górecki and his famous *Symphony of Sorrowful Songs*. Delightful performances by all the soloists constitute much of the enjoyment. Kim Kashkashian's resonant viola in *Ulysses' Gaze*, for example, lingers in the memory long after the disc has finished; as does Vangelis Christoulos's oboe in both scores. A complete absence of explanatory notes in either booklet seems almost deliberately calculated to deter the casual listener; although, given some small encouragement, they might be agreeably surprised by what they discover here.   **MW**

Also available:
Music for Films ECM 847 609-2

Aram Khachaturian

1903-1978 USSR

Aram Khachaturian played the tenor horn with the school band in his native Tbilisi, and taught himself to play the piano. He studied at the Gnesin Music Academy and the Moscow Conservatory, where Myaskovsky taught him composition. He continued postgraduate studies until 1937, but had already established himself as a composer before then. His music, informed by Armenian folk traditions, found its most popular expression in the ballets *Gayaneh* (1942) and *Spartacus* (1954); but his strongly pictorial style also found a natural outlet in films, and he wrote some 25 scores for Soviet films, beginning with *Pepo* in 1934 and ending in 1960 with *Men and Animals*.

The Battle of Stalingrad (1949) **Othello** (1956) **Bratislava Radio Symphony Orchestra / Adriano**.
Marco Polo Ⓟ 8 223314 (64 minutes: DDD). Recorded 1992.

This bright recording (with a slightly boomy bass) has five extensive tracks and 11 shorter sections, which admirably capture firstly the Slavic tone, might and imagery very idiomatically – heroic and noble, energetic and fatalistic – and secondly, the Moorish element with an almost historic feel of period, although there is an occasional reminder of *Kismet*. Khachaturian is outstanding in depicting death and despair, but also brings to life vividly the conflagration and nationalistic fervour of battle. There are fine solo violin and soprano tracks; but an unfortunate forced (intentionally) choral laugh at the end of track 15 has to be redeemed by the powerfully intense *Finale*.   **CT**

Wojciech Kilar

b. 1932 Poland

A native of Lvov, Wojciech Kilar studied piano and composition at the Katowice School of Music, before being taught composition by Nadia Boulanger in Paris (the city has remained a second home for Kilar). His compositions have won several prizes, including the Lili Boulanger Prize (1960), Juzykowski Foundation Prize (1967) and the Ministry of Culture Prize in his native Poland (1967 and 1976). His non-film work includes a *Petite Overture*, Symphony for Strings, *Ode in memoriam Béla Bartók* and *Riff 62*. Kilar has written extensively for Polish cinema, working particularly with directors Andrzej Wajda and Krzystof Zanussi. He rose to international prominence in 1992 with his score for Francis Ford Coppola's *Dracula*. and has been increasingly in demand outside of Poland.

Bram Stoker's Dracula (1992) **Original Soundtrack / Anton Coppola**.
Columbia Ⓜ 472746-2 (55 minutes: DDD). Includes *Love Song for a Vampire* (Lennox).

Gothic fantasy has always proved to be a fertile feeding ground for imaginative composers. Director Francis Ford Coppola's decision to musically get as close to the Carpathian mountains as possible paid off with his choice of the Polish Kilar. His middle-European sensibilities add a welcome seriousness to the often too fanciful trickery of the director and his visual effects crew. Even the love theme has a grimness about it. But what makes this music so interesting is that it is completely unlike a conventional Hollywood score. Through repetition and added layers of sound, Kilar slowly constructs his cues and the resulting level of intensity is quite extraordinary. A sort of monolithic minimalism. The centuries of old evil that is the essence of Dracula is well characterized by the insidiousness of Kilar's technique, making this score a difficult one to approach but well worth the perseverance. Annie Lennox's "Love Song for a Vampire" is tacked on to the end, but is in keeping with the mood of the score.   **DS**

New review
A Collection of His Work Original Soundtracks.
Milan Ⓕ 17638-2 (72 minutes: ADD).
La Chronique des Evenments Amoureux. La Ligne d'Ombre. Land of Promise (1975). Korczak (1990). Illuminations. Contrat. L'Année du Soleil Calme. Wherever You Are

(1988). Bilan Trimestrial. Hasard. Jealousy and Medicine (1973). Leper (1976). Bram Stoker's Dracula (1992).

In the wake of the success of Kilar's score to Coppola's *Dracula*, it is not surprising that compilations of his previous work should start to appear. This is welcome since so little of his film work is available on disc. This one is a lengthy collection of work written for such illustrious fellow countrymen as Andrzej Wajda and Krzystof Zanussi. A reasonable variety of styles is on offer and the disc opens with a sprightly cavalry march from *La Chronique des Evenments Amoureux* and continues with the bittersweet love theme from the same film. Waltzes and tangos sit side-by-side with grim dramatic statements, austere choral pieces and martial dirges. Kilar's fondness for sombreness and repetitive intensity in his music (or perhaps it is just the nature of the films?) means that listening to the whole disc in one sitting is rather draining. Sample a few tracks at a time and the frequently gripping nature of the music becomes more apparent; the romantic lyricism of some cues begins to stand out and the stark drama of others becomes more memorable. Occasionally, one is reminded of Morricone at his more grandiose – passionate melodies with spiralling climaxes. The last two tracks are from the aforementioned *Dracula* and fit perfectly well with the other music. The packaging only gives the film titles in French (despite most of them being Polish) and gives no clues as to their year of release. This is, nevertheless, a good reminder that strong, powerful orchestral film music doesn't just come out of Hollywood.   **DS**

New review
Film Music Original Soundtracks.
Olympia ℗ OCD602 (66 minutes: ADD).
Land of Promise (1975). Balance (1973). Hypothesis (1973). Polanieki Family (1978). The Silence (1963). The Taste of the Black Earth (1972). The Pearl in the Crown (1972). Salto (1965). Jealousy and Medicine (1973). Leper (1976).

Until *Bram Stoker's Dracula* brought his name to a wider audience little was known about Kilar's prolific film career in his native Poland. This CD, therefore, is a very handy resumé of ten scores Kilar composed between 1963 and 1978, and though none of the music matches the compelling Gothic intensity of *Dracula* the disc provides a valuable illustration of the composer's melodic flair. There is an impressive diversity of styles on display here ranging from the boisterous Rossini-esque scherzo and glittering valse from *Land of Promise*, to the tense, jazzy riffs of *Salto*. The concise eight-minute suites from *Balance* and *The Taste of the Black Earth* underline further Kilar's versatility. The former features a moody, suspenseful Barry-like mid-section framed by a romantic theme for piano and swelling strings that is very reminiscent of Michel Legrand; whilst *Black Earth* is a heartfelt homage to Kilar's forefathers, blending rustic dance rhythms with an elegiac adagio and a grave, portentous march. Considering the age of some of these recordings the sound throughout this rewarding collection is perfectly acceptable.   **RS**

Also available:
Death and the Maiden (1994) Erato 4509-99727-2
Fantome avec Chauffeur (1996) Auvidis Travelling K1024
Portrait of a Lady (1996) London 455 011-2

Erich Wolfgang Korngold

1897-1957 Austria

Perhaps the most precocious musical genius since Mozart, Korngold's impact on film scoring cannot be over-exaggerated. The son of eminent Viennese music critic Dr Julius Korngold, his first major orchestral work *Der Schneemann* (*The Snowman*) was written when he was just 11 years old. The grandiose *Sinfonietta*, Op. 5 was penned at age 14. "One shudders with awe to realize these compositions were written by a boy", commented an admiring Richard Strauss. Korngold arrived in Hollywood in 1934 to score an adaptation of Mendelssohn's music for the Warner Brothers film version of *A Midsummer Night's Dream*; his next film experience was on *Give Us This Night* (1935), a totally forgotten musical, which did, however, lead to an offer to score a swashbuckler starring newcomer Errol Flynn, *Captain Blood*. He went on to compose music for some 16 more films over a 12-year period. Korngold abandoned film scoring in 1947, when his speciality historical romances had fallen out of fashion, as had his music with the 'serious' critics. He returned only briefly to movies in 1955 to arrange Wagner's music for the biopic *Magic Fire*. Korngold's musical style was firmly rooted in the late Germanic romanticism exemplified by Wagner and Richard Strauss. His virtuosic, histrionic, grandiloquent music seemed tailor-made for the melodramas and costume epics of Hollywood's Golden Age. This style made an indelible impact on the infant art of film scoring, although it has too often been transformed by lesser talent into second-rate pastiche. His influence is still felt today, notably via composers like John Williams, whose own grandiose scores for *Star Wars*, *Superman*, the *Indiana Jones* trilogy and *Hook*, amongst others, owe a stylistic debt to Korngold. All but ignored at his death, Korngold's ever-increasing reputation is due largely to the efforts of his son, producer George Korngold, and conductor Charles Gerhardt, whose pioneering recordings of many of his classic film scores prepared the way for a critical reappraisal of his entire output. The serious musical establishment would do well to take heed: they ignored Korngold for years ("more Korn than gold" was one critic's contemptuous dismissal of the Symphony in F sharp) before being belatedly reminded of his genius by mere film music.

The Adventures of Robin Hood (1938) **Utah Symphony Orchestra / Varujan Kojian**.
TER Ⓕ CDTER 1066 / Varèse Sarabande Ⓕ VCD47202 (43 minutes: DDD). Recorded 1983.

Not just the archetypal Korngold score, but the archetypal film score of all time, few can doubt that here is to be found the very best of Korngold's film work. It is full of everything we associate with him: extraordinarily virtuosic, enormously bold, gorgeously melodic, it plays like a summary of everything else he ever wrote. The concert overture *Sursum Corda*, Op. 13, written some 18 years earlier, provided Korngold with a suitably heroic theme for Flynn's dashing, full-colour Robin. Not even an established composer of his stature could escape the time constraints under which Hollywood musicians have always laboured: "The Escape from the Castle" is distilled almost entirely from the overture. In this form, the concert work which – dare I say it – seems a little overlong, is transformed by the conciseness of film scoring into an even more thrilling piece. There are more than a few other touches of genius here: the playful pastoral of "Robin Meets Little John", with strings imitating the strumming of Will Scarlet's lute, before the *Sursum Corda* theme returns for the good-natured confrontation; the "Ambush in Sherwood", during which a bombastic march for the approaching Normans is interrupted by rapid descending motifs for brass and woodwinds as Robin and his men swing down from the trees; the impossibly, anachronistically grand Viennese waltz which accompanies the "Feast in the Forest" (it shouldn't work – somehow it fits perfectly); and on and on. Each episode is portrayed musically, so that the listener hardly needs to see the film to understand the action. Kojian and the Utah Symphony perform splendidly, ably negotiating the intricacies of this virtuosic piece. **MW**

Kings Row (1942) **National Philharmonic Orchestra / Charles Gerhardt**.
Varèse Sarabande Ⓕ VCD47203 (48 minutes: DDD). Recorded 1979.

"[His] combination of a certain spiritual naïveté with the most fantastic flights of melodic, harmonic and orchestral imagination equipped Korngold superbly for the medium of the film score", wrote Christopher Palmer in his book *The Composer in Hollywood*. Nowhere is Korngold's "spiritual naïveté" more apparent than in this utterly transparent score: here is a composer unafraid to expose his heart. A bold and grandiose fanfare – which to everyone under 30 must sound like an amalgamation of the *Star Wars* and *Superman* themes, only better – somewhat unexpectedly introduces a melodramatic fable of small town America. The innocent play of "The Children" is accompanied by a tender variation of the main theme, which skips and frolics along with them; the enduring love of Randy and Drake (a legless Ronald Reagan); the starkly cold music for Cassie's madness; and the warmth of Parris's grandmother all stand out as highlights of the score. As the music progresses, its initially optimistic mood shifts into darkness and melodrama, until the main theme bursts forth in passionate triumph once more. Produced by the composer's son George Korngold, the CD is sequenced into just two tracks (reflecting the original LP split) which form a condensed suite of the whole (running to 67 minutes in the film). Thus, the work can – and should – be approached as 'pure' music, without reference to the original. Gerhardt and the National Philharmonic were used to Korngold by this stage, and perform with evident pleasure. Less action-packed than his Errol Flynn movies, *Kings Row* is one of Korngold's most sincerely emotional works. **MW**

The Private Lives of Elizabeth and Essex (1939) **Munich Symphony Orchestra / Carl Davis**.
Milan Ⓕ 873 122 (66 minutes: DDD). Recorded 1991.

Unlike other abridged versions of Korngold scores, this marvellous recording features the complete score for *The Private Lives of Elizabeth and Essex*. Carl Davis has obviously done his homework well, managing to duplicate all of Korngold's original tempos – not easy when contemplating a score so rich in varying moods. All Korngold's music was splendidly opulent, but this score – with its heady mix of regal and martial ceremony and unbridled romanticism – must be one of his most sumptuous. Yet there is no extraneous material here: every cue, down to each minute phrase, is a delight. The score's final sequence, detailing the sorry events leading to Lord Essex's execution, has an emotional impact that might be more readily associated with a Mahler symphony than film music – indeed, Korngold later utilized this powerful thematic material as the core of the *Adagio* for his own symphony. The performance is exemplary, proving the Munich Symphony Orchestra a world class ensemble, and confirming Carl Davis as a masterly conductor. The sound mix by engineer Mike Ross-Trevor is of demonstration standard. **DW**

The Sea Hawk (1940) **Carol Wetzel** (mez); **Utah Symphony Chorus and Orchestra / Varujan Kojian**.
TER ⓔ CDTER1164 / Varèse Sarabande ⓔ VCD47304 (44 minutes: DDD). Recorded 1987.

Nobody could buckle and swash like Errol Flynn, but would he have cut such a dashing figure without Korngold's thrilling support? When he and his Sea Hawks boldly stride into Queen Elizabeth's court; when they break free of their bonds and capture the Spanish galleon, Korngold is with them, infusing their deeds with larger-than-life heroism. When Flynn crosses swords with the dastardly villain (for once, not Basil Rathbone) Korngold's music seems to set the screen alight; when the chorus breaks in with "Strike for the Shores of Dover!" even modern, hard-hearted cynics must relent and raise a cheer. The score for this blood-stirring nautical adventure is an irresistible treat. It has all the ingredients any film score could want: rousing fanfares, sombre marches, touching romance and spine-tingling action. This is even more of a roller-coaster ride than *Robin Hood*, and a treasure-trove of arresting themes (some of which have been 'borrowed' by more recent composers). The delightful "Doña Maria's Song" was later reworked by Korngold as *Alt-spanisch Lied*, Op. 38 No. 3 – thereby providing 'serious' critics with another nail for his coffin; and further proof that taking notice of critics impairs your enjoyment of seriously great music. **MW**

New review
The Sea Hawk The Classic Film Scores of Erich Wolfgang Korngold. [a]**Ambrosian Singers**; **National Philharmonic Orchestra / Charles Gerhardt**.
RCA Victor Ⓜ 7890-2 (70 minutes: ADD). Recorded 1972-74.
The Sea Hawk (1940)[a]. Of Human Bondage (1946). Between Two Worlds (1944). The Sea Wolf (1941). The Constant Nymph (1943)[a]. Kings Row (1942). Anthony Adverse (1936). Deception (1946). Devotion (1946). Escape Me Never (1947).

When RCA was first approached by producer George Korngold to record an album of his father's music, they were only interested in the untapped commercial possibilities represented by his film scores. The intuition of the RCA record executives was correct, as "The Sea Hawk" spent eight weeks at the top of the classical charts. The series was expanded to include other Golden Age masters such as Newman, Rózsa, Waxman, and Steiner. The end result was an improvement in the critical acceptance of Golden Age film music. Thanks to "The Sea Hawk" album, the once-proud reputation of Erich Wolfgang Korngold was restored. Ironically, it would be the very art form that Korngold was insecure about working in that became responsible for this revival. A plethora of excellent Korngold recordings have come out since, but it all began with this album.

The longer playing time offered by CDs allowed Charles Gerhardt and the late George Korngold (whom the conductor eulogizes in an explanatory note) to include previously unused selections on this disc. The National Philharmonic Orchestra – a much larger ensemble than the 54-piece one originally used by Korngold – add strength and definition to ten of the composer's best scores. The disc opens with *The Sea Hawk* itself, a late-romantic recipe of swashbuckling fanfares and broad, tonal melodies. Vienna is omnipresent throughout the program, as is Korngold's monophonic tendencies and distaste for dissonance. The music is operatic in its sense of a flowing, continuous drama, a parallel enforced further by his love of *leitmotifs*. The cine-music narrative is interrupted only by a choral break ("Strike for the Shores of Dover") and a brief excursion into exotica. The newly-expanded 12-minute suite from *Of Human Bondage* includes the lush theme for "Nora", a *scherzo* for "Christmas" and the lovely "Sally" music. *The Sea Wolf* finds the composer in a darker, more harmonically complex realm – Captain Wolf Larson would have approved. *The Constant Nymph* is represented by the tone poem "Tomorrow", featuring contralto Norma Procter and the Ambrosian Singers. The famous, albeit brief "Main Title" from *Kings Row* is an obligatory inclusion, as are the excerpts from the Oscar-winning score for *Anthony Adverse* (the first of his two statues). Sad music accompanies the death of Emily Brontë in *Devotion*, a dramatization of the literary sisters' lives. The disc ends with a suite from *Escape Me Never*, a film best left undiscussed. The score, however, is a seminar on melody writing, with no fewer than ten included in the suite. **KM**

The Prince and the Pauper (1937) – see **Steiner**: The Adventures of Mark Twain

Also available:
Another Dawn (1937) **Escape Me Never** (1947) (Moscow SO/Stromberg) Marco Polo 8 223871
Anthony Adverse (1936) (Berlin RSO/Scott) Varèse Sarabande VSD5285
Between Two Worlds (1944) **Symphonic Serenade** etc. (Berlin RSO/Mauceri) Decca 444 170-2
The Warner Brothers Years (original soundtracks – 2 CDs) EMI CDODEON13

see also Collections: **Captain Blood**

Francis Lai

b. 1932 France

Born in Nice, Francis Lai scored an early international hit with the film *Un Homme et une Femme* (1965), which also won him an Academy Award nomination. This led to further scoring assignments outside of France, both in Britain and Hollywood, although Lai continues to work mainly in French cinema. In 1970 he received an Oscar for *Love Story*. Other scores include *Mayerling* (1968), *Hannibal Brooks* (1969), *Bilitis* (1977), *International Velvet* (1978) and *A Man and a Woman: 20 Years Later* (1986).

New review

Un Homme et une Femme (1965) **Vivre pour Vivre** (1967) **Original Soundtracks / Francis Lai**.
DRG Ⓕ 12612 (59 minutes: AAD).

The theme from *Un Homme et une Femme* (*A Man and a Woman*), with its cheesy electric piano and husky 'da-ba-da-ba-da' vocals is so firmly rooted in the 1960s that today it almost sounds like a newly-written parody of the era. However, the music, like Claude Lelouch's film, was considered to be the height of French chic at the time and despite countless cover recordings it remains resolutely catchy. The score features a number of other songs with lyrics by Pierre Barouh, one of which, "Aujord'hui c'est toi" ("Today it's you"), would later become better known in the UK as the theme to BBC TV's *Panorama* (though not in the version heard here). Scored for an intimate grouping of instruments the overall sound could perhaps be described as minimalist cocktail music. Lelouch followed this international success with *Vivre pour Vivre* (*Live for Life*), and although neither this film nor its main theme (inevitably a close relative of the earlier hit) would mirror the popularity of *Un Homme et une Femme*, Lai's more liberal use of the orchestra and his more expansive scoring is still supremely evocative of the decade.   **RS**

Also available:
Love Story (1970) MCA MCLD19157

Michel Legrand

b. 1932 France

The son of French film composer Raymond Legrand, Legrand was born in Paris, and studied at the Conservatoire National de Musique. His penchant for popular music led him to become an accompanist, conductor and songwriter for artists such as Maurice Chevalier and Jacques Brel. His first film score came in 1955, although it was not until the 1964 film *Les Parapluies de Cherbourg* that he achieved international prominence. Several of his songs became international hits, including "I Will Wait for You" (English lyrics by Norman Gimbel) from *Parapluies*, "Watch What Happens" from *Lola* (1960) also with Gimbel, as well as "You Must Believe in Spring" from 1967's *Les Demoiselles de Rochefort* and "What Are You Doing the Rest of Your Life?" from *The Happy Ending* (1969) – both with lyrics by Alan and Marilyn Bergman. Legrand moved to Hollywood in 1968 and had further success with *The Thomas Crown Affair* ("The Windmills of Your Mind"). He won an Academy Award for *Summer of '42* (1971). He has also recorded several jazz albums, and scored the 1991 film *Dingo* with Miles Davis.

Never Say Never Again (1983) **Original Soundtrack / Michel Legrand**.
Silva Screen Ⓕ FILMCD145 (62 minutes: DDD).

By no means a classic, Michel Legrand's score for Sean Connery's Bond comeback vehicle does, however, contain some nifty orchestral sequences, and the familiar jazz riffs that are Legrand's speciality. Across some 26 cues – ranging in length from 25 seconds to five minutes – much typical James Bond-style music can be heard, reminiscent in places of that other non-Barry score, Burt Bacharach's *Casino Royale* (1967). The logic of playing an enjoyable Legrand/Bergman title song (sung by Lani Hall) over a shot of Sean Connery attempting to scale a well-fortified installation may have escaped us when watching the movie, but fortunately the song works perfectly well on its own. This is a disc that will appeal both to Bond fans and lovers of Legrand's music. It is just a pity that his magnificent *Wuthering Heights* (1970) score is not currently available on CD.   **JW**

Also available:
Le Monde est un Grand Chelm (1996) Auvidis Travelling K1023
Les Parapluies de Cherbourg (1964), **Summer of '42** (1971) **Yentl** (1983) **The Go Between** (1971) – suites. Auvidis Travelling K1020

Michael J. Lewis

b. 1939 Wales

Hailing from Aberystwyth, Michael Lewis began his musical career as a choirboy aged six; at ten he was promoted to church organist (thus enabling him to develop improvisation skills whilst filling in for brides late for their weddings). He studied harmony, counterpoint and composition at the Guildhall School of Music and Drama, London. Hearing Walton's oratorio *Belshazzar's Feast* for the first time convinced Lewis that his future lay in large-scale dramatic writing; a love for the classics of cinema, combined with seeing the new James Bond films during the early 1960s, naturally suggested to Lewis that he should try his hand at film scoring. His first score, *The Madwoman of Chaillot* (1969), was awarded the Ivor Novello Prize for Best Score. In 1973 his musical *Cyrano*, co-written with Anthony Burgess and starring Christopher Plummer, opened on Broadway. Lewis's first Hollywood picture came in 1982, Franklin J. Schaffner's *Yes, Giorgio* which starred Luciano Pavarotti. In 1995 he formed his own record label, Pen Dinas – named after a favourite Welsh hill of his boyhood – in order to release his past scores. He is currently based in Los Angeles.

Orchestral Film Music The First Twenty-Five Years, 1969-1994. **Berlin Radio Orchestra; Los Angeles Ensemble / Michael J. Lewis.**
Pen Dinas Ⓕ PD-951 (two discs, 117 minutes: DDD).
Julius Caesar (1970). The Medusa Touch (1978). The Naked Face (1985). Theatre of Blood (1973). The Madwoman of Chaillot (1969). The Passage (1978). The Hound of the Baskervilles (1983). 92 in the Shade (1979). Sphinx (1980). The Stick-Up (1974). The Rose and the Jackal (1990). The Unseen (1981). North Sea Hijack [Ffoulkes] (1979). Upon This Rock (1970).

When it was first issued, this double CD of music from the career of Michael J. Lewis attracted unreservedly enthusiastic reviews in the soundtrack press. Can it really be that good? Well, yes it can. This is the best compilation of music from films so far released. All of Lewis's films have a built-in flow of seemingly endless beautiful melody. *Julius Caesar* is on a par with John Scott's mammoth *Antony and Cleopatra*, so much so that the 11 or so minutes heard here makes one yearn for the complete score. *The Medusa Touch* with its organ climaxes and vibrant power is quite staggering and one of Michael's most requested scores, whilst *Theatre of Blood*, a horrific subject if ever there was one, is subtly contrasted by an exquisite piano and harpsichord theme. Bryan Forbes was responsible for Michael's first big break with *The Madwoman of Chaillot*. Three cues from that lovely score are presented here, including the superb "Aurelia's Theme", which must be one of the most beautiful themes ever heard in the cinema. It still packs a punch now as it did when it was first heard in 1969. The double CD finishes on a real cracker: a suite from *Upon This Rock*, a television documentary about St Peter's in Rome. This magnificent score is as powerful as anything that North or Rózsa could have ever done. As said, this is the best compilation of music ... until Michael brings out Volume 2. **JW**

Joseph LoDuca

USA

Trained as a guitarist, Joseph LoDuca's musical background is in jazz. After a stint touring the New York jazz clubs and studying music privately, he returned to his home state of Michigan (where he still lives) and began composing in addition to his concert activities. A record producer introduced him to director and producer Sam Raimi and Rob Tapert who were then planning to shoot an independent horror film called *The Evil Dead*. LoDuca was asked to write the score, which was recorded in an attic studio using five string players, one old synthesizer, some miscellaneous percussion and a prepared piano. He has since scored several other genre movies, in addition to the *Evil Dead* sequels – including *Crimewave* (1985), *Moontrap* (1989) and *Necronomicon* (1993) – and won eight Emmy Awards for his television work. His association with Raimi and Tapert has continued with the spooky TV series *American Gothic*, as well as the highly successful *Hercules: The Legendary Journeys* , and its spin-off *Xena: Warrior Princess*.

The Evil Dead (1982) **Original Soundtrack / Joseph LoDuca.**
Varèse Sarabande Ⓕ VSD5362 (36 minutes: ADD).
Army of Darkness: Evil Dead III (1992) **Original Soundtrack**, with the **Seattle Symphony Chorus and Orchestra / Tim Simonec.**
Varèse Sarabande Ⓕ VSD5411 (51 minutes: DDD). Includes *March of the Dead* (Danny Elfman).

Sam Raimi's ultra-low budget, tongue-in-cheek horror flick (originally shot in 16mm) was gruesome enough simultaneously to make fans ecstatic and censors apoplectic. LoDuca's chaotic score will undoubtedly provoke similarly opposite reactions. The colourless sonority of a small string-based chamber ensemble, the tuneless dissonance of percussion and synthesized effects, the deliberate avoidance of any warmth or melody – it all adds up to a distinctively original work which will either attract admiration or abhorrence. Taking full advantage of a significantly bigger budget for the third instalment, LoDuca penned a grandly epic score which musters all the energy of a full-sized orchestra and chorus. No longer are we confronted with unremitting horror: heroic themes, sumptuous orchestrations, and attractively full-blooded medievalisms make this a much more ear-pleasing work than his grim original. LoDuca's emphasis on action/adventure over horror inevitably means that *Army of Darkness* lacks the bone-chilling novelty of his first score, although for many this will be a reason to prefer it. Danny Elfman adds a small but characteristically gothic contribution.   **MW**

New review

Hercules: The Legendary Journeys (1994) **Original Soundtracks / Tim Simonec**.
    Varèse Sarabande Ⓕ VSD5660 (64 minutes: DDD).
    Hercules and the Circle of Fire. Hercules and the Lost Kingdom. Hercules and the Amazon Women. Hercules and the Underworld.
Xena: Warrior Princess (1995) **Original Soundtrack / Tim Simonec, Randy Thornton**.
    Varèse Sarabande Ⓕ VSD5750 (66 minutes: DDD).

It could only happen in America: the greatest hero of Greek mythology, the formidable, terrible Herakles transformed into a good-natured, musclebound all-American boy, living only to right wrongs, save small children from computer-generated monsters and flutter his eyelashes at admiring gaggles of scantily-clad women. *Hercules* the series may pack the intellectual clout of *Baywatch* meets *Jason and the Argonauts*, but it's all done with such naïve, empty-headed charm that even the most cynical of viewers can't help but enjoy it. Rather than go for the obvious and plunder Greek mythology for storylines, the producers often opt for gleeful take-offs of Hollywood movies (one episode featured a fearsome female Terminator, in an outrageous send-up of *T2*), and Joseph LoDuca's entertaining scores follow much the same path, the music lurching with carefree abandon from snatches of *Jurassic Park* to *RoboCop* to *The Omen*. The "Main Title" is rip-roaringly heroic in the *Indiana Jones* mould. But it's all executed with tongue firmly in cheek, and LoDuca adds his own more original contribution in the form of some 'exotic' instrumentation – is that a duduk? – an alternately heavenly and demonic choir, and even a few enjoyably silly bits of 'period' music. A presumably generous budget allows scope for a large, movie-sized orchestra considerably enhanced by synthesizers. So long as you don't take it seriously, this is seriously good fun.

    The *Hercules* spin-off, *Xena*, is apparently an admission that the series' principal attraction is the opportunity to see the above-mentioned scantily-clad (and well-endowed) females attired in interesting leather outfits outdoing their male counterparts in the high-kicking and carousing stakes. LoDuca's music is darker here than in *Hercules*, with jagged, percussive rhythms, fiercely chanting female choir and a harsher tone achieved by using more distinctively non-Western, non-Hollywood idioms. The sunny pastiche that was *Hercules* is replaced by a more distinctive sound, an extension of the 'ethnic' style developed for the original series, by turns strident and forbidding. It's a stronger disc as a result, with grandiose music of real drama and intense passion, though few touches of humour. The choral singing, modelled on traditional eastern European and Arabic styles is one of the disc's most evocative elements; a lack of strong, readily identifiable themes is its weakness, giving the ear little in the way of light relief. Xena herself, Lucy Lawless, adds her own vocal contribution, "Burial".   **MW**

Also available:
Evil Dead II (1987) TER CDTER1142

Mark Mancina
b. 1957 USA

Hailing from Santa Monica, Mark Mancina had his first piano lessons aged five, then took up the classical guitar. He studied music composition and solo performance (guitar) at California State Fullerton and Golden West College. But Mancina had grown up listening to British 'progressive' rock bands like Yes, Genesis, Emerson, Lake and Palmer and Jethro Tull, so his classical studies notwithstanding, he formed a rock band, Dexter. Yes guitarist Trevor Rabin was so impressed by Dexter's performance that he hired Mancina to play keyboards on his solo tour. Together, they wrote songs for the Yes album "Union". The Yes connection led to work with producer Trevor Horn, and further production work with Emerson, Lake and Palmer. He worked with Hans Zimmer on *Days of Thunder* (1990), which led to further collaborations with Zimmer – including producing some of the songs for his Oscar-winning *The Lion King* (1994). Mancina also wrote scores for the TV series *Millenium* and *Space Rangers*. As a result of his work on Zimmer's score for *True Romance* (1993) he was hired by director Jan De Bont to write his first full-length feature film score, *Speed* (1994). De Bont was so impressed he worked with Mancina again on his next picture, *Twister* (1996). Other scores include *Monkey Trouble* (1994), *Bad Boys, Assassins, Man of the House* (all 1995) and *Moll Flander*s (1996). Mancina composes entirely on synthesizers: using the latest technology he is able to produce a mock-up of the final score before it has even been seen by an orchestra. An album with Trevor Rabin is planned.

Speed (1994) **Original Soundtrack / Don Harper**.
    Milan Ⓟ 23465-2 (41 minutes: DDD).

From edge-of-the-seat tension to the all out adrenalin rush, Mark Mancina's joyfully unsubtle music is the perfect example of a contemporary action score. *Speed* successfully integrates a 'standard' orchestra within a predominantly synthesized framework. A simple main theme, usually stated by the conventional forces, is given extra impetus by underlying drums and sequencer figures. Mancina's score works best when he exploits the tension created by contrasting this broad orchestral theme with a punchy synth action motif, as in the cue "Rush Hour". Appropriately enough, Hans Zimmer's glorious *Backdraft* is obviously the model for this score, but Mancina is no slavish imitator. If certain 'atmospheric' synthesized cues are largely devoid of musical interest away from the screen, *Speed* is nevertheless a concrete demonstration that the marriage of synthesizers and orchestras does not always have to be one of convenience.   **MW**

New review
Twister (1996) **Original Soundtrack, with Trevor Rabin, Doug Smith** (gtrs); **L.A. Master Choral / Paul Salamunovich**.
    Atlantic Ⓟ 82954-2 (51 minutes: DDD). Includes *Respect the Wind* (Edward and Alex Van Halen).

For Jan De Bont's visually gripping but dramatically empty special effects extravaganza, Mark Mancina expanded on the orchestral/synthesizer approach of *Speed*, giving more prominence to the 120-piece orchestra whilst maintaining the very distinctive, Hans Zimmer-inspired synthesized action. The attraction of Mancina's music lies in his very approachable grasp of melody, in which well-defined solo lines are supported but not obscured by busy rhythmic underpinning (a result of his guitar training, no doubt). *Twister* features an attention-grabbing opening theme scored for conventional forces which, if not actually Coplandesque, is certainly a splendid piece of sunny Americana. A large choir, another feature familiar from Zimmer's work (*Crimson Tide*, for example), adds weight and depth to the musical depiction of whirling tornados, and percussive synthesizer patterns drive the action on. The orchestral writing is richer, more inventive than *Speed*, where it did little more than carry the main theme: here, Mancina's orchestration gives woodwinds, brass and strings different things to do, achieving some contrasting moods as a result: by turns threatening, hymn-like and celebratory. Combined with the awe-struck choir and excitable synths, this makes for a varied and often enthralling (but a little overlong) modern action score, enhanced in places by Trevor Rabin's guitar. "Respect the Wind", which functions as the "End Title" is an absorbing, if rather overlong piece of magical Eddie Van Halen axework.   **MW**

Also available:
Moll Flanders (1996) London 452 485-2

Henry Mancini
1924-1994 America

A gifted composer, arranger, conductor and pianist, Henry Mancini's melodies – from *The Pink Panther* theme to "Moon River" – have achieved enormous success around the world. Born Enrico Mancini in Cleveland, Ohio, Mancini took early flute and piano lessons, and studied with conductor Max Adkins, before enrolling at the Juilliard School in 1942. After war service he worked as pianist and arranger for the Tex Beneke 'Glenn Miller-style' Orchestra. Mancini studied privately in Los Angeles with Mario Castelnuovo-Tedesco and Ernst Krenek, and began an apprenticeship at Universal Studios in 1952. As one of a team of staff composers, Mancini worked – often uncredited – on over 100 films between 1952 and 1958; these included contributions to many B-movies like *Creature from the Black Lagoon* (1954) and *It Came from Outer Space* (1953) – collective efforts credited to Universal's music director Joseph Gershenson (see also Hans Salter). He adapted music for both *The Glenn Miller Story* (1954) and *The Benny Goodman Story* (1955) and scored Orson Welles's *Touch of Evil* (1958). In 1958 his contract was abruptly terminated; but producer Blake Edwards asked the recently unemployed composer to score his new TV show about a private detective, *Peter Gunn*. Mancini and Edwards continued their collaboration with *Breakfast at Tiffanys* (1961), which featured the first of a series of hit songs written with lyricist Johnny Mercer, "Moon River". The partnership continued with *The Pink Panther* (1964) and all subsequent sequels. Mancini's success with these light comedy pieces had the unfortunate effect of type-casting him. His dramatic, darker music for pictures like *The Molly Maguires* (1970) and *The White Dawn* (1974) were linked with box office failures; whilst his score for Hitchcock's *Frenzy* (1972) was rejected because it was "too menacing". Despite his wide-ranging talent and the sheer variety of his film work, Mancini will always be remembered as the composer who created the quintessential sound of the 1960s.

Breakfast at Tiffany's (1961) Henry Mancini Chorus and Orchestra / Henry Mancini.
RCA Ⓜ 2362-2 (35 minutes: ADD).

This was an early collaboration for the big screen between Henry Mancini and director Blake Edwards. *Breakfast at Tiffany's* was an international success, and went on to win Academy Awards for Best Song, the haunting "Moon River", and Best Score. Audrey Hepburn, plucking a guitar, sang Johnny Mercer's lyric on the soundtrack and though never issued commercially (it has surfaced recently outside this collection), its omission, though regrettable, was softened by Mancini's lovely choral arrangement, a trademark of so many of his title songs like *Days of Wine and Roses* and *Charade*. It was surely the star's gamin-like look on screen that inspired the dreamy glockenspiel-led title tune, this time with wordless chorus, and "Holly", where the melody floats along on muted trumpet. Other cues revelled in the current fashion for Latin rhythms and Mancini's exploration of percussion effects, which were taken a step further in *Hatari!*. Although the playing time is far from generous, this CD makes a happy introduction to a master practitioner of light music.   **AE**

Charade (1963) Henry Mancini Chorus and Orchestra / Henry Mancini.
RCA Ⓜ 2755-2 (30 minutes: ADD).

Stanley Donen's stylish comedy-thriller *Charade* represents a genre of movie making that has all but disappeared from our screens as the stars of that era, like Cary Grant and Audrey Hepburn, retired in quick succession: Grant in 1966 and Hepburn the following year (albeit she did reappear in *Robin and Marian* seven years later). Mancini's score mirrors the elegance and sophistication of the players in their Parisan setting, with the main title on electric guitar adding an air of suspense to the tight corners that Cary Grant is lured into. Other cues, like "Latin Snowfall", "Orange Tamouré" and "The Drip-Dry Waltz" don't disappoint in their mixture of inventive and colourful scoring whilst the bewitching title song, with Johnny Mercer's haunting lyric, probably only lost the Academy Award on account of there being three wins in a row for this team. Its appearance in the fairground scene as "The Happy Carousel" is an inspired idea. Personally, I'm happy to believe that there is no more entertaining CD of film music than this currently on offer.   **AE**

Mancini in Surround Mostly Monsters, Murders and Mysteries. Mancini Pops Orchestra / Henry Mancini.
RCA Victor Ⓕ RD60471 (61 minutes: DDD). Recorded 1990.
Surround Fantastique. The White Dawn (1974). Mommie Dearest (1981). Frenzy (1972). Creature from the Black Lagoon (1954). It Came from Outer Space (1953). Tarantula (1955). Fear (1990). The Man Who Loved Women (1983). The Prisoner of Zenda (1979). Nightwing (1979). Without a Clue (1988). Sunset (1988).

Mancini's craftsmanship and versatility were really quite remarkable, and yet it is very easy to pass him off simply as the writer of glossily packaged melodies without any regard for his intuitive talent for scoring drama. This disc is perhaps one of the most revealing Mancini ever recorded – for the emphasis here is just as much on character and mood as it is on light romance, with *Mommie Dearest*, *Fear*, *Sunset* and his rejected music from *Frenzy* all appropriately downbeat and far removed from the breezy and more recognizably high-spirited Mancini of *Without a Clue* and *The Prisoner of Zenda*. It is also interesting to compare the pounding histrionics of the monster movies he scored during his early and often anonymous career at Universal with the unsettling subtlety of *Nightwing*, a much later horror film. A highly rewarding tribute to a much-missed master.   **RS**

Mancini's Greatest Hits Cincinnati Pops / Erich Kunzel.
Telarc Ⓕ CD80183 (68 minutes: DDD).
The Pink Panther (1964). Breakfast at Tiffany's (1961). Days of Wine and Roses (1962). The White Dawn (1974). Mr Lucky (1959). Hatari! (1962). The Thorn Birds (1983). Charade (1963). Moment to Moment (1966). The Great Waldo Pepper (1975). Two for the Road (1967). The Molly Maguires (1970). Dear Heart (1964). The Great Race (1965). Peter Gunn (1958). Victor Victoria (1982). What Did You Do in the War, Daddy? (1966) plus Symphonic Soul. Drummer's Delight. Strings on Fire. March of the Cue Balls.

It might be thought that only the man himself could conjure that special Mancini magic, but Erich Kunzel, who can often be found offering his own individualistic interpretation of film music, here expertly duplicates the authentic Mancini 'sound' – tempos, playing, choral settings and ambience are all spot-on – it could be the composer himself at the helm. This is an album stuffed with goodies – all the Mancini standards seem to be here – and whilst Mancini will be primarily remembered for a profusion of haunting melodies and songs from "Moon River" to "Charade", this album also celebrates his uncanny knack for comedy scores, with the main theme for *The Pink Panther* a prime example; and illuminates his contribution to the big band via the irresistible *Peter Gunn*. Faced with this wealth of romantic melody, foot-stompin' jazz and comedic symphonic shenanigans it can be forgotten just how good a dramatic composer Mancini could be: vital cues from *Hatari!*, *The White Dawn* and *The Molly Maguires* redress the balance, although this last elegantly 'oirish' piece appears in a more commercial guise than that utilized for the film soundtrack. So, all facets of Mancini's talent are embodied, and at 67 minutes, with thirty selections all perfectly realized, this is as good a retrospective or a tribute as could be hoped for. It is essential Mancini. Without doubt, this is a desert island disc. **DW**

The Pink Panther (1963) **Henry Mancini Chorus and Orchestra / Henry Mancini**.
    RCA Ⓜ ND80832 (30 minutes: AAD).
Revenge of the Pink Panther (1978) **Original Soundtrack / Henry Mancini**.
    EMI Ⓕ CDP7 91113-2 (40 minutes: ADD).
The Trail of the Pink Panther (1982) **Original Soundtrack / Henry Mancini**.
    EMI Ⓕ CDP7 90627-2 (42 minutes: DDD).
Son of the Pink Panther (1993) **Original Soundtrack / Henry Mancini**.
    Milan Ⓕ 66319-2 (36 minutes: DDD).

The light jazz-tinged compositions that Henry Mancini gave us in Breakfast at Tiffany's were polished to perfection by the time he composed The Pink Panther, whose theme in all probability is the most readily identifiable in movie history. Style was of the essence first time round, not only in Mancini's music but in the deft playing of David Niven, his co-stars Capucine and Claudia Cardinale, dressed by Yves St Laurent, and in the meticulous sight gags director Blake Edwards constructed round them. But if it was Peter Sellers's portrayal of the bumbling detective that most likely gained this series immortality, Mancini's score put the gilt on the presentation. The humour of the Panther theme, the jolly Latin excursion to It Had Better Be Tonight, the smooth mixed choral group that re-inforces the melodic lines on certain numbers all became familiar trademarks as the sometimes uneven series progressed. Unlike the James Bond films, a series that commenced at roughly the same time, the Panther films have always been entrusted to one composer, Henry Mancini, who scored the last of them, The Son of the Pink Panther, shortly before his death. The film, alas, was a box office disaster in America and remains unknown in Britain. But, box office performance doesn't necessarily spell a poor soundtrack (witness Mancini's Darling Lili), and in The Trail of the Pink Panther, a virtual musical reprise of all that's gone before, we have most of the highlights including the otherwise unavailable "A Shot in the Dark", the jolly "Hong Kong Fireworks" and "It Had Better Be Tonight" from the first Panther. This happy compilation also includes the Inspector Clouseau theme – a charming little study in percussion scoring, and The Pink Panther theme in two fairly free jazz permutations. Much of that material can be heard on Revenge along with Peter Sellers's "Thank Heaven for Little Girls". Son of the Pink Panther has Bobby McFerrin with a new a cappella treatment of the Panther theme alongside much new material that shows no waning of Mancini's aural imagination in his final work for the movies. **AE**

New review
Touch of Evil (1958) **Original Soundtrack / Henry Mancini**.
    Varèse Sarabande Ⓕ VSD5414 (51 minutes: AAD).

Touch of Evil was Henry Mancini's first major film score after an extensive and largely anonymous career providing music for many of Universal's second-feature Westerns and Sci-Fi monster movies. Though it bears the master's unmistakable flair for melody, this is not the lushly romantic Mancini we know from scores like *Breakfast at Tiffany's* or *Charade*, nor is it a typical example of dramatic underscoring. As director and star, Orson Welles, was opposed to having a traditional Hollywood-style score much of the film's music is heard coming from radios or jukeboxes. With the emphasis therefore firmly on the popular music trends of the late 1950s – rock 'n' roll, Latin American and big band blues – the score is as entertaining as any of the celebrated band albums Mancini was recording for RCA during this period. But the hard, slightly sinister edge Mancini brings to his superbly-crafted arrangements, particularly on the nerve-jangling Afro-Cuban numbers Welles desired (as exemplified by the taut seven-minute cue "Background to Murder", an extended version of the music that accompanies the film's famous opening tracking shot), not only complements the Mexican border town setting but also infuses each scene with a unique and almost nightmarish sense of menace. *RS*

Also available:
The Adventures of the Great Mouse Detective (1992) Varèse Sarabande VSD5359
Hatari! (1962) RCA 2559-2

Lifeforce (1985) CDFMC256
Mr Lucky (1959) RCA 2198-2
Peter Gunn (1958) RCA 1956-2
Premier Pops Denon CO2320
Switch (1991) Varèse Sarabande VSD5312
Tom and Jerry: The Movie (1992) MCA MCAD10721
The Ultimate Collection RCA 74321 24283-2
Victor/Victoria (1982) GNP Crescendo GNPD8038

Brian May

b.1934 Australia

Born in Adelaide, Brian May studied the piano before receiving formal musical training at Adelaide's Elder Conservatorium. During a stint in the army May composed music for brass band. Becoming musical director for the Australian Broadcasting Corporation he achieved prominence as director of the ABC Show Band, with whom he made many award-winning recordings. It was May's symphonic arrangement of the musical *Hair* which led to offers of film work. He wrote scores for dozens of Australian films like *The True Story of Eskimo Nell* (1975), *Patrick* (1978), *The Day After Halloween* (1979) and *Harlequin* (1980), but it was the low-budget action movie *Mad Max* (1979) which brought him international fame. May now divides his time between Hollywood film assignments and domestic concerts. He is the composer of *A Gift of Life* for the Australian Ballet and the musical *Jewel of the Orient Express*.

Death Before Dishonour (1986) **Original Soundtrack**, with the **Melbourne Film Symphony Orchestra / Brian May**.
   Prometheus Ⓟ PCD118 (39 minutes: DDD).

Another forgettable B-movie is graced with a highly inventive Brian May score. The Marine's Hymn ("From the Halls of Montezuma") forms the basis of May's "Main Title", which is later repeated in a sombre arrangement in "Heroic Deeds". 'Exotic' percussion and woodwind are incidentally employed to establish a Middle-Eastern flavour, but it is the kinetic action scenes which remain memorable, with their stabbing chords, brass flourishes and pulsing rhythms which identify this score as coming from the same pen as the composer of *Mad Max*. The climactic "Ambush/Weapons Truck Chase" is the most effective. Admirers of May's *Max* scores will find much in a similar vein to enjoy here. **MW**

Mad Max (1979) **Original Soundtrack / Brian May**.
   Varèse Sarabande Ⓟ VCD47144 (38 minutes: ADD).
Mad Max 2 [The Road Warrior] (1981) **Original Soundtrack / Brian May**.
   Varèse Sarabande Ⓟ VCD47262 (35 minutes: DDD).

Mel Gibson's first major role was also the vehicle which propelled composer Brian May into the spotlight. May's energetic, all-action score belies its origins for what was an ultra low-budget movie by an unknown director, featuring an unknown lead man, and all of them Australian! The percussive main title hurls us straight into the thick of the action. An heroic horn call for the leather-clad Max is the score's principal theme, but the rest of the orchestra is too impatient to allow it any leisurely development. Menacing Bernard Herrmann-esque chords, jagged rhythms, propulsive string figures and angrily growling brass force the music ever onwards. A melancholy love theme (track 14) hardly has time to begin before it is cut short, and the music continues on its helter-skelter journey. The final track is a six-minute suite of outtakes.
   Mad Max 2 is a darker, grander work. The composer reprises little of the original music (Max's horn call resurfaces in a variant version) and the orchestration is thicker, intensified in places by electronics. The mood is enigmatic, not action-dominated, with murky bass strings, brass and woodwinds working in unison to generate a sinister atmosphere. The "End Title" is a sombre piece for strings over an ostinato bass. As the film itself is an amalgam of various genre influences, so May's score occasionally hints at its models: *Star Wars* being perhaps the most obvious. The concluding track is a 'suite' of sound effects, with the cue "Break Out" repeated so that the listener can hear how May has tailored his music to augment and enhance the FX. **MW**

Also available:
Dr Giggles (1992) Intrada MAF7043D
Nightmare on Elm Street VI (1993) Varèse Sarabande VSD5333

Toshiro Mayuzumi

b. 1929 Japan

Born in Yokohama, Toshiro Mayuzumi studied with Ikenouchi and Ifukube at the Tokyo Geijutsu Daigaku, graduating in 1951. His early compositions were cast in a traditionally late romantic mould, sometimes flavoured with jazz. *Sphenogrammes* brought him international success when it was performed at the 1951 ISCM Festival. Mayuzumi studied briefly at the Paris Conservatoire, before returning to Japan where he introduced several modernist and avant-garde techniques. He has worked extensively in Japanese theatre and written many film scores, including *Akasen-chitai (Street of Shame)* (1956) which was the first Japanese film to use electronic music, and 1965's *Tokyo Olympiad* which won the Mainichi Music Prize.

The Bible [La Bibbia] (1966) **Original Soundtrack / Franco Ferrara**.
RCA Ⓕ OST115 (45 minutes: AAD).

In the world of Biblical film scores, this is something of a fascinating hybrid. All the expected elements are here, the large orchestra, the heavenly choir, the marches and the fanfares, and yet *The Bible* sounds quite different compared to Hollywood companions like *Ben-Hur* or *The Robe*. Instead of emulating Rózsa and Newman, Mayuzumi plumps for an early twentieth-century style that combines the lush opulence of Respighi (as in the main theme) with an occasional Stravinskian astringency ("40 Days and 40 Nights") to end up sounding vaguely avant-garde, but always intriguing; the most striking moments being the ecstatic chorale that describes the creation of Eve and the effectively lugubrious march of the animals into the Ark.   **RS**

Dennis McCarthy

USA

Beginning his musical career as arranger and conductor for Glen Campbell, Dennis McCarthy also briefly worked as an orchestrator for Alex North. His first scores were for the television series *Enos* in 1980, followed by further TV assignments such as *Private Benjamin* and *Goodnight Beantown*. McCarthy's successful score for the Science Fiction mini-series *V – The Final Battle* led to him scoring the entire follow-up series. McCarthy has been associated with *Star Trek: The Next Generation* since its original pilot episode, *Encounter at Farpoint*, in 1987. McCarthy's music adorns over half of the entire 178-episode run: a total of some 80 hours of score over a seven-year period. He won an Emmy Award for his work on the episode *Unification Part 1*. McCarthy's association with *Trek* continues on both *Deep Space Nine* and *Voyager*.

Star Trek: Generations (1994) **Original Soundtrack /** Dennis McCarthy.
GNP Crescendo Ⓕ GNPD8040 (61 minutes: DDD). Tracks 16-38 are sound effects.

Dennis McCarthy's first big screen venture is a competent effort which will please admirers of his *Next Generation* TV scores. The best comes first, with an opening "Overture" which contains his own march-like principal theme, together with an atmospheric wordless chorus. The chorus returns, alongside synthesizers, to impart an impressionistic feel to "The Nexus"; whilst a driving beat propels the Enterprise D to its untimely fate. Alexander Courage's original *Star Trek* fanfare is unceremoniously drafted in at every possible opportunity, thereby negating its nostalgic impact. The accompanying booklet is lavish, even by GNP's commendably high standards. 15 minutes of sound effects from the film are included at the end of the disc (some of them "at 24th Century intensity!"). For serious *Next Generation* fans this is the opportunity they have dreamed about: position your favourite armchair in the middle of the room, put on track 28 ("Enterprise D Warp Out"), wave your finger in the air and cry "Engage!".   **MW**

Also available:
Star Trek: Deep Space Nine (1993) GNP Crescendo GNPD8034
The Utilizer (1995) Intrada MAF7067D

See also Collections: **Star Trek: The Next Generation**

Mark McKenzie

USA

Previously better known in Hollywood as an orchestrator, in the last few years Mark McKenzie has begun to build an impressive reputation as a composer to be reckoned with. McKenzie graduated in composition from the University of Southern California in 1984, when he was named "Outstanding Doctoral Graduate of the Year". He taught theory and composition part-time at USC, whilst devoting his talents initially to orchestrating film scores for other composers (his first job was Bruce Broughton's *Young Sherlock Holmes*, 1985). His orchestration credits encompass over 60 films, by composers as diverse as John Barry (*Dances with Wolves*, 1990), Danny Elfman (*Batman Returns*, 1992) and Dennis McCarthy (*Star Trek: Generations*, 1994). Despite these achievements, McKenzie's ambition was always to make it as a composer. His first original score was for *Son of Darkness: To Die For 2* (1991). In addition to his increasing film work, McKenzie has also written severa concert works. Alongside Joel McNeely, Mark McKenzie must surely be one of the most promising Hollywood composers to have emerged in the last couple of years. Keep an eye out for his name in the future.

Dr Jekyll and Ms Hyde (1995) Original Soundtrack / Randy Thorton.
Intrada Ⓕ MAF7063D (40 minutes: DDD). Includes "Habanera" from *Carmen* (Bizet).

Ignore the crass title, this score is Mark McKenzie's best work to date. The real strength of a composer like McKenzie (one he shares with only a few others) is that viewing the movie is entirely superfluous to the appreciation of his charming music. With so few of his assignments to date ever reaching the cinema, this is a distinct advantage. His score for the quickly forgotten *Dr Jekyll and Ms Hyde* is a case in point: a succession of ravishing melodies, lighthearted set-pieces, and tongue-in-cheek drama are all put together with a sureness, a lightness of touch that betrays the hand of a master orchestrator. A delicious main theme – which nods in the direction of Stephen Foster's "Beautiful Dreamer" – is put through its paces, contorted into a series of delightful variations. This is a comedy score, but McKenzie never sacrifices musicality for the sake of a joke. The music is shot through with humour – like the racy flute solo over *pizzicato* strings in "A Little Surprise" for example, or the jig at the end of "Charades" – but these elements only emphasize the sheer joy inherent in the music, not extra-musical slapstick. The cue "Taking Back My Chromosomes" is a sly take on John Williams's comically grand *1941* march. As has become customary on this composer's albums, a condensed suite of the score is included, the "Overture". It is a most welcome addition (pretty soon there will be enough of these suites to release a separate album of them – now there's an idea). If you can get beyond the self-consciously wacky packaging, this fun disc will certainly become a treasured addition to your collection. **MW**

Frank and Jesse (1994) Original Soundtrack / Mark McKenzie.
Intrada Ⓕ MAF7059D (39 minutes: DDD).

This is an attractive and eminently listenable work, firmly entrenched in the Western genre. The composer deftly alternates a 'folk' ensemble of recorder, harmonica, guitar and percussion with a full-bodied orchestra – the contrast adding extra poignancy to some of the music's more melancholy moments. A rousing main theme is not only memorable, but somewhat overly familiar. *Frank and Jesse*'s only real fault is that it lacks a truly personal touch. Although containing no surprises, this is a supremely well-constructed and pleasing score. The five-minute "Suite" which opens the disc would be a worthy addition to any future compilations of Western film music. **MW**

Warlock: The Armageddon (1993) Original Soundtrack, with the Southwest Symphony Choir and Orchestra / Mark McKenzie.
Intrada Ⓕ MAF7049D (41 minutes: DDD).

Ordinarily, a B-movie horror score might present the listener with little in the way of melody or smooth, rich orchestrations. This being a work by Mark McKenzie, *Warlock* turns out to be melodic, full of variety, and delightfully scored. The opening choral rendition of "Dies Irae" might seem to presage another dose of sub-*Omen* music, but the composer soon dispels our fears with the introduction of an unexpectedly light and sentimental love theme. There are plenty of horrific, spiky and discordant passages – in "Birth of the Warlock" for example – but it is the gentler music which lingers in the memory. McKenzie clothes his love theme in a series of attractive guises: strings, piano, flute, clarinet and horn all revel in its elegance, whilst the underlying harmonies shift and shimmer gracefully. The full theme is heard during "Samantha and Ken's Love" – a meltingly tender piece which is the highlight of this nasty horror score. The final cue – "A Warlock Fantasia" – succinctly distills the rest into a miniature suite. **MW**

Joel McNeely
USA

Joel McNeely, one of the most promising talents to have emerged in Hollywood in the last few years, was born in Madison, Wisconsin into a musical family. McNeely began playing instruments at an early age; his first love was jazz, and he played saxophone in several bands. Formal musical studies began at the Michigan Interlochen Arts Academy, where he studied composition, before moving to the University of Miami, during which time he began to write jazz arrangements.

Composition training continued under the tutorship of Rayburn Wright at the Eastman School of Music, where McNeely earned his Masters degree. After spending a frustrating period in Los Angeles working as a studio musician, McNeely hired a 30-piece orchestra with his own funds and recorded a demo of some film cues. As a result, offers of work began to arrive. McNeely's critically acclaimed work on George Lucas's *Young Indiana Jones Chronicles* (see Collections) won him an Emmy Award. His fresh and immediate scores, with their sweeping themes and rich orchestrations, clearly show him to be the inheritor of Hollywood's 'classic' film music style, with traces of Korngold, Alfred Newman and John Williams particularly apparent in his work. McNeely's score for *Samantha* (1992), a witty chamber music piece, featured his wife Margaret Batjer on violin. As well as composing, McNeely is increasingly in demand as a conductor of film music. David Slonaker is his usual orchestrator.

Gold Diggers. The Secret of Bear Mountain (1995) **Original Soundtrack / Joel McNeely.**
Varèse Sarabande Ⓕ VSD5633 (42 minutes: DDD). Includes *The Flying Song* (Hay/Fischer) performed by Colin Hay.

If Joel McNeely's way with family dramas like *Gold Diggers* and its stylistically similar predecessor *Iron Will* is all too apparently modelled on similar assignments from the pen of John Williams, it is worth noting that the resemblance is only skin deep. The various allusions (*Hook, Stanley and Iris*, a touch of Horner's *Field of Dreams* perhaps) quickly assume a secondary importance when considered alongside McNeely's own warm, likeable persona, which soon becomes evident beneath the surface gloss. There is much entirely of McNeely's own invention to enjoy here: the spectacular epic crescendos built over a racing four-note figure in "The Great Rescue"; and the elegant folk guitar introduction of "Into the Lake", which precedes a sudden shift of gear as we are unexpectedly caught up in another of the composer's orchestral whirlwinds. Little characteristic touches – rushing scales, tasteful chromatic slurs – enhance the impression that here is a highly talented, genuinely inventive composer, albeit one who is already beginning to suffer from a degree of typecasting, not to mention the stifling effect of the dreaded temp track. Only the exceptionally jaded will fail to respond to *Gold Diggers* with a quickening of the pulse and a sparkle in the eye – the enjoyment enhanced by McNeely's evident ability as a conductor, his broadly expansive manner not often encountered in music performed to such rigid time constraints. In the end, however, for all the composer's winning ways with melody and his exuberant use of the orchestra, *Gold Diggers* does give the impression that McNeely has outgrown the fairly limited challenges this kind of picture has to offer. Having cut his teeth on such lightweight family adventure movies, it is high time he was given some meatier fare. **MW**

Iron Will (1994) **Original Soundtrack / Joel McNeely.**
Varèse Sarabande Ⓕ VSD5467 (31 minutes: DDD).

Fresh from the Lucasfilm-produced television series the *Young Indiana Jones Chronicles*, Joel McNeely cast *Iron Will* very much in the mould of John Williams. McNeely clearly revels in the old-fashioned, expansive symphonic style as exemplified by Williams's grown-up *Indiana Jones* scores, with an additonal nod in this instance in the direction of Bruce Broughton's rousing Western music for *Silverado*. But, McNeely's skill as an orchestrator, coupled with his obvious zest for the work, removes any lingering misgivings about his music's antecedents. The joyful vivacity of the opening "Main Title", the flowing folk-like beauty of "Leaving Birch Ridge", these are concrete proofs that here is a composer ready to put his heart and soul into a score. *Iron Will* is a full-blooded piece of Hollywood-style Americana which breathes enthusiasm and excitement in every bar. Pure delight from beginning to end. **MW**

New review
Star Wars: Shadows of the Empire (1996) **Royal Scottish National Chorus and Orchestra / Joel McNeely.**
Varèse Sarabande Ⓕ VSDE5700 (66 minutes: DDD).

Spectacular space battles, lightsaber-wielding heroes, scheming minions of the evil Galactic Emperor – all the ingredients are here but this is not the long-awaited new *Star Wars* movie. Joel McNeely's latest score is not for a film at all. Instead, here is a novel experiment: conceived in exactly the same manner as a film score, *Shadows of the Empire* is actually inspired by a book, the latest of many spin-off novelizations. As in any film, McNeely's score follows the plot, underscoring certain key scenes which are usefully summarized in the booklet; but here the music exists independently of the book, requiring from the listener only a degree of imaginative participation to follow the action it vividly depicts.

In a brave attempt to amplify the episodic nature of a film score with the pictorialism of a tone-poem, McNeely has strived to portray musically some highly visual scenarios: during his 'tour' of

"Imperial City" splendid fanfares and ecstatic choral outbursts make it easy to picture the towering spires and awful grandeur of the palaces; every twist and turn of the action-packed finale is set to excitingly dramatic accompaniment. By such picturesque musical descriptions McNeely succeeds in investing the otherwise familiar *Star Wars* universe with a dash of his own personality. Inevitably, some of John Williams's original music appears – his *leitmotif* design dictates as much – although the score is most effective when avoiding such a comparison. "The Battle of Gall", for example, savours a little too much of Williams to be entirely satisfactory, whereas McNeely's new theme characterizing Darth Vader's rival, Xizor, is an evocative portrait of romantic decadence and lust without precedent in the *Star Wars* canon.

This disc doubles as an 'enhanced CD' with a CD-ROM track which includes a picture gallery of original artwork, background information on the creative team, session photographs, and even some of the composer's sketches. However, the best interactive entertainment on offer here is to be had by closing your eyes and using a little imagination when the music is playing. **MW**

Terminal Velocity (1994) **Original Soundtrack /** Joel McNeely.
Varèse Sarabande Ⓟ VSD5546 (32 minutes: DDD).

Another infectiously energetic offering from McNeely, grandly orchestrated and full to bursting with memorable themes, *Terminal Velocity* lacks only the fresh-faced charm of its predecessor *Iron Will*. This score once again shows the composer's complete confidence in orchestral writing – McNeely's music is written with the full potential of a symphony orchestra in mind. Some cues have the air of an old 1970s thriller, with a fretless electric bass underpinning orchestral strings and a sleazy saxophone on top. Electric guitar and synthesizers are also added to the mix ("Ditch's Dive" begins with quiet strings then suddenly explodes into a serious piece of heavy metal) However, it is the orchestra that ultimately makes most impression in the stunning action cue, "Cadillac Freefall", a six-minute showcase for McNeely's formidable compositional skill. **MW**

Also available:
Flipper (1996) MCA MCAD11445
Radioland Murders (1994) MCA MCAD1159

See also Collections: **The Young Indiana Jones Chronicles**

Richard G. Mitchell

b. 1956 England

Manchester-born Richard G. Mitchell took his degree in Fine Art and Film at St Martin's School of Art, where his interest in film scoring began. His early scores were written for student films at the Royal College of Music and National Film School. Much of his work to date has been for television, and he has written music for several documentaries and dramas including BBC1's *Harry* and Yorkshire TV's *Children of the Holocaust* amongst many others. In addition, he has composed themes for many well-known shows, such as *Masterchef* (BBC1), *Scotland Yard* (Thames) and *Eurosport* (Sky). His feature film credits include *Born American, Across the Lake, Worlds Beyond* and *Beastly Treatment.*

The Bridge (1992) **Original Soundtrack**.
Demon Ⓟ DSCD 5 (43 minutes: DDD).

To some viewers, the name of Richard G. Mitchell might conjure up the catchy theme he wrote for *Masterchef,* and whilst that theme is indeed memorable, perhaps I can bring your attention to a score he wrote for a Channel 4 film, *The Bridge*. Set in Suffolk, where a painter falls in love with a woman (Saskia Reeves) who is awaiting her husband's return from London, *The Bridge* features a score that is a balanced mixture of orchestral and electronic. Gorgeous is just too tame a word to describe it. At least three principal themes are showcased and merged as the film moves to its climax. Worth mentioning is the cue "Walberswick Fete", in which the composer begins with an original theme sounding, however, like an old tune, which merges into the love theme as the principal characters' eyes meet across the village green. It sounds marvellous on the CD, but I recommend trying to catch the film next time it is shown to appreciate the full dramatic effect of the music. *The Bridge* is the best British period score since Richard Rodney Bennett's classic *Far From the Madding Crowd* (1967), and testimony to the consistent talent of Richard G. Mitchell. **JW**

Also available:
The Tenant of Wildfell Hall (1996) KC KCCD4

Jerome Moross

Brooklyn-born Jerome Moross initially became involved in Hollywood simply to pay the bills. Moross was a gifted child – in music and everything else – who graduated from school four years early and finished University at 18. He met Bernard Herrmann at school in Manhattan and they became firm friends. Along with Herrmann, Moross studied at New York's Juilliard School. His first orchestral composition, *Paeans* (1931) was conducted by Herrmann. Throughout the 1930s Moross earned a living writing theatre music and playing the piano in pit orchestras (at George Gershwin's suggestion he was the pianist for the touring production of *Porgy and Bess*). He travelled to Hollywood in 1940, working primarily as an orchestrator, but his already highly individual style proved an impediment to getting work as a composer. He had to wait until 1948 to score his first film, *Close-Up*. Early films were mainly low-budget 'quickies' which earned him enough money to continue writing concert and theatre music back in New York. It was not until *The Big Country* (1958) that Moross really established himself as a film composer. Moross strived independently of Copland to create a unique and distinctively American style. It seems that he sometimes looked upon his film work as a distraction from other composing. Ironically then, his most evocative and lasting piece of Americana is a film score: *The Big Country*. Increasingly his crystal-clear style and beautiful folk-inspired melodies are being recognized for what they are: a significant part of America's musical heritage. Moross was not an American film composer, he was quite simply an American composer. A disc of some of his orchestral works – Symphony No. 1, *Variations on a Waltz* and *The Last Judgement* – has been recorded by the London Symphony Orchestra conducted by JoAnn Falletta (Koch International 37188-2); a second volume of his film music is due shortly from Silva Screen..

The Big Country (1958) **Philharmonia Orchestra / Tony Bremner**.　　　　　ARCAM
　　　Silva Screen ℗ FILMCD030 (55 minutes: DDD). Recorded 1988.

No other film score conjures up the rolling, dusty plains of the American West more convincingly than Moross's *The Big Country*. Without resorting to Coplandesque pastiche, the score's skilful mixture of bracing ruggedness and folksy gentility creates a sense of Americana that is totally individual; the swirling strings and ringing brass fanfares of the justly famous main title evoking magnificently the widescreen splendour of the film's dominating landscape. But this is not simply a one-theme score, Moross provides many other moments that are just as memorable, such as the invigorating "The Welcoming", the charming dance suite for "Major Terrill's Party", the savage, almost balletic "Attempted Rape" and a splendidly rousing "Cattle at the River" (a cue deleted from the final print). This vibrant and spectacularly detailed re-recording breathes new life into a score that was ill-served by the original soundtrack LP. Thrilling stuff! **RS**

The Valley of Gwangi The Classic Film Music of Jerome Moross. **City of Prague Philharmonic Orchestra / Paul Bateman**.
　　　Silva Screen ℗ FILMCD161 (78 minutes: DDD). Recorded 1995.
　　　The Adventures of Huckleberry Finn (1960). Five Finger Exercise (1962). Wagon Train (1957). The War Lord (1965). The Sharkfighters (1956). Rachel, Rachel (1968). The Mountain Road (1960). The Valley of Gwangi (1968).

A wholly invigorating foray into uncharted waters, this selection of suites is entirely new to CD (*The War Lord* suite recorded here has music not included on the Varèse reissue). Moross was notoriously shy of Hollywood, and rarely got the opportunity to tackle first-rate assignments. However, his music, no matter for what film, is always unfailingly delightful: the rhythms and textures of his own brand of Americana inform every work on this disc. Opening strongly with *The Adventures of Huckleberry Finn* – for which Moross unsurprisingly contributed a lilting idiomatic score – there is not one dull moment in an engagingly varied programme. The composer's thoroughly charming personality is omnipresent throughout. Distinctly run-of-the-mill performances have marred some earlier recordings with the City of Prague Philharmonic, but here at last is an undisputed winner. For some unfathomable reason the Czech musicians respond with previously unequalled enthusiasm to Moross's uniquely American style. The performances are polished and assured, making this the most convincing entry in the Silva Screen series so far: Volume 2 is eagerly anticipated. **MW**

The War Lord (1965) **Original Soundtrack / Joseph Gershenson**.
　　　Varèse Sarabande ℗ VSD5536 (31 minutes: ADD). Includes "The War Lord in Battle" and "The Death of Draco" composed by Hans Salter.

What was intended to be an introspective medieval epic with a difference was mutilated by the studio during post-production, resulting in a very ordinary costume potboiler, with – as the booklet succinctly puts it – "knights and vikings clanking around the North Sea coast countryside".

Moross, who had originally been allotted ten weeks composing time, found this period drastically reduced to just five. He still managed to produce a lyrical and moving score, derived from the characters' inner motivations and not from external pageant. Despite a gleeful ignorance of authentic medievalisms (Rózsa would have been appalled), Moross managed to convey a flavour of the period in his score, whilst steadfastly adhering to his own characteristic idiom. The central "Love Theme" is one of his most attractive creations. Veteran Universal Pictures stalwart Hans Salter was called in by the studio to beef up the score, and duly obliged with a few suitably bombastic military pieces. Despite the studio's tinkering, *The War Lord* is still a splendid score that has outlasted its film.   **MW**

Ennio Morricone
b. 1928 Italy

Ennio Morricone was born in Rome and studied trumpet and composition at the Conservatorio di Santo Cecilia. After graduating he wrote a series of experimental works and arranged many pop records before becoming involved in films through playing in an orchestra that regularly performed film scores.. Despite a prolific and diverse output, his name will forever be associated with the films of Sergio Leone. They had attended the same school, so when Leone established himself as a filmmaker it was only natural that he would turn to his old school friend for musical support. Beginning with *A Fistful of Dollars* in 1964, Morricone and Leone redefined the Western genre. Morricone abandoned Hollywood's traditional Americana in favour of a highly idiosyncratic style consisting of brief motifs and musical exclamations, scored for an eclectic mixture of whistles, chimes, electric guitars, harmonica and voices (sometimes singing, often just grunting). After the *Dollars* trilogy, he scored all of the director's later films, including *Once Upon a Time in the West* (1968) and Leone's last film, *Once Upon a Time in America* (1984). He won a British Academy Award for *The Mission* in 1986 (which was nominated for an Oscar), and achieved chart success when *Chi Mai* was used as the theme for the British TV series *The Life and Times of David Lloyd George* (1981). Morricone has remained based in his native city, dividing his time between Hollywood assignments and domestic Italian productions. He is one of the few film composers who insist on completing their own orchestrations.

Cinema Paradiso (1989) **Original Soundtrack /Ennio Morricone**.
 DRG Ⓕ CDSBL12598 (38 minutes: ADD).

Giuseppe Tornatore's nostalgic celebration of the magic of cinema could hardly fail to elicit a sympathetic response from any film composer, let alone one who has for so long been conjuring his own special brand of cinematic wizardry. Morricone's strikingly beautiful score is a thoroughly sentimental experience, although the sentiment is of a uniquely European kind: reflective and tinged with a bittersweet sense of regret not often encountered in the the sunnier climes of California. For such an unabashed display of emotionalism it is surprisingly sparsely scored, with much of the music assuming chamber-sized dimensions. An extremely close-miked, unflatteringly harsh recording only makes the contrast between this poignantly intimate piece and the enormously overblown gestures of Hollywood all the more telling. Solo strings, woodwinds, piano and saxophone share the principal themes, one of which – the heartbreaking "Love Theme" – was actually written by the composer's son, Andrea Morricone. This and the main *Cinema Paradiso* theme swirl and gyrate in an ecstasy of raw feeling; their wonderfully crafted completeness belying their movie origin. Just as the listener is beginning to believe that Morricone can eke no more intensity from his music, the montage cue "From American Sex Appeal to the First Fellini", achieves an emotional high-water mark not to be surpassed. This is deservedly one of the composer's most popular works.   **MW**

New review
Dario Argento Trilogy
L'Uccello dalle Piume di Cristallo (1969) **Il Gatto a Nove Code** (1970) **4 Mosche di
 Velluto Grigio** (1971) **Original Soundtracks / Bruno Nicolai**.
 DRG Ⓕ 32911 (78 minutes: AAD). Includes interview with Dario Argento.

Morricone is a composer who provides a wide range of music that can inspire pleasure and frustration in equal doses (usually within the same score). His voice is so distinctive that there is no mistaking one of his works, but that voice can range from the rhapsodic – making him one of the most popular composers for film – to the completely impenetrable, hence the frustration. The Italian 'giallo' genre, a term for the extreme psychological horror-thrillers that emerged during the 1970s, provided a valuable showcase for the talents of one of its leading exponents, writer-director Dario Argento. Probably better known for his association with the rock group Goblin, Argento's first three films, and, in fact, his most recent, *The Stendahl Syndrome*, were scored by

Morricone and these scores include examples of both ends of the composer's range. The first of the three is also the best known (the UK title is *The Bird With the Crystal Plumage*) and contains a "Main Title" theme that frequently turns up on compilations. Morricone's adroit use of the innocent lullaby format as a dramatic counterpoint to grisly on-screen occurrences was not particularly innovative but proved highly effective all the same and has since become associated with the genre. The melody line is strong and memorable, but it is the incidental score that proves somewhat challenging and this is true for all three films. Given the subject matter, perhaps it is not surprising that the composer's musical response to deranged states of existence should prove to be traumatic. Although they don't provide any easy listening, these sound pictures of the disturbed mind – consisting of layered textures of sound with frequent instrumental and/or vocal interjections – are fascinating. *Il Gatto a Nove Code* is the least interesting of the three. It has the same lullaby/dissonance structure but is just not particularly memorable. However, *4 Mosche di Velluto Grigio* presents a more interesting variation on this theme. The "Main Title" is more upbeat and percussive (as befits a film whose main protagonist is a drummer) but the central core of the work, a 19-minute suite which starts in a conventional ordered state and becomes increasingly unhinged as it unfolds, is fascinating in its complexity and range of sounds. The disc concludes with a brief interview with Argento in Italian but a translation is provided in the booklet which also contains detailed notes and illustrations. **DS**

The Good, the Bad and the Ugly (1966) **Various artists / Ennio Morricone.**
    Liberty Ⓜ CDP7 48408-2 (34 minutes: AAD).

The popularity of the 'spaghetti' Westerns was at its height when the third part of Sergio Leone's *Dollars* trilogy appeared. Each film had exhibited increasingly vivid and occasionally outrageous sequences with Morricone's musical contributions becoming even bolder. The title theme for this film with its striking use of unorthodox instruments and voices captured the imagination of listeners of the late sixties and inspired numerous cover versions. Now accepted as an obligatoryinclusion in any compilation of Great Western Film Themes, it is worth remembering just what an extraordinary score this is. Clint Eastwood's desert ordeal, Eli Wallach's frantic search for a certain grave in a massive circular cemetery, and the final showdown between Eastwood and Lee Van Cleef are visual and aural setpieces. An absolute minimum of dialogue and the maximum use of music and choreographed action render these memorable sequences almost balletic in their impact. The album is slightly disappointing in that the cues are re-recordings made at the time specifically for the soundtrack album and, in some cases, lack the harshness of the originals. Nevertheless, this is an important work not only in this composer's career but also in the whole genre of the Western. **DS**

The Mission (1986) **Original Soundtrack**, with **Incantation; London Voices;** `ARCAM`
    Barnet Schools' Choir; London Philharmonic Orchestra / Ennio Morricone.
    Virgin Ⓜ CDV2042 (49 minutes: DDD).

There is an aura of timelessness about this music: it stretches away into eternity. This is partly because of the Latin choral settings, which draw on a heritage of sacred singing over 1000 years old; partly because of the ageless attraction that any really exquisite melody exerts over us: the score's centrepiece, "Gabriel's Oboe", is a wondrous creation indeed and has deservedly become one of this composer's most famous theme. Even more than *The Good, the Bad and the Ugly*, even more than *Once Upon a Time in the West*, this score is perhaps Morricone's most resplendent achievement. Admittedly, the latter half of the disc is less effective, relying rather too much on shrill pan pipes. Incidentally, the stylistic similarities in John Williams's *Empire of the Sun* (1987) are reportedly a result of Steven Spielberg's great admiration for Morricone's score. **MW**

Once Upon a Time in America (1984) **Original Soundtrack**, with **Edda Dell'Orso** (sngr);
    Gheorghe Zamfir (pan flute) / **Ennio Morricone.**
    Mercury Ⓜ 822 334-2 (50 minutes: DDD). Includes *Amapola* (La Calle/Gamse).

Morricone's glowing, autumnal score for Sergio Leone's final epic movie stirs within the listener warm feelings of nostalgia for better times now lost. Notwithstanding the film's setting, the composer's lyrical, indelibly Italian melodic style inescapably evokes the long hot days and warm evenings of a balmy mediterranean summer; sensuously sunny moments, like the cue "Friends", and the delicate addition of mandolin are irresistibly Italianate. Big band jazz and swinging ragtime contribute the important American elements in keeping with the film's storyline, yet do not diffuse the score's overall ambience, which is further reinforced by an instrumental arrangement of the song "Amapola". Although lacking the immediately striking impact of its predecessor *Once Upon a Time in the West* (1968) – with its handful of distinctive character-themes – this late work, I suspect, will give longer-lasting satisfaction when played purely for listening pleasure. **MW**

The Thing (1982) **Original Soundtrack / Ennio Morricone**.
Varèse Sarabande Ⓕ VSD5278 (50 minutes: ADD).

The impression created by watching the movie that Morricone simply aped director John Carpenter's own distinctively minimalist style is largely dispelled by listening to this disc. Certainly, the ostinato synth motif so prominent in the film is well nigh indistinguishable from Carpenter's own scoring (on the disc it is relegated to track eight), but much of the (orchestral) remainder is significantly different. Spartan, string-based textures create a fittingly bleak and cheerless soundscape. The strict development of a fugue in "Bestiality" is an appropriate musical device to suggest a barren and sterile environment. Morricone's score is utterly frigid, quite deliberately avoiding any hint of warmth; quite consciously blood-chilling. The stark string writing is particularly to be savoured, making *The Thing* a successfully depressing experience.   **MW**

The Untouchables (1987) **Original Soundtrack / Ennio Morricone**.
A&M Ⓜ 393 909-2 (40 minutes: DDD).

Director Brian De Palma has proved adept at picking composers for his films: Bernard Herrmann (*Sisters*, 1973 and *Obsession*, 1975), John Williams (*The Fury*, 1978), and Pino Donaggio (*Carrie*, 1976, etc.). Ennio Morricone provided a dramatic and characteristically inventive score for De Palma's most mainstream and successful movie. The main theme is another memorable Morricone creation: a tick-tock drum pattern continually forces the pace, as complex syncopated motifs are developed above it; wailing harmonica – reminiscent of *Once Upon a Time in the West* – carries the unadorned melody. The disc actually opens with the "End Title", a celebratory fanfare which seems oddly premature as track one. Al Capone's Sicilian-style theme is almost comically sinister; by contrast, a delicate piece for flute and strings provides an affecting interlude in "Ness and His Family". For the film's climactic scene – De Palma's *Battleship Potemkin* homage – Morricone gradually overpowers an innocent child's lullaby with dark orchestral forces. This is a supremely effective tension-builder, but mistakenly sequenced as the disc's final track – the tension is never resolved. *The Untouchables* is a distinctly superior thriller score all the same.   **MW**

New review
Western Quintet Original Soundtracks / Ennio Morricone.
DRG Ⓕ 32907 (2 discs, 156 minutes: ADD).
Il Mio Nome è Nessuno (1973). Occhio Alla Penna (1980). Giù la Testa (1971). Tepepa (1969). Companeros (1970).

In the 30-odd years that Morricone has been composing for films, he has covered nearly every genre imaginable, but the one he will always be associated with is the Western. Of course, the novel appeal here was that these were not traditional Western scores but 'Italian' Western scores; a whole new film music style was born, and Morricone spearheaded the movement with his iconoclastic music for Sergio Leone's *Dollars* trilogy and the classic *Once Upon a Time in the West*. This generous double-disc set offers five complete soundtracks from the maestro that are fully representative of this style of music. *Il Mio Nome è Nessuno* is a minor classic of the genre and Morricone's score is an amusing send-up of his earlier works using the same elements but injecting some fun into the proceedings. Apparently, *Occhio Alla Penna* was the last Western he scored, but then the genre had all but died out by the early 1980s. This music, while not insubstantial, is only a reworking of all the familiar sounds from earlier scores. *Giù la Testa* (better known as *A Fistful of Dynamite*) is a much more heartfelt score, however, for this film is Leone's bridging work between *Once Upon a Time in the West* and *Once Upon a Time in America*. This score contains some of Morricone's most rhapsodic writing and there are less of the weirder sounds that one associates with Morricone's Western style. Mexican flavours dominate *Tepepa* which has a notably strong "Main Title" theme, while *Companeros* is somewhat more sombre but a rarity nonetheless and well worth the inclusion. Avoiding overly familiar material, this strong collection gives an overview of this unique genre from the perspective of the man who started it all.   **DS**

Also available:
Bugsy (1991) Epic EK48804
Butterfly (1981) Prometheus PCD108
City of Joy (1992) Epic EK52750
Classic Film Scores (City of Prague PO/Bateman) Silva Screen FILMCD148 / FILMCD171
Death Rides a Horse (1968) etc. RCA OST 107
Disclosure (1995) Virgin CDVMM16
The Dollars Trilogy RCA ND74021
Duck You Sucker [A Fistful of Dynamite] (1971) Alhambra A8917

El Greco (1966) **Giordano Bruno** (1973) RCA OST 111
Ennio Morricone Anthology DRG DRGCD32908
Ennio Morricone With Love DRG DRGCD32913
In the Line of Fire (1993) Epic EK57307
Jona che visse nella balena (1993) CAM COS015
Legendary Italian Westerns RCA 9974
Il Lungo Silenzio (1993) CAM COS014
Massacre in Rome (1973) **Battle of Algiers** (1967) RCA OST 105
Moses the Lawgiver (1975) RCA OST 113
Once Upon a Time in the West (1968) RCA 4736-2
Il Prato (1979) CAM CSE065
Sahara (1983) Intrada MAF7047D
State of Grace (1990) MCA MCAD10019
Tie Me Up, Tie Me Down (1990) Novus 3095-2

Mario Nascimbene

b. 1916 Italy

Born in Milan, Mario Nascimbene studied composition and conducting at the Giuseppe Verdi Conservatory; he also managed to become the Italian table-tennis champion. He wrote several concert works before his first film score in 1941, *L'Amore Canta*. After the war his film career continued with *I Fantasmi del Mare* (1948). His revolutionary score for *Rome 11 O'Clock* (1952) which incorporated a typewriter into the underscore won him the Nastri d'Argento (Silver Ribbons), the Italian equivalent of an Oscar. This score was reworked as the *Concerto for Four Typewriters and Orchestra*. Subsequently Nascimbene continued this penchant for unusual experimentation. In 1954 he took on his first Hollywood assignment, *The Barefoot Contessa*, which produced the popular "Song of the Barefoot Contessa". This was followed by the epic costume dramas *Alexander the Great* (1956) and *The Vikings* (1958). His score for *A Farewell to Arms* (1957) won him an Academy Award nomination. He also scored the 1959 movie *Scent of Mystery* which was filmed in "Smell-O-Vision"! Nascimbene's score for *Barabbas* (1962) continued his experimental approach, which he termed "suoni nuovi" (new sounds). Despite being slated to score the Spanish epic *El Cid* (1961) producer Samuel Bronston replaced him with Miklós Rózsa. Nascimbene went on to score three Hammer 'Stone Age' pictures, *One Million Years BC* (1966), *When Dinosaurs Ruled the Earth* (1970) and *Creatures the World Forgot* (1971). He has also written three operas, three ballets, theatre music and a television oratorio.

Barabbas (1962) **Alexander the Great** (1956) **Constantine and the Cross** (1960)
Original Soundtracks / Franco Ferrara.
Legend Ⓕ CD5 (67 minutes: AAD).

Rather like Mayuzumi's *The Bible* (1966), Nascimbene's music for *Barabbas* is also distinctly un-Hollywood. Here, the composer reveals his penchant for experimentation by overlaying tracks, slowing them down, playing them backwards, sideways, and so on to produce some rather unsettling and striking effects; the whipping of Christ (frighteningly amplified lashes interrupted by wailing chorus) being perhaps the most remarkable. The theme for Barabbas is a sombre, Hebraic dirge punctuated by the deathly, slowed-down tolling of a bell, and is heard at its best when taken up by the chorus during the impressive Crucifixion sequence. *Constantine and the Cross* is more traditional in style, whereas the spare orchestration of *Alexander the Great*, though not so interesting away from the film, does create a convincing sense of antiquity. A good alternative is the DRG coupling of *Barabbas* and *Alexander the Great* listed below.   **RS**

New review
The Vikings (1958) **Solomon and Sheba** (1959) Original Soundtracks / Franco Ferrara.
DRG Ⓕ 32963 (66 minutes: AAD).

It is fitting that the most popular of all Nascimbene's film scores, though not necessarily the finest, should be coupled together for their reincarnation on CD. The original United Artists LPs were consistently in print for nearly two decades, although the tracks here are actually from the composer's own archive. *The Vikings* (surely one of the most regularly aired films on TV) is a rugged comic-book adventure brought to life in ravishing Technicolor and it receives a busy and spirited score to match. The famous main theme, based on a three-note horn call, is an appropriately brawny, heroic *leitmotif* to rape and pillage by and is used most notably for the film's climax, where taken at half speed with wordless choral accompaniment it becomes a requiem for a dead Viking. In the ensuing "End Credits" its triumphant treatment enhances Saul Bass's clever animation designed in the style of the Bayeaux tapestry. Not surprisingly, Nascimbene also makes effective use of a large choir in *Solomon and Sheba*, particularly during the lushly exotic "Main Title" and the feverish "Orgy" (all pounding drums and wailing pagan worshippers punctuated by dramatic flashes of lightning), though the score as a whole is much more reflective than its predecessor. (Incidentally, Malcolm Arnold made several uncredited contributions to this film, but none appear on the CD). **RS**

Also available:
Barabbas (1962) **Alexander the Great** (1956) DRG DRGCD32964
The Barefoot Contessa (1954) **Room at the Top** (1958) **Quiet American** (1958) DRG DRGCD32961

Alfred Newman
1900-1970 USA

Recipient of nine Oscars and 45 Academy Award nominations, Alfred Newman was quite simply the most important composer in Hollywood. Korngold, Steiner, Waxman and Rózsa were significant figures, but Newman was more influential, and more powerful than all the rest. The eldest of ten children, Alfred Newman was born in New Haven, Connecticut into a poor family. His mother encouraged his early musical proclivity, and at age 14 Alfred was sent to study piano with Sigismond Stojowski in New York (although he could not afford the train fare, a kindly railroad conductor never once punched the boy's ticket). Newman's family could not pay for the luxury of full-time musical studies, so Alfred got a job as pianist at Broadway's Strand Theater. Eventually, he graduated to conducting matinée performances (he was still only 15), and soon took up conducting permanently. He was music director for Gershwin's *George White's Scandals of 1920*. A succession of other musicals followed, including Jerome Kern's *Criss Cross* of 1926, which was so admired by Fritz Reiner that he invited Newman to conduct the Cincinnati Symphony Orchestra. Irving Berlin's musical film *Reaching for the Moon* took Newman to Hollywood in 1930. His score for *Street Scene* in 1931 established his credentials as a composer – so successful was his film work that he never returned to Broadway nor fulfilled his ambition to become a symphonic conductor. Subsequently working on some 255 films over a 40-year period, Newman was the architect of the classic romantic Hollywood style of the Golden Age. Newman's talents lay not only in conducting and composing: he was appointed music director at United Artists; then from 1940 to 1960 was head of the music department at 20th Century-Fox. He proved to be as gifted at administration as he was at composing, and was responsible for furthering the careers of – among others – Bernard Herrmann, Alex North and Jerry Goldsmith. His brothers Emil and Lionel also became composer/conductors in Hollywood (the latter succeeding Alfred as head of music at Fox). His sons Thomas and David, and his nephew Randy, are all currently active film composers.

Airport (1970) **Original Soundtrack / Alfred Newman**.
Varèse Sarabande Ⓟ VSD5436 (30 minutes: AAD).

"Wildly anachronistic" was how one critic described Alfred Newman's final film score. What he had not appreciated was that Ross Hunter's production, with a cast of Hollywood heavyweights (Burt Lancaster, Dean Martin, *et al*), was itself an anachronism, or valentine if you like, to his own glossy 'soaps' made at Universal in the 1950s. No wonder it irked some when the fashion was for films of student and social unrest. *Airport* may have been honed by custodians of Hollywood's past, but its box office success was proof that there is always an audience for this kind of entertainment. Newman's score was a treat for his fans and sounds better than ever on CD. His "Love Theme", much recorded at the time, has that yearning feeling redolent of his work right back to *Wuthering Heights* (1939). A subsidiary theme for "Mel and Tanya", on piano with a lush string backdrop, is no less affecting, in fact a final refinement of his art. There's a humorous interlude for the octogenarian actress, Helen Hayes as the elusive "Stowaway", whilst the drama of the film is played out in "Emergency Landing!" and the brilliantly scored "Main Title", a mambo-driven theme that sets the ensuing drama alive as it surges along over the opening credits. Orchestrators, Leo Shuken and Jack Hayes, who had recently completed *Camelot* with Newman, turned up trumps again for his final opus. **AE**

Anastasia (1956) **Original Soundtrack**, with the **20th Century-Fox Studio Orchestra / Alfred Newman**.
Varèse Sarabande Ⓟ VSD5422 (40 minutes: AAD).

If one pauses to reflect on the output of Alfred Newman in 1956, perhaps it comes as no surprise to read that he wore himself out on behalf of the Hollywood studios. That year he supervised and conducted the music for *Carousel* and *The King and I* released in the spring and summer, and then went on to compose the lengthy score for *Anastasia*, which is full of incidental dance music, besides the memorable title theme. I find his piano demonstration track at the conclusion of this CD a touching memorial to his art – how many times must he have played in these circumstances so that a producer at Fox could hear his music for a new picture? The simplicity of the playing, with just a touch of rubato would surely have moved the hardest heart in the movie colony. "Anastasia's Theme" is quintessential Newman, veering from minor to major and back again, like the heroine searching for her identity. It is scored for a large body of strings with the full weight of the brass emphasizing the oppressive band of the Russian compatriots, out to convince her that she is the Czar's daughter. It comes in various guises, with the addition of an ethereal coda in the "Recognition Scene". Newman's dance music includes two swirling waltzes, a troika and polka, all most attractive, and there for the asking should a Christopher Palmer come along to arrange a suite.   **AE**

Captain from Castile The Classic Film Scores of Alfred Newman. [a]**Ambrosian Singers; National Philharmonic Orchestra / Charles Gerhardt.**
  RCA Victor Ⓜ GD80184 (45 minutes: ADD). Recorded 1973.
  How to Marry a Millionaire (1953). Captain from Castile (1947). Wuthering Heights (1939). Down to the Sea in Ships (1949). The Song of Bernadette (1943)[a]. The Bravados (1958). Anastasia (1956). The Best of Everything (1959). Airport (1970). The Robe (1953)[a].

This CD is a wonderful representation of one of the true Hollywood greats. Many of Newman's finest moments are here, opening, appropriately enough, with his immortal *20th Century-Fox Fanfare*, first heard in 1935, and the CinemaScope extension that was added in 1953. This introduces *Street Scene*, an evocative, Gershwinesque paean to the 'big city' originally from the 1931 film of the same name, but re-used countless times in Fox movies throughout the 1940s and 1950s, most notably in the "Prologue" to *How to Marry a Millionaire*, for which Newman conducted the piece on-screen in order to advertise the four-track stereophonic splendour of CinemaScope! Newman's trademark was his distinctive use of high strings, and the ethereal beauty of this keening sound is faithfully reproduced here in the love theme from *Captain from Castile*, Cathy's theme from *Wuthering Heights* and especially the radiant vision sequence from *The Song of Bernadette*. Also highly adept with a large orchestral canvas, the thrilling march *Conquest* and the score for the Biblical epic *The Robe* both create a magnificent sense of opulence. The "Main Title" from his final film *Airport* pulsates with a remarkably youthful and dynamic energy, proving that even at the age of 69 his skills remained undimmed.   **RS**

How Green Was My Valley (1941) Original Soundtrack / Alfred Newman.
  Arista 20th Century-Fox 11008-2 (49 minutes: ADD).

There have been few more enterprising releases than this: the original musical sessions for John Ford's 1941 Oscar-winning drama of the Welsh valleys – but in early stereo! And there is nothing phoney about this mix – there is genuine separation – although the liner notes give no clue as to source material, or how such an early experiment with stereo sound might have originated; it is as if the producers did not realize the historical significance of their own album. Of course, sound engineers at Disney had experimented with multi-channel musical recording the previous year for *Fantasia*, and it may be the recordists at Fox were simply following suit. The orchestra may not be presented in quite a standard symphonic set-up, and the overall sound, obviously from acetates, may be a little lean, but this is still an outstandingly well mastered album. Bravo to the pioneering engineers in 1941 and congratulations to their 1994 counterparts. The score itself is one of Alfred Newman's finest, characterized throughout by emotionally charged writing for muted strings (a regular Newman device for eliciting maximum sentiment) and wordless chorus, but with the lead often taken by an earthy flute, singing a song of the hills, conjuring a nostalgic, rustic ambience which perfectly complements the film's astonishing recreation of rural Wales. At John Ford's insistence the score's major theme is the Irish melody "The Sixpence". Whilst Newman had a passion for conducting he found composition arduous and emotionally draining – and his sincere, passionate music for *How Green Was My Valley* bears witness to how much of his inner self he obviously gave to his art. This is one of old Hollywood's great scores – and here it is presented in the best possible guise. An historic album in more ways than one.   **DW**

The Robe (1953) Original Soundtrack / Alfred Newman.
  Arista 20th Century-Fox 11011-2 (61 minutes: ADD).

The first CinemaScope epic is, in retrospect, a stiff and dramatically unconvincing tale which pales in comparison with the later splendour of *Ben-Hur* (1959). Alfred Newman, as head of Fox's music department, was the natural choice to score this flagship movie; his work on previous religious subjects such as *The Song of Bernadette* (1943) and *David and Bathsheba* (1951) proved him to be eminently qualified. Newman brings to *The Robe* a sincerely spiritual quality lacking from the film's narrative. He provides a martial horn call for the Roman protagonist, along with sundry fanfares, marches and bacchanalian 'Roman' music – none of which, however, attempts to emulate Rózsa's strident authenticism. Newman is more interested in matters of the spirit: his sincere love theme and several choral pieces representing the Hollywood-ized early Christians are infused with warmth, tenderness, and nobility. This disc is the very first issue of the Original Soundtrack recording in stereo: previous releases have been taken from the mono re-recording Newman made for Decca at the time of the film's release. As with all the Fox series of classic scores, sound quality and presentation are superb. **MW**

Also available:
How the West Was Won (1962) Rhino 72458 (2 CDs)

David Newman

USA

Eldest son of Alfred Newman, David Newman – as with his brother Thomas – clearly has film music in his blood. Like his father, David began with an early passion for conducting – he particularly admired Toscanini – and moved from playing the violin in an orchestra to conducting. Admiration of his father's vast command of technique, as well as his ability to conduct, inspired David Newman to follow his lead into film scoring. His scores include *The War of the Roses* (1989), *Bill and Ted's Excellent Adventure* (1989) and the follow-up *Bogus Journey* (1991), *Fire Birds* [*Wings of the Apache*] (1990), *Paradise* (1991), *The Flintstones* (1994), *The Nutty Professor* and *Matilda* (both 1996).

Critters (1986) **Original Soundtrack / David Newman**.
Intrada Ⓕ MAF7044D (48 minutes: DDD).

One of David Newman's first film assignments, *Critters* is a thoroughly entertaining comedy-horror score. Intrada's CD release restores some music not available on the original LP. A pre-title sequence consisting entirely of electronics introduces the sub-Gremlin-style Crites; thereafter, their unpleasantly amusing antics are accompanied by synths. Newman reserves his orchestral theme for the hapless family on whom the Crites (literally) descend. Several prominent passages for woodwinds add extra interest to the orchestration, which would otherwise rely a mite too heavily on dark string chords and other standard suspense devices. Newman's penchant for short, choppy motifs rather than full-blown melodies keeps the listener guessing as to what might happen next. The final track is an unexpectedly enjoyable synth-pop cue, "Critter Skitter". By no means a classic, *Critters* is nevertheless a quirky and inventive score with just the right balance of drama and fun. **MW**

I Love Trouble (1994) **Original Soundtrack / David Newman**.
Varèse Sarabande Ⓕ VSD5510 (36 minutes: DDD). Includes *You've Really Got a Hold On Me* (Smokey Robinson).

Despite being a last-minute replacement for a rejected Elmer Bernstein score, David Newman's smooth, relaxed music does not sound like it was written in a hurry. Smoochy saxophone and a mellow orchestral main theme keep things pretty laid back for much of the time. Even during racier moments – "Scoop de Jour" for example – the sax retains its cool. *I Love Trouble* is a nonchalant score with plenty of easygoing charm. Dim the lights, put your feet up, and enjoy. **MW**

Also available:
Heathers (1989) Varèse Sarabande VSD5223
Hoffa (1992) Arista 20th Century-Fox 11001-2
Mr Destiny (1990) Varèse Sarabande VSD5299
Operation Dumbo Drop (1995) Hollywood 162032-2
The Phantom (1996) Milan 35756-2

Randy Newman

b. 1943 USA

Singer/songwriter Randy Newman's acerbic, satirical and witty songs would alone be enough to establish his reputation; but, as if to prove there is indeed such a thing as destiny, Newman's family pedigree made it inevitable that he would turn his hand to film scoring as well. Nephew of the great Alfred Newman, Randy began piano lessons when he was seven, and started writing songs as a teenager: "Golden Gridiron Boy", produced by Pat Boone, was released in 1961. His first job was a staff songwriter for the Metric Music Company, for which he received a magnificent $50 a week. He studied music at UCLA, but elected not to complete the course. He began recording his songs in 1968, accompanied originally by his own lush orchestral arrangements. Sardonic humour is the trademark of such gems as "Political Science" ("They all hate us anyhow/Let's drop the big one now") and the million-selling "Short People", whimsy the predominant force behind "Simon Smith and His Amazing Dancing Bear". Newman provided some songs for the 1970 film *Performance*, and has since increased his involvement in film scoring, with *Ragtime* in 1981 being his first original score. This was followed by *The Natural* (1984), songs for the comic Western *Three Amigos!* (1986), *Parenthood* (1989), *Avalon* (1990) and most recently *Toy Story* and *James and the Giant Peach* (1995). He won an Emmy Award for his music for the TV series *Cop Rock* in 1991. His recent full-length musical, *Faust*, which took two years to record was released as an album with performances from James Taylor, Don Henley, Elton John, Linda Ronstadt and Bonnie Raitt; it opened in September 1995 at the La Jolla Payhouse, Los Angeles and a Broadway run is scheduled for 1997.

New review

Awakenings (1991) **Original Soundtrack**, with **Louise Ditullio** (fl); **Ralph Grierson** (pf) / **Randy Newman**.
 Reprise Ⓕ 7599-26466-2 (42 minutes: AAD).

Randy Newman truly has an exceptional gift for melody. It is perhaps due to his success as a lyricist and singer/songwriter that his music for film has such fluidity and lyricism. *Awakenings* is arguably the quintessential Newman score. This score blatantly wears its heart on its sleeve, it is music of unashamed sentimentality and melodrama. Newman unfolds a canvas that has the beauty and poignancy of a water-colour, a dreamy soundscape of vibrant colour and emotional resonance. His main theme has the charm and naïveté of a lullaby, often seamlessly drifting into waltz-like patterns. The fragile orchestrations for piano, flute, soprano saxophone, solo violin, harp and strings are warm and enveloping, embracing the listener. On the whole the music has a determined optimism and vitality, but occasionally a bittersweet air changes the mood and the score becomes dark and introspective. During these passages Newman delivers some particularly exquisite writing for solo violin, flute and saxophone. *Awakenings* is a score that, literally, brings a tear to the eye. Music loaded with such genuine emotion is rare in film. **PP**

Maverick (1993) **Original Soundtrack** / **Randy Newman**.
 Reprise Ⓕ 9362 45816-2 (42 minutes: DDD).

In a fit of marketing madness, Randy Newman's mature and eminently entertaining Western score was not issued to coincide with the film's release: a specious disc of "songs inspired by the film" was put out instead. Eventually, Warner Brothers relented and gave us what they should have given us all along. Newman's music trots along with a swinging pace, all the while treading that fine line between comedy and drama. The composer seizes every opportunity to indulge his fondness for ragtime rhythms and turn-of-the-century Americana, with a few additional tongue-in-cheek nods in the direction of Broadway and *42nd Street*. A suitably rumbustious theme for the eponymous hero, a pleasantly tender love theme, and some dark and dramatic music for the baddies constitute the score's conventional Western elements. Newman adds his own personality with large doses of characteristically wry humour. Comedy scores tend to work best when they are sparing with their attempts at wit: *Maverick* has an ideal combination of straight Western music and tuneful levity. The end credit song, "Tartine de Merde" is sung by one S. Bush – presumably the very same Singing Bush who appeared in *Three Amigos*? **MW**

The Natural (1984) **Original Soundtrack** / **Randy Newman**.
 Warner Bros Ⓕ 925116-2 (35 minutes: AAD).

With Alfred, Lionel and Emil Newman as his uncles it is hardly surprising that Randy would, after a successful career as a songwriter-performer, eventually find his way into the movies. All his scores revel in the glorious Hollywood orchestral sound of his illustrious forebears, but *The Natural* is arguably the most impressive: its broad, Coplandesque themes and warmly sentimental style eloquently underpinning the film's golden portrait of 1930s America, as well as the mystical events that shape the rise and fall of the enigmatic baseball-playing character portrayed by Robert Redford. **RS**

Also available:
Avalon (1990) Reprise 926437-2
James and the Giant Peach (1995) Walt Disney WD681202
The Paper (1994) Reprise 945616-2
Parenthood (1989) Reprise 926001-2

Thomas Newman
USA

Youngest son of the great Alfred Newman, nephew of Lionel Newman, brother to David Newman, and cousin to Randy Newman, Thomas has a firm pedigree on which to ground his film music career. He began his musical studies at the University of Southern California, which included classes with professor David Raksin, who had worked with Alfred Newman at 20th Century-Fox. Thomas moved on to Yale, where he studied with Jacob Druckman, Bruce MacCombie and Robert Moore. With the weight of historical inevitability upon his shoulders, Newman became involved in film scoring, beginning with *Reckless* in 1984. *Desperately Seeking Susan* (1985) was his first major success. Other rock and synthesizer-based scores like *The Lost Boys* (1987) followed before Newman began to refine his orchestrational style. With an increasingly busy schedule, Thomas Newman is regarded as one of the most interesting and original composers active in Hollywood today. In 1994 he received no less than two Academy Award nominations – *Little Women* and *The Shawshank Redemption* – although the prize ultimately went to Hans Zimmer (for *The Lion King*).

New review

How to Make an American Quilt (1995) Original Soundtrack / Thomas Newman.
> MCA Ⓕ MCAD11373 (43 minutes: DDD). Includes *Swinging on a Star* (Van Heusen/Burke), *Cherry, Cherry* (Diamond), *You Belong to Me* (King/Price/Stewart), *Riffin' at the Ritz* (Goodman/Miller), *At Last* (Warren/Gordon), *I Don't Want to Set the World on Fire* (Seiler/Durham/Marcus/Benjamin).

How to Make an American Quilt is the story of a young woman who spends a summer with her aunt and grandmother in an effort to bond, finish her thesis, and decide whether or not she should marry her fiancé. This is one of those well-intentioned, theatrical 'women's' films, but when the main woman is Winona Ryder, who can resist? The feast for the eyes is more than complemented by the subtlety of the accompaniment, in this case the music score by Thomas Newman. The classical approach taken by the filmmakers inhibits the composer's opportunity to experiment, but the listener will find no quarrel with the end result. Running 25'31" of the disc's playing time, the score opens with the pastoral "Quilting Theme". While oboes converse harmonically over strings and harp, Newman offers a I-V-IV-I progression that resolves in a plagal cadence (revisited in "An American Quilt"). Piano, electronics, guitars, and vocalese create an active contrast in "The Life Before", wherein the composer renders a Southern gospel feel and a sense of time being suspended.

This is an occasionally dreamy score in which synth-generated sounds are interpolated with acoustic magic. Newman's music displays an instinct for that critical dramatic moment when everything in the film stands still for the audience's contemplation. The ambient beauty is stolen, but there is no punishment – in Newman's world, music, character, and environment are peaceful allies. Melodic and poignant, the score features the composer's customary first-rate woodwind writing – the clarinets are smooth and even, the oboes are subjective and nasal, and the flutes are soft and feathery. Indeed, much of the score consists of winds moving over strings, piano, and bells. Newman is going more for texture than themes here, although a second major theme is introduced in "He Never Came Back". Meanwhile, "Hyacinth and Gladiola", "Night Orchard" and "Sophia" are mood-pieces that underscore the various patches of love stories told by the women. Gentle, fragile tracks like "The Sensation of Falling" and "Foolish Things" create the impression that the music could dissipate into nothingness without warning. Things only become solidified in "The Diver", the concluding track. It begins with the second theme in a typical arrangement, before closing with a strong thematic statement that suggests a resolution to the conflicts between/within the characters and the end of Ryder's journey of discovery. Fortunately, the songs on the disc are interspersed with the score to good effect, conjuring nostalgia in an idiomatically diverse manner.   **KM**

Little Women (1994) **Original Soundtrack**, with the **London Symphony Orchestra / Thomas Newman**.
> Sony Classical Ⓕ SK66922 (37 minutes: DDD). Includes *La Fayette's Welcome* (Francis Johnson), *Maria Redowa* (Gaetano Donizetti), *Port Royal Gallop* (Claudio Grafulla, arranged by Thomas Pasatieri), and *For the Beauty of the Earth* (Conrad Kocher).

Thomas Newman's continually evolving style here seems to suggest a cross-fertilization between an English pastoral idiom, and a broad Americana. The lightness of the orchestration, and the emotional restraint – only at pivotal moments does Newman allow his music to become expressively romantic – are all his own. Contrapuntal writing for brass in the carol-like "Main Title" is deceptively grand: much of the score is more intimate. A delightfully tender, pastoral theme, often stated by clarinet or strings, forms the backbone of the score. It is given a wistful variation for flute in "Learning to Forget". Copland's *Appalachian Spring* comes to mind, if only because Newman's score, like the ballet, contains the spirit (but not the substance) of nineteenth-century American spiritual and folk melody. The LSO, particularly their brass section in the opening and closing titles, give a model demonstration of the extra polish and unity of sound a first-class orchestra can bring to a film score.   **MW**

The Shawshank Redemption (1994) Original Soundtrack / Thomas Newman.
> Epic Ⓕ 478332-2 (54 minutes: DDD). Includes *If I Didn't Care* (Lawrence), *Lovesick Blues* (Hank Williams), and "Sull'aria" from *Le Nozze di Figaro* (Mozart).

The despair of confinement, and the irrepressible nature of the human spirit are expressed side by side in Newman's downbeat score. A grim theme for Shawshank prison and its brutal inmates, "Stoic Theme" – monochrome strings against a ground bass – is contrasted with warmer, gentler themes which convey the hope latent within – in the cues "Suds on the Roof" and "Workfield" for example. Murky, thudding synthesizer motifs and softly voiced piano chords reflect a mood of grinding hopelessness, whilst the score gradually works towards an optimistic and uplifting finale. A compelling mixture of styles, *The Shawshank Redemption* also features folksy Americana and, in the cue "And That Right Soon", a quasi-English approach recalling Holst's *St Paul's Suite*. The source music listed above really needs to be programmed out for full enjoyment of Newman's subtle and profound musical scheme. **MW**

New review
Unstrung Heroes (1995) **Original Soundtrack / Thomas Newman**.
    Hollywood Ⓕ HR62035-2 (27 minutes: DDD).

Thomas Newman certainly continues to develop his taste for the unusual with *Unstrung Heroes*. Newman's ensemble for this score includes vibraphone, jaw harp, zither, bowed brass dulcimer, indian banjo, pedal steel guitar and processed hurdy gurdy. As one might expect, such a bizarre collection of instruments produces an equally bizarre sound, especially when combined with some sprightly string effects. For the most part there is little that is tonal or melodic about Newman's writing, although there are some warmer cues which employ recorder and strings. Overall the music has a restless and rather edgy feel to it. There are no distinct themes, instead Newman patches together a series of pithy motifs, and many of his cues are simply brief expositions of the very individual sounds of his eccentric orchestra. There is certainly something very immediate and vibrant about Newman's colourings and its audacity is possibly its most endearing quality. **PP**

New review
Up Close and Personal (1996) **Original Soundtrack / Thomas Newman**.
    Hollywood Ⓕ HR62053-2 (42 minutes: DDD). Includes *Hong Kong Mambo* (Puente) and *Café* (Palmieri).

The listener can always be sure of a few surprises in every new score from Thomas Newman. Over the last few years he has achieved a staggeringly high degree of innovation in his music, and seems to have an unquenchable thirst for exploring new ideas and directions in film music. The most singular characteristic of Newman's music, however, is its simplicity and subtlety. *Up Close and Personal* is an ideal example of his passion for grafting wildly varied styles of music and instrumentation onto a conventional orchestral score. His orchestral palette is made up of such eclectic instruments as pan pipes, synthesizers, electric and acoustic guitar, electric percussion, steel drums and piano. The score has a sexy main theme, performed on chimes, steel drum, guitar and strings, which evokes a rather cool but erotic air of carnal pleasure. Indeed, much of the score has a sonorous flow of desire running through it, whether induced by lightly jazzy piano solos, or sultry transparent strings. During the more dramatic material, Newman introduces low brass, pan pipes, synthesizers and harp to produce a very unique and hot contemporary sound. He also uses jazzy mambo-style music, and this is reflected in the choice of two source music tracks. Above all, *Up Close and Personal* is a very tonal score, with many lyrical melodies and a real touch of class in the orchestration. **PP**

Also available:
Desperately Seeking Susan (1985) Varèse Sarabande VCD47291
Flesh and Bone (1993) Varèse Sarabande VSD5460
Fried Green Tomatoes (1991) MCA MCAD10634
Josh and S.A.M. (1993) Varèse Sarabande VSD5432
The Linguini Incident (1992) Varèse Sarabande VSD5372
The Player (1992) Varèse Sarabande VSD5366
Scent of a Woman (1992) MCA MCAD10759
The War (1994) MCA MCAD11160 [mostly pop songs]
Whispers in the Dark (1992) Varèse Sarabande VSD5387

Alex North

1910-1991 USA

Born of Russian parents in Chester, Pennsylvania, Alex North studied piano at the Curtis Institute in Philadelphia before winning a scholarship to the Juilliard School in New York. Lack of funds forced him to work as a telegraph operator all night so he could study music by day. In 1934 he went to the Moscow Conservatory, and became the only American member of the Union of Soviet Composers. Despite his Russian parentage, he could speak little of the language and soon decided to return home. Back in New York he studied composition with Ernst Toch and Aaron Copland, and wrote ballet scores for Martha Graham and others. During the Second World War he scored several documentaries for the Office of War Information. North's move to Hollywood was a result of his music for the stage production of Arthur Miller's *Death of a Salesman*, directed by Elia Kazan. Kazan's next project was a film version of Tennessee Williams's *A Streetcar Named Desire*, and he insisted that North should provide the music. This was the first major jazz-based score to be written in Hollywood, and it made North an overnight success. North's music is highly personal and distinctive, employing a wide palette of orchestral colour. Unusually for a film composer, his approach to scoring was often introspective and understated. His influence on a later generation of composers has been widespread. "Of all of us, he's the master", said Jerry Goldsmith. (In 1997, a disc of music from *Streetcar, Spartacus* and *The Bad Seed* performed by the London Symphony Orchestra conducted by Eric Stern will be released on the Nonesuch label).

Cinerama South Seas Adventure (1958) **Original Soundtrack**, with the **Norman Luboff Choir; Cinerama Symphony Orchestra / Alex North**.
Label X Ⓔ LXCD2 (48 minutes: ADD).

Cinerama South Seas Adventure serves not only as a nostalgic reminder of the long-gone days of the Cinerama travelogues, but also a rare example on CD of North's lighter, more romantic style. As the title suggests, the film took the audience on a journey around the South Seas and Australasia, all in the widest of widescreen Technicolored splendour *and* six-track stereophonic sound. The score is appropriately lush, without ever reverting to the stereotypical army of Hawaiian guitars and endless variations on "Aloha oe". This is North's own personal postcard view of the islands, a series of exquisitely exotic and often humorous snapshots as exemplified by "Surf Riding", "King Neptune" and "Kangaroo Roundup". The original LP was a popular demonstration disc in its day, and whilst the master tapes have inevitably deteriorated over the intervening 35 years, the sound still packs quite a wallop. The hackneyed source music recorded on location will soon outstay its welcome, but it can of course be programmed out quite easily. **RS**

New review

North of Hollywood Alex North and His Orchestra.
RCA Ⓔ 1145-2 (35 minutes: ADD). Recorded 1958.
A Streetcar Named Desire (1951). The Member of the Wedding (1953). The Racers (1955). Unchained (1955). The Rose Tattoo (1955). Hot Spell (1958). "Trick or Treat" and "Ticker Tape" from Wall Street Parade. "Ode to a Western" from American Road.

"Jazz has been sadly neglected", Alex North is quoted as saying in the programme notes for "North of Hollywood". Explaining the agenda behind the project, North elaborates: "Attempts should be made to extract its essence and spirit and to project it with all the resources and craftsmanship at one's command"."North of Hollywood" was the first of two collections North recorded for RCA in the late 1950's. The second album in this too-brief series, entitled "Film Music by Alex North", concentrated on his intimate, lyrical orchestral style (it was reissued on the now-defunct Bay Cities label). A keen student of twentieth-century forms and styles, North always had an affinity for jazz. When the time came for him to score his first film, he found a project that allowed to display this affection while also fuelling his desire to break with the aesthetics of his Golden Age predecessors. The film was *A Streetcar Named Desire*, a classic effort that represents the first time jazz was used in dramatic scoring for something other than source music. Since film music requires strict timings that run antithetically to jazz processes such as improvisation, North devised a form of compositional jazz that emphasizes structure over freedom. Three excerpts from that revolutionary score are presented here, including the sultry music written for Stan and Stella. In fact, this track was cut from the original print after pressure was applied by the MPAA and the Catholic Legion of Decency (it was restored for the film's 1993 re-release).

North has not used his original orchestrations for this recording, having eliminated the string section entirely and put together a group of about 30 players. There is little in the way of overlapping dialogue, the focus being on solo turns – though one never gets the sense that the members of the ensemble are going their own way. North's approach is to make musical statements and compose the responses, with each instrument carrying the torch forward as if performing in a relay. There is no rush to the finish, however, with North being content to allow his melodies and atmospheres to make their impact in their own good time. Only a few moods are presented here, but they are done with aplomb and virtuosity. Ironically, two of the disc's best moments aren't even film scores, but pieces from the composer's *Wall Street Ballet*. And in the last two tracks, "Jody's Lament" from *The Member of the Wedding* and "Blackjack" from *The Racers*, North displays his interest in another twentieth-century musical development: dissonance. **KM**

Spartacus (1960) **Original Soundtrack / Alex North**.
MCA Ⓜ MCAD10256 (41 minutes: AAD).

Only a handful of the costly blockbusters that sprawled across the wide screen during the late 1950s and early 1960s were endowed with the intelligence of *Spartacus*. Although the awesome visual spectacle made full use of the 70mm canvas, director Stanley Kubrick ensured that the human elements in this story of pre-Christian man's revolt against slavery were never dwarfed. Alex North's urgent, brass-dominated music gave the narrative a compelling contemporary resonance and it remains as potent now as it did in 1960. Throughout this pungent and intricately orchestrated score North employs staccato rhythms and augmented brass and percussion to galvanizing effect. The metallic brutality of the main title or the dynamic sequences illustrating Spartacus's growing army on the march never fail to send a thrill up the listener's spine. Large chunks of the score were omitted from the original LP in order to make room for the commercial exploitability of the beautifully limpid love theme (the only time the strings are allowed the upper hand), but the overall result is still one of the most exhilarating soundtrack albums in film music history, particularly as the stereo sound is still remarkably vibrant for its age. **RS**

A Streetcar Named Desire (1951) **Original Soundtrack / Ray Heindorf**. ARCAM
    Capitol mono Ⓕ 95597 (52 minutes: AAD).
    Also includes **Max Steiner:** Since You Went Away (1944). Now, Voyager (1942). The Informer (1935), conducted by **Max Steiner**.
A Streetcar Named Desire (1951) **National Philharmonic Orchestra / Jerry Goldsmith**.
    Varèse Sarabande Ⓕ VSD5500 (47 minutes: DDD). Recorded 1995.

From 1951 onwards, the mittel-European style of film scoring underwent a radical transformation after it received a potent injection of jazz via Alex North's ground-breaking music for Elia Kazan's screen version of *A Streetcar Named Desire*. This searing, claustrophobic score, with its bluesy brass and sultry strings, creates an air of raw sexuality rarely encountered in other scores of this period, and dramatically underlines the hothouse atmosphere of the Tennessee Williams play as well as the disturbed fragility of faded Southern belle, Blanche DuBois. The music still packs a huge punch more than 40 years later, and its reputation as a landmark film score remains undimmed. Although recorded on acetates, the sound is remarkably vivid. In direct contrast to the blazing modernism of *Streetcar* are Max Steiner's early 1950s recordings of his three Oscar-winners (which, incidentally, are quite different from Charles Gerhardt's later versions for RCA). These robust examples of traditional Hollywood film scoring at its best are, however, just as compelling, their strong, well-crafted melodies and sweeping romanticism quite impossible to resist. Jerry Goldsmith's new recording of *Streetcar* is a remarkably faithful reconstruction of the complete score and makes an invaluable supplement to the Capitol disc. The National Philharmonic, augmented by a select combo of such eminent session musicians as Ronnie Price and Tony Coe, capture all its moaning intensity with thrilling precision, as well as throwing into bold relief orchestral detail barely audible on the Original Soundtrack. **RS**

2001: A Space Odyssey (1968) **National Philharmonic Orchestra / Jerry Goldsmith**.
    Varèse Sarabande Ⓕ VSD5400 (36 minutes: DDD). Recorded 1993.

Since the release of Stanley Kubrick's epoch-making movie in 1968, with its instantly popular soundtrack comprising snatches of old and contemporary classics, legends have grown about a parade of composers who were asked to contribute an original dramatic score. Alex North, who had previously worked with Kubrick on *Spartacus*, was the only musician to actually get to compose and record a score for the Sci-Fi epic – although even he had his commission curtailed before he could tackle the all-important second half of the film – as by then Kubrick had decided to 'go classical'. North's part-score is here brilliantly re-recorded under the sure baton of his longtime devotee and old friend Jerry Goldsmith. The extant 35 minutes of music (which include an alternate cue for one sequence) are remarkable in every respect. North's opening stanza is an accomplished musical paraphrase of the awesome beginning of Richard Strauss's *Also sprach Zarathustra*, always Kubrick's preferred choice as the film's curtain-raiser. The music for the initial part of the film, "The Dawn of Man" sequence, when simians first encounter intervention from the stars, is spare, raw, rhythmically complex, modernistic, avant-garde even, evoking a primordial feel without any reference to Stravinsky's *The Rite of Spring*, the usual index for this kind of thing. Anyone familiar with North's output will recognize this music as quintessentially his, its bare primitiveness born of the major influences on this composer's work: South American folk idioms and North American jazz. The scoring of the later moon sequences maintains a strong rhythmic element, but the tone is here altogether different; there is a clarity, a purity, a simplicity even, the music higher in pitch, it is chaste and elegant – particularly personified by "Space Station Docking", a feathery waltz which spins and floats as blithely as the weightless space station. North typifies space travel itself with an unexpected stillness conjured by high strings and celeste, whilst he chaperones a journey across the surface of the moon with an elusive ethereal melody for wordless mezzo soprano.

    It is sad to contemplate what North might have summoned to accompany the bizarre and wondrous second half of the film, but at least we can now appreciate what was composed (and rejected) although during the interim North did not waste his thematic material: he later utilized the film's opening motif to lead his score for *The Shoes of the Fisherman* (1968), the waltz for the space station docking emerged in the music for *Dragonslayer* (1981), and the intermezzo framed for the intermission became the main title music for the ABC TV series *Africa* (1967). North's music for *2001* now looms as a masterwork: for those who still denigrate film composition as an imitative or impoverished relation of concert music, listen to this score and change your mind.   **DW**

Also available:
Cheyenne Autumn (1964) Label X LXCD4
Rich Man, Poor Man (1976) Varèse Sarabande VSD5423
The Sound and the Fury (1959) Varèse Sarabande VSD5297

Michael Nyman

b. 1944 England

Michael Nyman studied keyboard and composition at the Royal Academy of Music, and musicology (with Thurston Dart) at King's College, London. He began his career as a writer, and was the first to use the term 'minimalism' as applied to music. Nyman has written a great deal of distinctive and original music, much of it for the variable, partly electronic forces of his own group The Michael Nyman Band. He is the composer of five operas, including *The Man Who Mistook His Wife for a Hat* (1986). Nyman's film music career has been closely linked with the films of Peter Greenaway, although his most popular work, *The Piano* (1994), was in collaboration with Jane Campion.

Carrington (1995) **Original Soundtrack**, with the **Michael Nyman Band / Michael Nyman**.
    Argo Ⓟ 444 873-2 (67 minutes: DDD). Includes *Adagio* from String Quintet in C, D956 (Schubert).

On the face of it, there is no reason why the untold millions who rushed out to buy copies of *The Piano* should not do exactly the same for *Carrington*. That they will certainly not do so is no reflection on the fine polish of this score, but more a result of a lack of that certain indefinable spark which occasionally captures the public's – and the marketing executives' – imagination. *Carrington* is firmly embedded in the familiar Nyman manner: characteristically repetitive blocks of sound; restless, chugging rhythms; and overarching melodies carried by the obligatory saxophones are, in this instance, imbued with a wistful pastoral nostalgia. Material from the composer's Third String Quartet has been adapted as a recurring theme. Lacking the pianistic source music of his most popular score, *Carrington* is possibly a more coherent work as a result. This is a gentle and romantic piece, for which Nyman's modernist angularity has been significantly toned down.   **MW**

Drowning by Numbers (1988) **Original Soundtrack**, with the **Michael Nyman Band / Michael Nyman**.
    Virgin Ⓜ CDVE23 (45 minutes: DDD).

The minimalist school of music certainly has its detractors, and some would argue that it can never work as film music. Nyman's several collaborations with Peter Greenaway possibly would not alter that view, since the director's films can be seen as artistic contrivances rather than constructed narratives. Greenaway's work is never less than fascinating to watch, but *Drowning by Numbers* is probably his most accessible. The mournful nature of the opening music speaks of the murderous intent of the principal characters, the three Cissies, whereas other pieces deliberately underline the playful and somewhat irreverent approach to the grim subject matter. Nyman's score, artfully constructed around the slow movement of Mozart's *Sinfonia Concertante*, is a beguiling series of variations that match the mood of the film. It is less abrasive than, say, *The Cook, the Thief, His Wife and Her Lover*, but more involving than the rather clinical *The Draughtsman's Contract*. In this case, the music works as dramatic underscore, visual accompaniment to the sumptuous images, and as an entertaining musing upon the music of Mozart, which is much admired by both director and composer.   **DS**

The Piano (1994) **Original Soundtrack**, with the **Munich Philharmonic Orchestra / Michael Nyman** (pf).
    Virgin Ⓕ CDVE919 (57 minutes: DDD).

The heart of this score is the solo piano repertoire designed for Ada, the film's central character (played with such assurance by Holly Hunter in the film, but here performed by the composer). Taking as his cue Ada's Scottish origins, Nyman compiled a piano sourcebook for her based largely on traditional folk tunes. Using this as a foundation, he then constructed an orchestral underscore which is at its most effective when quoting or expanding upon the solo piano music. Listeners struck by the folk-like simplicity of the piano's themes may find Nyman's more characteristic contributions less appealing. Just as with the film, the piano is the focus of this album, making this not only the most popular, but also the most accessible of Nyman's film scores. (The composer's reworking of the score for concert performance, *The Piano Concerto*, is available on Argo 443 382-2). **MW**

New review
Prospero's Books (1991) **Original Soundtrack**, with **Sarah Leonard, Marie Angel, Ute Lemper** and **Deborah Conway** (sngrs); **Michael Nyman Band / Michael Nyman**.
Argo Ⓟ 425 224-2 (55 minutes: ADD).

"Be not afeard, the Isle is full of Noises, Sounds, and sweet Airs, that give Delight and hurt not; Sometimes a thousand twangling instruments will hum about mine Ears; and sometime Voices..." In the booklet notes, Michael Nyman confesses that his memory of this quotation from *The Tempest* only conjured the reference to voices. Still, the listener can find plenty of melodic lines, a variety of aural textures, and if not a thousand instruments, then certainly the 23-piece Michael Nyman Band. *Prospero's Books* – the sixth major collaboration between Nyman and Peter Greenaway – is one of the most unique films ever made. Scenes and characters from *The Tempest* are presented, but it is not a filmed adaptation. In fact, the film is difficult to describe. Perhaps it is best to say that it is a non-narrative work of art meant to be appreciated on its own terms. The same can be said for the score. One of the director's great visual accomplishments is the way he makes the film connect with the human body in the manner of the Renaissance masters – it's as if Titian had been hired as the director of cinematography. Greenaway, who presents every theme and interest as an obsession, has found a perfect musical partner in Nyman.

The music for *Prospero's Books* is not the music of Shakespeare's time or the music of the Mediterranean setting. It is a conflation of classical and modernist sensibilities, with the chief technique being minimalism. Nyman, of course, is one of the pre-eminent minimalist composers of our time. His highly stylized score employs brief cells of tonal material, often repeated obsessively. "Prospero's Magic", "Miranda", "History of Sycorax", and "Cornfield" are examples of this hypnotic approach. Vocals also play a prominent role, with music being provided for five of Ariel's songs performed by Sarah Leonard in what the composer describes as a "boy soprano voice". The vocal highlight of the score is "The Masque", a 12-minute setting of Act 4 in which Prospero gives his daughter to Ferdinand in marriage. Three spirits named Iris (Marie Angel), Juno (Deborah Conway), and Ceres (Ute Lemper) sing blessings to the young couple in three highly differentiated vocal traditions.

Argo's presentation is flawless, with impeccable sound, informative notes by the composer, and Shakespeare's text for the songs. If there is a problem, it might be that the intellectual and artistic properties of the Greenaway/Nyman aesthetic sometimes fail to make emotional connections. We are left gasping in admiration, but perhaps also feeling that the head is being addressed at the expense of the heart. **KM**

Also available:
The Cold Room (1985) Silva Screen FILMCD157
The Cook, the Thief, His Wife and Her Lover (1989) Virgin CDVE53
The Draughtsman's Contract (1982) Charisma CASCD1158
The Essential Michael Nyman Band Argo 436 820-2
Out of the Ruins (1989) Silva Screen FILMCD063
A Zed and Two Noughts (1985) Virgin CDVE54

John Ottman   USA

John Ottman's passion for movie music began with classic television Sci-Fi like *Star Trek* (the original incarnation of course) and flourished in the late 1970s during the rash of big screen spectaculars that followed *Star Wars*. A keen amateur filmmaker even as a schoolboy, Ottman edited his favourite film scores to fit his own home-made movies. He began writing original scores for student films, but later made a sideways move into film editing. Whilst working as editor on director Bryan Singer's first feature, *Public Access*, Ottman was unexpectedly asked to supply the music as well. This unique dual role of film editor and composer continued with Singer's next movie, *The Usual Suspects*. Ottman's close involvement in shaping these movies as editor enabled him to give a great deal of thought to his music well in advance of normal practice. Ottman hopes to expand his composing activities, but has resolved to continue as both editor and composer on all Bryan Singer's future projects, beginning with *Apt Pupil* (1997): thereby ensuring that an enlightened attitude to music is maintained in at least one small corner of Hollywood.

The Usual Suspects (1995) **Original Soundtrack**, with **Damon Intrabartolo** (pf) **/ Larry Groupé**.
Milan Ⓕ 30107-2 (54 minutes: DDD). Includes *Les Sons et Les Parfums Tournent dans l'Air du Soir* (Debussy).

Unusually for such a hip movie, *The Usual Suspects* dispenses with the almost obligatory string of trendy pop songs in favour of a handsome orchestral score. Ottman's potent combination of 1940s *film noir*, the cool ambience of a 1970s thriller, and resolutely 1990s action is informed throughout by a rare passion. Perhaps because he is more than just another hired hand, Ottman conveys a sense of conviction all too often lacking in scores from better known names. A mysterious motif for the equally mysterious Keyse Söze casts an elusive shadow across the rest. Dramatic moments like the chilling "Keyser Appears" are charged with an electrifying – almost Wagnerian – intensity. Piano, synths and even dobro guitar fill out sombre strings and woodwinds, adding a refreshingly different edge to the orchestrations. *The Usual Suspects* is an intelligent and thoughtful score, with a depth of psychological insight which is altogether unusual.   **MW**

Jean-Claude Petit
France

Jean-Claude Petit studied music at the Paris Conservatoire, but developed wide-ranging interests in contemporary music (with Pierre Boulez's Ensemble InterContemporain), Jazz (with Dexter Gordon and Kenny Clarke) and pop music (he has worked with Joan Baez, Julien Clerc and Claude François among others). Aware that writing music for the cinema is an art which requires "chameleon-like" abilities from the composer, Petit decided that his eclectic range of influences equipped him well for the job. Although he had been working in films since *Tusk* in 1980, Petit's big break came when director Claude Berri asked him to score his two films, *Jean de Florette* and *Manon des Sources* (1986), for which the composer made inspired use of the opening bars of Verdi's *La forza del destino* overture – a theme made even more popular by its later use in a popular lager commercial. In 1989, when Jean-Paul Rappeneau made his first film after a seven-year hiatus, *Cyrano de Bergerac*, he asked Petit to provide the score: they worked together again on *Le Hussard sur le Toit* – both scores distinguished by Petit's ability to write convincingly in the appropriate period styles. He has also worked with director Richard Lester on *The Return of the Musketeers* (1989–more period music), and with Claude Berri on *Fucking Ferdinand* (1987) and *Uranus* (1991). The composer also collaborated on the script as well as writing the music for Henri Verneuil's *Mayrig* (1991).

Cyrano de Bergerac (1989) **Original Soundtrack**, with the **Paris Opera Orchestra / Jean-Claude Petit**.
Colosseum Ⓕ CST348046 / DRG Ⓕ DRGCD12602 (50 minutes: DDD).

An enjoyable cross-fertilization this: the stately splendour of the high baroque blended with some much later romantic Hollywood-style swashbuckling, all written and performed with panache and a good deal of humour. A dotted rhythm main theme, given fanfare-like to trumpet, is the score's opening and most arresting 'ancient' music; although several other cues affect a jolly seventeenth-century air, none are ever serious or po-faced enough to be mistaken for straightforward pastiche. Chamber organ and lute crop up to reinforce the authentic atmosphere, whilst Petit gleefully undermines his own period-isms by straying into more familiar filmic territory: the excitement of "The Duel", for example, sounds uncannily like Danny Elfman's *Batman* of the same year (coincidence?); Cyrano and Roxane's love theme is unashamedly romantic. The finale abandons all pretence of baroque mannerisms, going straight for heart-tugging sentimentality. Both the orchestra's full-blooded performance and the warm ambience of the recording are an additional treat.   **MW**

Le Hussard sur le Toit (1995) **Original Soundtrack**, with the **Orchestre National de France / Jean-Claude Petit**.
Auvidis Travelling K10106 (55 minutes: DDD). Includes *Intermezzo*, Op. 116 No. 6 (Brahms).

Unlike *Cyrano de Bergerac*, where the composer's own musical inclinations were tempered by an unself-consciously tongue-in-cheek feel for period style, Petit's latest collaboration with director Jean-Paul Rappeneau allows him free reign to indulge in the most eloquent declarations of unadulterated romanticism. *Le Hussard sur le Toit* (*The Horseman on the Roof*) is, on the surface anyway – in the flow and texture of the scoring – a quite deliberate homage to the great composers of the last century: but elusively so, with only one overt quotation from Brahms. Indeed, what shines through this studied veneer is Petit's own warm, romantic personality. This score is not a copy of the past, but a continuation of its spirit ideally embodied by Petit in his own traditionally romantic form. If the musical language is careful never to stray beyond the confines of its period it is none the worse for that; and this is demonstrably a period in which the composer has found a natural home. The jolly dance suite towards the end – galops, quadrilles and waltzes all bubbling with *joi de vivre* – makes for a refreshing constrast. A beautifully voluptuous performance by the Orchestre National – obviously comfortable in this idiom – only makes the atmosphere of brooding passion all the more convincing. Like the movie. this is a disc which should give lasting pleasure. **MW**

Also available:
Jean de Florette (1986) **Manon de Sources** (1986) Milan CDCH378
Mayrig (1992) Milan 752 001

Basil Poledouris   USA

Basil Poledouris studied music under David Raksin at the University of Southern California, where he went on to earn a Masters degree in Cinema; he then completed his musical studies at California State University. He is thus a rare example of a composer schooled in writing, directing, editing and other aspects of filmmaking. His first film score was for *Extreme Close-Up* (1973). A student friendship with director John Milius resulted in him scoring *Big Wednesday* in 1978; their later collaboration on *Conan the Barbarian* produced what is regarded by many as one of the finest film scores of recent years. Later films with Milius include *Red Dawn* (1984) and *Farewell to the King* (1989). Another fruitful collaboration for Poledouris has been director Paul Verhoeven for whom he scored *Flesh and Blood* (1985), *RoboCop* (1987) and, in 1997, *Starship Troopers*. Poledouris often employs modal harmonies which add a distinctly Russian flavour to his music. Greig McRitchie is his regular orchestrator.

Conan the Barbarian (1982) **Original Soundtrack**, with the **Santa Cecilia Chorus and Orchestra; Rome Radio Symphony Orchestra / Basil Poledouris**.
Varèse Sarabande Ⓕ VSD5390 (68 minutes: ADD) / Milan Ⓜ 11126-2 (49 minutes: ADD).
Conan the Destroyer (1984) **Original Soundtrack**, with the **Unione Musicisti di Roma Orchestra / Basil Poledouris**.
Varèse Sarabande Ⓕ VSD5392 (33 minutes: DDD).

Conan the Barbarian is a glorious tribute to one of the few truly collaborative composer/director partnerships. What Eisenstein and Prokofiev achieved with *Alexander Nevsky*, Milius and Poledouris did with *Conan*. The director and composer worked together throughout production, Poledouris wrote music before and during principal photography. The result is an enormous, awe-inspiring creation that transcends the constraints of the picture's comic-book narrative to become a fully-fledged independent work. Every scene is given its own distinctive musical treatment: thundering timpani and unison French horns open the score in a manner worthy of comparison with *Alexander Nevsky*; the evil Thulsa Doom's arrival is heralded by a choral setting of "Dies Irae" that in mood and style echoes Orff's *Carmina Burana* but does not copy it; the young Conan's torment on the "Wheel of Pain" is expressed by a grinding, ever-rising motif comparable to Rózsa's "Rowing of the Galley Slaves" from *Ben-Hur*; and all this in just the first 15 minutes! The richness and variety of the orchestration is a joy from beginning to end – nowhere is it better demonstrated than during "Theology/Civilization": a delicious folk-like melody stated by cor anglais, clarinet and flute supported by gentle harp and tinkling percussion is taken over by sweeping strings, suggestive of the openness of the Russian steppes, before it is returned in sonata-style to the graceful cor anglais. Every scene is a fully-rounded composition. The Varèse Sarabande disc is a significantly expanded version of the original soundtrack album, adding such unmissable delights as "Mountain of Power Procession", "The Tree of Woe", "The Kitchen" and "The Death of Rexor". As such, it must be recommended over the shorter Milan version. The Milan disc has the advantage of being mid-price, but has no booklet notes. Whichever version you choose, this awesome score is an essential purchase.

The perfectly workmanlike and serviceable score for *Conan the Destroyer* suffers from an inevitable comparison with its gigantic predecessor. There is less variety, less inventiveness, less coherence than the original. The smaller orchestra sounds positively weedy; the omission of a chorus leaves an unfilled hole. Back to normal composer-unfriendly Hollywood working practices – and without the sympathetic encouragement of John Milius – Poledouris nevertheless came up with a score which manages to achieve some interesting variations on the original without relying on reprising too many of its best moments. **MW**

The Hunt for Red October (1990) **Original Soundtrack / Basil Poledouris**.
   MCA Ⓜ MCLD19306 (30 minutes: ADD).

This score's riveting centrepiece is the "Hymn to Red October", a rousing nationalistic choral anthem somewhat in the manner of Prokofiev's "Song about Alexander Nevsky". This and the extended chase sequence that follows ("Nuclear Scam") are the strongest parts of the score. Synthesizers add extra colour to the orchestral palette, whilst the chorus has a significant role beyond the opening "Hymn". Much of the interest comes from the composer's ability to invest fairly routine thriller material with a distinctly Slavic accent. The Russian lyrics are by the composer.   **MW**

New review

It's My Party (1996) **Original Soundtrack**, with **Basil Poledouris** (pf).
   Varèse Sarabande Ⓕ VSD5701 (32 minutes: DDD). Includes *Don't Cut Me Down* (Olivia Newton-John).

The traditional method of film scoring involved the composer performing his themes on piano to give the director an impression of the music before it was later realized by full orchestra at the recording session. Technology has now supplanted this, and computers linked to synthesizers are now able to give both composer and director a more realistic impression of the finished score before it is recorded. However, in asking Basil Poledouris to write a solo piano score for *It's My Party*, the director had remembered the simplicity of the original piano themes the composer had written for his previous films. He hoped that the simple approach would help eschew sentimentality in favour of "real emotional texture". The result is no mere album of cocktail lounge music, even though the cues have more of a 'real' structure than usual. Poledouris's themes are forlorn and meditative, but never depressing. This unusual approach to a film score makes for a quite pleasing listen.   **PP**

The Jungle Book (1995) **Original Soundtrack / David Snell**.
   Milan Ⓕ 24861-2 (48 minutes: DDD).

This live-action remake may not have won great acclaim – the 1942 Korda movie remains unbeaten, even by Disney– but Poldeouris's fairy-tale score has its own merits. Brimming over with ravishing melodies and imbued with the composer's most attractive mannerisms, *The Jungle Book* is yet another example of how a good score can survive the demise of a lacklustre film. Recorded in the glowing acoustic of London's Air Studios the score is as richly textured as an oriental rug. Bold Mowgli, the menacing Shere Khan, noble Baloo, and the impish monkeys are all given their own characteristic musical themes. Poledouris does not attempt to imitate Miklós Rózsa's 1942 original however, preferring to rely on his own ability to pen warm, memorable melodies. "Civilization", which juxtaposes a lilting treatment of Mowgli's theme and a ravishing love theme, is just one delight amongst many.   **MW**

Lonesome Dove (1989) **Original Soundtrack / Basil Poledouris**.
   Cabin Fever Music Ⓕ CFM972-2 (46 minutes: DDD).

The composer was rightly rewarded with an Emmy Award for this splendid television Western score. The main theme is a gloriously nostalgic piece for trumpet and orchestra, sumptuously scored. The music is by turns tender and delicate then bold and brash, without any of the usual genre clichés. Thoughtful orchestration adds dulcimer, guitar, banjo, mandolin and 'old-timey' fiddle to more conventional textures (during "Arkansas Pilgrim", for example, where a melancholy tune for clarinet, oboe and flute segues into a folk dance, before returning with the orchestra). Fiddle and harmonica are used to ravishing effect in "Gus and Pea Eye" – a beautifully authentic sounding folk tune which is at the same time an original and distinctive creation. The whole is an unmitigated old-fashioned wallow.   **MW**

Quigley Down Under (1990) **Original Soundtrack / Basil Poledouris**.
   Intrada Ⓕ MAF7006D (41 minutes: DDD).

After the folksy Americana of *Lonesome Dove*, Poledouris had another opportunity to show his affinity for Westerns in scoring this unusual tale of sharpshooter Matthew Quigley (Tom Selleck's best ever screen role) in the Australian outback. The music is pure, distilled Poledouris, with several distinctive themes which vie for attention. A quirky solo clarinet introduces the main character, this is taken up by trumpet and banjo with a delicious 'oompah' tuba before giving way to a full-blown Western theme; then a wistful tune for Cora appears on the flute. These themes function as *leitmotifs* throughout. "Marston's Murderers" introduces a fabulously exciting action theme played by the Poledouris favourite, unison French horns, backed by banjo and a hint of synthesizer. Another delightfully different twist on the Western genre.   **MW**

RoboCop (1987) **Original Soundtrack**, with **Derek Austin** (synths); **Sinfonia of London / Howard Blake, Tony Britten**.
TER Ⓕ CDTER1146 / Varèse Sarabande Ⓕ VSD47298 (41 minutes: ADD).
RoboCop 3 (1993) Original Soundtrack, with **Michael Boddicker** (synths) **/ Basil Poledouris**.
Varèse Sarabande Ⓕ VSD5416 (29 minutes: DDD).

Alongside Jerry Goldsmith, Basil Poledouris is perhaps the only composer who responds sympathetically – and musically – to the testosterone-driven silliness of movies like *RoboCop*. Like Goldsmith, Poledouris is able to see beyond the cartoon violence and penetrate to the heart of the story. In this case it is the half-machine's buried memories of his past life that evoke a sympathetic response from the composer. Typically warm melodies over minor-scale arpeggios signal the emotional core of the piece in the cue "Home". Elsewhere, action sequences are handled with unexpected passion: just occasionally – as with *Conan* before – a subject comes along which seems to grip Poledouris's imagination, and his music takes on additional intensity.
After being replaced by Leonard Rosenman for the sequel, Poledouris was given the thankless task of scoring the wearyingly unnecessary third feature. His *RoboCop* march, memorably introduced in the original, returns to good effect here, as does the tender "Home" theme. Through the synth-dominated brawn of many cues there remains much evidence of the fevered inspiration that gave the first score its impact. Even for such a dire sequel, Poledouris can still produce something exciting, distinctive – and musical. The absurdly short running time has the unlooked-for advantage of never allowing the music to run out of steam. **MW**

Also available:
Farewell to the King (1989) Milan CDCH375
Free Willy (1993) Epic EK57280
Hot Shots! Part Deux (1993) Varèse Sarabande VSD5426
Lassie (1994) Sony LK66414
On Deadly Ground (1993) Varèse Sarabande VSD5468
Red Dawn (1984) Intrada RVF6001D
Serial Mom (1993) MCA MCAD11052
Under Siege 2 (1995) Varèse Sarabande VSD5648
Wind (1992) For Life FLCF28209

Rachel Portman
England

Born in Haslemere, Surrey Rachel Portman began composing whilst attending Charterhouse School. She read music at Worcester College, Oxford where she gained experience composing for theatre and film, writing for Oxford Playhouse Productions and scoring her first film, a student production called *Privileged*. She began her professional career scoring David Puttnam's Channel 4 film *Experience Preferred But Not Essential* (1982). In 1988 she was the winner of the British Institute's Young Composer Award; and received BAFTA award nominations for her TV work on *Oranges Are Not the Only Fruit* (1989) and *The Woman in Black*. She has written several television scores, including all the music for the Jim Henson series *The Storyteller* (1986-8 and 1990). Her first full-length feature film score was Mike Leigh's *Life is Sweet* (1991), closely followed by Beeban Kidron's *Antonia and Jane* in the same year. *Where Angels Fear to Tread* (also 1991) received an Anthony Asquith Award nomination. Portman went to America to score Kidron's *Used People* (1992), and she has been increasingly in demand in Hollywood ever since. Her collaboration with Kidron has continued with *Too Wong Foo, Thanks for Everything! Julie Newmar* (1995). Rachel Portman's music is distinctively scored – often featuring clarinet and saxophone – witty, and full of delightful melodies. Her concern to capture every orchestral nuance means that she prefers to complete her own orchestrations.

New review
Emma (1996) **Original Soundtrack / David Snell**.
Hollywood Ⓕ MH62069-2 (43 minutes: DDD).

A comedy of manners and social mores, satirical but never mocking, sharp but never barbed, this screen adaptation of Jane Austen's greatest – and most subtle – novel required from its composer rare qualities of insight, wit and gentle empathy. Rachel Portman's delicate score meets the challenge adroitly. The often unspoken interplay between characters, the misunderstandings, the jealousies and deceits, all needed careful handling if the pointed effect of Austen's understated humour was not to be overstressed. Portman writes for a chamber orchestra led, as so often in her work, by clarinet, this time sharing solo duties with the appropriately period combination of flute and harp. Such a reduced ensemble, often providing the very simplest accompaniment for the soloist, gives the impression of being an eighteenth-century orchestra without ever actually sounding like one. Only the country dance is authentic – although not credited as such on the disc – and otherwise Portman makes no attempt to mimic rococo or classical mannerisms. Emma and Mr Knightley's developing love is accorded an unashamedly romantic theme, as strings take on the burden of emotional expression for the somewhat too heartwarming finale, which almost overbalances the score's previous restraint. **MW**

New review

A Pyromaniac's Love Story (1995) **Great Moments in Aviation** (1995) **Smoke** (1995) **Ethan Frome** (1993) Original Soundtracks.
Varèse Sarabande Ⓕ VSD5620 (60 minutes: DDD).

This CD showcases four totally different scores that reveal Portman as a composer of sophistication and wit. Although her style is far from conventional, her music always retains a strong tonality however bizarre the ensemble she employs. In *A Pyromaniac's Love Story*, for example, she draws on some comic and jolly playing from woodwinds for a toe-tapping tango-like score. Portman certainly enjoys playing with 'oom-pah' rhythms (just listen to her score for *The Road to Wellville*), and even though woodwinds are playing at very low registers here, the music retains an attractive, affable quality. The pace changes with *Great Moments in Aviation*, which features a sumptuous soprano voice performing a richly English pastoral-like theme backed by strings and horns. Those oom-pahs are back, this time for deep low brass and saxophone, but generally this is a more serious score, with a rather nostalgic feel given added depth by some haunting solo writing, particularly for violin. *Smoke* is slightly minimalist, both in development and instrumentation: a small string ensemble, xylophone, chimes and other percussion fuel her urgent ethnic-flavoured score, mounted around a pensive theme for clarinet. *Ethan Frome* is more downbeat and written primarily for strings and woodwinds. The sinister tone of the main theme is carried through most of the score, giving it a cold and unsettling edge. Four contrasting scores, then, all notable for their unusually intimate and colourful orchestral makeup. **PP**

Only You (1994) Original Soundtrack / David Snell.
Columbia Ⓕ 476818-2 (46 minutes: DDD). Includes *Only You* (Ram/Rand), *Some Enchanted Evening* (Rodgers/Hammerstein), *O Sole Mio* (Di Capua/Capurro/Mazzucchi) *Rondo* from Quartet in B flat (J.C. Bach), "Libiamo" from *La Traviata* (Verdi), and *Once in a Lifetime* (Bolton/Warren/Afanasieff).

Norman Jewison's true-love-by-accident film is pleasantly old-fashioned in its unashamed romanticism. Portman is no stranger to fairy-tale romance and there are moments in her score that hark back to the marvellously concise, but telling, scores she wrote for Jim Henson's TV series, *The Storyteller*. Simple, understated orchestrations with an achingly beautiful main theme do wonders for this film. It is one of her real strengths as a composer that, with admirable economy, she can suggest location, humour and emotion – and not wallpaper the film with music to get the point across. All her scores exhibit her penchant for bittersweet melodies that grab your attention, but this one is better than most. Normally, soundtracks that combine underscore with various songs heard, however briefly, in the film tend to come across as a mixed bag of sounds. Not so with this one, since the inclusion of – amongst others – Ezio Pinza singing "Some Enchanted Evening" and Louis Armstrong's "Only You" add much to the overall charm. **DS**

New review

Sirens (1994) Original Soundtrack / David Snell.
Milan Ⓕ 21302-2 (40 minutes: DDD). Includes "March Past of the Kitchen Utensils" from *The Wasps* (Vaughan Williams).

This is indeed a siren work – a score that is utterly beguiling and seductive. The folksy nature of the music is determined at the outset by Vaughan Williams's "March Past of the Kitchen Utensils" which is followed by Portman's "The Yearning", for which there is no better term to describe this exquisite piece. She introduces her own jaunty folk motifs soon after, but it is the ethereal nature of her opening cue that sets the overall mood of the album. The dreamlike inspiration comes from the film's setting of antipodean artist Sam Neill's mystical relationship with his three nubile models. The sustained serenity of Portman's music tempts one to nod off at times, but the Vaughan Williams excerpt plus two other folk music pieces, a lively dance and a solemn vocal refrain from Maddy Prior and June Tabor, add additional colour. **DS**

War of the Buttons (1994) **Original Soundtrack**, with the **Irish Film Orchestra / David Snell**. Varèse Sarabande Ⓕ VSD5554 (39 minutes: DDD).

Rachel Portman's characteristically melodic style speaks here with a lilting Irish brogue. A flageolet opens proceedings, playing a lilting, folk-like tune accompanied by a familiar chopping, rhythmic string figure. This is later transformed into a mock military march. Soon, Portman's favourite, the clarinet, takes up the theme. More toe-tapping, syncopated rhythms follow, as a delightful new theme is introduced in "Chasing the Fox". These off-the-beat rhythms are a pervasive feature of the score, even during the more dramatic moments; whilst the graceful clarinet soaring overhead is never far away. The score's dramatic centrepiece is the "Battle of Bunduff Castle" with its emphasis on heavy drum rhythms, accentuated by piano. The inventiveness and appeal of Portman's music never allows the listener to tire of such devices. Events take a nail biting turn in "Helicopter Rescue", before the chirpy clarinet returns, and the march theme is reprised with full orchestra.   **MW**

Also available:
The Adventures of Pinocchio (1996) London 452 740-2
Benny & Joon (1992) Milan 15168-2
Ethan Frome (1992) Varèse Sarabande VSD5620
The Joy Luck Club (1993) Milan 18456-2
The Road to Wellville (1994) Varèse Sarabande VSD5512
Smoke (1995) Hollywood MH62024-2
Used People (1992) Big Screen 924 481-2

Andrew Powell   England

Born in Worcester Park, Surrey, Andrew Powell is best known as arranger, musical director and co-composer for the Alan Parsons Project – a series of concept albums recorded under the guidance of producer Alan Parsons, beginning with *Tales of Mystery and Imagination* in 1976. Powell had attended classes at Darmstadt with Karlheinz Stockhausen and Györgi Ligeti before taking his Masters degree in music at King's College, Cambridge. At Cambridge he formed the electronic group Intermodulation with Roger Smalley and Tim Souster, and was also a founder member of the progressive rock band Henry Cow. After working as a session player, Powell was asked to arrange songs for Cockney Rebel's first three albums which were produced by Alan Parsons. He became involved in film scoring as a producer for composer Stanley Myers, and went on to 'ghost write' several cues for Myers. *Ladyhawke* (1985) was his first full-length score. This was followed by *Rocket Gibraltar* (1988), and he has contributed music to several other films and televison series, although the Alan Parsons Project has continued to be his mainstay.

New review
Ladyhawke (1985) **Original Soundtrack**, with **Richard Cottle** (keybds); **Ian Bairnson** (gtr); **David Paton** (bass); **Stuart Elliot** (drums/perc); **Philharmonia Orchestra / Andrew Powell** (keybds). GNP Crescendo Ⓕ GNPD8042 (70 minutes: DDD).

A Sword 'n' Sorcery movie with a rock score? Even taking into account the composer's contention that a traditional Korngold-style 'historical' score "would be some 700 years out of date instead of our 750", this still sounds like an absurd proposition. But for fans of the Alan Parsons Project (of which there are many, including, of course, Homer Simpson) and anyone not averse to the blend of rock band and orchestra popularized by innumerable progressive rock groups in the 1970s, this disc will be an experience to relish. The purely orchestral cues really do sound like dramatic underscore in the traditional sense, and there is no doubting Powell's ability to write excitingly in a symphonic idiom, but when the band joins in the music becomes closer in spirit to albums like Rick Wakeman's "Myths and Legends of King Arthur", or pretty much anything by Emerson Lake and Palmer, than ordinary film music. Beyond the novelty of its orchestration, however, the score contains some delightful melodies, and there are many moments to enjoy: the principal *Ladyhawke* theme, presented as a limpid love theme in several orchestral cues, is the music's outstanding centrepiece (try "She Was Sad at First" or the "Final Reunion" as examples). GNP's new CD reissue restores several cues – especially many of the straightforwardly orchestral ones – that were not present on the original LP, including an alternative orchestral treatment of "Turret Chase/The Fall" that was not used in the movie, the rock version being preferred. The result of these additions, whilst giving greater prominence to the orchestra, tends to accentuate the uneasy relationship between the two different groups. If *Ladyhawke* ultimately fails as a fusion of rock and classical – the rigid tempos of rock preclude easy coexistence with a symphony orchestra – it remains a fascinating footnote in film music history, and an enjoyable album for all of us who, like Homer Simpson, still cherish a fondness for 'dinosaur' bands.   **MW**

Zbigniew Preisner
Poland

Polish composer Zbigniew Preisner achieved international recognition with his score for Krzysztof Kieslowski's *La Double Vie de Véronique* (1991). He has also scored *Europa Europa* (1991) and *Olivier Olivier* (1992) for Agnieszka Holland and Kieslowski's *Three Colours* trilogy: *Trois Couleurs: Bleu* (1993), *Blanc* (1993) and *Rouge* (1994). His first Hollywood assignment was *At Play in the Fields of the Lord* (1991), and he is increasingly in demand internationally (in 1995 he composed the theme music for the TV series *People's Century*), although he continues to write and record in Warsaw and Katowice.

New review

La Double Vie de Véronique (1991) **Original Soundtrack**, with the **Silesia Philharmonic Choir; Great Orchestra of Katowice / Antoni Wit**.
Discovery Ⓕ DP1001 (31 minutes: DDD).

If one thing can be said about Zbigniew Preisner's music it is that the listener can never be sure what to expect. He is a mid-European composer in the modern film world, yet still retains the strengths of his Polish musical roots. Therefore, scores such as this one don't go the way a pair of western ears attuned to Hollywood scoring would anticipate. The main theme here is played almost solely by woodwinds, especially solo flute, and other tracks feature just piano and guitar. The cue "Childhood" is delightful, featuring a harpsichord played with remarkable fluidity. Not for Preisner the lush tones of a conventional orchestra: he uses just what he requires and nothing more. Approaching his scores with an open ear (if such an expression is permissible) will bring unexpected rewards. The booklet gives titles in French and English along with a few stills. The recording has a good, warm sound. **JW**

New review

Preisner's Music Original Soundtracks.
Virgin France Ⓕ VC8 40799-2 (69 minutes: ADD/DDD).
Eminent Domain. Decalogue (1991). Tu Ne Tueras Point. Damage (1992). The Secret Garden (1993). La Double Vie de Véronique (1991). Mouvements du Désir. Trois Couleurs (1993-4). Europa, Europa (1991). At Play in the Fields of the Lord (1991). Pour l'Amour d'une Femme. Quartet in 4 Movements (1994). Opéra Egyptien.

An ideal sampler of this composer's music. Preisner has, in an amazingly short period of time, risen from scoring films in his native Poland to writing for big-budget Hollywood features. If you are already aware of his eclectic and imaginative music, then this disc might provide an opportunity to expand your knowledge of his work as many of the items here are not available elsewhere. With his unmistakable string phrases, choral work and pervading atmosphere of wistful melancholy, Preisner is not a composer easy to categorize. This is therefore a good introduction to his world either for the casual listener or the avid collector. A remarkable album of music by a remarkable man. **JW**

New review

The Secret Garden (1993) **Original Soundtrack**, with the **Cracovian Philharmonic Boys' Choir; Sinfonia Varsovia / Wojciech Michniewski**.
Varèse Sarabande Ⓕ VSD5443 (31 minutes: DDD).

For such a quintessentially English tale as *The Secret Garden*, one would have expected a British composer to be automatically assigned to the project. This being a Hollywood production, no such logic applies, so Polish composer Zbigniew Preisner was chosen. Whilst Preisner's score is a good one, it does tend to sound like a European composer self-consciously attempting to write English-style music. The score revolves around a bewildering array of featured solo instruments, with the addition of a choir in "Awakening of Spring" and boy soloist in "Colin Opens His Eyes". Solo piano and acoustic guitar are also prominent. On record, this all gells together very well, and proves that there are many different ways to tackle a predominantly English subject. Sometimes the unexpected works very well indeed. **JW**

New review

Trois Couleurs Original Soundtracks, with the [a]**Silesia Philharmonic Choir**; [a]**Sinfonia Varsovia / Wojciech Michniewski**; [b]**String Quartet**; [b]**Preisner Light Orchestra / Zbigniew Paleta**.
Virgin Ⓕ CDVMM15 (three discs: also available separately: 39, 30 and 41 minutes: DDD).
CDVMM12 – Bleu[a] (1993). *CDVMM13* – Blanc[b] (1993). *CDVMM14* – Rouge[a] (1994).

Amid the surging, high voltage film scores produced by Hollywood these days, Zbigniew Preisner's music is a welcome breath of fresh air. His scores deal with love, death and everything in between. His music is always full of contrasting moods and styles, even within a single score, as his work for Krzysztof Kieslowski's *Couleurs* trilogy exemplifies.

The first installment of the trilogy finds the composer very much in a rare and wistful mood: short, broken cues full of sheer, sharp, resonant colours. The opening cue, repeated towards the end of the score is a rousing "Song for the Unification of Europe", surprisingly not heard elsewhere in other guises, to be followed by a woodwind-led cue, "Funeral Music". "Julie – in Her New Apartment" starts in melodic mood which then breaks up in an agitated climax. There is even some dialogue, and Preisner's trailer music for *Rouge* is also included: as ever with Preisner, the listener never knows what the next track will bring. His is not a mainstream approach to film scoring, and that is part of the attraction. A demerit is the amazingly short running time of some cues: "Ellipsis" runs a bare 20 seconds, and "Oliver's Theme", played on the piano, is only 30 seconds. Personally, I can't see the logic of including such cues, but for completists they are a useful addition.

In the second part, *Blanc*, the music is gradually evolving – certainly in terms of length, from 25 short cues in *Bleu* to 21 here. More importantly, the music itself is more structured and detailed. This may be due to the fact that the orchestrations are considerably different, bearing in mind the smaller forces Preisner has to work with here. The melancholy feel that permeates the first part remains – witness the opening cues where woodwinds dominate over a sinuous string section – but the addition of a string quartet gives the score a steelier edge, sharp and with sprightlier rhythms. "Home at Last" opens with a furious attack by the piano, again before woodwinds predominate; but it is the string quartet pieces that are etched into the memory by such eloquent playing.

In the final part of the trilogy the composer finds a more positive, melodic voice: his main theme, heard first in "Fashion Show", is absolutely gorgeous, vividly recorded with a warm violin tone. This must be one of the most attractive themes in all film music. Here, Preisner restrains his inclination to inject his scores with multiple themes, and lets this main theme do most of the work. "Psychoanalysis" is all solo guitar and swirling strings, whilst "Leaving the Judge" has a more expansive tone, but both are a variation of the main theme. From the haphazard, jagged cues of the first part, Preisner has moved towards a sustained and eloquent finale in *Rouge*. For those listeners seeking a more conventional, melodic score, therefore, *Rouge* is the disc to choose. But, whilst all three scores can be treated independently, they are part of a trilogy and each one is an extension of what has gone before. All three discs are the work of an imaginative and creative composer who is always ready to push back the frontiers of conventional film music.   **JW**

Also available:
Damage (1992) Varèse Sarabande VSD5406

Sergei Prokofiev

1891-1953 Russia

A rather spoilt only child, Sergei Prokofiev – one of the twentieth century's most gifted composers – was born in the town of Sontsovska in the Ukraine's Ekaterinoslav district. He was precociously musical and wrote his first piano piece at the age of five, and had written two operas by the age of 11. He entered the St Petersburg Conservatory in 1904 where he remained during a period of political turmoil for ten years. After the Russian Revolution Prokofiev spent much of his time either in the USA or Paris (where he worked with Diaghilev's Ballets Russes), but from 1936 settled permanently in Moscow for the last 17 years of his life. His first film score was for Alexander Feinzimmer's *Lieutenant Kijé* (1934) – which subsequently became one of his most popular works in the form of a five-movement concert suite. Soon after, Prokofiev had an opportunity to study film music techniques during a visit to Hollywood with a view to applying them to Soviet films. Returning to Moscow, he was asked by Sergei Eisenstein to write the music for his projected nationalistic epic *Alexander Nevsky*. Theirs was a truly two-way collaboration: in some places the director cut scenes to previously recorded music, in others the composer wrote to fit the final cut. The two teamed up again for *Ivan the Terrible* (1942-5). Both scores have entered the classical repertoire in their concert-hall arrangements. Alongside *Peter and the Wolf* and the *Classical Symphony*, Prokofiev's tiny amount of film music has become some of his best-loved work.

Alexander Nevsky (1938). **Evgenia Gorohovskaya** (mez); **St Petersburg Choruses and Philharmonic Orchestra /Yuri Temirkanov**.
RCA Victor Red Seal ℗ 09026 61926-2 (51 minutes: DDD). Recorded 1993. Reconstructed by William D. Brohn.
Alexander Nevsky – Cantata, Op. 78 (1938). **Linda Finnie** (mez); **Scottish National Chorus and Orchestra / Neeme Järvi**.
Chandos ℗ CHAN8584 (60 minutes: DDD). Recorded 1987. Also includes *Scythian Suite*, Op. 20.

For the original film, the perilous combination of primitive Russian recording techniques and Prokofiev's experimental tinkering (moving microphones closer to certain instruments instead of thickening the orchestration for example) yielded quite spectacularly substandard results, particularly when compared to, say, the lush splendour of *Gone With the Wind*'s soundtrack being recorded in Hollywood at about the same time. Prokofiev salvaged his score in an arrangement for full symphony orchestra and chorus, the *Alexander Nevsky* cantata, Op. 78, and it is in this form that the film music has endured, becoming one of the composer's most popular works. For RCA's handsome new recording orchestrator William D. Brohn has adapted the composer's concert hall version to fit once more with the visuals, transcribing some cues not present in the cantata. The result is a conflation of film score and concert transcription, with a few additions and amendments thrown in along the way. Yuri Temirkanov and his St Petersburg forces perform the whole with great gusto, and at Prokofiev's original speedy tempos. However, because the composer has already rescued everything of worth, the original version inevitably seems somewhat bitty and disjointed in comparison with the seamless flow of the cantata. "The Battle on the Ice", for example, is broken up into several short segments which collectively fail to make the same impact as the reworked single movement. The cantata, formidably performed in the Chandos recording listed above, may therefore seem preferable to some, although the attraction of hearing the 'complete' work is a powerful reason to acquire both versions. **MW**

Ivan the Terrible (1942-5) – Oratorio (arr. Stasevich). **Sergei Yursky** (narr); **Tamara Sinyavskaya** (mez); **Wolfgang Brendel** (bar); **Danish National Radio Choir; Frankfurt Children's Choir; Frankfurt Radio Symphony Orchestra / Dmitri Kitaenko**.
RCA Ⓔ 09026 61954-2 (78 minutes: DDD). Recorded 1993.
Ivan the Terrible (1942-5) – Concert scenario (arr. Palmer). **Linda Finnie** (mez); **Nikita Storojev** (bass-bar); **Philharmonia Chorus and Orchestra / Neeme Järvi**.
Chandos Ⓕ CHAN8977 (59 minutes: DDD). Recorded 1991.

Here is just one more reason to lament the passing of the late Christopher Palmer, whose death robbed film music of one of its most eloquent and intelligent advocates. Eisenstein's troubled masterpiece was suppressed by Stalin, left unfinished, and was not shown until 1958 when both director and composer were dead. Prokofiev was never able to fashion a concert hall version of the score as he had done for *Alexander Nevsky*; this task was carried out posthumously by Abram Stasevich who had conducted the original film soundtrack. In 1961, Stasevich produced an oratorio for narrator, soloists, chorus and orchestra: it is this version that has been recorded in a new live performance for RCA's '100 Years of Film Music' series. Given that the oratorio has often – and rightly – been condemned as overlong, excessively fragmented, and dominated by the (Russian) narration, this is a curious decision made all the more so by the same label's recent reconstruction of *Nevsky*'s original form. This ambitious performance is nonetheless appropriately grandiose and colourful, with the soloists giving due emphasis to the music's obvious operatic roots: an impression enhanced by the cavernous recording in Frankfurt's Alte Oper. If the thought of 78 minutes of brief 'cues' interspersed with long passages of spoken Russian fills you with dread, fear not: Christopher Palmer's shorter 'concert scenario' eliminates the narrator altogether, and considerably tightens up the musical action, transforming the work into a series of longer, well-structured scenes. Under the taught direction of Järvi, *Ivan* suddenly begins to sound like what it really is: a thrilling blend of film music and opera, with all the melodramatic gusto of both. **MW**

Also available:
Lieutenant Kijé, Op. 60. **Alexander Nevsky**, Op. 78 (Chicago SO/Abbado) DG 419 603-2GH

David Raksin
b. 1912 USA

David Raksin's father conducted the orchestra for silent movies in the Metropolitan Opera House in his native Philadelphia; the young boy was taken along to watch the movies, and listen to the music. As a teenager he worked part-time in his father's music shop, played in the school orchestra and taught himself to play the organ. The Dance Band he organised at age 12 was good enough to qualify him for admission to the Musicians' Union. He studied under composer Harl McDonald at the University of Pennsylvania, and took a keen interest in jazz. Moving to New York, Raksin got a job with music publisher Harms Inc., working under Robert Russell Bennett. He was recommended to Alfred Newman as the right choice to arrange the music for Charlie Chaplin's *Modern Times* (1936). Raksin soon disagreed with Chaplin about the music, and was sacked. However, Newman was so impressed with Raksin's work that he persuaded Chaplin to re-hire him. His score for the 1944 film *Laura* proved to be a turning point; his subsequent worked showed him to be a forward-looking, modernist composer of great skill. Raksin has also forged an important career as a teacher, taking courses at the University of Southern California and UCLA.

Laura (1944). **Forever Amber** (1947). **The Bad and the Beautiful** (1952) New Philharmonia Orchestra / David Raksin.
RCA Ⓜ GD81490 (47 minutes: ADD). Recorded 1975.

What we have here is a straight reissue of David Raksin's film music originally released in the same series of RCA albums that brought us many delights by Steiner, Newman, Rózsa, and others. Raksin's famous theme for *Laura* (that Fox classic starring Gene Tierney and Dana Andrews) is so much an integral part of the movie that it almost seems like another character. It will always remain a timeless classic. Also on this album is Raksin's score for a period potboiler called *Forever Amber*, although the score could hardly be so described. Bringing the recording to a close is *The Bad and the Beautiful*, one of Hollywood's frequent inward looks at its seamier side, featuring a superb saxophone solo by Ray Willcocks. David Raksin provides copious notes. Whilst we await a new recording of his music, we can rest assured that this classic album is everything a classic album should be. **JW**

Laura (1944) Original Soundtrack – see Herrmann: **Jane Eyre**
Also available:
The Bad and the Beautiful (1952) Rhino 72400

Graeme Revell
b. 1955 New Zealand

Although his mother was a singer and music teacher, and he took piano, trumpet and French horn lessons, Graeme Revell had no illusions about becoming a professional player. However, after studying political economy at University, Revell formed a 'new wave' band called SPK with one of the patients of the mental asylum he was then working in. With this group, Revell developed an abstract style known as 'Industrial music'. He moved to Europe in 1979 and formed a record label in order to release more experimental music, much of it incorporating ethnic elements; whilst in London he scored a National Film School feature, *The Malady*. Back in Sydney, Revell was asked to provide some source music for the Australian thriller *Dead Calm* (1989). As a result of this contribution, he went on to write the entire score. Revell soon moved to Hollywood. His eclectic blend of synthesizers, orchestral and ethnic instruments has been put to good use in several movies, including Wes Craven's *Spontaneous Combustion* (1989) and *People Under the Stairs* (1991), Wim Wenders's *Until the End of the World* (1991) and Jennifer Lynch's controversial *Boxing Helena* (1993).

Body of Evidence (1992) **Original Soundtrack**, with **Warren Hill** (sax); **Ellis Hall, Darlene Koldenhoven** (vocals); **Eberhard Weber** (electric bass); **Munich Philharmonic Orchestra / Tim Simonec**.
Milan Ⓕ 12720-2 (42 minutes: DDD).

Warren Hill's appropriately sultry alto-sax is the mainstay of this attractively low-key score (he even co-wrote "The Passion Theme"). Elsewhere, Revell relies primarily on a conventional orchestra to provide an understated atmosphere, which is by turns tension-filled and darkly passionate. Although never quite matching the ice-cold eroticism of Goldsmith's *Basic Instinct*, Revell adds some individualistic touches of his own: notably the sophisticated bass solo in "Hot Wax & Champagne", topped by Spanish-style guitar, and the intertwining voices of "The Handcuffs", built over keyboards and synths. Revell's uncanny knack of hypnotizing the listener with his variegated scoring is evident throughout, making *Body of Evidence* a compulsively attractive work to listen to. **MW**

The Crow (1994) **Original Soundtrack**, with **Bobbie Page, Darlene Koldenhoven, Chris Snyder** (voices); **Djivan Gasparyan** (Armenian duduk); **Kazu Matsui** (shakuhachi); **Oscar Brashear** (tpt); **Karl Verheyen, Philip Tallman** (gtrs); **M.B. Gordy** (perc); **Graeme Revell** (kybds) / **Tim Simonec**.
Varèse Sarabande Ⓕ VSD5499 (50 minutes: DDD).

Brandon Lee's ill-fated final film has been compared stylistically to a slick pop video; fitting then that Graeme Revell's richly textured score plays something like a modern-day concept album. All the soloists listed above are given significant roles, with some subdued orchestral playing in support. The exotic sonority of Armenian duduk is immediately arresting – and defines this score's fascination. Revell has a painter's eye for mixing his musical palette: duduk, shrill trumpet, breathy shakuhachi, tumultuous percussion, wordless voices and some delicate electric guitar: these are his raw materials, and he combines them with subtle skill. Revell is no tunesmith: sound and colour and exploiting the properties of different instruments are what interest him. There are pounding mechanistic elements here recalling Brad Fiedel's *Terminator*, and some effectively ambient atmospheric pieces too, but, ultimately, it is the unfamiliar mixture of sonorities that makes *The Crow* a mesmerizing musical experience.　　**MW**

Streetfighter (1994) **Original Soundtrack**, with the **London Symphony Orchestra / Tim Simonec**.
　　Varèse Sarabande Ⓕ VSD5560 (53 minutes: DDD). Includes *Attitude Adjuster* (Acogny/Brown/Lory).

This is probably the kind of score critics are thinking of when they bemoan the current state of film music. Big, blustering and bombastic, *Streetfighter* places less emphasis on the instrumental subtleties of earlier Revell scores and opts for all-out aural assault tactics instead. Yet, Revell's unique ear for musical texture – coupled with the always impressive forces of the LSO – make *Streetfighter* a surprisingly accessible score away from the childish and utterly ridiculous movie. In between innumerable brash action scenes, there is a good deal of diversity: an instrumental arrangement of Bizet's *Habanera* prompts Revell to endow some of his early cues with a similar Spanish tinge; there is slinky orientalism, tongue-in-cheek Russian nationalism, and languorous jazz. A growling tuba, accompanied only by pedal steel guitar, for the brief cue "Honda is Tortured" once again spotlights the composer's quirky approach to orchestration. For most of the time, this is a typical modern action score, albeit one distinguished by Revell's ability to fashion something of interest from conventional material.　　**MW**

Also available:
The Hand That Rocks the Cradle (1991) Hollywood 61304-2
Hard Target (1993) Varèse Sarabande VSD5445
Mighty Morphin Power Rangers (1995) Varèse Sarabande VSD5672
No Escape (1993) Varèse Sarabande VSD5483

Leonard Rosenman　　　　　　　　　　　　　　　b. 1924 USA

Born in Brooklyn, Leonard Rosenman originally set out to become a painter, but his musical interests gradually took priority. After war service, Rosenman studied composition with Schoenberg, Roger Sessions and Luigi Dallapiccola, and piano with Bernard Abramowitsch. By 1953, Rosenman had become composer-in-residence at the Berkshire Music Center. Whilst supplementing his income by giving piano lessons, one of his pupils introduced him to director Elia Kazan, who gave Rosenman the opportunity to score his first film. The piano student was James Dean, the film was *East of Eden* (1955). The resulting score is still regarded by many as Rosenman's most significant achievement. During the early 1960s, Rosenman lived and worked as a conductor in Rome. Returning to Hollywood, he wrote avant-garde scores for *Fantastic Voyage* (1966) and *Beneath the Planet of the Apes* (1970) amongst others. He has taught at the University of Southern California, and directed chamber music ensembles specializing in avant-garde music. Aside from film scores, Rosenman has produced a significant body of other works, including an early Violin Concerto (1951), and several chamber music pieces. Ralph Ferraro has been his usual orchestrator. Music from his two classic James Dean scores, *East of Eden* and *Rebel Without a Cause* performed by the London Sinfonietta conducted by John Adams is due for release in 1997 as part of the new Nonesuch film music series.

The Lord of the Rings (1978) **Original Soundtrack / Leonard Rosenman**.
　　Intrada Ⓕ FMT8003D (77 minutes: ADD).

The Lord of the Rings, Leonard Rosenman's granite-hewn edifice, consciously blurs the distinction between functional and absolute music. Intrada's extended CD release rightly emphasizes the purely musical value of the score over and above its association with Ralph Bakshi's truncated, incomplete animated film. They have resequenced and remixed the music to show the carefully designed structure, and highlight the composer's rich orchestral palette. Rosenman's score begins with a series of thematic fragments, which are gradually developed throughout, before being resolved in a final climactic statement of the main theme. Initially, the music contrasts a tonal, optimistic 'Hobbit' theme with the dark, dissonant 'Mordor' theme, as the Ringwraiths track our diminutive heroes across the Shire. A male chorus groans over chaotic, eerie orchestral textures. Relief is briefly to be found in a gentle choral lament for "Mithrandir", before the appearance of Orcs introduces a new and equally sinister march. To counter all this darkness, "The Riders of Rohan" appear to a rousing statement of the central part of the main theme. The gigantic battle of "Helm's Deep" forms a stupendous climax to all that has occurred previously, gathering force in a furious fugato (the chorus moans the words "Dranoel Namnesor" – the composer's name backwards). Eventually, when Rosenman can make us bear it no longer, he releases the tension with a glorious statement of the

"Riders of Rohan" theme – the cavalry has arrived in the nick of time! The score closes with a full rendition of *The Lord of the Rings* march, which, after all that has passed, brings a tear to the eye. Now, and only now, can we breathe again.   **MW**

Rebel Music from the Films of James Dean. **Czech Symphony Orchestra / William Motzing.**
    Edel Ⓕ CIN2206-2 (two discs, 96 minutes: DDD).
    Rebel Without a Cause (1955). East of Eden (1955). **Dimitri Tiomkin:** Giant (1956).

It's hard to imagine the excitement that was felt in film music circles when the scores of Leonard Rosenman burst upon the world. Film music then was what one leading critic described as "warmed-over Tchaikovsky" so Rosenman's (plus North's, of course) form of Americana must have seemed like a breath of fresh air. Coupled with the brand new star in the form of James Dean, Hollywood had come out of the forties with a vengeance. *East of Eden* actually is a very lyrical score, whilst the majority of *Rebel* is quite violent and in keeping with the teenage violence and rage portrayed on screen. Dimitri Tiomkin's *Giant* is the very opposite: film music from an earlier decade, typically Tiomkin and none the worse for that. Leonard Rosenman himself re-recorded extracts from these scores to form an LP, but this is the first time the full scores have been heard with today's recording techniques. Bill Motzing has said that this was one of his most rewarding projects, and it's not hard to see why. Rosenman is a much under-rated composer, but discs like this will certainly help keep his name where it should be – at the very top of film music circles.   **JW**

Star Trek IV: The Voyage Home (1986) **Original Soundtrack / Leonard Rosenman.**
    MCA Ⓜ MCLD19349 (36 minutes: DDD).

There is enough stylish and characteristically well-wrought music in this score to compensate for an apparent overall lack of direction. Rosenman's opening fanfare is the central set-piece, with the orchestra ringing bells of celebration and brass intoning a rousing theme, before a brief interlude for strings. When this music returns after an uplifting restatement of Alexander Courage's original TV theme in the final cue (as the credits begin to roll) some of the intervening weaknesses are entirely forgiven. These weaknesses include two entirely forgettable and inappropriate synth-pop cues co-written and performed by The Yellowjackets, whoever they may be. Some of the dramatic music, as in the extended "Crash-Whale Fugue", is highly inventive, but diffuse. The delightful main theme owes a little too much to his superior *Lord of the Rings* score. The two shortest cues are the most entertaining: "Chekhov's Run" – a frantic Russian polka – and "Hospital Chase" – riotously slapstick.   **MW**

Also available:
RoboCop 2 (1990) Varèse Sarabande VSD5271

Nino Rota   1911-1979 Italy

Precociously musical from an early age, Nino Rota began composing at the age of eight. He studied at the Milan Conservatory and the Accademia de Santa Cecilia, and received instruction on conducting from Fritz Reiner in Philadelphia. Rota wrote ballet, opera, oratorio and chamber works in addition to his 145 film scores. He achieved early international success with his music for the British film *The Glass Mountain* (1949); his most famous work, however, was in collaboration with director Federico Fellini. Rota and Fellini had a long-standing partnership which lasted from *Lo Sceicco Bianco* (*The White Sheik*) in 1952 to *Prova d'Orchestra* (*Orchestra Rehearsal*) in 1978. Rota's other work was hardly less remarkable, particular highlights being King Vidor's *War and Peace* (1956), Visconti's *Il Gattopardo* (*The Leopard*) of 1963, Franco Zeffirelli's *Romeo and Juliet* (1968) and Francis Ford Coppola's *The Godfather*.

New review
Film Music Original Soundtracks / Carlo Savina.
    CAM Ⓕ CVS004 (52 minutes: AAD).
    Napoli Milionaria (1950). The Glass Mountain (1949). La Dolce Vita (1959). Sunset Sunrise (1973). Le Notti Bianche (1957). War and Peace (1956). Romeo and Juliet (1968). Il Gattopardo (1963). Rocce e I Suoi Fratelli (1960). The Taming of the Shrew (1967). Purple Noon (1959). The Godfather (1972).

Ennio Morricone is often considered to be the most important film composer to have emerged in Italy. This is tough to argue against – although Nino Rota was undoubtedly a great artist who, at the peak of his powers, was second to nobody. And yet it seems that Rota has never achieved the recognition he deserves – this in spite of his lengthy and legendary collaboration with Federico Fellini. Thankfully, this release is a fine advertisement for the talents of a man whose art is in sore need of further appreciation.

The disc is actually a reissue of two previous CAM anthology LPs. Although it cannot encompass everything (Rota wrote around 80 scores), this is a reasonably comprehensive overview dating from 1949 to 1973. The sins of omission are outweighed by the virtues of commission, with 12 scores represented including the films of De Filippo, Anton, Cass, Kurahara, Visconti, Vidor, Zeffirelli, Clement, and Coppola. Only one Fellini score is included, but it is one of their more famous collaborations. Adding to the credibility is the conducting of Carlo Savina, undoubtedly the première interpreter of Rota's screen music.

A keen lover of drama, Rota's film music always emphasized melody without undue harmonic complexity. This is evident in the lovely Italian folk music performed by mandolins in the opening track, *Napoli Milionari*, or the timeless, beautiful main theme from *Romeo and Juliet*. There is a direct, immediate quality to his work, as well as solidly founded patterns of structure and rhythm – consider the melodramatic profile of *The Glass Mountain* or the orchestral grandiosities of *War and Peace*. The mod, decadent jazz/pop written for Fellini's *La Dolce Vita* is atmospheric without lapsing into excessive editorializing, while the romantic piano writing in *Sunrise Sunset* showcases the composer's discipline in refraining from sentimentality. Meanwhile, the tuneful waltzes of *Il Gattopardo* (*The Leopard*) are redolent of an era long since passed (one is actually a previously unpublished waltz by Verdi). This raises a point made by Rota's detractors, who accused him of not spending enough time in the present. Even if this is true, the composer resided in a home where he was most comfortable and lived there in a dramatically sensitive, musically authentic manner. The final touch on the disc is an excerpt from his most famous North American score: the traditional, haunting music composed for Francis Coppola's Oscar-winning Mafia epic *The Godfather*.

The only deficiency in this compilation is the booklet, which gives very little biographical information about Rota and no analysis of his career. This is one trend that is all too prevalent in film music recordings today. It is especially unforgivable in situations where there are no legalities or deadline pressures (as there are with new Hollywood films) for labels to deal with. Griping aside, this is an exemplary disc that should be in every film music collection. **KM**

The Godfather (1972) **Original Soundtrack / Carlo Savina**.
MCA Ⓜ MCLD19022 (32 minutes: AAD).
Includes *I Have But One Heart* (Farrow/Symes) and "Connie's Wedding"
(Carmine Coppola).
The Godfather Suite Milan Philharmonia Orchestra / Carmine Coppola.
Silva Screen Ⓕ FILMCD077 (41 minutes: ADD). Recorded 1975.
The Godfather (1972). The Godfather II (1974). The Godfather III (1990),
co-written with Carmine Coppola.

Nino Rota's *Godfather* theme – that proud, lonely trumpet solo – captures some ineffable part of the fiery Italian spirit. The score's consciously traditional mould – a waltz, a pastorale – wraps this innate Italianness in a preserving folk-influenced form; its very straightforward simplicity concealing layers of hot-tempered mediterranean complexity. The original film album contains little of substance beyond the two principal themes – the instantly recognizable "Love Theme" as famous now as Maurice Jarre's "Lara's Theme" or Francis Lai's theme from *Love Story* – but they both have more than sufficient strength of character to survive the disc's brief playing time. Francis Ford Coppola, an enthusiastic practitioner of nepotism who cast both his sister (Talia Shire) and daughter (Sofia) in his trilogy, hired his father Carmine to co-write the sequel with Rota. Coppola Senior had already supplied some dance music for the original, and went on to score the third film after Rota's death, meanwhile he shared an Academy Award with his co-composer for their joint efforts on *Godfather II*. His effective, if occasionally bland arrangements of pieces from all three films (or rather from the first two, some of which also appeared in the third) concentrates heavily on his own contributions. These are mostly ceremonial on-screen source music cues, as opposed to dramatic underscore, heard during the extended wedding and procession sequences. Continuing in the family tradition Coppola also includes arrangements of two songs by his father-in-law, Francesco Pennino, which featured in the second film. Given the sinister aspects of the movies, this selection is an unexpectedly light and attractive confection of Italian dances; therefore Rota's profound principal themes cannot help but dominate Coppola's more insubstantial items. The disc nevertheless is a pleasant complement to, but not a substitute for, the original. **MW**

The Symphonic Fellini/Rota Czech Symphony Orchestra / Derek Wadsworth.
Silva Screen Ⓟ FILMCD129 (69 minutes: DDD). Recorded 1993.
Lo Sceicco Bianco (1952). I Vitelloni (1953). La Strada (1954). Il Bidone (1955).
Le Notti di Cabiria (1957). La Dolce Vita (1959). Boccaccio '70 (1962).
Otto e Mezzo (1962). Giulietta degli Spiriti (1965). Fellini Satyricon (1969).
I Clowns (1970). Roma (1971). Amarcord (1973). Casanova (1976).
Prova d'Orchestra (1978).

There have been some productive composer/director partnerships over the years – Herrmann/Hitchcock, Jarre/Lean, Delerue/Truffaut – but none quite as prolific or as fertile as the one between Nino Rota and Federico Fellini, whose association spanned 16 films between 1951 and 1979. Rota's jaunty and unmistakably Italian melodies complement perfectly the director's heartily satirical view of modern society, his evocative use of solo trumpet and electronic organ flavouring scores like *Il Bidone, Cabiria, La Strada* and *La Dolce Vita* with a piquant air of tawdry decadence. The Respighi-influenced *Satyricon* and the jazz-tinged *Casanova*, on the other hand, provide a more sombre contrast but are just as haunting. Excerpts from each score are presented here as agreeably generous suites, making this an ideal introduction to one of the cinema's most individual composers. **RS**

Also available:
La Strada – ballet suite. **Il Gattopardo** – dances. Concerto for Strings. (La Scala PO/Muti) Sony SK66279

Miklós Rózsa

1907-1995 Hungary

Miklós Rózsa was the only survivor of the 'greats' from Hollywood's Golden Age to see his reputation begin once again to soar after a period of neglect. At the time of his death, several different record companies had embarked on projects to re-record his music. Rózsa only became a film composer after already establishing himself as a composer of concert works. Born in Budapest, he spent much of his childhood collecting Magyar folk songs in the countryside near his family estate. This music, which he noted in haphazard fashion in a little black book, formed his strongly personal compositional style. After receiving his doctorate in music from Leipzig University (he had originally gone to study chemistry at his father's insistence), Rózsa visited Paris. Here he met Arthur Honegger, who introduced the struggling young Hungarian composer to writing film music. In 1937, Rózsa, now in London, was asked to score his first film, the Sir Alexander Korda-produced Marlene Dietrich movie *Knight Without Armour*. A fruitful collaboration with the Korda brothers ensued, which took him to Hollywood, when war broke out, to finish work on *The Thief of Bagdad* (1940). Rózsa remained in Hollywood, although he has always disliked being known as just a film composer, even going so far as to call his autobiography *Double Life* to distinguish between his film and concert work. Initially typecast as an 'exotic' film composer (*The Thief of Bagdad, Jungle Book*, 1942) Rózsa went on to become associated with psychological thrillers (*Spellbound*, 1945, in which he introduced the theremin to Hollywood) and *film noir* (*Double Indemnity*, 1944, and many others). His 'historical' period began with *Quo Vadis* (1951) and extended across a dozen costume dramas, most of them for MGM, in which he attempted to add some historical authenticity to his scores by researching appropriate period music: Ancient Greek or Roman and early Christian (*Quo Vadis, Ben-Hur*, 1959, *King of Kings*, 1961) medieval troubadour songs and Latin hymns (*Ivanhoe*), Spanish *cantigas* (*El Cid*, 1961). Rózsa fell victim to the decline of the studio system and the trend for 'pop' scores during the 1960s. He finally retired from film scoring in 1982 after reprising his old *film noir* style for the Steve Martin spoof *Dead Men Don't Wear Plaid*. He won Academy Awards for *Spellbound, A Double Life* (1947) and *Ben-Hur* (1959). His regular orchestrator was fellow Hungarian Eugene Zador. Despite the enormous variety of his film and concert work, every Rózsa composition, with its dark-hued Hungarian folk influence, is instantly identifiable. His style is so distinctively personal that, his unrivalled reputation notwithstanding, his work has not been widely imitated.

All the Brothers Were Valiant (1953) **Original Soundtrack / Miklós Rózsa.**
Prometheus Ⓟ PCD131 (49 minutes: AAD).

Only recently made available on disc, and previously overshadowed by *Ivanhoe* and *Moonfleet*, this is actually one of Rózsa's finest adventure scores; the impressive early stereophonic recording adding to its impact. Colourful, packed with thrilling incident (the typically bracing main theme vividly describing all the excitement and danger of a nineteenth-century whaling expedition) and some gorgeously languid romantic interludes, this is the composer at his peak and a perfect example of well-crafted film scoring. **RS**

New review

Ben-Hur (1959) Original Soundtrack, with the MGM Studio Chorus and Orchestra / Miklós Rózsa. Rhino Ⓕ 72197 (two discs: 148 minutes: ADD) / EMI Ⓜ CDODEÓN18 (75 minutes: ADD).

Not only Rózsa's cinematic masterpiece, but the greatest of all his compositions, and arguably the finest film score yet written, *Ben-Hur* is a work which, as Tony Thomas comments in the 52-page illustrated booklet accompanying the Rhino set, "in another place, in another venue would have been the substance of a major symphonic cantata". From the opening *fortissimo* declaration of the centrally-defining Christ theme to the joyous "Allelulias" of the finale, this is music of truly epic stature, its enormous thematic variety and extraordinary range of emotional expression far outshining concert-hall staples like *Alexander Nevsky*; the restoration of this original soundtrack is indeed a cause for rejoicing. Rhino's attractively-packaged two-disc set of the complete score even goes so far as to include the 11-second "Shofar Call" at the end of the pre-credit Nativity sequence: meaningless completism some might think, before noticing that Rózsa's opening "Main Title" fanfare is a direct response to this plaintive solo horn.

Rózsa's Roman music may be his own very personal interpretation, heavily inflected with his distinctive musical accent as always – despite all that historical research – but no one else has rendered the glory and awe-inspiring power of the *imperium* so convincingly, and Rózsa never more so than here. Parading throughout the score, strident fanfares and grand marches bring the mighty legions alive in our imagination. If real Roman music didn't sound like this, it should have done. In opposition to all this heavy-handed militarism is the 'Jewish' music, representing the downtrodden house of Hur: the nobility of Judah Ben-Hur's spirit, the passion of his love for Esther, the gentle nature of his mother and sister. The conflict between these opposing forces is gloriously surmounted by the Christ theme itself: a redemptive force, the recurrence of which at certain key moments binds the score together more powerfully than any *leitmotif*. In one of the most important scenes – dramatically and musically – it is heard arising from the dissonant anguish of Judah's trek across the desert: soft organ chords, vibraphone and string harmonics constitute the musical voice of the Saviour, playing in counterpoint to Ben-Hur's own theme after a crucial intervention that has filled him with renewed hope.

The brilliantly remastered sound presented here even allows us to hear occasional extraneous studio noises, like pages turning or a discreet cough from a member of the orchestra. In between each track, the ambience of the studio has been retained instead of the usual "digital black", giving extra continuity to the sequence of cues. Unforgivably, however, EMI in the UK have opted only for a single-disc selection of highlights. Whilst not omitting the most memorable scenes, this abbreviated release fails to give due weight to certain parts of the score, including the darker, tragic music accompanying Judah's search for his mother and sister among the lepers. Stripped of the lavish packaging that makes the Rhino set such a treat for collectors, EMI's disc represents a compromise that I suspect anyone with the necessary means will not wish to make. Worse, it denies purchasers the opportunity to hear this great score as any great music should be heard: complete.   **MW**

---

12 Choruses from Ben-Hur and King of Kings Brigham Young University a Cappella Choir / Philip Woodward with Don Cook (org).
The Power (1967) Original Soundtrack, with the MGM Studio Orchestra / Miklós Rózsa.
    Prometheus Ⓕ PCD122 (70 minutes: ADD).

Why these beautiful choral pieces are not routinely programmed by church choirs and choral societies I cannot imagine. Can it be that their movie origin robs them of credibility? Music publisher Edward McCauley didn't think so when he asked Rózsa to adapt music from the Biblical epics *Ben-Hur* and *King of Kings*. The resulting 12 hymns, all with new texts, neatly form a cycle relating the life of Christ (one hymn is a new work, not from either film). The ravishing "Star of Bethlehem" and "Adoration of the Magi" from *Ben-Hur* are particularly effective. The Brigham Young Choir sing sympathetically, although their wide vibrato, which obscures Rózsa's delicate harmonies, might seem excessive to anyone used to English church singing. Clarity is not helped by an unfortunately murky recording.

Reportedly George Pal's film *The Power* was so impenetrable that not even the composer understood what was going on. His score is blustering and busy, but ultimately lacks conviction. An attractive gipsy melody is the centrepiece, and several cues are given a Romany flavour by including guitar, fiddle and dulcimer. The highlight is "Viva l'Amour", an idiomatic solo for Spanish guitar. An interesting fill-up, but it is the hymns which are the selling point of this disc.   **MW**

Dead Men Don't Wear Plaid (1982) Original Soundtrack / Lee Holdridge.
    Prometheus Ⓕ PCD126 (48 minutes: ADD).

At the very end of his career, Rózsa gave an affectionate adieu to the *film noir* style he had elaborated some 40 years earlier. Steve Martin's spoof relied on deadpan humour for its effect, so

– despite the composer's terse rebuttal "I don't do comedy" – Rózsa was eventually prevailed upon to provide a straight dramatic score. Although not overtly comedic, there is a touch of self-parody in this music: the wailing theremin in "Cleaning Woman!" is an amusing homage to *Spellbound*; and jazzy episodes like "Rigby Reardon, Cross Dresser" are written with tongue firmly in cheek. Otherwise, this score could almost as easily have been written in 1942 as 1982. The dark-hued harmonies and terse dramatic writing are familiar from any number of earlier Rózsa scores; whilst the gentle "Love Theme" is pure old-fashioned Hollywood. Only subtle touches of colour, and an absence of the acid harmonies that gave his old *noir* scores their bite, identify this music as being late rather than early Rózsa. *Dead Men Don't Wear Plaid* is a wonderfully nostalgic coda to a great career. **MW**

New review

El Cid (1961) New Zealand Youth Choir; New Zealand Symphoy Orchestra / James Sedares.
Koch International ℗ 37340-2 (66 minutes: DDD). Recorded 1995.

Although *Ben-Hur* is considered to be Rózsa's *magnum opus*, *El Cid* is in many ways just as triumphant an achievement. For here the pomp and pageantry are even more spectacular, setting this most pictorial of widescreen epics ablaze with colour. The thrilling "Overture" is one of Rózsa's most popular pieces, and yet ironically is never heard when the film airs on TV (along with the intermission and exit music it would have played to a closed curtain during its cinema screening). Framed by a resplendent fanfare, the music's rhythmic drive and glowing Spanish colouring never fails to set the heart racing. But the whole score is peppered with such similarly exhilarating set-pieces (the wonderfully vibrant "Fight for Calahorra" for example), and of course no one writes gripping, coherent battle music quite like Rózsa. Binding these opulent action highlights together are the ardent love theme for The Cid and Chimene (which was adapted into the song "The Falcon and the Dove" and performed as the film's exit music, though here it is heard without Paul Francis Webster's lyric), and the earnest, stout-hearted theme for the brave knight himself, which reaches a magnificently moving climax for the film's justly famous finale.

Despite grand and expansive sound, it is somewhat disappointing that James Sedares fails to match the spine-tingling vigour of both the original soundtrack (as demonstrated by selections on Cloud Nine's now deleted "Great Epic Film Scores" disc) and Rózsa's re-recording for MGM Records (briefly issued on CD but deleted at the time of writing). Furthermore, this is by no means a complete recording of the score, although it does include a number of cues missing from the composer's own version. Something of a missed opportunity then, but as the only disc currently available of this landmark score it is still an essential item for any film music collection. **RS**

New review

Epic Film Music [a]Crouch End Festival Chorus; City of Prague Philharmonic Orchestra / Kenneth Alwyn.
Silva Screen ℗ FILMCD170 (72 minutes: DDD).
The Golden Voyage of Sinbad (1973). El Cid (1961). Sodom and Gomorrah (1962). Quo Vadis (1951)[a]. King of Kings (1961)[a]. Beau Brummell (1954). Ben-Hur (1959). All the Brothers Were Valiant (1953). Madame Bovary (1949).

The musical voice of so many of Hollywood's glorious epics was, of course, Miklós Rózsa. For over a decade from *Quo Vadis* to *King of Kings* and beyond he endowed the mighty legions with pomp and splendour and opposed this military muscle with beautifully spiritual themes for his oppressed heroes and heroines. Silva Screen's latest Prague recording is a generous survey of Rózsa's 'historical' period which laudably stretches the definition of epic to include *Beau Brummell* and *Madame Bovary* – the former credited to Richard Addinsell in the film – and throws in a couple of rarities in the form of *Sinbad* and *Sodom and Gomorrah* . Kenneth Alwyn injects some necessary vigour into the proceedings, although the orchestra's apparent unfamiliarity with this bold and colourful music dilutes the blistering power of Rózsa's invention – only in the traditionally romantic *Madame Bovary* waltz do they sound completely at home. This disc nevertheless makes for a good introduction to what was the composer's most fertile period. Presentation and booklet notes are, as always, superb. **MW**

Ivanhoe (1952) Sinfonia of London / Bruce Broughton.
Intrada Excalibur Collection ℗ MAF7055D (62 minutes: DDD). Reconstructed by Daniel Robbins. Recorded 1994.

Described by the composer in his autobiography as "a typical Hollywood historical travesty", the film version of Sir Walter Scott's novel has long since been relegated to the Sunday afternoon TV graveyard. The original full music score no longer exists, so Daniel Robbins was faced with the task of reconstructing the orchestral parts from Rózsa's original sketches. *Ivanhoe* is one of the richest and most exciting of all Rózsa's scores: lacking perhaps only the epic scale of *Ben-Hur* or *El Cid*, it can nevertheless stand alongside its more famous siblings as an example of Rózsa at the height of his powers. Several important and memorable themes are based on authentic sources, but it is a seemingly impossible task to identify exactly where source music ends and Rózsa begins. Highlights include Rebecca's theme which, with its moody Jewish undercurrents, is reminiscent of some of the most tender moments of *Ben-Hur*. The fiendishly difficult battle music spread across two cues – "The Battlement" and "Saxon Victory" – are tackled with thrilling bravura by Broughton and his orchestra (just listen to the Norman and Saxon themes intertwining in furious counterpoint; or the pounding battering ram percussion). The difficulties of reproducing tempos and dynamics without making it sound like a mere mechanical exercise are many: Broughton and the Sinfonia, ably assisted by Mike Ross-Trevor, deserve the highest praise for their achievement in bringing *Ivanhoe* to life in glorious (digital) Technicolor. They really don't write 'em like this any more. **MW**

Julius Caesar (1953) **Jane Emmanuel** (sop); **Sinfonia Chorus; Sinfonia of London / Bruce Broughton.**
Intrada Excalibur Collection Ⓕ MAF7056D (53 minutes: DDD). Reconstructed by Daniel Robbins. Recorded 1995.

Released in August 1995, just a week or so after the composer's death, this second installment of Intrada's Excalibur Collection (the first being *Ivanhoe*) reunites conductor Bruce Broughton and the Sinfonia of London in the warm, open acoustic of Hampstead's Air Studios. Here they recreated Rózsa's sombre Shakespearian score for the film which starred Marlon Brando as Antony and James Mason as Brutus. Gone is the ceremonial of *Quo Vadis*; gone is the rumbustious energy of *Ivanhoe*. Responding to the universal relevance of Shakespeare's bleak political drama, Rózsa produced a thickly-scored, often melancholy work, which illustrates the machinations of men's minds more than their actions. This new recording should be regarded as a cornerstone of any Rózsa collection. *Julius Caesar* vindicates producer Douglass Fake's belief that good film music needs to be heard in its entirety to be fully understood: much of the score consists of fairly brief cues based around two principal themes; only by experiencing the whole from beginning to end can the stark power of Rózsa's music be realized. Twin themes for Caesar and Brutus dominate all else, each one vying for supremacy, until the final cathartic moment when noble Brutus is overwhelmed by an inexorable rendition of Caesar's (now Octavian's) march. Daniel Robbins and the Intrada team have restored all the music which was either severely truncated or dropped entirely from the finished film. Also recorded for the first time is the "Overture" specially composed by Rózsa for the film's première, which was bizarrely replaced in favour of Tchaikovsky's *Capriccio Italien*. Jane Emmanuel fills the (short) trouser role singing Rózsa's arrangement of Dowland's "Now, O Now I Needs Must Part" (the only 'authentic' music in the score) sung in the film by a boy soprano. Broughton's expert conducting brings a lightness to the score's dense textures, which in other hands might have become plodding and lugubrious. A very special recording indeed. **MW**

Lust for Life (1956) **Background to Violence Suite Frankenland State Symphony Orchestra / Miklós Rózsa.**
Varèse Sarabande Ⓕ VSD5405 (44 minutes: AAD).

Fired by the urgency and visual beauty of Vincente Minnelli's film biography of Vincent van Gogh, *Lust for Life* is one of Rózsa's most compelling scores. The dramatic thrust of the main title immediately conveys all the mental anguish of the tormented artist, whilst the rippling, impressionistic cues "Summer" and "Pastorale" beautifully evoke the sun-drenched landscapes of Southern France that inspired many of his best-known paintings. The *Background to Violence Suite*, a cogent adaptation of the powerful scores Rózsa provided for producer Mark Hellinger (to whom the suite is dedicated), namely *Brute Force* (1947), *The Killers* (1946) and *The Naked City* (1948), makes an equally impressive coupling and seethes with the brooding, monochromatic menace of *film noir*. The finale, however, with its serene introduction steadily building into a radiant, exhilarating paean to New York City, is not only quintessential Rózsa but also one of film music's greatest moments. **RS**

New review
Spellbound (1945) – Original soundtrack[a]; Suite[b] **Jungle Book**[c] (1942) [c]**Sabu** (narrator); [ab]**Samuel J. Hoffman** (theremin); [b]**Eadie and Rack** (pfs); [a]**Selznick Recording Orchestra**; [c]**RCA Victor Sympony Orchestra / Miklós Rózsa.**
Flapper mono Ⓕ PASTCD7093 (66 minutes: ADD).

Two versions of the composer's first Oscar-winner, *Spellbound*, may seem over-generous at first, but both of these very rare recordings present the score in a rather different guise and so rarely repeat each other. As the booklet explains in detail, there are some fascinating facts surrounding the original production and subsequent transfers of the four rather hastily prepared ARA discs which present the lengthier selection, but depite poor sound the score's romantic intensity – with its gorgeous love theme for Ingrid Bergman and Gergory Peck and the novel usage of a wailing theremin to underline the paranoia of Peck's character – still makes for enthralling listening. The 13-minute disc of excerpts from the original soundtrack was designed as a promotional tool for radio stations and is making its first commercial appearance here. Better played and recorded, this is a wonderfully concise souvenir of the score.

Jungle Book has the distinction of being the very first film score to be issued on disc as a set of three 78s. Spreading the score over six sides was accomplished so skilfully that it is often difficult to tell where the breaks occur on this superb transfer, for it all seems quite seamless. This beautifully-crafted score is certainly one of Rózsa's most melodically fertile, each one of Kipling's diverse cast of animals is treated to its own brilliantly characterized theme: sleek, sly strings for Bagheera the Panther, braying trombones and tubas for the elephants, a jocular contra-bass for Baloo the Bear and even a radiant hymn to the jungle itself. Some 50 years on Sabu's expressive narration remains surprisingly endearing, especially when coupled with such lively, colourful scoring. Despite the age of these recordings this is a disc of great historical value.   **RS**

The Thief of Bagdad[a] (1940) **Jungle Book**[b] (1942) **Nuremberg Symphony Orchestra /** [a]**Miklós Rózsa,** [b]**Klauspeter Seibel**.
Colosseum Ⓟ CST348044 (48 minutes: ADD). Recorded 1981.

Two magical scores on one disc, representing Rózsa's 'exotic' early Korda assignments. Both recordings are extended concert suites, originally issued on LP with an accompanying narration which has been dropped from this CD reissue. However, the music is too splendidly evocative of strange lands and far away places to require any additional spoken assistance. These are joyously sunny works, fairy-tale pieces, far removed from the threatening world of *film noir*, or the pomp and splendour of ancient Rome. There is a lightness and simplicity here that Rózsa would never return to in his later work; yet, they are undoubtedly two of his most appealing scores. Like the extraordinarily vivid Korda productions for which it was written, the music dazzles with kaleidoscopic variety, and sparkles with a youthful zest. *The Thief of Bagdad* is as richly colourful as an oriental rug, with dances, processionals, an airy flying theme, and a famously beautiful love theme. *Jungle Book* is a bewitching tapestry of interwoven character studies: the parade of jungle animals are all so expertly depicted by Rózsa that it is hardly necessary to have seen the film to hear the arrival of the elephants, the monkeys, the wolves, Kaa, Bagheera and Baloo. Under other circumstances, this music might have become as well-known as *Peter and the Wolf*. An enchanting album.   **MW**

Young Bess (1953) **Original Soundtrack / Miklós Rózsa**.
Prometheus mono Ⓟ PCD133 (56 minutes: AAD).

Another colourful 'historical' score, this time for a fictionalized acount of the traumatic adolescence of Elizabeth I. Lacking the stately solemnity of *Julius Caesar* and the swashbuckling excitement of *Ivanhoe*, *Young Bess* more than compensates with some gorgeously lyrical melodies, painted in the composer's characteristically broad brush strokes. Some particularly striking themes are a jolly tune for "Hatfield", the young princess's childhood home; a soaring "Love Theme" full of pathos; a warm and radiant piece representing Queen Catherine; and a toy march for the Prince of Wales. On top of this cornucopia of original invention, Rózsa sprinkles some sixteenth-century period flavouring – a little 'source music', a lot of incidental colouring to his own distinctive idiom – and rounds things off with a few obligatory fanfares and processionals. The mono recording vividly captures the warmth of this delightful score.   **MW**

Also available:
Classic Film Scores (National PO/Gerhardt) RCA GD80911
El Cid/Ben-Hur/King of Kings (Hamburg Concert Orch/Müller-Lampertz) Varèse Sarabande VCD47268
Film Music for Piano, Volumes 1 and 2 (Daniel Robbins) Intrada MAF7057D/7064D
Providence (1977) DRG CDSL9502

see also Collections: **Captain Blood**

Craig Safan   USA

Craig Safan's love of music stemmed from his family: his father loved musical theatre, his mother was a concert pianist and teacher, and his Uncle Joe had rubbed shoulders with Gershwin, George M. Cohan, Bing Crosby and Paul Whiteman during the 1920s when he worked as an agent. Safan played in bands and wrote songs from his early teens. He studied art at Brandeis University, but spent his spare time writing music – he wrote four musicals at college, and then travelled to London on a Watson Foundation Fellowship to continue writing for the stage. Back home in Los Angeles, he moved into scoring films with *The California Reich* (1975). Other scores for TV and feature films include *Angel* (1984), *The Legend of Billie Jean* (1985), *A Nightmare on Elm Street 4* (1988), *Major Payne* (1995), *Stinkers* and *Mr Wrong* (both 1996). He has continued working in musical theatre and writing songs: his show *Butterfly* was produced at the Goodspeed Opera House, and *Shangri-La Plaza* was a musical written for CBS Television; he is currently developing a new musical film with director Nick Castle and Mark Mueller.

New review

The Last Starfighter (1984) **Original Soundtrack / Craig Safan**.
  Intrada Ⓕ MAF7066 (49 minutes: ADD).

This lively and enjoyable score for a now almost forgotten Sci-Fi B-movie seemed to herald the arrival of a significant new talent in film music back in 1984. With the exception of his much-praised contribution to *Son of the Morning Star*, Craig Safan's career has, so far, not lived up to its early promise. *The Last Starfighter* previously appeared on disc in a truncated 30-minute version, which also included two songs from the movie; Intrada's new release dispenses with the songs and presents Safan's music in a more satisfyingly complete form. It might not rival the epic grandeur of its model, *Star Wars*, but this is a colourful and vivid film score nevertheless, with synthesizers judiciously incorporated into the orchestra to add their exotic 'alien' tones. Safan's principal march theme is rousing and heroic in the classic John Williams manner, whilst he adds interest and a sense of depth by giving prominence to the woodwinds in places. A welcome new release that may go some way toward reviving interest in this undoubtedly accomplished composer. **MW**

New review

Son of the Morning Star (1991) **Original Soundtrack**, with **Holly Gornik** (ob); **Ed Gornik** (tpt); **Tom Mauchahty-Ware** (fl) **/ Craig Safan**.
  Intrada Ⓕ MAF7037D (60 minutes: DDD).

Some films, and in rarer cases some television movies, can inspire a composer to produce music that might even surprise themselves. Such was the case with *Son of the Morning Star* and its composer Craig Safan. Not that Safan hadn't already written several good scores, just that here was a subject – the events leading up to Custer's last stand – that evidently both moved and inspired him. Scored for a large orchestra, the opposing forces of Custer's cavalry and the Native Americans are vividly evoked: a noble trumpet-led main theme (very reminiscent of Vaughan Williams) vies with some ethnic instrumentation, notably Tom Mauchahty-Ware's Native American flute. Richly expressive and played with great drive and vigour, the score culminates in a 17-minute *tour de force*, "Little Big Horn", where all the disparate musical threads are woven together in a luminous and irresistible tapestry. **JW**

Also available:
Angel (1983) Intrada MAF7047D
A Nightmare on Elm Street 4 (1988) Varèse Sarabande VSD5203

Ryuichi Sakamoto
b. 1952 Japan

Born in Tokyo, Ryuichi Sakamoto received his Masters degree in composition and electronic music from the Tokyo College of Arts. He formed the Yellow Magic Orchestra, achieving chart success in the UK with *Computer Game (Theme from the Invaders)* in 1980. He had two more UK hits with David Sylvian, as well as forging a career as a solo artist. He made his acting début in the film *Merry Christmas, Mr Lawrence* (1983) for which he also wrote the score. He received an Academy Award for *The Last Emperor*, written in collaboration with David Byrne and Cong Su.

The Last Emperor (1987) **Original Soundtrack / Gavyn Wright**.
  Virgin Ⓜ CDV2485 (50 minutes: AAD). Additional music by David Byrne and Cong Su.

With *Merry Christmas, Mr Lawrence* Sakamoto proved that he had a talent for producing an incredibly haunting theme from a few simple phrases. For the Oscar-winning *The Last Emperor*, he not only provided two equally unforgettable themes, but also had the opportunity of combining authentic Chinese instruments with a large orchestra, thus imbuing the film with a heady and hypnotic Oriental flavour as well as a sweeping sense of epic grandeur. With two other composers working on the score, the end result could easily have been an indigestible hodge-podge but each style blends remarkably well and makes for a convincing and genuinely exotic disc. **RS**

Merry Christmas, Mr Lawrence (1983) **Original Soundtrack**, with **Ryuichi Sakamoto** (synths).
Milan Ⓕ 22048-2 (41 minutes: AAD). Includes *Forbidden Colours* (Sakamoto/Sylvian).

Sometimes a wholly new sound emerges, and remains indelibly in the memory – this music has such an effect. Mostly synthesized (one track is played by a string section), it is composed by one of the main actors in the film, and completely entwines itself with the visual world of hot sun, torture, spiritual and mental struggle, memories of home, and hopes for the future. It is superbly engineered, with haunting effects, repetitive yet inventive motifs (melodic, harmonic and rhythmic), and a stylistic consistency which is potent and absorbing. The snatches of the old school mingle with the inexorable tread of oppression and 'justice', and the musical construction is memorably suited to the epic and intimate elements of the film. The disc stands up well on its own, as an ever-fascinating palette of tone and texture is explored.   **CT**

Also available:
Little Buddha (1994) Milan 35676-2
The Sheltering Sky (1990) Virgin CDV2652
1996 [compilation] Milan 35759-2

Hans J. Salter   1896-1994 Austria

Born in Vienna, Hans Julius Salter began his musical career conducting in Viennese theatres. Aged 23, Salter was hired to conduct a series of filmed operettas; he soon began to compose film scores. By 1929 Salter had moved to UFA studios in Berlin, but the encroachment of Nazism persuaded him to return to Vienna in 1933 and continue his film career there. When Hitler's influence extended even to Vienna, Salter emigrated to America in 1937. He was hired by Charles Previn at Universal Studios in 1938, and remained under contract for 25 years. Salter's name became indelibly associated with Universal's stock-in-trade horror movies: Dracula, Wolfman, Frankenstein and all their innumerable progeny terrified audiences to the strains of Salter's music. Many of these scores were composite creations, with Salter and other studio composers – including a young Henry Mancini – sharing the burden of scoring an endless stream of low budget flicks (in 1942, for example, Salter scored 30 films). He was occasionally able to diversify – as with his scores for Deanna Durbin musicals – but he will always be remembered as the musical voice of Universal's monster menagerie.

New review
Salter/Skinner The Invisible Man Returns (1940) The Wolf Man (1941).
Skinner Son of Frankenstein (1939) **Moscow Symphony Orchestra / William T. Stromberg**.
  Marco Polo Ⓕ 8 223747 (76 minutes: DDD). Reconstructed by John Morgan.
Salter/Dessau House of Frankenstein (1944) **Moscow Symphony Orchestra / William T. Stromberg**.
  Marco Polo Ⓕ 8 223748 (55 minutes: DDD). Reconstructed by John Morgan and William T. Stromberg.

When Hans Salter, a recent immigrant from Vienna, was hired by Charles Previn and put under contract at Universal Studios in 1938 he began a 25-year stint producing a succession of well-crafted if not always memorable scores principally for Universal's stock-in-trade output of low budget monster flicks. Often, tight production deadlines meant that these were composite creations written with other members of the music department. One of Salter's frequent collaborators was Frank Skinner, staff-composer at Universal whose 1939 *Son of Frankenstein* score was orchestrated by Salter, then the new boy on the block. Neither Skinner nor Salter were especially concerned with innovation, being content on the whole to traverse the furrow ploughed by others, particularly Franz Waxman's *Bride of Frankenstein* (1935) – the crippling deadlines they faced made experimentation almost impossible anyway. Skinner's *Son of Frankenstein*, as the follow-up to *Bride* inevitably suffers by comparison. Not that the music wants any additional polish, simply that the electrifying freshness of Waxman's earlier work is missing from Skinner's sequel. The same is broadly true of the other Salter collaborations recorded here. Paul Dessau's very un-Hollywood modernism contributes some added spice to *House of Frankenstein*, although the normally more traditionalist Salter should receive due credit for determining the music's overall tone. This complete score – only an abbreviated suite appeared on an earlier Marco Polo disc – is full of strong themes, occasional moments of pathos, and lashings of camp melodrama; it is in places very exciting indeed, and is easily the best of the music presented here.

Although Universal's hectic working practices too often robbed Salter's music of that sense of individuality, of a guiding musical personality, which makes some other scores of the period real classics, these enthusiastic and committed performances nevertheless make a strong case for this highly enjoyable, if occasionally workmanlike, music. **MW**

A Symphony of Film Music Original Soundtracks / Hans Salter.
Intrada mono Ⓕ MAF7054D (73 minutes: ADD).
Creature from the Black Lagoon (1954). The Black Shield of Falworth (1954). Hitler (1962).
The Incredible Shrinking Man (1957).

Presented here are four suites compiled from four of Hans Salter's typical Universal assignments, in their original flat and rather murky mono. *Creature from the Black Lagoon* (some of which was co-written with Henry Mancini and Herman Stein) is horrifically standard horror fare, with blaring brass, sudden crescendos, lurking strings, and much more 'monster' music of the type Salter did so well. *The Black Shield of Falworth* was a swashbuckling costume drama (starring Tony Curtis) with a pleasing pastoral feel to the music, and dramatic action aplenty which harks back to the Korngold/Flynn era. Salter's score for *Hitler* has a vivid immediacy and an emotional depth which is perhaps unsurprising coming from a first-hand witness of the rise of Nazism. Blustering marches and pompous militarism contrast with starkly sombre textures. *The Incredible Shrinking Man* is full of delicate shades, with a wistful love theme (by Fred Carling and Ed Lawrence) which makes a refreshing contrast to the more conventional thriller elements. Salter may never have been as gifted as his European-immigrant contemporaries Rózsa, Korngold or Waxman, but he was a thoroughly professional musician with a real flair for the dramatic – this disc is a fitting tribute to his skill. **MW**

Also available:
Music for Frankenstein (RTE Orch/Penny) Marco Polo 8 223477

Philippe Sarde

b. 1948 France

Born in Neuilly on the Seine, Philippe Sarde was introduced to music by his mother, an opera singer. He studied harmony, counterpoint, fugue and composition with Noël Gallon and later with Georges Auric. He has written extensively for French cinema – composing some 176 scores between 1969 and 1994 – and has worked both in France and elsewhere with directors including Jean-Jacques Annaud, Yves Boisset, Roman Polanski, Bertrand Tavernier and Roger Vadim. His score for Polanski's *Tess* (1979) recieved an Academy Award nomination.

New review
La Fille de d'Artagnan (1994) Original Soundtrack / Philippe Sarde.
Sony Classical Ⓕ SK66364 (53 minutes: DDD).

Philippe Sarde's score for *La Fille de d'Artagnan* represents his seventh collaboration with director Bertrand Tavernier (the pair previously worked together on films such as *L'Horloger de Saint Paul*, 1974, *Des Enfants Gâtés*, 1977, and *Coup de Torchon*, 1982). A baroque drama with comic elements, *La Fille de d'Artagnan* could have been scored in the stylistic framework of the Golden Age composers. After rejecting a traditional Hollywood approach, Tavernier and Sarde considered the possibility of using music from the actual baroque era. Reasoning that a pastiche score would have undermined the film's contemporary overtones, Sarde's solution was to assemble two orchestras, the first an ancient baroque ensemble to establish authenticity, the second being a modern version of the baroque orchestra updated with a mixed chorus, and, most interestingly, an ethnically diverse percussion section playing complex rhythms. The latter ensemble gave Sarde the flexibility to explore new expressive possibilities and addressed the director's desire to have an unconventional score that still marked the period.

The music for *La Fille de d'Artagnan* is all original, composed in the rigorously controlled, systematic forms created by the baroque school. Sarde maintains a balance between complexity and clarity, even in the score's polyphonic passages. Sounds from the past echo in friendly familiarity: the virtuoso recorder, the middle to high-range trumpet, the ubiquitous organ, the dextrous harpsichord playing, the drums, and the "festive" atmosphere of the orchestra. Before things become too comfortable idiomatically, Sarde throws in an anachronistic touch of percussion or an alternative sound that throws the listener into a different realm. This helps sustain interest over the course of the listening experience, and also offsets some of the problems people may have with baroque aesthetics. For example, there are no sharp contrasts in the rhythm or the dynamics within each piece, and the overall emotional impact borders on the impersonal. Sarde helps the situation by moving occasionally into harmonic and melodic territories that recall the composer's American work (Sarde's presence on the western side of the Atlantic is sorely missed – his outstanding scores for *Ghost Story* and *Quest for Fire* have not been forgotten). And in "Te Deum II", Sarde strays completely from his baroque stylings into the world of Cláude Debussy! Notwithstanding these diversions, this score is a consistent musical voyage that combines the baroque with a contemporary world view in a way that celebrates both traditions. Sony's presentation includes an interview with Sarde by Stephane Lerouge and photos of the leading actors in their film costumes. The disc was warmly engineered by John Timperley at EMI's world-renowned Abbey Road Studios. **KM**

New review
Le Petit Garçon (1994). **Original Soundtrack**, with **Andrew Marriner** (cl); **Michael Davis** (vn); **Howard Shelley** (pf); **London Symphony Orchestra / Harry Rabinowitz**.
Auvidis Travelling Ⓟ K1010 (42 minutes: DDD).

If Philippe Sarde's *Fort Saganne* (1984) is the one example of his work that I would not willingly live without, it is nevertheless worth noting that this French composer has quietly been turning in fine, at times classic, scores for many years far away from all the ballyhoo of Hollywood. His forays into international cinema – *Tess* (1979) and *Ghost Story* (1981) for example – notwithstanding, his finest work has been for homegrown product. For Pierre Granier-Deferre's delicate tale, *Le Petit Garçon*, about a young boy growing up during the German occupation, Sarde has written another finely-tuned score, subtle and haunting. As the booklet notes explain: "...the voice of a little girl 'with blue Hebrew eyes' will be heard ... for that voice we need a fragile violin. A limpid clarinet to answer it and a piano to defend them against the beautiful, terrifying waves of the War Symphony." Just listen to the soloists work magic with Sarde's music and open our eyes to the world of a nine-year old French boy, scared, but looking forward to better times. Not over long at 41 minutes, this is still a joy for anyone who cares about sensitive film music. **JW**

Also available:
The Music-Box (1989) Varèse Sarabande VSD5248

Lalo Schifrin
b. 1932 Argentina

Born in Buenos Aires, the son of the leader of the Buenos Aires Symphony Orchestra, Lalo Schifrin studied piano with Andreas Karalis and harmony with Juan Carlos Paz. After winning a scholarship to the Paris Conservatoire, Schifrin took lessons with Olivier Messiaen. But his real passion was for jazz. Returning to Argentina, he demonstrated his skill as composer, arranger and pianist equally at home with classical, jazz and pop music. He was the founder of an Argentine jazz band, modelled on the big band styles of Count Basie and Dizzy Gillespie. A meeting with Gillespie in 1957 resulted in Schifrin being invited to become his arranger, based in New York. He won acclaim for his jazz compositions and arrangements for Gillespie and others like Count Basie and Stan Getz. Schifrin had always been interested in film, and took a film course whilst a student at Buenos Aires University. His first film score was for an Argentinian art movie. Moving to Hollywood from New York, Schifrin began scoring television shows: his most famous work for TV – and one of TV's most enduringly popular themes – is *Mission: Impossible* (1966). His first major feature was *The Cincinnati Kid* (1965). Other scores include *Cool Hand Luke* (1967), *Bullitt* (1968), *Kelly's Heroes* (1970) and *Dirty Harry* (1971). Schifrin has never been solely a film composer, and continues to work in other musical forms. He is particularly noted for his jazz-based compositions.

A.D. Anno Domini (1984) **Original Soundtrack**, with the **Paris Philharmonic Choir and Orchestra / Lalo Schifrin**.
Prometheus Ⓟ PCD112 (62 minutes: ADD).

The TV mini-series has always given composers a wide-ranging palette to work from, and in scoring *A.D.* – a television story of the early days of Christianity immediately after the crucifixion – Lalo Schifrin produced a widely diverging score, ranging from anguished choral passages to grand fanfares for the Roman legions. The main theme is noble and devout; and across some 29 cues (13 of which did not appear on the original BBC album) a great variety and abundance of excellent scoring is heard, including several enjoyable period-style dances. Like so many composers who learnt their craft in the sixties – Dave Grusin is another – Schifrin is not heard so much of in the cinema as he was (but, like Grusin, his career has gone in more than one direction). *A.D.* is a timely reminder that he is still a force to be reckoned with. **JW**

Don Quixote (1993) **Original Soundtrack**, with the **Madrid Symphony Orchestra / Lalo Schifrin**.
Prometheus Ⓟ PCD132 (44 minutes: DDD).

From Purcell, through Telemann, to Richard Strauss and Manuel de Falla, Cervantes's quixotic hero has fascinated composers. He has also attracted the attention of filmmakers, but with conspicuously less successful results. By all accounts, producer Emiliano Piedra's Spanish television adaptation was one of the better attempts at bringing the Knight of the Doleful Countenance to the screen. However, in the final cut, Schifrin's score was mangled by the director Manuel Gutierrez Aragon; Prometheus have performed a valuable service in presenting the music as it was originally intended to be heard. Via a series of robust themes and delightful melodies, Schifrin offers a picturesque musical account of the knight's travels. The striking "Main Title" immediately sets the scene: a colourful pageant, with a strong vein of romance, and an appropriately Spanish tinge. The music for Don Quixote's homeland, "La Mancha", has a broad nostalgic hue normally associated (by film composers anyway) with the rolling prairies of America's midwest; the love theme for 'Princess' Dulcinea, and the mournful horn call for Quixote himself are especially poignant moments. Overall, this is an outstanding example of Schifrin's dramatic talent.   **MW**

The Four Musketeers (1974) **The Eagle Has Landed** (1976) **Voyage of the Damned**
(1976) **Original Soundtracks / Lalo Schifrin**.
Label X Ⓕ LXCD5 (62 minutes: AAD).

Schifrin's score for the second part of Richard Lester's romp through Dumas's period swashbuckler is a joy from beginning to end. Schifrin goes where Michel Legrand might have gone with the first instalment – jazz overtones and jangly harpsichord to the fore. His studio albums at this time combined period and jazz influences, and this score is a natural progression. The CD also features his exciting music for John Sturges's *The Eagle Has Landed*. Beginning with the main credits, soaring strings and cymbalom all add to the mystery of the forthcoming story. Sadly the love theme for Donald Sutherland and Jenny Agutter is mysteriously missing from this recording – it did appear on a Japanese single at the time of the film's original release – but that is a minor complaint. This is a gem of an action score. A more restrained and evocative work is Schifrin's score for Lew Grade's *Voyage of the Damned* which brings this recording to a satisfying conclusion.   **JW**

Also available:
Mission: Impossible (1966) MCA MCLD19320

Gerard Schurmann   b. 1928 The Netherlands

Dutch-born Gerard Schurmann was brought up in the Dutch East Indies, but settled in England. Although intending to pursue a career writing concert works, Schurmann was introduced to film scoring by Alan Rawsthorne; he acted as Rawsthorne's assistant, orchestrating and occasionally composing segments of his films. Much of his film work was as an orchestrator: aside from Rawsthorne scores like *The Cruel Sea* (1953), his credits include Mario Nascimbene's *The Vikings* (1958), Ernest Gold's *Exodus* (1960) and Maurice Jarre's *Lawrence of Arabia* (1962). Schurmann's first taste of film scoring was for a Dutch semi-docmentary called *Broken Dykes*; but his first score proper was *The Long Arm* (1956). Subsequently, Schurmann scored several pictures made at Ealing Studios. His highly modernist style tended to limit his assignments to horror movies, just about the only genre in which dissonance and serialism was (and still is) accepted.

Horrors of the Black Museum The Film Music of Gerard Schurmann. **Original Soundtracks**, with various conductors.
Cloud Nine mono Ⓜ CNS5005 (78 minutes: ADD).
Horrors of the Black Museum (1959). Cone of Silence (1960). The Bedford Incident (1965). Doctor Syn (1963). Konga (1961). The Lost Continent (1968). The Ceremony (1963). The Long Arm (1956). Attack on the Iron Coast (1967). Claretta (1984).

Though not a particularly prolific composer for the cinema, Schurmann was certainly a distinctive one. Alan Rawsthorne's chromatic, angular style spikes much of Schurmann's film work, injecting scores like *The Long Arm, The Bedford Incident* and *Horrors of the Black Museum* with a taut, chilling urgency that is very striking – the latter especially so considering the very small orchestra the composer had to work with. *Konga*, a cut-price British version of *King Kong*, is notable for the way in which Schurmann follows Max Steiner's lead by eliciting sympathy for the monster's demise. *The Ceremony* is more exotic (notably in the shimmeringly lovely cue "Freedom"); and for *Claretta* the icy menace of his earlier work is temporarily set aside as he paints a lushly Verdian portrait of Mussolini's mistress. Sound quality varies from track to track but does not detract from the many rewards this unusual retrospective has to offer.   **RS**

See also Collections: **The Red Shoes**

John Scott

b. 1930 England

Born in Bristol, John Scott was given early music lessons by his father, a member of the Bristol Police Band. Aged 14, Scott joined the army as a 'Boy Musician' where he studied clarinet and harp; a growing love of jazz – especially Charlie Parker – resulted in his also taking up the saxophone. After gaining performing experience with the Royal Artillery Band, he left the army and began touring with jazz bands. His skills as an arranger came to the fore during his time with the Ted Heath Band; as a result he was hired by EMI Records to arrange and conduct for artists like Tom Jones, Cilla Black and The Hollies (Scott contributed to their mega-hit "He Ain't Heavy, He's My Brother"). During this time he led a jazz quintet, and played on film soundtracks for composers like John Barry and Henry Mancini (he was principal sax on *Goldfinger*). In 1965 he wrote his first original score, *A Study in Terror*. In addition to film and television work, Scott has written several concert works, most recently a symphony commissioned to celebrate the city of Colchester. He is also in regular demand as a conductor. He formed his own record label – JOS Records – in order to make his own unjustly neglected output more widely available.

Antony and Cleopatra (1972) **Berlin Radio Symphony Choir and Orchestra / John Scott**.
JOS Records Ⓕ JSCD114 (58 minutes: DDD). Recorded 1987-92.

John Scott's music for Charlton Heston's little-seen epic (who so admired the score he mentioned it in his *Actor's Journal*) finally makes its appearance on CD in a new and much longer form than the original version issued by Polydor in 1972 (although many fans will remember its classy full-colour fold out sleeve). It is a wonderful score: the beautiful main theme – one of Scott's finest pieces – flows like the Nile, undulating gracefully through some memorable choral writing. The battle sequences have an excitement and style worthy of Alex North. The only let down is a rather bland sleeve design (which I understand is being re-vamped for future release). But don't be put off by the cover: this is John Scott's classic score. **JW**

Cousteau Documentaries –
Cape Horn[a] and **The Channel Islands**[b] **Original Soundtracks**, with the [a]**Royal Philharmonic Orchestra**; [b]**Berlin Radio Concert Orchestra / John Scott**.
JOS Records Ⓕ JSCD103 (61 minutes: ADD).
Parc Océanique Cousteau Original Soundtracks, with [a]**Colin Purbrook** (org); **Royal Philharmonic Orchestra / John Scott**.
JOS Records Ⓕ JSCD106 (60 minutes: ADD).
The Blue Whale[a]. Fire, Water, Life. Journey to the Depths of the Ocean[a]. Music for Shipwrecks.

These discs are just two examples of John Scott's colourfully illustrative music for Jacques Cousteau's famous nautical documentaries. This music is no less richly-orchestrated, dramatic and melodic than any of the composer's 'proper' film scores. Each Cousteau score presents a series of vivid tableaux, encapsulating the adventure, danger and fun of the different voyages. The Emmy Award-winning score on the first disc takes us to *Cape Horn*, with an arresting depiction of "The Violent Graveyard", followed by distinctive musical portraits of glaciers, seals, albatrosses and penguins (the "Penguin Gallop" is a real gem). *The Channel Islands* is less turbulent, with broad orchestral themes emphasizing the opening cue's title, "Islands of Beauty and Adventure". Scott's pellucid scoring gives the undersea movements a real sense of the wonder and mystery of exploration. As with all his Cousteau scores, each cue is a fully-developed portrait in miniature – able to be savoured individually, or as part of the whole. The grace and grandeur of *The Blue Whale* begins the second disc. Scott's music responds with awe and reverence: after full orchestral treatment, he introduces a lengthy solo movement for church organ. *Fire, Water, Life*, as the title suggests, shifts in mood from the drama of "Volcanoes" to the ethereal beauty of undersea life. *Journey to the Depths of the Ocean* is a musical voyage into the unknown in which Colin Purbrook is employed once again to evoke the unfathomable mysteries of the deep. *Music for Shipwrecks* is the shortest, and least convincing suite, if only because it includes a song – "Toll the Bell" – which unwittingly jars the listener, who has heretofore been mentally drifting beneath the ocean, back to dry land and reality. Throughout this series, the composer's vivid use of his orchestral palette to illustrate each different encounter is especially to be savoured. The absence of explanatory booklet-notes for any of the discs is the only quibble about these attractive and highly collectible discs. **MW**

John Scott Conducts His Own Favourite Film Scores Berlin Radio Concert Orchestra; [a]Royal Philharmonic Orchestra / John Scott.
JOS Records Ⓕ JSCD111 (59 minutes: ADD).
The Final Countdown (1980). The Shooting Party (1984). North Dallas Forty (1979).

England Made Me (1973). The People That Time Forgot (1977). Cousteau: Amazon[a]. Outback (1970). Greystoke (1984). Antony and Cleopatra (1972).

There is something so positively beguiling about John Scott's music – a succession of enchanting melodies, transparently orchestrated – that it requires no small effort of will to actually stop listening to a disc like this. Scott's output encompasses a diversity of styles, most of which are represented here: from the jazzy pre-war number "All on the Radio" (*England Made Me*), through the light pop of *North Dallas Forty*, to the electrified modernism of *Outback*. Scott's melodic skills are really shown to best advantage, however, in the unashamed romanticism of *The Shooting Party*, *Greystoke* and *Antony and Cleopatra*. The action-packed overture to *The Final Countdown* is an arresting reminder of his dramatic abilities. If you are not yet familiar with Scott's music, this is an excellent place to start exploring.   **MW**

New review
The North Star (1996) Original Soundtrack, with the Philharmonia Orchestra/ John Scott.
JOS Records ⒻJSCD120 (61 minutes: DDD).

All John Scott's film scores share an inherent and distinctive Englishness also to be found in the work of his contemporaries Ron Goodwin and John Barry; although *The North Star* was a multinational production with a Norwegian director and French leading man, this score is no exception. The broadly flowing, nobly heroic main theme is typical of Scott's music. As ever, his method was to compose several themes for the picture – more than he knew would actually be needed – and then build his score from a select nucleus. The result is a meticulously constructed piece which, while taking in a wide variety of styles from cowboy saloon music to American Indian chant, is solidly founded on recurring thematic material. Scott's crystal-clear orchestrations reflect his careful attention to detail: in the cue "Burn Out", for example, the evil McLennon's state of mind is suggested by violas playing *sul ponticello* without vibrato, and the effect is eerily reminiscent of Hollywood's favourite psychotic instrument, the Theremin; agitated string figures during "Blizzard Chase" vividly depict the swirling snowfall. Dramatic scenes are underscored with propulsive percussion, although Scott's astringent way with such angry musical outbursts remains a model of orchestral clarity. *The North Star* is a score full of admirable elements, not the least of which is the composer's ability to communicate his own passionate involvement in the project.   **MW**

The Shooting Party[a] (1984) Birds and Planes (1964) Original Soundtracks, with the [a]Royal Philharmonic Orchestra / John Scott.
JOS Records ⒻJSCD113 (52 minutes: ADD).

The elegiac qualities of Isobel Colegate's novel are perfectly taken up by Alan Bridge's film. A sense of loss and mourning for a time in English history when outside forces were beginning to change a way of life forever: the last year before the outbreak of the First World War. This amusing, but ultimately tragic film is blessed with an outstanding cast; fortunately it is also blessed with a superlative score by John Scott. Long-limbed, quintessentially English melodies flow with ease throughout the work. His music is imbued with refinement and elegance, but also sympathy and understanding for the countryside and those who live off it and for it. There is an additional autumnal stillness that permeates the work, which points to the immediate fate of the Gordon Jackson character, as well as the short destinies of the other principal characters revealed to us in the closing credits. The "Epilogue" is an extremely moving reprise of the "Main Title", but with a fragment of *The Last Post* underneath it. A lament for those lives to be lost in The Great War. Due to budgetary restrictions, the documentary *Birds and Planes* was scored for the odd combination of string quartet, piano and four double basses: such a curious sonority alone makes the inclusion of this short suite a welcome bonus.   **DS**

To the Ends of the Earth (1984) Original Soundtrack / John Scott.
Prometheus Ⓕ PCD102 (47 minutes: ADD).

John Scott has carved a niche for himself composing dramatic and evocative scores for documentaries. His Cousteau adventures are thoroughly chronicled on his own JOS Records; *To the Ends of the Earth* is the story of the Transglobe Expedition, led by Sir Ranulph Fiennes. Director William Kronick distilled 150 hours of raw footage into a 100-minute documentary. The composer's brief was to be operatic – he responded with a grandly conceived orchestral tapestry which spectacularly evokes the spirit of adventure and discovery. As with his Cousteau scores, each cue is a characteristic study of dangers, thrills and wonders. The whole is held together by an exhilarating "Main Title" theme, which recurs throughout in a series of delightful variations. The journey to and from both poles is vividly described in music, with portraits of cracking ice, white-outs and the long Antarctic night. Scott's use of orchestral colour to suggest mood and situation is once again to be marvelled at.   **MW**

New review
Walking Thunder (1994) **Original Soundtrack**, with the **Munich Symphony Orchestra / John Scott**.
JOS Records Ⓕ JSCD117 (62 minutes: DDD).

There are few film composers working today that can write a powerful and majestic theme like John Scott. Let loose on this large-scale adventure epic set in the American west in the latter half of the last century he has produced a score that is powerful and imposing, full of grandeur and expressive melody. The main theme, taken up by strings, woodwinds and occasional Native American instruments, is a masterful example of what a good composer can do with such a subject. This is fully developed in cues such as "Journey to Horsecreek" and "The Return Journey". We hear authentic Indian sounds in other cures, all researched by Scott while on a visit to Utah. A six-minute piece entitled "Horsecreek Rendezvous", strategically placed towards the centre of the disc, brings some light relief with a highly infectious suite of dance tunes. Yet it is the main theme of *Walking Thunder* that will be remembered long after the disc has finished. The Munich Symphony Orchestra respond well to the composer's direction, giving a warm and lucid performance. **JW**

Winter People[a] (1989) **Prayer for the Dying** (1987) [a]**Original Soundtrack**; Various artists; [a]**Graunke Symphony Orchestra / John Scott**.
JOS Records Ⓕ JSCD102 (69 minutes: ADD/DDD). Includes *Lightning in a Bottle* (Jimmy Webb).

Both scores on this disc are built around a nucleus of seven musicians. *Winter People* opens with a convincingly authentic bluegrass ensemble consisting of fiddle, mandolin and guitars, augmented by synthesizers – the latter assuming a more important role as the music becomes gradually darker. After previews of the film it was felt that a bigger emotional punch was required, so Scott re-scored the latter third for full orchestra: in this case, a happy decision on the part of the producers, as Scott's gorgeous melodies thereby gain an extra dimension (the final cue, "The Return of Jonathan", is ravishing). The composer's experience with *Prayer for the Dying* was less happy: his score was replaced (against the director's wishes) by one commissioned in Hollywood from Bill Conti. Rather than let his music languish in a drawer, Scott enterprisingly decided to record it, and issue it on his own label. This time the instrumentalists are centered around celtic harp and cello, with electric guitar and synths contributing a harder, 'urban' feel. Molly Simpson adds her own irresistible (wordless) soprano. There is plenty of dramatic writing here, but – as with the previous score – it is the composer's knack for penning attractive melodies that ultimately wins the listener's affection. Two such diverse and unusual scores on one disc – great value by any reckoning. **MW**

Also available:
The Deceivers (1988) RCA 7722-2
Far from Home: The Adventures of Yellow Dog (1994) JOS Records JSCD118
King of the Wind (1989) JOS Records JSCD109
Lionheart [A.W.O.L.] (1990) Intrada MAF7011D
William the Conqueror (1990) JOS Records JSCD110
Witchcraft (1996) JOS Records JSCD121
Yor (1983) Label X LXCD7
Jacques Cousteau Documentaries on JOS Records:
Amazon I: The River JSCD104
Amazon II: The Indians JSC105
Saint Lawrence/Australia JSCD107
The First 75 Years/The Warm Blooded Sea JSCD108
Papua New Guinea JSCD112

Eric Serra
b. 1959 France

Originally and primarily a rock musician, Eric Serra's involvement in film music has largely been a result of his friendship with director Luc Besson. Serra's first score was *Le Dernier Combat* (1983), and for Besson he has scored *Subway* (1985), the European version of *The Big Blue* (1988 – his score was replaced in the USA by Bill Conti's), *La Femme Nikita* (1990) and *Leon*. In 1995 he scored the latest James Bond movie, *Goldeneye* – Serra's penchant for synthesizers and electronic percussion made for quite a stylistic departure from the traditional approach to scoring Bond movies.

New review

Leon [The Professional] (1994) **Original Soundtrack / John Altman.**
  Sony ℗ 478323-2 (64 minutes: DDD).

Critical superlatives have become devalued coins in our hyperbolic society, but let's spend this one without guilt: Eric Serra's music for *Leon* (retitled *The Professional* for its US release) is one of the most effective scores in recent memory. Serra does everything in his power to support the film and to enhance this story of cold-blooded hitman (Jean Reno) who saves the life of a young girl (Natalie Portman) after her family is massacred by a psycho (Gary Oldman). She learns the tricks of the trade while he becomes a father (and at times a romantic) figure. *The Professional* continues Serra's ongoing association with director Luc Besson. This time the composer's musical approach is symphonic, although he has supplemented the orchestra with electronics and a diverse assortment of ethnic instruments. The score sets up a distinction between the ugly crime world of New York and the offbeat, gradually developing relationship between assassin Leon and his 12-year old apprentice, Mathilda. Equating the city's skyscrapers with Egyptian pyramids, Serra employs African and Arabian percussion in his city description. This is a refreshing change from the usual urban musical clichés, with the composer still managing to create the feeling of a melting pot. The music assumes a warmer shade when Serra turns to the Leon/Mathilda relationship. A solo oboe imparts a mournful quality to "Leon the Cleaner", while a toy piano sound and acoustic guitar conspire to create the beguiling "Ballad for Mathilda". A *boléro* is snuck into "What's Happening Out There?", while Serra slides into French mode in "How Do Your Know It's Love?". In the four-movement, climactic "Fight" tracks, the orchestra steps in and assumes a large presence that matches the violent drama. The final track, "Two Ways Out," ends things on a quasi-lyrical, wistful note – Leon has been killed, and Mathilda faces an uncertain future.   **KM**

Also available:
Atlantis (1991) Virgin 30687
The Big Blue (1988) Virgin CDV2541
Goldeneye (1995) Virign CDVUSX100

Marc Shaiman   USA

Born in New Jersey, Marc Shaiman had no formal musical training. Despite this, by the age of 17 he had moved to New York and was performing as part of Bette Midler's band. He began arranging and writing off-Broadway shows, then landed a job as arranger for the TV comedy show *Saturday Night Live* – this began his association with Billy Crystal, who brought the composer to Hollywood to arrange and score a number of HBO television specials featuring Crystal (Shaiman subsequently scored both *City Slickers* films). Another Billy Crystal assignment was acting as Music Director on *When Harry Met Sally* (1989). His early work with Bette Midler had also resulted in him taking on the same role for *Beaches* (1988). His first big scoring assignment was the Stephen King thriller *Misery* (1990) directed by Rob Reiner, who had also directed *When Harry Met Sally*.

City Slickers (1991) **Original Soundtrack / Hummie Mann, Mark McKenzie.**
  Varèse Sarabande ℗ VSD5321 (37 minutes: DDD). Includes *Young At Heart* (Richards/Leigh).

An agreeable send-up of just about every Western score ever written, *City Slickers* is also a good example of Shaiman's bright comedic manner. His principal Western theme is located somewhere on the border of the *The Big Country*, in the vicinity where *The Magnificent Seven* were last seen riding. Shaiman presents this theme in a series of different shadings: in one place a reflective guitar and harmonica arrangement, in others a more traditionally rumbustious version. Over-the-top comedy is served up in "Cowabunga", a jazz/gospel/r'n'b hoedown for clarinet, sax, orchestra and 'Hallelujah brother!' chorus, whilst the score is given some dramatic bite in "The River". But a Hollywood comedy is not complete without some life-affirming schmaltz, consequently Shaiman gives us a convincingly tender lullaby, sentimental yet never too syrupy. The inclusion of Jimmy Durante's "Young at Heart" is much more of an asset than the yawn-inducing MOR song "Where Did My Heart Go?".   **MW**

Also available:
The Addams Family (1991) Capitol C21298172
Addams Family Values (1993) Varèse Sarabande VSD5465
An American President (1995) MCA MCAD11380

City Slickers II (1993) Columbia CK66183
A Few Good Men (1992) Columbia CK53391
First Wives' Club (1996) Varèse Sarabande VSD5781
Hearts and Souls (1993) MCA MCAD10919

Howard Shore

b. 1946 Canada

Toronto-born Howard Shore played saxophone from an early age, and was heavily influenced by jazz. He studied composition at Boston's Berklee School of Music with John Bavicci. Later, he toured extensively with a rock group called Lighthouse, before beginning to write music for CBC-produced theatre and radio plays. In 1975, Shore, now in New York, became Music Director of the hit comedy show *Saturday Night Live* on NBC. Shore began scoring films for fellow Canadian, director David Cronenberg. Their first collaboration was *The Brood* (1979); and they have since worked together on several other movies, including *Scanners* (1981), *The Fly* (1986), *Naked Lunch* (1991) and the controversial *Crash* (1996). Unlike many of his contemporaries, Shore does not live in Los Angeles, preferring New York, and carefully limits his movie assignments.

New review
Before and After (1996) **Original Soundtrack**, with the **London Philharmonic Orchestra / Howard Shore**.
Hollywood Ⓕ 162039-2 (41 minutes: DDD).

One of Howard Shore's more tonal works, *Before and After* exhibits all the characteristics of an elegy. Although written for full orchestra, strings and woodwinds carry most of the music. Shore draws on a number of pastoral-like themes that have a rich autumnal texture. Of course, as with all his scores, there is darkness as well, although this time not achieved through dissonance. Instead he brilliantly tints his themes with the most subtle shadows of unease and pain. The overall effect is to produce a bleak but always animated score. The expansive string writing is particularly memorable, filling practically every bar of the thick and rather linear orchestrations. A highlight is the acutely moving "Before and After" which concludes the disc. Here, Shore greatly expands on a theme briefly heard earlier. Whilst at the same time musically resolving other themes, this new theme pushes towards a sparkling resolution of its own, causing a rare tingle down the listener's spine. Any music that produces 'the tingle factor' needs little recommendation from me.   **PP**

New review
David Cronenberg Films
Scanners (1981) **The Brood** (1979) **Dead Ringers** (1988) **London Philharmonic Orchestra / Howard Shore**.
Silva Screen Ⓕ FILMCD115 (63 minutes: DDD).

The music Howard Shore has written for the many films of David Cronenberg is often as challenging and jarring musically as the director is visually, as these three scores certainly attest. *Scanners* is strikingly atonal and modern: a small orchestra of strings and percussion is fused with pre-synthesizer electronics to produce a startling and aggressive sound. Instruments play at the extreme high end of their range amidst screaming electronic sounds looped in repetitive bursts. A contemporary string ensemble of 12 players performs the music for *The Brood*, which is again fiercely atonal and based on an anxious three-note ostinato. For *Dead Ringers*, however, the highlight of this disc, Shore has written a much more tonal score for full orchestra. Strings are prominent once again, though harp and low woodwinds also contribute. Shore adds lustre to the strings with subtle electronic embellishment. Befitting a film dominated by suicide, the music has a bitter sense of tragedy, Shore's main theme is dark but sensuous. The most moving cue, "Suicide", accompanies the film's final scene and brilliantly evokes release as well as pain. An eclectic collection.   **PP**

Ed Wood (1994) **Original Soundtrack**, with **Lydia Kavina** (theremin); **Cynthia Miller** (ondes martenot); **London Philharmonic Orchestra / Howard Shore**.
Hollywood Ⓕ 162002-2 (44 minutes: DDD). Includes *Kuba Mambo* (Perez Prado) and *Nautch Dance* (Korla Pandit).

An eccentric orchestral tango, augmented by the agonized wailings of theremin and ondes martenot, begins Howard Shore's witty pastiche of innumerable B-movie scores. Ed Wood, the man who directed what is widely regarded as the worst movie ever made (*Plan 9 from Outer Space*), is the subject of Tim Burton's biopic; the trashy B-movie director would probably have sold his own grandmother to have a Howard Shore score of this quality adorning one of his own lamentable efforts. The tone may be tongue-in-cheek, but Shore's music has enough sincerity to forestall any accusations of glibness, and the LPO play with real conviction. The delicate theme for cross-dressing "Glen or Glenda", for example, manages to be affectionate, yet humorous simultaneously. The 'Swan' theme from Tchaikovsky's *Swan Lake* stands in as a notional love theme. Scattered dialogue excerpts enhance the overall affectionately tacky effect. **MW**

New review

The Fly (1986) **Original Soundtrack**, with the **London Philharmonic Orchestra / Howard Shore**. Varèse Sarabande ⓕ VCD47272 (38 minutes: ADD).

Howard Shore's score for David Cronenberg's shocker starring Jeff Goldblum and Geena Davis is unapologetically modernistic film music. Hearing what a full symphony orchestra can do with such a score is a quite mind-blowing event. Whilst breaking no new ground in modern music *per se*, in cinematic terms its effect is spellbinding. This is music full of attack, with extreme bursts of energy, especially in the highest registers of the strings. Yet within this harsh and sometimes nightmarish modernism, Shore retains a melodic base that comes as a relief for the listener when not contemplating the full horror on screen. *The Fly* is not a score that should be played on a regular basis (at least by me anyway), but it has a power and style that is compelling nevertheless. **JW**

New review

M. Butterfly (1993) **Original Soundtrack**, with the **London Philharmonic Orchestra; Royal Philharmonic Orchestra / Howard Shore**. Varèse Sarabande ⓕ VSD5435 (41 minutes: DDD). Includes "Entrance of Butterfly" and "Un bel dì" from *Madama Butterfly* (Puccini), *Drunken Beauty* and *Sha Jia Bang* (Chinese Traditional).

Of all his work for David Cronenberg, *M. Butterfly* is Howard Shore's most tonal by far. It appears on this disc alongside some Chinese Opera selections performed by the Beijing Opera Company and extracts from Puccini's *Madama Butterfly*. Dramatically relevant, these selections are also very in keeping with the score. Shore's own music, performed as ever by the LPO, has a strong oriental flavour, even at times when no oriental instrumentation can be heard. It is a rare gift for a composer to be able to evoke the music of another culture by using his own musical vocabulary. The orchestrations are focused on strings, woodwinds and some elaborate and quite enchanting writing for harp. A supple four-note theme forms the core of the material, sometimes strident, sometimes delicate. There is an unusual fragility to some of the music, which is hauntingly tender and elegant. Shore also uses one of his most effective dramatic devices: he slowly develops some of his cues, building a fiery and passionate anticipation which is suddenly squashed as Shore gently deprives the listener of the expected musical resolution, ending instead on an utterly devastating note of disappointment and failure. This seamless combination of beauty and dissonance is the essence of Howard Shore's music. **PP**

Mrs Doubtfire (1993) **Original Soundtrack / Howard Shore**. Arista ⓕ 07822 11015-2 (41 minutes: DDD). Includes *Papa's Got a Brand New Bag* (Brown).

A typically light and fluffy Hollywood comedy score completely unlike this composer's 'horrific' assignments, *Mrs Doubtfire* therefore makes for an effective demonstration of Howard Shore's versatility. The music is transparently orchestrated, and attractively scored for an ensemble which highlights flute, clarinet, keyboard, harp and strings. A breezy main theme bubbles along nicely, pleasantly pointing up the affectionately comical nature of the central character; whilst Shore does not neglect the necessary emotionalism: the finale is sweetly sentimental, of course, but not overly mawkish. **MW**

Naked Lunch (1991) **Original Soundtrack**, with **Ornette Coleman** (sax); **London Philharmonic Orchestra / Howard Shore**. Milan ⓕ 262 732 (49 minutes: DDD). Includes five compositions by Ornette Coleman, and *Misterioso* (Thelonius Monk).

Music for an hallucinatory movie which includes graphic scenes of shooting up with bug powder and conversations with unpleasant insectoid typewriters must necessarily be a weird experience in itself. Howard Shore's score – considerably augmented by Ornette Coleman's jazz – is an essay in oddities. To say that the music never develops, to say that each cue invents itself anew, to say that there is a sense of aimlessness and lack of form is no negative criticism. The music holds an eerie fascination: it is not particularly difficult to listen to, just plain and simply odd. Hypnotically, trippingly odd. The mixture of static orchestral textures and free-style jazz may irritate or illuminate, depending on your state of mind, your personal preferences, and just how bad your bug powder habit is. **MW**

New review

Nobody's Fool (1994) **Original Soundtrack**, with the **London Philharmonic Orchestra; London Metropolitan Orchestra / Howard Shore**.
Milan Ⓟ 35689-2 (39 minutes: DDD).

By this composer's standards, the score for *Nobody's Fool* is practically featherweight. Shore explores the emotions associated with the innocence of childhood, the adventure of parenting, and the joys and insecurities of old age. Each of these strands is embodied in a distinct theme, woven together to form the score. The "Main Title" features the charming and catchy principal theme, scored for full orchestra with solo recorder, flute, banjo and accordion. Initially this suggests an earthy evocation of 'the country', but as one listens further, that subtle Shore melancholy begins to creep in: Shore is musically representing the spirit of the story, that nothing in life should be taken for granted. However, for the most part this is a light-hearted and warm score which even exhibits some child-like energy through sprightly interchanges between plucked strings and recorder. With some 20 cues in 40 minutes, it's somewhat pithy on disc, but no less essential listening than the composer's more weighty efforts. **PP**

New review

Seven (1995) **Original Soundtrack / Howard Shore**.
Edel Ⓟ 0022432CIN (57 minutes: DDD).

You would be hard pressed to find a piece of music to match the depiction of unadultered evil which Howard Shore's music for *Seven* evokes. Shore has a quite unique ability to delineate musically the darkest side of the human psyche with frightening clarity, and has done so on many occasions. As well as being dramatically effective, *Seven* is musically significant: Shore has the most original and distinctive sound in cinema today; his orchestrations are almost impossibly complex, remarkably elaborate and detailed, thick with layers of sound. Shore utilizes a conventional orchestra, but his sound is far from conventional. In musically defining the character and life of a serial killer, he has created a simple two-note principal theme and a range of other equally pithy motifs. They impart to the music a feeling of falling, slowly descending out of control. There is no warmth in the score, brass and woodwinds perform at their lowest registers, and waves of strings and synthesizers pierce the murky soundscape with clinically cold exactitude.

Sadly this CD features only 20 minutes of score, the rest of the 57-minute running time is padded out with classical selections and songs. Many will find the score impenetrable, but the sheer scale and audacity of Shore's approach will not fail to exhilarate. **PP**

New review

The Silence of the Lambs (1991) **Original Soundtrack**, with the **Munich Symphony Orchestra / Howard Shore**.
MCA Ⓟ MCAD10194 (57 minutes: DDD).

Howard Shore's music for *The Silence of the Lambs* has deservedly earned a place in history, joining such luminaries as Bernard Herrmann's *Psycho* and John Williams's *Jaws* as evocations of terror. Indeed, this score was so effective – the film practically trembled beneath it – that, like its predecessors, it has been repeatedly copied to the point of cliché. However, there is nothing to match the quite overwhelming and devastating power of Shore's original. The orchestrations are almost incomprehensible, densely packed with instruments often performing at their lowest registers. There are no quick transitions or sudden crescendos in this score, instead it has a chillingly premeditated pace which is agonizingly cumbersome. Other than the ascending eight-note theme of the main title there are no recognizable themes, just motifs of differing shapes and sizes. This is not, however, a flat, monothematic score: there is a great deal of instrumental colour, but all is very dark and pensive. There are many moments to savour: in "Lecter Escapes" the orchestra assimilates the rhythm of a feverishly beating heart, careering with rampant aggression toward a screaming conclusion; the atmosphere of "The Moth" is almost nauseatingly painful, as Shore manipulates near heart-wrenching tension through nervously high strings. Murky and unpleasant electronics join the orchestra for "The Cellar", a remarkably bleak and compelling piece of suspense. In "Finale" an oscillating rhythm for strings and woodwinds is juxtaposed against a long-limbed theme for high strings, musically suggesting that the evil has gone, but will return. There is an addictive quality to Shore's desperate score for this film that fans of modern music will find themselves returning to again and again. **PP**

Also available:
The Client (1994) Elektra 61686-2
Crash (1996) Milan 40198-2
Prelude to a Kiss (1992) Milan 11125-2

Dimitri Shostakovich

1906-1975 Russia

Dimitri Shostakovich is regarded as this century's greatest exponent of the symphony, producing 15 in all from the First in the mid-1920s to his last in 1971. A native of St Petersburg, he took piano lessons from his mother, a professional pianist, and studied piano and composition at the Petrograd Conservatory (he supported his family by playing as a silent film pianist in a local cinema). Although best remembered for his massive symphonic utterances charting his epic struggle to find expression within the confines of Soviet ideology (he was indicted in 1948 by the Union of Soviet Composers for "formalistic perversions and anti-democratic tendencies in music"), he also wrote a great deal of dramatic incidental music for both stage and screen. His first film score was for Grigori Kozintsev's *New Babylon* (1929) and he wrote scores for 34 films in all. These provided a source of income for the composer during his times of strained relations with the Soviet authorities, and left a legacy of music that is too often overlooked.

New review

Hamlet (1964) **The Gadfly** (1955) **Berlin Radio Symphony Orchestra / Leonid Grin.**
Capriccio Ⓟ 10 298 (79 minutes: DDD). Recorded 1988.

Shostakovich first tackled Shakespeare's *Hamlet* in his score for a 1932 stage production. Thirty-two years later he returned to the State of Denmark in Grigori Kozintsev's laudable 1964 film version (the Shostakovich/Kozintsev association had begun in 1929 with *New Babylon*). The director, known for his experimental post-revolutionary cinema, came to be stifled by Stalin's cultural policies, and eventually turned to literary adaptations. On the other hand, Shostakovich (a former silent film pianist) strived to compose within the framework of official Soviet aesthetics. For the most part he was successful, but his film scoring record is somewhat spotty. Fortunately, the composer saved some of his finer film music pages for Kozintsev's *Hamlet*.

The hallmarks of the composer's style resonate throughout the score. An eclectic progressive who loved tradition and tonality, Shostakovich was willing to make infrequent albeit effective trips into dissonance and atonality. Russian influences mingle freely with Germanic/Austrian characteristics. The style is not in the Hollywood tradition, but neither is it a statement against Hollywood. In fact, Shostakovich is remarkable in his ability to create the kind of directly communicating effect demanded by film music. The musical coverage in the film is fairly minimal, but Shostakovich does not hold back when called upon to enhance a scene or to make a point. The portentous "Introduction" defers to the neo-classical "Ball at the Castle" in which Hamlet ruminates about his mother's sudden marriage to the brother of his dead father. When Hamlet's father appears in "The Ghost" an otherworldly mood is fashioned. "In the Garden" is a diverting set-piece that revels in pastiche, while the functional quality of "Poisoning Scene" proves that Shostakovich could rival the Golden Age composers in his mastery of cine-music synchronization. The tragic-romantic aspect of "Ophelia" is not represented so much as her madness, with minor-mode, harmonically centreless music taking over from the lyrical cello opening. In the climactic "Duel and Death of Hamlet" powerful brass fly over scurrying strings as Laertes and Hamlet exchange blows.

The Gadfly is of secondary interest to *Hamlet* cinematically, but holds its own musically. Romantic, lyrical, and colourful, Shostakovich's score for Alexander Fainzimmer's film is a different creature. Framing a love story of people from different classes against the fight for a unified Italy, Shostakovich's score navigates a course between war and romance (has one ever existed without the other?). "Overture" and "Finale" frame the suite with their warlike intonations and fateful, heroic qualities. The elegantly stylized "Counter Dance" is a contrast, while the beautiful "Romance" and "Nocturne" details the ups and downs in the love affair between Gemma and Arthur (codename: The Gadfly). In the hands of Shostakovich, the music achieves a form of considerable structure. The darkly tragic, achingly beautiful "Introduction" is a more familiar example of the kind of effect a film composer needs to be able to generate. Capriccio's presentation features committed playing from Leonid Grin and the BRSO. Robert Usaczyk and Elmar Johanson provide the lengthy and informative programme notes. **KM**

Also available (none are original soundtracks):
The Gadfly (1955) CfP CD-CFP4463
The Golden Hills (1931) **New Babylon** (1929) Russian Disc RDCD11064
King Lear (1970) Capriccio 10 397
King Lear (1970) RCA RD87763
'Maxim' Trilogy (1961) Capriccio 10 561
Odna (1931) Capriccio 10 562
Zoya (1944) **The Young Guard** (1948) Russian Disc RDCD10002

Alan Silvestri

b. 1950 USA

Born in New York, Alan Silvestri studied at Boston's Berklee College of Music. He initially began scoring low-budget pictures, and worked on the television series *Chips*. This led to early film assignments including *Las Vegas Lady, The Amazing Dobermans* (which starred Fred Astaire) and *Par Ou Tes Rentre?* (1984). Much of Silvestri's best work has been for director Robert Zemeckis, scoring blockbusters like *Romancing the Stone* (1984), *Who Framed Roger Rabbit?* (1988) and all three *Back to the Future* films (1985, 1989, 1990); the enormously successful Zemeckis-directed *Forrest Gump* won the composer an Academy Award nomination in 1994. He was awarded the BMI's Richard Kirk Award for career achievement in 1995.

The Abyss (1989) **Original Soundtrack / Alan Silvestri**.
   Varèse Sarabande Ⓕ VSD5235 (47 minutes: DDD).

Silvestri's music for *The Abyss* is a deeply emotive depiction of the film's mysterious undersea enviroment. The literally uplifting choral theme which receives its fullest statement in the "Finale" is used sparingly by Silvestri beforehand: the most effective example being a key sequence in the movie, "Resurrection", where its hesitant orchestral reappearance is tender and joyful after the disturbing "Lindsey Drowns". Those cues which cover the early encounters with aliens are inevitably reminiscent of *Close Encounters of the Third Kind*, although Silvestri is never so dissonant. That the final scenes in which the aliens reveal themselves manage to avoid this obvious comparison is largely due to Silvestri's very distinctive melodic gifts. There are small doses of dynamic action, whilst synthesizers add an otherworldly ambience to much of the score; but it is the wordless chorus which really sticks in the memory long after the disc has finished. The intial impression that this music works better with the movie is dispelled by repeated playing.   **MW**

Back to the Future III (1990) **Original Soundtrack / Alan Silvestri**.
   Varèse Sarabande Ⓕ VSD5272 (45 minutes: DDD). Includes *Doubleback* (ZZ Top).

Freed from the Rock 'n' Roll restraints of the earlier movies, Silvestri was able to provide an exuberant orchestral adventure for the third instalment. There is no denying that a touch too often his score is simply marking time until the main theme comes around again; but equally there is no denying Silvestri's gift for snappy melodies and bold gestures. If the composer plentifully reprises his catchy, foot-tapping *Back to the Future* theme, he also adds some new elements which are just as attractive: a big rousing Western theme, and a delicate lullaby for Doc and Clara. Much loud and brash action music accompanies the frenetic train ride (sensibly split into three separate cues here). ZZ Top's cameo appearance in the movie is represented by the composer's tongue-in-cheek barn dance arrangement.   **MW**

New review

Eraser (1996) **Original Soundtrack / Alan Silvestri**.
   Atlantic Classics Ⓕ 82957-2 (43 minutes: DDD).

Alan Silvestri has proven time and time again that his skill and talent for writing action music is second only to that of Jerry Goldsmith. For Silvestri, like Goldsmith, has an uncanny and riveting grasp of rhythm. Much of contemporary action music is simply loud and cacophonous, devoid of any sense of form or direction. Silvestri's scores admittedly have more bombast than most, but the mercurial and dynamic rhythms which he employs possess an almost mechanistic physicality. The steely coldness of Silvestri's early action scores have recently been superseded by a more refined and heated sound, but the razor-sharp clarity and muscular definition of his orchestrations remain. For *Eraser*, Silvestri raises the temperature to almost unbearable levels with an exhibition of utterly mindless orchestral violence. Thunderous snare drum and timpani, slicing brass, brooding woodwinds and agile strings combine with electric guitar and synthesizers to form a weighty palette. Set-piece cues such as "Kruger Escapes", "Cyrez Break In", and "Dock Fight" are catapulted towards the listener with such energy and force that the result is practically euphoric.   **PP**

Forrest Gump (1994) **Original Soundtrack /Alan Silvestri**.   **ARCAM**
   Epic Ⓕ 477369-2 (39 minutes: DDD).

Shamelessly manipulative and sentimental, Alan Silvestri's *Forrest Gump* will bring a tear to the eye of even the hardest-hearted cynic. The score opens with a tender piano lullaby which is then given to the orchestra. It lacks only a chorus of angelic voices to make it truly maudlin (these unexpectedly appear in the final "Suite"). Much of the rest of Silvestri's music is pleasantly quiet and understated. As it is sandwiched in the film between a chronological procession of pop songs (all relegated to a separate two-disc set), many cues are therefore very brief and have little opportunity to develop beyond the basic lullaby theme. An energetic 'running' motif for strings and brass recalling Goldsmith's superior *Rudy* score appears throughout – in "Run Forrest, Run" and "The Crimson Gump" for example – which gives the album some much needed uplift. Overall, an inoffensive work, the enjoyment of which may be coloured by your attitude to the film.   **MW**

The Quick and the Dead (1995) **Original Soundtrack / Alan Silvestri.**
Varèse Sarabande Ⓟ VSD5595 (34 minutes: DDD).

For Sam Raimi's quirky Western Alan Silvestri came up with a suitably quirky score, in which he successfully exploits a range of familiar Western influences. Syncopated rhythms deliberately point to a Morricone-like 'spaghetti' style; whilst strident 'south-of-the-border' trumpet recalls *The Magnificent Seven.* A moodily romantic theme for Spanish guitar suggestive of Rodrigo's *Concierto de Aranjuez* is, however, the music's most endearing feature. This is an action score that is – unusually for Silvestri – not at all action-dominated. A classically restrained solo guitar piece, "I Don't Wanna Die", is a central and defining moment. The loud music which surrounds it is always tempered by subdued and expressively melodic writing, never allowing the score to degenerate into mere noise (unlike his cacophonous *Judge Dredd*, for example). This is a further demonstration of Silvestri's burgeoning talent, and perhaps an indication of his growing musical maturity.   **MW**

Voyages The Film Music Journeys of Alan Silvestri **Original Soundtracks / Alan Silvestri;** [a]**Seattle Symphony Orchestra / Joel McNeely;** [b]**Royal Philharmonic Orchestra; John Scott.**
Varèse Sarabande Ⓟ VSD5641 (70 minutes: DDD).
Silver Pictures Logo. Forrest Gump[a] (1994). Father of the Bride (1991). Back to the Future III (1990). Ricochet (1991). Romancing the Stone (1984). Soapdish (1991). Who Framed Roger Rabbit?[b] (1988). The Abyss (1989). Clan of the Cave Bear (1986). Death Becomes Her (1992). Predator 2 (1990).

The first retrospective of Alan Silvestri's career is a thoroughly enjoyable record of his particular strengths – snappy, memorable melodies presented in sunnily optimistic colours – which contrives to avoid the weaknesses of some of his full-length soundtrack albums. By concentrating largely on opening and closing title music, Silvestri's tendency to plug musical gaps with noisy bombast or uninteresting repetition is neatly sidestepped. Inevitably, this collection gives due prominence to the composer's work with Robert Zemeckis: every one of these assignments has produced some memorable music, from the up-tempo "End Title" of *Romancing the Stone* (previously unreleased on disc) to the comic caperings of *Death Becomes Her.* By far the two most impressive Silvestri/Zemeckis items featured here, however, are the non-soundtrack suites from *Who Framed Roger Rabbit?* and *Forrest Gump.* The former is a jazzy 11-minute fairground ride given a rollicking reading by John Scott (previously issued on *Screen Themes* VSD5208); the latter is Joel McNeely's sensitive rendition of the nine-minute *Gump* suite from his *Hollywood '94* album (VSD5531) – this sweetly sentimental music is summed up here in a far more cogent form than the annoyingly bitty soundtrack album. Silvestri's gift for comedy is evident in the jolly excerpts from *Father of the Bride, Soapdish* and *Richie Rich;* whilst *The Quick and the Dead, Ricochet, Clan of the Cave Bear* and *The Abyss* add strong dramatic contrast. Only the lengthy excerpt from *Predator 2* threatens to introduce some of that overly bombastic material avoided elsewhere. Overall, an impressive summary of an impressive career.   **MW**

Also available:
Back to the Future (1985) MCA MCLD19151
Back to the Future II (1989) MCA MCAD6361
Clan of the Cave Bear (1986) Varèse Sarabande VCD47252
Death Becomes Her (1992) Varèse Sarabande VSD5375
Father of the Bride (1991) Varèse Sarabande VSD5348
Ferngully (1991) MCA MCAD10619
Judge Dredd (1995) Epic 480855-2
Predator 2 (1990) Varèse Sarabande VSD5302
Richie Rich (1994) Varèse Sarabande VSD5582

Mark Snow
b. 1946 USA

Born in Brooklyn of musical parents – his father a Broadway percussionist and mother a music teacher and pianist – Mark Snow began piano lessons aged 10. He took up the oboe, and learnt to play the drums as well. He began composing whilst attending New York's Music and Art High School, then moved on to the Juilliard School. It was here he met a kindred spirit in fellow student Michael Kamen, and together they formed the innovative rock/classical fusion group The New

York Rock 'n' Roll Ensemble. The band enjoyed five years of success with Snow as the drummer. In 1974, he moved to Los Angeles to begin a career composing for film and television. He wrote themes and scored episodes of, among others, *Hart to Hart, Cagney and Lacey* and *Crazy Like a Fox*. In addition, he has written scores for over 70 television films and mini-series, including *The Boy in the Plastic Bubble* (1976) and *Vietnam War Stories* (1987), and feature films including *Ernest Saves Christmas* (1988) and *Born to Be Wild* (1995). His biggest success, however, has been with *The X-Files*. Snow writes all of the show's electronic scores at his home studio. His collaboration with *X-Files* creator Chris Carter has continued on Carter's new series, *Millenium*; and Snow's paranormal tendencies were also heard in the pilot episode of the alien invasion series *Dark Skies*.

New review
The Oldest Living Confederate Widow Tells All (1994) **Original Soundtrack**, with **Kelly Parkinson** (vn).
Milan Ⓕ 35672-2 (46 minutes: DDD).

For everyone who thought Mark Snow just did 'spooky'. This score for a US mini-series is a delightful piece of nostalgic, sentimental Americana performed by a full orchestra, with hardly a synthesizer in sight. Snow's attractive melodies are shaped by folk music, and their rustic appeal is emphasized by the orchestration – harmonica, piano and especially Kelly Parkinson's plaintive violin solos. The principal theme which recurs throughout has an especially wistful quality: the cue "Having the Baby/All About Ned" for example, in which piano states the theme and is then gently supported by strings, is typical. There are several dramatic incidents in which Snow lets loose with all of his orchestral forces, but much of the score is more low-key, and the modest folk-like themes tinged with gentle nostalgia – you can almost smell the apple pie baking – create the strongest impression. It is good to have such an example of Mark Snow's other work available on disc as proof that there is more to this composer than just *The X-Files*. **MW**

New review
The X-Files (1994-6) **Original Soundtracks**, with **Teri DeSario** (vocals); **Erika Duke-Kirkpatrick** (vc); **Mark Snow** (electronics)
Warner Bros Ⓕ 9362-46448-2 (53 minutes: DDD).

Not to be confused with an earlier best-selling Warner Bros disc entitled "Songs in the Key of X", this is actually the score album X-Philes everywhere have been awaiting. Mark Snow's moody, sometimes downright scary music is a prominent feature of the show – one of its distinctive hallmarks – and as such has already attracted much praise. Snow's dramatic and atmospheric contributions have, however, taken a long time to materialize on CD. Conspiracy theorists should not get too excited: there is no real mystery here, just the same familiar story of a record company wanting to maximize the commercial potential of such a hit show. Hence, the "Songs in the Key of X" album, and hence the frustrating format of this disc. Instead of those well-beloved washes of sound, those sombre textures occasionally disturbed by eerie electronic cries of horror presented in their unadulterated gloom, each is served up with a generous helping of dialogue excerpts from the show. The listener's sense of entering the weird world that is *The X-Files* is undoubtedly heightened, the inventive mixing dovetails words and music with care, and the disembodied voices of Mulder and Scully *et al* rising then fading from the soundtrack makes for a fascinating experience first time around. But the end result of adding dialogue is, of course, to push the music once more into the background, and repeated playings reveal the voices in their true light as a distraction from the score (the integral mixing precludes the option of programming them out). It is as if someone is afraid of allowing this music to stand alone, as if some shadowy figure has decreed the public is not yet ready to accept the truth: that Mark Snow is a gifted composer whose *X-Files* scores show a real knack for unsettling and disturbing his audience. **MW**

Also available:
Born to Be Wild (1995) Milan 35705-2

Ronald Stein
1930-1988 USA

Before coming to Hollywood, aspiring film composer Ronald Stein had written to Lionel Newman, head of 20th Century-Fox's music department asking for advice: Newman replied pithily "Don't come." But Stein found a niche for himself scoring a succession of B-movies: his first assignment, setting the scene for the rest of his career, was Roger Corman's *Apache Woman* (1955). He went on to write music for over 90 films over the next 30 years at American International Pictures, the last being *Razzle Dazzle* in 1985. His ability and professionalism meant that Stein never gave less than his best for all of these diverse assignments. Highlights include *Reform School*

Girl (1957) *She Gods of Shark Reef* (1958), *Diary of a High School Bride* (1959), *Dinosaurus!* (1960) and –his penultimate assignment – the unforgettable *Frankenstein's Great Aunt Tillie* (1984).

New review

Not of This Earth! The Film Music of Ronald Stein. **Original Soundtracks.**
Varèse Sarabande Ⓟ VSD5634 (63 minutes: ADD).
Attack of the 50 Foot Woman (1958). The Terror (1963). Dementia 13 (1963). Not of This Earth! (1957). Attack of the Crab Monsters (1957). The Devil's Partner (1959) Spider Baby (1964).

Sixty-three minutes of B-movie heaven. From the immediately gripping opening of *Attack of the 50 Foot Woman* through to the infectiously catchy "Song from Spider Baby" (sung by Lon Chaney, Jr. no less), this disc provides every type of variation of mood/horror/suspense cue in the time-honoured tradition of 1950s and 1960s low-budget genre films. Growling brass, pounding percussion and urgent strings (plus the occasional electric organ) bring these tawdry tales to life. Stein captures the mood of the moment with swift economical gestures that display a remarkable virtuosity and imagination in orchestration skills. The forces used belie the low budgets employed by the film makers, since he frequently used the Munich Symphony Orchestra for his scores and they provide a big sound. He always treated the films with the utmost respect – an extraordinary feat given how laughable most of them were. These are not classic scores and nor are they classic films but this disc should bring a lot of enjoyment to those with a fondness for the genre.   **DS**

Max Steiner

1888-1971 Austria

Max Steiner was the personification of Hollywood's musical Golden Age, and is often called the Father of Film Music. The warm nineteenth-century romanticism of his music set a precedent in Hollywood that is still being followed today. Born in Vienna of a musical family (his godfather was Richard Strauss), Steiner studied at the Imperial Academy of Music where he was taught composition by Robert Fuchs and conducting with Felix Weingartner. His first operetta, *The Beautiful Greek Girl*, written at age 15, had a year-long run in Vienna. He made a successful career conducting operettas throughout Europe and England, before the outbreak of the First World War suddenly turned him into an enemy alien in London. He moved to the USA. In New York he arranged and conducted Broadway shows, working with George Gershwin, Victor Herbert, Jerome Kern and others. On Christmas Day 1929 – right at the very beginning of the sound era – Steiner arrived in Hollywood. Initially he was expected to work as an orchestrator, but soon began composing original scores. At this period, films just required beginning and end title music; Steiner – along with Alfred Newman – was one of the first to grasp the importance of dramatic underscore. *Symphony of Six Million* (1932) was his first full score, and introduced many of the techniques that were to become standard for the infant art of film scoring. *King Kong* the following year proved to all just how much a musical score can enhance the film's drama; as such it was a watershed for film music. After working for RKO, Steiner moved to Warner Brothers in 1936, composing an incredible average of eight major film scores every year for a decade (in 1939, the year of *Gone with the Wind*, he wrote 11!). Steiner wrote in excess of 200 scores until failing health forced him to retire in 1965. Even more than Newman, Korngold and Waxman, Steiner was responsible for shaping the 'classic' Hollywood sound. It is suprising therefore that very little of his enormous output has been issued on CD.

New review

The Adventures of Mark Twain (1944) **Brandenburg Choir; Brandenburg Philharmonic Orchestra / William T. Stromberg**.
RCA Victor Red Seal Ⓟ 09026 62660-2 (74 minutes: DDD). Recorded 1995. Disc also includes **Korngold:** The Prince and the Pauper (1937).

Steiner was audaciously adroit at weaving traditional melodies or popular songs into his scores to underline a film's locale or emotional resonance, and so the heavily romanticized screen 'biography' of one of America's most beloved authors gave him ample opportunity to embellish his score with liberal references to "My Darling Clementine", "Oh Susanna", "Battle Hymn of the Republic", as well as "Aloha oe" and "Rule Britannia" for the sequences describing Twain's tours around the world. Though this all seems rather clichéd today, it certainly adds to the overall flavour of one of Steiner's most vibrant and characterful scores. The author's many colourful encounters – the river steamboats, the frog-jumping competitions, the gold rush, etc. – are scored with Steiner's customary melodic exuberance and typically there are themes for each of the major characters, human and otherwise (even the Mississippi has its own distinctive *leitmotif*). Korngold's effulgent score for the 1937 adaptation of Twain's popular tale makes an ideal companion, and its appeal is summarized most eloquently by the composer's son, George Korngold: "The score is reminiscent of music for a *commedia dell'arte*; it is sparkling, humorous and heart-warming, capturing all the naïvete of childhood, the regal splendour of the court and the demeaning poverty of Tudor England." Throughout this delightful disc Stromberg's readings are vigorous and warm, and are matched by suitably expansive sound. **RS**

New review
Gone With the Wind (1939) Original Soundtrack / Max Steiner.
> Rhino mono Ⓟ 72269/ EMI Ⓟ CDODEON27 (two discs: 148 minutes: ADD).
Gone With the Wind (1939) National Philharmonic Orchestra / Charles Gerhardt.
> RCA Victor Ⓜ GD80452 (44 minutes: ADD). Recorded 1973.

The confrontations that threatened to make *Gone With the Wind* as tempestuous off-screen as on carried over from choice of director and leading actors to the music. Although Max Steiner was under contract to Warner Brothers at the time, he was always David O. Selznick's first choice. But, after bombarding the composer with curt memos regarding the character themes and various snippets of source music to be used, and increasingly concerned by Steiner's legendary tardiness as the première approached, Selznick almost dropped him and hired Herbert Stothart, fresh from *The Wizard of Oz*, instead. Spurred on by the rumour of his imminent replacement, Steiner set to work – fast. It is remarkable that he achieved what he did, considering that he was given just three months to write over three hours of music (not all of which appeared in the final picture), whilst simultaneously scoring three other movies. It is hardly surprising, therefore, that many connoisseurs do not consider *Gone With the Wind* his finest work; yet there is no doubt it his most enduringly popular. This is partially explained by the timeless fascination of the film, but has more to do with the score's immortal signature, the "Tara" theme. Nothing since has surpassed its soaring, heart-stopping romantic appeal. This is music for lovers, but of no ordinary kind. It strikes a chord in everyone who hears it because it speaks of the nostalgic, affectionate love – not of a person – but of home.

Rhino's attractive presentation of the complete soundtrack is another fine issue in the exceptional Turner Classic Movies series of restored treasures from the MGM vaults (although not technically an MGM production, the film was distributed by Metro). Accompanied by the now-familiar booklet packed with fascinating background notes and splendid illustrations, Steiner's score is vividly presented in its original form, complete with all the arrangements of period music insisted upon by Selznick – Stephen Foster songs, Civil War tunes and even a dash of Wagner. These latter constitute a significant minority of the score, but it is to Steiner's credit that his character themes – for Scarlett, Rhett, Melanie, Ashley and, of course, Mammy among others – provide continuity throughout, and give unity to the other elements. When it appears, "Tara" dominates all.

For those who wish to forgo the pleasures of Rhino's admittedly expensive collectors' edition, or prefer their Steiner unadulterated by "Dixie" and "Massa's in de cold, cold ground", the single RCA disc is a worthy alternative. Charles Gerhardt's recording edition of the score was prepared with the approval of the composer: short in comparison to the soundtrack version, it nevertheless contains all of the music's principal themes and was performed by the same scale forces as the original (although, sadly, it does not include a choir). Gerhardt's expansive, concert-hall approach fits Steiner's score perfectly, and if the packaging is nothing like as lavish, as a musical experience this suite, unencumbered by period music, is arguably more satisfying than the soundtrack. This pioneering recording was one of a series which paved the way towards a greater appreciation of film music. Notwithstanding the availability of the original, it still deserves to be a cornerstone in every collection. **MW**

New review
Gone With the Wind The Classic Max Steiner. Westminster Philharmonic Orchestra / Kenneth Alwyn.
> Silva Screen Ⓟ FILMCD144 (52 minutes: DDD).
> The Adventures of Mark Twain (1944). A Distant Trumpet (1964). Casablanca (1942). A Summer Place (1959). The Treasure of the Sierra Madre (1948). Helen of Troy (1955). The Caine Mutiny (1954). Gone With the Wind (1939).

The Westminster Philharmonic Orchestra may have a few uncomfortable moments during this excellent concert (the strings just lacking that certain expressive sweep during the suites from *Gone With the Wind* and *Casablanca*, and the two excerpts from *A Summer Place*), but the enthusiasm of the young players cannot be faulted. Under the firm guidance of Kenneth Alwyn they give lively, glowing readings of familiar titles like *Sierra Madre* and *The Caine Mutiny*, as well as such unjustly ignored delights as the eight-minute "Overture" from *The Adventures of Mark Twain* (a flavourful slice of Americana composed for and originally performed live at the film's première), the brief but rousing cavalry march that opens *A Distant Trumpet*, and – best of all – the splendidly rich 11-minute suite from *Helen of Troy*. This was Steiner's only foray into the widescreen sword-and-sandal genre, and his characteristically lush approach to the drama stands some way apart from the more 'archaic' tonality of, say, Newman's *The Robe* or Rózsa's *Quo Vadis* from the same period. Bright, robust sound and informative packaging make this a highly appealing sampler of Steiner's massively melodic output. **RS**

King Kong (1933) **National Philharmonic Orchestra / Fred Steiner**.
Label X ⓕ LXCD10 (48 minutes: ADD). Recorded 1976.

Whilst many commendable original scores had been composed for the Cinema prior to *King Kong* in 1933, here, finally, was a marriage of film and music which was indisputably great, undeniably potent. Film music had come of age. From here on and throughout the thirties it was de rigueur for movies to be invested with non-stop musical accompaniment. King Kong, with its massive canvass, unbridled exoticism and pioneering special effects could not have succeeded without a substantial score: and here, like the eponymous ape, the music is of gigantic proportions. Max Steiner, more often to be found composing in a comfortable late romantic idiom, here excels with sterner, decidedly harsher stuff: here, dynamism is everything – from the truly tumultuous opening music with its barbarous brass and frenzied percussion to the raw vehemence of Kong's New York rampage, Steiner is closer to the modernism of the Parisian school than the candied Viennese swirl of his Austrian heritage. Oases of calm are few, only "Sea at Night", with its lilting love theme for winsome heroine and beefy hero is totally free of energetic elements. Inevitably the sledgehammer impact of so much determined music is tiring to the extent that it is probably best to approach this album in two separate sittings; except, of course, for anyone who really relishes their music loud, dramatic and unrelenting. The 20-year old recording by veteran engineer Bob Auger is sensationally on a par with modern digital counterparts, whilst the National Philharmonic under Fred Steiner (no relation to the composer) attack the score with a fervour and an exuberance which is awe-inspiring: this is meaty music played with a vengeance. A landmark score here receives a landmark recording. **DW**

Now, Voyager The Classic Film Scores of Max Steiner. **National Philharmonic Orchestra / Charles Gerhardt**.
RCA Victor ⓜ GD80136 (54 minutes: ADD). Recorded 1973.
Now, Voyager (1942). King Kong (1933). Saratoga Trunk (1945). The Charge of the Light Brigade (1936). Four Wives (1939). The Big Sleep (1946). Johnny Belinda (1948). Since You Went Away (1944). The Informer (1935). The Fountainhead (1949).

The daddy of them all, and perhaps the most perfect example of the old style Hollywood film composer. It is impossible to sample Steiner's massive output on just one CD, but this selection sums up his long career admirably. His wonderful gift for melody often reached Korngoldian heights of sumptuousness, and yet he also had a remarkable knack for milking the drama to its full effect. *King Kong* is a typical example, pounding, exotic but also invoking great sympathy for the fate of the monster. Redolent of the Warner Brothers years are the impossibly romantic *Now, Voyager*, the gently lilting *Johnny Belinda*, the irresistibly melting *Saratoga Trunk* and, perhaps most atypically, the jangling angularity of *The Fountainhead*. Gerhardt is the composer's most ardent advocate and with beautifully rich sound to boot, who indeed needs to ask for the moon! **RS**

Also available:
Band of Angels (1957) etc. Label X LXCD3
The Lost Patrol (1934) **Virginia City** (1940).**The Beast With Five Fingers** (1947) (Moscow SO/Stromberg) Marco Polo 8 223870

see also Collections: **Captain Blood**

Toru Takemitsu
b. 1930 Japan

Tokyo-born Toru Takemitsu is a largely self-taught composer whose eclectic style is drawn from contemporary Western as well as traditional Japanese sources. His early compositions were praised by Stravinsky, and Western avant-garde composers like John Cage admired his work as truly cross-cultural. His best known concert works are *November Steps* (1967) and *Eclipse* (1966) both scored for traditional Japanese instruments biwa and shakuhachi. Beginning with *Kurutta Kajitsu (Crazed Fruit)* in 1956 he has written extensively for Japanese cinema, with occasional forays to Hollywood. Amongst a host of prestigious awards for his concert works, he was the recipient of the Los Angeles Film Critics Award for *Ran* (1985).

Rising Sun (1994) Original Soundtrack / Hiroyuki Iwaki.
Arista 11003-2 (39 minutes: DDD). Includes music written and performed by Seiichi Tanaka and the San Francisco Taiko Dojo drums.

The skill of Takemitsu's orchestration is outstanding, and the opening and closing tracks (performed by the Taiko Dojo drums) are exhilarating. Unfortunately there is no sense of the music going anywhere, and the frequent motivic interjections over interminable low drones do not convey momentum, even though they signal 'events'. The combination of 'West tolerates East' is evident in the rough juxtaposition of some classic jazz against contemporary orchestral effects. There is one track, however, (number nine) which is very arresting, and it shows to brilliant advantage how a masterful 'classical' composer can integrate popular and avant-garde styles in an extended and purposeful passage. **CT**

Tangerine Dream Germany

Formed by Edgar Froese, Connie Schnitzler and Klause Schultze in 1968, the innovative Tangerine Dream were named after a line in the song "Lucy in the Sky With Diamonds". The group recorded one album, *Electronic Meditation* (1970), before Schnitzler and Schultze departed. Replaced by Christopher Franke and Peter Baumann, the group continued their experimental forays with the new technology of synthesizers throughout the 1970s. They developed an abstract but firmly melodic style that can now be seen as a forerunner of New Age music. Their first film soundtrack was *Sorcerer* (1977) and the group continued to compose for films in between recording studio albums. Their approach to scoring a film is unusual in that they do not deliberately tailor their music to fit the picture, but compose stand-alone pieces designed to evoke appropriate moods. Other scores include *Firestarter* (1984), Ridley Scott's *Legend* (1986 – replacing Jerry Goldsmith for the film's American release) and Kathryn Bigelow's *Near Dark* (1987). Franke left the band in 1988 and has since pursued an independent career as a film composer (see separate entry).

New review
Dream Music The Movie Music of Tangerine Dream, Volumes 1[a] and 2[b]. [a]Original Soundtracks, with **Tangerine Dream**; [b]**Mark Ayres**, [b]**John Beal**, [b]**Daniel Caine** (synths). Silva Screen Ⓕ FILMCD125/166 (two discs: 54 and 60 minutes: DDD).
FILMCD125 – The Park is Mine (1985). Dead Solid Perfect (1988). Deadly Care (1987). *FILMCD166* – Legend (1986). Intersection – trailer music (1993). Dead Solid Perfect (1988). Heartbreakers (1984). Streethawk (1985). Catch Me If You Can (1989). Risky Business (1983).

The film music of Tangerine Dream represents a unique contribution to the medium. Most film composers strive to write music which first and foremost serves the dramatic needs of a film. If the end result has enough strength to stand on its own away from the film, this is a pleasing bonus, but it is not the composers' first priority. Tangerine Dream, however, take a completely different approach. Whilst they are certainly sympathetic to the needs of the drama they are not concerned with 'scoring' in the traditional sense. Instead, their music is aimed from the outset at the listener. Indeed, filmmakers hire them for precisely this reason: they work to establish mood and atmosphere rather than character or blow-by-blow detail of dramatic situations. The music featured on these two compilations is, therefore, much more linear than most film music. Working exclusively with synthesizers, they produce a distinctive sound that is rarely harsh or jagged; instead they are often able to create warm textures and colours, as in *The Park is Mine*, *Catch Me If You Can* and *Legend*. Their more dramatic material is typically quite minimalist, with even quite lengthy cues based on only one or two motifs. Scores such as *Heartbreakers* and *Dead Solid Perfect* are fiercely contemporary, with percussive effects and relentless rhythms best described as rock influenced. By their very nature, the scores featured on these discs have very little emotional resonance; the music will not appeal to everyone, but it is illustrative of an approach that breaks every rule in the book. **PP**

Also available:
Catch Me If You Can (1989) Edel CIN2213-2
Dead Solid Perfect (1988) Silva Screen FILMCD079
Deadly Care (1987) Silva Screen FILMCD121
Firestarter (1984) Varèse Sarabande VSD5251
Legend (1986) Varèse Sarabande VSD5645
Sorcerer (1977) MCA MCLD19159

Mikis Theodorakis

b. 1925 Greece

Born on the island of Chios, Mikis Theodorakis began writing chamber music for violin and piano in his early teens, and was heavily influenced by Byzantine and Cretan music (his father was a Cretan), although he received little formal musical instruction. His family settled in Athens in 1943 where he studied compostion at the Conservatoire. In 1954 he enrolled at the Paris Conservatoire to study with Olivier Messiaen. Although he had achieved international recognition with his works for the concert hall – his ballet *Antigone* was produced at Covent Garden in 1959 with Fonteyn and Nureyev – in the early 1960s he increasingly turned his attention to popular Greek music and cinema. *Zorba the Greek* (1964) produced one of film music's most popular themes (Theodorakis later reworked the music as a ballet in 1988). But his revolutionary doctrines and vituperative attacks on the state of Greek music proved unpalatable to the military Junta: in 1967 all performances of his music were banned and Theodorakis was placed under house arrest and subsequently exiled. He has written over 700 songs and 100 larger-scale works, including oratorios, ballets, operas and symphonies.

New review

Phaedra (1962) **Original Soundtrack**, with **Melina Mercouri** (sngr) / **Mikis Theodorakis.**
 Sakkaris Ⓕ SR50060 (34 minutes: AAD).

Mikis Theodorakis's music for yet another Jules Dassin film is one of those 1960s soundtracks that is a delight divorced from its accompanying images. Dassin's attempt to bring Greek tragedy into the twentieth century got mixed reviews at the time and today is little seen. Luckily, the score has been rescued by the Greek label Sakkaris, and whilst no additional music has been added – indeed the whole CD package is a virtual copy of the original LP – the music is a joy, brim full of exciting, typically Theodorakis melodies. Whatever the setting, the music always sounds Greek, and therein lies its charm. A cue called "London Fog" sounds nothing like you might expect, but who's complaining? Not many films produce such memorable melodies as these that live on long after the film has slipped by. I must admit though that I could well have done without Melina Mercouri warbling her way through the main theme, but that is a small price to pay to hear the work of a master composer who wrote many more effective scores than he was given credit for. **JW**

Also available:
The Day the Fish Came Out (1967) Sakkaris SR50088
Elektra (1962) Sakkaris SR50090
Serpico (1973) Sakkaris SR50061
State of Siege (1973) Sakkaris SR50063
Z (1968) Sakkaris SR50062

see also Collections: **Classic Greek Film Music**

Dimitri Tiomkin

1894-1979 Russia

Born in the Ukraine, Dimitri Tiomkin studied at the St Petersburg Conservatory when Alexander Glazunov was its director. Although he learned composition, Tiomkin's real interest was the piano, and he was instructed by Felix Blumenthal (who also taught Vladimir Horowitz). As a result of the Russian Revolution he moved to Berlin, continuing his studies with Ferruccio Busoni. After a brief visit to the USA in 1925, Tiomkin gave the European première of Gershwin's Piano Concerto in Paris in 1928. The following year he returned to America, but the stock market crash and subsequent Depression made life difficult for an itinerant concert pianist. Tiomkin's wife, the choreographer Albertina Rasch, suggested they try their luck in Hollywood devising ballet sequences for musical films. In 1930 Tiomkin composed some short ballets for MGM musicals: *The Rogue Song, Devil May Care, Lord Byron of Broadway* and *Our Blushing Brides*. His first original score was for *Resurrection* (1931), but it was not until Frank Capra's *Lost Horizon* (1937) that Tiomkin was established. He scored several other Capra movies, including *You Can't Take it with You* (1938) and *Mr Smith Goes to Washington* (1939). Tiomkin's real forte unexpectedly proved to be for that most American genre, the Western (apparently he saw little difference between the broad open spaces of the Russian steppes, and the plains of America). After *The Westerner* (1940) he went on to provide his own brand of Russian 'Western' scores for, amongst others, *Duel in the Sun* (1946), *The Big Sky*, *High Noon* (both 1952) and *Giant* (1956). *High Noon* was notable for its effective integration of a ballad, "Do Not Forsake Me", into the score (which won him two

Academy Awards). He later repeated the ploy in *Gunfight at the OK Corral* (1957). Following the death of his wife in 1968, Tiomkin turned his back on Hollywood and settled in London.

The Fall of the Roman Empire (1964) Original Soundtrack / Dimitri Tiomkin.
Cloud Nine mono/stereo Ⓕ ACN7016 (45 minutes: ADD).

As no one really knows what 'authentic' Roman music might have sounded like, it is hardly surprising that few composers have adopted Miklós Rózsa's historical approach to music of this period. For what was to be the last gasp of the great Hollywood epic, Dimitri Tiomkin relied on his own innate epic sensibilities which had served him well on previous assignments like *55 Days at Peking* (1963) and *The Guns of Navarone* (1961). *The Fall of the Roman Empire* may have been unhistorical nonsense, but Tiomkin's contribution is everything an epic score should be: lively, stirring, romantic, filled with grand fanfares and even grander gestures. Yet there is little to suggest to the ear that we are notionally in Imperial Rome: the use of mandolins to underscore moments of pomp and celebration, for example, adds delightful colour to the orchestra, but irresistibly recalls Italy some 1500 or so years later than the date of the film's action. Tiomkin's Rome, unlike Rózsa's, is evoked in spirit, not in (purported) fact. The "Prelude" was recorded in Westminster Central Hall in order to include that most grandiose of all instruments, the organ. Cloud Nine's version of this score differs significantly from the original re-recorded CBS album version. Aside from containing additional music, this is the Original Soundtrack performance, albeit derived mostly from a mono source, with only the opening "Fanfares and Flourishes", the "Prelude" and the choral statement of the love theme, "Intermezzo: Livius and Lucilla", in stereo. The somewhat muddy and lugubrious sound, however, does not detract from the enjoyment of one of Tiomkin's greatest scores: audiences would have to wait until *Star Wars* in 1977 before they were to hear anything even remotely approaching this magnificence again. **MW**

High Noon Original Film Scores of Dimitri Tiomkin.
Berlin Radio Choir and Symphony Orchestra / Lawrence Foster.
RCA Victor Red Seal Ⓕ 09026 62658-2 (78 minutes: DDD). Recorded 1994-5.
Cyrano de Bergerac (1950). High Noon (1952). The Alamo (1960).
55 Days at Peking (1963).

The above sub-title is something of a misnomer, as all the selections on this generous anthology are in fact concert suites arranged by Christopher Palmer. *High Noon*, the shortest item here, gets top billing, presumably becuse it is the most familiar (and makes for an eye-catching CD cover). It is undoubtedly exciting music: this ten-minute suite is substantially the same as that featured on Unicorn's earlier *Western Film World* compilation, albeit unaccountably shorn of its centrally important title song, "Do Not Forsake Me". *The Alamo* is the longest item on the disc and, to my mind, the least interesting: although Tiomkin's battle music always contains much agreeable larger-than-life bluster, and his principal themes are always characteristically strong-willed, they are badly let down here by the sugary nineteenth-century sentimentality of "The Green Leaves of Summer" and the hollow insincerity of "The Ballad of the Alamo". Fortunately, RCA's disc has other delights, most especially *Cyrano de Bergerac*: the jolly tinkling of a harpsichord tells us that this music is ostensibly baroque in style; Tiomkin's habitual grand gesturing is anything but, however, and the resulting clash of cultures makes for a richly over-the-top experience, delightfully summed up in some memorable set-pieces: Roxane's theme, the witty "Seventeenth-Century Blues"; the fugal "Street Fight"; and the sincerely sentimental "Requiem". Rounding things off is a suite from *55 Days at Peking*, another somewhat patchy affair with a soap opera plot allowing for plenty of melodrama, and a welcome chance to revisit that exotic meeting place of occident and orient originally revealed in *Lost Horizon* (1937). Performances are good without ever seeming exceptional. **MW**

Lost Horizon The Classic Film Scores of Dimitri Tiomkin. [a]John Alldis Choir; National Philharmonic Orchestra / Charles Gerhardt.
RCA Victor Ⓜ GD81669 (46 minutes: ADD).
Lost Horizon (1937)[a]. The Guns of Navarone (1961). The Big Sky (1952). The Four Poster (1952). Friendly Persuasion (1956). Search for Paradise (1958)[a].

Director Frank Capra took a risk in entrusting the score for his mammoth *Lost Horizon* to a relatively untried composer, but after nearly 60 years this extraordinary music – here brilliantly distilled into a bountiful 23-minute suite, still radiates a power and a lustre rarely matched in movie scoring since. For this magical tale of a wonderland sheltering amidst the impenetrable mountains of Tibet, Tiomkin effects a potent quasi-oriental ambience by employing an array of ingenious devices – outlandish percussion, ethereal chanting, curious woodwind groupings, and ample use of the (Chinese) pentatonic scale. This monumental music might only be a clever concoction, a spicy confection, yet it sounds authentically of The East. Tiomkin was often chided for displaying too much bravura, for being too profuse, for using all the instruments, all together, all the time – but whilst much of his output was expansive (and wonderfully so), he was equally capable of the constrained simplicity of *The Big Sky*, a score possessing an austerity, a clarity, which sings of the pioneer spirit, and conjures all the grandeur, all the majesty of a proud untamed land (the music also begins and ends in trembling *pianissimo* – a murmering rebuff to all who might dare dub Tiomkin the master of cacophony). *Friendly Persuasion* also has a hushed simplicity; Tiomkin's main theme, the languorous "Thee I Love", was a hit for Pat Boone, whilst a second melody "Coax Me a Little", is every bit as winning. The raucous "Prelude" to *The Guns of Navarone* is a theme so strong, so indestructable, and so versatile, it even engendered a reggae version. Conductor Charles Gerhardt's handling is masterly throughout – or perhaps that should be General Gerhardt, given the massed forces he commands here – deploying a truly huge ensemble to effect much of Tiomkin's monumental music. An epic album. **DW**

The Western Film World of Dimitri Tiomkin ªBob Saker (bar); **John McCarthy Singers; London Studio Symphony Orchestra / Laurie Johnson**.
Unicorn-Kanchana Ⓜ UKCD2011 (48 minutes: ADD). Recorded 1980.
Giant (1956). Red River (1948). Duel in the Sun (1946). High Noon (1952)ª. Night Passage (1957). Rio Bravo (1958).

It is remarkable that Dimitri Tiomkin, born and musically educated in Russia, should have become Hollywood's leading exponent of the Western score. When movies were young, and there was no definite approach to scoring films set in the Old West, Tiomkin unexpectedly established an idiom. This style, expansive, densely orchestrated, hinting at – and sometimes drawing on – folk elements, is fully epitomized by the well-chosen selections on this disc. The prelude for *Giant*, welling into being like oil gushing from the Texas subsoil, is nothing less than a hymn to the Lone Star State; whilst the music for *Red River* deliberately evokes a rugged folk element, with a male chorus dispensing burly cowpoke ditties dotted about some robust symphonic soundscapes. *Duel in the Sun*, still the cinema's most successful, and notorious Western, is riveting from its flamboyantly regal opening to the terse modernism of the final fatal shootout between the tale's two star-crossed lovers. *High Noon* has since passed into history as *the* Western score – the suite recorded here mainly consists of the fully scored final ten minutes of the film: a thrilling, raucous *tour de force*, with fractured variants on the theme song "Do Not Forsake Me" tossed relentlessly from one section of Tiomkin's massive ensemble to another. There is also a vocal version of the song, well sung by Bob Saker, but inevitably it is difficult to cast aside memories of how potent both Tex Ritter and Frankie Lane were with this same material. *Night Passage* is embodied by the ballad "Follow the River", here in a splendid setting for male chorus by Jester Hairston, Tiomkin's long-time choral arranger. The disc is rounded off with *Rio Bravo*, a more low-key score, but featuring the stirring trumpet-led "De Guello" (which would find a further flourishing in *The Alamo*) and occasion for an unexpectedly sensuous and decidedly contemporary sounding love theme for saxophone. Conductor Laurie Johnson brings much necessary vigour to the proceedings, but the recording is somewhat cavernous and ill-focused, and whilst Tiomkin liked to pitch his music into a large acoustic, some closer, more detailed miking might have been better here. Still, classic music for a classic genre. **DW**

Also available:
The Alamo (1960) Columbia CK66138
Giant (1956) Capitol 92056 – see also **Rosenman**: Rebel

Colin Towns
England

Colin Towns began his career as a film composer when he was equally busy as keyboard player and songwriter with ex-Deep Purple frontman Ian Gillan's eponymous rock outfit Gillan. In 1976 he was hired by producer Peter Fetterman to provide a soundtrack demo for a projected low-budget feature called *Full Circle*. Towns's haunting, ethereal score proved instrumental in attracting potential backers to finance the making of the film. Since then, television and film work has accounted for a large proportion of the composer's output. In addition to numerous commercials, Towns has provided music for several British TV shows, including *Blind Justice, The Fear, Capital City, Black Heath Poisonings, Clarissa, Cadfael, Pie in the Sky* and *The Buccaneers*. His British film credits include *Bellman and True, Rawhead Rex, Vampire's Kiss,*

Shady, Slayground and *Getting it Right*. Fully conversant with many different musical styles, Towns has also written several pieces for the concert hall; both his Concerto for Trumpet and String Orchestra and *1930 Cityscape* are featured on the *Full Circle* soundtrack disc (below). His abiding passion for jazz resulted in the formation of The Mask Orchestra, with whom he has successfully toured and recorded.

The Buccaneers (1995) **Original Soundtrack**, with **Olive Simpson** (soprano); **London Filmworks Orchestra / Colin Towns**.
Mercury ℗ 526 866-2 (48 minutes: DDD).

A typically lavish BBC costume drama, adapted from Edith Wharton's last novel, has produced a typically fine score from Colin Towns. The backbone of this music is a wistful setting of the song "Lov'd I Not Honour More", which instantly transports the listener back to those Victorian drawing rooms where – as a succession of filmmakers have assured us – darker passions lurked beneath the decorous exterior. Using a small orchestra, with prominent solos for violin (Rolf Wilson), cello (Andrea Hess) and piano (presumably the composer), *The Buccaneers* consists of a series of romantic chamber music pieces, all deftly orchestrated in a manner befitting the period. These charming melodies bear comparison, in mood if not in style, with Patrick Doyle's sprightly *Much Ado About Nothing*: both scores share a lightness of texture; and both composers share an ability to create delicious tunes. Later cues emphasize the girls' loss of innocence by shading previously optimistic themes with more sombre orchestration. A delightful piece of Victoriana for the 1990s.   **MW**

New review
Cadfael (1996) **Original Soundtrack**, with **James Bowman** (alto) **/ Colin Towns**.
EMI ℗ CDEMC3735 (54 minutes: DDD). Includes Gregorian chant.

This is the music for the Central Television series starring Derek Jacobi as Brother Cadfael, the medieval monk with a knack for detective work: a sort of whodunit in a habit. Colin Towns's score utilizes modern samples of such distant times, with wonderfully authentic music performed by percussion, solo voices, recorders and flutes. Add Gregorian chants written by the composer and so subtly is this original music merged with some genuine Gregorian chanting, that the whole disc sounds like a unified whole. Colin Towns is one of that elite group of British composers who are acccepted in Hollywood and is capable of writing scores of integrity and distinction. *Cadfael* is a good example of why.   **JW**

Full Circle [The Haunting of Julia] (1978) **Original Soundtrack**, with **Colin Towns** (keyboards/synths).
Koch Screen ℗ 38703-2 (72 minutes: AAD). Disc also includes Concerto for Trumpet and String Orchestra and *1930 Cityscape*.

The composer's earliest film score is a subtle and highly atmospheric synthesizer-based work, which would these days probably be filed under 'Ambient' or 'New Age'. A typically memorable Townsian melody constitutes the main theme, which was released as a single at the time by Virgin Records. The rest of the score is more reminiscent of those 1970s instrumental albums by Mike Oldfield or Rick Wakeman than a film soundtrack. By contrast, both the concert works which act as fill-ups are fascinating examples of the composer's versatility: a classical three-movement Trumpet Concerto, and a New York-style Gershwinesque piece for saxophone and orchestra, *1930 Cityscape*. The disc can be recommended for these works alone.   **MW**

The Puppet Masters (1994) **Original Soundtrack**, with **Colin Towns** (electronics); **London Filmworks Orchestra / Alan Wilson**.
Citadel ℗ STC77104 (50 minutes: DDD).

A deceptively beguiling opening characteristic of Towns's more tuneful scores is rudely interrupted by a burst of electronic noise. *The Puppet Masters* is standard monster movie fare, executed with rare panache. The composer recorded the electronic parts of the score in his own studio, before adding an 80-piece orchestra; the combination of the two gives this music an unsettling quality entirely unlike his other soundtracks. Wherever possible Towns introduces gentle orchestral melodies to alleviate the bleaker episodes, although rarely is a tune allowed to develop before being swamped by harsh electronic effects. Some of the wilder passages for orchestra have an almost improvisatory feel to them: furious bursts of energy that overpower even the hissing, percussive electronics. Better music than any B-movie has a right to expect.   **MW**

The Wolves of Willoughby Chase (1988) **Original Soundtrack**, with the **Graunke Symphony Orchestra / Allan Jones**.
TER Ⓟ CDTER1162 (39 minutes: ADD).

For this children's fantasy the composer has fashioned a fairy-tale score – music for children of all ages in the mould of *Peter and the Wolf* and *The Nutcracker*. After a nostalgic main theme, Towns conjures up the playfulness of the nursery in "The Rocking Horse". Here, and throughout a variety of delightful themes, the music maintains its naïve appeal. Orchestrations demonstrate the composer's care and attention to detail: trumpets and brass suggestive of a colliery band herald the arrival at the grim industrial town of Blastburn. As the two young heroines suffer their inevitable share of vicissitudes the music turns a darker corner, although Towns is careful never to make his score dissonant or too 'adult'. Perhaps the most dramatic cue on the album is "The Ski Sledge", which briefly hints at the violence of Mussorgsky's *Night on the Bare Mountain*, albeit complete with all that music's Walt Disney associations. **MW**

Vangelis

b. 1943 Greece

Vangelis Odyssey Papathanoussiou was instrumental in bringing western pop music to Greece in the 1960s, and was a founder member of Aphrodite's Child, which also featured singer Demis Roussos. Between 1969-74 he was based in Paris, where he had the opportunity to produce more experimental works. He scored his first film, *Sex Power* in 1969 – the original LP is now a collector's item. Vangelis began working with French documentary film director Frederic Rossif, one of their earliest films being *L'Apocalypse des Animaux* (the album appeared in 1973), and their collaboration continued until 1990. Back in the pop world, he produced several hit singles and album with his friend Yes lead singer Jon Anderson, including "I'll Find My Way Home" from the album *The Friends of Mr Cairo* (1981). Based in London between 1975-85, he composed some of his most popular film scores, including *Chariots of Fire* (1981), the theme of which was an international hit. Although primarily known as an exponent of the synthesizer, Vangelis often incorporates acoustic instruments, especially percussion, into his compositions. In addition to his film work, Vangelis has written several large-scale works, theatre and ballet scores, and acted as a producer for albums by other artists. He has an unusual approach to film scoring, preferring to compose and perform his music 'live' as the picture is running.

Blade Runner (1982) **Original Soundtrack** etc, with **Mary Hopkin, Don Percival, Demis Roussos** (sngrs); **Dick Morrissey** (sax); **Vangelis** (synths).
East West Ⓟ 4509-96574-2 (58 minutes: AAD/DDD).

Ridley Scott's atmospheric depiction of the future had to wait over a decade for it to be released in its intended form; fans of the composer's futuristic music had to wait even longer for the soundtrack album to be released. This disc is a conflation of music heard in the film – overlaid in places with snatches of dialogue – with other soundtrack excerpts recorded at the time but not used and some newly-recorded itmes (instrumental fantasies on themes from the film if you will). The whole package is an evocative experience, less a soundtrack, more an ambient journey through one of the richest of Vangelis's sound worlds. Old collaborator Demis Roussos helps out with a striking vocal on "Tales of the Future", an oriental-flavoured piece in which the singer cries out like a muezzin calling the faithful to prayer. The wistful saxophone-led "Love Theme" is the heart of the score. Curiously, despite the presence of a straightforward jazz-style number, "One More Kiss, Dear", co-written with Peter Skellern, the least effective cue is in fact the jarringly up-tempo "End Titles". **MW**

1492: Conquest of Paradise (1992) **Original Soundtrack**, with **Bruno Manjarres, Pepe Martinez** (Spanish gtrs/sngrs); **Francis Darizcuren** (mandolin/violin); **Didier Malherbe** (flutes); **English Chamber Choir / Guy Protheroc**; **Vangelis** (synths).
East West Ⓟ 4509-91014-2 (55 minutes: DDD).

A decade after *Blade Runner*, Ridley Scott and Vangelis present a rather more verdant soundscape to explore. Vangelis might not have been the obvious choice to musically depict Medieval Spain and the Americas, but this full-blooded, tuneful score removes any misgivings: the stirring main theme, with its cod-latin singing, has become almost as popular as *Chariots of Fire*. Augmenting his own synths with acoustic instruments and choir, Vangelis has produced a series of distinctive musical impressions which somehow conjure up the spirit of the times, whilst retaining his unmistakably modern ambience (for example, doubled mandolin and violin over a synthetic background for the beginning of "City of Isabel"). The choral singing is a welcome addition to the composer's usual palette of sound colours, although the somewhat restricted timbre of the synthesizers fails to provide sufficient interest in the final 13-minute cue.   **MW**

Also available:
Antarctica (1983) Polydor 815 732-2
L'Apocalypse des Animaux (1971) Polydor 831 503-2
Chariots of Fire (1981) Polydor 800 020-2
Entends-Tu les Chiens Aboyer? (1975) CAM CSE005
La Fete Sauvage (1976) CAM CSE067 / Polydor 841 198-2
Opéra Sauvage (1979) Polydor 829 663-2
Themes [compilation] Polydor 839 518-2

see also Collections: **Classic Greek Film Music**

Ralph Vaughan Williams   1872-1958 England

Born in the Gloucestershire village of Down Ampney, Vaughan Williams was related on his mother's side to Josiah Wedgwood III and Charles Darwin. He was taught the piano by a Wedgewood aunt, and played in the school orchestra at Charterhouse. He received instruction in composition at the Royal College of Music from Hubert Parry, Charles Stanford and Henry Wood; and later studied with Bruch in Berlin and Ravel in Paris. His work, informed in part by a revival of earlier Elizabethan and Jacobean models, brought about a renaissance in English music. Muir Mathieson, the music director of London Films, invited him to write the first of his 11 film scores, *49th Parallel* (1941). This was followed by other scores which were also part of the propaganda effort during the Second World War. Music from the film *Scott of the Antarctic* (1948) found its way into his Sixth Symphony (which also has echoes of *Story of a Flemish Farm*, 1943) and formed the basis of his Seventh, *Sinfonia Antarctica*.

Film Music RTE Concert Orchestra / **Andrew Penny**.
Marco Polo Ⓔ 8 223665 (68 minutes: DDD).
49th Parallel (1941). Story of a Flemish Farm (1943). Coastal Command (1942). The England of Elizabeth (1957).

Played with warmth and persuasive flowing phrasing and panache, only just missing the great Boult-Vaughan Williams tone and style, this orchestral balance is well handled by both conductor and engineer, and the music has great charm and symphonic stature. VW confessed he was incapable of doing other than "to ignore the details and intensify the spirit of the whole situation by a continuous stream of music". Thank heavens he did, for these extracts are wholesome and extensive. The pastoral simplicity of the *Prelude* from *49th Parallel* returns in other tracks; but what is striking is the sense, in *Coastal Command* of the glorification, rightly, of the 'heroes' of the film, the sea-planes themselves, then of the spirit of their pilots, and not least of the seascapes and battles. In the *Three Portraits*, taken from the almost continuous score for *The England of Elizabeth* which accompanied a visual parade of historic images with commentary, VW neatly evokes the pageantry and culture of Drake, Shakespeare and Elizabeth I, quoting an occasional sixteenth-century tune, but nevertheless succeeding in its own vigorous independence.   **CT**

see also Collections: **The Red Shoes**

Sir William Walton   1902-1983 England

The son of an Oldham choirmaster, William Walton sang in his father's church choir; aged ten he won a place at Christ Church Cathedral, Oxford as a chorister. He had begun to compose by the age of 12. He enrolled as an undergraduate at Christ Church College, but left in 1920 without a degree. His early compositions include *Façade*, based on Edith Sitwell's verse, the Viola Concerto and the grand choral work *Belshazzar's Feast*, but it was not until he began writing music for films that Walton was able to earn a living by his composing. His first score was *Escape Me Never* (1935); he later scored several propaganda films during the Second World War, but his greatest film successes came with Laurence Olivier's Shakespeare adaptations *Henry V* (1944), *Hamlet* (1948) and *Richard III* (1955). Despite his prominent status as one of Britain's finest living composers, much of his score for *Battle of Britain* (1969) was rejected – allegedly because there was not enough of it to fill an LP – and replaced by Ron Goodwin's music (only the "Battle in the Air" sequence was retained after Olivier threatened to have his name removed from the credits unless the producers reinstated Walton's music). Like most concert composers who also worked in films, Walton adapted several scores for concert hall use, including the "Spitfire" Prelude and Fugue from *The First of the Few* (1942).

Film Music, Volumes 1-4 [a]Sir John Gielgud, [b]Christopher Plummer (narrs); **Academy of St Martin in the Fields / Sir Neville Marriner.**
Chandos Ⓟ CHAN8842/70/92/41 (four discs, 52, 65, 67 and 61 minutes: DDD). Recorded 1989-90.
CHAN8842 – Hamlet[a] (1948). As You Like It (1936). *CHAN8870* – "Spitfire" Prelude and Fugue (1942). A Wartime Sketchbook. Escape Me Never (1935). Three Sisters (1970). Battle of Britain (1969). *CHAN8892* – Henry V (1944)[b]. *CHAN8841* – Richard III (1955)[a]. Macbeth (1941). Major Barbara (1941).

The late Christopher Palmer is to be thanked most royally for his inestimable service in preparing the materials for all these recordings; the William Walton Trust have assisted Chandos to produce these four excellent discs; and the performances are first-rate. A real treasure-trove. With the added pleasure of narrations by Sir John Gielgud and Christopher Plummer, the scores consistently excite and delight. From the first film score *Escape Me Never* to his last *Three Sisters*, Walton displays a remarkable skill of mood control through purely musical means – orchestration mainly, but also structurally, as sharply pointed out by Hans Keller, who admired the manner in which the human voices of the actors seemed almost to have been orchestrated into Walton's scores, so carefully and sensitively does he dovetail the rhythm and scale of the music preceding and underlying the dialogue. Most famously, there is the war music – instantly striking the heroic, frenetic and deadly activity, and the all-time greats *Henry V* and *Hamlet* – superb writing which conveys not only the sense of history and regency, but also entering the world of psycho-drama, where *leitmotifs à la* Wagner intertwine and develop to convey with apparent inevitably and powerful logic the character developments of the principal roles. All these discs are worth hearing and owning, for they are very fine in every way, but by a short head, I would plump for *Hamlet* as being the most wonderfully written of them all – its pairing, *As You Like It*, is more lightweight (indeed was given a poor review by the 22-year-old Benjamin Britten after the première in 1936 – he expected no doubt that the great hope of *Escape Me Never* would be consolidated, whereas this later film needed no more than appropriate background music). There are première recordings of *Henry V, Richard III, Macbeth, Major Barbara* and *Three Sisters*, as well as the delightful dances of *A Wartime Sketchbook* – a suite compiled by Christopher Palmer from various scores (*Went the Day Well?, Next of Kin, The Foreman Went to France* and *Battle of Britain*). This is truly a great collection.   **CT**

Ken Wannberg   USA

Better known as one of Hollywood's finest music editors – especially because of his long-standing collaboration with composer John Williams – Ken Wannberg has also found time to write some of his own scores. He took music lessons privately as a youngster, and later played in bands during his three years in the Air Force. Introduced to music editing by a friend, Wannberg's first assignment was for Bernard Herrmann's *Journey to the Centre of the Earth* (1959). His first original score, *The Tender Warrior* (1971), was directed by Stewart Raffill, who went on to direct another Wannberg-scored picture, *The Philadelphia Experiment* in 1984. He has worked with John Williams since *Valley of the Dolls* (1967).

The Philadelphia Experiment[a] (1984) **Mother Lode** (1982) **Original Soundtracks**, with the [a]**National Philharmonic Orchestra / Ken Wannberg**.
Prometheus Ⓟ PCD121 (76 minutes: AAD).

An imaginative score, *The Philadelphia Experiment* shows Wannberg emerging from the shadow of John Williams as a distinctive musical personality in his own right. Based on a Sci-Fi premise worthy of *The X-Files* – with attempts to make US Navy ships invisible to radar resulting in time anomalies – there is plenty of opportunity for musical experiment. Wannberg adds electronics to depict the disastrous consequences of the failed project, although he generally prefers to rely on conventional forces. If little of the music is immediately memorable, there is plenty of dramatic variety to sustain interest. Wannberg's rhythmic action cues, enlivened by spiky percussion, are the score's strongest elements. *Mother Lode* – starring and directed by Charlton Heston – is the stronger of the two scores, despite being given second billing on the disc. A warm, folk-like theme opens the score; expansive strings impart a pleasingly old-fashioned mood – in "The Flight" for example, a gentle piece which was not actually used in the film. Overall, the music is far more subdued than its companion. A sinister six-minute cue, "The Price of Greed" – with *glissando* strings, muted brass and percussion – comes closest to the Williams manner. The curious strains of a synthesized bagpipe can be heard in "Magee's Lament". Neither score is a neglected masterpiece, but both are well worth investigating nevertheless. Sound quality is somewhat uneven. Prometheus have enterprisingly issued a further two volumes of Wannberg's music. **MW**

Also available:
Draw! (1984) **Red River** (1988) Prometheus PCD129
The Amateur (1982) **Of Unknown Origin** (1983) **The Late Show** (1977) Prometheus PCD137

Franz Waxman
1906-1967 Germany

Franz Wachsmann (as he was originally known) studied at the Dresden Music Academy, then at the Berlin Conservatory. He played piano in a jazz orchestra called the Weintraub Syncopators, who were asked to perform the soundtrack for Marlene Dietrich's *Der blaue Engel* (*The Blue Angel*) in 1930. Waxman's skill as an arranger for the band resulted in him orchestrating and conducting Friedrich Hollaender's score. He penned his first original score for Fritz Lang's *Liliom* (1933), before moving to Paris after being beaten in the street by Nazis (Waxman was Jewish). Producer Erich Pommer then asked Waxman to come to America and arrange the music for the film version of Jerome Kern's *Music in the Air* (1934). With the success of his score for James Whale's *Bride of Frankenstein* a year later, Waxman's position in Hollywood was assured. He was appointed Head of Universal's music department, but preferring composing to administration, he resigned, eventually becoming freelance in 1948 after a period on the staff at MGM and Warner Brothers. He was the founder and principal conductor of the Los Angeles Music Festival at which he gave the West Coast premières of many important works including Britten's *War Requiem*, Debussy's *Le Martyre de Saint Sébastien* and Stravinsky's *The Nightingale*. Non-film compositions include a Sinfonietta for Strings and Timpani (1955 – available on Koch International 37152-2), an oratorio *Joshua* (1959), a large-scale song-cycle for soloists, chorus and orchestra *The Song of Terezin* (1965), and the famous *Carmen Fantasy* (1947) written for Jascha Heifetz. He remains the only composer to win an Academy Award in two consecutive years: 1950 for *Sunset Boulevard* and 1951 for *A Place in the Sun*. Waxman's German romanticism stemmed from the same source as Korngold's, although he constantly strived to expand his musical style by incorporating more contemporary idioms (Christopher Palmer, in his book *The Composer in Hollywood* notes how Waxman's score for *A Place in the Sun*, 1951, bears a striking similarity to the fugal *Allegro* in the second movement of Shostakovich's Eleventh Symphony – despite predating the symphony by some seven years). Like Korngold and Rózsa, the quality of Waxman's music is only gradually being rediscovered by the serious musical establishment, thanks in part to the recordings of his film music listed below.

The Bride of Frankenstein (1935) **The Invisible Ray** (1936) **Westminster Philharmonic Orchestra / Kenneth Alwyn**.
Silva Screen Ⓟ FILMCD135 (47 minutes: DDD). Recorded 1993.

Waxman's first Hollywood assignment proved to be an auspicious beginning. So successful was his music that Universal constantly recycled portions of it in innumerable B-movies and serials like *Flash Gordon* thereafter. *The Bride of Frankenstein* must count, along with Steiner's *King Kong* (1933), as one of the very first fully developed film scores ever written for a Hollywood movie. It employs many devices that were quickly accepted as standard practice, not least the use of *leitmotifs* to delineate particular characters. Waxman's motifs for the monster, for his 'bride', and for the morbid Dr Pretorius are so strong and distinctively memorable that it is not hard to see why they were thought too good not to use again (and again). In the movie they bring stiff and unreal creations to life; they also help to unify the score, making this disc play like a thrilling 'monster symphony'. To modern ears some other devices – sinister chromaticisms, galloping chase music – tend towards cliché, but only because Waxman's use of them was so good that they were widely imitated. The music is rich, varied and full of incident, with the famous creation scene only one highlight amongst many: a period minuet, a solemn processional march, a contrapuntal "Danse Macabre" also deserve particular mention. Silva's ambitious recording restores music cut from the final version of the film, and orchestrator Tony Bremner has taken the pardonable liberty of expanding the orchestration to symphony-sized proportions. Kenneth Alwyn directs the Westminster Philharmonic with conviction and vigour (not to say obvious enjoyment) both for *Bride* and in a short suite from another Boris Karloff vehicle, *The Invisible Ray*, which rounds off this enthralling disc. The illustrated booklet, with detailed notes and music examples, is exemplary. **MW**

New review

Legends of Hollywood, Volumes 1-4. **Queensland Symphony Orchestra / Richard Mills.**
Varèse Sarabande Ⓟ VSD5242, VSD5257, VSD5480 and VSD5713 (69, 70, 69 and 75 minutes: DDD). Recorded 1983-1993.
VSD5242 – Task Force (1949). Objective, Burma! (1945). Come Back, Little Sheba (1952). Peyton Place (1957). The Paradine Case (1947). The Horn Blows at Midnight (1945). Sorry, Wrong Number (1948). Demetrius and the Gladiators (1954). *VSD5257* – Anne of the Indies (1951). Captains Courageous (1937). The Pioneer Suite – Red Mountain (1951); Cimarron (1960); The Indian Fighter (1955). Huckleberry Finn (1939). The Nun's Story (1958). Botany Bay (1953). Possessed (1947). Mister Roberts (1955). The Bride of Frankenstein (1935). *VSD5480* – Elephant Walk (1954). Night and the City (1950). Night Unto Night (1949). The Furies (1950). Hotel Berlin (1945). Destination Tokyo (1944). Mr Skeffington (1944). The Silver Chalice (1955). *VSD5713* – Untamed (1955). On Borrowed Time (1939). My Geisha (1962). The Devil Doll (1936). My Cousin Rachel (1952). The Story of Ruth (1960). Dark City (1950). A Christmas Carol (1938).

Four discs which stand as a tribute not only to Waxman's genius, but also to the efforts of those who have strived to bring his music wider recognition, particularly the composer's son John Waxman and the late Christopher Palmer, whose meticulous arrangements from the composer's original sketches considerably enhance this collection. Richard Mills and the Queensland Symphony Orchestra also deserve the highest praise for their commitment to a recording project which has taken a decade to complete.

Consciously modelled on Charles Gerhardt's pioneering RCA recordings of a decade or so earlier, *Legends of Hollywood* presents suites from many scores that have not been recorded since the original soundtrack versions. Highlights from Volume 1 include the tender *Reminiscences for Orchestra* derived principally from *Come Back, Little Sheba*, and the gorgeous – if now unfortunately clichéd – *Peyton Place* ("The Wonderful Season of Love") which amply demonstrates Waxman's melodic gifts: the old world charm of small-town New England prompted the composer to create one of his most ravishing tunes. Volume 2 opens with two swashbuckling, somewhat tongue-in-cheek, tributes to Korngold – *Anne of the Indies* and the rollicking *Captains Courageous. Huckleberry Finn*, reconstructed by Christopher Palmer, is a grand hoedown, delightfully scored, with a whimsical middle section featuring some of the composer's favoured contrapuntal writing. Volume 3 begins with Christopher Palmer's *Elephant Walk* suite, containing yet another romantic Waxman melody, "Many Dreams Ago". Waxman's devotional, sincerely spiritual music for the Biblical story of *The Silver Chalice* – themes from which were re-used in his oratorio *Joshua* – closes the disc.

Recorded in 1993, but not issued until 1996, the fourth volume explores some curious filmic backwaters: the music for *On Borrowed Time* in particular is an odd mix of jollity, whimsy and sentiment which apparently impressed David O. Selznick so much that after hearing it he immediately hired Waxman to score *Rebecca*. The brassy fanfares and languid love theme from *Untamed* are typical Waxman; *My Cousin Rachel* revisits *Rebecca* territory – but then he was so good at such full-blooded melodrama. A three-part suite from the Biblical epic, *The Story of Ruth*, is the strongest item, full of vivid instrumental colour and contrast: angular brass and brittle percussion opposed by impassioned strings – solo violin giving a Jewish tinge – but without any of Rózsa's deliberate archaisms. The frenzied climax of the *film noir* score for *Dark City* is built over an ominously treading ground bass – a favourite Waxman device – before concluding with a gentle coda for strings. This final disc ends with an all too brief suite from the 1938 version of *A Christmas Carol* which Waxman had to write in just five days: it is an enjoyable blend of Christmas carols, a Purcellian prelude (in "Mr Scrooge, Ghost and Spirits"), some dark-hued drama and sprightly *scherzos* – and is just long enough to whet the appetite for more.

Performances are of a generally high standard across all four discs, the orchestra and conductor becoming perceptibly more comfortable with the music as the series progresses. On the negative side, they too often lack dramatic flair, and the pace does flag in places, draining the music of some of its inherent vitality. But such weaknesses are a small price to pay for such an impressive collection of fine music. These discs should go a long way towards increasing awareness of Waxman's enormous contribution to cinematic music, and help clear the way for a long-overdue critical reassessment of his great talent. **MW**

Rebecca (1940) **Bratislava Radio Symphony Orchestra / Adriano.**
Marco Polo Ⓟ 8 223399 (72 minutes: DDD). Recorded 1990.

Listening to this newly recorded version of Waxman's classic score, it is fascinating to note just how different it sounds after years of being locked into Hitchcock's classic and timeless movie of 1940. Away from the visuals there seems a great deal more of this amazing music than one remembers. This was one of Waxman's own favourites, and it is easy to see why: drama, romance, murder, and a happy (?) ending all contribute to a Hollywood classic. Congratulations to Marco Polo and the Bratislava Radio Symphony Orchestra under Adriano for bringing this great score out in new digital glory: this is a reminder of the days when Hollywood movies were just magical, and had scores to match. Good sleeve-notes and a fine performance make this one not to miss. Franz Waxman was a giant amongst film scorers, and the more of his scores that find their way onto compact disc, the more I for one will be delighted.   **JW**

Sayonara Orchestral Suites. **Berlin Radio Symphony Chorus and Orchestra / Elmer Bernstein.**
RCA Ⓟ 09026 62657-2 (67 minutes: DDD). Recorded 1994-5.
Taras Bulba (1962). A Place in the Sun (1951). Hemingway's Adventures of a Young Man (1962). Sayonara (1957).

An extremely well-chosen selection which displays Waxman's multifarious gifts to brilliant advantage, this disc is yet another indication of the renaissance his previously undervalued reputation is experiencing. Four extended concert suites showcase the composer's art in a form guaranteed to please both film music fans and a broader classical audience. High adventure, dark melodrama, romantic lyricism and exotic orientalism – all are here to be savoured in Waxman's inventive and colourful scoring. The disc opens with *Taras Bulba*, reconstructed by Arnold Freed and Steven R. Bernstein, which amply lives up to the promise of its oft-performed showpiece,"The Ride to Dubno". An expressive *Pastorale* and a spiky fugal *scherzando* are both just as exciting, whilst "The Battle for Dubno" itself – complete with furiously galloping Cossacks – is a thrilling *tour de force*. Christopher Palmer's *Symphonic Scenario* from *A Place in the Sun* takes us behind the syrupy theme and delves deep into chilly psychological drama by restoring some of the composer's more astringent music which was cut from the film. *Hemingway's* sunny, lyrical opening recalls the gorgeous autumnal colours of *Peyton Place*, although Arnold Freed's *Symphonic Suite* soon twists and turns into less welcoming regions, with Waxman's clean contrapuntal writing succinctly pointing up the drama. The longest item here is Christopher Palmer's *Sayonara* suite, an enticing blend of Hollywood romance and authentic Japanese melodies which also freely incorporates Irving Berlin's title song with characteristically unassuming generosity. The choral "Finale" makes for a ravishingly sentimental end to an excellent disc. The Berlin orchestra are captured in fine form, and Elmer Bernstein ably articulates all the intricate detail of Waxman's scoring.   **MW**

Sunset Boulevard The Classic Film Scores of Franz Waxman. **National Philharmonic Orchestra / Charles Gerhardt.**
RCA Victor Ⓜ GD80708 (54 minutes: ADD). Recorded 1974.
Prince Valiant (1954). A Place in the Sun (1951). The Bride of Frankenstein (1935). To Have and To Have Not (1945). Sunset Boulevard (1950). Old Acquaintance (1943). Mr Skeffington (1944). Objective, Burma! (1945). Rebecca (1940). The Philadelphia Story (1940). The Two Mrs Carrolls (1947). Taras Bulba (1962).

Franz Waxman scored over 120 films in Hollywood over a period of 27 years, beginning in black and white with *The Bride of Frankenstein* through to *Lost Command* (1966). This magnificently played collection leaves one in no doubt as to his versatility in whatever genre he tackled. It opens with music from an early CinemaScope production of Arthurian times – *Prince Valiant*, one of four extended selections on this well-planned CD. The swagger and pomp of the prelude topped by an eloquent love theme makes for an invigorating introduction. Further highlights include *A Place in the Sun* with its wailing saxophone melody and languorous love theme, and *Rebecca's* journey from ethereal "Prelude" to the pandemonium of "Manderley in Flames" – a virtuoso Scherzo. Of more than passing interest are Waxman's scores for *The Philadelphia Story* and *Sunset Boulevard*, both later subjects for musical treatment. Shorter pieces make no less of an impression as the eloquent "Elegy for Strings" from *Old Acquaintance* or the highly charged "Ride to Dubno" from *Taras Bulba*, which would make a marvellous concert encore, testify. This is an essential film music CD from this classic RCA series.   **AE**

Also available:
The Spirit of St Louis (1957) **Ruth** (1960) – suites with narration (Berlin RSO/Foster) Capriccio 10 711

Roy Webb

1888-1982 USA

Born in New York, Roy Webb studied at Columbia University and went to the Metropolitan Opera whenever he was able. Despite a thoroughly classical musical education, Webb's interest was in light music and musical shows (his first professional conducting job was on Broadway).

After arranging and conducting a series of musical comedies, RKO hired Webb in 1929, initially as an orchestrator on the film *Rio Rita*. He stayed with the studio until its demise in the 1950s, making *film noir* a particular speciality. He later worked for the TV company Desilu (producers of the original *Star Trek*). In total he wrote over 300 film scores.

The Curse of the Cat People The Film Music of Roy Webb 1942-49. **Original Soundtracks /** **Constantin Bakaleinikoff.**
Cloud Nine mono Ⓜ CNS5008 (73 minutes: AAD).
Out of the Past (1947). Bedlam (1946). Crossfire (1947). Sinbad the Sailor (1947). Journey into Fear (1942). Dick Tracy (1945). Mighty Joe Young (1949). Notorious (1946). The Ghost Ship (1943). They Won't Believe Me (1947). The Locket (1946). Cornered (1945). The Curse of the Cat People (1944).

Despite scoring the majority of RKO's most important productions of the 1940s, Roy Webb remains the most under-rated Hollywood film composer from the Golden Age. Overshadowed by his legendary contemporaries, Steiner, Newman, Tiomkin, etc, he nevertheless possessed the same melodic gifts and the same flair for dramatic underscoring, as this unique and quite invaluable CD amply demonstrates. Webb's name is most closely linked to the imaginative psychological thrillers of producer Val Lewton for which he provided tense, atmospheric scores without ever resorting to clichéd hysteria. However, as a great romantic, he could supply a sweeping love theme to rank alongside the best of them, and many of the studio's great *films noir* were given added lustre by Webb's rhapsodic style, as in *Out of the Past, The Locket, Cornered* and, most notably, Alfred Hitchcock's *Notorious*. Recordings have been taken from acetates, but the sound is extremely good.   **RS**

John Williams
b. 1932 USA

To write music for films which is nonetheless 'absolute' music away from the images has been the special achievement of only a few composers: Korngold and Rózsa were both classically trained European immigrants who adapted their pre-existing concert hall style to films. Copland, Prokofiev, Walton and Vaughan Williams only dabbled in film music. Trained in the Hollywood studios, John Williams is arguably the only practising film composer who can claim to have done, regularly and successfully, what all these great names aimed to do.

Born in New York, the son of a jazz drummer, John Williams originally trained to be a concert pianist. Moving to Los Angeles in 1948, he studied with pianist-arranger Bobby Van Eps. A three-year stint in the US Air Force from 1951-4 saw Williams orchestrating for and conducting service bands. Returning to New York, he continued his pianistic studies at the Juilliard school with Rosina Lhévinne, before heading back West to enrol at UCLA. Here he took private lessons in composition from, amongst others, Mario Castelnuovo-Tedesco (as had Jerry Goldsmith). From 1956, Williams worked as a studio pianist, initially for Columbia Pictures, then 20th Century-Fox. At Fox, he worked under Alfred then Lionel Newman, playing piano for composers like Franz Waxman and Dimitri Tiomkin, and sharpening his compositional abilities under the guidance of orchestrator Conrad Salinger. It was not until this time that Williams decided to abandon his concert-playing ambitions and concentrate on composition. Beginning with television shows like *Wagon Train, Gilligan's Island, Checkmate* (the first show to have his main title music) and *Lost In Space* (produced by Irwin Allen, who later asked Williams to score his 1970s disaster movies *The Poseidon Adventure*, 1972 and *The Towering Inferno*, 1974), Williams gradually moved into feature film scoring – his first being *Daddy-O* (1959). Many of his early films were comedies – *Bachelor Flat* (1961), *John Goldfarb, Please Come Home* (1964) and *How to Steal a Million* (1966). His first film with director Mark Rydell, *The Reivers* (1969), established Williams as a composer of significance. A British television adaptation of *Jane Eyre* (1971) produced one of the composer's own favourite scores. His famous collaboration with Steven Spielberg began in 1974 with *The Sugarland Express* – Spielberg's first major film – which the director had temp-tracked with music from *The Reivers* and *The Cowboys* (1972). The rest, as they say, is history.

John Williams has received one Academy Award for his film adaptation of *Fiddler on the Roof* (1971) and no less than four for his original scores: *Jaws* (1975), *Star Wars* (1977), *E.T.* (1982) and *Schindler's List* (1993). So far he has received 33 Academy Award nominations. From 1980 to 1995 Williams was principal conductor of the Boston Pops Orchestra. His concert works include a Symphony (1966), and concertos for Violin (1974) and Flute (1969) – both recorded on Varèse Sarabande, VSD5345 – a Cello Concerto premièred by Yo-Yo Ma, and *Five Sacred Trees*, a Bassoon Concerto recorded by Sony Classical with soloist Judith LeClair.

Close Encounters of the Third Kind (1977) **Original Soundtrack / John Williams**.
Varèse Sarabande Ⓕ VSD5275 (41 minutes: AAD).

At the 1977 Academy Awards, John Williams faced serious competition from just one man: John Williams. He won his Oscar that year for *Star Wars*, but it would have been equally well deserved for this quite overpowering score. *Close Encounters* could not be more different from the familiar romanticism of *Star Wars*: rigorous and atonal for much of its running time, the music taps into our primeval fear of the unknown. This is a side of the composer rarely revealed in his other Spielberg collaborations: modernist, uncompromising. But, as the finale approaches, a magical transformation occurs: the music develops towards a sumptuously romantic, solidly tonal climax, in which Leigh Harline's "When You Wish Upon a Star" is put to inspired use. The five-note 'spaceship' signature has passed into legend; even more notable, though, is the composer's audacious decision to make the alien ship speak with the voice of a solo tuba. The only complaint here is the poor CD sound quality – this is a classic score badly in need of the kind of loving remastering and restoration bestowed on its Oscar-winning brother. **MW**

The Cowboys (1972) **Original Soundtrack / John Williams**.
Varèse Sarabande Ⓕ VSD5540 (30 minutes: ADD).

The composer's second collaboration with director Mark Rydell – the others being *The Reivers* (1969), *Cinderella Liberty* (1973) and *The River* (1984) – is at once an exuberant display of Americana and an example of Williams's developing personal style. The combination of an ageing John Wayne and 11 schoolboys out on the cattle trail gave the composer scope to indulge in boyish displays of extravagance – with an everything-bar-the-kitchen-sink approach to orchestration – as well as moments of quiet pathos. Like other early Williams scores, the music is very busy: a robust "Main Title" alternates a flashy brass-led theme and a lyrical string passage. The disc also includes an alternate "Main Title" and the "Overture", which is an early version of Williams's concert-hall suite. With informative booklet notes and cover art by Bob Peak, *The Cowboys* is an essential purchase for all admirers of this composer's work. **MW**

Dracula (1979) **Original Soundtrack**, with the **London Symphony Orchestra / John Williams**.
Varèse Sarabande Ⓕ VSD5250 (37 minutes: AAD).

A series of grand variations on a wild and stormy main theme, *Dracula* is redolent of the lush neo-gothic romanticism that characterizes Bram Stoker's original. Williams confessed to director John Badham that he had never seen a vampire film; thus, freed from any preconceptions, he was able to craft a highly distinctive piece entirely devoid of cliché. Closer in spirit to *The Fury* than his more familiar Spielberg collaborations, *Dracula* can be an intense, claustrophobic experience. The music glowers and broils and thunders overhead; it is both broodingly romantic and astringently modern. A superb gothic melodrama. **MW**

New review
The Eiger Sanction (1975) **Original Soundtrack / John Williams**.
Varèse Sarabande Ⓕ VSD5277 (36 minutes: ADD).

A respected composer since the 1960s, Williams didn't hit the big time as far as the public was concerned until *Star Wars*. His score for *The Eiger Sanction* dates from a little before then and was from a very peculiar film starring and directed by Clint Eastwood concerning espionage double-dealings and mountain climbing. Despite this, *The Eiger Sanction* is well worth investigating as a soundtrack because it neatly encompasses all the characteristics of Williams's work during the 1970s before he got embroiled in the big symphonic post-*Star Wars* material. This is a modest but thoroughly entertaining disc which offers a wide spectrum of styles; the light jazz-influenced title theme, the propulsive action music in "Fifty Miles of Desert", the classically inspired serial writing of "The Icy Ascent" and the baroque classical-style of "Training With George". The CD transfer from the old MCA tapes is not terribly brilliant, with noticeable hiss on some tracks, but it is acceptable. **DS**

Empire of the Sun (1987) **Original Soundtrack / John Williams**.
Warner Bros Ⓕ 7599-25668-2 (55 minutes: DDD). Includes *Suo Gan* (Welsh traditional).

Undoubtedly owing a debt to Morricone's gorgeous *The Mission* of the previous year (Spielberg reportedly asking Williams to "lean on it" when writing this score), *Empire of the Sun* is nevertheless a fine work in its own right. Spielberg's sprawling account of the Japanese occupation of China was a subject rather different to the comic-book epics that he and Williams were used to; critics responded negatively to both film and score (not until *Schindler's List* would they admit that the Wunderkind director had finally grown up). Listening to the disc, however, it is hard to think of this music as anything less than another first-rate achievement. There are some wonderful set-pieces: the tripping Scherzo "Jim's New Life", the choral celebration "Exsultate Justi", the lyrical "Cadillac of the Skies". Nerve-jangling dramatic episodes such as Lost in the Crowd recall the 'adult' music of *The Fury* and *Dracula*. The composer's decision to use a Welsh traditional hymn, "Suo Gan", for certain key moments in the film is nothing less than inspired. Elsewhere, the youthful main character, Jim, elicits from Williams some of his most sincere, yet playful music. The multi-part choral writing in the end credits reprise of "Exsultate Justi" is alone worth the price of this disc.　　**MW**

New review

E.T. The Extra-Terrestrial (1982) Original Soundtrack / John Williams.
　　MCA Ⓜ MCLD19021 (40 minutes: AAD) / MCA Ⓔ MCAD11494 (71 minutes: ADD).

John Williams relaunched the tradition of symphonic scoring for motion pictures with *Star Wars* in 1977. Five years later came *E.T.*, for me the summit of his formidable output and another box-office smash. Since *E.T.* was issued, the "Flying Theme" has become a 'standard' in film programming, likewise "Adventures on Earth", where Williams brings together all that has gone before in an imposing conclusion. The contrast between the symphonic weight of this finale, and the gossamer scoring of earlier scenes, conjuring up images of indigo skies round a lunar landscape, brings home Williams's penchant for the colours of wind and brass, already manifest in his scoring of *Goodbye, Mr Chips* (1969). The little concertino, "Over the Moon", with two pianos, glistens away like some far-off cluster of bright stars. Superb playing by the studio orchestra make this amongst the most desirable of film recordings.

The newly-issued 'special edition', running for an impressive 71 minutes, finally presents the complete score, sympathetically remastered by Shawn Murphy, who has done away with the harsh, over-bright sound of the original and restored a more natural studio ambience in which greater orchestral detail can clearly be heard. This disc contains the score in chronological order – including delicate cues from early in the film like "Toys", and later more dramatic pieces such as "Invading Elliott's House" – but omits the composer's concert arrangements that graced the original album, so "Flying" and "Over the Moon" are missing. The benefit of having all of Williams's music is offset somewhat by the sacrifice of the musically very satisfying structure of the first album. Anyone who loves this score will want both albums, of course, although many will remain satisfied with the original.　　**AE/MW**

The Fury (1978) London Symphony Orchestra / John Williams.
　　Varèse Sarabande Ⓔ VSD5264 (44 minutes: ADD).

Not, in fact, a soundtrack at all, this album came into being only because Williams found that, when he was in London with the LSO putting the music to *Superman*, he had sufficient sessions left with the orchestra to enable him to record another album. For this we should be truly thankful because, not only is this a much superior reading of the score than that in the film (which was recorded in America) but it gives the composer the opportunity to build on the music and adapt it so that the album feels less like a soundtrack and more like a demonic symphony, each movement concentrating on a particular aspect or section of the story. The end result being that there is music not heard in the film. This is film music on a big scale and the composer's flamboyant gesturing of Wagnerian proportions is a perfect match for Brian De Palma's operatic treatment of what is, it has to be said, completely over-ripe nonsense. There are sequences in the film where extravagant slow-motion exercises are cut to fit the music, but the final one, where Amy Irving uses her psychic powers to cause John Cassavetes to explode, is a marvellous example of music and film working together splendidly. The effect is, literally, mindblowing. Here Williams is clearly enjoying himself and has said in interviews that De Palma loves to have lots of big music in his films, a good early example being Bernard Herrmann's score for *Obsession*. The inclusion of the original version of "Death on the Carousel" is of interest but adds nothing to the impact of the album.　　**DS**

Home Alone (1990) Original Soundtrack / John Williams.
　　Sony Ⓜ MK46595 (57 minutes: DDD). Includes *White Christmas* (Berlin), *Please Come Home for Christmas* (Brown/Redd), *O Holy Night* (Adam), *Carol of the Bells* (Wilhousky), *Have Yourself a Merry Little Christmas* (Martin/Blane).
Home Alone 2: Lost in New York (1992) Original Soundtrack / John Williams.
　　Arista 20th Century-Fox Ⓔ 11002-2 (64 minutes: DDD).

Although Williams cut his compositional teeth on comedies, it was the opportunity to write Christmas music that attracted him to *Home Alone*, not the slapstick action. The first disc mixes underscore with a Christmas selection of standards (the Adam and Wilhousky carols were newly recorded for the film). The principal theme is the enchanting "Somewhere in My Memory"; a jolly chromatic melody, heard first on celesta, provides comedic contrast. A bubbling Tchaikovsky-style *scherzo* appears in "Holiday Flight" (just compare it with the "Trépak" from *The Nutcracker*). The two hapless villains lurk about to the strains of a mock sinister march. Much cartoon-like action ensues, tempered by the festive feel of the main themes.

Even more of a cheerful Christmas pageant, the score album for *Home Alone 2* was never issued in the UK (although a separate disc of songs and carols was). If it is therefore slightly harder to obtain, it is well worth the extra effort. Reprising all the original themes in expanded form, with additional, more elaborate orchestrations, the second film also includes much that is utterly delightful and new. The new New York music sparkles with a child's excitement of Christmas in the big city. There is danger and drama lurking, but the composer is mindful that this is cartoon danger: Central Park in the dark, and the "Haunted Brownstone" are appropriately scary; the two thieves are once again accompanied by their ponderous motif. Boisterous and comedic music, conceived in the same unashamedly overblown manner as *Hook*, whirls them, and us, along. Two delightful new carols – "Christmas Star" and "Merry Christmas, Merry Christmas" – both have lyrics by the redoubtable Leslie Bricusse. There is a lightness of touch about these two scores, a sure feel for the right tone that distinguishes this composer's best work. Williams possesses the rare ability to reach back and – through his music – to remind us of the wonder of childhood. **MW**

Hook (1991) Original Soundtrack / John Williams.
Epic Ⓔ EK48888 (75 minutes: DDD).

Hook is an unadulterated, naïvely joyous experience: one in which Williams once again allows us to relive the wide-eyed amazement of the child within. The score has a lithe, balletic grace – even more than *Home Alone* – that is strongly reminiscent of Tchaikovsky, with an additional hint of Stravinsky's *Firebird* (appropriately enough for the firefly-like Tinkerbell). Ravishing, deceptively unsophisticated, unashamedly sentimental, swashbucklingly over-the-top in the best tradition of Korngold (compare the cue "Hook-Napped" with *The Sea Hawk* for example), listening to this score is a reminder of just how much fun great music can be. When the 'flying' theme bursts forth, or Captain Hook is introduced with that wonderfully pompous march, there is no option but to smile. Only the excessively saccharine lyrics and earnest moppet rendition of the song "When You're Alone" (words by Leslie Bricusse again) temporarily spoil things: such a dreamy tune deserves better treatment. Generous running time precludes quibbling that the "End Title" suite is not included. Something like *E.T.* meets *Indiana Jones*, this score is another not-to-be-missed Williams treasure. **MW**

Jaws (1975) Original Soundtrack / John Williams.
MCA Ⓜ MCLD19281 (35 minutes: AAD).
Jaws 2 (1978) Original Soundtrack / John Williams.
Varèse Sarabande Ⓔ VSD5328 (41 minutes: AAD).

There is much, much more to this music than just that two-note 'heartbeat' shark theme, with its echoes of Stravinsky's *Rite of Spring*. Due to the technical limitations of Spielberg's mechanical monster, Williams's music is instrumental in suggesting the presence of the shark, even when it is not actually seen on screen – in this respect *Jaws* is often, and rightly, compared to Bernard Herrmann's *Psycho*. In both cases, the music is required to do far more than 'underscore' a scene: it becomes one of the main characters in the film. But, the remainder of the score is not to be neglected. The dissonant horror of "Chrissie's Death" is no less an integral part of the music than the jaunty "Promenade (Tourists on the Menu)", the optimistic "Out to Sea", or the fugue which underscores "Preparing the Cage" (later reworked as a concert piece). The composer's depiction of the sea – with rushing harp textures and intricate fugal passages – is perhaps the strongest argument for this score's classic status.

Aside from the obligatory shark theme, *Jaws 2* borrows little from the original. It is not therefore an adjunct to the first film, but an independent work in its own right. Just a year after *Star Wars* and *Close Encounters*, and the same year as *The Fury*, this score shares much of the intensity of the latter two and the pulse-racing drama of the former. There are lighter moments: "The Menu", another version of the original "Promenade", and "The Catamaran Race", an optimistic sea-going *scherzo* of the kind Williams does supremely well. The haunting "Ballet for Divers" employs harp arpeggios to suggest the delights and the dangers underwater; another fugue is heard in "The Big Jolt!". Overall, this score is a thrilling compendium of Williams's style at this period, unjustly overshadowed by its predecessor. **MW**

Jurassic Park (1993) **Original Soundtrack / John Williams**.
  MCA Ⓕ MCD10859 (70 minutes: DDD).

The monsters that inhabit *Jurassic Park* are the fantastic inhabitants of our childhood dreams; the movie's success trades on our memories of their juvenile fascination. Appropriately then, Williams's music reminds us just what it is that makes dinosaurs such objects of wonder: his *Jurassic Park* theme begins like the first amazed intake of breath on seeing a real, live dinosaur. We are not scared, we are overcome with awe. One cue – "Journey to the Island" – exemplifies exactly how he draws us into this impossible bestiary, like children being taken on an adventure: a giddy, 'flying' motif begins the journey, pitching and yawing in imitation of the helicopter's movement; a major-key statement of the 'Island Fanfare' warns us to expect grand things ahead; this in turn gives way to an excited 'travelling' motif – complete with bells – as if for a modern sleigh ride; then, the dinosaurs appear, and the minor-key theme (heard in the film, but not on the album for the first time) fills us with wonder. There are other neat touches – the dragging brass aping the clumsy, yet sinister gait of the 'raptors; the synthesizer portraying computer nerd Dennis (the only electronics in the score); the Brachiosaurus lullaby – but the simplicity of the main theme overcomes all, even the ferocious virtuosity of the finale. With all the familiar elements of a Spielberg/Williams collaboration, *Jurassic Park* is a musical treat, guaranteed.   **MW**

New review
Nixon (1995) **Original Soundtrack / John Williams**.
  Hollywood Ⓕ HW162043 / Polydor Ⓕ 162043-2 (68 minutes: DDD). Enhanced CD, with CD-ROM tracks.

Unlike the albums for *Born on the Fourth of July* and *JFK* – Williams's previous collaborations with Oliver Stone – this disc is mercifully free from interpolated songs and miscellaneous snatches of whatever else happened to crop up in the movie (a brief burst of *The Battle Hymn of the Republic* excepted). Both those films elicited from the composer a strongly masculine response, with music of purposeful nobility and righteous anger subsumed by elegaic main themes. *JFK* especially was the tragedy of greatness lost; *Nixon* is the reverse side of the coin. However, few could have predicted just how dark and forbidding Williams's portrait of the fallen President would be. Even for the nostalgic reminiscence of "Growing Up in Whittier" – a lyrical trumpet solo for the wonderful Tim Morrison – the composer paints middle America under leaden skies. His treatment of "The Ellsberg Break-in and Watergate" is unrelentingly oppressive, and throughout the orchestral writing is extraordinarily dense. Dark sonorities abound (the extremely low bass frequencies will probably make your speakers rattle), and the addition of growling synthesizers colour the score in even gloomier hues. The principal theme, even when marking Nixon's moment of triumph at "The Miami Convention, 1968" is strident rather than celebratory; for the finale it becomes a lament – a telling contrast with the elegy for *JFK* – and the score closes with an appropriate air of resignation.   **MW**

Raiders of the Lost Ark (1981) **Original Soundtrack**, with the **London Symphony Orchestra / John Williams**.
  Silva Screen Ⓕ RAIDERS001 (74 minutes: ADD).
Indiana Jones and the Temple of Doom (1984) **Original Soundtrack / John Williams**.
  Edel Ⓕ TCS102-2 (40 minutes: DDD). Includes *Anything Goes* (Porter arr. Williams).
Indiana Jones and the Last Crusade (1989) **Original Soundtrack / John Williams**.
  Warner Bros Ⓜ 925 883-2 (59 minutes: AAD).

The three-way collaboration between George Lucas, Steven Spielberg and John Williams was a momentous and, in retrospect, inevitable event in the annals of film scoring. Movie music fans had good reason to be ecstatic: here were the three people who more than anyone else were responsible for rekindling the glorious flame of old Hollywood and displaying its light to a new generation with even greater brilliance. Just as Flynn's Robin is now unimaginable shorn of Korngold's kinetic accompaniment, so too would Harrison Ford's *alter ego* be a mere shadow of his heroic self if deprived of that immortal fanfare. The music's infectious spirit of adventure cannnot be resisted: here is Williams the inheritor of Korngold's mantle, producing orchestral writing on a grand scale, creating music of unparalleled exuberance and wit.
  Silva Screen's restored *Raiders* soundtrack (remastered from the original session tapes), which contains some 30 minutes of previously unreleased music, is – not to put too fine a point on it – quite stupendously good: the massed brass of the LSO blazing forth in superb glory during the central cue, "Desert Chase". True, the music relies very heavily on the then novel thrill of Indy's fanfare, but there is so much else to savour – "Marion's Theme", the *Ark* theme, the dazzling

orchestral fireworks display – that its past neglect on disc seems all the more inexplicable. This disc will doubtless be guaranteed a place on every film music lover's shelf.

Edel's CD release of the second score – a straight reissue of the original LP – is, in comparison, less impressive. Both the harsh, exceedingly bright sound (not remastered) and the monochrome booklet are something of a disappointment. The music is not: several new themes are presented amidst the expected rip-roaring action, most notably the "Parade of the Slave Children", subsequently extracted as a concert work. A good deal of much-needed humour is also introduced: the grand opening production number, "Anything Goes" (is that really Kate Capshaw singing Cole Porter in Cantonese?) and the tip-toeing *pizzicato* bustle of "Nocturnal Activities" being especially fine.

Probably the most musically satisfying of the *Indiana Jones* saga, *The Last Crusade* is a near-perfect example of what Williams does so well. As ever, he seeks out the spiritual centre of what is ostensibly a two-dimensional story, imbuing his music with utter conviction. The *leitmotif* approach of the earlier films is again employed, although the fanfare is used sparingly. A lovely pastoral theme associated with the Holy Grail is heard several times as a contrast to the more boisterous moments, which include sinister military marches and a blistering Chaconne-like piece for the tank rescue. A colourful scene tracing Young Indy's exploits opens the disc, with some splendidly frenetic, but lighthearted chase music. There is an abundance of excitement to follow. Particular mention must go to the "Scherzo for Motorcycle and Orchestra", perhaps the most impressive of all Williams's *scherzos*. More than excitement, there is humour: mandolins chiming in during "Escape from Venice"; more tip-toe antics in "No Ticket" (another perfectly-formed piece); the joyously overdone "Keeping Up with the Joneses", with its progressively tender treatment of the father-son theme. Climaxing with the complete "End Credits" suite – as do the previous two discs – this is an invigorating experience from beginning to end.   **MW**

The Reivers (1969) Original Soundtrack / John Williams.
Columbia Ⓜ CK66130 (33 minutes: AAD).

John Williams's early score for *The Reivers* – a fortuitous last-minute replacement for Lalo Schifrin's rejected score – at once succinctly captures the mood of William Faulkner's coming-of-age story set in 1905 Mississippi, and utterly transcends it. Guitar, harmonica and banjo weave bluegrass melodies through the orchestral textures; a trad jazz ensemble evoke the exciting ragtime sleaze of the city. The principal themes utilize 'blue' notes and fiddle-style slurs, whilst the inventive orchestration prevents them from ever seeming like pastiche. The whole is encapsulated by an achingly nostalgic waltz, one of the most heart-tugging pieces in the Williams canon. Although deriving its initial impetus from Stephen Foster's music – *Camptown Races* is briefly quoted at the beginning of the "Finale" – *The Reivers* is far more emotionally compelling than anything Foster produced. Ultimately, *The Reivers* relies less on the effect of particular elements within it than on the success of the whole in creating for the listener an emotion-filled sound world all of its own. This is not just the hallmark of good film music, but of *all* music. There are significant differences between this original and the concert suite version (see Collections: "Music for Stage and Screen"). The suite's orchestration is less eclectic, dispensing with harmonica, guitar and most of the jazz elements; it also omits entirely the above-mentioned waltz. The soundtrack album includes a previously unreleased track, "Reflections", but does not have the jolly solo tuba representing grandad's Winton Flyer, the quite delightful horse-race *scherzo*, or Burgess Meredith's charming narration. Anyone who possesses one version would therefore do well to have the other. The only disappointment here is the CD sound which is no better than LP quality.   **MW**

Schindler's List (1994) Original Soundtrack, with Itzhak Perlman (vn); Boston Symphony Orchestra / John Williams.
MCA Ⓕ MCD10969 (65 minutes: AAD).

How to provide musical accompaniment to a film depicting in graphic detail one of the worst atrocities in history? Perhaps only Steven Spielberg could have made such a film, yet still manage to celebrate our frail human virtue of compassion; certainly only John Williams could provide such beautiful, yet fitting music. Restraint and dignity – qualities not often associated with Spielberg/Williams collaborations – characterize this poignant and moving score. A deceptively simple theme communicates aching, anguished pathos, but never overstates it. The substitution of recorder for violin, to highlight a child's suffering, is just one example of the gentle empathy Williams brings to this subject. Itzhak Perlman's contribution makes this music cry the pure, compassionate tears of incomprehending humanity. Certainly a disc that no Williams fan should be without; perhaps a disc no lover of genuine, heartfelt music should be without either.   **MW**

Stanley and Iris (1989) **Original Soundtrack / John Williams**.
Varèse Sarabande Ⓕ VSD5255 (29 minutes: DDD).

Just for once never mind the ridiculously brief running-time, this score is a miniature gem. A truly heart-warming piece of chamber-sized dimensions, *Stanley and Iris* is far removed from the bombast of *Star Wars* or *Indiana Jones*. Piano, flute and strings sketch a delicate portrait of blossoming romance; scaled-down forces reveal all the intricate beauties of the composer's orchestration. Williams's greatest gift – his ability to reach out and touch his audience with displays of genuine emotion – is laid bare before us, unobscured by big action scenes or commercial gloss. **MW**

The Star Wars Trilogy `ARCAM`
Star Wars: A New Hope (1977) **Original Soundtrack**, with the **London Symphony Orchestra / John Williams**.
RCA Victor Ⓕ 09026 68746-2 (deluxe CD); 09026 68772-2 (two discs: 106 minutes: ADD).
Star Wars: The Empire Strikes Back (1980) **Original Soundtrack**, with the **London Symphony Orchestra / John Williams**.
RCA Victor Ⓕ 09026 68747-2 (deluxe CD); 09026 68782-2 (two discs: 128 minutes: ADD).
Star Wars: Return of the Jedi (1983) **Original Soundtrack**, with the **London Symphony Orchestra / John Williams**.
RCA Victor Ⓕ 09026 68748-2 (deluxe CD); 09026 68792-2 (two discs: DDD).

Notwithstanding the unprecedented influence of these seminal scores, the thrilling bravura of the original soundtrack performances and the sheer listening pleasure to be had from them, it might be thought that even dedicated collectors would baulk at being asked to purchase yet another version of the *Star Wars* soundtracks so soon after the issue of an apparently definitive four-disc box set from Arista. That these new discs are certain to exceed even the record company's most sanguine expectations, however, seems to be in little doubt, given the heightened interest in the saga now that the 'new' originals have been re-released at the cinema and the second trilogy (or rather the first) is currently in production at Leavesden studios.

These three separate two-disc sets contain all the music sequenced in film order, plus a mind-boggling total of 88 minutes of previously unreleased music (including nine minutes of newly-composed music for the new *Return of the Jedi* finale). Unlike the Arista set which opted for an 'extra' disc of outtakes, all the music cues are presented here in sequence, with concert versions mostly grouped at the beginning of each second disc. The original *Star Wars* album was sequenced by the composer to produce a satisfactory musical experience away from the film; but it is a tribute to the enduring appeal of this music that its now 'authentic' incarnation is no less pleasing. New here is the first version of the "Binary Sunset" cue, plus about six minutes of extra music which was dropped from the film, and (in a "hiddden" track at the end of Disc 1) all five raw takes of the "Main Title", complete with the engineer's voice noting the take number. The only (purely musically) less than ideal feature is the loss of the opening "Main Title" recapitulation (which on the original album functioned as an overture). On all three discs, track titles have been changed to clarify their position in the film.

The Empire Strikes Back set has an additional 20 minutes of music notably expanding upon the early Hoth sequences and the Cloud City finale. "The Battle of Hoth" now becomes a continous 15- minute 'suite', one of this composer's most glorious set-pieces. *Return of the Jedi,* although not available for review at the time of going to press (January 1997), contains almost an hour of newly-issued material and, most exciting of all, a newly-written, extended finale. The remastered sound, an improvement even on the much-improved Arista issue, has been taken from "newly-discovered multi-track source elements", leaving the listener to ponder where all this "newly-discovered" material has been hidden all these years.

The bad news is that *Star Wars* fans and serious collectors can now no longer be satisfied with their suddenly obsolete Arista boxes (let alone their copies of the original albums). So, for those of us who bought the LPs, then the reissued CDs, then the four-disc box, it is time once again to dig deep for Mr Williams and Mr Lucas. The good news is that each of these splendid sets comes in two versions: the expensive deluxe edition, boasting laser-engraved discs and luxury booklets, and a plainer, slightly cheaper package, although all are CD-sized unlike the outsized Arista box. Completists' heaven, and they fit on your shelves. **MW**

Superman: The Movie (1978) **Original Soundtrack**, with the **London Symphony Orchestra / John Williams**.
Warner Bros Ⓕ 3257-2 (73 minutes: ADD).

As if by accident, not design, during the course of his film career John Williams has created a corpus of splendidly rousing marches and parades which have come almost to rival the preeminence of Sousa in the public's affection. *Midway* (1976), *1941* (1979), *Raiders of the Lost Ark* and *The Empire Strikes Back*, to name but a few, have all provided foot-stompingly impressive examples; *Superman* is perhaps by general consent the favourite. The crowd-pleasing appeal of the "Superman March" never seems to pall; its chest-swelling patriotism bursts with a virile energy that never becomes tiresome. This lengthy score has plenty to offer besides, not all of it as brash and showy as the theme. The early Krypton scenes have a brooding power darker than the rest; "The Fortress of Solitude" is subtle and poignant; whilst, in contrast to the main theme, "The March of the Villains" is another of those witty toy marches the composer manages to create with apparently effortless ease. The overarching "Love Theme" ("Can You Read My Mind") is spoiled only by Margot Kidder's flat, toneless recitation of lyrics by Leslie Bricusse that were surely intended to be sung. In order to fit the score on one disc, two cues from the original double LP are missing, although the "End Title" suite remains intact. **MW**

Also available:
Always (1990) MCA MCAD8036
Earthquake (1974) Varèse Sarabande VSD5262
The Empire Strikes Back (1980) (National PO/Gerhardt) Varèse Sarabande VSD5353
Far and Away (1992) MCA MCAD10628
Filmworks [compilation] MCA MCD32877
JFK (1992) Elektra 7559-61293-2
Presumed Innocent (1990) Varèse Sarabande VSD5280
Return of the Jedi (1983) (National PO/Gerhardt) RCA GD60767
The River (1984) Varèse Sarabande VSD5298
Sabrina (1995) A&M 540 456-2
Schindler's List: Classic Film Music (City of Prague PO/Bateman) Silva Screen FILMCD160
Sleepers (1996) Philips 454 988-2
The Spielberg/Williams Collaboration (Boston Pops/Williams) Sony SK45997
Star Wars Trilogy (Utah SO/Kojian) TER CDTER1067 / Varèse Sarabande VCD47201
Star Wars Trilogy (Skywalker SO/Williams) Sony SK45947
Williams on Williams: Classic Spielberg Scores (Boston Pops/Williams) Sony SK68419

Debbie Wiseman

b. 1963 UK

Debbie Wiseman studied composition (with Buxton Orr), piano (with James Gibb) and conducting at the Guildhall School of Music and Drama. She has worked extensively in television, with credits including *The Upper Hand, A Week in Politics, Children's Hospital* and *People's Century*. Her music for *The Good Guys* won the TV Theme Music of the Year Award in the 1993 Television and Radio Industry Club Awards; in addition to other accolades, her score for *Tom and Viv* was nominated for an Academy Award. She has appeared on Radio 3 and presented the Channel 4 documentary *Backtracks*. In addition, she is Visiting Professor at the Royal College of Music for their Masters degree course in Composition for the Screen.

Haunted (1995) **Original Soundtrack**, with **Andrew Bottrill** (pf); **Debbie Wiseman** (pf).
Silva Screen Flimtracks Ⓟ TRXCD2002 (45 minutes: DDD).

In contrast to the sensitive period setting of *Tom and Viv*, Debbie Wiseman's score for this supernatural thriller (based on James Herbert's novel) includes some pretty astringent writing in places, sparsely scored for vibrato-less flute and harp over icy string harmonics, ominous chords and (synthesized?) voices. The real substance of the album, however, is not the starkly chilling atmosphere generated by these spartan textures, but the romantic solo piano themes for Juliet and Christina – the former a delicate, fragile piece that is quite hauntingly beautiful, the latter a moodily songlike Minuet – both of which are given warmly expressive readings by the composer. This is a subtle, evocative, and distinctively personal score, in which some memorably melodious writing is shrouded in the romantic semi-darkness of shifting shadows. **MW**

Tom and Viv (1994) **Original Soundtrack**, with the **Palm Court Theatre Orchestra /** **Debbie Wiseman** (pf).
Sony Ⓟ SK64381 (53 minutes: DDD). Includes *The Wibbly Wobbly Walk* (Long/Pelham).

For admirers of the music of Debbie Wiseman, it was indeed rewarding to hear her first major score for a feature film. *Tom and Viv*, starring Willem Dafoe and Miranda Richardson, is set in a period much loved by British film and television producers – the early part of the twentieth century. Wiseman's well-constructed score employs solo piano, at times blended with a string orchestra. Although some period-style music is included – "Tom and Viv's Dance" and "Pianola Rag" for example – this is not a lightweight subject, and as the story moves to its dramatic conclusion so the music becomes more introverted, with the solo piano more to the fore. On the strength of *Tom and Viv* there seems to be no reason why Debbie Wiseman will not become one of our major screen composers in a very short space of time. **JW**

Christopher Young USA

Acclaimed by connoisseurs as one of the most interesting and innovative of today's film composers, Christopher Young is only just beginning to break into Hollywood's major league (recent scores include *Species* and *Murder in the First*). The popularity of his highly original and imaginative music amongst collectors is attested, however, by the relatively large proportion of his scores available on CD.

The composer's parents being both non-musical, Young got his earliest musical training as a member of a local choir. Some of his first compositions were for this medium. Moving from the East Coast to UCLA, Young took David Raksin's film music classes, but spent as much time as possible working with student directors. His first feature came about as a result of his student scores – a low-budget horror movie called *Pranks* (1982 – re-released as *The Dorm that Dripped Blood*). Between 1982-85 he composed for a variety of forgettable pics like *Oasis* (1984 – aka *Savage Hunter*), *Wheels of Fire* (1985) and *Barbarian Queen* (1985). Young's first 'major' score was for *Def Con 4* (1985). Subsequently, Young continued in the low-budget exploitation market working with directors like Roger Corman and Tobe Hooper (who rejected Young's avant-garde *Invaders from Mars* score in 1986). Outstanding scores for *Hellraiser* and *Flowers in the Attic* (both 1987) finally established him as a significant new force in the world of film music. His television work has included episodes of the new *Twilight Zone*, and full-length TV movies *American Harvest* (1987), *Last Flight Out* (1990) and *Max and Helen* (1990). Jerry Goldsmith and Bernard Herrmann were his primary influences, although he quickly developed a distinctive style of his own, derived in part from his interest in *musique concrète*: music made by recording and manipulating sounds. In parallel with his film career, Young has written avant-garde concert works – including *Masses* (1992) inspired by his rejected *Invaders from Mars* – and he also teaches classes on film music at USC.

New review

Copycat (1995) **Original Soundtrack**, with **Gary Nesteruk** (pf) **/ Pete Anthony.**
  Milan Ⓟ 33742-2 (64 minutes: DDD).Includes *Get Up to This* (New World), *Carabu Party* (Steven Ray), *Techno Boy* (Silkski), "Largo al factotum" from *Il Barbiere di Siviglia* (Rossini) and "Vissi d'arte" from *Tosca* (Puccini).

John Amiel's serial killer on the loose thriller *Copycat*, is, in a very cunning way, a look back at the classic *film noir* movies of the the 1940s, brought bang up to date with all the excesses of the 1990s. Christopher Young's score blends high-voltage orchestral forces with his characteristic synthesized sounds. The result is an effective mix of the two, full of nervy, jumpy, scary music contrasted with some finely-tuned quieter passages. This is familiar territory for the composer, and previous scores like *A Nightmare on Elm Street 2* (1985), *Flowers in the Attic* (1987) and *The Vagrant* (1992 – see below) have all demonstrated Young's gift for writing particularly effective scores for this genre. Although *Copycat* is a more mainstream and high profile film, he still succeeds in conjuring up a world of fear and danger. Not a score to be listened to alone. **JW**

Haunted Summer (1988) **Original Soundtrack**, with **Mark Zimoski,**
  Tom Calderaro (synths).
  Silva Screen Ⓕ FILMCD037 (54 minutes: DDD).

'Mood music' might be thought a pejorative description, but in the case of this enchanting, epicurean and erotic score the term is entirely complimentary. Young's voluptuous synthesizer textures, drawing on sampled sources of acoustic instruments, entice the listener into a sensual world of shifting shades. Intricate, multi-part melodies inspired by Renaissance lute music are reinvented in a modern electronic idiom; formless synthesized sound combines with early nineteenth-century classicism. The effect is appropriately Byronic in its darkly romantic intensity. "Hauntings", the final cue, is an 18-minute electronic collage of music from the film, which forms a hauntingly dreamlike montage of the whole score. **MW**

Hellraiser (1987) **Original Soundtrack / Paul Francis Witt.**
  Silva Screen Ⓕ FILMCD021 (43 minutes: ADD).
Hellbound: Hellraiser II (1988) **Highpoint** (1984) **Original Soundtracks**, with the **Graunke Symphony Orchestra / Alan Wilson.**
  GNP Crescendo Ⓕ GNPD8015 (74 minutes: DDD).

Both these discs should carry a health warning: not suitable for people of timid or nervous dispositions. It is no exaggeration to describe them as shockingly, disturbingly terrifying. They also happen to make musically fascinating, endlessly compulsive listening. Young begins with a rich vein of dark-hued, melodramatic romanticism which proves to be unsettling but, initially at least, not too extreme. Once he has enticed the unwary listener into his oddly distorted sound world, however, he tightens his grip remorselessly. Leading us ever on, gently at first, the composer begins his inexorable descent into infernal regions; like Virgil in Dante's poem he guides us through each increasingly gruesome level, insisting we view every writhing, screaming, agonizing torment – every fell creation of his own dark imagination. The hugely gothic orchestral writing – greatly expanded and augmented by chorus for the second score – has precedents only in seminal horror works like Goldsmith's *The Omen* and Williams's *The Fury*; the grim chaos of Young's sampled *musique concrète*, however, has no equal this side of the Black Gate of Mordor. The composer exercises his hypnotic will over the hapless listener: time and again they must return to these discs seeking to re-experience the seductive wickedness of this hellish music. Only the suite from *Highpoint*, generously added to GNP's disc, with its sunny guitar-led "Love Theme", allows some chink of natural light to penetrate this hidden world of secretive pleasure and pain. "All hope abandon, ye who enter here." **MW**

Invaders from Mars (1986) **Oasis**[a] (1984) **Original Soundtracks** etc, with **Mark Zimoski** (synths); [b]**Meredith Snow** (viola) / [a]**Paul Francis Witt.**
  Edel Ⓕ 0022032CIN (72 minutes: DDD). Includes *Holy Matrimony*[b] for viola and toys.

The mutant offspring of an unwanted parent might seem an unkind description of Chistopher Young's incredible *Invaders from Mars* score, but this is a work which lends itself readily to metaphorical comparisons with distorted Dr Moreau-like creations. After suffering the anguish of having his radical *musique concrète* score rejected by Tobe Hooper, Young reworked some of the material inspired by the film as a 32-minute independent piece, *Masses* (1992). This is in itself an extraordinary experience – chaotic sampled voices, ominous tolling bells, fierce electronic waves of sound exploring the demented realm where madness and spirituality collide – but there the matter did not rest. Approached by Edel Records with a view to giving his unused score a CD release, Young decided to take a fresh look at his original tape sources and reconstruct (or de-construct?) the film score in an entirely new form. This time the spiritual battleground is disputed by choirs intoning snippets of Gregorian chant whilst fending off soundtrack selections from the film which are 'invading' their notional cathedral. Further complications arise with the introduction of 'crazies' – a cacophonous medley of clamouring voices representing the underworld – and the addition of some otherworldly percussion effects. The whole runs continuously for 34 minutes; it is summed up by the composer as resembling an "exotic Christian ritual". By any standards this is extraordinarily audacious, ultra-experimental music; that it should have originated in Hollywood (albeit as a rejected score) will seem almost inconceivable to those who still decry film music as derivative and conservative.
  Oasis, written two years earlier whilst Young was still a student, is by his standards at least a slightly more conventional score, although still a difficult and challenging piece. A chamber-sized group of 'normal' instruments shares unequal house room with a disproportionately large percussion ensemble. The result is a psychological study of confinement and confrontation during which the composer mercilessly peels away our civilized veneer to reveal the savage primitive lurking below. As if these two terrifyingly inventive pieces weren't enough, the disc closes with a ten-minute concert work, *Holy Matrimony*, scored for viola and "toys". Conceived as a companion to his avant-garde score for *The Vagrant*, this is also related to his earlier concert work *Black Dragon*. The whole amazing 71 minutes is a mind-expanding, possibly mind-bending, journey into unexplored regions. A lengthy illustrated booklet, with notes by the composer, is a model of presentation. **MW**

Judicial Consent (1995) **Original Soundtrack**, with Mark Zimoski (synths) / **Lex de Azevedo.**
  Intrada Ⓕ MAF7062D (35 minutes: DDD).

A *film noir* score for the 1990s, *Judicial Consent* hints at dark passions and terrible deeds, without indulging in histrionics. Positively dripping with atmosphere, this score abundantly demonstrates Young's ability to create and sustain mood: here he evokes a dangerously erotic climate. Smouldering orchestral strings play tense arpeggios, whilst a solo piano carries the sensuous principal theme. Support comes from the synths; harp adds gentle colour, but it is the low register strings and insistent solitary piano that prey on the imagination. Electronic percussion effectively terrifies in the finale ("Gavel On"), before the theme is restated and developed. As with his earlier score for *Jennifer 8* (1992), no light is allowed to illuminate the shadows. **MW**

New review

Norma Jean and Marilyn (1996) **Original Soundtrack / Pete Anthony**.
Intrada Ⓕ MAF7070 (33 minutes: DDD).

Christopher Young has often proven particularly adept at reflecting the emotional contradictions and tensions of characters in the films he has scored. *Norma Jean and Marilyn*, a television movie in which both personas of the tragic actress appear on screen together, affords him a further chance to demonstrate this skill. Young's primary thematic material simply but surely evokes Marilyn Monroe's dual personality – an adored sex symbol who was also tormented and disturbed throughout both childhood and adulthood. His score reflects the mood and music of the times, with solo soprano saxophone and trumpet juxtaposed with warm sultry strings. His main theme, like the character, ascends and descends simultaneously, perfectly combining moments of glamour and adulation with fear and despair. This motif is usually heard in piano, harp and vibes. For the most part the music is lyrical and flowing, but beneath this deceptively simple veneer lies an uneasy dissonance. A well-rounded work, glistening with melody, that confirms Young's skill as both composer and dramatist. **PP**

New review

Set It Off (1996) **Original Soundtrack**, with **Lori Perri**, **Peggi Blu**, and **Roy Galloway** (sngrs); **Brandon Fields**, **Mike Vacarro** (saxes); **Nick Kirgo**, **George Doering** (gtrs); **Carl Vincent** (electric bass); **MB Gordy**, **Steve Scheafer** (drums) **/ Pete Anthony**.
Varèse Sarabande Ⓕ VSD5779 (35 minutes: DDD). Includes *Up Against the Wind* (D. Goldsmith/Young).

There are, it seems, no limits to Christopher Young's versatility. This unusual score – well, unusual for anyone other than this composer – is a compelling combination of Young's sampled experiments, a soulful ensemble credited above, standard orchestra and breathy vocalese. The resulting score is an audacious mix of styles: dramatic Hollywood action, hip R 'n' B, Jazz and something that is uniquely Christopher Young: all of the above yet not quite resembling any one of the above. The wordless vocals seem to sing Motown Soul, but the insistent breathing and finger-snapping accompaniment unseat any preconceptions. The thriller material might have come from a 1970s Lalo Schifrin score, were it not for the odd vocal interjections. Raucous saxophone and electric guitar solos alternate with more restrained tones of classical guitar (apologetically referred to in the booklet as "nylon string guitar"). Bookended by two versions of the song "Up Against the Wind" the score runs for a short 27 minutes, although such brevity makes for an ideally compact creative whirlwind, showcasing yet another facet of this enigmatic composer. **MW**

The Vagrant (1992) **Original Soundtrack / Christopher Young**.
Intrada Ⓕ MAF7028D (42 minutes: DDD).

"Scary, yet not horrific; humorous, but not comedic ... quirky, without being too insane", thus the composer describes his surreal, *musique concrète* comedy-horror score. It is a masterpiece of its kind; in fact, it is the only one of its kind! The scoring is unique, and probably unrepeatable: a flexible string ensemble augmented by voices, melodica, accordion, bansuri flute, deowah, kalimba, toy pianos, marimba and a mind-boggling variety of percussive sounds obtained by using pots and pans, wind-up toys and other oddities. Vocalized breathing, and rhythmic finger snaps push the music even further over the edge. Utterly crazy, but it works wonderfully. This is film music straining at the barriers of convention, and triumphantly surmounting them. It is also another demonstration that low budget does not necessarily equal low quality: financial constraints force the composer to be even more inventive. The final, lengthy piece – *Vagrant Rhythms* – is an independent suite derived from sampled fragments of the musical material written for the film – "manipulated through transpositions and outboard gear mutations". Outrageous fun. **MW**

Also available:
Cinema Septet [Invaders from Mars etc.] Intrada VJF5001D
The Dark Half (1993) Varèse Sarabande VSD5340
Dream Lover (1994) Koch Screen 38700-2
The Fly II (1989) Varèse Sarabande VSD5220
Rapid Fire (1992) Varèse Sarabande VSD5388
U-Boats: The Wolfpack (1993) Cerberus 0214

Victor Young

Born in Chicago of Polish extraction, Victor Young spent his formative teenage years in Poland. He was precociously musical, and studied at the Warsaw Conservatory, graduating with honours. His tutor was Roman Statlovsky, who had been a pupil of Tchaikovsky. After graduating, Young performed as a solo violinist with the Warsaw Philharmonic. He returned to the USA in 1920, and appeared as soloist with the Chicago Symphony Orchestra before taking a full-time post as concertmaster (leader) for the Central Park Movie Theatre. As a result, Young gained experience in accompanying silent movies; before long he was arranging and composing for radio and films. In 1936 he moved to Hollywood and signed a contract with Paramount Pictures, one of his earliest scores being *Champagne Waltz* (1937). Altogether, Young either wrote, arranged or conducted music for over 350 pictures until his untimely death in 1956. Due to ill health that year he suggested the virtually unknown Elmer Bernstein should take over on *The Ten Commandments*, thereby giving Bernstein's fledgling career an enormous boost. His last, unfinished score, *China Gate*, was completed by Max Steiner. He was nominated for an Academy Award 19 times, but only won posthumously for *Around the World in 80 Days*. Victor Young's music is in the best tradition of Hollywood's Golden Age – richly melodic and highly romantic.

Around the World in 80 Days (1956) **Original Soundtrack / Victor Young.**
    MCA Ⓜ MCAD31134 (44 minutes: AAD).

The release of this film produced by Mike Todd in his Todd-AO widescreen process ushered in a new fashion for theatrical presentation in first-run movie houses, with one performance a day and two weekday matinées. Like a live show, all seats could be booked in advance, at higher than average prices. *Around the World in 80 Days* ran for two years in London in this manner. The music, including the lengthy "End Credits", which runs here for six minutes, would have been heard in six-track stereophonic sound emanating from speakers mounted round the auditorium: a thrilling experience in those early days of the medium. This record makes a fitting memorial to Young who died before the work received an Oscar for Best Score. It is superbly transferred from analogue tape, complete with that authentic Hollywood brashness. The main title "Around the World" with lyrics by Harold Adamson, literally went around the world in dozens of recordings. It is presented several times in full orchestral glory. At the start a drum and fanfare announce its arrival on strings, leading to a treatment on piano in Latin style. Then in three-four, it serves as a prelude to the "Sky Symphony", depicting an aerial sequence with Jules Verne's intrepid hero, Phileas Fogg, in a hot air balloon. Young draws on traditional tunes for some of the episodes, like the "Invitation to a Bull Fight" (preceded by a pavement café orchestra in a "Spanish Dance"), "Passepartout", and "Land Ho!", with its echoes of British sea songs. These are presented through the eye of a traveller, mid-fifties fashion, when the airlines were just opening the possibilities of long distance flights. What we hear is travelogue music, lushly designed and beautifully played. Try for instance the track "India Countryside", where Young's shimmering strings take us gently on our way. If the film now has a distinctly musty air, the music still glows brightly on, 40 years later. **AE**

The Quiet Man (1952) **Dublin Pub Singers; Dublin Screen Orchestra / Kenneth Alwyn.**
    Scannán Film Classics Ⓟ SFC1501 (46 minutes: DDD). Recorded 1995. Includes
    The Isle of Innisfree (Farrelly), *The Wild Colonial Boy* and *Galway Bay*
    (Traditional).

The spontaneous charm of folk music – with its instantly recognizable structure and unpretentious appeal – has been of great service to film composers: a well-placed folk tune can establish both locality and mood in the space of a few brief bars. The audience immediately knows we are in Texas, South of the Border, or gazing out across Galway Bay; the melodies come with their own ready-made emotional associations. Hence John Ford's insistence on using folk music in his films, nowhere more delightfully assimilated than by Victor Young in *The Quiet Man*. This score is a marriage made, if not in Heaven, then certainly in Hollywood: traditional Irish tunes and beautifully syrupy Golden Age romanticism intertwine with gorgeous results. Young's treatment of his folk sources is easily as convincing as anything by Grainger or Britten – and markedly less inhibited. Perhaps Young's happiest selection, however, was not a traditional melody at all, but a song written by Richard Farrelly in 1949, "The Isle of Innisfree", which is heard here in both the original vocal and Young's orchestral versions. This première recording of the complete score makes an apt and impressive début for Alwyn's Dublin orchestra, who perform with great gusto. **MW**

The Quiet Man[a] (1952) **Samson and Delilah**[b] (1949) [a]**Victor Young Orchestra**; [b]**Paramount Symphony Orchestra / Victor Young**.
Varèse Sarabande mono Ⓕ VSD5497 (40 minutes: AAD).

The Oscar-nominated *Samson and Delilah* is one of Victor Young's most impressive scores and certainly the finest of the six he provided for director Cecil B. DeMille. The composer's richly melodic style was well suited to this Technicolored slice of Hollywood kitsch, and the themes for the two title characters are amongst Young's most memorable, with the boldly heroic and sturdy horn call for Samson and the lush, deliciously perfumed, string-laden theme for Delilah skilfully interwoven to accentuate their passionate love affair. An orgiastic pagan ritual was a staple ingredient of most DeMille costume spectaculars and here they are scored with a flair for rhythmic drive and exotic colour that rivals Rimsky-Korsakov. Unlike the concise 23-minute suite from *Samson*, which presents the music much as it was heard on the soundtrack, the six separate selections from *The Quiet Man* are performed in slightly modified arrangements. With the bulk of the music freely adapted from songs such as "Isle of Innisfree" and "I'll Take You Home Again, Kathleen" and other traditional Irish melodies, the result is an unashamedly sentimental valentine to the Emerald Isle; the sweetly romantic strings of "My Mother" and "Forlorn", along with the rustic high spirits of "The Big Fight" and "St Patrick's Day", once again providing a perfect illustration of Young's innate craftmanship.   **RS**

Rio Grande (1950) **Original Soundtrack / Victor Young**.
Varèse Sarabande mono Ⓕ VSD5378 (46 minutes: ADD). Includes songs by Stan Jones performed by The Sons of the Pioneers.

In the 1950s many classic Victor Young scores were released by Decca (with few available now), but this is the première outing for *Rio Grande*. The score is endearingly awash with the folk elements (mostly Irish) so beloved of director John Ford; the main theme is "I Dream of Jeannie With the Light Brown Hair", previously favoured by Ford for *Stagecoach*, and here afforded a whole roster of sterling orchestral arrangements from the rousing to the poignant. And then there is "I'll Take You Home Again, Kathleen", sung by The Sons of the Pioneers, who also weigh-in with "Erie Canal" plus a selection of quasi-folk ditties penned by Stan Jones – we even get Ben Johnson, Harry Carey Jr. and Claude Jarman Jr. singing the wacky "Aha San Antone", a song by Dale Evans no less. All this is winning stuff, but there is also a good measure of dramatic scoring – vintage Western action music – incorporating a batch of standard movieland Red Indian motifs, and some hefty chunks of beefy chase music. Horns and trumpets are enlisted to evoke expansive Western plains whilst plaintive strings and woodwind edged with accordian conjure more intimate moments. The mono sound, although recorded nearly 50 years ago, is here excellently reproduced, with a full sonorous quality. Victor Young was one of Hollywood's finest musical exponents, and although his music was never as complex or inspired as many of his contemporaries, it was always unfailingly captivating. The music featured on this album is no exception. *Rio Grande* is the real McCoy!   **DW**

Shane A Tribute to Victor Young. **New Zealand Symphony Orchestra / Richard Kaufman**.
Koch International Classics Ⓕ 37365-2 (59 minutes: DDD).
Shane (1952). For Whom the Bell Tolls (1943). Samson and Delilah (1949). The Quiet Man (1952). Around the World In 80 Days (1956). Tribute to Victor Young (arranged by Henry Mancini).

Finally, a retrospective of Victor Young's extraordinary contribution to film music! Young's unpretentious, memorably melodic, and, in their day, incredibly popular movie scores have been standing in line too long for a modern digital recording. Here, at last, we are treated to an outstanding overview of Young's faultless facility.

Shane sports one of the screen's great melodies – "The Call of the Faraway Hills" – but the score has oodles more to offer; the stirring formality of "The Tree Stump", the brief but boisterous "Rodeo Music", the delicately expansive "Wyoming Sketches", and the masterly "Cemetery Hill" – the final showdown – although the resolute *basso ostinato* should dominate, but here it is shyly hidden within the main body of the orchestra – the only dramatic *faux pas* in an otherwise faultless reading. *For Whom the Bell Tolls* (rather lamely ushered in on this disc by the meagre ping of a ship's bell rather than the stonking clang obviously demanded by the score) is one of Young's finest creations; he seemed to have a particular affinity for Spanish subjects – witness his scores for *Golden Earrings* (1947), *The Brave One* (1956), and the Spanish selections in *Around the World in 80 Days*. Here a gloriously sweeping love theme dominates – romantic Hollywood at its most unbridled – the scoring vibrantly infused with rhythmic Hispanic counterpoint. *Samson and Delilah* is orchestrally and rhythmically the most florid of Young's scores. Here again, an expansive love theme holds sway, but the true centre of the score comprises a series of symphonic dances: infectiously energetic and wholly, gloriously Hollywood in concept: prime kitsch. *The Quiet Man* is about as roistering and Oirish as you get: the composer weighs-in with the double-distilled "St Patrick's Day" and breathlessly leaves us with the rollicking "Innisfree". In between we are treated to the wholesome respite of "I'll Take You Home Again, Kathleen". A knockout!

There just is not room enough on one disc to do justice to all Victor Young's timeless melodies, so a useful resumé courtesy of arrangements by Henry Mancini is included; this includes brief glimpses of *Golden Earrings* (1947), "When I Fall in Love" from *One Minute to Zero* (1952), *Love Letters* (1945) and "Stella By Starlight" from *The Uninvited* (1944) among others; the arrangements are alternatively cutesy and smooth – and wholly captivating. The complete "End Credits" from *Around the World in 80 Days* segues directly from Mancini's suite, as a fuller alternative to Mancini's shorter version. This is a *tour de force* – and a true overture – albeit after the event rather than before it, a musical dash around the globe, interspersed with the now famous love theme "Around the World", and with a few *misterioso* asides alluding to the underhand activities of the nefarious Inspector Fix – forever hot on the trail of Phileas Fogg.

Despite the occasional niggles, and although it could be argued the interpretations are a little too reverent, too portentous – with some of the composer's straightforward unfussy appeal lost in the overly classical readings – this is still a disc to die for! **DW**

Also available:
Johnny Guitar (1954) Varèse Sarabande VSD5377

see also Collections: **Captain Blood**

Hans Zimmer
b. 1957 Germany

The most conspicuously successful film composer of the 1990s, Hans Zimmer's rock-inspired scores have profoundly changed the accepted 'Hollywood sound', brought the art of movie scoring bang up to date with the very latest synthesizer technology, and produced a 'techno' style perfectly suited to the all-action, surround-sound multiplex movies that have come to dominate our viewing.

Zimmer is the new face of Hollywood: a precociously musical child from Frankfurt, he had already decided he wanted to be a composer by the age of six. A composer without any formal musical education, he served his apprenticeship working with rock bands like SPK, Ultravox and The Damned, exploring to the full the use of synthesizers. He learnt the craft of film scoring whilst working in England as assistant to composer Stanley Myers, with whom he scored *Blind Date* (1984), *My Beautiful Laundrette* (1985) and *The Wind* (1987) among others. His big break came when director Barry Levinson heard Zimmer's music for *A World Apart* (1987) and asked him to score *Rain Man* (1988). His much-admired score for Ridley Scott's atmospheric *Black Rain* (1989) introduced the now familiar Zimmer blend of computers, percussion and orchestra. Although he has written many scores for conventional forces, and collaborated on a number of diverse projects including Disney's *The Lion King* (1993) for which he received an Academy Award, his principal innovation has been to discern the dramatic potential inherent in rock music, and incorporate its raw energy into his scores. Like those film composers of the 1950s who found inspiration in jazz, Zimmer has refashioned Hollywood film scoring to suit contemporary tastes. By using all the modern technological resources available to him, he has also helped develop new techniques of scoring and recording: he uses his synths to digitize and enhance sound effects, exploiting the capabilities of modern cinema sound systems. Zimmer frequently works with collaborators: Fiachra Trench, Shirley Walker and Nick Glennie-Smith have all assisted him. Mark Mancina, with whom he worked on *Days of Thunder* (1990), *Thelma and Louise* (1991), *Where Sleeping Dogs Lie* (1992) and *The Lion King* amongst others, has now gone on to compose independently (see separate entry).

Backdraft (1991) **Original Soundtrack / Shirley Walker.**
Milan Ⓟ 262 023 (43 minutes: DDD). Includes *Set Me in Motion* and *The Show Goes On* (Bruce Hornsby & the Range).

A militaristic march introduces this rousing score, Zimmer's macho anthem for orchestra and synthesizers. It is the grand sweep of the conventional orchestra, augmented by a choir, that steals the show however. Zimmer's mix of electronic and acoustic instruments is always effective: a tender theme for piano and strings in "Brothers" is interrupted by sinister synths, before the orchestra returns to weave in and out of the electronic soundscape. Track 5, "335", enhances the sound effects of the firemen's breathing apparatus during a suspenseful series of rising chords underpinned by a throbbing bass, which then breaks out – track 6, "Burn it All" – into a muscular action motif for orchestra, choir and synthesizers. Events rise to fever pitch in "You Go, We Go", interrupted only by the return of the tender "Brothers" melody. An exciting, adrenalin-pounding experience which characteristically never sacrifices musicality in favour of mere noise. Thrilling.   **MW**

Beyond Rangoon (1994) **Original Soundtrack**, with **Richard Harvey** (ethnic pipes) / **Nick Glennie-Smith**.
Milan Ⓔ 28665-2 (39 minutes: DDD).

Wraith-like, the haunting strains of Richard Harvey's wooden flute rises from the swirling synthesized mists of Zimmer's ethereal score; a wordless female voice sighs over gentle, tinkling percussion. Zimmer's enchanting music reinvents the film's Burmese setting in electronic topography. The most compelling cue is the nine-minute "I Dreamt I Woke Up", co-written with frequent collaborator Nick Glennie-Smith, during which the impassioned voices of pipes and singer are gradually replaced by increasingly urgent synthesizer figures, which finally resolve into the ominous sound of whirling helicopter blades. This album shows Zimmer at a peak of inspiration and creativity. Richard Harvey's irreplaceable contribution helps make *Beyond Rangoon* a wondrous evocation of the Orient.   **MW**

New review

Broken Arrow (1995) **Original Soundtrack**, with **Duane Eddy** (gtr); **Hans Zimmer** (synths) / **Bruce Fowler, Don Harper**.
Milan Ⓔ 34865-2 (59 minutes: DDD).
Crimson Tide (1995) **Original Soundtrack** / **Nick Glennie-Smith**.
Hollywood Ⓔ 162025-2 (61 minutes: DDD).
The Rock (1996) **Original Soundtrack** / **Nick Glennie-Smith, Bruce Fowler, Don Harper**.
Hollywood Ⓔ HR62062-2 (61 minutes: DDD). Co-written with Nick Glennie-Smith and Harry Gregson-Williams.

Received critical opinion, as expressed in the pages of **Gramophone** during the early 1960s, summed up Miklós Rózsa's *Ben-Hur* (1959) as "ear-splitting exotic nonsense", and *El Cid* (1961) as "meaningless". In the late 1990s, critical reactions to Hans Zimmer's wall-to-wall synth/rock scores have been startlingly similar in tone. Our tolerance for "ear-splitting" noise may have increased, but attitudes towards "meaningless" contemporary film music seem stuck three decades behind the present.

Broken Arrow, *Crimson Tide* and the collaborative score for *The Rock* represent everything that critics loathe about Hans Zimmer's work, and contain everything that makes it so hugely popular. Stylistically, they are all very similar – if you like one you will like them all and vice versa – so it is appropriate to discuss them together. Overwhelmed by electronic percussion and swamped by multi-tracked synths, the traditional orchestra is relegated to a supporting role, or dispensed with altogether in favour of more easily manipulated sampled instruments. There is little musical development in the classically accepted sense; instead the technique is adapted from rock: powerfully simple riffs achieve their effect by repetition, melodies are ideally short, easy to grasp on first hearing and memorably hummable, packing the kind of emotional wallop delivered by the chorus of a Bon Jovi song; transitional passages are covered by near-continuous drum patterns, maintaining the often breakneck pace even when the music is otherwise static. Judged by the old standards this must indeed appear "meaningless", but the supercharged energy of these scores has an attraction that has nothing to do with music criticism and everything to do with gut impact. All three discs can be unreservedly recommended for their aggressive dynamism, their speaker-shattering power, and their energetic vitality.

Chronologically the earliest, *Crimson Tide* incorporates a ready-made emotionally-charged tune, the sailors' hymn "Eternal Father Strong to Save", sung by a male voice choir who provide Zimmer with more material for his electronic samples. His own themes are characteristically robust, and he shows an often overlooked pictorial sensibility in his synthesized depiction of the murky undersea environment. *Broken Arrow* uses an eclectic array of instruments and samples – not just Duane Eddy's twanging guitar, but banjo, harmonica, children's choir, wordless soprano, a cracking whip and other assorted "weird noises" credited in the booklet – to produce what is described as a "techno western" score, replete with tongue-in-cheek references to the Leone/Morricone 'spaghetti' style. The three-note motif for John

Travolta's character creates interludes of unexpected calm dignity amidst the otherwise continuous loud action. *The Rock* may have had at least two other composers, but it is indistinguishable from Zimmer's other action scores, with a principal theme almost borrowed from *Crimson Tide*. Like *Broken Arrow*, electric guitar set against a pounding backbeat is a prominent element – the modern equivalent of those rock concept albums of the 1970s. Given the film's title, this is hardly inappropriate.

Although Miklós Rózsa is now (posthumously) enjoying critical acclaim, Hans Zimmer will probably have to wait more than three decades before his zestful, ebulliently noisy creations even begin to enjoy similar acceptance. He should worry.   **MW**

Driving Miss Daisy (1989) **Original Soundtrack**, with **Hans Zimmer** (synths).
Varèse Sarabande Ⓕ VSD5246 (36 minutes: DDD). Includes *Kiss of Fire* (Louis Armstrong); *Santa Baby* (Eartha Kitt) and "Song to the Moon" from *Rusalka* (Dvořák).

Sandwiched between two songs and an operatic excerpt, Hans Zimmer's uplifting music runs to just 23 minutes. However, that tick-tock 'driving' motif and the bluesy solo clarinet (a little too slick to be a real one) are alone worth the price of this disc. The composer has captured the winsome charm of Miss Daisy and her chauffeur in delicate synthesized textures. Additional themes are attractive – a poignant melody in "Home" for instance – but it is the main theme that rightly dominates. For once, neither the additional songs nor the opera aria seem out of place.   **MW**

K2 (1991) **Original Soundtrack**, with **Pete Haycock** (gtr) and various artists / **Fiachra Trench**.
Varèse Sarabande Ⓕ VSD5354 (41 minutes: DDD).

A potent blend of synths, standard orchestral instruments and searing electric guitar, *K2* distills Zimmer's multifarious talents into just two tracks, "The Ascent" and "The Descent". Pete Haycock's (presumably) improvised Eric Claptonish guitar-licks punctuate a quintessentially rich aural landscape; significant additional contributions come from Richard Harvey (ethnic pipes, etc.), Graham Ward (drums), Anthony Pleeth (cello) and David Emanuell (viola). This is a varied, consistently fascinating musical journey which never seems like an uphill struggle.   **MW**

The Power of One (1992) **Original Soundtrack**, with the **Bulawayo Church Choir** and various artists.
Elektra Ⓕ 7559-61335-2 (47 minutes: DDD). Lyrics by Lebo M. Includes *Limpopo River Song, The Funeral Song* and *Wangal Unozipho* (Khabo), *The Power of One* (Clegg), *Southland Concerto* and *Senzenina* (Trad arr. Clegg).

A choral celebration of Africa, *The Power of One* features authentic Zimbabwean music and performers. Surprisingly then, it is Zimmer's own compositions that stand out as the album's great strengths (he was to revisit this territory for the Oscar-winning *The Lion King*). His ability to grasp ethnic idioms without sounding like pastiche is remarkable. Assisted by lyricist, singer and choirmaster Lebo M. (who was later to collaborate on *The Lion King*), Zimmer beautifully captures the soaring, spiritual quality of African choral singing, and combines it with his own very western, synthesized music. The result is by turns uplifting ("Mother Africa") and moving ("Of Death and Dying"). The other music is hardly less attractive, only the title track (not by Zimmer) turns out to be disappointing – a thoroughly routine pop song.   **MW**

Also available:
Assassin [Point of No Return] (1993) Milan 14302-2
Black Rain (1989) Virgin CDV2607
Days of Thunder (1990) Epic 467159-2
Green Card (1991) Varèse Sarabande VSD5309
I'll Do Anything (1994) Varèse Sarabande VSD5474
The Lion King (1994) [mostly songs by Elton John and Tim Rice] Mercury 522 690-2
Muppet Treasure Island (1995) [+ songs] EMI PRMCD5
Nine Months (1995) Milan 30110-2
Pacific Heights (1990) Varèse Sarabande VSD5286
Rain Man (1988) Capitol CDP7 91866-2
Renaissance Man (1993) Varèse Sarabande VSD5502
Something to Talk About (1995) Varèse Sarabande VSD5664
Thelma and Louise (1991) MCA MCLD19313
Younger and Younger (1993) Varèse Sarabande VSD5456

Collections

New review

Arnold Schwarzenegger Action Collection Original Soundtracks.
Varèse Sarabande Ⓟ VSD5398 (48 minutes: DDD).
Brad Fiedel: Terminator 2: Judgment Day (1991). **Randy Edelman:** Kindergarten Cop (1990). **Jerry Goldsmith:** Total Recall (1990). **Harold Faltermeyer:** The Running Man (1987). **Ennio Morricone:** Red Sonja (1985). **Cinemascore:** Raw Deal (1986).

The Greatest Themes from the Films of Arnold Schwarzenegger Mark Ayres (synths); **City of Prague Philharmonic Orchestra / Nic Raine.**
Silva Screen Ⓟ FILMCD164 (71 minutes: DDD).
Alan Silvestri: Predator (1987). **Jerry Goldsmith:** Total Recall (1990). **James Horner:** Commando (1985). Red Heat (1988). **Randy Edelman:** Kindergarten Cop (1990). **James Newton Howard:** Junior (1994). **Randy Edelman, Georges Delerue:** Twins (1988). **Cinemascore:** Raw Deal (1986). **Harold Faltermeyer:** The Running Man (1987). **Brad Fiedel:** The Terminator (1984). Terminator 2: Judgment Day (1991). True Lies (1994). **Basil Poledouris:** Conan the Barbarian (1982). Conan the Destroyer (1984).

Whilst the films of Arnold Schwarzenegger may not be everyone's idea of great cinema they, and films like them, afford composers an opportunity to explore and experiment with their own styles. Indeed, some of the scores featured on these two discs are amongst the best work of the composers represented. Both Alan Silvestri's music for *Predator* – the angular and militaristic main theme included on Silva Screen's compilation – and Basil Poledouris's scores for the two *Conan* films are modern classics. Jerry Goldsmith's *Total Recall*, with its massive and quite mesmerizing fusion of orchestra and electronics, is arguably the best action score of his career. Randy Edelman has seldom been in finer form than with his jaunty and unforgettable melodies for *Kindergarten Cop*: the "Astoria School Theme" has a real child-like innocence and vitality.

Varèse Sarabande's compilation consists of original soundtrack recordings, many of which are electronic. Brad Fiedel's music for *Terminator 2* is one of the most complex and sophisticated electronic scores of recent years: a myriad of sounds, including clanking percussion, drive the urgent and steely rhythms with a great deal of energy and verve. Harold Faltermeyer's aggressively percussive score for *The Running Man* has a similar if less sophisticated impetus. *Raw Deal* achieves a thicker contemporary sound with electric guitar and drums relentlessly pounding the listener. The orchestral selections provide a contrast: Ennio Morricone's quietly heroic theme for *Red Sonja* features trumpet and mixed chorus against a pulsating backdrop of strings. The inclusion of *Total Recall*, although welcome, does tend to overshadow the other items on this disc. Notable on Silva Screen's selection of re-recordings are Brad Fiedel's relentless theme for the original *Terminator* movie, here performed by Mark Ayres, and James Horner's theme from *Commando* with its infamous steel drums, again performed by Ayres. The City of Prague Philharmonic otherwise deliver a competent performance of even the most difficult material. Both discs are certainly full of contrasts. **PP**

Blood and Thunder Parades, Processionals and Attacks from Hollywood's Most Epic Films.
Seattle Symphony Orchestra / Cliff Eidelman.
Varèse Sarabande Ⓟ VSD5561 (39 minutes: DDD). Recorded 1994.
Miklós Rózsa: Ben-Hur (1959). **Alfred Newman:** Captain from Castile (1947). **Alex North:** Cleopatra (1963). **Jerry Goldsmith:** The Wind and the Lion (1975). **Bernard Herrmann:** North by Northwest (1959). **Elmer Bernstein:** The Ten Commandments (1956). **Franz Waxman:** Taras Bulba (1962). **Bronislau Kaper:** Mutiny on the Bounty (1962).

Despite the portentous title, "Blood and Thunder" is a varied and often enthralling collection of some classic scores. These are avowedly concert-hall interpretations, not painstaking attempts to recreate every nuance and tempo of the originals, "to be interpretive without being revisionary" as the booklet puts it. This deliberate treatment of these pieces as independent concert works is apparent throughout – particularly notable is Eidelman's idiosyncratic version of Herrmann's *North by Northwest* main title. A three-movement suite from Alex North's *Cleopatra* focuses more on the love music than the processional; the late Christopher Palmer is remembered in his concert suite of Elmer Bernstein's grand *The Ten Commandments*; Franz Waxman's "Ride of the Cossacks" from *Taras Bulba*, with its Russian folk music motifs, is perhaps the most thrilling item on the disc (even if this reading doesn't come close to Charles Gerhardt's for sheer excitement – see Waxman). The Seattle Symphony Orchestra perform adequately under Eidelman's direction, although the feeling that some more rehearsal time would not have gone amiss is never far away. Combined with a percussion and brass-heavy recording, this detracts somewhat from the enjoyment of an otherwise fine disc. **MW**

Captain Blood Brandenburg Philharmonic Orchestra / Richard Kaufman.
Marco Polo Ⓟ 8 223607 (65 minutes: DDD). Recorded 1994.
Miklós Rózsa: The King's Thief (1955). **Victor Young:** Scaramouche (1952). **Erich Wolfgang Korngold:** Captain Blood (1935). **Max Steiner:** The Three Musketeers (1935).

Korngold's *Captain Blood* is well-known from Charles Gerhardt's recordings for RCA's Classic Film Scores series, though the bulk of this colourful, gloriously descriptive 20-minute suite is making its first appearance on disc. The composer's surging, athletic romanticism made the ideal companion for Errol Flynn's dashing screen image: little wonder Korngold would work on six other films for the charismatic star. The same year, Korngold's compatriot, Max Steiner, was scoring one of the many screen adaptations of *The Three Musketeers*. Though this particular version is not well-remembered, Steiner's score is a spirited and highly melodic gem that fully deserves its resurrection here. The swashbuckler made a comeback during the 1950s and for MGM's brisk, Technicolored remake of *Scaramouche* Victor Young produced one of his most accomplished and lushly melodic scores, featuring a boisterous Rossini-esque theme for Scaramouche and a delicious waltz-like love theme. Though *The King's Thief* was rather humdrum as an adventure yarn, Miklós Rózsa's delightful score provided all the excitement and romance the film lacked. Performances throughout are terrifically idiomatic and with a luxurious recording to match, this is a disc to treasure.   **RS**

Classic Greek Film Music Mark Ayres (synths); City of Prague Philharmonic Orchestra / Nic Raine.
Silva Screen Ⓟ FILMCD165 (67 minutes: DDD).
Mikis Theodorakis: Z (1968). State of Siege (1973). Phaedra (1962). Honeymoon (1959). Serpico (1973). Zorba the Greek (1964). **Vangelis:** 1492: Conquest of Paradise (1992). Missing (1982). Chariots of Fire (1981). Blade Runner (1982). **Manos Hadjidakis:** Topkapi (1964). Never On Sunday (1959). Blue (1968). The 300 Spartans (1962). **George Hadjinassios:** Shirley Valentine (1989). **Yanni:** I Love You Perfect (1989).

Whilst many soundtrack collectors would never come up with a combination of such titles in a month of Sundays, this compilation bears closer examination. To older cinemagoers, Greek film music means Theodorakis, whilst the younger generation would cite Vangelis as the chief exponent. Whichever camp you fall into, this varied selection of themes and mini-suites from the world of Greek film music – from Henry Mancini's arrangement of the "Theme from Z" to a bonus vocal version of the theme from *Phaedra* nicely sung by Haris Alexiou – will have something of interest. Such favourites as *Topkapi, Never On Sunday* and *Serpico* are performed with vigour by the City of Prague Philharmonic, sometimes with considerably larger forces than heard on the original soundtracks. Standout tracks include Hadjidakis's stirring Western music for *Blue* (sometimes a non-American perspective on the genre can produce something quite unexpected and unusual); a truly 1950s feel permeates Theodorakis's theme from *Honeymoon*, orchestrated here by Philip Lane, who is also responsible for all the percussion and drums in that gem of a march from Hadjidakis's *The 300 Spartans*. Competent notes, along with mini colour posters of all the major films, make for an informative booklet. An entertaining collection for those wishing for something just a bit different.   **JW**

Classic Republic Serials and Westerns
Cliffhangers! Classic Republic Serials. **Cinemasound Orchestra / James King**.
Varèse Sarabande Ⓟ VSD56658 (60 minutes: DDD). Music by Victor Young, Mort Glickman, Arnold Schwarzwald, Paul Sawtell, William Lava, Cy Feuer and Alberto Colombo.
Perils of Nyoka. Adventures of Captain Marvel. Dick Tracy's G-Men. Zorro's Fighting Legion. The Fighting Devil Dogs. King of the Royal Mounted. Daredevils of the Red Circle. Mysterious Dr Satan. Hawk of the Wilderness. Drums of Fu Manchu. Adventures of Red Ryder.
Shoot 'em Ups Classic Republic Westerns. **Cinemasound Orchestra / James King**.
Varèse Sarabande Ⓟ VSD5666 (67 minutes: DDD). Music by Cy Feuer, William Lava, Mort Glickman, Alberto Colombo, Paul Sawtell and Karl Hajos
The Three Mesquiteers. The Border Legion. Don Barry Series. Republic Chase Montage. The Painted Stallion. Adventures of Red Ryder. Republic Action Trilogy. Republic Suspense Montage. The Lone Ranger. Under Western Skies.

These albums, originally released by Intersound, have now been reissued, with less than inspired artwork, by Varèse Sarabande. Conductor James King has affectionately recreated the music of

Hollywood's 'B-movie' composers – Mort Glickman, Arnold Schwarzwald, William Lava, Cy Feuer, Alberto Columbo, Karl Hajos and Paul Sawtell (best known for his TV theme for *Voyage to the Bottom of the Sea*). On listening it is not difficult to see why these composers never graduated to 'A' movies as their music now sounds terribly hackneyed, derivative and dated – but there is a certain joy and naïvete in the music which makes it (almost) irresistible. King has done a first class job in not only reconstructing the original scores for titles such as *The Three Mesquiteers* and *Adventures of Captain Marvel*, but also in recreating the original sound, style and feel of the period by remaining scrupulously faithful to the original orchestrations and size of orchestra.   **PC**

New review

Classic Western Film Scores, Volumes 1 and 2. [a]Daniel Massey (narr); City of Prague Philharmonic Orchestra / [b]Nic Raine, [c]Paul Bateman, [d]Derek Wadsworth.

Silva Screen Ⓕ FILMCD173/6 (two discs: 78 and 67 minutes: DDD).

FILMCD173, "How the West Was Won" – **Elmer Bernstein:** The Magnificent Seven[c] (1960). **Dee Barton:** High Plains Drifter[d] (1972). **Randy Edelman:** Gettysburg[ab] (1993). **Maurice Jarre:** The Professionals[b] (1966). **Lee Holdridge:** Buffalo Girls[b] (1995). **Jerry Fielding:** The Wild Bunch[b] (1969). **Jerry Goldsmith:** Wild Rovers[b] (1971). **Alfred Newman:** How the West Was Won[b] (1962). *FILMCD176*, "Lonesome Dove" – **Basil Poledouris:** Lonesome Dove[b] (1989). **David Mansfield:** Heaven's Gate[b] (1980). **Lee Holdridge:** Old Gringo[b] (1989). **Elmer Bernstein:** The Sons of Katie Elder[b] (1965). **Jerome Moross:** The Proud Rebel[c] (1958). **Maurice Jarre:** El Condor[c] (1970). Red Sun[c] (1971). **Richard Hageman:** She Wore a Yellow Ribbon[b] (1949). **Manos Hadjidakis:** Blue[b] (1968). **Dimitri Tiomkin:** Red River[b] (1948). **Dominic Frontiere:** Hang 'em High[d] (1967). **Jerry Fielding:** The Outlaw Josey Wales[d] (1976).

The first two volumes of a projected six-CD survey of this perennially popular genre, Silva Screen's generous and attractively presented discs contain a refreshingly eclectic selection, from Elmer Bernstein's old warhorse, *The Magnificent Seven*, to Jerry Fielding's untypical, jazz-influenced *The Wild Bunch*. Dimitri Tiomkin and Jerome Moross, both featured on the second disc, are representatives of an earlier generation largely responsible for defining the familiar Western style that – with few exceptions – remains the benchmark by which newer scores are still measured. Moross's perky and entirely characteristic *Pastorale* from *The Proud Rebel* is performed here in a version arranged by the composer for his concert suite, *Music for the Flicks*; Tiomkin's typically robust score for *Red River* is an early example of this Russian composer's inexplicable affinity for the genre that was to culminate with *The Alamo*. Whilst *Gettysburg* is neither generically nor geographically a 'Western', Randy Edelman's stirring music, accompanied by Daniel Massey's recital of the Gettysburg Address, is a welcome newcomer – spoiled only by a painfully turgid performance – as is the opening item on disc two, Basil Poledouris's simple and affecting theme from the television series *Lonesome Dove*. Maurice Jarre's jolly Spanish-American influences reflect a distinctively European approach, best exemplified, however, by Ennio Morricone who has yet to make an appearance in this series. A 24-minute suite from Alfred Newman's *How the West Was Won* which concludes the first disc sums up Hollywood's celebratory Americana with delightful folk-song melodies, fierce attacking Indian rhythms, and a "Finale" full of the old Pioneer spirit (a two-disc set of the full score has now been reissued by Rhino records in the USA). The City of Prague orchestra, although enthusiastic as always, lack cohesion in the more rumbustious items, making their performances adequate but never distinctive; nevertheless, the breadth of repertoire encompassed here promises well for the series as a whole.   **MW**

New review

Dark Shadows: The 30th Anniversary Collection. The Robert Cobert Orchestra; The Charles Randolph Grean Sounde; The First Theremin Era; The Vampire State Building.

Varese Sarabande Ⓕ VSD5702 (56 minutes: ADD)

1996 saw the 30th anniversary of a TV series that, in its own way, generated as much of a cult following as *Star Trek*, also 30 years old. *Dark Shadows* never had the same impact in the UK as it did in US so the appeal of this disc will remain elusive to many non-American readers. In celebration, there have been two discs released. One, on Rhino, contains the soundtracks from the two films that were made, but this Varèse disc is more enterprising and is a treasure trove of tracks taken either directly from the series or inspired by it. Various cover versions of Robert Cobert's "Quentin's Theme" are included and these, along with other tracks, particularly from The Charles Randolph Grean Sounde are all nostalgically cheesy with their electric organ and 'pop' arrangements. Some balance is maintained with previously unreleased extracts from Cobert's original scores and the inclusion of opening and closing voice-overs, radio commercials and a wonderfully yucky romantic duet between two of the cast add to the fun. Possibly this is strictly only for fans but the music is so much of its time that it should have wider appeal.   **DS**

The Fantasy Film Worlds of Irwin Allen Original Soundtracks.

GNP Crescendo Ⓔ GNPBX3009 (six discs: 58, 45, 34, 44, 43 and 78 minutes: ADD).
GNPD8044, "Lost in Space" (1965) Volume 1 – **John Williams:** Main Title. The Relcutant
Stowaway. Island in the Sky. The Hungry Sea. *GNPD8045*, "Lost in Space" (1966-8)
Volume 2 – **John Williams:** Main Title, Season 3. **Alexander Courage:** Wild Adventure. The
Great Vegetable Rebellion. **Joseph Mullendore:** The Haunted Lighthouse. *GNPD8046,*
"Voyage to the Bottom of the Sea" (1964-5) – **Paul Sawtell:** Main Title. Eleven Days to Zero.
Jerry Goldsmith: Jonah and the Whale. *GNPD8047,* "The Time Tunnel" (1966-7) – **John
Williams:** Main Title. Rendezvous with Yesterday. **George Duning:** The Death Merchant.
GNPD8048, "The Land of the Giants" (1968) – **John Williams:** Main Title, Seasons 1 and 2.
The Crash. **Alexander Courage:** The Crash. *GNPD8049* – Special Bonus Disc: Sound
Effects and Interviews.

Now that 1960s kitsch is back in vogue, doubtless fuelled by the need for low-budget cable and
satellite channels to fill their schedules with cheap programming, shows that we once thought forever
consigned to the happy oblivion of nostalgic reminiscence have been miraculously resurrected. The
once-derided figure of producer Irwin Allen has re-emerged into our televisual consciousness as a
giant in what the programme schedulers are trying to persuade us was a golden age of television.
True, the many and often hilarious weaknesses of these shows – their risible plots, wooden acting,
fake scenery and endless re-use of stock footage – only confirm the extraordinary and exploratory
status of their contemporary, Gene Roddenberry's original *Star Trek*, but at least Allen's over-
ambitious experiments provided audiences at the dawn of the space age with a regular diet of small-
screen Sci-Fi unsurpassed until our modern saturation of worthy-but-dull *Star Trek* spin-offs.

Like the shows, the music has also been dusted off and repackaged; unlike them, its attempts
at ambitious, genuinely involving dramatic writing are on the whole successful. But then, Allen
was never one to do anything by halves, so naturaly he hired the very best musical talent then
available in television. "Johnny" Williams scored the pilot for *Lost in Space* and four of the first
seven episodes, as well as providing the show with both of its distinctively quirky main titles.
Despite growing film commitments, Williams later contributed main titles for both *The Time
Tunnel* and *Land of the Giants*, as well as scoring their pilot episodes. Because of his later fame,
these early Williams scores would be of particular interest even if their intrinsic musical merit was
not as high as it is. The all-Williams *Lost in Space* disc (Vol. 1), containing as it does many
premonitions of his later, greater work – with much densely-textured writing in that now-familiar
idiom – is indeed far more interesting than some of the composer's contemporary movies
assignments, many of which, like the modish comedy *How to Steal a Million* (1966), now seem
rather dated.

Jerry Goldsmith's dark and brooding music for *Jonah and the Whale*, the second season opener
of *Voyage to the Bottom of the Sea* (Vol. 3), is grippingly dramatic, employing a characteristically
eclectic ensemble to produce music that is serious in intent and full of anxious tension.
Unfortunately, *Voyage to the Bottom of the Sea*, even if it aspired to more, never rose above the
level of light entertainment, and Goldsmith's sombre new theme was unsurprisingly deemed
inappropriate. His brief contribution represents the serious adult drama *Voyage* might have been;
Paul Sawtell's more upbeat "Seaview Theme" better defines what it actually was.

Alexander Courage, better known for his work on *Star Trek*, also did stints on *Lost in Space*
and *Land of the Giants*. For the famously silly third season episode of *Lost in Space*, *The Great
Vegetable Rebellion* (Vol. 2), he displays a sensitivity not reflected by the camp space comedy
being enacted on screen. As with *Trek*, Courage's music is always well-crafted, always listenable,
but not always memorable (the original *Trek* pilot, *The Cage*, stands out as a fine exception).
Contributions from Joseph Mullendore and George Duning to *Lost in Space* and *The Time
Tunnel* respectively are workmanlike and unexceptional.

GNP have surpassed themselves with their lavish presentation: copious notes in fully-
illustrated booklets accompany each disc, which are available separately or in a six-disc box set,
a real collector's item for nostalgia buffs. The sixth 'bonus' disc, a collection of interviews and
sound effects, is a must-have for devotees of Allen's shows, and quite the reverse for everyone else.
Musically, however, the John Williams *Lost in Space* (Vol. 1) perhaps rather predictably stands
out as the best single purchase. **MW**

François Truffaut Films
Les Aventures d'Antoine Doinel Original Soundtracks etc.

Milan Ⓔ 887 790 (38 minutes: ADD).
Georges Delerue: Les 400 Coups (1958). Antoine et Colette (1961). L'Amour en Fuite
(1978). **Antoine Duhamel:** Baisers Volés (1968). Domicile Conjugal (1970).

Les Passions Amoureuses Original Soundtracks etc.
Milan Ⓕ 887 974 (74 minutes: ADD).
Georges Delerue: Jules et Jim (1961). La Peau Douce (1963). Deux Anglaises et le Continent (1971). La Femme d'à-Coté (1981). **Maurice Jaubert:** L'Histoire d'Adèle H. (1975). L'Homme Qui Aim Ait les Femmes (1976).

Récits d'Apprentissage et d'Amour Original Soundtracks etc.
Milan Ⓕ 887 975 (56 minutes: ADD).
Maurice Le Roux: Les Mistons (1957). **Bernard Herrmann:** Fahrenheit 451 (1966). **Vivaldi** (arr. Duhamel): L'Enfant Sauvage (1969). **Georges Delerue:** La Nuit Américaine (1973). Le Dernier Métro (1980). **Maurice Jaubert:** L'Argent de Poche (1975). La Chambre Verte (1977).

Les Films Noirs Original Soundtracks etc.
Milan Ⓕ 887 976 (71 minutes: ADD).
Georges Delerue: Tirez sur le Pianiste (1959). Une Belle Fille Comme Moi (1972). Vivement Dimanche! (1983). **Bernard Herrmann:** La Marié Etait en Noir (1967). **Antoine Duhamel:** La Sirène du Mississipi (1968).

The late François Truffaut was one of the world's finest film makers; his subject was always the human condition – and it followed that the musical scores for his films were almost invariably intensely personal and intimate in tone. His favoured composers – Georges Delerue, Antoine Duhamel, Maurice Jaubert, and Bernard Herrmann – were all adept at reflecting the basic humanity intrinsic to Truffaut's vision. Milan Records have now laudably collected together themes and suites from all Truffaut's films, compiling four superb albums which are not only a tribute to the director's memory and talent, but stand as the finest ever collections of Gallic film music.

The first disc chronicles the saga of Antoine Doinel, the wayward lad introduced in Truffaut's first feature *Les 400 Coups*, and whose life adventures the director detailed through four other productions. From Georges Delerue's lilting and sometimes jazzy *Les 400 Coups* through Antoine Duhamel's perky and occasionally dramatic *Baisers Volés* to Alain Souchon's earthy vocal for *L'Amour en Fuite* the disc conjures fond memories of some of Truffaut's most personal, most searching films – the fictional Antoine surely being in many respects the director's *alter-ego*.

The following album brings together music from six of Truffaut's most heartfelt, if sometimes ironic tales of love. Georges Delerue claims the lion's share here, storming in via his raucous *à la cirque* main theme for *Jules et Jim* (we are also treated to Jeane Moreau's delicious vocal of *Le Tourbillon*), before offering the yearning melancholy of *La Peau Douce, Deux Anglaises et la Continent* and *La Femme D'a-Coté*, three of the composer's most profound scores. But Maurice Jaubert is also well represented, bringing a charming and restrained period ambience to *L'Histoire D'Adèle H* and a more celebratory flavour to *L'Homme Qui Aimait les Femmes*.

Third out of this magical hat is a compendium of films more difficult to categorize – but here is Georges Delerue's wonderfully mock-baroque music for *La Nuit Américaine* (*Day for Night*), and his pervasively mysterious score for *La Dernier Metro*, plus Bernard Herrmann's celebrated music from *Fahrenheit 451* (in a performance licensed from Decca with the composer conducting), and some arresting Vivaldi mandolin music utilized for *L'Enfant Sauvage*.

Last, but certainly not least, comes music for thrillers – *film noirs*. Delerue is again to the fore, from his early quirky *Tirez Sur le Pianiste*, with its irresistible honky-tonk piano, to the soundly dramatic *Vivement Dimanche!* – and Bernard Herrmann is well in evidence too – with *La Marié Etait en Noir* (in a suite arranged by Christopher Palmer and conducted by Elmer Bernstein), one of the most evocative of this composer's later scores.

It would be difficult to recommend any one of these discs over the others; all are excellent. Sound quality, despite the differing years of recording, is good, with only the "Main Title" music from Maurice Le Roux's *Les Mistons* of inferior quality (but at least it has been included for completists) and with the suite from *The Bride Wore Black* mastered at much too low a level, this despite the performance being a new digital recording! The entire set of four discs is highly recommended – to lovers of Truffaut's films, certainly – but more especially to aficionados of the very finest of French film music. **DW**

New review
Great British Film Music National Philharmonic Orchestra / Bernard Herrmann.
Decca Phase Four Ⓕ 448 954-2 (56 minutes: ADD). Recorded 1974-75.
William Walton: Richard III (1955). Escape Me Never (1935). **Constant Lambert:** Anna Karenina (1948). **Arnold Bax:** Oliver Twist (1948). **Arthur Benjamin:** An Ideal Husband (1947). **Ralph Vaughan Williams:** 49th Parallel (1941). **Arthur Bliss:** Things to Come (1936).

Herrmann's series of recordings for the Decca Phase Four label in the mid-1970s were a source of great joy for his many admirers, for the simple reason that so little of his music had previously been available. Now, of course, we are awash in it but one of the lesser known items from this period was an album called "Great British Film Music". It didn't contain any of Herrmann's own material, but was the result of his own love of English music and literature. It made for an interesting collection of pieces by some of the most illustrious names in British music – Bax, Bliss, Walton and Vaughan Williams – together with two scores from Constant Lambert and Arthur Benjamin. Herrmann's other recordings have undergone many re-issues in one form or another but this one was always something of a forgotten album and this is the first time it has been re-issued complete (the "Prelude" from *Richard III* actually comes from Herrmann's Shakespearian film music album but is no less welcome here). Although some of these tracks have turned up on other compilations it is good to have them all together, and, at last , we have Lambert's gorgeous "Suite" from *Anna Karenina* preserved on disc. This is a real gem of a score and sits well with the other better known works. The clarity and dynamic range of these Phase Four recordings is truly remarkable and the whole disc would be a joy from start to finish if it were not for the question of Herrmann's interpretation of these scores. The *Richard III* is painfully slow and the "March" from *Things to Come* sounds more like a funeral dirge. There may be a case for suggesting that the music benefits from letting it 'breathe'. With unfamiliar pieces, this is not a problem since the tempo of the actual soundtrack is unknown and the Vaughan Williams has more *gravitas* than usual because of this. But don't let such worries about the conducting put you off, because so much of this disc contains sterling music-making. On the packaging side, it is a pity that there is no mention made of Christopher Palmer's fine work in assembling and re-constructing some of these works and Decca have also seen fit not to reprint his original sleeve notes. **DS**

The Great Fantasy Adventure Album Cincinnati Pops Orchestra / Erich Kunzel.
Telarc Ⓕ CD80342 (66 minutes: DDD). Recorded 1993-4.
Miklós Rózsa: El Cid (1961). **John Williams:** Hook (1991). Jurassic Park (1993). **Michael Kamen:** Robin Hood, Prince of Thieves (1991). **Patrick Doyle:** Henry V (1989). **James Horner:** Willow (1988). The Rocketeer (1991). **Alan Silvestri:** The Abyss (1989). **Laurence Rosenthal:** Clash of the Titans (1981). **Bernard Herrmann:** The Seventh Voyage of Sinbad (1958). **Danny Elfman:** Beetlejuice (1988). **Jerry Goldsmith:** Total Recall (1990). **Mark Knopfler:** The Princess Bride (1987). **Lee Holdridge:** Wizards and Warriors (1983). **Basil Poledouris:** Conan the Barbarian (1982). The Hunt for Red October (1990). **Brad Fiedel:** The Terminator (1984).

This is a fun album done seriously. The 'fun' is served up in the form of Telarc's gimmicky sound effects: from the twanging of Robin Hood's bowstrings to the belching of a Tyrannosaurus Rex (mildly amusing on first acquaintance, rather wearing thereafter). The playing is another matter: Kunzel and his accomplished orchestra treat the listener to a generally higher standard of performance than such loose assemblages of miscellaneous film themes normally attract. There is a judicious mix of unfamiliar pieces among the better-known items, including a brief but previously unrecorded cue from *El Cid*, and Lee Holdridge's *Wizards and Warriors*. Both James Horner and Basil Poledouris should win new admirers as a result of this disc, whilst Brad Fiedel's unprepossessing *Terminator* theme provides the only moment when the silly noises actually enhance the music. The ubiquitous Spielberg/Williams partnership is represented by brief suites from *Hook* and *Jurassic Park* (the former disappointing; the latter, I suspect, served up only as an *hors d'oeuvre* for the T-Rex!). A new opportunity to hear Patrick Doyle's uplifting "Non nobis, Domine" prevents me from questioning the classification of *Henry V* as Fantasy/Adventure? Overall, a well-chosen selection of themes from (mostly) recent films, distinguished by the obvious commitment of the performers. **MW**

The Great Waltz Hollywood Bowl Orchestra / John Mauceri.
Philips Ⓕ 438 685-2 (74 minutes: DDD). Recorded 1993.
Dimitri Tiomkin: The Great Waltz (1938). **Richard Rodney Bennett:** Murder on the Orient Express (1974). **Bernard Herrmann:** The Snows of Kilimanjaro (1952). **Frederick Loewe:** Gigi (1958). **Miklós Rózsa:** Madame Bovary (1949). **Franz Waxman:** Hotel Berlin (1945). **Max Steiner:** Jezebel (1939). **Erich Wolfgang Korngold:** The Prince and the Pauper (1937). Also includes **Maurice Ravel:** La Valse. **Richard Strauss:** Der Rosenkavalier. **Sergei Prokofiev:** Cinderella. **Stephen Sondheim:** A Little Night Music. **Leonard Bernstein:** Candide.

An album of lush waltzes from the opera, ballet but mainly the movies is a nice idea, especially one that includes an intriguing number of pieces that are new to CD. Particularly enjoyable are Dimitri Tiomkin's flamboyant reworkings of Johann Strauss for MGM's lavish film 'biography', *The Great Waltz*, the selection of evocative "Café Waltzes" from *Hotel Berlin*, in which Franz Waxman recalls the salons of his homeland in happier times, and – receiving its first recording for some years – Rózsa's brilliant set-piece from *Madame Bovary*, a steadily accelerating waltz that mirrors to thrilling effect Emma Bovary's exhilaration as she savours the high romance for which she's been yearning. The other waltzes are more familiar, but it's always a pleasure to hear Steiner's sumptuous waltz from *Jezebel*, Herrmann's wistful "Memory Waltz" for *The Snows of Kilimanjaro* and Richard Rodney Bennett's affectionate concerto-style pastiche from *Murder on the Orient Express*. **RS**

A History of Hitchcock, Volumes 1 and 2 **City of Prague Philharmonic Orchestra / Paul Bateman**.
Silva Screen Ⓟ FILMCD137/159 (two discs: 64 and 60 minutes: DDD). Recorded 1993 and 1994.
FILMCD137, "Dial M for Murder" – **Gounod:** Marche funèbre d'une marionette (The Alfred Hitchcock Theme). **Franz Waxman:** Rebecca (1940). Suspicion (1941). **Miklós Rózsa:** Spellbound (1945). **Richard Addinsell:** Under Capricorn (1949). **Dimitri Tiomkin:** Dial M for Murder (1954). **Bernard Herrmann:** Marnie (1964). North By Northwest (1959). Psycho (1960). Vertigo (1958). **Maurice Jarre:** Topaz (1969). **Ron Goodwin:** Frenzy (1972).
FILMCD159, "To Catch a Thief" – **Lyn Murray:** To Catch a Thief (1955). **Jack Beaver:** The Thirty-Nine Steps (1935). **Charles Williams:** The Lady Vanishes (1938). **Hugo Friedhofer:** Lifeboat (1944). **David Buttolph:** Rope (1948). **Leighton Lucas:** Stage Fright (1950). **Dimitri Tiomkin:** Strangers on a Train (1951). **Franz Waxman:** Rear Window (1954). **Bernard Herrmann:** The Trouble with Harry (1955). Vertigo (1958). North By Northwest (1959). Torn Curtain (1966). **John Williams:** Family Plot (1976).

Such an obvious idea you might think: a musical history of Alfred Hitchcock, with suites and themes from the majority of his movies. Not so. Apart from an early Varèse Sarabande CD which included a handful of themes, it has taken the enterprising British label Silva Screen to fully realize this exciting project, even if all the recordings were made in Prague. Some of this orchestra's earlier recordings were somewhat hesitant, a fact that is hardly surprising given that they were totally unfamiliar with film music. Silva's perseverance has finally paid off however: with these recordings the orchestra really comes up trumps (their performances rival – or surpass – the RPO under Elmer Bernstein in a similarly structured collection of Bernard Herrmann's scores – see Herrmann). Before Herrmann, there were Waxman and Tiomkin. Volume 1 has a spirited rendition of Tiomkin's *Dial M for Murder*, a lengthy suite from Waxman's *Rebecca* and his "Prelude" from *Suspicion*. Ron Goodwin's *Frenzy* (which replaced a rejected Henry Mancini score) is also well served. The real revelations here, however, are Paul Bateman's definitive interpretations of Bernard Herrmann's Hitchcock scores. His versions – particularly of *North By Northwest* and *Psycho* – are much nearer to the film versions than even Herrmann's own recordings. (Not that it necessarily matters if a performance differs from the film – only that, in the case of Hitchcock, his films are so familiar and popular that it is certainly an advantage to be pretty close.) Volume 2 begins with a very underrated film – and score – *To Catch a Thief*. Lyn Murray's music almost sounds Herrmannesque in places, and this before Herrmann ever wrote a note for Hitch! For lovers of British film music, there are some great vintage scores here, including Jack Beaver's *Thirty-Nine Steps* and Charles Williams's *The Lady Vanishes*, not forgetting Leighton Lucas's *Stage Fright* (Lucas wrote several other fine scores, including *Ice Cold in Alex*, 1958, and *The Dam Busters*, 1955. It's about time his music was re-evaluated). Additionally, there is another cue from *Vertigo* and the delightful "Conversation Piece" – for the scene when Eva Marie Saint and Cary Grant make small talk in the dining car of the 'Twentieth Century' train – from *North By Northwest*. Silva Screen have been recording in Prague for several years now, and there are many more recordings in the pipeline. As these discs represent their best efforts so far, we can only wait with baited breath for more goodies.   **JW**

New review
Hollywood '95 Royal Scottish National Orchestra / Joel McNeely.
Varèse Sarabande Ⓟ VSD5671 (52 minutes: DDD).
Elliot Goldenthal: Batman Forever. **James Horner:** Apollo 13. Casper. Braveheart. **Alan Silvestri:** Judge Dredd. **Jerry Goldsmith:** Judge Dredd – trailer music. First Knight. **James Newton Howard:** Waterworld. **Miklós Rózsa:** That Hamilton Woman (1941).

The first of Joel McNeely's yearly round ups of blockbuster film music, "Hollywood '94" (VSD5531), was strong on repertoire – *Schindler's List*, *The Age of Innocence*, *The Shawshank Redemption* among others – but let down by some routine playing from the Seattle Symphony Orchestra. In 1995, Varèse Sarabande visited Glasgow with appreciably better results: the RSNO are enthusiastic collaborators, and McNeely has little trouble in coaxing from them a vivid performance of some of the year's most prominent film scores. Pride of place goes to Elliot Goldenthal's refreshingly insane *Batman Forever* suite, a characteristic piece, even if not this composer's best work. Ever in demand, James Horner scored three of 1995's biggest movies: these selections, which demonstrate the attractive melodic appeal and lush textures of his music, make the reasons for his popularity self-evident. *Judge Dredd* had two composers: Jerry Goldsmith was forced to pull out due to a scheduling clash after providing some boisterous trailer music which McNeely and the Scots breeze through in under 50 seconds; Alan Silvestri's full score seemed diffuse and incoherent, but distilled into a taut five-minute suite its weaknesses are almost forgiven. Goldsmith's other work is represented by his martial *First Knight* – although not included here is the theme he lifted from the opening of Vaughan Williams's Sixth Symphony. James Newton Howard landed the biggest assignment of the year, and produced something surprisingly attractive from the shipwreck that was *Waterworld*. To conclude this enjoyable survey, Miklós Rózsa, who died in August 1995, is remembered with a sensitive rendition of the "Love Theme" from the 1941 Laurence Olivier/Vivien Leigh potboiler, *That Hamilton Woman* (known in the UK by the more genteel title *Lady Hamilton*).   **MW**

Hollywood Dreams Hollywood Bowl Orchestra / John Mauceri.
    Philips Ⓟ 432 109-2 (76 minutes: DDD). Recorded 1991.
    Richard Rodgers (arr. Newman): Carousel (1956). **Max Steiner:** Gone with the Wind (1939). **Alfred Newman:** How to Marry a Millionaire (1953). **Franz Waxman:** A Place in the Sun (1951). **Leonard Bernstein:** On the Waterfront (1954). **Harold Arlen** (arr. Stothart): The Wizard of Oz (1939). **Erich Wolfgang Korngold:** The Adventures of Robin Hood (1938). **Michael Gore:** Defending Your Life (1991). **John Barry:** Dances with Wolves (1990). **John Williams:** E.T. (1982). Also includes **Arnold Schoenberg:** Fanfare for the Hollywood Bowl. **Igor Stravinsky:** Firebird Suite. **Sergei Prokofiev:** Semyon Kotko.
Hollywood Nightmares [a]Stephen Hough (pf); Hollywood Bowl Orchestra / John Mauceri.
    Philips Ⓟ 442 425-2 (72 minutes: DDD). Recorded 1993.
    Domenico Savino/William Perry: The Phantom of the Opera (1925). **Max Steiner:** King Kong (1933). **John Williams:** Jurassic Park (1993). Dracula (1979). **Bernard Herrmann:** Vertigo (1958). **Miklós Rózsa:** Spellbound[a] (1945). **John Barry:** Body Heat (1981). **Franz Waxman:** Sunset Boulevard (1950). Dr Jekyll and Mr Hyde (1941). **Jerry Goldsmith:** The Omen (1976). Also includes **Igor Stravinsky:** The Rite of Spring.

"Hollywood Dreams" is an extremely attractive programme of excerpts from several Hollywood classics, plus music by some of the distinguished emigrés who sought refuge in the film capital during the Second World War. Much of the material will be familiar from the superb recordings made by Charles Gerhardt for RCA's Classic Film Scores series, but Mauceri's readings are just as idiomatic and in some cases (as in the opening to *Gone with the Wind*) are actually an improvement. The disc's chief pleasures, however, derive from the rarely recorded titles like Bernstein's blossoming love theme from *On the Waterfront*, Alfred Newman's blazing arrangement of the "Carousel Waltz" and, most cherishable of all, the 11-minute suite of Herbert Stothart's incidental music from *The Wizard of Oz*; its nostalgic impact and authenticity heightened by the knowledge that the original score was recorded on the same MGM sound stage some 50 years earlier.

    The companion volume, "Hollywood Nightmares", makes for an entertaining selection of nerve-jangling music from movies that deal with various manifestations of horror, from giant monsters and diabolical intervention to less visible psychological disturbances, executed with Mauceri's customary flair. Apart from the well-respected thrills and chills of *The Omen, Vertigo* and *Dracula*, the chief delights here are the bold, dramatic "Overture" that Steiner wrote specifically for the première of *King Kong*, Rózsa's sweepingly romantic *Spellbound Concerto* (a beautifully shaded performance led by a fluent contribution from pianist Stephen Hough that fully deserves the "Bravo!" expressed by the composer as the music fades away), and the two compelling Waxman suites from *Dr Jekyll and Mr Hyde* and *Sunset Boulevard*, whose lush but appropriately *noir*-ish acerbity clearly influenced David Cullen's superb orchestrations for the current Lloyd Webber stage hit.   **RS**

New review
Horror! Westminster Philharmonic Orchestra / Kenneth Alwyn.
    Silva Screen Ⓟ FILMCD175 (45 minutes: DDD).
    Gerard Schurmann: Horrors of the Black Museum (1959). Konga (1961). **Humphrey Searle:** The Haunting (1963). The Abominable Snowman (1957). **Buxton Orr:** Corridors of Blood (1958). Fiend Without a Face (1957). **Clifton Parker:** Night of the Demon (1957). **Paul Ferris:** Witchfinder General (1968). **Carlo Martelli:** The Curse of the Mummy's Tomb (1964). **James Bernard:** The Devil Rides Out (1968). **Benjamin Frankel:** The Curse of the Werewolf (1961).

From Franz Waxman's groundbreaking *Bride of Frankenstein* (1935) to more recent experimental scores like Christopher Young's avant-garde *The Vagrant* (1992), horror movies have given film composers an opportunity to stretch the boundaries of their art not often available in more mainstream assignments. The British cinema, just before its fatal decline into an interminable cycle of *Carry On* films, produced a whole crop of imaginative low budget horror movies in the 1950s and early 1960s, the scores for several of which have been enterprisingly resurrected by Silva Screen. Undoubtedly the pick of this thrillingly spine-tingling compilation is Benjamin Frankel's predominantly serial score for Hammer's *The Curse of the Werewolf*, which despite its ferocious climax also contains a sprightly and charming "Pastorale". In other places, too, the luridly atonal accompaniment to things that go bump in the night is softened: Buxton Orr's "Love Theme" from *Fiend Without a Face* or the folksong-like "Romanza" from Paul Ferris's *Witchfinder General*. Most of the selections are extremely short, although as the choice of music and the sequencing of tracks avoids highlighting any one item over another, the disc can be usefully experienced as a whole, a single symphony of the macabre. The Westminster Philharmonic negotiate some tricky twists and turns with confidence under Alwyn's direction; the recording is warm and spacious, and the notes are first-rate.   **MW**

New review
The Italian Horror Films Collection Original Soundtracks.
DRG Ⓟ 32903 (76 minutes: AAD).
Marco Werba: Dario's Theme. **Bruno Nicolai:** Il Trono di Fuoco (1970). **Giorgio Gaslini:** La Notte dei Diavoli (1972). Profondo Rosso (1975). **Franco Bixio/Fabio Frizzi/Vince Tempera:** 7 Note in Nero (1977). **Carlo Savina:** La Cripta e l'Incubo (1964). **Gianni Ferrio:** L'Isola Misteriosa e il Capitano Nemo (1973). **Piero Piccioni:** Il Monaco (1972). **Gino Marinuzzi, Jr:** Terrore Nello Spazio (1965). **Riz Ortolani:** Passi di Morte Perduti Nel Buio (1976).

Music from Italian Westerns has a great reputation and is highly cherishable but the same cannot be said for music from Italian horror films. Nevertheless, this disc should be welcomed since it offers an interesting range of styles which, while not providing any great revelations with previously undiscovered gems, is never less than absorbing listening. Bruno Nicolai's *Il Trono di Fuoco* has an arresting "Main Title" but a rather sombre incidental score; Giorgio Gaslini's nine-minute suite from *La Notte dei Diavoli* is lively; Carlo Savina's *La Cripta e l'Incubo* is effectively grim, while the Gianni Ferrio piece has an attractive theme that makes you regret that more of the score wasn't included. The disc is mostly mood music as befits the subject matter, but there is certainly variety here and it offers the listener a good overview of Italian horror film music without including any tracks by Goblin, the rock group who, at one time, seemed to be scoring every other film.   **DS**

New review
Jacques Tati Films Original Soundtracks.
Auvidis Travelling mono Ⓟ K1504 (43 minutes: ADD). Includes dialogue and sound effects. **Jean Yatove:** Jour de Fête (1947) **Franck Barcellini/Alain Romans:** Mon Oncle (1958). **Alain Romans:** Les Vacances de Monsieur Hulot (1953). **Francis Lemarque:** Playtime (1967).

There is an inherent daftness about this release that I suspect Tati himself would have enjoyed. Given that so much of his inspired humour came from the observation of the foibles of other people and that it is largely visual in nature, a disc containing music, dialogue and sound effects seems somewhat perverse. It's almost like having a CD of Marcel Marceau routines. Without having seen these films, the unwary listener will find most of this completely bewildering (music only tracks from all four films have been released on a French PolyGram disc). But, it has to be said, if you are a fan of these films, then this is a wholly delightful purchase. The humour was mostly visual, but the disc makes you realize how important sound was to Tati. Small sound effects together with the original music creates instant images from many classic sequences – even brief dialogue exchanges in French with bits of English thrown in remind you that Tati was interested in the way people spoke, not in what they actually said. It would not be possible to recommend this disc to anyone not interested in the films, but the nostalgic spell that it weaves makes it hard to resist for admirers.   **DS**

New review
Monstrous Movie Music Cracow Radio Symphony Orchestra / Masatoshi Mitsumoto.
Monstrous Movie Music Ⓟ MMM1950/1 (two discs: 69 and 59 minutes: DDD). Recorded 1995.
MMM1950 – **Herman Stein/Heinz Roemheld:** The Mole People (1956). **Bronislau Kaper:** Them! (1954). **Herman Stein/Irving Gertz/Henry Mancini:** It Came from Outer Space (1953). **Mischa Bakaleinikoff:** It Came from Beneath the Sea (1955). *MMM1951* – **Herman Stein/Henry Mancini:** Tarantula (1955). **David Buttolph:** The Beast from 20,000 Fathoms (1953). **Irving Gertz:** The Monolith Monsters (1957). **Angelo Francesco Lavagnino:** Gorgo (1960).

That these two discs represent the exhaustive labours of a production team very much in love with their source material is obvious before you even play them. Both contain hefty booklets with highly detailed notes on the films, the scores and their composers, plus lots of incidental information about genre music in general. Most of the films are classics of the genre and would appear in any enthusiast's top-ten list, but none of the scores are ever likely to be issued as original soundtrack recordings and so we should offer thanks to producer David Schechter for starting this series. Apart from *The Mole People* and *The Monolith Monsters*, all the scores are represented by suites of around 20 minutes. Using close-miking techniques, Schecter has taken his Polish orchestra and Japanese conductor and extracted a sound that is remarkably faithful to that of a Hollywood studio in the 1950s. The performances are good, too, with lots of energy and vigour. But what of the music? The films may be classics but the scores have never merited much attention until now, and on the evidence of these discs, I would suggest that there is only one that retains its impact after the music has stopped: Bronislau Kaper's *Them!* This is a splendidly bustling score that never rests for a moment and contains many exciting passages that demand a second listen. It is crowned by the kinetic "Ant Fugue", a piece written for the film but subsequently dropped, that, within its three-and-a-half minutes, conveys all the relentless purposeful energy that is the world of the ant. The other scores all have points of interest but all share the same basic features that single them out as 'monster movie' music – they are threatening and suspenseful and contain much destructive monster-on-the-loose histrionics. The energy level is always high and so an onslaught of this type of music is quite tiring after a while. Not that there aren't pleasures en route. The opening of *It Came from Outer Space* is highly evocative with excellent use of the theremin; *It Came from Beneath the Sea* has a lot of solid, gutsy brass writing; *Tarantula* has a thumpingly good "Main Title"; *The Beast from 20,000 Fathoms* conjures up mayhem in Manhattan in its finale with great force, and *Gorgo* provides a fresh dynamic sound with an accordion giving a nautical edge to the music. Within the booklet notes, there is mention of recordings from *This Island Earth* and *The Deadly Mantis* as future projects. If they are of the same standard, then one can only welcome them with open claws!　　**DS**

Music for Stage and Screen [a]Burgess Meredith (narrator); [b]Tim Morrison (trumpet); **Boston Pops Orchestra / John Williams**.
Sony Classical Ⓕ SK64147 (69 minutes: DDD)
Aaron Copland: The Red Pony (1949). Quiet City[b]. **John Williams:** Born on the Fourth of July (1989)[b]. The Reivers (1969)[a].

"Those days were like an endless summer, stored with pleasure in my memory", recalls the narrator of William Faulkner's *The Reivers*. The two main items on this disc evoke that warm American summer, when the broad horizons of a young country seemed limitless in their possibilites. Copland's jaunty *Red Pony* suite positively skips along towards its "Happy Ending". Williams's orchestra attack the music with gusto: you can almost smell the greasepaint and sawdust during the "Circus March". The extended suite with narration from *The Reivers* reveals a side to the film composer often overshadowed by his bigger box-office assignments. Burgess Meredith narrates, as he did for the original film: his avuncular, occasionally mischievous persona lends itself perfectly to this nostalgic tale. The scoring is subtle and witty, with many refinements on the original soundtrack version: a chugging tuba depicts grandfather's automobile (the first in town); a banjo accompanies the ebullient drive across country; the horse-race *scherzo* seems to encapsulate in miniature the whole of Williams's artistry. If *The Red Pony* and *The Reivers* embody the optimism of America's past, then the suite from *Born on the Fourth of July* represents the flip side of that country's aspirations. It is a pastoral elegy for the death of the American dream in the dark jungles of Vietnam. In both this and Copland's *Quiet City*, Tim Morrison's eloquent trumpet speaks with a sadder, more reflective voice. This thoroughly delightful album demonstrates that, in the person of John Williams, the rare breed of composer/conductor is not yet extinct.　　**MW**

New review
The Paradine Case Hollywood Piano Concertos. **David Buechner** (pf); **New Zealand Symphony Orchestra / James Sedares**.
Koch International Classics Ⓕ 37225-2 (55 minutes: DDD).
Franz Waxman: Rhapsody for Piano and Orchestra (from *The Paradine Case*, 1947). The Charm Bracelet (1947). **Bernard Herrmann:** Concerto Macabre for Piano and Orchestra (from *Hangover Square*, 1944). Prelude for Piano (1935). **Alex North:** Concerto for Piano and Orchestra with Trumpet Obligato (1939/1957).

The perfect crossover disc! Where does movie music end and classical composition begin? Although conceived for concert performance, Franz Waxman's *Rhapsody* never tries to hide its cinematic roots (Hitchcock's 1947 overripe courtroom melodrama *The Paradine Case*); this is good old-fashioned movie music – a splendidly romantic wallow utilizing the quasi-concerto style to devastating effect; a three-handkerchief tear-jerker of a piece! Previous recordings of this work have benefited from good performances but have been lacking in sound quality; happily here we are provided with an outstanding reading and superb sonics. Bernard Herrmann's *Concerto Macabre* is much sterner stuff – uncompromising in its bleak austerity – but still damned dramatic. The film *Hangover Square* told the woeful tale of a homicidal composer driven to murder whenever hearing discords: this powerfully oppressive concerto was his master opus – the music virtually dripping with despair, with mania, with blood ... With only minor adjustment, Herrmann was able to convert the work into an extraordinary concert piece; this is its third recording – and whilst its previous outing (on RCA GD80707) with Joaquin Achucarro as soloist and Charles Gerhardt as conductor might remain the definitive performance, the present recording is still technically dazzling.

Koch International confidently tell us this performance of the Alex North concerto is a world première recording – but seasoned film music buffs will know this concerto had an outing on record 40 years ago under Joseph Gershenson's baton with André Previn as soloist, with the work foisted on the public under the guise of being the music to the film *Four Girls in Town* (1956 – the movie did sport a good deal of the concerto as the basis for its score). The handling here is considerably more relaxed and reserved in tempi than the Gershenson version, but all to good effect – this is a superb reading: easy, jazzy, dramatic and winning.

If soloist David Buechner excels in the three concertos he truly comes into his own with Franz Waxman's simple but brilliant miniatures for solo piano *The Charm Bracelet*; Buechner's facility seems stunning (on a par with the noted Eric Parkin who previously recorded these pieces), the virtuosity carried over for Bernard Herrmann's brief but pithy *Prelude*, dating from 1935 but already displaying all the vigour and venom which was to permeate much of the composer's subsequent work. Buechner is ably abetted by conductor James Sedares and the New Zealand Symphony Orchestra in seamless performances presented in flawless sound. An outstanding disc.   **DW**

The Red Shoes Classic British Film Music. **Philharmonia Orchestra / Kenneth Alwyn.**
Silva Screen Ⓜ FILMCD713 (57 minutes: DDD). Recorded 1990.
Ralph Vaughan Williams: Coastal Command (1942). **Brian Easdale:** The Red Shoes (1948).
Gerard Schurmann: Attack and Celebration. **Sir Arthur Bliss:** Conquest of the Air (1936).

An impressive array of composers supplied scores for British films from the mid-1930s, and Vaughan Williams was especially enthusiastic about the challenges the medium had to offer. His music for *Coastal Command* is a rugged reflection of the harsh conditions in which the flying-boat patrols operated during the Second World War, and in many ways pre-echoes the austerity of his Sixth Symphony. Sir Arthur Bliss scored *Conquest of the Air* a year after his remarkable début on *Things to Come*, and although this music is rather more lightweight, the suite's six brief movements are no less expertly crafted and provide some very attractive moments (namely the sunny waltz "Gliding", and "Stunting" with its rip-roaring brass figures), whilst Gerard Schurmann's *Attack and Celebration* is a powerfully heroic concert piece adapted from his music for *Attack on the Iron Coast* (1967) and *The Two-Headed Spy* (1958). The undoubted highlight though is Brian Easdale's ravishing ballet for one of the most fondly-regarded of all British films, *The Red Shoes*, a skilful and quite magical combination of elements from Stravinsky and Prokofiev that takes on an identity all its own.   **RS**

New review

Star Trek, Volumes 1-3 (1966-67). **Original Soundtracks / Alexander Courage, Gerald Fried, Sol Kaplan.**
GNP Crescendo Ⓕ GNPBX3006 (3 discs, also available separately: 43, 53 and 47 minutes: ADD).
GNPD8006 – **Alexander Courage:** The Cage. Where No Man Has Gone Before.
GNPD8025 – **Sol Kaplan:** The Doomsday Machine. **Gerald Fried:** Amok Time.
GNPD8030 – **Fried:** Shore Leave. **Courage:** The Naked Time.
Star Trek – music from selected episodes of the original TV series (1966-8). **Royal Philharmonic Orchestra / Fred Steiner.**
Varèse Sarabande Ⓕ VSD5762-2 (two discs, also available separately: 41 and 42 minutes: ADD). Recorded 1985-6.
VCD47235–**Fred Steiner:** The Corbomite Maneuver. Charlie X. Mudd's Women. **Sol Kaplan:** The Doomsday Machine. *VCD47240*–**Steiner:** By Any Other Name. Mirror, Mirror. **Jerry Fielding:** The Trouble With Tribbles. **George Duning:** The Empath.
Star Trek: The Next Generation, Volumes 1-3 (1987, 1990-92). **Original Soundtracks / Dennis McCarthy, Ron Jones.**
GNP Crescendo Ⓕ GNPBX3007 (three discs, also available separately: 36, 47 and 46 minutes: DDD).
GNPD8012 – **Dennis McCarthy:** Encounter at Farpoint. *GNPD8026* – **Ron Jones:** The Best of Both Worlds, Parts 1 and 2. *GNPD8031* – **McCarthy:** Yesterday's Enterprise. Unification 1 and 2. Hollow Pursuits.

Rescued from an obscure corner of Paramount Studios, after languishing in obscurity for 20 years, and lovingly remastered by GNP, the original *Star Trek* soundtracks play like a library of motifs and themes from the series. Here is the original version of Alexander Courage's "Main Title", the threatening two-note 'danger in space' motif from Sol Kaplan's *Doomsday Machine*, and the perennial 'fight' music – used whenever Kirk got into a sticky situation and had the front of his shirt ripped – which originally appeared in Gerald Fried's *Amok Time*. Volume 1 is the most interesting musically, with Courage's experimental and highly-listenable score for *The Cage*. The remaining two volumes consist mainly of a series of generally very brief cues written for a small ensemble, but the strength of the themes and the dramatic writing is always compelling. All three discs will be of interest to musically-inclined fans of the series, although Volume 1 stands out as a clear recommendation. Booklet notes and presentation are characteristically excellent.

Aside from a brief extract from *The Doomsday Machine*, Fred Steiner's re-recordings made in the 1980s and now reissued on two Varèse Sarabande CDs, do not overlap with GNP's enterprising selection. Of course, when Steiner recorded these suites the spectacular resurrection of the *Star Trek* phenomenon was just beginning, its multiple reincarnations still some years in the future, as was the belated discovery of the original soundtracks. Between them, the Varèse and GNP sets give *aficionados* a pretty comprehensive selection of the themes and *leitmotifs* used with increasing frequencing as the show's budget was steadily reduced before it was finally axed. Just listen, for example, to Steiner's own score for *Charlie X* to hear several familiar motifs that were to crop up again and again. Not that these scores function simply as a 'theme library': they all have their own character and work well as self-contained suites, as the RPO's smooth, designedly symphonic performance and the sequencing of short cues into longer tracks emphasizes. Inevitably, perhaps, Steiner has chosen to conduct several of his own scores, many of which are founded on short, spiky ostinatos, with plenty of added dynamic contrast – try *Mirror, Mirror*, for example (another one of *those* themes). The standout item, however, is Jerry Fielding's modern but lighthearted music for one of classic *Trek*'s most fondly-remembered episodes, *The Trouble With Tribbles*, a frenetic rough and tumble *scherzo* that incidentally features the only theme ever written for Scotty!

Unlike its original low-budget incarnation, *Star Trek: The Next Generation* could afford to commission new scores for each and all of its 178 episodes. Unexpectedly, perhaps, this turns out to be a weakness: the recurring library of themes made for musical continuity in the original series; here much of the music seems deliberately unmemorable. Dennis McCarthy was the principal composer, with over half the entire run being scored by him. His approach throughout – exemplified by the music available here – was consistently understated, bordering on the bland. McCarthy favours diffuse textures, consisting typically of unison strings supported by synthesizer, with the occasional muted French horn left to carry the theme (his work on the *Star Trek* spin-offs *Deep Space Nine* and *Voyager* continue this trend). Dramatic sequences are handled with rhythmic chordal passages, although with little in the way of dynamic contrast, nothing in McCarthy's music ever quite sets the pulse racing. The double episode scored by Ron Jones is in quite a different mould: Captain Picard's near-disastrous encounter with the machine-like Borg affords Jones ample opportunity to be dramatic. Mixing synthesizers with his orchestra, *The Best of Both Worlds* is dynamic and exciting, featuring the kind of loud, *Star Wars*-inspired battle music which should grace any self-respecting space adventure. Once again, GNP's presentation is of a high standard. **MW**

True Grit Music from the Films of John Wayne **City of Prague Philharmonic Orchestra / Paul Bateman**.
Silva Screen Ⓟ FILMCD153 (65 minutes: DDD). Recorded 1994.
Richard Hageman: Stagecoach (1939). She Wore a Yellow Ribbon (1949).
Victor Young: The Quiet Man (1952). **Dimitri Tiomkin:**
The High and the Mighty (1954). The Alamo (1960).
Max Steiner: The Searchers (1956). **Alfred Newman:** How the West Was Won (1962).
Paul Anka: The Longest Day (1962). **Jerry Goldsmith:**
In Harm's Way (1965). **Elmer Bernstein:** True Grit (1969).
John Williams: The Cowboys (1972).

This terrific CD is not just a convenient reminder of many of the Duke's best known movies but also a very distinguished round-up of Hollywood's most famous musical greats. The star's films certainly contained some marvellous music and the robustly recorded excerpts here make for rousing entertainment. Amongst the highlights are Alfred Newman's stirring "Main Title" from *How the West Was Won*, the suite from the Oscar-winning *Stagecoach* (film scoring at its most elementary but extremely effective nonetheless), John Williams's bracing concert overture for *The Cowboys*, Goldsmith's dynamic *In Harm's Way* and Tiomkin's ever-haunting whistling theme from *The High and the Mighty*. **RS**

New review
Wanted Dead or Alive Original Soundtracks.
CAM Ⓟ CVS900-020 (70 minutes: ADD)
Ennio Morricone: Duello Nel Texas (1962). La Banda J&S – Cronaca Criminale del Far-West (1972). **Angelo Francesco Lavagnino:** 5,000 Dollari Sull'Asso (1964). **Piero Piccioni:** Minnesota Clay (1965). **Gianni Ferrio:** Un Dollaro Bucato (1965). Vivo o Preferibilmente

Morti (1969). **Benedetto Ghiglia:** Adios Gringo (1965). **Stelvio Cipriani:** The Bounty Killer (1966). Un Uomo, un Cavallo, una Pistola (1967). **Francesco de Masi:** Arizona Colt (1966). Quella Sporca Storia Nel West (1968). **Carlo Rustichelli:** Dio Perdona ... Io No! (1967). **Bruno Nicolai:** Corri, Uomo Corri (1968). **Domenico Colarossi:** All'Ultimo Sangue (1968). **Luis Bacalov:** Il Prezzo del Potere (1969). **Daniele Patucchi:** Los Amigos (1973).

This is an absolute corker of a disc and a must-have for anyone with any interest in traditional 'Spaghetti' Western music. What is really refreshing about this collection is that while Ennio Morricone is the only composer's name on the front of the album, he is only represented by two films, neither of which are well known and one of which is *Duello Nel Texas* from 1962 – his first Western score! Music from the really famous Spaghetti Westerns are so well covered on numerous other compilations that it is a relief not to find them here. However, all the classic names associated with the genre are here and the selections are all good ones. Themes and suites cover all the trademarks of this type of score: choirs, solo trumpets, harmonicas, galloping snare drums, daft songs and mucho electric guitar. The compiler has chosen well for there isn't a dud track to be found. There are many favourites, but top marks go to Stelvio Cipriani's *Un Uomo, un Cavallo, una Pistola*, which has a great tune plus all the whistles, bells, whips and chimes that you could want. Sound quality is variable and the packaging is uninspired but this is great stuff from an era of energetic and inventive film scoring that has sadly passed on. **DS**

The Young Indiana Jones Chronicles, Volumes 1-4 (1992-4) **Original Soundtracks,** with the **Munich Symphony Orchestra; Munich Philharmonic Film Orchestra; West Australian Philharmonic Orchestra / Laurence Rosenthal, Joel McNeely, Charles Ketcham.**
Varèse Sarabande Ⓟ VSD5381/91/401/421 (four discs: 76, 76, 70 and 76 minutes: DDD).
VSD5381 – **Laurence Rosenthal:** Main Title. Peking 1910. Barcelona 1917. **Joel McNeely:** Verdun 1916. Paris 1916. *VSD5391* – **Rosenthal:** Main Title. Vienna 1908. British East Africa 1909. **McNeely:** German East Africa 1916/The Congo 1917. London 1916. *VSD5401* – **McNeely:** Indiana Jones and the Scandal of 1920. Indiana Jones and the Mystery of the Blues. **Rosenthal:** Princeton 1916. *VSD5421* – **Rosenthal:** Ireland 1916. Northern Italy 1918. **McNeely:** Indiana Jones and the Phantom Train of Doom.

Like his mature big-screen counterpart, Young Indy's television adventures are accompanied by lavish wall-to-wall music. With Yoda-like wisdom, producer George Lucas shared most of the scoring assignments between just two composers – Laurence Rosenthal and Joel McNeely – and *their* efforts have been chronicled by Varèse Sarabande on four highly impressive releases.

Laurence Rosenthal is the veteran, whose long experience of musical theatre, film and television is quite apparent in these well-crafted and witty scores. Rosenthal's dotted-rhythm "Main Title" theme for the series is a jaunty juvenile equivalent of Williams's grand *Raiders* march. He uses this "Main Title" in much the same way as in the big screen adventures, to act as Indy's theme whenever he is doing something exciting or heroic. Where appropriate, Rosenthal adds suitable 'ethnic' colouring: Chinese (Volume 1), Viennese (Volume 2) or Irish (Volume 4). Sometimes, as in *Peking 1910*, the effect is so delicate and low-key as to be almost completely overshadowed by the other items on the disc. Perhaps the finest example is *Barcelona 1917*, in which Rosenthal delightfully weaves quotes from Rimsky-Korsakov's *Scheherazade* (Russian) into the heavily Spanish-tinged underscore. As he says in the booklet-notes, "the composer is given seeming unlimited licence to have fun". Rosenthal is a craftsman who has refined his abilities and style over a period of years; Joel McNeely is a new and rising star. If McNeely doesn't quite demonstrate a cohesive overall approach to match Rosenthal's efforts, he more than compensates with unbounded energy and enthusiasm. McNeely draws much of his inspiration for these scores from outside sources, but he is as skilful at adapting as he is at inventing anew. Volume 3 features two foot-tappingly enjoyable arrangements of Gershwin and New Orleans jazz respectively. Although containing a smaller proportion of original music, they are nevertheless two of his most memorable contributions to the series (McNeely received an Emmy Award for *The Scandal of 1920*). The episode *London 1916* (Volume 2) has an exquisite love theme which sounds like a cross between Holst's "I Vow to Thee, My Country" melody and Vaughan Williams's *Lark Ascending*. Volume 4's grandiose centrepiece, *The Phantom Train of Doom*, is predominantly John Williams-inspired – quite blatant borrowings from *Hook* and *Raiders* especially – with some Korngold thrown in for good measure. What McNeely fashions from all these diverse influences, however, indicates that he may very well live up to his promise of being one of the most talented composers to have emerged in Hollywood in recent years. With unusually generous playing times, booklet-notes by the composers, and a great deal of top-quality music, these CD *Chronicles* carry their own recommendation. **MW**

Record companies and distributors

Entries are listed as follows: **Record company** or **Label** – UK Distributor.

A&M PolyGram

Argo PolyGram

Arista BMG Conifer

Auvidis Harmonia Mundi

Cabin Fever Silva Productions

Cappricio Target

Chandos Chandos

Charisma EMI

Cloud Nine Silva Productions

Colosseum Pinnacle

Columbia Sony

Demon Demon

DRG New Note

EastWest WEA

ECM New Note

Edel Pinnacle

Elektra WEA

EMI EMI

Epic Sony

Flapper Pinnacle

Fox Arista (BMG)

Geffen BMG Conifer

GNP Crescendo BMG Conifer/Silva Productions

GRP New Note

Hollywood Silva Productions

Intrada Silva Productions

Island PolyGram

JOS JOS

Koch Koch International

Label X Silva Productions

Legend Silva Productions

Marco Polo Select

MCA BMG Conifer

Mercury PolyGram

Milan BMG Conifer

Morgan Creek PolyGram

Olympia Priory

Philips PolyGram

Preamble Silva Productions

Prometheus Silva Productions

RCA BMG Conifer

Real World Virgin

Sakkaris Pinnacle

Scannan Silva Productions

Scotti Bros PolyGram

Silva Screen BMG/Silva Productions

Sonic Images Pinnacle

Sony Classical Sony

Spectrum Karussell (PolyGram)

Stax Pinnacle

Telarc BMG Conifer

TER MCI

Unicorn-Kanchana Harmonia Mundi

Varèse Sarabande Pinnacle

Verve PolyGram

Virgin EMI

Warner Bros WEA

Record company and distributor addresses

A&M Records
136-140 New Kings Road, London SW6 4LZ
Telephone 0171-705 4343 Fax 0171-731 460

Arista Records (UK)
Cavendish House, 423 New Kings Road,
London SW6 4RM
Telephone 0171-973 8040 Fax 0171-373 9324

Arista Records (USA)
6 West 57th Street, New York, NY 10019, USA
Telephone 212 489 7400 Fax 212 489 7400

BMG Conifer/RCA
Bedford House, 69-79 Fulham High Street,
London SW6 3JW. Telephone 0171-973 0011
Fax 0171-371 9571

BMG (UK Distribution)
Lyng Lane, West Bromwich, West Midlands,
B70 7ST Telephone 0121 500 5545 Fax 0121 553 6880

BMG (USA)
1540 Broadway, New York, NY 10036-4098, USA
Telephone 212 930 4000 Fax 212 930 4263

Cabin Fever Entertainment
100 West Putnam Avenue, Greenwich,
CT 06830, USA

CAM
Via Cola di Rienzo, 152-00192 Roma, Italy.
Telephone 396 687 4220 Fax 396 687 4046

CEMA Distribution
21700 Oxnard Street, #700, Woodland Hills,
CA 91367, USA Telephone 818 587 4000

Chandos Records
Chandos House, Commerce Way, Colchester,
Essex CO2 8HQ
Telephone 01206 794 000 Fax 01206 794 001

Citadel
– see Klavier International

Cloud Nine Records
– see Silva Productions

Colosseum Records
Bayernstrasse 100, Postfach 44 02 52,
8500 Nurnberg 44, Germany Fax 911 474 0160

Columbia
– see Sony Music Entertainment

Demon Records
Canal House, Stars Estate, Transport Avenue,
Brentford, TW8 0QP
Telephone 0181-847 2481 Fax 0181-568 8223

DRG Records
130 West 57th Street, New York, NY 10019, USA
Telephone 212 265 4050

Edel
PO Box 520151, Wichmannstr. 4, Haus 2, 22607
Hamburg, Germany
Telephone 40 89 08 50 Fax 40 89 65 21

Elektra
– see WEA

EMI Records
(Customer Services) EMI House, 43 Brook Green,
London W6 7EF
Telephone 0171-605 5000 Fax 0171-605 5050

EMI
(Sales and Distribution Centre) Hermes Close,
Tachbrook Park, Leamington Spa,
Warwickshire CV34 6RP
Telephone 01926 888 888 Fax 0181-479 5992

Epic
– see Sony Music Entertainment

Fox Music Group
c/o Twentieth Century-Fox Film Corporation,
10201 W. Pico Boulevard, Building 222 South,
Los Angeles, CA 90035, USA
Telephone 310 369 1000 Fax 310 369 2735

Geffen
– see MCA

GNP Crescendo
Suite 4A, 8400 Sunset Boulevard, Los Angeles,
California CA 90403, USA
Telephone 213 656 2614 Fax 213 656 0693

GRP Records
555 West 57th Street, New York, NY 10019, USA
Telephone 212 245 7033

Harmonia Mundi (UK)
19-21 Nile Street, London N1 7LL
Telephone 0171-253 0863 Fax 0171-253 3237
Harmonia Mundi (USA)
2037 Granville Avenue, Los Angeles,
CA 90025-6103, USA
Telephone 310 478 1311 Fax 310 996 1366
Hillside CD Productions
"Hillside House", 1 Woodstock Road, Strood,
Rochester, Kent.
Telephone 01634 711053 Fax 01634 294 176
Hollywood Records
500 South Buena Vista Street, Burbank, CA
91521, USA Telephone 818 560 5670 Fax 818 845
9705
Intrada Records
1488 Vallejo Street, San Francisco, California
CA 94109, USA
Telephone 415 776 1333 Fax 415 776 2666
Island Records
22 St Peter's Square, London W6 9NW
Telephone 0181-910 3333 Fax 0181-748 1998
JOS Records
34 Grantley Close, Copford, Essex, CO6 1YP
Telephone/Fax 01206 213 057
Klavier International
PO Box 177, San Juan Capistrano, CA 92675,
USA Telephone 714 248 7234
Koch International UK
24 Concord Road, London W3 0TH
Telephone 0181-992 7177 Fax 0181-896 0817
Koch International USA
2 Tri-Harbour Court, Port Washington, New
York, NY 11050-4617, USA
Telephone 516 484 1000 Fax 516 484 4746
Label X
– see Fifth Continent
Marco Polo
– see Select
MCA (UK)
139 Piccadilly, London W1V 0AX
Telephone 0171-957 8600 Fax 0171-957 8560
MCA (USA)
70 Universal City Plaza, Universal City, California
CA 91608, USA
Telephone 818 777 4018 Fax 818 397 8726
Mercury
PO Box 1425, Chancellor's House,
72 Chancellor's Road, Hammersmith,
London W6 9QB
Telephone 0181-910 5678 Fax 0181-741 1616
Milan
- see BMG (UK)
Milan (France)
S.E.P.A.M, Z.A. Kleber, 165 Bd de Valmy, F-
92706 Colombes Cidex, Paris
Telephone 47 86 36 19 Fax 47 86 36 31
Morgan Creek
4000 Warner Boulevard Building 76, Burbank,
CA 91522, USA
Telephone 818 954 4800 Fax 818 954 4770
New Note
– see Pinnacle
Olympia
31 Warple Way, London W3 0RX
Telephone 0181-743 6767 Fax 0181-749 1300
Pen Dinas Productions
12525 Victory Boulevard, Suite 121,
North Hollywood, CA 91606, USA
Telephone 818 786 0844 Fax 818 781 5751

Philips
– see PolyGram Classics and Jazz
Pinnacle Records
Electron House, Cray Avenue, St Mary Cray,
Orpington, Kent BR5 3RJ
Telephone 01689 873144 Fax 01689 878269
PolyGram Classics and Jazz (UK)
22 St Peter's Square, London W6 9NW
Telephone 0181-910 5000 Fax 0181-748 4104
PolyGram Classics and Jazz (USA)
Worldwide Plaza, 825 Eighth Ave., New York,
NY 10019, USA
Telephone 212 333 8000 Fax 212 333 8118
PolyGram Record Operations
PO Box 36, Clyde Works, Grove Road, Romford,
Essex RM6 4QR
Telephone 0181-590 6044 Fax 0181-597 1011
Prometheus Records
Astridlaan 171, 2800 Mechelen, Belgium
Telephone 15 41 41 07 Fax 15 43 36 10
RCA
– see BMG
Rhino Records
10635 Santa Monica Boulevard, Los Angeles,
CA 90025, USA
Telephone 310 474 4778 Fax 310 441 6578
Select Music and Video Distributors
34a Holmethorpe Avenue, Holmethorpe Estate,
Redhill, Surrey RH1 2NN.
Telephone 01737 760020 Fax 01737 766 316
Silva Productions Ltd.
Silva House, 261 Royal College Street,
London NW1 9LU
Telephone 0171-284 0525 Fax 0171-482 2385
Sonic Images
8908 Appian Way, West Hollywood, CA 90046,
USA Telephone 213 650 1000 Fax 213 650 1016
Sony Music Entertainment (UK)
10 Great Marlborough Street, London W1V 2LP
Telephone 0171-911 8200 Fax 0171-911 8600
Sony Music Entertainment (USA)
550 Madison Avenue, New York, NY 10022, USA
Telephone 212 833 8000 Fax 212 833 8659
Sony Music Operations
Rabans Lane, Aylesbury, Buckinghamshire
HP19 3RT Telephone 01296 395 151 Fax 01296 395
551
Spectrum
Karussell, PO Box 1425 Chancellor's House,
72 Chancellor's Road, Hammersmith,
London W6 9QB
Telephone 0181-910 5692 Fax 0181-910 5892
Stax
– see Ace Records
Target Records
23 Gardner Industrial Estate, Kent House Lane,
Beckenham, Kent BR3 1QZ
Telephone 0181-778 4040 Fax 0181-676 9949
Telarc
23307 Commerce Park Road, Cleveland,
OH 44122, USA
Telephone 216 464 2313
TER (That's Entertainment)
107 Kentish Town Road, London NW1 8PB
Telephone 0171-485 9593 Fax 0171-485 2282
Unicorn-Kanchana Records
PO Box 339, London W8 7TJ

Telephone 0171-727 3881 **Fax** 0171-243 1701

Varèse Sarabande

– see Pinnacle (UK)

Colosseum (rest of Europe)

Varèse Sarabande Records Inc.

11846 Ventura Boulevard, Suite 130, Studio City,CA 91604, USA **Telephone** 818 753 4143 **Fax** 818 753 7596

Virgin Records

Kensal House, 553-579 Harrow Road,

London W10 4RH

Telephone 0181-964 600 **Fax** 0181-964 6073/0386

Warner Music (Distribution)

PO Box 59, Alperton, Middlesex HA0 1FJ

Telephone 0181-998 8844 **Fax** 0181-998 3429

WEA/Warner Music (UK)

The Warner Building, 28 Kensington Church Street, London W8 4BP

Telephone 0171-937 8844 **Fax** 0171-937 6645

WEA (USA)

Dealers and mail order services

UK

Backtrack

The Old Grammar School, Rye, East Sussex TN31 7JP **Telephone** 01797 222777

58 Dean Street Records

58 Dean Street, London W1V 5HH

Telephone 0171-437 4500/0171-734 8777

EMS Imports

18 Kings Park, Primrose Hill, King's Langley, Herts WD4 8ST **Telephone** 01923 267060 **Fax** 01923 260078

Farringdons Records

64-72 Leadenhall Market, London EC3V 1LT

Telephone 0171-623 9605

Royal Festival Hall

South Bank Centre, London SE1 8XX

Telephone 0171-620 0198

HMV

150 Oxford Street, London W1N 0DJ

Telephone 0171-631 3423

HMV

363 Oxford Street, London W1R 2BJ

Telephone 0171-629 1240

Movie Boulevard Ltd.

3 Cherry Tree Walk, Leeds LS2 7EB

Telephone 0113 242 2888 **Fax** 0113 243 8840

Soundtrack Deletions

"Hillside House", 1 Woodstock Road, Strood, Rochester, Kent.

Telephone 01634 711053 **Fax** 01634 294 176

Soundtracks Direct

Silva House, 261 Royal College Street, London NW1 9LU **Telephone** 0171-284 0525 **Fax** 0171-482 2385

Tower Records

1 Piccadilly Circus, London W1R 8TR

Telephone 0171-439 2500 Mail Order –

Telephone 0171-287 1510 **Fax** 0171-434 2766

Tower Records

62-64 Kensington High Street,

London W8 4PL **Telephone** 0171-938 3511

Virgin Megastore

14-16 Oxford Street, London W1R 1DD

Telephone 0171-491 8582

Virgin Megastore

527 Oxford Street, London W1R 7DD

Telephone 0171-580 5822/0171-631 1234

Information on the major retailers who stock soundtracks, and the location of your nearest local branch, can be obtained by contacting the following:

HMV	**Telephone** 0171-439 2112
Music and Video Club	**Telephone** 0181-424 0101
Tower Records	**Telephone** 0171-938 3625
Virgin/Our Price	**Telephone** 0181-400 4000
WH Smith	**Telephone** 01793 616161

In addition, the *Gramophone Blue riband* dealer scheme contains comprehensive listings of specialist classical UK record dealers, many of whom also stock soundtracks

USA

Footlight Records

113 East 12th Street, New York, NY1003, USA **Telephone** 212 533 1572

Intrada

1488 Vallejo Street, San Francisco, CA94109, USA

Telephone 415 776 1333 **Fax** 415 776 2666

STAR (SoundTrack Album Retailers)

PO Box 487, New Holland, PA17557, USA

Telephone 717 656 0121

Reference books and magazines

The Film Composers' Guide

[Editor: Vincent J. Francillon] Lone Eagle Publishing Company, 2337 Roscomare Road, Suite Nine, Los Angeles CA90077-1851, USA.

Telephone 310 471 8066 **Fax** 310 471 4969

Film Score Monthly

[Editor: Lukas Kendall] 5967 Chula Vista Way, Number 7, Los Angeles, CA90068,USA

Telephone 213 464 7919.**Fax** 213 464 5916

Music from the Movies

[Editor: John Williams] 1 Folly Square, Bridport, Dorset DT6 3PU. **Telephone** 01308 427 057 **Fax** 0117 923 8153

R.E.D. Soundtracks Catalogue

Retail Entertainment Data Ltd., Paulton House, 8 Shepherdess Walk, London N1 7LB.

Telephone 0171-566 8216 **Fax** 0171-566 8259

Soundtrack!

[Editor: Luc Van de Ven] Astridlaan 171, 2800 Mechelen, Belgium. **Telephone** 15 41 41 07 **Fax** 15 43 36 10

The Soundtrack Collector

Phil Nohl, 5824 West Galena, Milwaukee, WI53208, USA

Tele-Tunes

Mike Preston Music, The Glengarry, Thornton Grove, Morecambe, Lancs LA4 5PU.

Telephone 01524 421172 **Fax** 01524 421172

Index

End Credits:

Thanks are once again due to all the contributors for their hard work and boundless enthusiasm; to all the various record companies without whose willing cooperation this book could not have been written; to all the various people who have helped with biographical information, including Mark Ayres, Rachel Portman, Kevin Mulhall (Mychael Danna), Oliver Barder (Yoko Kanno), several of the artists's agents, and interviews appearing in various magazines, particularly Soundtrack!, Music from the Movies and Film Score Monthly. A thousand thanks to David Arnold for his flattering Foreword and to his irrepressible and ever-helpful agent, Trish – and finally, of course, to David and all his fellow composers, without whose continuing efforts, this book would not exist.

Specialist Arcam Dealers

Location	Dealer	Phone		Location	Dealer	Phone
ABERDEEN	Holburn Hifi	01224 585713		LEEDS	Image Hifi	0113 2789374
ABERDEEN	Sevenoaks Hi Fi	01224 587070		LEEDS	Superfi	0113 2449075
ALDERLEY EDGE	Aston Audio	01625 582704		LEICESTER	Cymbiosis	0116 2623754
ALDRIDGE	Musical Approach	01922 57926		LEICESTER	Leicester Hi Fi Co	0116 2539753
BANBURY	Overture	01295 272158		LEICESTER	Richer Sounds	0116 255 4656
BARNSLEY	Barnsley Hi Fi Centre	01226 205549		LEICESTER	Sevenoaks Hi Fi	0116 2557518
BARNSTAPLE	J & A Cameras Ltd	01271 75037		LINCOLN	Superfi	01522 520265
BARROW IN FURNESS	Sevenoaks Hi Fi	01229 838757		LIVERPOOL	Better Hi Fi	0151 227 5007
BASINGSTOKE	Audio T	01256 24311		LIVERPOOL	Richer Sounds	0151 708 7484
BATH	Radford Hi Fi	01225 446245		LLANDUDNO	Peters Hi Fi	01492 76788
BECKENHAM	Musical Images	0181 66337772		LONDON NW6	Audio T	0171 794 7848
BEDFORD	Richards Audio Visual	01234 365165		LONDON N7	Bartletts Hi Fi	0171 6072296
BEDFORD	Sevenoaks Hi Fi	01234 272779		LONDON SE13	Billy Vee Sound Systems	0181 318 5755
BELFAST	Lyric Hi Fi	01232 381296		LONDON W1	Cornflake Shop	0171 631 0472
BIRMINGHAM	Empire	0121 633 4962		LONDON N1	Grahams Hi Fi	0171 226 5500
BIRMINGHAM	Griffin Audio	0121 692 1359		LONDON W1	Hi Fi Experience	0171 580 3535
BIRMINGHAM	Music Matters	0121 429 2811		LONDON W1	K J West One	0171 486 0552
BIRMINGHAM	Sevenoaks Hi Fi	0121 233 2977		LONDON SW5	Listening Rooms	0171 244 7750
BIRMINGHAM	Superfi	0121 631 2675		LONDON W4	Martin-Kleiser Limited	0181 400 5555
BISHOPS S'FORD	Audio File	01279 506576		LONDON WC2	Musical Images	0171 497 1346
BLACKBURN	Romers Hi-Fi	01254 887799		LONDON SW20	O'Brien Hi Fi	0181 946 1528
BLOXWICH	Sound Academy	01922 473949		LONDON SW11	Oranges & Lemons	0171 924 2040
BOLTON	Cleartone	01204 531423		LONDON EC2	Richer Sounds	0171 626 8006
BOURNEMOUTH	Movement Audio	01202 529988		LONDON SE18	Sevenoaks Hi Fi	0181 855 8016
BOURNEMOUTH	Suttons Of Bournemouth	01202 555512		LONDON SW10	Sevenoaks Hi Fi	0171 352 9466
BRADFORD	Cleartone	01274 309266		LONDON SE1	Sound Organisation	0171 403 2255
BRIGHTON	Jeffries Hi Fi	01273 609431		LONDON NW1	Superfi	0171 388 1300
BRIGHTON	Power Plant	01273 775978		LONDON NW6	Studio 99	0171 624 8855
BRIGHTON	Richer Sounds	01273 673333		LONDON W4	Uxbridge Audio	0181 400 5000
BRIGHTON	Sevenoaks Hi Fi	01273 733338		LOUGHBROUGH	Stuart Westmoreland	01509 230465
BRISTOL	Audio Excellence	0117 9264975		LOWESTOFT	Audio Images	01502 582853
BRISTOL	Radford Hi Fi	0117 9240878		MAIDSTONE	Sevenoaks Hi Fi	01622 686366
BRISTOL	Richer Sounds	0117 973 4397		MAIDSTONE	Unilet Audio	01622 676703
BROMBOROUGH	Peters Hi Fi	0151 334 2825		MANCHESTER	Audio Counsel	0161 4287887
BROMSGROVE	S.M. Spain Ltd	01527 872460		MANCHESTER	Hi Fi Stereo	0161 973 5577
BURTON ON TRENT	Grange Hi Fi	01283 533655		MANCHESTER	Richer Sounds	0161 480 1700
BURY ST EDMUNDS	Sevenoaks Hi Fi	01284 724337		MANCHESTER	Richer Sounds	0161 773 0303
CAMBRIDGE	Audio File	01223 368655		MANCHESTER	Superfi	0161 835 1156
CAMBRIDGE	University Audio	01223 354237		MELTON MOWBRAY	Stuart Westmoreland Hi Fi	01664 63366
CANTERBURY	Q Audio	01227 462787		MIDDLESBOROUGH	Gilson Audio	01642 248793
CARDIFF	Audio Excellence	01222 228565		MILTON KEYNES	Technosound	01908 604949
CARDIFF	Radford Hi Fi	01222 398121		MONTROSE	Rob Ritchie Hi Fi	01674 73765
CARLISLE	Tysons	01228 46756		NEW MALDEN	Unilet Audio	0181 942 9567
CASTLEFORD	Eric Wiley	01977 553066		NEWARK	Peter Ellis Audio	01636 704571
CHATHAM	Sevenoaks Hi Fi	01634 846859		NEWCASTLE	Bainbridges	0191 232 5000
CHELMSFORD	Rayleigh Hi Fi	01245 265245		NEWCASTLE	Richer Sounds	0191 230 1392
CHELMSFORD	Richer Sounds	01245 355 666		NORTHAMPTON	Listen Inn	01604 37871
CHELTENHAM	Audio T	01242 583960		NORWICH	Basically Sound	01508 570829
CHELTENHAM	Sevenoaks Hi Fi	01242 241171		NORWICH	Martins Hi Fi	01603 627010
CHESTER	Audio Excellence	01244 345576		NORWICH	Richer Sounds	01603 620 860
CHESTER	Acoustica	01244 344227		NORWICH	Sevenoaks Hi Fi	01603 767605
CHESTER	Peters Hi Fi	01244 319392		NOTTINGHAM	John Kirk Hi Fi	0115 9252986
CHESTERFIELD	Audioscene	01246 204005		NOTTINGHAM	Nottingham Hi Fi Centre	0115 9786919
COLCHESTER	Grayston Sound & Vision Ltd	01206 577682		NOTTINGHAM	Stuart Westmoreland Hi Fi	01664 63366
COVENTRY	Frank Harvey Hi Fi	01203 525200		NOTTINGHAM	Superfi	0115 9412137
COVENTRY	Superfi	01203 223254		OLDHAM	Audio Counsel	0161 633 2602
CROYDON	Sevenoaks Hi Fi	0181 665 1203		OXFORD	Audio T	01865 65961
CROYDON	Spaldings	0181 654 1231		OXFORD	Radford Hi Fi	01865 511241
CROYDON	Zebra Hi Fi	0181 688 2093		OXFORD	Sevenoaks Hi Fi	01865 241773
DARLINGTON	Hi Fi Experience	01325 481418		OXFORD	Westwood & Mason	01865 247783
DERBY	Stuart Westmoreland	01332 367546		PETERBOROUGH	Hi Fi Company	01733 341755
DERBY	Superfi	01332 360303		PLYMOUTH	Hi Fi Attic	01752 669511
DUMFRIES	T N Mckay	01387 54117		PLYMOUTH	Radford Hifi	01752 226011
DUNDEE	J D Brown	01382 226591		POOLE	Movement Audio	01202 730865
DUNFERMLINE	Andrew Thomson	01383 621803		PORTSMOUTH	Jeffries Hi Fi	01705 663604
DUNFERMLINE	Andrew Thomson	01383 724541		PRESTON	Audio Excellence	01172 253057
DUNSTABLE	Technosound	01582 663297		RAYLEIGH	Rayleigh Hi Fi	01268 779762
EAST GRINSTEAD	Audio Designs	01342 314569		READING	Audio T	01734 585463
EASTBOURNE	Jeffries Hi Fi	01323 731336		READING	Richer Sounds	01734 591 111
EDGWARE	Musical Images	0181 952 5535		READING	Sevenoaks Hi Fi	0118 959 7768
EDINBURGH	Bill Hutchinson Hi-Fi Ltd	0131 2200909		RICHMOND	Riverside Hi Fi	0181 892 7613
EDINBURGH	Hi Fi Corner	0131 220 1535		ROCHDALE	Helen Koczur	01706 42107
EDINBURGH	Hi Fi Corner	0131 556 7901		ROTHERHAM	Moorgate Acoustics	01709 370666
EDINBURGH	Russ Andrews Hi Fi	0131 557 1672		RUGBY	Sounds Expensive	01788 540772
ENFIELD	Audio T	0181 367 3132		SAFFRON WALDEN	Chew & Osborne	01799 523728
ENFIELD	Sevenoaks Hi Fi	0181 342 1973		SALISBURY	Salisbury Hi Fi	01722 322169
EPPING	Chew & Osborne	01992 574242		SCARBOROUGH	Audio One	01723 355654
EXETER	Audio Excellence	01392 491194		SEVENOAKS	Sevenoaks Hi Fi	01732 459555
EXETER	Radford Hi Fi	01392 218895		SHEFFIELD	Moorgate Acoustics	0114 2756048
FALKIRK	Hi Fi Corner	01324 629011		SHEFFIELD	Superfi	0114 2723768
GATESHEAD	Lintone Audio	0191 460 0999		SHREWSBURY	Creative Audio	01743 241924
GATESHEAD	Lintone Audio	0191 477 4167		SKIPTON	John Phillip Hi Fi	01756 793388
GLASGOW	Bill Hutchinson Hi-Fi Ltd	0141 204 4433		SOLIHULL	Music Matters	0121 742 0254
GLASGOW	Glasgow Audio	0141 332 4707		SOUTHAMPTON	Hampshire Audio	01703 252827
GLASGOW	Hi Fi Corner (Glasgow) Ltd	0141 248 2840		SOUTHAMPTON	Richer Sounds	01703 231 101
GLASGOW	James Kerr Home Hi-Fi	0141 226 5711		SOUTHEND ON SEA	Rayleigh Hi Fi	01702 435255
GLASGOW	Stereo Stereo	0141 248 4079		ST ALBANS	Darbys	01727 851596
GLOUCESTER	Audio Excellence	01452 300046		STAFFORD	Musical Approach	01785 55154
GRIMSBY	Manders Hi Fi	01472 351391		STIRLING	Stirling Audio	01786 479958
GUILDFORD	P J Hi Fi	01483 504801		STOKE ON TRENT	Living Design	01782 260047
GUILDFORD	Sevenoaks Hi Fi	01483 36666		STOKE ON TRENT	Superfi	01782 265010
HALIFAX	Huddersfield Hi Fi	01422 366832		STOURBRIDGE	Music Matters	01384 444184
HARPENDEN	Studio 82	015827 64246		STRATFORD U'AVON	Stratford Hi Fi	01789 414533
HARROW	Harrow Audio	0181 863 0938		SWANSEA	Audio Excellence	01792 474608
HEREFORD	English Audio	01432 355081		SWINDON	Audio T	01793 538222
HERTFORD	Ultimate Audio Visual	01992 583399		TUNBRIDGE WELLS	Sevenoaks Hi Fi	01892 531543
HIGH WYCOMBE	Sound Gallery	01494 531682		UXBRIDGE	Uxbridge Audio	01895 465 444
HITCHIN	David Orton Audio Visual	01462 452248		WAKEFIELD	Image Hi Fi	01924 200272
HOUNSLOW	Musical Images	0181 569 5802		WARRINGTON	Doug Brady Hi Fi	01925 828009
HUDDERSFIELD	Huddersfield Hi Fi	01484 544668		WATFORD	Richer Sounds	01923 218 888
HULL	Superfi	01482 324051		WATFORD	Sevenoaks Hi Fi	01923 212736
HULL	Zen Audio	01482 587392		WELWYN G'DEN CITY	Video Vision	01707 323610
ILFORD	Audio T	0181 518 0915		WEYBRIDGE	Cosmic	01932 854522
INVERNESS	Telly On The Blink	01463 233175		WEYMOUTH	Weymouth Hi Fi	01305 785729
IPSWICH	Eastern Audio	01473 217217		WINDSOR	Radford Hi Fi	01753 856931
ISLE OF MAN	Island Cd And Hi Fi Centre	01624 815521		WITHAM	Sevenoaks Hi Fi	01376 501733
KILMARNOCH	Laser Audio	01563 540292		WOKING	Bartletts Hi Fi	01483 771175
KINGS LYNN	Martins Hi Fi	01553 761683		WOLVERHAMPTON	Superfi	01902 772901
KINGSTON	Infidelity	0181 943 3530		WORCESTER	Sevenoaks Hi Fi	01905 612929
KINGSTON	Sevenoaks Hi Fi	0181 547 0717		WORTHING	Phase 3 Hi Fi	01903 245577
KIRKCALDY	Andrew Thomson	01592 205997		WREXHAM	Acton Gate Audio	01978 364500
LEAMINGTON SPA	Hi Fi Company	01926 888644		YEOVIL	Mike Manning Audio	01935 79361
LEAMINGTON SPA	House Of Music	01926 881500		YORK	Sound Organisation	01904 627108
LEEDS	Audio Projects	01132304565				

Also available at branches of John Lewis.